THE EDUCATION OF JOHN DEWEY

JAY MARTIN

The Education

Columbia University Press
New York

# of John Dewey

A BIOGRAPHY

Columbia Universtiy Press
Publishers Since 1893
New York   Chichester, West Sussex

Copyright © 2002 Jay Martin
All rights reserved
All photographs courtesy of:
Special Collections / Morris Library
Southern Illinois University, Carbondale,
except photograph of Alice Chipman (fig. 5)
courtesy of:
Collegiate Sorosis records
Bentley Library
University of Michigan

Library of Congress Cataloging-in-Publication Data
Martin, Jay
The education of John Dewey: a biography / Jay Martin
p. cm.
Includes biographical references and index.
ISBN 0–231–11676–4 (alk. paper)
1. Dewey, John, 1859–1952. 2. Philosophers–United
States–Biography. 3. Educators–United States–Biography.
I. Title
B945.D44 M29 2002
191–dc21
[B]2002073883

Columbia University Press books are printed on
permanent and durable acid-free paper.
Printed in the United States of America

c 10 9 8 7 6 5 4 3 2 1

To my beloved Helen
"Your love fills everything"

Contents

Criticism of philosophy must begin with the motives and interests which actuate the philosopher, not with problems of logical consistency and considerations of truth. The biographical element must be stressed if we are to study motives and interests of philosophers. We must know his temperament, his personal problems, times, biases, etc. . . . We must also take cognizance of the particular social environment of the philosopher, as well as his [experience and] native sensitiveness.

—John Dewey, *Lectures on Types of Philosophic Thought*

Near the end of his life, Mr. Dewey spoke at an affair at Columbia; when the applause died down, he got up, not to take a bow, but to add a word of caution, *to be a philosopher takes guts.*

—Jack C. Lamb, "John Dewey: A Look Back"

THE EDUCATION OF JOHN DEWEY

BOOK I

Emergence

All biographies are interpretations of their subjects. The best biographers compose accounts that make use of every possible resource of representation that narrative can offer. They are concerned with a judicious dispersal of the facts of a life but also, much more important, with devising a form, a style, an attitude, and a perspective that can come as close as a book may do to paralleling the life of its subject. If this is done well enough, the book can truly resemble the man or woman it is describing.

The biographer is the life's second author or, perhaps, its editor. A biography of John Dewey demands that its author represent Dewey as and how he lived. Because Dewey's main occupation in life was thinking, his biographer must not only write about Dewey's thought but also reflect and inquire with Dewey into the processes of thinking. Dewey's main entry into the life of thought was through his emotions. He was not a thinking machine but a vibrant person-who-thought. His biographer can succeed only if he, too, conveys in his own narrative the continuous activity of Dewey's strong emotions.

Dewey once said that the two sources of his happiness were his work (or play) of thinking and his family. His biographer must give attention to Dewey's family, or the portrait of the thinker will be incomplete.

Dewey actively responded to the character and condition of the times in which he lived. His biographer, too, must represent the changing face of history during Dewey's life. Because Dewey experienced a large part of his nation's history and was enmeshed in it, so must his biography be.

Dewey was one person. But he prepared many faces to meet the opportunities offered by both his own inner capacities and the possibilities of his time and place. For philosophers, he was a philosopher, immensely learned and technically brilliant. For those people engaged with issues of education, whether experts in the field or anguished parents, he was the leading exponent of the new learning. For the citizenry, he was an advocate and combatant in the rough-and-tumble of American politics, public affairs, and public policy, as well as a powerful controversialist for liberal causes.

Dewey moved effortlessly from any one of these roles to the others. His biographer thus must be ready to portray his many activities and explain how they all emanated from one person. Dewey's many faces are like the facets of a crystal that, as it turns, reflect the various angles of a single life.

My biography of John Dewey is constantly in motion, just as he was. Dewey's life was his best education. By making his life an inquiry, he did not so much *find* meaning as he *made* meaning. In this book I move from one facet of Dewey's life to another—as son and brother, husband and father, student and professor, contemplative philosopher and political activist, educator and disputant, a man of deep thought and of yet more profound emotions, a person accustomed to joy yet one who was sometimes plunged into excruciating misery.

By inquiring into Dewey's life, I have made meanings of which he himself might not have been aware. It is the province and privilege of a biographer to create meanings, and meanings in turn create values. Yet I have attempted to be as true to Dewey's activities as possible:

writing as a philosophic commentator about his thought; as a historian about his times and his involvement in them; as a psychologist examining the shape and form of his habits and arrests in development as well as his creative advances; as a political scientist to represent his active engagements in politics; as a remembrancer of his family and his affectionate involvements; and, above all, as a guarded optimist who believes that his life was worth living once and is worth saving now.

Biographers have a privileged knowledge that is hidden from their subjects. They know how their subject's life turns out before beginning to write about it. Biographers are not the slave of time but are free to move their narrative backward and forward in order to convey the meaning of their subject's life. This book is not identical with its subject; it merely condenses Dewey's life into a few hundred pages. Still, I dare to hope that I have constructed this biography in such a way that my portrait of Dewey will disclose his person.

Dewey made his life. He continually learned what he was making precisely by making it. Using the bricks of style, the architecture of form, and the ever refocused camera of perspective, I have remade his life. If I have done it well enough, Dewey will breathe again and renew his life in these pages.

CHILDHOOD

In 1856 Archibald Sprague Dewey, grocer, and Lucina Artemisia Rich Dewey, his wife, became the parents of a boy. They named him John Archibald, after his father. A second son was born two years later and was named Davis Rich after Lucina's father. Both boys flourished. Then, on January 17, 1859, there was a tragic accident. The Burlington, Vermont, *Daily Free Press* carried the news:

Distressing Accident.—We learn, with pain, that our friend and townsman, A. S. Dewey, has lost his oldest child by a distressing casualty. The child, a fine little boy, between two and three years old, was fatally scalded last evening, by falling backward into a pail of hot water. The customary appliance of sweet oil and cotton batting was made, when, by some accident the cotton took fire, and burst into flames upon the person of the child. The last mishap added to the pain of the little sufferer, as well as to his parents' distress, and death resulted (from the scalding principally, as we understand), about seven o'clock this morning. The afflicted parents have the sincere and tearful sympathy of the community, in their sudden and most painful bereavement.

It was a horrible sequence of accidents. John Archibald suffered an excruciating death, and his parents were devastated.

Forty weeks later, on October 20, 1859, Lucina gave birth to a boy. His parents named him John, after his deceased brother. Clearly they thought of him as replacing the dead son, but Archibald could not bear to confer his own name on this second child. So he was not named John Archibald but simply John, John Dewey.

Most of us live and act for others as well as ourselves. But replacement children inherit a duty to live not just for themselves and their parents but for the lost child as well. They have to bear anxieties in their parents that for a long time they cannot understand and perhaps never will understand, but they will certainly feel behind them the shadow of another. Having to replace another made for the first crisis of his life.

The living child may experience his or her special duties as burdens. If he is melancholy by temperament, this is unlucky, for he will feel the responsibilities of replacement to be a weight too heavy to bear. But if he is lucky and if his temperament is sunny and optimistic, he can enjoy as a gift the extra attention he receives. After he lives past the age at which his sibling perished, he may feel invulnerable, the darling of fate. Perhaps he will carry lightly the burden of living for others and even turn it into a talent for relatedness and deep compassion.

John Dewey was lucky. He made the most of his parents' and his loss. They always treated him as if he were their first child, and in many ways, he went ahead of his brother Davis. Like an older brother,

John counseled Davis (who eventually became a famous economist, but not until after John achieved fame). Like the oldest brother, it was John who tried to help his younger sibling, Charles Miner, when he floundered. Lucina, especially, was always preoccupied with John's health and safety, more so than with her other two boys, and Charles Miner suffered from her relative inattention to him. Instead, Lucina doted on John as if he really were the firstborn who had fortunately survived a terrible accident. When she wrote to John, she packed the pages with news and inquiries, and when the page was filled, she continued to write all around the margins until all the blank places were used up. Before Archibald's death, she and he came to live with John, not Davis, her oldest child, or Charles, her youngest. And she always had a greater attachment to John's children than to Davis's.

If John had had a frail disposition, this extra attention might have crushed him. There is abundant evidence that he did feel the difficulties of its weight. But he shouldered his responsibilities and learned to enjoy living for his parents first and for others later, until eventually he committed himself to representing the needs of the American people.

One issue with which John had to deal was his father's complicated response to John Archibald's death. On August 20, 1859, seven months after John Archibald's death, Lucina, Archibald, and Davis moved into a new house at 186 South Willard Street in Burlington. This house was a gift from Lucina's father, who had bought it for $2,000 five months earlier from the original owners. The house had three stories, a gabled roof, and a front porch. With no purchase price recorded in city hall, Davis Rich transferred the house to the Deweys. No doubt they needed a new house, since they were expecting a child. But perhaps they also wanted a new location for the arrival of their next child, a place not associated with John Archibald's death.

John Dewey was born in this house. The Deweys settled in, Archibald's business prospered, Davis thrived, and baby John was watched over nervously by his parents. January 17, 1861, was the second anniversary of John Archibald's death and nearly the second anniversary of John's conception. In nine more months John would reach the age of two, the same age at which John Archibald had died. Simultaneously, history was getting ready to provide Archibald with the grounds for a surprising decision.

In the presidential election of 1856, the Republican Party candidate John C. Fremont had outpolled all other candidates in the North. But he received only a handful of votes in the South, and so he lost narrowly to the Democrat James Buchanan of Pennsylvania.

The nation was as sharply divided as the election. The campaign had been fought against the background of several compromises that everyone knew would not last. The Compromise of 1850 had been hailed as "final and irrevocable" by President Millard Fillmore when he signed it. But anyone who was willing to look at it carefully could see that the legislation that had been cobbled together to admit California as a free state but allow slavery in other territories and to introduce new, more effective fugitive slave laws would not bring about sectional reconciliation or end the controversies between North and South, free and slave states. Only economic interests kept open conflict down and the states together. The Kansas-Nebraska Act, using the mask of popular sovereignty to determine whether a state would enter as "slave" or "free," was a mere juggling act and had no beneficial effect. It produced only the breakup of the old political alliances and the outbreak of violence in Kansas, where the fierce abolitionist John Brown came to fame through mayhem in the name of the humanitarian ideal of ending slavery.

Despite inheriting all this, President Buchanan lacked the one instrument that had previously kept the nation together—economic prosperity. Hardly had he taken the oath of office when a financial panic, partly due to the national strife, ran through both the North and the South. The economic recession soon turned into a prolonged depression, and American agriculture was hit particularly hard. American farmers had prospered by selling produce to Europe, but the Europeans' own production now met their needs, and American farmers were left with debt and overproduction. In the Northeast and the Midwest the depression was severe. The economic distress in Vermont, where John Dewey was born, was followed by social problems, as many farmers began to move to the cities, especially Burlington, where the infrastructure was unprepared for such a rapid influx of people. In a time of division and indecision, President Buchanan was conflicted and indecisive. The country wavered, and so did he.

The many separate opinions that were written in the U.S. Supreme Court's decision in *Dred Scott v. Sanford* shows how divided the Court itself was. But the majority of the justices generally coalesced around the opinion of Chief Justice Roger Taney that African Americans had almost no constitutionally mandated rights, that the federal government could pass no laws regulating slave property in the territories.

At about the time that John Dewey was born, in the fall of 1859, John Brown raided the U.S. arsenal at Harpers Ferry, Virginia, and stole enough weapons to begin what he hoped would become a widespread slave rebellion. The Virginia courts, however, did not share his passion for freedom through violence, and after Robert E. Lee captured him, he was promptly convicted and hanged.

In the 1860 election in the following year, four candidates received electoral votes. Like John C. Fremont earlier, Abraham Lincoln received almost no Southern votes and only about 40 percent of the popular vote. But he won handily in the electoral college. Temporizing, undecided, and ambiguous, Buchanan announced in December 1860 that it was unconstitutional for a state to withdraw from the Union but also illegal for the federal government to intercede in order to prevent secession. Just before Christmas, South Carolina seceded from the Union, with other states not far behind. In 1861 Lincoln was inaugurated president; Fort Sumter was captured; and federal property was seized.

In April 1861, the war between the states finally broke out. Archibald Sprague Dewey was fifty years old at the time. He had a wife who was pregnant with their fourth child, two young boys, and a successful business. Everything indicated that he was too old and too settled to go off to war.

But suddenly in the summer of 1861, Archibald sold his grocery business and enlisted as quartermaster in the First Vermont Cavalry. Soon he was gone, joining the Union Army in Northern Virginia and leaving Lucina to care for two children and prepare to give birth to another. She managed to keep the household together for a while, using some of the funds realized from the sale of the store. But she finally had to sell the house on Willard Street and go to live with relatives.

Archibald had been swept up in the national conflict. Was it abolitionist or patriotic fervor that persuaded him to enlist? Or was he still mourning the death of his namesake and uneasy as the second John approached the age at which the first one had died? In any event he was gone, and all Lucina could do was wait for news about the First Vermont Cavalry. For John, his father's departure was the second crisis in his life.

Archibald's entry into military service meant that Lucina became closer to her sons, especially John, than she would have otherwise. Archibald also was not available for John to identify with, except as a distant ideal, at the time that he was ready to separate from his mother. On July 14, 1861, Lucina gave birth to another boy, Charles Miner Dewey. So even though John had an older brother, Davis, he was encouraged to act like a still older brother, John Archibald; and in addition, he had to adjust to the departure of his father and to a mother distracted by a new infant.

It was a scary time for everyone in the country. "My father was in the army most of the civil war period," John remembered in 1933, "and [I and] my mother and brothers lived with other members of the family." During this time, war hysteria was high, even far from the battle lines. John remembered that while they were living with his uncle Matthew H. Buckham, there was a false alarm of a Confederate attack in Burlington, and his uncle went to the fort to stand guard all night. The gates were open, everything was unsettled, and the future was even more uncertain than the present.

The particular uncertainty of the Dewey family and Lucina's parents and extended family was the fate of Archibald. The First Vermont Cavalry was deeply engaged in the conflict. Although bulletins from the front were always sketchy and unreliable, in many areas in the North they were regularly posted on a bulletin board in the city center and then published in the newspaper. Lucina could follow the sporadic war engagements of her husband's unit whenever there was news to report. Between December 1861 and the end of 1864, the First Vermont Cavalry fought in seventy-two battles and skirmishes; it was at Gettysburg and Richmond. Archibald himself wrote an account of the regiment's retreat from the Confederate forces at Strasburg, Virginia, in the early summer of 1862:

> The baggage train was taken across Cedar Creek early in the morning of May 24th by orders from headquarters. . . . About ten o'clock word came that the trains in front were cut off and we should soon be attacked; this caused a slight flurry, which a word from my wagon master C. P. Stone of Company F. instantly quieted.
>
> About 4 o'clock a battery of 4 guns, followed by our regiment under Col. Tompkins as a support, came up and took a position a short distance to the right and front of our train. The firing was brisk for over half an hour, when the battery, being threatened by a flank movement of the enemy . . . was forced to limber up and retire. . . .
>
> The train was put in motion, each driver taking his proper place in the line in the most perfect order. We had no sooner commenced to move than the enemy's skirmishers showed themselves emerging from the timber within half rifle range, and the hiss of bullets soon became familiar; but not even now did confusion arise—in proof of which I will say that three drivers dismounted to chain their wheels in descending a steep hill. . . .
>
> Four teams crossed the stream unhurt, the others got into the water where several horses fell by the fire which was poured in by largely increased numbers; there being now from 75 to 100 within 20 to 25 rods.
>
> Still not a man left his seat while his horses kept their legs. When one horse fell, another was cut loose, the driver would mount and be off. In this way seventeen horses out of seventy-six were saved.

When the passage through the water was obstructed by dead or disabled horses the order was given to the drivers to save themselves by cutting out each a horse for himself; and I have reason to hope that all are alive, though two were wounded and four are prisoners.

I have written nothing on hearsay; the whole movement was made under my own observation and direction.

Archibald survived, and for "faithful and meritorious service," he was promoted to captain. By the fall of 1864, he had not even been wounded. In late 1864, just before the war ended, the First Vermont Cavalry was assigned duty in the Cumberland, in the loyal western counties of Virginia. This area had seceded from Virginia in June 1861 and had been admitted into the Union as the state of West Virginia in 1863.

The war was slowly ending. In any event, it seemed relatively safe for the occupying soldiers to receive visitors, so Lucina set out with her three children to join her husband for Christmas 1864.

John had not seen his father for more than three years. Now he was four years old, and it was like meeting Archibald for the first time. All his life he remembered the first night he spent with his father after this long separation. In 1931, sixty-six years later, a friend asked him about his childhood. Although he usually was reticent about his past, one memory leaped out:

The Xmas I remember best was one when I was four years old I think; my father was stationed in West Va in the war and mother took us down to spend a winter there, and one of the few things I remember is waking up and seeing their bed across the room, it seemed a mile, and then getting some things; one of them was a little wooden churn. Afterwards my mother told [me], it must have been many years [later], that they thought we would be so disappointed because it was so impossible to get things there, and yet how happy we were with what we got.

Lucina and the boys returned to Burlington where they were living with relatives. The war ended at last in early 1865, and then on
April 14, 1865, President Lincoln was assassinated. The nation was
plunged into mourning. One of John Dewey's earliest recollections was
"seeing the buildings in Rouses Point draped in black for Lincoln's
death." He was five years old. For him, this began a memory of
America's vicissitudes that continued until, at the age of ninety-two, he
read about the beginning of the Korean War.

Archibald was discharged in the spring of 1865. Although most of
the First Vermont Cavalry immediately returned home, Archibald
remained in the South. Was he reluctant to return? Or was it that he
had found some commercial opportunities that were too promising to
abandon? In any event, he stayed in the South, engaged in various
business ventures in Virginia and southern Illinois, and did not settle
down in Burlington until 1867.

In the summer of 1867, shortly after Archibald's return, the
Deweys moved into their own house, on George and Pearl Streets in
Burlington. At the same time Archibald reestablished his grocery and
cigar business close by on Pearl Street. Family life resumed and, with
it, came the third crisis in John Dewey's early life.

John's parents were very unlike each other. They had very different, almost opposite, temperaments; each reacted quite differently to
children; each had very different interests and was driven by different
needs. How was John to reconcile the influences of parents so different
from each other?

Born on September 12, 1830, in Shoreham, Vermont, Lucina grew
up on her father's prosperous farm where she learned all the skills of
home industry required of an independent, self-sustaining farm family. At this time in America, such skills were rapidly disappearing as the
population moved from the farm to the city. But John Dewey idealized
his mother's skills and had them in mind years later when in *The
School and Society* (1899) he celebrated the "discipline and . . . character-
building involved in . . . training in habits of order and of industry, and
in the idea of . . . obligation to do something, to produce something in
the world" cultivated by farm families until the mid-nineteenth

century. He told Joseph Ratner that in stressing these skills in his own writings on educational theory and practice, he had been influenced "by the Vermont environment, especially of my [maternal] grandfather's farm . . . where all these occupations were still common." In a late essay, he described what he had experienced that children of the 1920s and 1930s were denied:

> There in the village was the old-fashioned sawmill, the old-fashioned gristmill, the old-fashioned tannery; and in my grandfather's house there were still the candles and the soap which had been made in the home itself. At certain times the cobbler would come around to spend a few days in the neighborhood, making and repairing the shoes of the people. Through the very conditions of living, everybody had a pretty direct contact with nature and with the simpler forms of industry. As there were no great accumulations of wealth, the great majority of young people got a very genuine education . . . through real contact with actual materials and important social occupations.

John Dewey admired Thomas Jefferson above all other Americans, for several reasons, one being that he shared with Jefferson an idealization of rural life. In his writings Dewey tried to give children raised in cities or working in factories a sense of the creative, productive, independent life of a farming family like his mother's.

But Lucina's father was not only a farmer. Davis Rich had also been a member of the Vermont General Assembly for five years. His father, Lucina's grandfather, Charles Rich, had served in Congress in Washington for five terms. Prosperous and public-spirited, engaged in public service, and influential in public policy, for three generations the Rich family had been connected by blood and interests to many important citizens in Shoreham and Burlington. Lucina's cousin Matthew H. Buckham was the president of the University of Vermont when John Dewey was a student there. Lucina and the boys sometimes lived with the Buckhams during and after the Civil War, and John and Davis were good friends with the two Buckham boys. In short, Lucina identified with the older Burlington elite in politics and university life.

Lucina viewed the world through her strong sense of moral rectitude deepened by continuous self-examination and accompanied by a
commitment to social welfare and reformist activities. Her values
centered on the soul. She was, in the terms of the day, "a Partialist,"
believing that because not everyone could be saved, she should be
deeply concerned about the souls of her loved ones. Many years later,
John wrote to his wife that his early experience with his mother had
made "it necessary for one to formulate [my] . . . whole self, past &
future, . . . having been brought up . . . with the true evangelical interest in my own soul's welfare & development." He was a serious, shy,
introspective child.

Dewey's father conferred on him the other side of American life—
the brash, vigorous, pious, but not spiritually reflective, business-class
life that was oriented toward social action and a rapid rise to prominence. As Henry James and other commentators portrayed these
Americans, they may not have had education, the power of reflection,
or even manners—but they had confidence in themselves, and they
seized power whenever they could. The social class based on the
University of Vermont in Burlington reflected an older democracy
centered on teaching people. By contrast, the new business class reflected a commercial democracy that bought from anyone and sold to
anyone.

Archibald Sprague Dewey was born on a farm in Fairfax,
Vermont, on April 27, 1811, into an old New England family, his family's eleventh and last child. Like Lucina's, his family had lived in New
England for several generations and also had made distinctive contributions to American life. His grandfather's father, Parson Dewey, had
played a role in the Revolutionary War and was buried at Bennington.
Whereas Lucina's ancestors were English, Archibald had some Dutch
blood in his otherwise Scots-Irish heritage. His ancestors were weavers
who had fled Flanders in the sixteenth century; their original name
was de Wei ("of the meadows"). In later years, John associated
England with rigid Puritanism and preferred to claim his Dutch

ancestry: "I rejoice in the fact however that I am Dutch by descent & not English. And in western Mass. where Deweys most do congregate there are two proverbs—one to the effect 'as industrious as a Dewey' . . . and the other that no one could get a Dewey drunk." Whether the reason for the latter talent lay in "abstemiousness" or the "absorptive powers" of the Deweys, he added, was unclear. He liked the Dutch strain he had inherited from Archibald. As a boy and long after, he wished to be like his father.

Archibald was one of the wave of New Englanders who moved from the country to the towns when the region's commercial expansion made it possible to develop successful service businesses. He made an easy transition from the farm to the town by choosing to work as a grocer, opening a grocery store in Burlington in the early 1840s. By the time he married and brought his twenty-five-year-old wife from Shoreham to Burlington in 1855, he was a mature man of forty-four. Although he stammered in speech—a condition that John Dewey much later realized was "psychiatric and not [due to] any trouble with [his] vocal organs"—he had an absolute genius for advertising, demonstrating how useful humor could be in attracting customers. As soon as the Burlington *Daily Free Press* started publication in April 1848, he began to place ads in it, his first one reading: "Those who prefer darkness to light are advised not to purchase oil or sperm candles" at Dewey's store. In 1850, under the heading "Links from the 'Chain of Events,' " Archibald Sprague Dewey offered for sale a quantity of sausages. In 1852, he made advertising fun of religious prophets. Under the heading "In the name of 'Profit' Phigs," he announced, "A Phew Phresh Phigs Phor Sail." "Dewey has armed himself with Hams, for the promotion of 'Family Broils.' " As for his hams, he assured his customers: "Dewey's hams are smoked only by himself; His cigars are smoked by everybody." Sometimes he varied this ad with "Hams and tobacco, smoked and unsmoked." His cigars, he said, in turn, were "a good excuse for a bad habit." These advertisements continued unabated all through the 1850s. He was a friend of the poet John G. Saxe and persuaded him to write a comic parody about some salmon he had for sale. Archibald himself composed a poem for the *Free Press* entitled "Owed to Dewey."

In 1860, the year following John's birth, the growth of Burlington had increased Archibald's business to the point that he had to move into a much larger store on Church Street in the university area, between College and Main Streets. He wrote to his clients that he had moved his goods there, "and he hopes they may keep moving." The new store, which was extensively remodeled and considerably expanded, was, he pronounced with satisfaction, "spacious and elegant." But he sold this store the next year to join the crusade for abolition.

For all the fun in his advertisements, Archibald was a serious businessman. As early as 1851 he was promulgating the motto of his establishment in the *Daily Free Press*: "All goods not otherwise represented are warranted perfect and failing to give satisfaction may be returned." In addition to the store, he also owned a brick kiln at Marbles Bay and was in the "hay commission business" with a partner in Boston. Finally, he was a member of the board of directors of the American Telephone Company for Northern New England. Archibald's talent clearly bloomed in commerce, whereas Lucina's, by contrast, flourished in moral action.

In some superficial ways, this contrast between Dewey's parents is typical of the situation that many commentators on American social life have portrayed, with the mother taking charge of the children while the father was away in his office or store. Both Henry James and Henry Adams described women carting children around Europe in search of culture while their husband stayed behind in some industrial town making contact mainly through letters of credit. George Santayana saw this split as the chief deficit of the genteel tradition. But the split between Lucina and Archibald was different. Lucina was no genteel flower but a truly vigorous woman fully committed to the so-called masculine virtues of Puritanism. She equipped Davis and John with moral purpose and committed them to the pursuit of responsibility.

John Dewey's parents treated their children very differently. Archibald was a businessman and had little time for the boys. He tended to be closer to Davis than to John, and in becoming an economist, Davis reflected this affiliation with his businessman father. With John, Archibald was always rather cautious. In all outward forms, their relationship was respectful, but there was always an affective gap between them. When he later filled out a form for inclusion in a cyclopedia of national biography, John's remark that his father was "noteworthy" for "wit" and "geniality" has a condemnation underneath its commendation. Archibald was awkward with his son and used his wit to keep him at arm's length when intimacy threatened. This is nowhere better exhibited than in a very strange passage in a letter from Archibald to John dated October 21, 1885, the day after John's twenty-sixth birthday. Archibald wrote rather pointedly at first: "I didn't forget yesterday—[the] anniversary of your burglarious entrance into the family circle, but the weather was so fine that I did not like to lay aside the spade for the pen. . . . If mother's correspondence don't miscarry you will receive a trifling reminder that we both thought of you." In addition to the suggestions that he *had* forgotten the birthday or that the weather was too fine to trouble himself with writing on his son's birthday or that the gift he was sending would be a "trifle," there is the odd word *burglarious*. John had come like a burglar into the family circle, stealing a place that was not his by right; that is, it rightfully belonged to John Archibald. What word or metaphor could convey better than *burglarious* that he was a replacement child who would never have been named John Dewey had not his father's true son and namesake, John Archibald, died? However we interpret these and other exchanges between Archibald and his son John, there is always a sort of off-putting distance on Archibald's part.

Lucina, by contrast, was overly involved in John's life, the likely result of her being his sole caretaker from the time he was a year and a half until he was five. The fact that he seemed frail as a child also may have drawn her to him. More than her other sons, John bore a striking resemblance to Lucina. A frequent visitor in the Dewey household in the 1870s remarked in 1947 that "Lucina looked then exactly as [John Dewey] looks now—the resemblance is striking." Like hers, his dark eyes were his most prominent feature. She was somewhat frail physically, as John was also, yet she worked very hard, even at "immense cost to her." John, too, became a tireless worker. He was always at his duties shortly after seven o'clock. As late as 1918, when he slept until eight o'clock one morning, he confessed to his children that on this day he had broken his "record" for sleeping late.

John Dewey, then, had one parent who was allied with intellectual development, public service, and moral values and another who was steeped in business and economic expansion. One was concerned with thoughtfulness, and the other was preoccupied with action in a manly world. One remained rather remote from involvement in his children's lives, and the other was intensely involved. What would he make of these two personalities? What personality would he form for himself from these influences?

After John Dewey's death, his second wife, Roberta, wrote about this question. She told the philosopher George Axtelle in no uncertain terms that John had "often told me about his parents and his life in Vermont." He invariably insisted, she said, that his "father was a greater influence than his mother." This was one of Dewey's masks, a barely hidden wish. In fact, however, the influence of his mother was very strong, so strong that he had to learn how to resist it. Although he was influenced by his mother, he yearned to be affected by his father. He was loved intensely by his mother, but he hungered for his father's affections. His father's attempt to influence him was as minimal as his mother's wish to influence him was great. But while he resisted hers, he would absorb any influence he could get from his father. Because he remembered what he wished for when he insisted that his father had been the greater influence, in fantasy he began to resolve the crisis of possessing two different parents: choosing to identify with his distant father left him space to become himself.

THE CHRISTIAN INFLUENCE

John's fourth early crisis was his relation to Christianity. His father's view of Christianity was, like the rest of his life, defined by his business relation to it. He was a member of the First Congregational Church of Burlington. During Archibald's formative years, the First Congregational Church of Burlington was untroubled by theological

disputes or schisms, and he grew up understanding religion to be sole-
ly a Sunday affair. When he became a church member, he devoted
himself to the administrative aspects of church business. In 1849, he
was appointed "collector" (or treasurer) of the Prudential (budget)
Committee of the Congregational Society. In 1852, he became its chairman and, for the first time, put the committee's finances on a "knowl-
edgeable"—meaning "intelligible"—basis and made it keep within its
budget. He was a fine businessman and a dutiful member. But he
showed little spiritual drive.

Lucina was the opposite. While she was growing up in Shoreham,
the Congregational Church there underwent a profound transformation through its division into Trinitarian and Unitarian wings.
Upheavals in Congregationalism were common throughout New
England in the first half of the nineteenth century, the main conflicts
being between the orthodoxy represented by the Yale School of
Divinity and a growing liberal trend. The conservative group tended
to interpret the Bible rather literally, to stress personal introspection,
and to emphasize the individual. The liberal group insisted that
human intelligence must be applied to the interpretation of the Bible,
that social welfare was an appropriate goal of ethical action, and that
mutual concern in a group had moral value. This conflict reached each
New England congregation at a different time, depending on the dispositions of the pastor and the leading personages of the church.

The liberal thrust came to Lucina's hometown of Shoreham in
1814 when Rev. Daniel D. Morton became the pastor, and it continued
under his successor, Rev. Josiah Goodhue, who was appointed in 1833,
when Lucina was three years old. But the triumph of liberalism was
not unopposed, and the Shoreham congregation was in turmoil for a
long time. In contrast to the placid Burlington congregation,
Shoreham was a hotbed of theological controversy, and every member
of the congregation had to take sides. Religion was a powerful force in
Shoreham and a decisive influence on Lucina's life.

Lucina, who grew up under Goodhue's direct influence, also was
affected by Morton's influence on her parents. She was admitted to the
United Congregational Church of Shoreham by a formal confession of

faith, followed by baptism, on January 5, 1850. Her mature activities show what kind of theological and moral amalgam she put together for herself. She combined the older, conservative emphasis on individual introspection—being good and possessing a rigid personal morality—with a loose interpretation of scripture, an intense liberal emphasis on doing good through social welfare, and a reformist drive. By the time she married, transferred her membership to the First Congregational Church of Burlington, and bore children, this conservative-liberal combination of personal rectitude and social concern was well established. She fused personal austerity with an interest in social improvement. John Dewey kept some of her favorite books with him all his life, including Edmund H. Sears's *Pictures of Older Times, as Shown in the Fortunes of a Family of the Pilgrims* (1857) and Edward Young's melancholy reflections in *The Complaint: or, Night Thoughts* (1875 edition).

Lucina's personal piety emerged in her continuous preoccupation with the spiritual welfare of her children. She was the enemy of all frivolity—drinking, playing pool, gambling, playing cards, or dancing. She made it clear to her boys that they could not even play marbles on Sunday. Sunday was for Sunday school and church. Lucina taught Sunday school and, in the case of her own sons, taught it all week. She did not give up easily. As late as 1883, she was still pressing Davis to seek Jesus Christ. "I have been reading a book by Dale on *The Atonement* which it does seem to me if Dave would read [it] candidly he would find convincing," she sighed. Monday was for prayer and prayer meetings. She continually asked the boys: "Are you right with Jesus?" She reached beyond her own family in advising college students about their personal morality. The Congregational Sunday-School and Publishing Society issued a didactic story entitled *Freshman and Sophomore* in which Lucina identifiably appears as the character Mrs. Carver in giving beneficial moral counseling to students at the University of Vermont. Her emphasis on introspection was doubtless helpful to college students who saw her only infrequently. But her steady inspection of her boys made introspection undesirable for them. Every Christmas she gave John a diary. Dutifully, he kept it, but all he

ever entered in it was "it was a hot or cold day" and "I went outdoors
or read a book." He remained wary of introspection all his life, seldom
talking about himself or his past—and *never* kept a diary after Lucina
stopped giving him one. Still, as a child he was, as he later described
himself, "a highly 'self-conscious' youngster hypersensitive [and] morbidly [inclined to] thinking of others['] alleged opinions of me, which I
really knew were mostly imaginary anyway."

Lucina was equally earnest about the ideal of service. Very early
she became deeply involved in the church's mission work and eventually became the president of Burlington's Woman's Home Mission
Society, later called the Adams Mission. Indeed, she was "one of the
earliest and staunchest" friends of the mission. Her obituary in the
Adams Mission Monthly tells us, "She gave her last thoughts to the problems which are still pressing on our philanthropists. 'How can we
make Burlington a temperate and moral city, a safe, clean place for
young men, a city of virtuous and happy homes?' " Lucina was "especially solicitous . . . for the protection of the . . . poor and unfortunate."
It was she who came up with the idea that the Burlington churches
should be organized to support the mission, and she did the work to
organize them, forcefully telling Rev. E. P. Gould, the head of a church
delegation, that "the work is of God. If the churches of Burlington do
not seize this opportunity to take up a vital work . . . they will make the
mistake of their lives."

In the account of the hundredth anniversary of the founding of the
First Congregational Church in Burlington, published in 1905, Lucina
is categorized as "The Idealist":

> Her thought was always reaching out to something beyond,
> something which might be done for those who needed help in
> body, or soul. . . . She gathered the children of Water Street
> into a Mission Sunday School. She tried to establish a coffee
> house in that part of the city. She was the earnest ally of Mrs.
> Adams. . . . She had an eager, questioning mind, which was
> ever seeking the answer to some unsolved problem. . . . She
> was always looking forward from things as they *are*, to what
> they ought to be, and might be.

In the Dewey family, Lucina's evangelical pietism had obvious consequences. Late in his life John Dewey remembered what Easter was like
in his house:

> Maybe we had dyed eggs but that was the limit [of frivolous
> play]—I have a vague recollection . . . of dying eggs. But New
> England Congregationalists didn't pay much attention to east-
> er except to go to church and hear a sermon on the resurrec-
> tion. We weren't so Puritan as to cut out Christmas but it was
> always stockings and getting up before daylight to see what
> was in them, not a tree.

Lucina herself did not make a declaration of faith and become a member of the church until she was twenty. But in her concern with her
sons' spiritual welfare and her eagerness to bring them forward into
the spiritual life, on June 15, 1871, when John was eleven, she herself
composed and actually wrote out short declarations of faith for Davis
and John to present to the church as part of a formal request to be
admitted to communion. John's read: "I think I love Christ and want
to obey Him. I have thought for some time I should like to unite with
the church. Now, I want to more, for it seems one way to confess Him,
and I should like to remember Him at the Communion." John continued to be an active member in the Burlington church from this time all
through his college years, until he left the city in 1879 to teach in
Pennsylvania. In 1881, when he returned to Vermont to teach high
school in Charlotte, he immediately resumed his participation in
church activities.

Charlotte is located about fifteen miles south of Burlington, but
John made the journey back every week. In November 1881, not long
after his return, he and four other young men met with the pastor to
form an official young people's society at the church. At the first meeting, on December 5, he was elected president. Forbidden by the rules
of the organization to continue as president beyond six months, he next
became vice-president and was a member of the arrangements committee that planned young persons' events. Every weekend he traveled
to Burlington to attend the young people's Saturday night "sociables"

and to go to services with his parents on Sunday. He attended church festivals, too, such as the Strawberry Festival in June 1882.

If personal piety and moral commitment were constant themes in the Dewey household, these emphases were given equal weight as the ideal of service to which Lucina had committed herself. If her austere piety turned the young John Dewey inward to focus on himself, her social ideals turned him outward to the world. There is no doubt that John felt uncomfortable with Lucina's intrusive emphasis on personal introspection. He squirmed whenever his mother inquired whether he was "right with Jesus." In a news article in 1886 on religion, he showed his anti-Puritanical uneasiness about emotion in religious introspection:

> Religious feeling is unhealthy when it is watched and analyzed
> to see if it exists, if it is right, if it is growing. It is as fatal to be
> forever observing our own religious moods and experiences, as
> it is to pull up a seed from the ground to see if it is growing.

Dewey resisted his mother's efforts to make him morbidly introspective. "I am so far from the proper gifts for edification," he told his friend Max Otto in 1941, "that yielding to a certain propensity in the direction of preaching would have ruined me."

Nonetheless, Lucina's liberal devotion to public service and her stress on intelligence and experience in interpreting the Bible—concerns that turned her outward to the world—appealed to John early in life and continued to hold his attention until he died. Lucina's bent in these directions was given extra force by the appointment of Rev. Lewis O. Brastow as pastor of the First Congregational Church in 1873, when Dewey was thirteen years old. With his pastorship, Burlington arrived at the liberal position that Lucina had experienced with Goodhue years earlier at Shoreham. But twenty years had made a difference. Gone, with Brastow, was the pietism that Lucina had learned. Brastow was thoroughly committed to an enlightened liberal evangelism. "Liberal evangelicism [*sic*]," he wrote, "assumes that human intelligence may venture to deal with the facts of revelation and of religious experience." That he preached two parts of the three ideals

to which Lucina was committed is evident. Well trained philosophically, Brastow dropped the older theme of personal piety and stressed
intelligence and social action. "One should rise to 'spiritual manhood,'"
he asserted, but "the rescue and reconstruction are not wholly of individual men in their isolation from their fellows, but of men in their
associate life. . . . No man ever finds completeness in himself, . . . only
in our associate life. Men must be won to a common life." Brastow's
emphasis on religious "reconstruction" rather than "conversion" planted that word in Dewey's mind, and years later, in many books and articles, it was "reconstruction," he argued, that was needed in philosophy
and society. It remained one of Dewey's favorite words.

Brastow was an important figure in New England. His appointment to a professorship at Yale Divinity School in 1884 signaled the triumph of liberal over orthodox Congregationalism. He was Dewey's
pastor all during John's high school and college years, and when John
turned away from Lucina's piety, he could still keep the rest of his
mother's faith by allying himself with Brastow's preaching. Lucina,
who had been waiting for liberal theology to arrive in Burlington,
rejoiced at Brastow; and John clearly understood that his pastor's
philosophic bent was the very one that he himself was yearning to find.
If he was not, in Lucina's sense, right with Jesus, he was perfectly right
with Brastow, and that was good enough. Dewey later summarized the
character of his religious training: "I was brought up in a conventionally evangelical atmosphere of the more 'liberal' sort."

The fourth crisis of Dewey's early years was eventually resolved
through the liberal branch of Congregationalism, but until he got away
from his parents, he did not find a way to get enough distance to
resolve his conflicts over the divided elements of his spiritual life.

THE BEGINNING OF JOHN DEWEY'S EDUCATION

Meanwhile, with the war over, the country was still experiencing its
own crises—one after another. The war had been the worst of times
for the thousands of families that had lost loved ones in it or that had
been uprooted and economically devastated by it. But the 1870s seemed

like the finest of times. In the North, the military conflict had started prosperity rolling, and with the need to rebuild after the war, the economy was booming: "Reconstruction" was in the air, in rebuilding and reunifying the nation and in the so-called Reconstruction occupation of the South by federal troops to ensure compliance with the constitutional protection of former slaves.

As John Dewey was going through school, the country was changing quickly. By the time he graduated from college at the end of the decade, the world in which his mother and father had grown up had been radically reconstructed, and with the nation, he faced unprecedented new conditions.

The increase in wealth was remarkable—and rapid. It started during the war itself. Needs in meatpacking, transportation, clothing, and weapons created several new millionaires before the conflict ended. Before the war, only a handful of millionaires existed in America, but by the early 1890s, there were four thousand. Early on, Lincoln noticed this new condition and wrote to his friend W. R. Ellis:

> I see in the near future a crisis arising that unnerves me and causes me to tremble for the safety of my country. By a result of war, corporations have been enthroned and an era of corruption in high places will follow, and the money power of the country will endeavor to prolong its reign by working upon the prejudices of the people, until all wealth is aggregated in a few hands and the Republic is destroyed.

Lincoln was soon silenced. But if his prophecy needed confirmation, it came very soon. In *The Court Circles of the Republic*, Mrs. E. F. Ellet noted that despite the president's death the year before, "the fashionable season of 1866 [in Washington] was almost a carnival." Note the phrase "Court Circles": a new money-aristocracy was being born. When Herbert Spencer came to America, even he, whose version of social Darwinism perfectly suited American businessmen, recommended a "Gospel of Relaxation" instead of the "Gospel of Work and Wealth" embraced by the business elite.

When industrial wealth grows, cities must follow. The urban population grew almost four times as quickly as the rural population. In contrast to such prewar American writers as Emerson, Whitman, and Whittier, the authors who began writing in the 1870s, like Howells and Henry James, were city men and turned as naturally as the population was doing to city occupations and preoccupations. Americans hoped to find in urban life what the historian Arthur M. Schlesinger described: a place where people could realize "all those impulses and movements which made for a finer, more humane civilization," including "education, literature, science, invention, the fine arts, social reform, public hygiene[, and] the use of leisure." All these elements were pressing concerns in the 1870s. But while some fortunate persons achieved them, poverty, illiteracy, the exploitation of labor, the misery of disease, and crime-infested slums were the fate of others.

The increased number of immigrants helped form the "other half" and how they lived. Cities and factories were often the first and last stop for the new immigrants. Before the war, émigrés found little difficulty in adjusting to rural conditions, as farms in the United States were not so different from those in Europe. But adjustment to the cities was harder. Urban conditions allowed for workers' exploitation, and the contrast between the haves and the have-nots was greater and more noticeable in the cities.

Education and reform movements provided two obvious paths out of the problems, which became apparent as early as the 1870s. Congress created the first Department of Education in 1867 to disseminate the gospel of the free school. In 1872, when the U.S. Supreme Court upheld the city of Kalamazoo's right to establish a free school, Charles Frances Adams Jr. wrote in the *North American Review*: "The state, therefore, says to the rich: you shall contribute of your abundance for the education of your poor neighbors' children." Adult education also boomed, and free libraries were established. Founded in 1874, the Chautauqua movement sent lecturers all over the country. Thomas Davidson established his summer philosophic schools in Farmington, Connecticut, and later in Keene Valley, New York. Education seemed to be a prime necessity in a time when immigration was growing and literacy rates—on which Americans had prided themselves and American industry depended—were falling. Progress was the watchword after the depression of the 1850s and the hiatus of the war, and progress seemed to be related to good education. It came to be seen as a necessary acquisition in a modern world, especially as the transition from rural to urban life was separating children from many of the practical educative elements of the family farm. With the invention of the rotary press, the number of newspapers increased tenfold, and with the organization of book distribution—wholly ineffective until the 1870s—cheap, good books became widely available. Textbooks for all grades through college were being produced and selling well. Above all, the continuation and expansion of democracy rested on education and called for its steady advance.

Education nourished the appetite for reform, and reform stressed the significance of education. The triumph of moral idealism in the war left a heritage of reform. With the cause of abolition having been won, in 1865 William Lloyd Garrison suspended publication of *The Liberator*. Now other problems needed to be solved, and these were much more difficult to end. As Thomas Wentworth Higginson said of the problems that began appearing in the 1870s: "You could not settle[, for instance,] the problems of capital and labor off-hand, by saying, as in the case of slavery, 'Let my people go'; the matter was far more complex. It was like trying to adjust a chronometer with no other knowledge than that won by observing a sun-dial." This was because questions of reform were no longer abstract or moral; they involved social and economic relations and demanded knowledge of these. In the postwar period, the older reformers were ineffective, because, as William Dean Howells remarked of the powerful abolitionist poet John Greenleaf Whittier, he (and they) had not "appreciated the importance of the social movement." But moral idealism did live on, and when it fused with knowledge of society, it produced powerful champions. John Dewey was one of them, and like the best sort of reformers who were to appear, he was noteworthy for the range of his interests and his ability to envision and then promote change on all levels of a densely interconnected society.

The last of the developments that began to affect postwar citizens was the rapid rise of science, with the inevitable consequence that a naturalistic test of truth steadily undermined the religious test of truth that had prevailed before the war. Before 1860, the president of every major American college was a clergyman; every professor of philosophy, similarly, had a guarantee of moral rectitude through a ministerial degree. Both changed. Now intellectuals, with John W. Draper's *The Conflict Between Religion and Science* (1874) as their guide, saw science as rivaling theology. In the 1860s alone, twenty-five scientific schools were founded, a movement that culminated in 1876 with the establishment of Johns Hopkins University on the German research model, free from all religious connections and obligations. Its president was not a clergyman.

Darwin's *Origin of Species* played a major role in this by becoming the match that lighted a firestorm of controversy. It was published in 1859, the year in which John Dewey was born. Americans either condemned the book wholly or swallowed it whole, but it was, everyone saw, part of a general revolt in America against Calvinism. The immense number of war dead rendered strict predeterministic Calvinism untenable, and the ideal of progress that took hold after the war made evolution a desirable alternative. At Yale, the conservative clergyman president, Noah Porter, took a volunteer class through Herbert Spencer's *First Principles*, with a view toward refuting them— and every member of the class departed a convinced evolutionist. Spencer—who coined the phrase adopted by Darwin, "survival of the fittest"—sold 370,000 authorized copies of his books in America between 1860 and the turn of the century. The widespread opposition to Darwinism served only to publicize it. But such mediators as Minot J. Savage articulated perfectly what most Americans really wanted to believe: "If you accept [evolution], you will have to surrender your belief in 'the fall of man.' Evolution teaches the *ascent of man*: that the perfect Adam is ahead of us, not behind." Soon most people were persuaded that God worked through natural selection.

God seemed to work through the machine too, for machines were improving human life at a great rate. Technology was the child of science, and technology called for more and more science. Inventions were the toys of the age. Elbert Hubbard went around proclaiming that "a well-appointed factory is a joy," and inventors spread the joy freely. In 1876, the social gospel minister Washington Gladden discovered the "thoughts of God" in the machine room of the American Institute. The new American mythical figures were men like Casey Jones who were associated with the power of the new machines. The joining of the Union Pacific and the Central Pacific Railroads in 1869 to form the first transcontinental railroad was an event of epic proportions, and it was treated like one. The industrial frontier was already bidding to replace the westward frontier of settlement in American development.

These were the major changes taking place in America during the 1870s when John Dewey was receiving his education. An older and more sophisticated American, Henry Adams, confessed in his *Education* that he was nearly struck dumb by the rapidity and vastness of these changes. What could John Dewey, a naïve schoolboy, make of them? How would he contrive to make a vocation and a place in life for himself among them?

The issue of vocation formed the last of John Dewey's inner crises, and he stumbled toward a vocation rather than pursuing one. But he eventually found the one for which he was destined, and he became one of the heroes of the age in carrying it to its end. He was the person for his time, the one who learned to think about wealth and its consequences, the turmoil of the cities, the need for a new kind of education, the obligation to reform and reconstruct, and the importance of science and its practical applications in method and thought. All these, so crucial to his time, were at the very heart of his existence, perhaps more than of any other person in America.

But this was not easy to achieve, and at first it looked as if Dewey would fail to become this new American, this *newer* man.

The final crisis that John Dewey had to resolve concerned the complex relation between his education in Burlington and the choice of vocation in his life. We know that he eventually chose to become a philosopher-teacher. But how did he decide on that?

That Lucina found many reasons for social welfare tells us something about Dewey's birthplace. Burlington certainly needed the attention that Lucina lavished on it, for it was not the idyllic New England
town of American legend. When Dewey's first biographer, George
Dykhuizen, wrote about Dewey's birthplace, he was intent on creating
a special New England myth. Dykhuizen himself taught at the
University of Vermont, and he described the "charm and the natural
beauty of Burlington as 'unmatched' by most other New England
communities." He continued:

> Situated on the slopes of the hill, which rises gently from the
> shores of Lake Champlain, it overlooks the Green Mountains
> to the east and Lake Champlain and the Adirondacks to the
> west. The majority of the people belonged to the middle class,
> and were neither exceptionally rich nor unusually poor.

Irwin Edman, Dewey's student and, afterward, colleague at Columbia,
stated this legend most concisely and most incorrectly when he spoke
of Dewey as "a homespun, almost regional character . . . a Vermont
countryman." Contrary to the facts, Edman reported that Dewey had
been born "on a Vermont farm," even though he had been born in a
sizable city. And Burlington, he said, had a homogenous pattern of culture. Dewey's dissertation student Sidney Hook agreed. Dewey, he
claimed, was raised in "a community in which no great disparities in
wealth or standards of living were to be found." But this was not true.

Burlington was certainly beautiful scenically. On seeing the Bay of
Naples William Dean Howells exclaimed that this was "the most
beautiful view in the world except one—a Lake Champlain sunset as
seen from Burlington." But the realities of Burlington as a city were far
different. Like many other American cities, it was undergoing rapid
change around the time Dewey was born. Owing to its position on
Lake Champlain, it was a center of water transportation and commerce. For the lumber trade, it was the second largest port in the
United States. The rivers that flowed into Lake Champlain brought to
the town not only logs but also rivermen, immigrants, strangers, and
temporary residents, mostly Irish and French Canadian. The city's

waterfront was a place for boatmen, transient toughs, and roustabouts. It was no wonder that a mere five years after Dewey was born, the city council approved "an ordinance in relation to common prostitutes," imposing a jail term of sixty days, a fine of forty dollars, or both, for the offense. In 1866 in his "Report of the Health Officer," Samuel N. Thayer asserted that Burlington's South Ward consisted largely of "overcrowded tenement houses . . . one [of them] occupied by 51 persons of a low and filthy class." In the Middle Ward, "there are tenements where men, women, and children are herded together in violation of all the laws of decency and morality . . . hideous diseases and fatal pestilence [that is, cholera] will most surely be engendered" there. These were "haunts of dissipation and poverty," "abodes of wretchedness and filth." Because of Burlington's speedy growth, all its facilities were inadequate.

Of particular concern to the Dewey parents were the schools. The sorry social state of Burlington obviously had its impact on the schools there. Eldridge Mix's 1866 "Report of the Superintendent of Common Schools," published just before John started school, declared that the schools were severely overcrowded because of the rapid "transformation" of Burlington from a "town to a city" during the previous ten years. The schools, he observed, are "neither well-managed, nor effective." "The school buildings are so poor," Mix noted, that "I doubt whether any gentleman who owns valuable horses would long tolerate for them such a building . . . as a certain schoolhouse in our city." To make matters even worse, "the teachers were not the very best talent." Mix concluded that if nothing else, self-interest should persuade Burlington's city fathers to improve its schools. Burlington might be the leading commercial city in the state, but the "neglect" of the schools was "suicidal to our true interests." Therefore, "a radical change is necessary," in which "an entirely new [school] system ought to be inaugurated."

Mix's charges may have displeased some of the city fathers; he was soon replaced as superintendent. But two years later, his successor, L. G. Ware, offered essentially the same assessment. He found that the instruction consisted "too much of [rote] learning and teaching parrot-wise." And he saw the effects on the students: "I have noticed among

the older boys and girls a languid and shiftless way, and a trifling, friv-
olous way of study."

This was the school system that was educating John Dewey. The
condition of the high school was of particular concern to the Deweys.
In 1866, Mix declared the Union High School to be "in every respect a
disgrace to the city." But it was not until after twenty years of debate
that a new high school was approved by the city government in 1870,
shortly before John was ready to enter it. Even so, its construction was
not complete until well after he began high school.

John Dewey grew up in a city that was in transition and turmoil.
The older, rural, still-wild America could be found all around
Burlington in the sparsely populated hills and farms settled mostly by
English and Scots-Irish. In Burlington, Anglo-Saxon America could
also be found in an older generation of settlers, as well as in the university community. Founded in 1791, the University of Vermont was
the fifth oldest college in New England. In Dewey's youth it was
regarded as a distinguished center of learning, especially for philosophy, rivaling or surpassing the curricula of the four earlier—also
all-male—New England colleges: Harvard, Yale, Brown, and
Dartmouth. So the University of Vermont brought an elite to
Burlington: a Protestant, Congregational, freethinking, educated class,
which absorbed the more affluent and better-educated members of the
city's ruling business class. As was common elsewhere, the university
was built on the hill rising up from the lakeshore. Gathered around the
university were the older residential areas with neat New England
homes and estates that contrasted strikingly with the lakeport's slum
districts. Here could be found, as one Burlington citizen wrote, "the
homes of many wealthy persons, who, with the people of refinement
always to be found in a college town, form a cultured society which
keeps the city rich in social attractions." Entrance to this society,
Lucina's cousin Matthew H. Buckham claimed, required only "intelligence, virtue, and good manners," no matter what the "rank or occupation" of the newcomer. One had only to walk around Burlington
and its surroundings to see what America had been and to receive an
education in what it was becoming—a very mixed, stratified, and complicated country.

John Dewey's entry into the university community was assured and assumed. Some of his mother's relatives held important posts in the school, and his father was acquainted with most of the administrators. At the First Congregational Church most of the professors were regular communicants. Still, the secondary schools that were supposed to prepare him for college were marginal. In later years Dewey complained frequently about their deficiencies. Although he was destined to go to college, the schools did not do a good job at preparing him for it.

In September 1867, John entered District School No. 3, located at the corner of North Street and Murray Street, a short walk from his new house. At that time, the school, and indeed the area in which the Deweys lived, was largely French Canadian, so not all the students spoke English. When John entered it, the school was still ungraded. At that date in Burlington, each local district regulated its own schools, with the result that the classrooms in this district were overcrowded. The ungraded class in which Dewey enrolled had fifty-four pupils, ranging in age from seven to nineteen. The teachers were often poorly qualified; the standards were low; and after years of neglect, even the buildings were falling down. The result was predictable: the instruction consisted largely of "a mere pronouncing and mispronouncing of the words, a lifeless, monotonous, droning utterance of syllables, [rather] than the intelligent, appreciative, sympathetic experience of thought."

Fortunately, by September 1868, the schools throughout the city were completely reorganized; the classes were graded; and the teaching staff was rejuvenated. Instruction was still reported to be rather tedious, but at least the division of the curriculum into required subjects—reading, writing, rhetoric, geography, and spelling—meant that John would be adequately introduced to the basics. Very early, his grades showed his interests and capabilities. His deportment was perfect. He excelled in reading but scored low in recitation, then an important part of the curriculum.

John spent five years in grammar school, skipping from grade to grade until he graduated at the appropriate age. Although this was a fine arrangement chronologically, it left him with few friends outside his family. Everyone noticed that in contrast to Davis and Charles, who were friendly and sociable, John was shy and withdrawn. It was his bashfulness that affected his grades for recitation.

In the fall of 1872, John began attending the old, dilapidated high school at College and Willard Streets—"a poorly built structure," he wrote, "which was [soon after] condemned as a hazard" and "replaced by a newly built school." On the few occasions when he later talked about his experience in high school, the sense of his accounts is one of confinement. The stress on regulation must have reminded him unpleasantly of Lucina's home rules, from whose austerity he might have hoped to escape in school. The new high school may have been better than the old one, but the teaching, as he remembered it, was just as poor and intellectually as dilapidated. The teachers simply moved from the old building to the new, and what was called education continued. He remembered that at first he

> went to the old high school building on College St, [where] . . . the principals were Messers. Bartley and Halsey. The latter was a specialist in English grammar; he was also famous among the pupils for his saying "There is a rule against that." Mr. French the author of a series of arithmetics was supt. part of the time; his arithmetic books was full of puzzles in percentage; sometimes even the teachers differed as to the correct answer.

High school, as Dewey seems to have experienced it, was simply a continuation of the basics—reading, composition, and arithmetic—on a more demanding though more pedantic level. Bored and restive, anxious for something new, Dewey probably did learn more than he realized at the time. He was a voracious reader all his life. His composition skills were highly developed by the time he went to college, and he wrote correctly, swiftly, and easily, in a very natural plain style. He thought with mathematical precision, and indeed, he eventually wrote a philosophic work on arithmetic.

Although he did well in school, he didn't like it, a perhaps remarkable fact in light of his later activities in early education. His second wife, Roberta Dewey, speculated that his interest in education was a reaction to his negative experiences in grammar and high school. She told Pearl Weber that "in Vermont he saw a teacher beating a child who became adversely conditioned so that the child was never normal again." This was true. Dewey himself told a correspondent:

> It may be of some educational interest to know that I remember one teacher who whipped some body practically every day, sometimes with a ruler on the hand and sometimes with a rawhide on the body. Once she and some of the older boys hauled in a truant from the street and she gave him such a beating that I think it permanently affected him.

Of course, Dewey didn't spend all his time at school. He roamed the hills that surrounded Burlington. He, Davis, and their Buckham cousins went far afield, often crossing over into French Canadian territory and sometimes getting caught in rainstorms and spending the night in a barn. But excursions to Mount Mansfield and beyond gave him no direction for his life. He also got odd jobs during his school years. During grade school, he made a dollar a week delivering papers. At the age of fourteen he got a salaried job—six dollars a week—tallying lumber. But these menial jobs did not give him any indication of what he should do with himself.

Dewey took the college preparatory curriculum in high school, which included four years of Latin—which he finished in three years—three of Greek, and two of French, as well as English grammar, English literature, and arithmetic. Charles Darwin's *Origin of Species* had been published more than a decade earlier, in 1859; Karl Marx's *Critique of Political Economy* appeared that same year. But Dewey's high-school preparation included no real natural science or political theory. He was prepared to go to college only as such preparation was then defined, and no more.

When John graduated from high school in 1875 at the age of fifteen, he had not yet resolved the major issues of his youth. The pressures of having a replacement child had distanced his father and overinvolved his mother. More generally, in his family life, John was influenced by his mother's values and her hopes for him while at the same time yearning to be like his father. Pastor Brastow's influence, beginning in 1873, helped him work out a rational version of Christianity free from Lucina's Puritanism while retaining her commitment to reform and social service: the "social gospel," as it was soon called. But when John graduated from high school, he had not yet been liberated from the orthodoxy of personal piety. In fact, the orthodox-liberal strains that were fused in his mother's spiritual synthesis seem to have confused John Dewey about what beliefs were essential to Christianity. In response to a query about Christianity put to him by his student Joseph Ratner, Dewey wrote: "Impossible to say what a Christian believer 'believes' and what he is conventionally attached to." Dewey admitted that he "never had much interest in theology." He had been educated and education held a high value for him, but he was dissatisfied with the rule-driven, pedantic education that he had received. The internal pressures on him were evident not just in his shyness but also in psychogenic symptoms—respiratory problems, bodily aches, and possibly even in his recurring eyestrain.

John's four years in college offered a time and place to resolve these issues, but even college did not give him a direction in life to which he could commit himself. At the time he entered the University of Vermont, fewer than one hundred students were in attendance, among whom was John's brother Davis. Eight professors, teaching classics, rhetoric, moral philosophy, political economy, natural sciences, mathematics, and modern languages, led the students through a prescribed sequence of courses. Until John's senior year, no student could choose an elective.

A large part of Dewey's education was his reading some of the sixteen thousand books then in the university library. He remembered that "I was in those days an omnivorous reader as the Library records would show." The library books were fiercely guarded by John Ellsworth Goodrich, librarian and professor of rhetoric, English literature, and classical languages. John's brother Davis, himself an avid reader, remembered his own frustration over the difficulty of getting at the books:

> The library was open . . . only twice a week, and then for a limited number of hours. To me its contents were the most precious gift which the University had to offer, and I utilized its privileges to the full. My selection of books probably was not always wise, and I chafed under the scrutiny and solicitude of the librarian, who seemed to me to be unnecessarily concerned over the quality of my reading. At home my reading had been unrestricted, and I saw no reason why I should not indulge my curiosity in regard to any book which the University thought proper to house.

Of course, both Davis and John had access to books from their home, from the collections of their relatives, from sympathetic faculty, and from the recently renovated Burlington city library. From these varied sources, they were likely to have borrowed a conventional selection of light reading, novels, and poetry, but the books and periodicals that John borrowed from the university library during his four college years are a good indication of his serious interests. The fact that no single subject matter predominates among his choices suggests both the variety of his interests and, possibly, that he had found no central interest because he had not yet found a center in himself.

During his freshman year John checked out fifteen books from the library. Of these a third were political, including Argyll's *Reign of Law* (1872), Bagehot's *Physics and Politics* (1873), MacKinstosh's *History of the Revolution in England in 1688*, Hinton's *English Radical Leaders* (1875), and both volumes of Henry Reeves's 1844 translation of Tocqueville's *Democracy in America*. Of special interest in light of his subsequent career is that as a freshman he took out the first volume of the *Journal of Speculative Philosophy* (1868), the very periodical in which his earliest writings later appeared.

What can we find out from his choices at this early time? Of the fifteen books checked out, seven had been published since 1870. Clearly, Dewey's personality was not disposed to antiquarianism. Rather, he wanted the new, the up-to-date, the experimental. This also shows up in his subject choices: few if any of the books that he chose were on subjects that he had studied in high school. He was looking for new knowledge. The years that he spent studying Latin, Greek, and French held no power over him, and he even read Tocqueville in translation. Then too, we find few American works among his selections. Although he read Eckermann's *Conversations with Goethe*, most of the books were British or concerned England.

Much of this pattern continued in his sophomore year, with some further developments. For a brief time Dewey was passionate about William Makepeace Thackeray, for after he read *Roundabout Papers*, he rushed on to *The History of Samuel Titmarsh* and *The Book of Snobs*, finishing all three in three weeks. (The next year he read *Pendennis*.) George Eliot was also a favorite novelist. The other noteworthy development was that he began to read journals assiduously, including the *North American Review*, *Edinburgh Review*, and *Atlantic Monthly* in his sophomore year. During his last two years, he checked out *Bibliotheca Sacra*, *Fortnightly Review*, *Blackwood's Magazine*, *Westminster Review*, *Nineteenth Century*, *Littel's Living Age*, *Princeton Review*, and *Quarterly Review*. If anything exhibited his devotion to the new, the journals did, giving him the latest news from the intellectual front.

Although he was enrolled in the classical curriculum, Dewey showed no interest, outside his classes, in ancient authors. Even in his courses themselves, his interest in the classics was flagging. In his course on Herodotus he received a grade of 69, and he checked out William Cowper's translations of *The Iliad* and *The Odyssey* rather than attempting to read the originals. Instead, as his immersion in contemporary journals shows, he was increasingly interested in current knowledge and the controversies of his day. In her *Biography of John Dewey*, his daughter Jane remarked that these journals "affected him more deeply than his regular courses in philosophy." Joseph Ratner once asked him whether he read the *Andover Review*, in which controversies over Congregational theology raged, but he had not the slightest interest in these disputations and pointed Ratner toward such political journals as "Eng. Contemporary, 19th Century, and Fortnightly" for his real influences. Beyond the periodicals, he sought out authors with new points of view affected by evolutionary theory, such as John Fiske's *Myths and Myth-Makers* (1873) and Richard Prochris's *Other Worlds Than Ours: The Plurality of Worlds Studied Under the Light of Recent Scientific Research* (1871). It was not easy to straddle the two worlds of the classical curriculum at the University of Vermont and of modern political, philosophical, scientific thought. He had not yet joined his education to his interests.

The rate at which Dewey checked books and periodicals out of the university library speeded up in his junior year, when he borrowed twenty-six books. This year he made two discoveries: Matthew Arnold and historical narrative. He read Arnold's *Essays* (1873 edition), *Literature and Dogma* (1873 edition), *God and the Bible* (1875), and *The Popular Education of France* (1861), along with two of Frances Parkman's histories, and accounts of Roman, German, Greek, and English history. Arnold's attempt to reconcile humanism and religion attracted Dewey and remained a strong influence. (Years later he wrote a fine essay on Matthew Arnold.) His growing interest in history seems to have been fostered by the spirit of evolution to which he had been introduced and hastened to embrace.

This last interest bloomed in his senior year with Herbert Spencer, Darwin's coworker in philosophy and psychology. Dewey read the two large volumes of Spencer's *Principles of Psychology* (1872 edition), which he checked out twice, and eventually went on to Spencer's *First Principles*, which was the first volume of Spencer's *A System of Synthetic Philosophy*.

Dewey had little luck finding serious works of science in the university library, but he checked out whatever he could find. In his senior year, he borrowed Austin Flint's *Physiology of the Nervous System* (1873) and John Tyndall's *Fragments of Science for Unscientific People* (1871). But we know that his readings in science went beyond these. The British periodicals that he read regularly contained many articles on new scientific theory and scientific controversy. He also took courses on natural and physical science. Dewey remembered that in his junior year he had taken Professor Perkins's course in physiology, "without laboratory work," for which the text was T. H. Huxley's *Elements of Physiology*, based on evolutionary principles. He told George Dykhuizen, "I imagine that was the beginning of my interest in philosophy—the organic character of living creatures impressed me deeply." In this physiology course he received a grade of 92, remarkably high at that time (and far above his 69 in Herodotus).

Dewey's reading in science led him to become interested in positivist approaches to philosophy and social analysis. He read August Comte "while an undergraduate—and undoubtedly got the idea of science as organized intelligence and the need for intelligent direction of social affairs from Comte." Davis Dewey also was interested in Comte and positivism, and the two brothers often talked about social analysis.

The curriculum of the senior year at the University of Vermont "included courses in political economy, international law, history of civilization (Guizot), psychology, ethics, philosophy of religion, . . . logic, etc."—that is, "serious intellectual topics of wide and deep significance—an introduction into the world of ideas." It was the senior year with its special opportunities toward which Dewey was striving.

Dewey was correct in assigning the origin of his interest in philosophy to T. H. Huxley and his other scientific reading. Following his reading of *Elements of Physiology* in his senior year, his interest in philosophy grew. His library borrowings in his senior year included books by Richard Hooker, George Berkeley, Edmund Burke, John Stuart Mill on William Hamilton, David Hume, Plato, Schwegler's *Handbook of the History of Philosophy*, and additional volumes of the *Journal of Speculative Philosophy*.

John's concentration on philosophy was not surprising. Since 1826 when James Marsh had been inaugurated as its fifth president, the University of Vermont had been regarded as the preeminent academic center in America for the study of philosophy. Marsh was one of the first persons in the United States to introduce German thought— Kant, Schelling, and Herder—into American intellectual life. His bridge to German idealism came through Coleridge. "Though I have read a part of the works of Kant," Marsh wrote to Coleridge, "I am indebted to your own writings for the ability to understand what I have read." Marsh brought transcendentalism into American thought by editing an edition of Coleridge's *Aids to Reflection* in the hope, he said, "that [it] will help to place the lovers of truth and righteousness on better philosophic grounds." He then went further and translated Herder's treatise on *The Spirit of Hebrew Poetry*.

A decade after he was admitted to college, Dewey recalled that "the University of Vermont . . . used to rest its fame mostly on its teaching of philosophy, which was that of Coleridge, never having bowed the knee to the Baal of Locke or the Scotch school." Dewey read an essay that had been published by Marsh in the *North American Review* in 1822 while Marsh was still teaching at the famous Andover Seminary. Here Marsh allied himself with the "romantic" school of philosophy, opposing the classic, and therefore enrolling his efforts on the side of the moderns. More than fifty years later, in 1929, Dewey returned to a reconsideration of Marsh's piece in a talk that he gave on "James Marsh and American Philosophy." He noted that Marsh's "readings in the scientific literature of his day were wide and influenced his speculations." As Dewey understood him, Marsh modified Kant by way of Aristotle and Newtonian physics to arrive at the conclusion that space and time are not merely, as Kant argued, mental forms but "forms of actual and external things of nature." The received real, Marsh believed, could be distinguished from acts of the mind, and the "rational psychology" that he developed was there, in the still active philosophic tradition of the University of Vermont, for Dewey to take the next step to a naturalistic psychology. But he did not yet understand how to do that.

Later in life, Dewey often was asked by those who knew little about the American transcendental movement if he had been influenced by Emerson. His answers were always a bit tepid, surprisingly so to most of those who inquired. Although he did read Emerson's essays while he was in college, there were two reasons that Emerson had little impact on Dewey. The first was cultural: Emerson had made a break with his Congregational background and was not a great favorite in Dewey's milieu. The second was much more important. In

Dewey's eyes, Marsh, not Emerson, was *the* transcendentalist. To this philosophically inclined Vermonter, Marsh's technical reach in philosophy went far beyond Emerson's. It was no wonder that when Dewey named the work by Emerson that he admired most, it was not the essays or other works that contemporaries regarded as characteristically Emersonian, but the late psychological work, *The Natural History of the Intellect*, in which Emerson's position was most akin to Marsh's of a few decades earlier. Marsh's work stayed in Dewey's memory for a long time.

Herbert Schneider, one of Dewey's students at Columbia and later a colleague, recalled that when he started on his history of American philosophy, Dewey "handed me a volume [Marsh's *Memoir and Remains*], with the remark, 'This was very important to me in my early days and is still worth reading.' " On another occasion when Columbia's philosophy department held a birthday party for Dewey at the famous old Lafayette Restaurant, his admirers presented him with a copy of Marsh's edition of *Aids to Reflection*:

> He was obviously pleased; said he hadn't seen the book for many years; . . . it was still dear to him. Then he began reminiscing a bit, contrary to his usual habits. He said Marsh and Coleridge were emancipating spirits to him and to his generation. They conceived the spirit as a form of life, the essence of life, and they freed belief in the spiritual energies from the doctrines both of the churches and of the Enlightenment: spirit and reflection were the traits of free living; both became intimately associated with actual life and natural being. Then he said: "My ideas on religion have not changed since then; I still believe that a religious life is one that takes the continuity of ideal and real, of spirit and life, seriously, not necessarily piously. Such 'common faith' became a commonplace fact for me. But I soon discovered that nobody had much interest either in Coleridge or in my idea of religion, and so I kept quiet about it." It was a basic conviction of Dewey's that religion should not be institutionalized any more than life itself could be institutionalized.

An advanced thinker, Marsh commenced his course on philosophy with a discussion of physiology and psychology. Indeed, he wrote eleven chapters of an uncompleted work entitled "Remarks on Psychology." An educational innovator as well, he opposed instruction in which "rules were . . . too limited and inflexible," insisting that "the business of education is to develop the mind, and to make it conscious of its own powers." Joseph Torrey's edition of Marsh's *Memoir* was assigned in one of Dewey's philosophy courses, and it seems clear that Marsh's ideas about philosophy, psychology, physiology, and education were part of the seedbed of Dewey's earliest intellectual progress in philosophy.

More personally influential was Dewey's teacher in mental and moral philosophy, Professor H. A. P. Torrey, himself the nephew of Marsh's editor, Joseph Torrey, a philosopher who became the president of the university from 1862 to 1866. H. A. P. Torrey, a Congregational minister, was wholly in the liberal camp of Congregationalism. He had been a "very active" member of Dewey's church since 1868, the year that he resigned his ministerial post at Vergennes to replace Joseph Torrey in the chair of philosophy at the university. Dewey described H. A. P. Torrey as "a man [with a] genuinely sensitive and cultivated mind, with marked esthetic interest and taste . . . he was an excellent teacher, and I owe him a . . . debt, that of turning my thoughts definitely to the study of philosophy as a life-pursuit." The texts Torrey assigned in the classes that Dewey took were to some degree remnants of his uncle's course—Marsh's *Memoir*, Noah Porter's *Elements of Intellectual Science*, and Joseph Torrey's *A Theory of Fine Art*—but in his private preferences Torrey went well beyond these. A few decades earlier, Marsh approached Kant chiefly through Coleridge, but Torrey was well acquainted with Kant and combined Kantian idealism with Scottish intuitionalism, placing prime importance on the moral significance of the emotions. "Thanks to my introduction under your auspices to Kant at the beginning of my studies," Dewey wrote to Torrey, "I think I have had a much better introduction into phil. than could be had any other way. . . . It certainly introduced a revolution into all my thoughts, and at the same time gave me a basis for my other reading and thinking."

Torrey had no interest whatsoever in politics, but Dewey did. At the same time he was reading Scotch Common Sense philosophy and American intuitionalism with Torrey, on his own he was making his way to the English idealists, especially T. H. Green and Edward Caird. He and his brother Dave both came at these through their critiques of individualistic economics and politics. Especially important to him as an undergraduate was Harriet Martineau's translation of Auguste Comte's positivist sociology and Edward Caird's book on Comte. From Comte, John first got the idea that science is organized intelligence and that sociology is the scientific investigation of social affairs. Thus at his University of Vermont commencement when Dewey was chosen to deliver the student oration, he selected the subject "The Limits of Political Economy."

John and Dave took the same classes and read and discussed the same books, especially those dealing with political philosophy, analysis of society, and political economy. If John had not been so influenced by Torrey, he might have gone in Dave's direction into some study of social life. And if Dave had found what John did in Torrey, he might have gone into philosophy. But in college, neither had yet settled on a vocation, and they both drifted for a while before choosing a career.

Had John Dewey not experienced the conflicts that are nearly inevitable for the replacement child; had his parents had a more harmonious marriage; had he been brought up in a faith about which no controversy existed; had his experience in school been unambiguous; or had he had a solid, single goal in life, he would still have experienced the stresses felt by every adolescent. But these other complications gave him additional burdens. Perhaps no one who had suffered these conflicts could have resolved them by the age of nineteen when Dewey graduated from college. He ranked second in his class of eighteen and was elected to Phi Beta Kappa, with a cumulative grade point average of 86 percent.

By the time he graduated, Dewey had not reconciled the historical, emotional, spiritual, and intellectual crises of his early years. Rather, he was more conflicted than ever. He was full of dualisms, and his philosophical studies only added more conflicts to his internal life. Self and others, personal morality and social good, pessimism and optimism, piety or reform—on these were piled the philosophical dualisms of God and the world, idealism and materialism, intuition and reason, faith and science, the infinite and finite, the soul and society, spirit and sense, or soul and body. From any move that he made toward unity and commitment, he was called to its opposite, whose claims seemed equally persuasive.

For the reader wishing to understand Dewey's development, the principal importance of these conflicts, however they existed in the world or in philosophic speculation about it, was that they existed so pervasively in nineteen-year-old John Dewey. How could he rid himself of philosophic dualisms when he could not resolve his own conflicts? He tried to discern unity, but it lay beyond his grasp. Dewey acknowledged this to Joseph Ratner. His "dualisms," he wrote, "were not so much intellectual formulations as they were an emotional sense of restrictions and barriers." "There were a lot of dualisms, gaps, barriers, in my intellectual make-up," he wrote in another letter.

Dewey had two minds about everything. Nearly twenty, a college graduate, his thoughts and motives, his whole being, went in so many directions that he couldn't take a step. He had no vocation. He had no job. He had no destination. He was a bundle of dualisms. He didn't know where to go.

Consequently, he went nowhere. Or rather, he went to what must have seemed the ultimate nowhere to this Vermont boy: Oil City, Pennsylvania.

A CAREER IN TEACHING?

Oil City was Burlington's worst nightmare. All the social and cultural ills that came to Burlington with river commerce were underscored in Oil City. Before the lumber trade boomed, Burlington had been a relatively established town with a settled population, a university, and stable churches. Oil City, however, was a town created by an oil boom that had begun less than thirty years before Dewey's arrival there.

Oil City got its name from its trade. When oil was discovered in Pennsylvania in the 1850s, Oil City was born at the confluence of the Allegheny River and the newly named Oil Creek. This was the area of the highest production of oil, with up to fifteen million barrels a day shipped out of Oil City. It had the development and the character of any boom town. The oil men came first—transients, toughs, teamsters, quick-buck guys. Tents went up for housing. Then came the oil paraphernalia—drills and derricks. Next the storage and shipping facilities were constructed—oil basins, warehouses, wharves, then docks, sailors, boatmen, muscle men. The wharves stretched out for nearly a mile around the point. Then came the flatboatmen to float the bulk oil down in barrels to Pittsburgh for refining. Prostitutes and con-men followed. The big money was always there—investors, brokers, speculators, frauds, gamblers, those who preyed on the oil, and those who preyed on the oil men. This was where John D. Rockefeller created Standard Oil by driving out all the small-fry producers. The Oil City Exchange was opened in 1878. Next came the construction of a town, board houses thrown up in a day, hardly better than tumbledown shacks; makeshift facilities brought sanitation problems. Then moneyed managers and owners built better houses and demanded some gentility. Sheriffs were hired. Finally came wives, which meant children, followed by schools and a few churches, an Oil City Opera House, a thin fringe of civilization scattered among the drilling rigs, set in mud and barely holding its own amid the frenzied finance. The population had swelled to nearly eight thousand by the time John Dewey arrived.

He had sat out the summer after graduation waiting for someone to hire him and tell him what to do. And when no job had come his way by late September, he took a job teaching high school in Oil City. This job was a favor from a cousin, Affia Wilson, the principal of the Oil City High School, which had been established only four years earlier when Oil City's new moneyed elite demanded that their children be provided a high-school education. When Dewey arrived, the school occupied a brick building whose construction had been completed only in the previous year. The large building on Central Avenue could have accommodated a couple of hundred students, but during the two years that Dewey taught there, only forty-five students attended and nineteen graduated. For forty dollars a month he became the assistant principal and taught algebra, natural sciences, and Latin.

Dewey was almost twenty when classes began. He knew Greek and Latin and French and a little German but nothing about girls. He later told his wife that before he fell in love with her, he had felt a "youthful ardour" for a cousin. He was more forthright with his student Max Eastman: "I tried to work up a little affair with my cousin [Affia Wilson] when I was nineteen. . . . I thought something ought to be done. But I couldn't do it. I was too bashful. I was abnormal." If he hadn't been so shy, he might have lived out his life as a high-school teacher in Oil City, married to Affia Wilson.

With little to satisfy him in his teaching, with only a few acquaintances and no friends in the town, with no ability to form an intimate relation with a woman, what was Dewey to do? He would do what he had always done—withdraw into himself and entertain himself with his own thoughts. In this case, there is plenty of evidence that this is precisely what he did. Dewey lived at a boarding house in South Oil City, across the street from the Y.M.C.A. One of the other boarders, E. V. D. Selden, then a young member of the Oil Exchange, remembered him. Dewey, he said, was "studious, serious, and reserved. At the table, he was not talkative and did not socialize much with the other boarders. Dewey read in his room at night and appeared to be absorbed with his thoughts when the boarders dined." Selden told a story about an April Fool's joke in which Dewey was served pancakes made of a woolly material. Absentmindedly he tried to eat them. "John did not join in the laughter . . . and was not amused in the least," Selden remembered. He and others advised the young teacher to invest part of his salary in a new Oil City company, John D. Rockefeller's Standard Oil. But Dewey showed no interest.

Perhaps in this boarding house story Dewey cut a somewhat comic figure, a sort of Ichabod Crane. But away from his parents and seeking something inside himself on which he could rely, he made personal breakthroughs with regard to two areas of his discontent: his Christianity and his vocation. The time he spent in Oil City came at just the right time. These years gave him a moratorium, a relaxation of the pressures that he could not resolve at home. He started to become himself; and his old conflicts, arising from outside himself, started to fall away. His mother's old query about whether he was "right with Jesus" still haunted him when he arrived in Oil City. As he put it, he was still uncertain about his "spiritual sincerity" when he prayed. Then one night in Oil City, he told Max Eastman, he suddenly experienced a feeling of harmony with existence, an unquestioning confidence in the adequacy of his spiritual well-being. Eastman saw it as a "mystical experience," but it was not mystical. "There was no vision, not even a definable emotion—just a supremely blissful feeling that his worries were over." Such an experience comes out of the self and signals an internal solution to a long-standing problem. He had finally answered his mother's question. Dewey told Eastman: "I've never had any doubts since then, nor any beliefs. To me faith means not worrying.... I claim I got religion and that I got it that night in Oil City." Once the question of personal sincerity was answered, he could enjoy the intellectual and social remains of liberal Congregationalism without conflict. He was right with Jesus because he was right with himself.

The other problem that he had not yet reconciled was that of a vocation. Still, he was teaching now, and teaching seemed to be something he could do. The nights he spent in his room began to lead to a solution of that problem, too. True to the purposefulness of his parental training, he was reading dutifully in his room, but with a difference. No one told him what to read. There was no course schedule. He had no assignments. He would receive no grades. He didn't have to live for anyone else, please anyone else, compensate for anyone else. There was nothing he had to read, no idea he had to think, no thought he was obliged to pursue except what arose out of his own desires, so far as he was able to discern them.

He was thinking most about a subject related to resolving his spiritual struggles. Once these were set right, a philosophic subject opened up for him. He started to think about writing an article. The metaphysical assumptions of materialism may not seem to be a subject to stir one's soul, but it stirred Dewey's. Having resolved the personal issue of faith, Dewey settled into the idea that religion is a mental and social good. Although contemporary discussions of materialism left no place for Christianity, Dewey was bent on preserving what he had saved. His way of doing so was not to prove the validity of Christianity but to attack the assumptions of materialism. He entitled his article "The Metaphysical Assumptions of Materialism." Through straightforward logical analysis, he showed that the primary assumption of materialism—the monism of matter—was contradicted by the underlying secondary assumption "that the ultimate form of matter has dualistic 'mind' and 'matter' properties." If matter was associated with mind, Dewey concluded, this contradiction would be "suicidal" for materialists. Nothing could have better stated his personal case than the dichotomy between his own wish for internal unity and the fact of his dual-mindedness about everything. In attacking the materialists, he stated his own problem.

Part of his critique of materialism reads like the books he had taken out of the University of Vermont library:

> If there be no knowledge of substance as such, there is . . . only knowledge of . . . phenomena entirely unrelated to any substance whatever (Humean scepticism), or of those related only to objective spirit (Berkeleian idealism), or of those related to an unknown and unknowable substance (H. Spencer), or of thought brought into unity by the forms of knowledge which the mind necessarily imposes on all phenomena given in consciousness (as Kant).

Dewey developed these ideas in a short intuitionalistic essay. He sent it to W. T. Harris, the editor of the *Journal of Speculative Philosophy*, the leading philosophical journal in the United States and one that Dewey had read as an undergraduate. Harris was a sophisticated thinker and one of the few philosophers in the United States who was not a clergyman. Nationally, he was the best known of the St. Louis school of Hegelians. At this time, Dewey knew scarcely anything about Hegel.

But Harris's spiritualized "Right" Hegelianism gave Dewey the direction he was seeking. Dewey was a theist who accepted Hegelianism because it "rendered creation and providential oversight rational instead of merely supernatural events."

For Dewey to have sent his first philosophic article to Harris was a bold move. Just a few weeks before he was to leave Oil City, he began to resolve the issue of his vocation. If Harris approved of his work, he would become a philosopher. Dewey wrote:

> Enclosed you will find a short article on the Metaphysical Assumptions of Materialism, which I should be glad if you could make use of in your Review. . . .
>
> I suppose you must be troubled with many inquiries of this sort, yet if it would not be too much to ask, I should be glad to know your opinion on it, even if you make no use of it. . . .
>
> An opinion of as to whether you considered it to show ability enough of any kind to warrant my putting much of my time on that sort of subject would be thankfully received, and, as I am a young man in doubt as to how to employ my reading hours, might be of much advantage.

Dewey's new confidence must have been evident. One of his high-school pupils, J. Berrell Porterfield, told his family that Mr. Dewey "was a brilliant man" and "too big to stay here." After two years of teaching in Oil City, he left in 1881.

For now, he went back to Burlington to think further philosophic thoughts and to await Harris's reply. But first there was the problem of a job. Back in Burlington, he accepted a job teaching in a high-school academy in Charlotte, Vermont. Since the job would not start until January, he would be free for six months. He decided to read philosophy and study philosophic German with his college teacher, H. A. P. Torrey, for Dewey now was determined to try to make a career as a philosopher. He had already asked W. T. Harris to give him an opinion about his philosophic capabilities. But Harris, as Dewey already knew, was very slow to answer his mail. Torrey took him under his wing as Dewey's first real mentor, the first man who believed in him. Yet it was clear to Dewey that true philosophic speculation troubled Torrey because it threatened to conflict with the religious faith so important to him. Torrey's timidity provided a powerful cautionary lesson, and even as Dewey was taking lessons from him, he was preparing to go beyond his teacher as a philosophic experimentalist.

One of the earliest books that Torrey recommended they study was Spinoza's *Ethics*. By October, after nearly three months of study, Dewey wrote an article on Spinoza's pantheism. Harris had still not rendered an opinion about Dewey's qualifications for a philosophic career, but Dewey was already quite ready to make his own decision, and he sent the Spinoza article to Harris, accompanied by a note that struck a tone entirely different from his first tentative, uncertain letter of a few months earlier. Now he sounds confident and professional:

Enclosed you will find some thoughts upon *Spinoza's Pantheism*, tending to show its inadequacy as a theory of knowledge. As they seem to me to bring out one or two things commonly overlooked in criticisms of Spinoza, I send it to you thinking perhaps you may find it a suitable article for your journal.

Like his first submission to the *Journal of Speculative Philosophy*, this article had a very personal origin and reflected his relationship to Torrey. Torrey had confessed to him, "Undoubtedly pantheism is the most satisfactory form of metaphysics intellectually, but it goes counter to religious faith." This comment, Dewey remarked, "told of an inner conflict" in Torrey "that prevented his native capacity from coming to full fruition." In "The Pantheism of Spinoza" Dewey side-stepped Torrey's impasse by asserting that Spinoza's pantheism was itself epistemologically inadequate. So, he concluded, Torrey was wrong about the suitability of pantheism as a basis for metaphysics.

Dewey always went beyond his teachers. He would adopt a mentor, absorb his ideas, and then attempt to supersede him. It was a solution he had learned from his father. It had its benefits, for Dewey would never really be anyone's disciple for long, but it also had its shortcomings, for it tended to drive Dewey into negative solutions, or reactions against mentors, which cut him loose from the teachers who had supported him.

The day after Dewey mailed his Spinoza article to Harris, the editor's response finally arrived. Harris accepted Dewey's article on materialism for publication and encouraged him to think of a career in philosophy. "Thanks for your favorable opinion," Dewey wrote back to Harris, adding that he expected no pay for either of the articles he had sent. Years later Dewey remarked to William James that "by some sort of instinct, & by the impossibility of my doing anything in particular, I was led into philosophy & into 'idealism.' "

Harris led him to both. Five years later, when Dewey published his first book, *Psychology*, he acknowledged to Harris what he had felt in 1881:

When I sent you my first article for the J. S. P. I was a school teacher with not much time for work of that sort. But I ventured to ask you your opinion of it. Your very kind judgment turned the scale in favor of a plan which I had been considering but rather feared by my own ability to carry through—the special study of philosophy with a view to teaching it. So in one sense you are a progenitor.

Dewey's plan to pursue a career in philosophy was indeed audacious at this time, and he needed a good deal of inner conviction of his own in addition to Harris's encouragement. Until this time, nearly all academic professors of philosophy in America had been clergymen, and many of them exhibited the same sorts of conflict and restraints as Torrey had between religious faith and philosophic speculation. Dewey never intended to study for the ministry. Harris's journal, Dewey wrote, was "the only philosophic journal in the country at that time," and Harris and his group of St. Louis Hegelians were among the few laymen devoted to philosophy for nontheological reasons. Torrey's philosophy went as far as Kant, while Harris was the country's leading Hegelian. Dewey read Harris's voluminous work, one sentence taking him a decade to understand, even though it influenced him all that time. Eventually, Dewey acknowledged to Harris: "When I was first studying the German Philosophers I read something of yours on them of which one sentence has always remained with me—you spoke of the 'great *psychological* movement from Kant to Hegel.'"

"The remark," Dewey said, "was rather a mystery to me at the time." His attempt to unravel it worked its way into Dewey's Ph.D. dissertation on Kant's psychology, as well as into several articles, and found its final expression in Dewey's first book. Accordingly, through this casual remark, Harris became Dewey's second teacher. Harris was a prolific writer, the author of nearly five hundred publications. Above all, he was interested in the crucial problem of the second half of the nineteenth century: education. He was, one scholar wrote, "the preeminent figure in the world of education" in this period, becoming the national educational commissioner in Washington, D.C. Personally and as an exemplary figure, Harris brought Dewey first to Hegel and then to the field of education. Hegel remained an influence for a long time, and Dewey never abandoned Harris's conviction that a socially humanistic education was essential to the maintenance and extension of democracy.

Harris's group was not the only independent school of philosophic thought in America at that time. Another philosophic group then operating outside the academies was Thomas Davidson's School of Philosophy and Culture Sciences, with a summer outpost first in Farmington, Connecticut, and then, in the 1880s, in Keene, New York. Davidson was a close friend of William James and the mentor of Morris Cohen. With Davidson, serious laypersons were studying philosophy without seeking degrees. Dewey spent many summers in Hurricane in the Adirondacks. He built a cabin near Hurricane Mountain in 1891 and spent most of his summers there until 1907, lecturing and discussing philosophy. One of the problems in forming a serious philosophic fellowship in America was the vastness of the country. Widely separated in space, philosophers could find no easy way to congregate and talk to one another. Davidson's summer school provided that by establishing a center in which many of the leading intellectuals of the time could congregate. William James, Felix Adler, and W. T. Harris made long visits here in the summer. Years later, Dewey's friend and contemporary Max Otto described the feeling of exultation that young secular thinkers began to feel around this time: "What a grand period it was. . . . Those were *men* who in those days engaged in the philosophic enterprise." Dewey would have agreed.

But Dewey wanted a paying job, and for this he needed a degree, for he did not have the financial resources that would enable him to study philosophy for its own sake. Dewey could scarcely hope to pursue a philosophic career as a teacher in a high school. Besides, he had to admit that he had very few of the talents required of a high-school teacher. He had succeeded only moderately well at his post in Oil City, and just as he had there, he had trouble maintaining discipline at the Lake View Seminary in Charlotte, Vermont. By June, the townspeople who had organized the Lake View Seminary to educate the local children were glad to see him depart, judging him to be below average as a teacher, and Dewey was just as glad to go.

No matter how many articles he placed in the *Journal of Speculative Philosophy*, the only way Dewey would get a job in a university would be by getting an advanced degree, a doctorate that might be the modern equivalent of a degree in theology, as a qualification to teach philosophy in America. Another possibility was to go abroad to study. In England and on the Continent, philosophy was flourishing in the universities and was being taught by secular scholars inspired by the rise of science. Philosophers were looking to biology, geology, and chemistry for hints about human thought; they were working in laboratories. Friedrich Überweg had written his important *History of Philosophy*. Americans were going to Germany to study psychology with Wilhelm Wundt or neo-Kantian and neo-Aristotelian thought with F. A. Trendelenburg or were traveling to England to be tutored by Bernard Bosanquet and others.

But that choice was not available to Dewey because he did not have the financial resources to spend two or three years as a peripatetic philosopher in Europe or England. Each in a different way, Lucina and Archibald had taught him to make his own life and to depend on himself. His parents and especially his mother's affluent relatives could have given him the money he needed. But no one, least of all John Dewey, considered this proposition.

If he could not go to Europe, he still might be able to collect enough money to go to Baltimore to study philosophy at the one and only school in America that was based on German principles, Johns Hopkins University. This new school and its new president, Daniel Coit Gilman, were dedicated to bringing scientific research into graduate study in the United States. Even Baltimore itself was reputed to be a little fragment of Germany that had resettled on the eastern seaboard. Dewey remembered it this way: "The distinctive traditions and customs of the American college are unknown [in Baltimore]. Were one to ask where college life [in Johns Hopkins] was centered, he would be pointed to a little club room where students and teachers meet to drink German beer, and sing German songs."

The young philosophers of Dewey's generation were making philosophy into a new scientific discipline. Many of them believed that a new way of looking at the world was just around the corner and that those who ran fastest would find it first. Dewey, as it turned out, would run the fastest of all, but that was by no means apparent as yet. He had been teaching for barely a month at Lake View Seminary when he learned that Johns Hopkins was offering twenty graduate fellowships of $500 each. Dewey wanted to win one, and his mentor Torrey offered to help. In the second week of February 1882 Torrey wrote to one of the professors of philosophy at Hopkins, George S. Morris, seeking his assistance in securing a fellowship for Dewey: "While in college he showed a decided aptitude for philosophy, and since his graduation he has made it his special study. With a marked predilection for metaphysics, Mr. Dewey seems to me to possess in a rare degree the mental qualities requisite for its successful pursuit."

Dewey had every hope of receiving one of the coveted fellowships from Hopkins. At the age of twenty-two he had had an article accepted by the leading American journal of the new philosophy, and he had already submitted another. In the winter of 1882 he started work on a third article, "Knowledge and the Relativity of Feeling," in which, at the very outset of his career, he declared himself to be an advocate of Darwin's theory of evolution and insisted on the validity of objective experience. Increasingly confident, he offered to help Harris edit the journal, and he even declared himself already competent enough in philosophic German to translate the works of contemporary German philosophers for the journal. And finally, well aware of Harris's commitment to Hegel, he asserted that he too had plunged into Hegel and claimed to have reached a perfect understanding of his work. "I have been reading recently K. Rosenkranz's brief introduction to Kirchmann's ed. of Hegel's Encyclopädie, which seems to bring out clearly both Hegel's relation to Kant & his own leading principles. If you desire, I should be glad to send a translation." Dewey was moving so quickly that he did not wait for Harris's response but went ahead and translated Rosenkranz's introduction, which Harris added to the July issue of the *Journal of Speculative Philosophy*.

Harris wrote to say that Dewey's first two articles were about to appear: "Expect to print your article on Materialism in the Apr. no J. of P., & w'd like to put the Spinoza article in Notes & Disc. July." Here, then, was good support for Dewey's fellowship application to Johns Hopkins. But in the summer's announcements of grantees, Dewey's name did not appear. Gilman was the sole judge of the recipients, and in retrospect it appears that Dewey had gone about his application in exactly the wrong way. A letter from a clergyman, Torrey, and especially one stressing Dewey's metaphysical talents, was not likely to impress Gilman, with his scientific enthusiasm. Support from George Morris, who taught at Hopkins one semester a year and was himself a clergyman, may only have reinforced the impression that Dewey was a genteel Christian, not a Hopkins type. Dewey's article on the limitations of materialism may have sealed the impression.

One of Dewey's great personal qualities was perseverance. Undeterred by his failure, he immediately wrote to Gilman to request a $300 presidential scholarship. He was anxious, he told Gilman, to "continue my studies in Philosophy and Psychology." Although he knew little about psychology beyond Herbert Spencer's work, he was aware that at Hopkins, psychology formed part of the philosophy curriculum and fit in well with the emphasis in the school on experimental research. He continued to Gilman: "I would not make the request [of a scholarship] if I were not so situated pecuniarily as to make it almost impossible to go on without aid." Then, with a new inner security that suggests his increasing ability to see beyond his inner crisis and conflicts, Dewey added: "I feel confident that if I were to secure that aid, I could render a good account . . . of myself." As proof, he told Gilman that he had read over the list of books recommended to prospective graduate students in philosophy as suitable preparation for the coming year: "I have read almost all the books. . . . And others, more than an equivalent for those which I have not." The Department of Philosophy had three emphases, and Dewey covered all bases by applying to study in all three, "History of Philosophy, Psychology, and Logic."

Dewey had pressed the right buttons, but Gilman was not impressed. (In fact, he never was much impressed by Dewey, and he also refused aid to Thorstein Veblen.) Again, he rejected Dewey's application. But Dewey had made up his mind: he *would* go to Hopkins. His aunt Sarah Rich in Richville had promised him that if all else failed, she would lend him $500. He accepted her offer and sent in his application for admission. (He repaid this loan, about $50 at a time.) Only days before the fall term of 1882 began, he received word that he had been admitted. Promptly, on September 4, he wrote to Gilman to accept the offer. In those days the president of a university involved himself in all aspects of its life, and Dewey also asked Gilman for information "regarding board—places, prices, &c—that would help me on arriving there?" Before a reply could come back, he started out for Baltimore and a university culture whose spirit would influence his whole professional career.

A CAREER IN PHILOSOPHY?

He traveled to Baltimore by a circuitous route, passing through West Point, New York, in order to visit his younger brother, Charles Miner Dewey, who was a freshman at the U.S. Military Academy there. Partly, this visit represented his ties to the family even as he was leaving it. Partly, it was Dewey acting like the older brother whom he had replaced and also substituting for a father who by now was in his seventies. But it mostly reflected the concern that everyone in the family had for Charles Miner. He had never gotten the attention from Lucina that her other children received, and already Charles seemed to be a lost child—easily fatigued and easily discouraged, struggling at school, and having few reserves of confidence. Both Lucina and Archibald wrote to John to thank him for this encouraging visit to Charles, for they both feared "lest he grow discouraged, as he is now *en*couraged." Charles needed constant encouragement, but as it would turn out, no amount of encouragement would be enough. He never succeeded at anything; the successes of his two older brothers discouraged rather than inspired him. His admission to West Point was the high point of his success. The family already was pessimistic about his future.

Charley found the academy "monotonous." In June 1883 he failed math and placed last in his class, and on June 24, 1884, he was discharged from the academy. After leaving West Point he returned to Burlington where he followed what Lucina called "his willful way" and got into debt. Lucina told him that if he did "not turn squarely around," she would put him out of the house and he would "have to board himself." She was perplexed about how to deal with him, sometimes thinking to leave him to heaven and then worrying about his inaction:

> when I see the plainest duties of morality disregarded by C—
> & know he is only going further & further away from the right
> & making it harder for himself I ask, my self is *this* right, & can
> I expect God, to send the blessings of a new heart, when I take
> no step which a responsible person ought to take. . . . I am at
> my wit's end, Father's patience sometimes gives out & I do not
> dare trust advice given in the spirit of impatience.

This early in John's life Lucina was asking him to be wise, wiser than his father or his older brother, Dave. She confessed to him that she believed he understood Charley better than she did, "& know that what I want . . . is his best good, reformation & not his punishment." But

Charley didn't go to church to hear the healing gospel, and "his reading is the trashiest kind of stories which I know he is ashamed of as he keeps them in the drawer." He also went "to the opera house, *very often*." Given past evidences of his cheating, too, Lucina was worried that he would "run into open dishonesty." Or would his complete degradation be "God's way of bringing him to his right mind"? She begged John to write him, to be his "Helper and Friend," to urge Charley to "let Christ come into" his life and to pray for her and Archibald as well as Charley. But John didn't know any more than his mother did about how to rescue Charley. The youngest son of Lucina and Archibald drifted away from Vermont, ended up in Oregon, married, occasionally sent a letter to John, and died in 1926.

In 1882, all the boys had moved away from home. Davis was teaching in the Hyde Park High School in Illinois. He was taking classes in Hebrew and teaching Latin and Greek. Like Charles, he was uncertain about his prospects and wrote to John that he was "taking [life] . . . as it comes for the present." John Dewey had lived away from home for two school years in Oil City, but now he was really alone for the first time, for even his residence in Oil City had been associated with a member of the family. He had taught in Charlotte for the spring semester but went back to Burlington every weekend. Now he was going to a strange city, where he knew no one. No sooner had he left than the whole family seemed worried about him. His aunt in Richville sent him another installment of the money she was lending him: "I had wanted to hear of your plans, what you were deciding to do, &c, &c, I felt sorry that we had not talked more on this subject, in fact was rather troubled lest I had given foolish and hasty advice." His mother asked, "Have you met any of the Professors? Your letter from West Pt. was *very* satisfactory. . . . Remember you cannot be too explicit or minute in your letters. Wish I knew everything all the time about you. . . . Good bye my dear son. Be careful of yourself—." His father soon joined the chorus of concern, remarking on more practical matters but not entirely concealing his worries: "We rejoiced some over the fact of your safe arrival. Let me say here & now, compel them to give a muskeetoe bar to your bed: the 'Euta House' should be indicted for 'musketoecide' for putting a man unprotected into the power of

Southern Cannibals." Finally, Archibald enclosed a group letter from Dewey's female cousins expressing the hope that "you will find your quarters agreeable and the weather not too warm for comfort."

The Euta House where he boarded in Baltimore was located at 66 Saratoga Street. He settled down there, presumably with a mosquito netting, and began classes while a flurry of letters continued to rain down on him all fall. His mother nearly always closed her letters: "Good bye my dear son—be careful of yourself. Mother." Lucina urged him to write every day, and when she did not receive a letter, she worried. Even as late as February, in his second semester, the absence of a letter from him caused panic in the family:

> My dear John, What is the reason we do not hear from you? Not a word this week. Have you taken any precautions with regard to small pox? If you have not, will you . . . *please* to do so *at once*? Do not think dear John that it is any light matter and laugh it off—your landlady's ideas are no doubt good as far as they go, but do not cover the whole ground. Dirt is not the *only* evil in the world, Carlyle & your landlady to the contrary.

Lucina was concerned not only about John but also about Charles's academic difficulties and about Dave, who was doubtful in his faith, even though he sometimes thought of studying for the clergy. Lucina complained to John that in the last month she had had only one letter from Dave: "I need not say how it hurts, to have him so silent," she told John. Meanwhile, both Dave and Charley were writing to John, mostly about things that Lucina would not have wanted to hear. Dave confessed:

> I have been laboring . . . [under] mental exhaustion for about three weeks. Head trouble again. . . . so I just sleep an ever-lasting amount and read none but what is necessary. . . . Haven't said any of this to those at home, as it just worries them needlessly. . . . It almost convinces me however that I can do no professional work in life.

By contrast, Dave believed that John's "success is now . . . well assured." Charley was writing to John that he was failing in his studies: "French is hard and long," he said, and kept him up to eleven or twelve at night to finish. He had barely passed algebra in the fall; he was having difficulty with geometry now, and a little later he declared himself "wofully ignorant" in "trig. & analytics." Charley, too, predicted that John would soon be a "Prof. at Johns Hopkins. . . . I wish you all the highest success & feel sure that you will reach it too." Clearly, John had to bear the mantle of the family success. He was assigned to "rescue" Dave, which he did by encouraging him to become a graduate student at Hopkins in the fall of 1883. But Charles was beyond saving. Writing to John in May 1883, his father acknowledged, "I shudder to think what failure would do for him." Charley never recovered.

By early October of his first year John Dewey was able to sketch his impressions of Johns Hopkins for Professor Torrey, who, Archibald subsequently told John, "expressed much pleasure" in this letter:

> Things have just reached the point where it is possible to have & give some definite idea of them. They were rather slow about beginning, and even after they had nominally commenced it was some time before Prof. Morris' books and papers came so his first lectures were of a quite general character. But now we have settled down to work. My work under him is four hours a week in the history of Phil. in Great Britain—from Bacon to Spencer; and twice a week in the Philosophical Seminary, as it is called. The latter I think will, in many ways, be the more profitable. It is "for the study of texts, relating to the Science of Knowledge." The method of working is this. We begin by reading Plato's Theatetus (in translation) and along with it are given subjects relating to the matter suggested by the text—the writings of Heraclitus, Democritus, Protagoras &c—one subject is given to each & he is expected to look up the fragments that remain of that

author[']s writings, consult leading authorities &c, and then give an account of it before the class.—We then take up Aristotle's 'De Anima' & treat it in a similar manner. By the time of finishing we will be supposed to have a pretty good knowledge of Greek Phil. & from original sources as much as possible—at least of Gk. Phil. in so far as it relates to the origin, meaning &c of knowledge.

Dewey was learning from Morris what Morris had learned in Germany about the new philosophic method of instruction. Gilman had brought Morris to Hopkins to represent the scholarly study of the history of philosophy in relation to theory. Dewey, as it turned out, was the only graduate student in his class specializing in the history of philosophy, and so Morris's classes were of particular interest to him. As he wrote to Torrey,

> Prof. Morris, as one would judge from that article in the Princeton [Review], on Phil & its problems, is a pronounced idealist—and we have already heard of the "universal self." He says that idealism (substantial idealism, as opposed to subjectivistic, or agnosticism) is the only positive phil. that has or can exist.

In trying to explain Morris's ideas about the science of being to Torrey, Dewey stumbled over Morris's favorite terms but concluded correctly that for Morris subject and object "are in organic relation, neither having reality apart from the other. Being is within consciousness. And the result on the side of Science of Being is substantial idealism." This means, as Morris himself put it elsewhere, that as the study of organic wholes, philosophy was the "Science of Science itself."

Dewey was fascinated by Morris and his central aim of defending idealism as a science. He had been discussing these matters with him, for he already predicted that when Morris took up positivistic philosophy, his lectures would have a critical character. With the enthusiasm of the first-year graduate student, Dewey asked whether Torrey had seen Morris's work on Kant's *Critique of Pure Reason*, about which Morris's opinions were quite well developed.

Dewey's response to Morris showed the seriousness of his own aims. What he failed to reveal was even more important because it shows how far Dewey's own metaphysical dispositions and capacities had blinded him to other streams of philosophy and stuck him in idealistic controversies from which he found it difficult to extricate himself. One of Dewey's blind spots provides a good example of how much he missed and what his limitations were at this time. He mentioned Charles Sanders Peirce to Torrey:

> I am not taking the course in logic. The course is very mathematical, & by Logic, Mr. Peirce means only an account of the methods of physical sciences, put in mathematical form as far as possible. It's more of a scientific, than philosophical course. In fact, I think Mr. Peirce don't think there is any Phil. outside the generalizations of physical science.

But his inability to grasp Peirce's importance had one positive effect. If he did not register for Peirce's course, he would have to find a substitute, which pushed him outside the philosophy department and introduced him to social and political subjects. In the history and political science departments, he studied world history with Herbert Baxter Adams, and in another course he read Hegel's *Philosophy of History* with Morris. Morris's idealist emphasis on the unity of all knowledge, letters, and science as parts of one organic whole had a profound influence on Dewey, for he came to believe that being a philosopher meant unifying every discipline—history, literature, economics, political science, sociology, and anthropology—into one body of knowledge.

Dewey worked very hard to follow Morris's idealism and learn Bosanquet's logic, which Morris favored. He studied the eight public lectures that Morris delivered in the fall at the Union Theological Seminary in New York and at Hopkins under the general title of "Philosophy and Christianity." For Morris, who liked to talk of "the catholicity of science," science and religion were one, and he began to work out a neoidealist version of philosophy that could become the fountainhead of a "symmetrical and catholic culture . . . [fusing] Church and State, . . . science, literature and religion" and creating "leaders capable of recognizing the true ideals and of intelligently directing the nation's energies."

Dewey applied to his course work the ideals that Morris set forth in his teaching. In the spring semester he registered for the "seminary" in history and political science taught by Herbert Baxter Adams and Adams's course on comparative constitutional history. He listened to six lectures by the novelist George Washington Cable on a subject that would always be close to his heart, "The Relations of Literature to Modern Society," in which Cable stressed the reciprocal duties of literature and society. Most important, he registered for the advanced course in psychology taught by G. Stanley Hall, attending the class sessions four times weekly and also enrolling in the laboratory work of "observation and experiment." Dewey soon pronounced Hall's course "purely physiological" but thought Hall himself a "fine man & certainly a thorough master of psychology." Dewey designed two experiments on "attention," one of Hall's favorite topics. In one experiment, he tried to determine "what effect fixing attention upon one thing very strongly, has upon a 'remainder' in consciousness," while in a second experiment he considered "the effect attention has in producing involuntary muscular movements."

Dewey's relation to Hall was always troubled because Hall was competing with Morris for the unfilled chairmanship of the department. Gilman was testing both to see which (if either) fit better with the spirit of Hopkins. Most students chose Hall, as did Dewey's classmate James McKeen Cattell, who became a famous psychologist. It would not be easy to be a student of both—an idealist and an experimentalist—but Dewey tried.

One aspect of Hall's interest aroused special attention in Dewey. Hall was fascinated with the psychology of education, as were the European psychologists. During the spring of 1883, in addition to his classroom and laboratory work with Hall, Dewey attended Hall's eight public lectures, entitled "Principles and Methods of Intellectual Training." Hall began with practical observation: "Present educational needs and interests. The Methods of Pedagogy Illustrated by a systematic study of children in Boston Public Schools." Then he turned to such topics as the "training of attention and will" and the "study of language," topics that would engage Dewey himself for decades.

Dewey was so absorbed in his course work and so driven to succeed that he made few friends at Hopkins. But one, James McKeen Cattell, remained his friend for more than fifty years. "Who that has ever met John Dewey is not his friend?" Cattell asked. Dewey, on his part, envied Cattell's chance to have studied logic with Hermann Lotze at Göttingen, for Lotze was one of the logicians Dewey most admired at this time. In his second year, Dewey was given the fellowship first assigned to Cattell, and Cattell himself approved of the choice.

Dewey could become, at least temporarily, Hall's follower, since Morris spent only the fall semester at Hopkins. In the spring, Morris returned to the University of Michigan at Ann Arbor, where he had held a full-time position for several years before being invited to Hopkins. This made it a bit easier for Dewey to take advantage of both Morris and Hall, separately, in alternating semesters. With Morris back in Michigan, too, there was no one to teach the history of philosophy. Dewey had proved himself to be an apt pupil in the fall semester. His two articles had appeared in the *Journal of Speculative Philosophy* even before he arrived at Hopkins, and in December 1882 he delivered his paper "Knowledge and the Relativity of Feeling" to the Hopkins Metaphysical Club with Morris in attendance. Again, in this paper Dewey took the position of a critic of philosophers, especially of Spencer's sensationalism, and ended with his own defense of "self-consciousness" as the "true absolute." Since Dewey had proved himself to be a disciple of Morris, it was only natural that in Morris's absence he should occupy his position. At Morris's suggestion, this second-semester graduate student took over the guidance of undergraduate students in the history of philosophy course in the spring semester and was paid $150 for his instruction. He was a teacher at Hopkins!

Charley's prediction had already come true! John described the class to Torrey:

> Ueberweg's Hist. [in Morris' translation] is used as the text-book, omitting, of course, a good deal.—The object is to give them as much as possible a knowledge of what different phils. have held—as matter of fact, and not critically so that they will have at least a knowledge of some of the questions of phil. and the answers that have been given.

Dewey added modestly, "as I am the only [graduate student] . . . making a specialty of the hist. of phil. it was not such a very great honor." Two of Dewey's seven undergraduate students were also registered in Peirce's "Logic," and we can only wonder how they understood both courses to be part of the same discipline. After all, as Dewey wrote to W. T. Harris, Morris gave "special attention" to the "fact" of "the difference between mathematical & philosophic procedure and method" while Peirce took precisely the opposite position.

"It is a commonplace of educational history," Dewey later wrote, "that the opening of Johns Hopkins marked a new epoch in higher education in the United States." It also was important to his own history. Dewey's admission to Johns Hopkins and his rapid success there opened a door for him to a professional life. His success and his academic studies at Hopkins, however, did not help him resolve his personal conflicts and crises. Successful as he was on the surface, he remained as full of conflicts as ever, and if anything, the varied influences at Hopkins only exacerbated the demands on him of contradictory forces. Although he kept it well concealed, what Dewey faced at Hopkins left him, in his inner life, more muddled than ever; for the influences on him there mirrored the conflicts that he had started to resolve in Oil City and Charlotte but that now came back with renewed force. Represented in his graduate education by the differences among his teachers, the tentative resolutions that he had made flew apart and set him back where he had started, merely at a higher intellectual and thus at a more difficult emotional level. As he later said of himself, he was driven by "an intense emotional craving" for inner unity; but at this stage of his life he could seek satisfaction for emotional "hunger [only in] . . . an intellectualized subject-matter." In H. A. P. Torrey, he found a man who could briefly give him the semblance of emotional peace in galvanizing his intellectual life through a philosophic vocation. It was a narrowly focused intellectual unity, but it was something. At Hopkins he sought out other mentors who could teach him how to hold his fragments together, at least superficially. But it turned out that the longer he stayed there, the conflictual situation in the faculty and their ideas intensified his own intellectual questions and therefore renewed his interior irresolutions. We now look a little deeper into the influences claiming his attention and allegiance.

Dewey's Philosophic Influences

George Sylvester Morris was the first of Dewey's greatest influences. In 1877, when President Gilman invited Morris to give an annual series of public lectures—and, after a time, courses—at Johns Hopkins, it was because Gilman saw Morris as the leading research-oriented philosopher in America. Morris's 1872–73 translation of Überweg's *History of Philosophy*, Neil Coughlin remarked, was "one of the largest endeavors in pure scholarship [as] yet undertaken by an American philosopher." In addition, from Gilman's point of view, Morris had the "right" credentials: he had studied at the University of Halle with Hermann Ulrici and in Berlin with Friedrich A. Trendelenburg, then the most prominent philosophic mediator between empirical science and metaphysics. Given Morris's training by Trendelenburg, Gilman must have thought his new lecturer was an Aristotelian and thus a philosopher of science. Indeed, both Ulrici and Trendelenburg believed that philosophy was centrally engaged in an evolving investigation into the nature of truth itself and thus of all truths—in short, philosophy was not a metaphysic but a science. This is certainly what

Gilman expected to find in Morris, and Morris truly followed his teachers when he spoke about his belief in the "demonstrated," a "favorite word of his," Dewey recalled.

But Gilman had mistaken Morris's thought. Early in his life, Morris studied for the ministry at Union Theological Seminary, beginning at about the time that Dewey's earlier teacher, H. A. P. Torrey, had completed his studies there. Morris experienced a severe crisis of faith at the seminary. He abandoned his plan for a ministerial career and left Union after his second year to begin three years of philosophic study in Europe, chiefly in Germany. These years in turn left him so full of doubts that he considered abandoning his choice of philosophy as a profession and sought to be appointed a U.S. consul in some European city. In this hope he was also disappointed and arrived back in the United States with no aim and no job and was reduced to accepting a position as a tutor to the children of a wealthy New York banker. Only after two years did he find a position at the University of Michigan, not as a philosopher, but as a professor of modern languages and literature. During the next decade there, his biographer says, "he took little, if any, part in the general affairs of the university" and impressed students as "strange" or "queer." Evidently he had retreated from Trendelenburg's mediational logic and found himself unsure about both naturalism and metaphysics. His crisis of faith persisted into middle age and was still active when he began teaching at Hopkins.

From 1877 on, Morris divided his academic year, spending the fall semester at Hopkins and returning to Michigan for the spring. Then, hardly more than two years before John Dewey arrived at Johns Hopkins, Morris made a momentous discovery. Through the writings of the British philosopher Thomas Hill Green he discovered Hegel! Green and Hegel gave him a way of combining empiricism and idealism in the reconciling concept of Mind. In 1889, Dewey summarized what he had learned from Morris about Green and Hegel: "There is a principle, spiritual in nature, at the root of ordinary experience and science which is also the basis of ethics and religion . . . [and] any fair analysis of the conditions of science will show certain ideas, principles, or categories . . . that are not physical and sensible, but intellectual and metaphysical."

This idea—that in attending to nature humans were, pari passu, learning about God—brought Morris back to humankind. His prolonged spiritual crisis disappeared, and he was soon writing the books he could not write before, such as his *Hegel's Philosophy of the State and History* (1887). Hegel's dualisms allowed Morris a logic by which he could unify himself and especially by which he could return to the easy confidence of his youth that intelligence could end in an affirmation of God, or at least of Hegel's "Absolute Self Consciousness."

If Morris's fifteen-year turmoil over whether he was right with God recalls the period that John Dewey spent anguishing over whether he was "right with Jesus," the danger for Dewey when he arrived at Johns Hopkins and began to study with Morris was evident. The religious uneasiness that still lingered in Morris's embrace of Hegel affected Dewey. If he was thrown back to his earlier conflicts over Christianity, he also was disposed to adopt Morris's solution, and he became a Hegelian in the manner of his mentor.

By 1882, when Dewey arrived in Baltimore to study with Morris, President Gilman seems already to have become disillusioned with him, whom he had originally appointed with the expectation that Morris would assume the university's chair of philosophy. But the five years that Morris spent visiting Hopkins convinced Gilman that he had been mistaken and that Morris was not dedicated to empirical, objective scientific ideas and the goal of scholarly production that he wanted in his chair. Indeed, his disappointment almost certainly lay behind his reluctance to offer Dewey, who planned to study with Morris, a fellowship.

Two other philosophers on his faculty were proving themselves to be more in accord with the experimental ideal. In 1882, the year that Dewey began his graduate studies, Gilman appointed G. Stanley Hall to the Department of Philosophy. Four years younger than Morris, Hall seems almost to have lived in his wake. Like Morris and Dewey he was born in Vermont. Like Morris he prepared to secure a post in philosophy by first studying theology. A year after Morris left Union Theological Seminary, Hall enrolled there and remained, as Morris had, for two years and then proceeded, similarly, to Berlin.

There the similarity ended. The new science of psychology was just then ascending in Germany, and philosophers were looking to experimental psychology for insights into the problems of mind, perception, and intention in order to get new perspectives on old philosophical problems. Philosophy thus naturally became allied with the new science of psychology. Hall studied only long enough with Morris's teacher Trendelenburg to absorb his view that no conflict existed between science and metaphysics, and then he turned to the study of anatomy, medicine, and physiology in the newly established psychological laboratories. With none of Morris's scruples concerning ultimate truth, Hall rode the wave of the future. Shortly after his return to the United States and an inspiring reading of Wilhelm Wundt's *Physiological Psychology*, Hall went to Harvard, where he earned the first American doctorate in psychology and the approval of his dissertation director William James. Hall returned to Germany and there, with remarkable prescience, grasped the truth that psychology and, with it philosophy, was going in two directions: toward both experimentalism and educational psychology. They were familiar subjects in Europe but had just appeared in America. In Europe, Hall established his dual credentials: he did laboratory work on the physiology of the muscles, and understanding that in America "the most promising line of work would be to study the applications of psychology to education," he visited the schools in which the new ideas of education were being tried.

Hall had guessed right. In 1882, President Charles Eliot of Harvard invited him to give a course of lectures there, and in January of the following year Hall arrived at Johns Hopkins just as Morris was returning to Ann Arbor. As a second-semester graduate student, John Dewey naturally registered in Hall's classes. From the clutches of idealist philosophy, he was dropped suddenly into the laboratory of the physiologist and the schoolroom of the educationalist. Hall was necessarily Morris's rival on many grounds. Morris had languished for five years, waiting for Gilman to appoint him to the chair of philosophy. Within two years of Hall's arrival, the chair went to him. On hearing that the chair long promised to him had gone to Hall, Morris, always gracious, wrote to President Gilman that Hall's appointment as one of the "full & permanent instructors . . . seems to me a subject for congratulations on every ground. I have sent him my sincerest congratulations."

Dewey was torn between them. Morris encouraged Dewey's unfortunate disposition to seek truth in systems. By contrast, Hall's focus on experimental psychology appealed to Dewey, who had been fascinated at the University of Vermont by Huxley's physiology and Spencer's psychology. Hall was prickly where Morris was empathic. He aspired, one commentator pointed out, "to become known as the 'Darwin of the Mind.' " He was staking his claim to leadership in philosophy at Johns Hopkins on fact, data, and research—not on Truth. For him, philosophy had to get out of the library and into the laboratory. When Hall arrived at Hopkins, he sized up the graduate students in philosophy and found the demon of idealism in many; John Dewey was certainly on the list of suspects.

For Dewey, the rivalry between Morris and Hall simply exacerbated his own conflicts. Dewey was not easily won over to Hall's ideas—and never to Hall personally. He wrote to Torrey shortly after he started to study in Hall's lab: "I don't see any very close connection between it & Phil. but I suppose it will furnish grist for the mill, if nothing else." By contrast, he was greatly attracted to Morris the man as well as the thinker. Obviously he respected Morris's learning and adopted his Hegelianism. "I have never known a more single-hearted and whole-souled man," Dewey later remarked. Morris, he said, "deeply affected [him], to the point of at least a temporary conversion, by [his] . . . enthusiastic and scholarly devotion." In turn, Morris held Dewey to be his star pupil. Although Dewey needed to follow Morris at a certain distance, his scientific passions allied him with Hall. After all his personal anguish about religion, it was a relief simply to work in the laboratory running experiments, not to run after truth. Moreover, Hall's interest in fusing philosophy with psychology and psychology with education found a ready response in Dewey, whose disillusion with conventional educational practice was clear. To the young Dewey, Morris's passion for "big questions" was more admirable than Hall's collections of physiological data. But it was Hall's way with philosophy, not Morris's, that Dewey was destined to pursue in his early professional work.

Charles Sanders Peirce was the third lecturer in philosophy at Hopkins when Dewey arrived there. His specialty was "philosophic logic." Dewey was deeply interested in logic and intended to study it, except as Dewey found, Peirce was intensely absorbed with mathematical logic and the application of scientific methodology to logical analysis. This was not what Dewey considered to be logic, but it was easy to see why Gilman had appointed Peirce to the department, for he exemplified a third stream of philosophic development. In Morris's historical scholarship, Hall's psychological experiments, and Peirce's quantitative logic were assembled for this new research university a triad of philosophic approaches. But the department was never integrated, because Morris, Hall, and Peirce never connected their work. It seemed to the students that they had to choose one of them. Dewey chose Morris's person even as he followed Hall's way, but he decided against Peirce.

Although Dewey did take Peirce's mathematical logic course during his second year, he was still dubious about its contribution to his philosophic education. But Peirce's more informal Emersonian examination of "the psychology of great men" seems to have had a lasting effect on Dewey. For a long time he continued to question Peirce's mathematical approach. Dewey told W. T. Harris, who himself had little interest in Peirce's sort of logic, "Mr. Peirce lectures on Logic, but the lectures appeal more strongly to the mathematical students than to the philosophical." In the last paper that Dewey wrote before he left Hopkins, he even took a swipe at Peirce. Led by Hegel and the "new psychology," Dewey wrote, modern philosophy "abandons all legal fiction of logical and mathematical analogies and rules; and is willing to throw itself upon experience." Thus casually, Dewey consigned Peirce to the dustbin of outmoded philosophers. It took him thirty years to begin to appreciate Peirce, and then Peirce became the philosopher who influenced him most.

Dewey chose Morris, followed Hall, and ignored Peirce. Today it would be easy to say that he should have dismissed Morris, nodded to Hall, and followed Peirce, the only original philosopher of the three. In truth, during his next thirty years, Dewey rejected Morris's idealism, went far beyond Hall, and finally understood Peirce's importance. What always was characteristic of John Dewey is evident here. He took much in and winnowed it slowly, clarifying his ideas and only cautiously coming to understand himself.

Becoming a Philosopher

Always attentive to financial matters, Dewey had two things on his mind in addition to his studies during the spring of 1883. First, he now believed he had enough support and a good enough record of accomplishment to apply for a teaching fellowship for 1883–84. In December 1882 he sent his paper "Knowledge and Relativity of Feeling" to Harris, explaining that he had "attempted to apply to one of the phases of Sensationalism the same kind of argument which I used regarding Materialism." By March, when he had still not heard back from Harris, Dewey wrote to ask whether Harris would accept it: "The reason I inquire is that I wish to make application for a Fellowship . . . and . . . published original works count very largely. . . . Otherwise I should not have troubled you." In fact, the article appeared in the somewhat delayed January issue, at almost the same moment that Dewey wrote. To ensure that his application was successful, Dewey also wrote a paper for the April meeting of the Metaphysical Club. Although Morris was back in Michigan, Dewey was still very much under his influence, as this paper shows. In "Hegel and the Theory of Categories" he argued that Hegel's method, which arrived at dynamic truth through dialectics, was the solution to earlier idealist quandaries. Morris would have appreciated the argument. The final paper that Dewey wrote as part of his fellowship application was entitled "Kant and Philosophic Method." Parallel to his talk on Hegel, this reflected the persistent influence of Torrey (and even Marsh) and showed that

Dewey was still shuffling from one mentor to another even as he tried to put them together. Generally following the critical method that he had earlier applied to the works of Spinoza and Spencer, he contended that Kant's separation of subject and object necessarily led to subjectivism and agnosticism. But bowing to Torrey, he noted that Kant had introduced "the notion of an intuitive understanding which is the ultimate criterion of all truth." Kant's insight, he concluded—now with a nod to Morris—was left to Hegel to develop into an organic system.

With these remarkable accomplishments in philosophy behind him by the end of his first year as a graduate student, it might seem that Dewey would be awarded a fellowship. But Gilman's suspicions of Dewey now seem to be concentrated on Dewey's personal capacity as a teacher. Gilman wrote to Matthew Buckham, president of the University of Vermont, for advice. Dewey had made a "very favorable impression upon our teachers of philosophy," Gilman acknowledged, but "if we invite him to a post as a teacher, next year, his instruction will be given to undergraduate students. I have doubted, whether with his recognized mental power, he had enough pedagogic power." Buckham responded immediately that he was aware that Dewey "is very reticent, as you see—probably lacks a due amount of self operation," but he recommended that an appointment "would reinforce his own confidence in himself." Buckham referred the query to Torrey, who added, two days later: "From early youth he has manifested a deeply reflective turn of mind, accompanied by the reticence which often attends it." But, Torrey added, Dewey was unusually gifted in "clearness and penetration," and "certainly his pupils could not complain of want of clearness in his instructions." Finally, Gilman decided to award him the fellowship for his second year that Cattell had held in his first year. But his misgivings suggested that in his view, a new, less genteel philosopher would carry the future. What the president of Hopkins did not realize was that Dewey, above all his contemporaries, would be precisely the sort of philosopher he wanted.

Dewey wished to finish his degree at the end of his second year of courses. All he needed was a completed dissertation. He brought home a draft of his paper "Kant's Philosophic Method" during the summer to show to Torrey, with a view toward developing it into a dissertation topic. During the fall semester of 1883, Dewey again enrolled in both of Morris's courses. One was on the development of German philosophy, "with special reference to the movement from Kant to Hegel," and the other was on Spinoza's *Ethics*. Morris also delivered four public lectures, "The Philosophy of Social Relations," which Dewey dutifully attended. Finally, Morris invited a young Harvard Hegelian, Josiah Royce, to deliver two lectures at Hopkins on "The Religious Aspects of Philosophy."

In spring 1884 Dewey enrolled again in Herbert Baxter Adams's seminary in history and political science and even engaged in a lively debate with another student in the class, Woodrow Wilson. The subject was the Blair bill, which proposed using federal funds to improve education in the South. Wilson argued that the bill was unconstitutional, based on states' rights. Dewey took the opposing side. Records of the seminary note that Dewey wished to "direct attention to the facts of education in the South, and gave some statistics from the Census of 1880, which seemed to show, by the increasing percentage of illiteracy . . . a retrograde movement in education" there. This early Dewey was insisting that law—even constitutional law—had to reflect social needs. Moreover, he already was exhibiting a clear sense of the importance of education to social progress. He said in the debate with Wilson "that history proved that educational advance always came from *above*" and that therefore education was necessarily a *federal* question. Obviously Dewey's passions showed, for the recording secretary noted that he spoke with "emphatic eagerness," and the "quite interesting" discussion that followed his remarks prompted the members to vote to extend the class by one hour, and it did not adjourn until 11 p.m.

By this time Dewey had also been subjected to the influence of G. Stanley Hall, in both the classroom and laboratory experiments. During Dewey's second year, he enrolled in Hall's course on "Psychophysics," mainly concerned with "the physiology of the senses . . . as introductory to a course on psychology, beginning with instinct." Dewey was one of six students who "engaged in special investigations in the room set apart for psycho-physic research." He also attended Hall's lectures on "psychological ethics," beginning with the Greeks and concluding with Kant, with particular attention given to "inductive methods of studying ethical problems." (This subject was one that Dewey himself regularly taught throughout his career.)The result was that as the focus of his dissertation evolved, Dewey found himself trying to meld the various influences on him into one. Torrey's interest in Kant, Morris's Hegelianism, and Hall's psychological focus—itself drawing on Kant—all were fused in his dissertation, "The Psychology of Kant." While he was still writing it, he described it to W. T. Harris. Since Dewey's dissertation has been lost, this is the best account we have:

> Personally, I am endeavoring to get my Ph.D. this year, and my own work is being done largely upon my thesis, whose subject is "Kant's Psychology"—that is his philosophy of spirit (so far as he has any), or the subjective side of his theory of knowledge, in which besides giving a general acc't of his theory of Sense, Imagination &c, I hope to be able to point out that he had the conception of Reason or Spirit as the centre and organic unity of the entire sphere of man's experience, and that in so far as he is true to this conception that he is the true founder of modern philosophic method, but that so far as he was false to it he fell into his own defects, contradictions &c— It is this question of *method* in philosophy which interests me most just at present—

How were these to be integrated? Dewey made the idea of philosophic method the linchpin of the three entities: Kant's "conception of Reason or Spirit as the centre and organic unit of the entire sphere of man's experience," Hegel's clarifying focus on the dialectical method through which to achieve organic unity, and Hall's emphasis on the conscious and unconscious states lurking in the background. This was a nice unifying strategy and provides an early example of the skill in technical philosophy that would always be a hallmark of Dewey's work. The thesis was finished around the end of April and approved in May. By then Dewey was already at work on a more important paper.

Hall's influence was more apparent in this new paper, entitled "The New Psychology," which Dewey delivered to the Metaphysical Club as he was completing his dissertation. Full it is of Kantian idealism, neo-Hegelianism, Hall's laboratory, and even Herbert Baxter Adams's political historicism, this paper suggests the first genuine blossoming of the kind of original philosopher that Dewey would become. In the old psychology, Dewey said, "we find every mental phenomenon not only explained" but explained reductively. The "rich and colored" particularized experiences of individuals, groups, and nations, even in "two moments of the same life," were schematized and categorized.

> We now know better. We know that . . . [an individual's] own life is bound up with the life of society . . . [and] connected with all the past by the lines of education, tradition, and heredity; we know that man is indeed the microcosm who has gathered into himself the riches of the world. . . . We know that [in] our mental life . . . large tracts never come into consciousness; that those which do get into consciousness, are vague and transitory, with a meaning hard to catch and read; are infinitely complex . . . ; in short, that we know almost nothing about the actual activities and processes of the soul.

In a few phrases, Dewey disposed of the intuitionalist faculty psychology, common sense, and positivistic thinkers on whom he had been raised philosophically—William Hamilton, Mill, Hume, and Reid—and asserted "the best we can do is thank them, and then go about our own work . . . for *our* work is in the future."

To physiology, Dewey explained, we owe the idea that the mind is not a storehouse of ideas but "lines of activity." To biology, we owe the full conception of organic life, especially mental life, "as an organic unitary process developing according to the laws of all life." To the environment, we owe the understanding that "psychical life . . . [is not] an individual, isolated thing."

This idea of the organic relation of the individual to that organized social life into which he is born, from which he draws his mental and spiritual sustenance, and in which he must perform his proper function [leads to the necessary investigations of] . . . the social and historical sciences,—the sciences of the origin and development of the various spheres of man's activity.

All areas of human activity are thoroughly "permeated with psychological questions and materials," he concluded.

In the spring of his second year, he continued to study history and economics with Adams and Richard T. Ely and talked with Dave about the political books his brother was reading. After his debate with Woodrow Wilson, he predicted that Wilson "could . . . go far in politics if he wished." Dewey told W. T. Harris: "I am taking . . . the theory of the state, international law in the historical department, & am in pretty close contact with the men there." Well he might have been, for although John's historical and political interests had predated Dave's arrival, Dave's presence sharpened them and (along with Morris's understanding of Hegel) inspired in John a "special interest in the philosophy of history and the study of social ethics." Now, in his article on the new psychology, he asserted that "history in its broadest aspect is itself a psychological problem, offering the richest resources of matter," while more particularly the data of everyday normal or abnormal life offer rich concrete material for psychological investigation: "The cradle and the asylum are becoming the laboratory of the psychologist." It was a grand synthesis.

In this first important article, Dewey seemed poised to create from the new psychology a logic of fact, of process, of life. But at that crucial juncture, he lost courage and suddenly fell back on the old influences of Lucina, Brastow, and Torrey, owing to a reading of Newman Smyth's quasi-theological "dynamic intuitionalism." Under Smyth's influence, Dewey suddenly—in a great leap backward to his old pieties—discerned the new psychology to be "intensely ethical," suffused with "devotion, sacrifice, faith, and idealism" and leading ultimately to God: "It finds no insuperable problems in the relations of faith and reason, for it can discover in its investigations no reason which is not based upon faith, and no faith which is not rational in its origin and tendency." At the edge of a new direction, Dewey regressed to dutiful affirmations of his earliest faiths. Here was the young Dewey's uneasy situation: he had proved himself capable of philosophic thought; he had completed a dissertation; he was soon to give a very "creditable" performance on his comprehensive examinations; and he had thoroughly absorbed Hall's physiological instruction. He was poised for a creative leap, but at the last moment, his personal reticence, his family faith, his allegiance to his mother's piety, and the reactionary influence of Smyth all drove him to defending New England church culture.

Gilman's misgivings seemed to have been borne out: Dewey really did seem to lack the drive to become an original philosopher, even to the extent of being unable to follow the implications of the new psychology that he himself had outlined. When the crucial test came, all his old conflicts held him fast. He left Hopkins still very much a man in doubt, one who could too easily be pulled back to the areas of his earliest conflicts. He had a mind, and he could have a future. But did he have the courage to go all the way? All in all, did the reticence that everyone saw in him reflect a lack of confidence and an unwillingness to go all out? What he had made was not the breakthrough statement he hoped it would be. He spoke of the "rich and colored experience" of mankind, but was he himself doomed to be colorless? He had a brand-new doctorate, but what did he have inside him?

FINDING BOTH A PHILOSOPHIC NICHE AND A JOB

The presidential election of 1876, contested by Rutherford B. Hayes, a Republican, and Samuel Tilden, a Democrat, was decided by one electoral vote. While the contested election was still in doubt, Archibald remarked that if Tilden were the winner, the Civil War would have been "fought in vain." (Both John and his brother Davis voted for Tilden.) Hayes won, but the two major parties continued to divide voters almost equally.

The federal government tended to be weak, and patronage—the awarding of jobs—still flourished at all levels, from the federal government to the municipalities. Everyone spoke of governmental corruption, but no one, it appeared, could do anything about it. President James Garfield announced his support for civil service reform, but four months later he was shot by a deranged and frustrated office seeker; and suddenly Chester Arthur was president. An accomplished Tammany Hall machine politician and a defender of the spoils system, Arthur surprised everyone, possibly even himself, by taking a reformist turn and supporting and signing a civil service reform bill.

The 1880s was a decade of political unrest and a rising desire for reform, but few sustainable gains for reform were achieved. The caretakers of the national government were devoted to minimal government, even as popular sentiment increasingly inclined to the view that the federal government needed to take a more active role in solving some of the main issues of the day. But in the tradition of Hayes, the presidents who followed him—James A. Garfield, Grover Cleveland, and Benjamin Harrison—all held that the federal government had only a small legitimate sphere for activity, and they let the issues of the day fester until action was unavoidable.

Perhaps the foremost of these unsolved issues was the rapid expansion of industrialization that followed the war, when the new inventions and new systems designed for war needs were carried over into civil life and accelerated as former troops became civilians. No one doubted that in a very short time America would surpass England as the world's leading manufacturing nation. Now the population was organized by industry; jobs depended on machine production; and upward mobility depended on technical skill and the possession of capital, each bringing abuses in its wake. The growing number of people consolidated into small areas soon produced industrial slums. Miners were relegated to terrible living and work conditions. Work in factories and sweatshops strained the ability of humans to keep up an inhuman pace. Depressions came and went, and those who lived on the margin were driven into the ground whenever one struck. Socioeconomic classes were moving apart as never before in America, and the title of Henry George's great work, *Progress and Poverty* (1879), accurately described the conditions in America.

New industries based on innovations in production and the centralization of ownership sprang up. Perhaps the most important new invention was both the best known and the least visible: the corporation. It could be seen nowhere but was felt everywhere. City dwellers might sometimes have idealized the farm, but farm life could be even more arduous than industrial employment and often less rewarding. In the South, white farmers were almost as poor as black farmers, and sharecropping was the norm. In the Northeast, the exodus from the farm continued without pause. By the end of the decade, those who stayed were being studied for inbreeding, imbecility, and addiction to alcohol or opiates disguised as medicines. In the West, the best lands had been taken by the 1880s. The Homestead Act (1862), which awarded 160 acres to each settler, proved to be more enticing than helpful. The acreage was too small for a truly productive farm, and later modifications of the act improved it only a little. Almost all the farmers who had moved to the less productive, marginally arid lands of western Kansas in the early 1880s had returned east before the end of the decade because of the severe droughts.

William Dean Howells saw the time as one "groping for fairer conditions," which was a good description of the 1880s. But what was a "fairer condition"? Entrepreneurs believed that it was their freedom to conduct business with few or no restrictions. Industrial workers defined "fairer conditions" as better pay and improved working conditions. Inventors believed that it was an opportunity to derive a large profit from their inventions. Consumers believed that "fairer" meant low prices for new products that now seemed essential. "Fairer conditions" meant "free enterprise" in the promotional literature of business; but in boardrooms "fairer conditions" meant the ability to cut the throats of competitors and to eliminate competition. Fairer conditions meant the ability of J. P. Morgan to create trusts without legislative interference, but the public had its own suspicions that "fairer" and freer for the bankers meant fouler and foolish for ordinary people. "Fairer" meant genuine economic growth, and this, in some sense, helped everyone; but it also meant insecurity, anxiety, and uneasiness for almost everyone who had not gotten to the top of a heap. Factory or mine owners felt that "fairer" included their freedom to provide sanitary conditions at their discretion. Laborers increasingly believed that it would be fair for them to be free to unionize and even strike if the need arose.

Who was to decide where fairness lay? Was private wealth a public blessing? What was the responsibility, as Henry Demarest Lloyd phrased it, of "wealth" to "commonwealth"? Should trusts be regulated? Should unions be established and allowed to become powerful? Could a citizenry be expected to abide by the four gospels when a gospel of wealth responded, for some, so well to earthly desires? Should immigrants be welcomed or rejected? Should 1 percent of the nation's families control 88 percent of its wealth? Were the wealthy entitled to ride in the gilded coach of luxury while the laboring masses strained to pull it along? In this metaphor, Edward Bellamy, in his utopian novel *Looking Backward* (1888), found an image for his time. Dewey read Bellamy's book, and more than fifty years later, when asked what books of the previous fifty years he considered the most influential, Dewey named William James's *Principles of Psychology* and *Looking Backward*. Since Dewey completed his schooling and came to maturity during this time, it was not surprising that he himself would be preoccupied all his life with ethical questions and questions of ethics, in both books and numerous articles. Certainly the moral bent of his mother and his early education, as well as his continuing commitment to Christianity, played a part. For most Americans, major questions would have to wait to be answered in the 1890s. Dewey concentrated on ethical questions and began finding answers a little sooner.

Dewey's difficulty when he graduated from Hopkins was that he had not yet found a philosophic point of view that satisfied him emotionally, and so his emotional impulses kept intruding on his thinking.

His commitment to Hegelianism consisted not alone in his temperamental inclination to appreciate well-organized, coherent systems; it also allowed him to accept a rational basis for his continuing wish to believe in God. His commitment was also, of course, derived from his devotion to George Morris. The divisions in Dewey's own identity made any dualistic system attractive. He called this state of distress "an inward laceration" when, years later, he tried to account for the spell that Hegel and Morris held over him in 1884.

> There were, however, also *subjective* reasons for the appeal that Hegel's thought made to me; it supplied a demand for unification that was doubtless an intense *emotional craving*, and yet was a hunger that [then] only an intellectualized subject-matter could satisfy. . . . [The] divisions and separations that were . . . borne in upon me as a consequence of a heritage of New England culture . . . were an *inward laceration*. . . . Hegel's synthesis . . . operated as an immense release, a liberation.

The needed "liberation" provided by Hegelian idealism was temporary in its intensity, though long lasting in its duration. Some critics find traces of Hegel's influence even in Dewey's last works. His friend Arthur Bentley claimed that in every intellectual of their generation, a "deposit of Hegel" could be discerned. By the same token, even in Dewey's early works it is clear that he was never entirely satisfied with Hegelian solutions. His emotional needs rebelled against his rational, systematic programs. In the summer of 1884 Dewey was still in the grip of so many emotions that even Hegelian dialectics could not unify them. Each of his attempts left him with only more emotional impulses and only intellectual positions with which to resolve his emotional cravings.

In the summer of 1884, what seemed even worse with regard to the immediate demands of his life was that he had not yet found a job. George Morris had hinted that the University of Michigan might hire Dewey. After all, Morris himself spent each half-year at Hopkins, which required him to supply a substitute in Ann Arbor. Morris's

current assistant there, George W. Howison, a Harvard-trained idealist, had accepted a job at the University of California at Berkeley, to
begin in the fall. Dewey heard that in May 1884 Morris told President
Gilman that Dewey's name "is under serious consideration for a subordinate appointment here," which raised his hopes.

By June 5, 1884, the date of the Hopkins commencement when
Dewey's Ph.D. was conferred, Michigan had not yet made a decision,
and Dewey went home to Burlington to contemplate his future. One
possibility other than a job had been offered, but he had already rejected it. Apparently, Gilman had finally been convinced that his newest
graduate in philosophy might have talent. Owing to Dewey's work
with Hall, Gilman now saw him in a somewhat better light: as a scientific researcher. And so before Dewey left Baltimore, Gilman called
him into his office and offered him a postdoctoral traveling fellowship
that would allow him to study in Germany. Anxious to begin his
career, however, he rejected Gilman's offer.

Finally, the president of the University of Michigan, James B.
Angell—who had been the U.S. ambassador to China and also president of the University of Vermont before Buckham—wrote to Dewey
of his pleasure in remembering his parents and him as a boy. On the
same day that he received Angell's offer, Dewey wrote back that he
took "pleasure in accepting" the job and also relished Angell's "kind
and friendly words" and "good wishes": I "esteem it an honor to have
been remembered by you for so many years." In the late summer,
Morris traveled east to Hopkins and Dewey went west to Michigan.
There Dewey took up his duties as that semester's entire philosophy
department. He took rooms in a boarding house at the corner of
Maynard and Jefferson Streets and made his final preparations to teach
his four fall classes, which included "Empirical Psychology" and
"Special Topics in Psychology."

As the oldest and most distinguished institution of higher learning
in the West, the University of Michigan was sometimes called the
"Athens of the West." It was already well enough established that the
University of California at Berkeley had begun to "raid" Michigan's
faculty, as had happened with Howison. Moreover, it was a routine

stop for national lecture tours by major speakers. In the semester that Dewey arrived, for instance, Mark Twain and George Washington Cable lectured there. But as a place to live, Ann Arbor was not so well developed: it was in the midst of changing from a rural town into an intellectual center. A distinctly pastoral tone still prevailed in Ann Arbor, and President Angell himself kept a flock of sheep on a nearby farm.

In 1884, Ann Arbor had a population of eight thousand, which swelled by nearly fourteen hundred students during the academic year. The faculty numbered around sixty-five and already included some scholars who later distinguished themselves. The young radical historian Henry Carter Adams joined the Ann Arbor faculty at the same time as Dewey. Charles Horton Cooley, still a student, was soon recognized as the father of American sociology. Dewey frequently gathered together with Adams and Cooley in several reading clubs, as well as meeting them individually. But to Dewey's New England eyes, Ann Arbor was just emerging from the wilderness and had barely achieved the sophistication of a frontier outpost. Years later, during his travels in China when Dewey tried to describe Manchuria to his family back in the United States, he said it was "something like our western frontier . . . [in] the U.S. Except that the frontier . . . is more conservative." Ann Arbor was deeply conservative, and Dewey had been well prepared by his mother to be conservative with it.

When Dewey arrived, he gave no indication that he understood or cared about the student discontent that had been decisive in determining his appointment. During the previous year the Michigan students had criticized the narrowness of the philosophy department. Equipped by Harvard with a strong dose of Hegelianism as well as a degree in theology, Howison, like Morris, had been intent on justifying the ways of philosophy to Christianity. When Howison had arrived at Michigan in October 1883, the student *Argonaut* published a column in which it was predicted that "nothing in his teaching will be very different from what we have long been accustomed to. We may expect to have Mill and Spencer and the whole modern scientific school of Philosophy made little of and Bishop Berkeley and the like set up for our admiration and instruction." By contrast, many of the Michigan students were much less committed to traditional pieties and instead were interested in the contributions of science to empirical philosophy. No one could have rebelled against the persuasive, genteel, and sincere Morris himself, but the assistant was an easy target. The students' discontent had bubbled over into the pages of the student newspaper during the 1883–84 school year. They complained that Morris and Howison neglected to teach Herbert Spencer, George Henry Lewes, and other empiricists. The students suspected that the curriculum in philosophy was calculated to "counteract" any irreligious tendency by the student body, and they added the charge that the two idealist philosophers were intellectually timid: "What we hold is in short that proper instruction is not given in religious subjects in a fair, comprehensive and completely undogmatic way, and based upon data." This expressed the conflict between religion and science that so many intellectuals were feeling in the 1880s. The students added: "When young men see . . . [philosophers] whom they have been taught to respect in science [courses], contemptuously left unnoticed, an idea that perhaps it is a disinclination [of the professors] to grapple with them . . . is liable to take possession of their minds." Fortunately, Howison was called to Berkeley.

Dewey was the perfect replacement. His psychophysiological training under Hall and his own interest in modern science allowed him to be exactly what the Michigan students were clamoring for. Morris understood the students and responded to them perfectly. He assigned Dewey almost entirely scientific courses, even as he revamped his own offerings to stress British and European empiricism, along with Hegelian logic, in addition to designing a new course, "Philosophy of the State and of History." No freethinking Michigan student could have asked more of either Morris or, especially, the new instructor. One course that Dewey announced for the fall was "Special Topics in Psychology (Physiological, Comparative, and Morbid)." Dewey even imitated Hall in replicating his psychological laboratory. Over the years Dewey added such courses as "Psychology and Philosophy," "Experimental Psychology," "Speculative Psychology" (this was, he told Torrey, "discussing philosophical problems from the psychological side"), "History of Psychology," "Greek Science and

Philosophy," and "The Philosophy of Herbert Spencer." As early as 1886, even Morris's class on ethics could be advertised as "a course . . . which may be advantageously taken . . . [by those students] who have first finished Murray's Psychology with Professor Dewey." Dewey's appointment smoothed Morris's friction with the students by bringing a new person with advertised and evident scientific interests into the department. More important, Dewey's training in psychology situated him at the beginning of the alliance of philosophy and psychology in America. Philosophers looked to the new psychology to provide further insight into human thinking and an expanded understanding of each in the traditional conception of the tripartite soul: intellect, will, and emotion. When Dewey's science replaced Howison's theology at Michigan, a new chapter in American philosophy was opened.

Some of this change was more superficial than real. Morris knew Dewey well enough to know that he still sought a secure basis in Hegel's system. In academic circles, this was clear, and soon Michigan's philosophy department under Morris and Dewey was identified as the center of scholarly neo-Hegelian thought in the United States. Dewey walked a fine philosophic line: he satisfied the scientific students and also appealed to the idealism of the large body of Christians at Michigan. He seemed to be a tough scientist to some and a genteel idealist to others. Although he had to satisfy the new empiricists, the Student Christian Association was still one of the largest organizations on campus, and for its members he had to exhibit enlightened orthodoxy. Dewey taught the new science at the same time that he practiced philosophy within the theistic framework established by Morris. It would have been enough for him to demonstrate that science did not *conflict* with religion, but he wanted to go further and to show that science *confirmed* religious faith.

Dewey's seriousness was then, and always remained, one of his chief virtues. It was no wonder that a writer in a student publication, the *Palladium*, declared: "I never knew so young a man with so old a head." One of Dewey's first acts after his arrival was to form a Bible class in cooperation with the Student Christian Association (S.C.A.). The *Monthly Bulletin* reported:

A Bible class has been formed . . . for the accommodation of those persons who . . . desire to pursue a critical course of study of the Bible and of Christian doctrines. The first subject of the study is the life of Christ, with special reference to its importance as an historical event. The class is to be led by Dr. Dewey.

Dewey soon also scheduled Sunday lectures to the S.C.A. students. The first talk that he delivered shows where he initially felt obliged to situate himself. He spoke on "The Obligation to Knowledge of God," in which he began: "The scriptures are uniform in their treatment of scepticism. There is an obligation to know God, and to fail to meet this obligation is not to err intellectually, but to sin morally. Belief is not a privilege, but a duty." The final sentence of the talk was equally stern: "God is everlastingly about us, and to fail to know Him is to show that we do not wish to know him." Somehow, in Dewey's mind, Lucina's pietism had mixed with Morris's Hegelianism, bringing Dewey to the bewildering conclusion that the "religious evangelist, ignorant though he may be," is likely to be closer to the truth than the speculative "man of science." This conclusion may have comforted the S.C.A. students, but *that* idea was not appropriate for the students in his lab. And it could not bear much examination by Dewey himself, who was leading a double life. Dewey's attempt to be all things to all people—his parents, his students, himself—could not long survive the contradictions it entailed. Still, over the next few years Dewey gave several talks to the S.C.A., conducted Bible studies, and frequently addressed the Congregational society. As one newspaper article stated, "These [talks] were so satisfactory, no one can miss the privilege of hearing him." His piety did not fail to elicit criticism, however, and his religious ideas sometimes did encounter objections. In an article, "The Revival of the Soul," published in *The University*, Dewey claimed that "it is absolutely impossible for science to settle any religious question." This statement brought a letter to the editor refuting Dewey and concluding that "science in its true, broad sense has as much to do with religion as with any other department of knowledge." This was the same position that Dewey himself eventually adopted.

On another occasion when he had a chance to make a public presentation—this time not under the auspices of a Christian organization—he gave a very different talk. In the spring of 1884, Morris organized the Philosophic Society at Michigan. In Morris's words, this group was formed "with the purpose of encouraging personal study in philosophical matters, the application of philosophy to literature and history, and the awakening of an interest in philosophical discussion." With Morris back in Baltimore for the 1884 fall semester, it fell to Dewey to run the society meetings. He led the first meeting with a talk entitled "Mental Evolution and Its Relation to Psychology." Here were the code words of the new scientific philosophers: "Mental" (not spiritual), "Evolution" (not religion), and "Psychology" (not theology). The Dewey who was a traditionalist for the S.C.A.. became a modernist for the Philosophic Society, and the modernist got a splendid reception. The *Argonaut* for October 18 entitled its report on the occasion "An Able Paper by Dr. Dewey":

> Room 21 was filled on Wednesday evening by a select audience of upper-classes, professors, and a few townspeople. The main discourse of the evening was given by Dr. Dewey, the new professor of Philosophy. It was without a doubt the ablest discussion that has been given in Ann Arbor for some time. He showed that life must be looked upon as an organic whole, whose parts are interdependent and in close relations, and [that] self-consciousness [is] . . . the leading principle of mind; that mental evolution consists in enlarging our environment; in placing ourselves in proper organic relations with the spiritual universe.

In this talk Dewey played it safe, essentially repeating his paper "The New Psychology." Obviously, he had not yet read Chauncey Wright's essay "The Evolution of Self-Consciousness," which would have helped to enlarge his argument. But Dewey already saw that his work on psychology and empirical philosophy would win him the approbation of Michigan students. If he wanted to pursue idealism, it would have to be united somehow with the new science, not with religious piety and genteel persuasion.

Dewey had reason to be satisfied with his reception during his first year at Ann Arbor. Even by the end of his first term, he wrote to W. T. Harris, he found his work "very enjoyable." He was bulging with ideas—on religion, morals, Hegel, psychology, self-consciousness, and social and political change. How would he link all these together, and what would serve as their center? Would he find a new male mentor, a new father, to help him toward a solution, as he had always done in the past?

DEWEY IN LOVE

But it was a woman whom he found, a woman who saved him. The inward laceration of New England piety had come to him through his mother. His solitary existence in Oil City had done a great deal to release his energy and replace his pious self-examination with philosophic thought and the appeal of self-consciousness. Now it took another woman to release his stored-up capacity for emotional richness and an inner life, someone who could heal his inward laceration and ease his mind about the connections among his disparate thoughts. Undoubtedly to him, John Dewey's experience was much more straightforward and seemed more simple than this description of it. He simply fell in love, which brought a new center and new purposes to his life. What he called his "intense emotional craving" set him on fire:

> I am thinking of you, and my darling I do want you so this
> evening. . . . Oh, sweetheart, you are the centre of everything,
> so that my being would be torn by its attraction to its centre,
> were you not the circumference of everything also. My own
> self, I love you—and it is hard to be without one's self. My own
> life, I love you—and it is hard to live without one's life.
> But darling you *are* my self and my life and so I can be and

live. . . . Darling, how did you ever manage to do away with and put out of sight so thoroughly my old doing & my old thinking, and fill my self so full of you? [You] . . . found a home for me, who had been homeless before, because I was always looking for you.

Dewey was not exaggerating when he told Max Eastman many years later that "no two people were ever more in love." Such an overflow of emotion is likely to seem repetitive and overdone, but Dewey was indulging the pleasure of attaching his "intense emotional craving" to a person who could return his love, as mere Hegelian logic could not do.

This person was Harriet Alice Chipman, a junior majoring in philosophy who boarded at the same house on Jefferson Street as John did. She sat on his left at the dinner table, and she took his classes. While discussing involuntary motor reactions related to will in the lab and Aristotle and Herbert Spencer in class and then passing the boiled beef and mashed potatoes during meals, they fell in love.

Coeducation had not yet arrived at the University of Vermont when Dewey was an undergraduate there. No female graduate students attended Johns Hopkins, except for the brilliant logician Christine Ladd who was allowed to take classes as a special nonregistered student there in 1879. But Ann Arbor had admitted female students since 1870. The student newspaper reflected on the importance of admitting women to the university: "American civilization and liberty" offered women "the opportunity to struggle for existence and renown." It had been settled, a writer for the *Argonaut* boasted, that the female mind was "as capable of the reception of abstract truth as that of the male." Six of the thirteen philosophy majors graduating in 1886 were women. Dewey's access to women and his comfort with them were eased by the intellectual basis on which he could start a relationship. The obligations of the dinner table provided another, and Harriet Alice Chipman's own evident talents sealed it.

Like John, Alice was a serious person, truly interested in ideas; one of her classmates remembered her "serious and earnest nature and her exceptional mind." She had been born about a year before John, on September 3, 1858. Beyond philosophy they discovered many things they had in common. Like John, she had taught in high school, and the Chipman family were originally Vermonters like his own family. Although he had a Ph.D. and an academic position while she was still an undergraduate, on another level she already possessed qualities that were still incipient in John, and so she could become her teacher's teacher. She was one of the freethinking, radical students who had complained about the lack of scientific attitudes in her department. Alice had a "deeply religious spirit," her daughter Jane later wrote, but a general, nonsectarian one. Never once did she ask John if he was "right with Jesus." Rather, as Jane said of her, she herself "never accepted any church dogma." Her sister claimed that she may have even ridiculed John's scrupulous attendance at prayer meetings in the Ann Arbor church. In Jane's view, her father acquired from her mother "the belief that a religious attitude was an indigenous natural experience and that therefore theology and ecclesiastical institutions had benumbed rather than promoting it." She did not, of course, join the S.C.A., but she did become a member of two secular groups that showed the bent of her thought. Alice helped found the Michigan chapter of an international society, the Collegiate Sorosis, an intellectual and feminist sorority that numbered among its members Lucretia Mott, George Sand, and George Eliot. The local society named John Dewey a "Sorosis brother." With John she was also among the founders, in the fall of 1885, of the Samovar Club, which devoted itself to discussions of Tolstoy, Turgenev, and Russian thought in general while its members sipped tea poured from a genuine Russian samovar. Before the 1884 fall semester began, she eagerly awaited the arrival of the new scientifically trained philosophy instructor, and she enrolled in all his classes. Soon she found that he was also sitting at her right at the boarding house, offering her apple pie.

Her sister Pett called her Hattie, her friends called her Chippy, and John called her Alice. She came from nearby Fenton, Michigan. Her father, Gordon Orlen Chipman, had been a cabinetmaker by trade and a Jacksonian Democrat by political enthusiasm. In accordance with the rules of the spoils system in effect after Franklin Pierce's election as president, Chipman was rewarded in 1854 with the postmastership of Fenton. Alice's mother, Lucy Riggs, was the daughter of Frederick Riggs and his wife Evaline. Born in 1810, Evaline Bishop Riggs "worked a home from the wilderness, for Michigan was an unsettled territory when she came here," the *Fenton Independent* reported in her obituary. Alice's grandfather's history was remarkable. A true frontiersman, he was born in Livingston County, New York, in 1810. He became a surveyor for the U.S. Army Engineering Corps, mapping the territory between Saginaw and Mackinaw. A fur trader for the Hudson Bay Company, he lived with the Chippewas, learned their language, and was made a member of the tribe. Later, he was a vigorous defender of Native American rights against the Bureau of Indian Affairs. He traveled all over the West, explored the Kansas prairies, and passed easily from the first stage of frontier life—trapping and trading—to the next stage—prospecting and mining—and even registered mining claims in Colorado. John Dewey was referring to Fred Riggs when in 1917 he told Horace Kallen that he had known "one American pioneer . . . who made & was made by the settling of the West," adding, "I do not see how just that type of character is ever to be produced by this country again." On the paternal side, another of Alice's ancestors, John Logan Chipman, was married to a Native American, so both sides of her ancestry were authentically associated with the frontier.

Four years after Gordon became postmaster, Lucy fell ill and suddenly died. Gordon was inconsolable, falling deeper and deeper into melancholy. From the moment of his wife's death, he thought of nothing but dying. Before the year was over, he had mourned himself into the grave, dying of tuberculosis and leaving Harriet Alice, her sister Augusta, and a new baby as orphans. It is likely that the severe depressions from which Alice periodically suffered originated in the early loss of her parents. Indeed, Alice seems to have been particularly disturbed by loss, and each one that she suffered as an adult cut more deeply into her spirit. At the same time, she was fiercely determined to remain independent. She was an early feminist and remained committed to women's liberation. But she also needed continuous reassurance from John that she was loved and cared about.

Their parents' deaths left Harriet and Augusta in the care of Evaline and Fred Riggs, their grandparents. Influences in families are always diffused and hard to trace, but in this case it is roughly accurate to say that Fred had a major influence on each of his granddaughters. Augusta was attracted by the frontiersman's life, and she eventually married Isaac Topping, an itinerant showman who traveled with a sort of circus, performing with a "singing donkey." Augusta wrote sketches and composed songs for the show. Harriet Alice was influenced by her flamboyant grandfather's iconoclasm. He defended the oppressed Chippewas against Washington's policy of encroachment, and she became a lifelong advocate for the politically, socially, and economically oppressed. Fred's refusal to join any church, unusual even on the frontier, disposed her to freethinking in religion and on social issues. Some townspeople in Fenton regarded Alice as "headstrong and exasperating," especially in her defense of women's rights. Not long after she arrived at the University of Michigan, she joined three of her women friends to protest against the policy of the library's reading room, from which, the *Argonaut* reported, women "are practically debarred." Their protests won the use of the "South dressing room," and they took possession of it and fitted it out as a reading room for women.

When Alice graduated from Fenton High School in the mid-1870s, she, like John, was uncertain about her future. She spent a year studying music in Fenton's Baptist Seminary and then taught high school for a while in nearby Flushing. After studying French with the intention of going to the university, she entered the University of Michigan in 1883 with advanced status and became a philosophy major. As for her own seriousness, her casual reading ranged from the English poets to Aristotle, Montaigne, and Spinoza (whom she found perfectly "comprehensible"). For fun, she read and wrote Greek. In the spring of 1886 she delivered a paper to the Philosophy Club, "Pantheism and Modern Science," which reviewed four articles appearing in the current issue of the *Journal of Speculative Philosophy*.

The central event in 1885 for John Dewey was his falling in love with Alice and becoming a new person. President Gilman had been right in declaring him to be too bookish. Dewey's passions had been channeled into ideas and strict personal rectitude. "My wife used to say quite truly," Dewey wrote in later years, "that I go at things from the back end, . . . hampered by too much technical absorption." Alice refocused him. In 1885 he started to go at things from the "front end," that is, from the perspectives of human desire and social need. In this regard, Alice reinforced other influences exerted on him, from Henry Carter Adams to his brother Dave. Dewey started to move from technical methodology to practical absorption; from idealism to social statics in the Herbert Spencer sense; from the absolute to the individual; from the abstract to the particular; from Hegelian logic to the logic of inquiry; from system to pluralism and experiment; and from pietistic "ethics" to "ethical culture."

Some of these changes were soon manifested at a second remove in the articles he wrote. But the best evidence of the internal changes in John Dewey is in the letters that he wrote to Alice during their separation for school holidays. The first came in the summer vacation following Dewey's first year at Michigan. Dewey returned to his parents' house in Burlington, but his thoughts remained with Alice. "It feels curious enough to be back again," he told Alice:

> I started to write home, instead of "back," but really I can't
> find that this is my home any more. . . . Where my parents live
> is like home enough, but Burlington, otherwise, isn't my home
> anymore. I am weaned. . . . For the first time in the six years of
> coming back, I feel as if I were only visiting.

The crucial word is *weaned*. He loved his mother as much as ever—her home was still his "home"—but by finding Alice he had been weaned from New England culture in Burlington. In Michigan, not New England, he told Alice, he "expected . . . [and] wanted to make a permanent home." (In his long life he never lived in New England again, not even during vacations.) If he was not yet conscious of it, Alice had become the center of his emotional family. That is illustrated by the next thing he told her, that he was doing research to discover the Chipman family roots in his own birth state of Vermont, for he still took a distant pride in the state of his birth. Soon, he reported, he discovered the existence of a Chipman who was "the first town clerk in Vergennes," as well as an "Old Nathaniel Chipman," whose existence, he informed Alice, "makes you intimately related to the state of VT." and thus related, statewise, to the Vermonter John Dewey. He actually found and bought for her Nathaniel Chipman's *Sketches of the Principles of Government*, published in Rutland, Vermont, in 1793. (Dewey did not do enough research to discover that in fact, the Chipmans had been in Vermont longer than the Deweys, as John Chipman [1620-1708] had immigrated from Barnstable, England, in the seventeenth century.) They also discovered another common link: they both had relatives in Oil City.

John confessed to Alice that he had set aside some of his own old passions in order to adopt hers. He put his Plato on the shelf and began to read Goethe's poetry aloud for an hour a day in the original German. He reminded her of "a little conversation we had . . . regarding nature and poetry, Wordsworth's in particular." He browsed through Mrs. Oliphant's *Literary History of the Nineteenth Century* and then read Browning's poetry as a "sauce." For the first time in his life, he began to wax poetical. He told Alice that even though he had grown up in Burlington, he hadn't realized until now how beautiful it was; and he romantically described the "purple, bronze & sage green" sunsets and the "four ranges of mountains varying from the darkest purple in the foreground to a greenish opal in the background visible across a flame colored lake streaked with orange." Soon, he delivered a lecture on Browning's poetry to the Unity Club.

In case Alice missed the fact that all of this was a shy New Englander's way of saying he liked her, he became bolder and expressed "my pleasure and thanksgiving that you are going to be in Ann Arbor another year. It adds greatly, I cannot say how greatly, to the enjoyment of the prospect of my own return, to reflect that the pleasures of last year may be renewed, and I hope added to." He kept up the correspondence all during the summer. With only two weeks remaining before school was to resume, he made a philosopher's appeal to Alice. He had done no work, he told her, for his scheduled fall class on Plato's *Republic*. He urged her: "If you would kindly spend your time between now and the 30th, in reading the *Republic*, noting down good subjects for discussion and investigation, looking up references, and laying out a course generally, you will remove a burden from my mind." In the nineteenth century, a philosopher who asked an intelligent woman to lay out a philosophic course for him was certainly on the verge of proposing marriage.

John Dewey had been transformed. His mother had helped him with his first statement of "conversion." Now, through Alice, he went through a second conversion. Everything romantic blossomed for them during the fall term of 1885. Dewey's classes continued to draw a large number of students. As for his philosophic writing, he was still trying to reconcile Hegelianism with Christianity and both with experimental psychology—he called this "speculative psychology"—and also to use all three to analyze social problems. Alice was interested in both philosophy and politics, but she had no difficulty resolving the conflicts among her interests. On December 31, 1885, John told Alice that in the morning he wrote "some on that Hegel idea," and in the afternoon he brushed up on "statistics of the cotton and wool & iron trades." These two interests could certainly be joined, and Alice was ahead of him in doing so.

John's thoughts and his researches went in many directions. The easing of his inward laceration that came with his deepening relation to Alice started him into unanticipated areas of research. In "Doctor Martineau's Theory of Morals," published in the early fall of 1885, he began to investigate the search for moral principles undertaken by a prominent intellectual woman. Next he began to assemble a sociological critique of the widespread assumption that female delicacy could not tolerate without ill health the stresses of higher education. In "Education and the Health of Women" and "Health and Sex in Higher Education," both written in 1886, one published in *Science* and the other in E. L. Youmans's *Popular Science Monthly*, Dewey disputed that negative assessment and offered impressive statistical data to prove that education did not harm women's health. As a bold empiricist, he stated in the first of these articles: "The tendency to apply the exact methods of science to problems of education, is one of the most hopeful signs of present pedagogy." In both articles his main concern was to see that adequate scientific research was conducted before any sociological conclusions were reached: "Education must follow the example of the special sciences. *It must organize.*"

DEWEY'S PHILOSOPHY EXPANDS

His new interests, mostly influenced by Alice, did not stop with women's health. W. T. Harris had stimulated his interest in educational theory, and G. Stanley Hall had given it a another push. Now Alice was interested in education and was preparing at the University of Michigan for a career in teaching. These influences combined to start John on a vital part of his own career. His growing awareness of the pressing need in America to reorient education led Dewey to join the Michigan Schoolmasters' Club and to begin a philosophic study of education and educational theory in Europe. He soon found himself addressing the Michigan schoolmasters on "Psychology in High-Schools from the Standpoint of the College." Before long, Dewey was assisting the University of Michigan in making accreditation visits to high schools in Fenton, Owosso, and Muskegon. He was starting to use in educational theory what he had learned to be operational ends; enlarging his concept of philosophy, he began to apply psychology to the study of how we learn, how we focus attention, and how we think. With the growth of American's population in the 1880s, public education was becoming a national topic, and educational reformers were making names for themselves. In the nineteenth century, under the sentimental influence of romanticism, Americans idealized childhood. This led to a concomitant interest in early education, and the new science of psychology led naturally to educational research. Moreover, the industrial and information revolutions meant that public schools became more and more necessary to educate the citizenry for high-level economic mobility and success. A free high-school education was a relatively recent and rare development in the United States, as it had no system like the German *gymnasium* to prepare qualified students for higher education. Now Americans had to ask: What should a secondary school teach? How should high school be taught? What should be the basic and the vocational curricula? College education influenced high schools, but colleges were in flux and moving toward electives. Conversely, as high-school curricula expanded, college instruction changed also. Similarly, elementary education was modified as well. Americans were uncertain on all three levels about how a democratic education should differ from a traditional European education. As a consequence, educational specialists were in demand and quickly achieved fame. During Dewey's first term at Michigan, Colonel Frances Parker, a well-known educational theorist and innovator, addressed the state meeting of Michigan teachers on the topic "Learn to Do by Doing," an idea that Dewey further developed in his work with Parker in Chicago only a few years later. In 1885, Dewey's turn to education was a promising one, and it began to bring him national attention.

Humanistically and dynamically based morals, women's health, and early education were new subjects for Dewey, and he used them to conduct experiments aimed at inward unification. But Christian concerns, as well as his continuing devotion to Morris and Harris, also kept him at his Hegelian endeavors, as evidenced by his talk delivered to the Philosophical Society on "Hegel and Recent Thought." It was not yet clear to Dewey that his commitment to philosophic idealism was an unconscious attempt to hold onto Christian fundamentalism. He believed instead that he could find a way to combine them all in a grand new synthesis, just by adding new ones.

It seemed to Dewey that his greatest asset—his training as a psychologist—was the glue to make all these interests cohere. As early as the middle of his first year at Michigan, he started to plan a book on psychology. His first thought was practical. All the textbooks on psychology were outdated, including the textbook by Murray that he used, and he believed that he could make up for the deficiency. But what should its point of view be? If he followed Morris and wrote a text on psychology as placed in the Hegelian structure—in the subsidiary position between "organics" and "mechanics" within the category of the "Idea-Outside-Itself"—he would not satisfy the needs of teachers of the new psychology. If he followed his other Hopkins mentor, Hall, and wrote a text on such specific physiological subjects as muscular discharge or verbomotor reactions, he would puzzle most academic philosophers searching for a way of teaching psychology as a new branch of philosophy. Dewey's unspoken answer was that he would do both—combine German idealism with German experimentalism to produce an American psychology.

He started to work out this idea in two articles that he wrote during 1884–85. Both were soon published in Mind, then the most distinguished philosophical journal in the English-speaking world. In them he argued that "perception"—the subject matter of psychology—could be extended to include "memory, imagination, conception, judgment, [and] reasoning." If this was so, then philosophy's concern with self-consciousness could be merged with psychology's emphasis on perception, the source of self-consciousness. In this way, psychology and philosophy would meet in the real world of human striving and even subsume the concerns of history, politics, and art. In the first of the articles, "Psychology as Philosophic Method," Dewey's conclusion stands out:

> There is no possible break: either we must deny the possibility of treating perception in psychology, and then our "purely objective science of psychology" can be nothing more than a physiology; or, admitting it, we must admit what follows directly from and upon it—self-consciousness. Self-consciousness is indeed a *fact* (I do not fear the word) of experience, and must therefore find its treatment in psychology.

The best philosopher, therefore, must be the best psychologist. William James, beginning to develop his own ideas about psychology at Harvard, took in Dewey's point, and he eventually wrote a better book about psychology than Dewey's was. But Dewey's seminal perception concerning self-consciousness influenced James before James influenced him. In one stroke, Dewey completed the phase of his intellectual life that had started years before when he read Harris's cryptic remark concerning the "great psychological movement from Kant to Hegel." Now, it was a triple play: Kant to Hegel to Dewey. Dewey said as much to Professor Torrey:

> Whether I can succeed in bettering the existing text-books, or even in getting it published remains to be seen. I am simply trying, however, to write one with the greatest possible unity of principle, so that without ceasing to be a psychology, it shall be an introduction to philosophy in general.

Dewey was very clear about what he wanted to achieve in a book about psychology, and the clarity shows in the book he produced. He wanted to *use* psychology for the sake of philosophy and, by setting forth a concept of mind as a genetic, active unit, to breathe new life into "philosophic ideas that were becoming exhausted."

Dewey's book—the first book on modern psychology published in America—has been largely forgotten now, but in 1885–86 it constituted a brilliant intellectual move on his part. The originality of his work lay in his successful fusion of philosophic idealism with psychological experiment, to show their relation and then to assert that philosophy *must be* psychological. His argument was simple: everything that exists, exists in consciousness; therefore, the psychological study of consciousness is the key to understanding all existence. Psychology explored the depths of self-consciousness and philosophy dealt with self-consciousness; that is, they were one. By a neat tautology, Dewey taught his colleagues, as well as his own students, that remaining a philosopher meant becoming a psychologist. In addition, in his book Dewey provided scientists and philosophers with a common language: to be a true philosopher-psychologist, one would speak like neither Morris nor Hall but like Dewey.

Dewey completed a draft of *Psychology* in early December 1885, after a year and a half of teaching at Michigan. He sent it to Harper & Brothers, a leading publisher, and almost immediately received their promise of "our careful consideration." Like all first authors he waited nervously for further news. His mind was full of psychological ideas, and not just in the lab; he saw psychology everywhere. Reading Browning again, he observed that his dramatic lyrics "are almost all a study of motives." Revising his book on the day before Christmas, he also began to investigate a new, perplexing area: "My studies of infant psychology have now brought me to the point where I regard a young one as a compound of mechanical imitation and his majesty Mephistopheles—not in the way of wickedness, in this case, but of supernatural and unholy wisdom." But what would his research in psychology mean for early childhood education?

Concerns about the publication of *Psychology*, however, were displaced by missing Alice, who had gone home to Fenton for the holidays. As they said their good-byes, John experienced a nonphilosophical moment of abandon and—gave Alice five kisses. Then their letters started. "My sweet one," Alice began her missives, "I found your dear letter yesterday . . . and my heart was so happy as it listened to the voice of its love speaking sweet words of life and peace. . . . All the way from the office there it kept saying to me 'my darling loves me' and the grayness of the day all vanished and there was sunshine and springtime all around me." John responded in a self-effacing, mock-philosophical manner: "Sweetheart, I have found out that I am only an abstractly subjective standpoint without you." Only her love, he meant, made him a real person. This Christmas, for the first time, he did not go back to Burlington but stayed in Lapeer, Michigan, with his mother's sister, who strongly resembled Lucina. From there he could sometimes run over to see Alice in Fenton.

On the days when they were apart, John resumed his reading of Browning, undertaking the difficult *Sordello*. Both he and Alice admired Browning for his poetic modernism and especially for the legendary story of his and Elizabeth's love. Philosophy took a backseat to thoughts of marriage. On the day before Christmas 1885, Alice opened a package from John and inside it found an opal engagement ring. In her excitement she fancied that she "saw little loves shining out of every color of the stone, and I know they were kisses from you, and I am going to sleep with this on my finger." "Next Christmas," she happily wrote him, "we shall be together." Her pointed remark was a resolution, not just a prediction. John's New England will found its match in Alice's power of determination.

During the holidays, he informed his parents and brothers of his engagement, and when he got back to Ann Arbor, he wrote to his father to ask him to send a welcoming letter to his fiancée. Even on this occasion, the joking tone toward John that Archibald always used produced a remarkable reply:

> You suggest a letter to Miss Chipman. I forgive you John for you do it in ignorance. Over 30 years ago I wrote to an estimable young woman and what came of it? You yourself are one of the consequences of the manouver: you dont remember it, nor many more that followed in reckless succession, but you see how I thwarted the high possibilities of your excellent mother. But seriously John, if I could write a letter that would not shame you I would gladly introduce my self to the chosen girl of your manhood. . . . Perhaps I may write a line to Miss Chipman *some* time, til then let her think as well as she can of your Father.

He did not get what he wanted from his father, but otherwise John Dewey was triumphing on all sides. He was greeted with warm admiration from his students. President Angell supported him and invited him to join the New England Society. Alice loved him. Crowning these was his new book. After considerable revision, *Psychology* was accepted by Harper & Brothers in April, almost as soon as he finally finished revising the last chapter. The book proved to be an international sensation, calling Dewey to the attention of the philosophical world. Academic philosophers in the same bind as Dewey, struggling to blend idealism with empiricism, welcomed Dewey's solution not just in America but also in Great Britain and Germany. This gave him and his text instant fame, for it was the only available one suitable for instruction in psychology in American colleges. The intention that Dewey expressed in his preface and carried out in his book was decisive in establishing its usefulness as a textbook. "I am sure," Dewey wrote, "that there is a way of raising questions, and of looking at them, which is philosophic; a way which the beginner can find more easily in psychology than elsewhere, and which, when found, is the best possible introduction to all specific philosophic questions." Moreover, as Dewey's notes show, *Psychology* is a work of extraordinary scholarly erudition. Within a short time the book was adopted at Williams, Brown, Smith, Wellesley, the University of Minnesota, the University of Kansas, and the University of Vermont.

A second edition was published in 1889, and a third one, two years later. In each, Dewey modified and improved on the idealist terminology and increased the experimental illustrations. The 1891 edition even incorporated Dewey's important identification of the reflex or adjustive arc as the basis of thinking. The influence of the book was immediate. In the first edition of his own work on educational theory, James A. McLellan acknowledged Dewey "whose work in Psychology has been so well received by students of philosophy." Dewey's *Psychology*, which firmly established psychology as a basic instrument of philosophy, continued to serve as the standard textbook through the turn of the century. It was just the sort of book that American philosophers had been hoping to find. James Rowland Angell, then a student, found that the book "instantly opened up a new world which it seemed to me I had been waiting for."

The book was, however, criticized by philosophers observant enough to see the tautology at its core. Dewey had converted physical perception-as-self-consciousness into metaphysical idealism and idealism back into self-consciousness, as if these were the same. Even the sympathetic H. A. P. Torrey, reviewing the book in the *Andover Review*, remarked that to make his argument work, Dewey had used "psychology" where "metaphysical" should have appeared. William

James confided to his friend Croom Robertson that at first glance he was "enthused," "hoping for something really fresh," but found the work to be too systematically Hegelian to be adequate as philosophy.

Psychologists attacked the book for the opposite reason—its deficiency in scientific particularization. Dewey's teacher Hall was aghast (and perhaps a bit envious) at what his student had produced and did not hide his disapproval. In his review he wrote: "That the absolute idealism of Hegel could be so clearly adapted to be 'read into' such a range of facts, is indeed a surprise as great as when Geology and Zoology are ingeniously subjected to the rubrics of the six days of creation." He believed that "very few of [the facts] . . . are satisfactory, and many we believe to be fundamentally wrong and misleading," since Dewey was "more intent on the mutual interpretation and coherence of his network of definitions than on their relation to the facts." Hall's review appeared in the first number of the new *American Journal of Psychology*. It must have stung, coming from his mentor in psychology. Even several years later, Dewey was uncharacteristically harsh in commenting on Hall, telling Alice in 1894 that Hall was "parading a kind of psychology with a pious swish," which was good only for "a mental emetic." Now he understood what William James had meant when he said that "Hall threatened harm to our culture with his combination of crude fact & edifying piety." In 1903, Dewey remarked that Hall's rivalry with others and his claims to have originated ideas that were theirs

> have ultimately made it impossible for him to retain harmonious cooperative relations with other investigators, even the stronger ones among his own students. . . . It is a matter of common repute that Dr. Hall is incapable of either permitting men near him to work freely along their own lines of interest, or to keep from appropriating to himself credit for work which belongs to others.

Perhaps Dewey's kindest critics were the Michigan students. Their satire magazine, *The Oracle*, reported slyly that students were "vending the only authorized translation of Dewey's *Psychology* at fabulous prices." A student wit defined "Dew[e]y" as "Adj. cold, impersonal, psychological, sphinx-like, anomalous and petrifying to flunkers." An imitation of Keats's "La Belle Dame sans merci" teased Dewey:

O what is the matter with you, lank girl,
A pale and wild and haggard she,
Oh, don't you know, the old man said,
She's taking Dewey's Psychology.

The final student judgment of *Psychology* was that it was "one of the 'stiffest' text books in existence." But his classes were always full. Obviously, Dewey took his teaching very seriously and demanded a lot of his students. Even without these comments, that would be clear to anyone who examined his preparation for every course. On the first day of class, he passed out to the students a synopsis of the expected content of each class session, not merely the reading for the semester, but a detailed précis of each subject to be investigated, along with guidance to further reading and reflection. This usually amounted to a handout of about 120 pages, in which he provided the notes the students might have taken. In turn, this allowed him to roam freely in discussion and lectures, well beyond the fundamentals of the course.

All the approbation that Dewey was accorded on every side had led him to feel confident in 1886 that the regents of the university would act favorably on Professor Morris's recommendation that Dewey be promoted to assistant professor and have his salary increased to $1,600. President Angell himself told John that he had "almost no doubt" that he would be promoted. Based on that expectation, John and Alice planned to marry. When he confided his marriage plans to George Morris, John told Alice, "I never saw Mr. Morris so enthusiastic. He gripped my hand and shook it—really shook it—said that was *good*, was *splendid*—he was so glad to hear it; it pleased him ever so much." Their anxieties began when the regents delayed. John urged Alice not to fret—"we shall not be separated from each other another year." Still, April, while the regents debated, was a time of uncertainty. Alice had not yet told her grandfather, or anyone else, about their engagement, worried that they would not be able to afford to marry.

"I am rather doubtful about the wisdom of getting married next summer dearest," Alice wrote in mid-April. Even Dewey's mother was
worried that he could not marry on his present salary. But he remained
both confident and determined. "What are you doing this night sweet
one?" he asked Alice. "Doing things so that we can get married next
summer, aren't you, my love?" By April 12, Dewey heard a rumor
from Morris that President Angell had argued Dewey's case with one
of the regents. Another period of uncertainty. Finally, in June the
appointment went through.

On July 28, 1886, John and Alice were married in Fenton. Rev.
Thomas Wright officiated, and Evaline Riggs and Mrs. G. J. K. Stoner
were witnesses. When John's mother received the news, she wrote to
John:

> I shall take a little time, to write a few words to you, to express
> however faintly, my deep interest and sympathy in this new
> phase of your life. I am deeply and tenderly moved on your
> account, my dear son, and full of the most eager interest in not
> only yourself but in the object of your affections.

She begged him to send her Alice's photograph and to give her permission to write her daughter-in-law. John and Alice moved out of the
boarding house at 315 Packard Street into their own quarters at 441
Thompson Street and started their married life.

Dewey's Reputation Builds

No further development was possible concerning the fusion of idealist
thought with empirical psychology that Dewey had accomplished in
Psychology. For a long time—as late as *How We Think* (1910) and
beyond—Dewey used these empirical insights. But the idealist language and Hegelian influence began to fade. By April 1886, Dewey's
interest in applying psychology to social issues was growing while
Hegelianism lingered, but now with little original spark. Other interests were building parallel to psychology. He wrote to Alice that he was

"reading up on machinery & wages. . . . It has opened up a new field to me—I almost wish sometimes I were in pol. ec.; it is so thoroughly human." At the same time he reviewed Samuel Tilden's *Public Writing and Speeches* in *The Christian Union*. Tilden had lost the disputed election to Rutherford B. Hayes, but when Hayes became president, he was saddled with the sobriquet "Fraudulent Hayes" while Tilden earned respect for his political sagacity. Forgotten today, Tilden's essays on democratic, activist politics were Dewey's practical introduction to the conditions of political life in America. Around the same time Dewey also looked at "a number of French and German histories of the laboring classes," which aroused his democratic enthusiasms.

This reading was partly done in preparation for a talk that Dewey was scheduled to give two weeks later. On April 14, he addressed the Political Science Association (PSA) on "The Rise of Great Industries." With this talk, Dewey began to edge out of his effort to unify science, religion, and psychology-as-self-consciousness and to turn his philosophy toward the psychological investigation of economic society. His subsidiary interest at Hopkins in the historical and political sciences complemented his personal experience. Dewey knew at first hand about the industrial progress of Burlington and, from his residence in Oil City, even more about the rise of Rockefeller's Standard Oil. In his Political Science Association talk, he spoke with passion on the degradation of democracy through rampant industrial development. A report of the speech classed it as "a masterly study of the economic, industrial, social, and moral effects . . . of the great corporate undertakings of modern times." Although there had been abuse, Dewey declared, "the future is full of hope for all classes." In a recasting of this talk two years later, he wrote: "Democracy is not in reality what it is in name until it is industrial as well as civil and political." "Workers have the right," he told the rather conservative members of the PSA, "to organize trade unions in order to re-democratize the industrial system."

Dewey's interest in democracy and its vicissitudes was deepening. He followed his critique of the great industries with a talk to the Philosophical Society on "Sir Henry Maine's Conception of Democracy," in which he used Maine's critique of democracy to present his own, more positive view that democracy "approaches most nearly the ideal of all social organization; that in which the individual and society are organic to each other." A few months later he spoke more pointedly in a talk at Ann Arbor in Delphi Hall, asserting that "the aim of the educated man . . . should be to keep in sympathy with the people," and he bewailed the increase of economic-class thinking in America.

It is characteristic of John Dewey's mind that he never resolved intellectual quandaries so much as he simply left them behind or looked differently at them. When questions became "old," he transformed or recalibrated them. As his interest in politics grew, his philosophical idealism faded. His second book, *Leibniz's New Essays Concerning the Human Understanding* (1888), shows only traces of the influence on him of neo-Hegelian logic. Leibniz, of course, was a favorite of H. A. P. Torrey, and Dewey's book was commissioned by George Morris for a philosophic series he was editing. In fact, the departed Howison was originally scheduled to write the volume, but Dewey replaced him. So in some sense, this second book of Dewey's looked backward. But the volume shows how good Dewey's training and development as a technical philosopher was. It was warmly reviewed for its clear handling of philosophical issues and enhanced Dewey's reputation. Even years later he was regarded as America's foremost authority on Leibniz, and for a series he was editing, Ralph Barton Perry invited Dewey to write the Leibniz volume.

Two results of Dewey's growing fame were immediately apparent. First, he began to receive many more invitations to attend conferences, write books, submit articles, or collaborate on monographs. From this time forth, for the rest of his life, Dewey was always in demand. Invitations now came from strangers who knew him only through his writings. "I have just finished making a kind of abstract of my psychology," he wrote to Torrey. "A gentleman [James A. McLellan] in Toronto Canada, Director of Normal Schools for Ontario & Professor of Pedagogy in the University of Toronto, is writing a book on Education theory and practice [entitled *Applied Psychology*] and wanted a psychological introduction, and so I have been working in conjunction with him." This became Dewey's third book and one of the few cowritten by him; in the second edition of *Applied Psychology*, Dewey is listed as coauthor. This book started Dewey's reputation as a theorist of educational method.

The major means by which educational innovations were brought quickly to the attention of educationists, psychologists, and philosophers was through lectures. About this time, Dewey began to receive numerous invitations to put his most recent thoughts into talks. At first he offered these free, asking compensation only for his expenses. But soon he began to charge $25 per lecture. Instead of reducing his invitations, this only multiplied them.

Another consequence of Dewey's growing fame was that he now began to attract the attention of schools that wished to create or improve their philosophy departments. The regents' delay in promoting him in the spring of 1886 left John and Alice somewhat resentful, and he was looking at other job possibilities. Dewey's name came up as a potential appointment at Johns Hopkins in 1886, but G. Stanley Hall, still suspicious of Dewey, told Gilman he was "skeptical of his work." The idea was dropped. In 1887, Alice encouraged John to talk to President Cyrus Northrop about a job at the University of Minnesota. He did so, but at that time nothing came of it. Thomas Peebles, a student of James McCosh at Princeton and an advocate of the old-fashioned Scottish Common Sense school of philosophy, was hired temporarily. But for Dewey the seed of departure was planted, and Northrop did not forget about Dewey.

Perhaps Dewey forgot for a while about Minnesota, for as Dewey's third year at Michigan drew to a close, all attention was focused on another kind of production. Alice was pregnant.

FRED DEWEY

Frederick Archibald, usually called Fred, sometimes known as "dear Freddie boy" by his father, was born on July 19, 1887, in Fenton, Michigan, at the home of Fred and Evaline Riggs, where Alice had grown up. "Frederick" was for Alice's grandfather, and "Archibald" was for Dewey's father.

Now began the many legends about Dewey's curious behavior as a father. Lillian W. Johnson, who boarded at the Deweys, recalled one time, during "Sunday dinner, [when] Fred was making a great racket in the hall. Mrs. Dewey said, 'John, go and make Fred keep quiet.' 'Oh, Alice, I can't, it's too hard work,' he drawled." Another tale recounts how Fred overflowed the upstairs' bathroom playing at the biblical flood. Finally the water dripped into Dewey's study. Rushing upstairs, he stood silent with amazement until the boy spoke up: "Don't say anything John," he ordered. "Get the mop."

Many tales were circulated in several versions and were eventually applied to most of his children. In an often repeated story, Dewey had rolled a baby carriage with a baby in it down to the bank, parked it outside, came out preoccupied with counting his money, and strolled happily home—without the carriage. The child, in all versions, slept contentedly until John remembered his mistake. Such are the legends about philosophers, which, in Dewey's case, were sometimes true.

From the time of his birth, except for a brief period when he was seven, Fred was the perfect child, devoted, dependable, good spirited, independent, and caring. When Fred was six, John visited his first-grade class in Ann Arbor "two or three times" and took great pleasure in seeing the beautiful look on Fred's face: "he was the only person there who looked really socially placid and at the same time full of business." Fred was by nature "always so generous." His father adored him and expected much of him. John and Alice shared a great burden: they both were interested in the education of young children, they both felt that they were on the cutting edge of educational and child-raising reform, and therefore they both assumed that they must train their children to be exceptional creatures. Any misbehavior caused them lots of worry, and often they asked themselves, "Where have we gone wrong?" forgetting that a child's developmental path is not always straight.

When Fred was seven, the Dewey family moved from Ann Arbor to Chicago, and at the same time Alice prepared to go abroad with the children to give them the European "experience" that neither she nor John had been able to have. Suddenly, Fred went "to pieces," experiencing what later would be called "separation anxiety"—that is, losing

Ann Arbor without yet having a home in Chicago; leaving his father behind, even though he promised to join them in a few months; and going to a strange land where people didn't speak English. Fred was nervous, overwrought, depressed. He began to convert some of his stress into physical symptoms: he had bad headaches, and he suffered from eyestrain so severe that he couldn't read from the blackboard.

John himself was ready to downplay the psychogenic disorders. "I used to have [headaches] . . . during school hours," he told Alice. And he had eyestrain too, but in "10 or 15 minutes" after he got out of school, the symptoms would evaporate. (Unfortunately, Fred had inherited John's temperamental tendency toward conversion, and so did all his other siblings until nearly all, with their father, got a treatment that mostly cured them.)

But what made John feel guilty was that if Fred was so prone to go to pieces, it must be because John had put too much pressure on him. Fred seemed to have no ability "to fix himself," that is, calm himself, when he became anxious. John felt that he had "antagonized" Fred, pushing him to become interested in science. It was, John thought, "too much." "Fred seems," he wrote to Alice, to have "a crisis with every marked change in his surroundings." Dewey wished that he could "start all over" in raising his child, worrying that Fred was fragile and had too great a need "for continuity of action." After much introspection, John concluded that it was all his fault: "I abused him fearfully all the earlier days of his life" by expecting too much of him. All that could be done for the poor boy now, John believed, was to give him simple tasks; he should be "taught a trade, like carpentry," since more reflective study "stimulates without affording any normal channel for the stimulation to get out." John felt remorse, for he believed that in Fred he had taken into his care a blank slate tinged with brilliance—and made a mess of it.

John's own rather long-lasting crises made him stronger once he overcame them, and he thus began to feel that he could do anything, pass through any turmoil, and come out smiling. The same thing happened to Fred, but Fred's crisis of anxiety was much shorter. He never again lost confidence. By the age of nine, he was writing chatty, loving letters to his parents, who left him on his own quite a lot. Often he stayed at his great-grandparents' house in Fenton, and sometimes he remained with acquaintances in Hurricane, New York, where the Deweys had a cabin in which they spent many summers. Never again did he have separation anxiety. He wrote joyful letters and surrounded his signature with Xs and Os for his parents. When he became a teenager, he occasionally babysat for his siblings for a few days at a time and sent engaging reports of their behavior to the absent parents. For instance, in 1902, when he was fifteen, he informed John and Alice: "Every body is well except that Lucy has developed a streak of 'I can do anything I please . . .' and so proceeds to raise a general roughhouse—Janie is good as pie and Gordon is good too." On occasion, he even gave his dad advice. "It is too cold to wear linen," he told John, "so you might bring another pair of corduroys." Fred was enthusiastic about everything. When he visited New York City in 1902 with friends from Hurricane, he couldn't wait to walk over the Brooklyn Bridge and visit the Statue of Liberty. Fred also turned out to be a precocious student. In January 1904, his parents went over to University High School to listen to Fred and his team debate Armour Academy before an audience of three hundred. Fred stood right up, calm as could be, and spoke in the affirmative on the topic "Joseph Chamberlain's tariff proposals should be adopted by the British government." And Fred's side won.

In 1904 Alice took the children to France. Fred registered for the fall semester at the University of Grenoble to study French while Alice and the other children went to the coast. Then, when the fall semester was finished, he moved to the University of Jena, where he studied German and Latin. Fred did well in German itself but had a bit of difficulty in Latin, because he was used to translating Latin into English, not Latin into German or German into Latin. Naturally, with this stress his eyes acted up again, and he could read for only brief periods. As soon as he took up fencing, though, his eyestrain cleared up speedily.

When Fred returned to the United States, he spent the 1905–6 academic year at the University of Michigan. The following year he transferred to the Massachusetts Institute of Technology where his uncle, Davis Rich Dewey, was teaching economics. All went smoothly, but his parents experienced some anxiety over one incident that occurred while he was a junior at MIT. He wrote his mother one of those dreaded letters that open ominously: "Let me break the news gently." The news was "I am engaged." He explained that on just the previous night "a dandy girl" named Alice Hamilton O'Connell abandoned her resolution not to marry outside her religion and accepted his proposal. Alice Dewey must have held her breath, for Alice O'Connell was a Roman Catholic. Already, at the age of twenty, she had graduated from the state normal school and was teaching second grade. According to Fred, she had a head on her shoulders and was "without any foolish romantic delusions as to the ethical value of cold cash." Alice, who hated dogmatism of any kind, was concerned. She sent a letter back full of both "reproofs and encouragements." Fred complained at this time, as he often did, that Alice didn't understand him. However, Fred's passion for Miss O'Connell did not last until his graduation in 1910. Instead of marrying, he became a graduate student and eventually a university fellow in sociology at Columbia, graduating with a Ph.D. in 1913. His dissertation was entitled "Some Aspects of Behavior in Social Groups." He promptly went off to teach sociology and economics at Bryn Mawr and there met a young alumna of the college, Elizabeth Braley, whom he married in 1915. She was not a Catholic. Alice was relieved, and John loved her and treated her just like one of his own daughters. After marrying, Fred resigned from Bryn Mawr and went into business.

When Liz gave birth to their first child, Gordon Chipman, in 1918, John declared himself "crazy" to see the baby. "I can hardly wait," he wrote to Alice. Other children followed—Elizabeth Anne in 1919, then John—another John Dewey. But John was killed in an automobile accident during a vacation from his military academy in Colorado Springs in 1934, and Fred and Liz decided to have another child to replace John. In 1936 Liz gave birth to JoAnna. John was living with Fred and Liz at their apartment on 320 East 72d Street at the time JoAnna was born, and he made the connection: "They lost a boy in an accident two years ago and so are very happy—it is really lovely."

Fred joined the army in World War I and, because of his scientific training, was assigned to the Chemical Warfare Service Gas Defense Plant in Long Island City, New York. In September 1918 he was promoted to major and put in charge of the plant. After the end of the war, he remained in charge for several months as the plant was demobilized. Although he began writing a book on America's manufacturing of lethal gas, he was prevented by the army from publishing the material he had gathered as he closed the plant.

In 1919, as John Dos Passos put it, the "Big Money" was on the horizon in America because another war had pumped up the economy. Fred saw the future clearly and took a job in Philadelphia at Montgomery and Company, dealing in stocks and bonds. But he also traveled back to New York to teach a course at the New School for Social Research. He left Montgomery and Company and became vice-president of the Farmer's Loan and Trust Company. He proved to be a successful investment broker and became an organizing partner of his own firm of Dewey and Bacon. John got him some business occasionally, referring S. O. Levinson to him, for instance. An enthusiastic yachtsman and ocean racer, Fred was a member of the New York Yacht Club. In the 1920s, he moved to Long Island and commuted into the city from Great Neck until the mid-1930s when he moved back to the city. From 1936 until his death in 1967, he was a director of several corporations and a consultant.

Fred always remained close to his father. He prepared his tax return; he gave him investment advice; he arranged an annual Christmas dinner; and finally he brought John to live with him. He talked to John Dewey as if he, Fred, was his father's older brother, and John, "a kid brother of whom [Fred] . . . is very fond." Whenever his dad needed a bit of rest, he'd go out to Great Neck for a breather. As the years went by, if John ever remembered those days in 1894 when Fred went to pieces and John blamed himself for overstimulating him, he must have wondered how he had gone so wrong in his assessment of the boy. True, Fred devoted himself to making money instead of improving society, but he was a good son, a good husband, and a good citizen.

To Minnesota and Back to Michigan

In the early winter of 1888, Professor Thomas Peebles resigned from the University of Minnesota. Dewey was almost immediately offered a full professorship and the chair of mental and moral philosophy and logic there, to begin in the 1888–89 school year. He was torn and explained his conflicts to Torrey. In Minnesota, he would be the entire department, which would limit advanced work; the students would not be as well prepared as those at Michigan; and there would be fewer of them. But there also were good reasons for accepting the job:

> The institution in Minn. is growing rapidly and Pres. Northrop is very ambitious to see it in the front rank. There are some advantages also in a new institution where its policy is still to be shaped, especially for a young man. Then the attractions of a large city like Minneapolis are, I confess, great.

These are the sorts of explanations that a young man may give to a still revered mentor, but there were others that an ambitious young man might not acknowledge. Professor Morris was only forty-eight years old, and Dewey could be his subordinate at Michigan for nearly twenty years. Another inducement that Dewey also left out weighed rather decisively: at Minnesota his salary would be raised to $2,400.

He accepted the job and submitted his resignation at Michigan, where the regents expressed "sincere regret" in losing "so bright a light." Clearly, Dewey left Michigan with a large repository of goodwill. As a university publication noted, Dewey "has shown by his ability, learning, and skill as a teacher, that his promotion to a full chair is merited." At Minnesota, President Cyrus Northrop and Dewey's new colleagues were highly gratified at the arrival of "a young man, [who] . . . has a clearer grasp of philosophic truth than many who have spent a lifetime in its study. His advent . . . will mark the end of the McCosh School." Once again, Dewey was fortunate in the dissatisfaction with his predecessors. At Minnesota he was poised for success.

Dewey had scarcely arrived at his new university and moved into a house at 925 Fifteenth Avenue, S.E., when he was being praised by one and all. "Professor Dewey," a writer for the *Ariel* remarked, "has made his department one of the most interesting and successful in the institution, and with the bright prospect before us, a few years' growth will enable us to take our rank with any first-class college in the country."

But Dewey was not to be connected with this hoped-for progress for long. In late February 1889, Professor Morris made the mistake of going on a winter fishing trip, caught a cold that developed into pneumonia, and on March 23 he died. Dewey, shocked deeply, suspended classes and departed for Ann Arbor. Immediately, the administration at Minnesota was concerned that he would be offered Morris's job and was "glad to learn on his return that no such arrangements had been contemplated." But in fact that very arrangement was not only contemplated but completed as well, for by the time this comforting news appeared in the *Ariel*, Dewey had already been offered Morris's chair, had conferred with President Northrop (who was "very kind in the matter"), and accepted the "high compliment" of Michigan's offer at its top salary of $2,200.

Eighteen days before George Morris's death, Alice gave birth to a daughter, whom they named Evelyn, and Dewey was now taking Morris's place. The next issue of the *Ariel* expressed regret over Dewey's resignation. Dewey's loss would be felt especially by those who had started to study with him and also by those who anticipated taking his courses in the future: "As a profound thinker and scholar Professor Dewey stands in the foremost rank, and is eminently successful as a teacher. He possesses the faculty of making a difficult subject easy and interesting, and his fair, genial treatment has made him loved and respected by all." Not long afterward, S. C. Griggs and Co., publishers of Dewey's *Leibniz*, asked Dewey to take over the editorship of the German philosophic series that Morris had started. In a nice turnabout, Dewey was soon writing to W. T. Harris, whom Morris had commissioned to write on Hegel's *Logic*, urging him to complete his work, which now would be under Dewey's editorship.

That summer, and in many thereafter, Dewey took his family to Thomas Davidson's philosophic "camp," Glenmore, in Keene, New York, for the chance it gave him to meet America's philosophical luminaries, with whom he could talk over his new ideas. With Morris's death, there was one less reason for Dewey to hold on to Hegelianism. Bubbling over with original ideas, he was already intent on building a new kind of department at Michigan. He started to assemble a cadre of like-minded colleagues. He identified James B. Tufts as the philosopher who should fill the vacancy in the department. Tufts took over the general psychology course, using Dewey's textbook, while Dewey taught some of Morris's courses and created others, such as political philosophy, to reflect his newest interests. To expand the offerings in philosophy still further, Dewey persuaded an instructor in literature, Fred Newton Scott, to offer courses in aesthetics. When Dewey offered an advanced course in psychology in 1891, he dropped his own textbook in favor of James's new *Principles of Psychology*. When Tufts left that same year to study philosophy in Freiburg, he was replaced by George Herbert Mead, who had already studied in Leipzig and at Harvard under James and Royce. Alfred Henry Lloyd, another Dewey appointment, had studied at Göttingen, Berlin, and Heidelberg and had also earned a Ph.D. under the guidance of James and Royce. All those whom he appointed were, like Dewey, Congregationalists, and all were on paths similar to Dewey's, from absolutism to experimentalism. In a natural, almost unnoticed way, Dewey was creating the first philosophic school in America from this gathering of like-minded thinkers. At the University of Michigan all the elements, conditions, and persons were already in place that would bring Dewey to the forefront of American philosophers a few years later at the University of Chicago.

Upon his return to Michigan, Dewey resumed his close association with the Student Christian Association, continued his regular attendance at the Ann Arbor Congregational Church, spoke frequently to the "Ministerial Band" on biblical interpretation, and participated in Bible study institutes. His attachment to the church, which had been so important to his mother, was given a renewed impetus in early 1891 when Lucina and Archibald moved from Burlington to Ann Arbor and settled in John and Alice's new house at 15 Forest Avenue. Archibald was eighty years old and ill and came to his son's house to die. On April 10, 1891, he died of heart failure. No record exists of Dewey's reaction to his father's death. Lucina remained with John and Alice.

WRITING ABOUT ETHICS

Dewey's involvement with his mother's twin passions still influenced him. Although he continued to support Christian religion at Michigan, he was also at work full time on his advancing concern with freedom and social justice. His passion for social reform, his sense of the psychological dynamics of intention and the social fluidity of conviction, and, perhaps above all, his participation in the character and condition of his times brought him to reflect seriously on ethical questions. As the department's new chair, he offered such courses as "Anthropological Ethics" and "Ethics of Human Relations." Believing that the traditions of ethical writing in philosophy were inadequate, he set about to correct them and did so with such success that he became the leading exponent in America of an ethics based on modern science, especially on psychology. He soon published two books on the subject. Although neither book received much attention in the press, both were read carefully by philosophers. In early May 1891, William James wrote Dewey a "hearty note" about his *Outlines of a Critical Theory of Ethics* soon after it was publicly issued. Dewey replied that the book had received only a little "favorable comment" or "the reverse," but James was the first person "to see the point," and "when one man like yourself expresses what you wrote me[,] the book has already succeeded." James had discussed the *Outlines* with the chair of his Harvard department,

George Herbert Palmer, who also praised it highly. Modestly titled though they are, *Outlines of a Critical Theory of Ethics* (1891) and *The Study of Ethics: A Syllabus* (1894) revolutionized the subject.

Both books were issued by a printing house in Ann Arbor to serve Dewey's preparation for his classes in ethics, psychological ethics, and the history of ethical thought. Both were also meant to be independent "critical" contributions. His intention, as he expressed it in the first book, was exemplary. His *Outlines*, he said, was "an analysis of individuality into function including capacity and environment." Dewey's indebtedness to the British empiricists shows, but he had already worked through to his own conception of what he called "ethical science"—consisting of the "growth of freedom" as the guide to moral development and the basis for moral choice—and he had moved beyond his influences by associating ethics with the evolution of democracy. Similarly, he followed Caird's interpretation of Comte in teaching ethics in relation to the social meanings of scientific investigation and aesthetic appreciation. But he also indicated in his preface that he viewed the social bearings of science and art through the lens of intelligent action; and therefore again he reached an understanding of ethics that came to be his own.

Dewey's method shows Morris's lingering influence. To get at ethical issues, he contrasts opposite views and then exhibits the narrowness of each as he drives toward a more inclusive position. For instance, in part 1 ("Fundamental Ethical Notions") he begins with a long analysis of the theory of hedonism that the ethical "good" or aim is "pleasure." To this he counterposes the theory, as Kant did, that locates the good in the act of will itself; the "good will is the will which acts from regard to its own law," without an object of desire outside itself. Both theories are subjected to intense analysis in which the two central characteristics of Dewey's early work as a philosopher reach their height: his truly impressive scholarship in the history of philosophy and the rigor of his intensive reading of philosophic texts. Dewey's conclusion is that neither pleasure nor the realization of the law of the will is the "good" of ethical choice; instead, the moral end is the realization of a community of wills, at one and the same time both inside and outside the individual self. Through such dialectics, Dewey was able to arrive at a conception of a two-poled ethical unity in the fusion of the individual's aim with the community's common good. Just as individual intelligence makes for social knowledge, moral experience issues into the world of social action.

Dewey followed the same procedure more briefly in examining ideas of "obligation" and "freedom" as he had done in looking at the "good." These investigations allow Dewey to assert that ethics (or moral actions) are not something to be superadded to behavior; they *are* behavior and suffuse behavior in the "here and now." For a clarifying analogy, Dewey reaches into his own industrial culture in a way that shows him to be a true American of the late nineteenth century:

> The existence of this moral world is not anything vaguely mysterious. Imagine a well-organized factory, in which there is some comprehensive industry carried on—say the production of cotton cloth. This is the end; it is a common end—that for which each individual labors. Not all individuals, however, are doing the same thing. The more perfect the activity, the better organized the work, the more differentiated their respective labors. This is the side of individual activity or freedom. To make the analogy with moral activity complete we have to suppose that each individual is doing the work because of itself, and not merely as drudgery for the sake of some further end, as pay. Now these various individuals are bound together by their various acts; some more nearly because doing closely allied things, all somewhat, because contributing to a common activity. This is the side of laws and duties.
>
> This group of the differentiated and yet related activities is the analogue of the moral world. There are certain wants which have constantly to be fulfilled; certain ends which demand cooperating activities, and which establish fixed relations between men. There is a world of ends, a realm of definite activities in existence, as concrete as the ends and activities in our imagined factory.

In his later work, as Dewey moves out of the ideal moral world into the social and economic world, where pay *does* count, ethics must become more relational and thus more complicated.

In the preface to *The Study of Ethics: A Syllabus*, Dewey explains that this book does not duplicate the earlier one. The *Syllabus* is a continuation of *Outlines*, and in both books he argues for "a theory which conceives of [ethical] conduct as the normal and free living of life as it is." In the *Syllabus* he focuses on the psychology of "active experience." This is, he asserts, "a task, so far as I know, not previously attempted" in ethical theory.

Psychology leads Dewey to counterpoise the Judeo-Christian conception of morality as law and justice to the psychological conception of the affections. In the *Syllabus* he follows the same logical procedure that he pursued throughout *Outlines* and now finds in the dualisms of justice and desire ethical positions confined too narrowly in separate spheres. "Love," he points out, is "justice brought to self-consciousness"; love is affection unified. Thus, love is "not simply the supreme virtue; it is virtue," the complete identification of "subject and object" or "agent and function." Psychologically, love is the unity of freedom and responsibility, power and justice. It is a conclusion to which logic—and Alice—led him.

In writing to Thomas Davidson about the courses he would offer in the summer school at Keene, Dewey wrote about the *Outlines*, but his comments apply to both books:

> There is no morality in my ethics. There is no *apart* morality. . . . But when you say that I have no answer to the question, "Why am I *bound*" I rise up in protest. Why, what am *I*? *I am* nothing but this binding; it is my bindings [in conduct] which make me what I am. "Why am I bound to do good?" Because that is what *I am*.

Bad ethics, then, is simply the failure of a person to be himself.

Dewey's work on ethics inevitably led him from an "imagined" factory to the real factory and so formed the logical basis and paved the way for concern with social justice in an industrial world. Now,

regularly going beyond his earlier influences in finding his own position, he rejected Comte's *systeme de philosophie positive* while accepting
the *systeme de politique positive* and endorsing Comte's "honest desire to
better society." More and more closely engaged with the need to use science as an analytic method and to reform society in a scientific manner,
Dewey followed a logical path from neo-Hegelianism to social concern,
replacing ideal spirit with ideal society and understanding thought as a
social act. Like Comte and Caird, Dewey was disposed to personalize
justice, seeing it as emanating from powerful, scientifically disposed
leaders. At the conclusion of his review of Tilden's speeches, Dewey
quoted Tilden on America's urgent need for "a man who was qualified
to reform the government from inside . . . by the active, intelligent
agency of the executive." From this time on, Dewey appears to have
had an eye out for a suitable man with an intelligent plan to reform politics in order to establish a new level of justice in America.

A UTOPIAN DECEPTION

Unfortunately, throughout Dewey's life, his wishes often deceived his
intelligence. This was certainly the case concerning his gross misjudg-
ment of a newspaperman named Franklin Ford. In the early 1880s, as
a writer for *Bradstreet's* commercial paper in New York, Ford had
decided that the defects in America's democratic progress, associated
with the rise of frenzied finance and rapacious capitalism, were due to
the lack of journalistic intelligence in analyzing and reporting the
news. Certainly, Ford had hit on a fertile idea and was a bit ahead of
the progressive journalists who would soon try to bring about social
reform through muckraking articles. Infected by the utopianism of
that decade—when scores of utopian novels were published and hundreds of utopian schemes were floated—Ford decided that he needed
to find a man, a man of thought, a person of social sympathy and science, to enact his reformist plan to create what he came to call "thought
news." In 1888, he started on a year-long tour of major universities—

Columbia, Harvard, Yale, Johns Hopkins, Cornell, and the University of Michigan—in the hope of finding his man among the faculties of philosophy, history, or social science. He was, he later said, looking for "a man and men who would give more than a passive assent to the principle" of "thought news." In this, he grandly concluded, "I succeeded at the University of Michigan. I got to John Dewey." For his part, Dewey was astonished by Ford's pitch to him: " I never saw anything like his mind except the Corliss engine," he told Alice. "I can feel it work."

Ford possessed the utopian idealism of Edward Bellamy, the magnetic persuasive power of a tent preacher or a snake-oil salesman, and the rampant eccentricity of his time. For Dewey, the combination was irresistible. He reveled in Ford's eccentricities, as when Ford predicted to Alice "that the time would come when there would really be metaphysicians in [therapeutic] practice; when the cure of souls perplexed with intellectual questions & burdened with personal matters would be seriously undertaken as a business." When Dewey and Ford met, their individual quests fit together like the pieces of a puzzle. Dewey, the philosopher, was concerned with intelligence; Ford said that reporting needed to be raised to intelligence; and both concluded that intelligent news would reform politics and establish justice. Alice, who was even further advanced in radical utopianism than her husband, was also entranced by Ford.

Ford saw Alice's utopian susceptibility at once. He told her she was "the bravest man" he knew and said to John that Alice was "nearer to [being] . . . ready for action" than John was. In fact, Ford was a fabulous salesman of radical ideas. His pitch involved the kind of visionary wonderment that inevitably caught John and Alice in its spell. (Neither would ever be entirely immune to that kind of enchantment.) John described what Ford told him. In an exquisite pastiche of visionary mumbo jumbo, Ford declared that "the problem of men" has always been more than that of thought. Then he rhapsodized in his vision. He had seen an "immense spiritual belt revolving & unrolling in the swiftest & most powerful way" and "a great material pulley revolving too." In this hypnotic, somewhat daffy vision, he saw himself caught in the belt and pleaded that men should put the spiritual belt on the material pulley in order to ground idealism. He had "found" Dewey and said to him:

> Now it is your turn. You have helped me work out the thought—that's done. Our relationship on that basis is ended tonight. The question is whether you are going to have it go on[,] on the basis of action—The thought is ended & the scheme has begun. You haven't taken the latter on your will yet and I'm not free until you do.

In his foolish enthusiasm Dewey promised Ford "that I stood beside him and that my relationship to the university would have to take care of itself as subordinated to the primary relationship."

Dewey's closest friend at Michigan, Henry Carter Adams, whose own radicalism would have made him fair game for Ford, somehow missed meeting him, and yet he was so taken by reports of the remarkable man that he wrote to Dewey to inquire about Ford's "real meaning." Dewey's reply described Ford as the embodiment of Comte's *systeme politique* Americanized by way of John Dewey: "Now Ford's idea is not that of simply telling the truth . . . but that of *finding* out which the truth is; the *inquiry* business in a systematic, centralized fashion." For Adams's sake, Dewey typed out a précis of what he believed Ford meant. It had several principles: first, that journalism should be scientifically and systematically organized; second, that journalism should seek to "*centralize the intelligence of the country, and then to distribute it again*"; third, that to be successful, scientific "thought news" must be sold for a profit, like any other commodity. Above all, intelligence must be organized through an efficient exchange of information. Finally, "thought news" would create a public for politics, its means being truthful thought, and its end, intelligent action. "The newspaper in giving publicity to public matters (not for reform, or for any other purpose excepting that it is its business to sell facts) becomes the representative of *public interests*."

For Dewey, Ford was a dream come true. Dewey told William James that to know Ford was "a wonderful personal experience." Ford's plan to start a great news organization moved by idealism allowed Dewey to hold onto his Christian faith through social gospel, Christian positivism, political progressivism, and even Hegel. With regard to the last, Dewey, via Ford, was soon contending that American democracy was the realization of Hegel's "achieved organism" and that far from being "transcendental," Hegel was the philosopher of "the rationality of fact," political fact. Ford provided Dewey the opportunity he dreamed of, to hold onto everything he ever believed. In this way, he could convince himself, as he always wanted to do, that he was unified, not a bundle of incompatible fragments—the fate he always feared. He confessed to his former student and future colleague James Rowland Angell that the plan for "thought news" would "sound more or less crazy to a professor of philosophy," but, he added, "I intend henceforth to act on my convictions regardless."

On March 16, 1892, Dewey allowed the *Michigan Daily* to report that on "April next will appear the first issue of the 'Thought News.' " Was it doubt that made him hold off the announcement of the paper's name to the last? If so, Dewey does not seem to have registered this consciously, any more than when he told Thomas Davidson that the paper was simply a "project, with which I shall while away my leisure hours." Inwardly, however, he was glorying in this press release in the way that *Thought News* would unify all his wayward interests. He told the press: We "shall treat questions of science, letters, state, school, and church as parts of the one moving life of man." When Dewey's democratic idealism was added, it made this mélange complete. The next announcement of the impending publication came soon after. The writer, very likely Ford himself, reported: "Mr. Dewey calls the paper 'A Report of the Social Fact.' The social fact is the social organism. . . . [The] social organism is here . . . the social organism is a fact . . . the reporter, the fact man, becomes scientific."

Then the bubble burst. The Ann Arbor correspondent for the *Detroit Tribune* ridiculed Dewey's idea of publishing *Thought News*

randomly whenever a spark of intelligence was ignited: "It is generally understood," he noted, "that Mr. Dewey proposes to get out an
'extra' every time he has a new thought." Then in another issue, the
Tribune sarcastically suggested that *Thought News* devote its attention
to the most urgent intellectual puzzle of the day: why do University of
Michigan male students exhibit such an intense and abiding interest in
Ypsilanti factory girls? For the first time in his life, Dewey was news,
and he didn't like it. A reporter showed up at his door, and he soon dis-
avowed all that Ford had announced on April 8. He hadn't written
that release, Dewey stated firmly. He wished only "to show that philosophy has some use." In no uncertain terms, Dewey impressed on the
reporter that he himself was no revolutionary.

Next, Ford and his brother Corydon appeared at Dewey's door
and castigated him for timidity. They *had* wanted to start a revolution,
but their promising professor had turned tail. In his memoirs, *The
Child of Democracy*, Corydon indicated that they now regarded Dewey
with contempt. Dewey was unable to put his political convictions into
practice. He refused to challenge the Michigan Supreme Court. He
wouldn't even criticize "the disorder of the [Detroit] city government";
he was too timid to "put the cross upon President Angell who stood
against progress on the campus"; he "refused to denounce as a Judas his
[Congregational] pastor falsifying Christ." Even worse, he was a time-
serving hypocrite: "his salary meant that he was to keep quiet."
According to the angry brothers, Dewey should have chosen to forgo
"his bribe" and become "a tramp upon the highway that he might have
a voice," but instead he had chosen the salaried "sop of convention."
Such bitter recriminations plunged Dewey back into his old dark
uncertainties. Not since Lucina had plagued John about being right
with Jesus had he been so questioned, and never, even to himself in his
worst moments, had he experienced such vituperation. The first issue
of *Thought News* never appeared, although as late as April 25, Dewey
was still embarrassedly explaining to friends that "we have postponed
publication of *Thought News* for the present; will take it up later on a
larger scale & with more adequate financial outfit." But Dewey was
finished with the project. He had done little technical philosophical

work while Ford was nearby, and he yearned to get back to the excite-ment—and the safety—of technical philosophy and psychology. For a while, it had been fun to spin grand plans with Franklin and Corydon; now it was a relief to return to "studies of time reactions, rhythm, time perception & attention." Ford made one last attempt to reenchant Dewey, but by that time Dewey was free of his spell. Ford continued his search for "a man" and soon fell into oblivion.

The Ford fiasco, though humiliating to Dewey, cannot be separat-ed from the crucial developments to which it led. Dewey never forgot the principles of "thought news" and Ford's captivating visions. More than four decades later, it is not surprising to find Dewey a leading fig-ure at a Harvard conference

> in which seventy-two of the world's leading scientists and scholars in all major fields of learning constituted a "micro-scope" of living brains focused on man and his universe . . . [aiming at] organizing the intelligence of man into a unified "world mind," which would give the nations of the world the benefit of man's collective wisdom.

The article's subhead reads: "Dewey and Others Say America Must Lead in Move to Free All Men's Minds." Ford's spirit must have stalked Dewey's memory as he participated in this Harvard assemblage.

More specifically, the exuberance that Ford spawned in Dewey tilted the balance that Dewey had been keeping between "spirit" and "fact." He had been shifting his emphasis from the aim of the right Hegelians to justify the ways of Christianity and democracy to human-ity, to the effort of left Hegelianism to improve society. Every letter of any substance that Dewey wrote during the last months of his involve-ment with Ford stressed a new assertion: that thought must be realized in facts, that language must be expressed in acts, that meaning is inex-tricably connected to consequences, and that ends are derived from means. These moves in Dewey's philosophical development were, ironically enough, stimulated by Ford's harebrained scheme.

Writing at length to William James in anticipation of seeing him in Davidson's camp, Dewey summarized what Ford had meant to him: "What I have got . . . is first the perception of the true or practical bearing of idealism—that philosophy has been the assertion of . . . unity of intelligence & the external world *in idea* or subjectively, while if true in idea it must finally secure the conditions of its objective expression." He was, of course, redefining and refining and improving and finally attenuating his Hegelianism, so that with not the slightest acknowledgment, it was fading into pragmatism or instrumentalism. In the late fall of 1891 Dewey returned to this theme with James, from whom he had reason to think he would receive a sympathetic hearing. Dewey remembered James's complaint that Dewey's *Psychology* had been too suffused with neo-Hegelianism. Now Dewey referred to James's Harvard colleague Josiah Royce, a leading philosopher of idealism, to show how and why idealism had to be reformed. Royce believes, Dewey said, in the organic character of intelligence, meaning that the individual is the "instrument of truth but not its author." But, Dewey went on to assert, the individual *is* the author of truth, and truth lies in its realization. He refused to accept Royce's conclusion that (in Dewey's terms) philosophy is "a Pickwick club where things are true in some special sense—where the organic character of intelligence is true *as philosophy*, but not in specific action." On the contrary, Dewey asserted, an idea is true and truth is organic only in "specific action." He challenged James, who, he said, had "never joined" the Pickwick club: "If the organic theory of intelligence is true as theory isn't it time something was done to make it true as fact, that is as practice?"

In another letter in early 1892, Dewey wrote to Joseph Denny about one of the ways that he increasingly saw organic intelligence passing into practice, in early education. All thought is unified, Dewey argued in typical organicist fashion, but then he took the next, pragmatic, step: "Seeing the common objective fact, we get [a] . . . unified language—the language of action." And with that assertion another insight followed: the discovery that dynamic thought could be expressed only in the language of action. *"This,"* Dewey said, "is democracy—the appropriation of the store of intellectual spiritual wealth in all directions." In short, he was driving at what he named to James Rowland Angell a "philosophic idea of activity" related to "political movement & organization." He gave talks on this same subject at Ann Arbor's Unity Club and Jane Addams's Hull House in Chicago in late 1891 and early 1892. His title was "Psychology and History," and he concluded that philosophers were just beginning to understand "the relation of idea to action, or that ideas find their actual expression in material things." Peirce came to pragmatism through Kant, James through British empiricism, and Dewey through Hegel. All three were influenced by the Darwinian concept of humanity as an evolving organism. Each conceived of scientific investigation in a somewhat different way, but all similarly emphasized inquiry as an instrument. Younger than Peirce and James, Dewey went further then they to create the largest and most varied pragmatism "of use." But in the 1890s his full achievement was still decades away and would not be completed until he was eighty years old.

For all the visionary, eccentric strains in Franklin Ford's utopianism, he too, this latest of Dewey's many teachers, contributed to Dewey's development. Always ready to be influenced, Dewey thought so hard and felt so much that eventually he shaved the rough spots off the ideas of others, smoothed them into sense, and rendered them personal. He never really forgot any intellectual or personal passion that he felt strongly, but he never allowed his varied influences to remain separate and to render him a broken bundle of mirrors. He stored up all he learned and, forgetting its individual sources, made it all his own. So even though Ford was forgotten and the humiliation he brought to Dewey laid aside, Dewey was transformed by him. Dewey learned how to absorb Ford's influence, as he absorbed many others, and to become himself through all he took in.

Dewey treated his experience as a mine from which he could extract philosophy. All his life he continued to dig and to unearth, and at last he brought up a truly original and personally satisfying philosophy. But this was never to be easy work.

FAMILY LIFE

During the 1880s and 1890s, Dewey put a lot of effort in a war of attrition with his old ideas. He was lost in thought, but he was also raising a family. The interest that he was developing in early education came directly from his experience with his own children. An old friend of the Deweys described the family in action. Thomas Trueblood, who had lived in the same boarding house with Alice Chipman and John in the fall of 1884, described a dinner at the Dewey house after the births of Fred and Evelyn. Trueblood told Willinda Savage "that John and Alice Dewey were developing some interesting theories and practice on the education of children." Little Fred Dewey was evidently rambunctious. "When, from self-protection, Mrs. Trueblood attempted to restrain [him]. . . from using her as a target, Mrs. Dewey shook her head and whispered, 'leave him alone. His father is studying him.' " Dewey used Fred's and Evelyn's early acquisition of vocabulary for data in his article "The Psychology of Infant Language." John was certainly intent on gathering psychological material; and Alice, clearly, had very advanced, fiercely held ideas about the proper way to raise children. She wanted them to be "natural," unrestrained, and therefore unconflicted, which produced some curious results. Even in the winter, the Dewey children often went without shoes and socks. Once a policeman stopped Mrs. Dewey to remind her of the severe weather and was told "that it was none of his business as she was quite capable of bringing up her own children." The children's doctor soon refused to treat the Dewey children. Alice went further. Burke Hinsdale, a professor of history who lived next door to the Deweys, was shocked to learn that when the third Dewey child, Morris (named after George Sylvester Morris), was born in October 1892, Fred and Evelyn were "given an opportunity to stand by during the birth while Mrs. Dewey explained the process." One "liberated" practice that would surely have shocked their Ann Arbor neighbors, had they known of it, was alluded to much later in a letter by Dewey to W. E. Hocking. He told the somewhat genteel philosopher that "during the critical years of the sex-development of their children, Mrs. Dewey and he would go about the house in the nude." (Joseph Ratner believed that this was the reason the children talked about sex so freely.) John and Alice shared the children's upbringing: she believed in the benefits of their frequent separations from their parents. It was not uncommon, therefore, for her to take one or more of the little ones on a trip and leave John with their youngest child. When Dewey said in the 1892 syllabus for his course "Introduction to Philosophy" that "our experience is simply what we do," he could have been thinking of Franklin Ford, politics, pragmatism, educational theory, or raising his own children.

In the 1890s Dewey was writing books and publishing a steady stream of articles in the major journals, conducting an extensive correspondence, chairing a popular department, directing Ph.D. dissertations, serving on university committees, teaching large classes, continuing to give dozens of lectures to student and university organizations, and offering philosophy courses at Davidson's summer school. Two women were among his first doctoral students. One, Bertha Wolfe Levi, wrote to him years later to tell him that she had "never forgotten the joy and inspiration" that she had received from his courses in 1891–92. In 1893 Dewey lectured at the Philosophy Congress of the World's Columbian Exposition on "The Reconciliation of Science and Philosophy." Royce and Harris were on the same program; Henry George, Hamlin Garland, Edward Everett Hale, and Frederick Jackson Turner talked there to other groups. Dewey was becoming so well known as a speaker that he gave the commencement address at Smith College in 1890 when he was barely thirty years old.

A wholly unexpected adventure of a completely different sort occurred in August 1892. Dewey himself could not have anticipated that any philosopher would find himself in a mining camp in Colorado. But there he was by the middle of the month, and by early September he wrote to Alice: "I am beginning to feel myself quite a miner." This came about in the most remarkable way.

Alice's grandfather, Fred Riggs, was nearly ninety years old by this time. Still vigorous, he began to think about the old days when he had gone west, as far as Colorado, mined for a few years, and staked a claim before returning to Michigan to raise children. As recently as 1889, he had returned to Colorado and established more claims. Now he wanted to return once more to assure himself that his claims had not been "jumped" and then sell them. A fine plan, but he could not go alone. Obviously, Alice herself could not go, as she was due to deliver her third child (Morris) in the middle of October. She settled down in the Dewey cottage in Keene, near the Davidsons, and spent her time reading Zola. Without hesitation, John Dewey volunteered to accompany Grandpa Riggs. On August 4, Dewey put aside his preoccupations with organic intelligence, and the next day he and Fred Riggs were on the train to Colorado. They arrived in Del Monte on August 9. John was exhausted by this time and at first found the Rockies "disappointing."

Fred Riggs had clearly been an excellent businessman. When they arrived in Summit Camp on August 10, he found that his claims were intact, although there was evidence that at least one of his mines had been worked by a poacher. Now that he was back again in Colorado, he was as excited as in the old days and even started to do a bit of prospecting again. Dewey wrote, "In a claim he found [silver] . . . in some fine clay. . . . He thinks he knows where the main vein is." John was watching a real frontiersman and prospector operate naturally, and he was full of admiration: "I believe he has the instinctive sense in everything of this kind," he told Alice. Within a week, Fred had an exploratory tunnel run through his property at a cost of about $500, and immediately he hit two veins of silver.

Suddenly, John Dewey was a prospector's sidekick.

> I don't wonder at the fascination this sort of thing has had for gpa. You have the general fascination of being out in the woods & mountains, and besides the scientific interest of keeping the lay of the land, the knowledge of minerals, &c and the hope of striking something rich. I shouldn't want anything better than to wander 'round here summers, if you & the children were only here.

The speculative fever got to the philosopher, and he was soon talking of figures—silver ore that would produce from $5 to $6 a ton, a sale of the mine at $20,000—maybe as high as $35,000—25 percent down, $5,000 advance at least. Riggs assured him that this would be a productive strike, and John was convinced that "there isn't one chance in a thousand that he is wrong." A surveyor came up to determine the property line, and the assayer ran samples. Everything was lining up for a strike and a sale.

Between flurries of activity, John read most of Shakespeare's plays and Shelley's poems; he thought that one of Shelley's lesser-known long poems contained "one of the greatest expressions of democracy I have ever read." In his heart, he was fast becoming a democratic entrepreneur waiting for a big strike. But the strike didn't come. The mining equipment broke down; the one potential buyer was slow; and although many deals were discussed, none was completed.

Grandpa took it all with the patience of an old prospector, but he was obviously frail. Dewey saw how much Fred's health was failing. "This is undoubtedly his last trip west," he told Alice, "& he may want to go to some of the places he hasn't been in." They had made no strike, but Dewey had gained a new perspective on the man of action. Fred Riggs had become another of Dewey's many teachers and expanded his education in another direction, entrepreneurship, exactly opposite the one into which Franklin Ford had led him. By the time that Fred died of heart failure, Dewey's education as a businessman was complete, and he was able to settle Grandpa's affairs easily.

Dewey was engrossed in all these business activities when letters from Franklin and Corydon Ford followed him to Colorado. They were ready to give him another chance. But Dewey's mind was made up, and he wrote back that he had no further interest in anything connected with "thought news" or the Ford brothers. Years later, when Horace Kallen asked Dewey about Franklin Ford, John said only, "He turned out to be a scoundrel."

The prospecting foray concluded around the same time, and further negotiations concerning the sale or lease of the mine would have to be continued by mail. On September 9, 1892, Dewey was back in Fenton with Alice, and without a day's hesitation he started to answer his accumulated correspondence and to prepare for the opening of school.

"Our experience is what we do." John Dewey was doing a great many things and thereby becoming a complicated young man. Yet in the midst of this multiplicity, his inner life consolidated. Through the varieties of his activities, he arrived at an identity that was fluid, not fixed, an evolving self that needed to keep developing in order to sustain its central truths. He was finding a center in himself, a confidence and tone of authority.

Others saw this, too. Charles Horton Cooley, who attended Dewey's Michigan lectures on political philosophy as both an undergraduate and graduate student wrote almost forty years later that Dewey

> certainly left a lasting mark [on me] rather by his personality, I think, than by his lectures. . . . In the group to which I belonged [in 1893–94], his character was deeply admired, for its simplicity . . . and for a gallantry, which, one felt sure, would never compromise the high purpose by which he was visibly animated.

Soon European students started coming to America to study the philosophy of education with Dewey. European professors studied his work, too. As early as 1899, a professor established a school in Zurich, Switzerland, to work out educational problems "in the way suggested by Dr. Dewey." With the rapid creation, development, and expansion of universities in the United States, it was only a matter of time before Dewey would be besieged by requests to move to another university. A new group of university presidents, academic promoters, and entrepreneurs with plenty of money for recruitment was forming in America. For the first time, universities were competing for talent. Both higher-education circles and the public at large were realizing that information and technical knowledge would be crucial to the coming "American Century." University presidents were becoming national figures.

HARPER AND THE UNIVERSITY OF CHICAGO

One of these academic figures was William Rainey Harper, recently a professor of Hebrew and Semitic languages at Yale, but now the first president of John D. Rockefeller's newly endowed University of Chicago. He had already hired Dewey's former assistant James Tufts when Tufts returned from study in Germany, and he had also recruited another young psychologist-philosopher, Charles A. Strong, from Clark University.

Tufts's reasons for going to Chicago instead of returning to Michigan were personal and did not reflect any discontent with Dewey's department at Michigan. He explained:

> I came to the University of Chicago through my personal acquaintance with President Harper who was when I met him a professor at Yale. Before entering Yale Divinity School I had taken Hebrew by correspondence for a year, and then attended the summer school at Newton where [Harper] taught for part of a session. I continued my work with him for a year at Yale.

When Tufts returned from Germany, he became one of Harper's earliest appointments. But Harper was determined to make his philosophy department nationally and internationally important, and neither of his junior instructors measured up to his plans. He wanted a "star," a man to put Chicago "on the map." Without consulting either of his faculty in philosophy, Harper went out shopping on his own. First he looked to Harvard and offered George Herbert Palmer the chair of philosophy and the deanship of the graduate school. It would have been a sound choice, for although Palmer was scarcely an original thinker, at Harvard he had led in the creation of the best philosophy department in the United States. Perhaps he would do the same at Chicago? But Palmer refused. Next, Harper went to Jacob Gould Schurman, but he was about to become the president of Cornell and to compete with Harper as an academic promoter. Harper then turned to

F. Benjamin Andrews, but he had already become president of Brown and rejected Harper's offer. Charles Sanders Peirce, still at Johns Hopkins, was the next possibility that Harper considered, but in June 1892, when Harper consulted George Herbert Palmer about that, Palmer strongly advised Harper against recklessly choosing an unreliable man. Harper had nearly exhausted the possible candidates in the East, the area to which he instinctively looked.

At this point, Harper's philosophy department became involved. Charles Strong suggested to James Tufts one day: "I propose that we recommend to the President to appoint Professor John Dewey as the head of the department." Tufts "cordially agreed" and embraced the suggestion, since, as he replied, he had "the highest opinion of [Dewey's] ability." Tufts sat down at once and wrote a long and completely unqualified letter to Harper on Dewey's behalf. He spoke of Dewey's reputation first, which was a good move, since Harper was explicitly interested in celebrities: "He is well known on both sides of the Atlantic. Although as yet a young man he has been for nearly ten years one of the most frequent and vigorous contributors to the various philosophical periodicals, and has produced three books." Dewey's *Psychology*, he said, "at once made him known as an original and acute observer as well as an able thinker. It has been very widely used—at nearly all the Eastern institutions." The reference to eastern universities also was a good selling point for Harper. Tufts followed that by describing the reception of Dewey's *Leibniz*—a book "which Prof. Ladd of Yale spoke of in the *New Englander* as the clearest and most useful of the series." In Tufts's own opinion, the book showed "a mastery of philosophical principles." Tufts knew what Harper wanted: a good organizer who would encourage research in his faculty. Would Dewey cooperate with Harper? Tufts noted: "He is withal a delightful man to work with," and besides that, he was popular as a teacher. Then Tufts ended with the obligatory final moral wrap-up: Dewey is "a man of religious nature, is a church-member and believes in working with the church. He is moreover actively interested in practical, ethical activity and is a valued friend at the Hull House of this city."

Harper had already met Dewey in the summer of 1890, when Harper taught a biblical institute in Ann Arbor. He was receptive to

Tufts's assessment, and now as an administrator he acted decisively. Early in 1894 he asked Dewey to consider becoming the chair of philosophy and psychology at Chicago. Aware of the rumors that had been circulated about Harper's search, Dewey knew that Harper's urgent and frustrated desire to appoint a distinguished scholar in philosophy had so far failed, and he negotiated hard. Many conditions were favorable, Dewey wrote: Mrs. Dewey's desire to move, the chance to build up a department "whose main interest is in advanced research," and the "living in Chicago": all these "weigh greatly with me." But, he stated firmly, Harper's offer of a $4,000 salary did not afford him "an adequate basis for living" in such an expensive city as Chicago.

Harper countered with the proposal that Dewey could be on leave with pay during the spring semester of 1895, so that the family would not have to settle in Chicago for that first year. Dewey replied that if he were assured of $5,000 for the second year, he would "accept with pleasure; and come to Chicago in condition to throw my best powers into helping strengthen the university." However, he still urged Harper to give him "definite statements . . . regarding the succeeding stages in the development of the salary."

Harper merely replied that he empathized with Dewey's concern about costs in Chicago and waited for Dewey's answer. Dewey then placed the matter on principle: "I should hardly think the University would want a man . . . who would leave a place like the one I now hold, for $4000." Harper proposed that Dewey start teaching in the summer session of 1894 as soon as his contract with Michigan expired, teach in the fall, then have nine months free, and to pay him a summer salary plus $4,000 for the academic year. As to $5,000 in "the second year," Harper remained uncommitted, but Dewey was by now yearning to make the change, and he knew he had bargained as far as he could. "I regret that it was not possible to arrange definitely for the future increase," he wrote, "and I accept in the expectation of having the full salary in due season." (His expectation was, in fact, fulfilled.)

With the appointment settled, Dewey took Harper at his word and started to plan a strong department. Philosophically speaking, Dewey was a better choice than any of the other philosophers whom Harper had tried to recruit earlier. Dewey was anxious to create a great department; he was full of energy; and above all, he was committed to science and scientific research, a continuing result of his Hopkins training. "Harper's ideal," Dewey himself soon saw, resembled Gilman's: it was "the inductive method, the laboratory method." As long as Dewey stuck to experiment, Harper backed him with promises. When the time came, he was as good as his word and gave Dewey the resources to appoint his Michigan colleague George Herbert Mead as assistant professor of psychology at a salary of $2,000. Mead, Dewey assured Harper, 'is above all, a man with original ideas in philosophy . . . the most original of all the young men of the last six years output whom I have run across." When Charles Strong resigned because "the ill health of his wife made it undesirable for her to reside in Chicago," Dewey was able to call his former student, James Rowland Angell, from Minnesota to become assistant professor of psychology, also at $2,000. The result was that the Chicago department quickly acquired four philosophers who had all been together at the University of Michigan. "It was regularly harmonious," Tufts wrote, "and from the date of its organization . . . there has never been a serious difference of opinion in the department."

Dewey continued to nag Harper about money. He needed a lab assistant for Mead, $1,000 for the departmental library, and $2,500 or $3,000 for "apparatus" for the psychology laboratory. Even before he began his appointment, Dewey reminded Harper that "competition is sharp"—for instance, "Harvard has a full professor, Münsterberg, of great reputation besides James in general psychology"—and that Chicago should not "start out with anything less than the best available talent in the experimental laboratory." He also expected "further development," as Harvard had five full professors and Cornell, seven. Clearly, Dewey was sensing that with Harper's support and the continued research development of his Michigan team, he might fast become the head of the first real school of philosophy in America.

The *University of Chicago Weekly* was soon boasting:

The appointment of Professor John Dewey of Michigan, to the chair of philosophy and the head professorship of the department of philosophy, is another of the series of brilliant moves the University has made. He is among the foremost thinkers in ethics and metaphysics. He is a brilliant writer and his work on psychology is famous. Then he is a young man. As the philosopher grows in years he gains in wisdom. His best work may be expected yet to come. But the world knows his name already and if we are proud of the reputation of our faculty we are proud of the association of a scholar who enhances and brightens that reputation greatly.

Dewey left Michigan not only for the increase in salary and the possibility that he could create a department that would make him the foremost of American philosophers but also because he—and, even more, Alice—was chafing under the increasing pettiness and bureaucracy of the University of Michigan, by now a well-established institution that had fallen into a rut. "It is a great relief," he told Alice, "to think of getting out of this mire of pettiness." Alice declared herself anxious to leave. "I hope we both experience the same relief over leaving AA tho' probably mine is greater and more physical." Upon leaving Ann Arbor, she confessed that after being away from it, she did not miss it at all. She disliked the faculty gossip, and both she and John agreed that the president's wife was responsible for much of it. A note of dissatisfaction even with the president crept into John's report that Alfred Lloyd's wife said: "Angell reminded her of Pilate, always washing his hands of something." John gave Alice several reports of pettiness. It will be a "relief" to go to Chicago, John said, "after the dead level of everybody trying to find fault with everything & everybody that prevails here." Faculty meetings were "funerals." The faculty at Ann Arbor were too cautious for him. He had learned in Ann Arbor, he told Alice, "that a too continuing & insistent attitude of self-protection isn't the most 'successful' thing in the world, to say nothing of the most generous." No wonder that he could "easily" "contemplate a final farewell."

The University of Chicago was new and not yet set in its ways; religious orthodoxy was not looked for or expected there, as it was in Ann Arbor; and Dewey looked forward to broad horizons for his research and his life. His family was growing; his philosophy was expanding in all directions; and his social interests were deepening. When Alice and John made the break, it was final. Both admitted that memories of their Ann Arbor years faded rapidly: "I never saw anything disappear so fast as Ann Arbor has, by the way," John said after only a few months in their new home. Even Mead agreed; Irene Mead told John that George declared it "a tremendous personal relief . . . to get away from Ann Arbor & have a chance to begin afresh." When the son of President Angell became the new assistant in psychology at Chicago, he even seemed to be relieved and invigorated by the "prospects" of a "chummy department." John summed it up for all of them in October 1894: "Ann Arbor seems to be a shell easily shaken off."

Michigan could not come close to matching Harper's offer. During the panic and depression of 1893, the university's enrollment had dropped, and it was having financial difficulty. The best that President Angell could do was to offer Dewey the promise of a nice corner office on the ground floor of the newly built Tappan Hall. After Dewey's departure, philosophers around the country seemed to agree that Michigan was no place to go. With a nearly empty department on his hands, President Angell scoured the country to rebuild it, but as Alice characterized it, the university was "not a maid with crowds of suitors," and Angell had a difficult time building up the department again.

Dewey also eagerly accepted Harper's offer because it made possible his and Alice's plan to go to Europe. There, the doting parents believed, their three children would quickly learn foreign languages, and Alice would fulfill her dream of plunging into the rich life of European culture. John's motives were more diffuse and more complicated. Foremost, he was a truly good father and wished his children to have the experiences and the broad education he himself had not had. He knew how restive Alice had become, and he wanted her to have a chance to spend a long time in Europe. For himself, he was entering the international scene as a philosopher. Almost every other philosopher he knew had been to school in Europe; his own staff—Tufts, Mead, and Angell—all had been to Germany and been immersed in German philosophic thought, an experience that he himself had turned down when it had been offered to him by President Gilman. But he did not go to learn philosophy from Europeans; to his American mind, Tufts and Mead and Angell had brought the best of Europe back with them, and the center of the philosophic world was his own office at Chicago. As he looked from his college desk over the tops of the remaining buildings of the World's Columbian Exposition, he mused, "The idea of going to Germany to study philosophy is, objectively viewed, the most ridiculous joke conceivable—when a man can come to Chicago." He knew German well and he wanted to learn to speak French and Italian, but it was not language learning that drew him to Europe. After all, he could read French well enough to race through Daudet's *Sappho* and Zola's novels as each new one appeared. His Latin allowed him to pick up Italian easily. Rather, he was most like an American in one of those novels that Henry James was still writing: a transatlantic traveler with a truly grasping imagination prepared to seize Europe for American uses.

Dewey's first public act at the University of Michigan had been to create a Bible class for the Student Christian Association, and his last public act there was to speak on "Reconstruction" to the same organization. But he did not ask the Ann Arbor Congregational Church to send a letter to the Chicago congregation. He never again joined a church.

BOOK II

Experience

Once he arrived in Chicago, Dewey no longer took an active role in Congregational religion, but he maintained his interest in religious experience, and he never saw a reason to abandon the name "God" as an instrumental sign in the semiotic system of a spiritual life. This distinction between a religion and religious attitudes and his conviction that "God" denoted the "uniting of the ideal and actual" are the main themes of a short book that he wrote many years later. *A Common Faith* (1934) was Dewey's only extended examination of the subject. It accurately describes the position at which Dewey arrived around 1894, seeing religious experience as a crucial part of human life, inner and outer, but explaining spirituality in a wholly naturalistic manner. Dewey had already come far in creating a flexible philosophic method for examining the varieties of mental experience in general. Philosophy was inquiry by way of logical method, and art was a non-pragmatic inquiry into imagination and its representations. Because the religious experience lent itself to both sorts of inquiries, Dewey asked, what part of our experience does the religious attitude seek to know logically and scientifically? What different part of our experience does the religious imagination seek to represent? Religious experience, as he now understood it, shares in the modes of both knowing and representing, science and art. Like these, but in its own special, integrative way, it connects person with person and thus allows people to feel at home in the universe. For Freud, the religious experience was a defensive illusion, but for Dewey, since religious attitudes have the capacity for realization in action, they are as real as any other experience and certainly far from illusory. Religious experience provides aspirations toward values, and aspirations lead to the actualization of values in social life. Religious values, Dewey said in his conclusion to *A Common Faith*, which is repeated on his tombstone, "exist by grace of the doings and sufferings of the continuous human community in which we are a link. Ours is the responsibility of conserving, transmitting, rectifying and expanding the heritage of values we have received."

Dewey waited forty years after severing his connections with an institutional church to explain his religious views of 1894. Finally, *A Common Faith* allowed Dewey the scope to touch more fully than elsewhere on Bergson's theme of the evolution of consciousness and to expand it. But the reception of the book in 1934 showed Dewey that his audience was far less ready to understand, much less embrace, his method of inquiry into faith than it was to grasp such other inquiries as he had made with logic, social life, politics, or art. He said no more publicly on the topic, although he continued his personal engagement in his own version of faith. In private, when a young student at a small college wrote to him to ask whether it were true, as her teacher said, that "pragmatists deny the existence of God," he could not resist replying immediately: "The statement you quote is absurd," he began, since pragmatism is "concerned with testing of statements and beliefs," not with proofs of existence. Indeed, I know one Catholic," he added, "who wrote an article saying that the pragmatist test—of consequences—was a proof of the existence of God" since the universe "*works* so well."

For himself, Dewey insisted that the development of his philosophic point of view was not determined by religion, nor were his religious attitudes modulated by way of his philosophic investigations. For him, religion was not a philosophical problem, or philosophy a religious problem, but both were fused in his "feeling that any genuinely sound religious experience could and should adapt itself to whatever beliefs one found oneself intellectually entitled to hold." "I have not been able to attach much importance to religion as a philosophic problem," he observed. But in *A Common Faith* he attached a great deal of importance to it as a human need for otherness that resembles the needs satisfied by art and philosophy but goes beyond both to touch the human community and the experiences of friendship, brotherhood, and even the emotion so important to Dewey: love.

WEALTH AND POVERTY

In the 1890s, America turned a corner. After a decade of peace, everything seemed to break loose. Clouds of uncertainty gathered, although on the surface everything seemed fine. Progress had been so evident in the 1880s that even some social reformers could assume that it would solve poverty and bring about at least some of the conditions that such hopeful utopian commentators as Bellamy and Howells envisioned.

In Chicago especially, hopes ran high. The city was booming. Louis Sullivan describes this period in his *Autobiography of an Idea* (1924). In Chicago, he, Frank Lloyd Wright, LeBaron Jenny, Daniel Burnham, and John Wellborn Root developed a new American aesthetic, which Sullivan characterized in his famous phrase "form follows function." Using new materials, steel framing, and innovative technologies such as the elevator, they created a whole new sense of space in designing the tall buildings for which Chicago became famous.

Caught in the euphoria of the time, the city fathers decided that for the coming celebration of Columbus's discovery of America, Chicago should create the greatest world's fair the universe had ever seen. Gathering together a national consortium of architects, artists, and construction workers and supported lavishly by businessmen, entrepreneurs, bankers, and promoters, they created a monumental fair, which soon became popularly known as the "White City" for its pure white buildings and was officially known as the World's Columbian Exposition. It was always unclear whether the fair was a celebration of the four-hundredth anniversary of Columbus's voyage of discovery or a very expensive toast to the triumph of business enterprise centered in Chicago.

But underneath it all, the future of the 1890s was already present. The grand buildings were mostly made of staff—a kind of plaster— and were constantly in need of repair. It was all an illusion, and many critics looked beneath the surface grandeur and saw deception. Thorstein Veblen found in the fair a perfect illustration of his theory of the dominance of pecuniary over aesthetic considerations characterizing (and creating) middle-class taste. Just after the fair closed, in November 1893, W. T. Stead announced a conference with the theme "If Christ Came to Chicago!" What would he see?—municipal corruption, rapacious capitalism, vagrancy, and prostitution—that was the Soiled City that Stead saw behind the White City's mask.

A participant in creating the fair, Louis Sullivan, saw in its "bigness, organization, delegation, and intense commercialism a parallel to the rapidly increasing mergers, combinations, and trusts in the industrial world" and therefore not the beginning of Atruria but the enlargement of the "feudal idea" in America. When Ward McAllister, gadfly to New York's wealthy "Four Hundred," declared that the fair proved Chicago society to be "moving in the right direction," he unintentionally corroborated the analyses by Veblen and Sullivan of the fair's meaning.

Right next to the White City, another set of buildings was rising, John D. Rockefeller's recently founded University of Chicago, with its Gothic, distinctly feudal architecture. Here was another confirmation of Veblen and Sullivan. Soon, John Dewey would occupy an office in the university from which he could see the fair's buildings rapidly decaying. When the businessman Charles T. Yerkes donated the world's largest telescope to the university, W. T. Stead remarked: "It is much better for people like Mr. Yerkes that the scrutinizing gaze of the public should be turned to the heavens than to the scandalous manner in which he neglects his obligations to the people."

The most striking contrast with the magnificent White City lay in the depression of 1893. The aging socialist Thomas Morgan described this contrast. Every day, he said, the unemployed "assemble peacefully on the lake front, begging for work, and with the strong arm of the law are driven back into their tenement houses, [so] that the visitors who come to see the White City might not see the misery of the Garden City which built it." One of the favorite places for the unemployed to congregate was around the statue of Columbus just outside the fairgrounds. So was it this—poverty and despair caused by rampant money capitalism—that Columbus's voyage and discovery were all the while making for and meaning? After the fair closed, its ruined and deserted buildings were soon taken over and inhabited by poverty-stricken bohemian artists and writers. Was this a symbol of the low place assigned to art by the new gospel of affluence? Was Richard Morris Hunt's marble Fair Administration Building, modeled after St. Paul's Cathedral, the exemplary building of the new Chicago? Or was it Jane Addams's Hull House, where some of Chicago's poor could be saved from starvation each day?

The panic of 1893 ushered in an economic depression that lasted much longer than the fair did. The bankruptcy of overexpanded railroads, the collapse of several large companies, a stock market sell-off, and a tide of bank failures leading to the virtual disappearance of credit created massive bankruptcies and widespread unemployment. There was agrarian devastation, too, for farmers also had overextended themselves, seeking credit after the decline in European purchases. Then, when the loans were called in, foreclosures followed. In farming areas, several protest parties sprang up, increasing in numbers and stridency as the agricultural depression grew—the Grange, the Greenbacks, the Farmer's Alliance, and the People's Party, otherwise known as the Populists. Ignatius Donnelly's famous preamble to the party's first national platform was: "A vast conspiracy against mankind" is in progress, and "if not met and overthrown at once, it forebodes terrible social convulsions, the destructive of civilization, or the establishment of an absolute despotism." In rural areas, the stage was being set for William Jennings Bryan's "Cross of Gold" speech and his campaign for the presidency, in which the business and working classes were pitted against each other, and business won. Things were bad enough, but when foreign investors withdrew their investments, the American economy almost totally collapsed. A million workers who had had jobs in 1892 now found themselves out of work. Many people attended the fair because they were unemployed or underemployed and were looking for an escape into the delusion that prosperity was just around the corner. But the depression did not ease until 1896 and was not officially ended until two years later.

American citizens who were not deluded by the fair were desperate, and their desperation showed itself in a number of zany schemes. For example, Jacob Coxey rose out of obscurity by advocating a large-scale federal public works program along with government-planned inflation that would allow "cheap" money to circulate and make the paying off of debts easier. The president ignored Coxey, and Congress showed no interest in passing his "Good Roads and Non-Interest-Bearing Bond" bills, and so Coxey formed an army of the unemployed and marched on Washington. Jack London joined the big parade of Coxey's army. Following a banner on which was emblazoned a portrait of Christ and the motto "Peace on Earth, Good Will to Men, He Hath Risen, but Death to Interest on Bonds," Coxey's "Army of Peace" marched. The few who finally arrived in Washington drifted about aimlessly and were promptly arrested for walking on the grass. Nonetheless, the idea took hold, and soon Fry's army and Kelley's army were on the move, streams of tramps that formed a growing river of the discontented unemployed.

A simple arithmetic formula was exhibited in the depression of the 1890s. Financial panic plus unemployment plus reductions in wages plus the decline of working conditions equaled the rise of unions and the onset of strikes. In fact, a strike in Chicago at the McCormick Harvester Company lighted the torch that often appeared in the 1890s. To protest the harassment of the McCormick strikers, union leaders called for a demonstration in Chicago's Haymarket Square. When the police tried to disperse the crowds, the protesters rioted. A bomb was thrown that killed seven policemen and injured dozens of others. The police responded by firing on the mob, killing four. A frightened city administration demanded justice, and the judiciary complied by sentencing seven demonstrators to death.

Other unions arose and other strikes followed. Andrew Carnegie and Henry Clay Frick decided to break the Amalgamated Association of Iron and Steel Workers at the Homestead plant in Pennsylvania. The police rounded up eight suspects. Frick hired the Pinkerton Detective Agency to open the plant to nonunion workers. A furious battle broke out between the Pinkertons and the strikers, and men on both sides were killed. Finally, the governor of Pennsylvania sent the entire state militia to Homestead and broke the strike.

War between capital and labor was declared. The next battle took place in the town of Pullman, Illinois, where George M. Pullman had established a company town for the production of railroad sleeping and passenger cars. Although Pullman saw himself as the benevolent lord of his town, he charged high rents and high prices in the company stores, and the workers were convinced that he wanted to be not their steward but their master. In the first year of the depression of 1893, when railroads were failing and Pullman's profits declining, he cut wages drastically while maintaining the same high costs for rent and food. The result was inevitable. The Pullman employees struck and enlisted the American Railway Union and its president, Eugene V. Debs, to support them by refusing to service Pullman's cars. Debs agreed. Instantly, railroad workers went on strike in twenty-seven states and territories. Pullman appealed to the governor of Illinois, J. P. Altgeld, to follow Pennsylvania's example by sending in the militia, but he refused. Astonished (but not stymied) the railroad barons persuaded a reluctant President Grover Cleveland to send in federal troops to restore interstate commerce. Debs was arrested; the strike was crushed; and the workers returned to their jobs and homes in Pullman, seething impotently.

America had gone to great expense to reeducate this young idealist philosopher, John Dewey. Leaving Ann Arbor to move to Chicago at the beginning of the strike, Dewey got on one of the last trains to run for weeks to come. Because he read the papers, he knew about the panic, the depression, urban poverty, agrarian unrest, exploitation of workers, child labor, social disorder, clash of classes, and industrial strikes elsewhere. But the Pullman strike was distinctly "his": the occasion for another part of his education and an extension of his identity. In the 1880s there was plenty of thought but no action, and in the 1890s, there was plenty of action but almost no thought. It would be up to men like Dewey to put thought and action together and thus create something solid from the chaos they encountered.

EVELYN DEWEY

Dewey's education had numerous sources. He and Alice produced six children, and from each, in a different way, he learned something. Evelyn Riggs, named after Alice's grandmother, was born in Minneapolis in 1889. Just as John had visited Fred's school and observed him to be so happy and placid, he later went to five-year-old Evelyn's but got just the opposite impression. "Poor Evelyn," he wrote to Alice, her class was "playing with cubes, to find out about the edges & surfaces," and he could see in her expression of "complete boredom" an "inner perplexity as to why they were doing all these unreal things to find out what she [already] knew."

But when they moved, Evelyn did not have the distress that Fred experienced. She easily progressed through school, even though Alice took her and her siblings to Europe more than once. When the family moved from Chicago to New York in 1904, she began attending Horace Mann High School in New York City and graduated in 1906.

At the age of eighteen she was admitted to Smith College, and she graduated in 1911.

At first her training at Smith and the general atmosphere of the Dewey household inclined Evelyn to become a social worker in New York City, where massive immigration and poverty were rife and social workers were greatly needed. She was an independent person and lived in her own apartment at 66 Montague Street in Brooklyn from 1918 to 1919 and then, in 1920, moved to 135 East 56th Street in Manhattan. In the early 1920s she taught at the Lincoln School, associated with Columbia Teachers College. She was on the governing council of the Bureau of Educational Experiments. For a while she worked as an advertising copywriter at the most famous of the early agencies, J. Walter Thompson. She succeeded at everything she tried. Max Eastman said of Evelyn that early in her life, she developed a "poised and sagely humorous good sense." She assisted her father on several of his educational investigations during this time and then started to write articles and books on education herself. In 1914 Dewey sent her to the Gary, Indiana, schools "to get some material for me regarding modern illustrations of educational principles."

She and her father collaborated on *Schools of To-Morrow* (1915). Evelyn did all the field research, visiting schools and interviewing parents, teachers, administrators, and students; and she wrote most of the book's sections involving observation. She visited and observed the best—or sometimes simply the best-known—experimental schools in the nation, showing how they applied various educational theories, by Rousseau, Herbart, Froebel, Pestalozzi—and Dewey. These included Mrs. Johnson's school in Fairhope, Alabama; Public School 45 in Indianapolis; the Parker School in Chicago; and William Wirt's Gary, Indiana, school system. Evelyn and her father examined experimental schools and used the data to imagine how to reconstruct public education. "We have tried to show," the two Deweys wrote in the book's preface, "what actually happens when schools start out to put into practice . . . some of the theories that have been pointed to as the soundest and best ever since Plato." Most of the schools that Evelyn chose to visit and include are likely to be considered "child-centered" schools—that is, teaching at the place where the child's readiness resides, schools in which learning occurs by doing and doing flourishes through liberty.

Evelyn went on from her part of *Schools of To-Morrow* to write *New Schools for Old* (1919), examining another experimental school, Mrs. Harvey's Porter School, this time in a rural setting. In her conclusion she argued, as her father had done, that "the schools are the only place where it is possible to give everyone alike [the] . . . necessary groundwork of social and democratic consciousness." That is, the schools are the laboratories in which experiments in democratic evolution are conducted, and therefore educational progress must "keep pace with the government's progress." E. P. Dutton published *New Schools for Old* as well as Evelyn's next book, *The Dalton Laboratory Plan* (1922). The Dalton Laboratory Plan was "an experiment in an environment that permits character development." She published articles in the *Nation*, *Progressive Education*, and other journals concerning education and testing of children. Indeed, Evelyn became the leading authority on educational experiments in America, her theme being "as long as man develops, his education must develop."

When she was five years old, on her way to Europe with Alice, her father wrote her: "I love you dear little girl of mine. Pappy." All through their lives, he was close to her. After her mother died in 1927, father and daughter lived together, and in 1928 they went on the same educational mission to the Soviet Union.

Like her mother, Evelyn suffered periodically from depression, along with the same sort of psychogenic conversions that all the Deweys experienced. But instead of seeking help through the physiologically oriented "Alexander method," as her father and siblings did, she chose treatment from a psychoanalyst in the late 1920s following Alice's death. It was a complete success. She considered herself the "best living example" of what "facing your troubles and doing something about them can do to change a person from an unhappy one."

Most Dewey children tended to marry early, but Evelyn remained single until she was forty-five years old. Then she fell suddenly in love

with Granville Smith, the owner of a three-thousand-acre cattle property, Spring Creek Ranch, in Missouri. They married in haste on the
morning of May 26, 1934, because her father and Jane were scheduled
to sail to South Africa that afternoon. In her usual good-natured,
humorous way, she quickly arranged to have her father's friend John
Elliott of the Ethical Culture Society perform the ceremony. He "said
a lot of swell home truths and was very nice and short to boot," she
said. But still, "this business of getting married is distracting," she
added. As soon as the ceremony ended, "Jane and Dad got off in pan-
demonium as the boat first changed to sailing [early,] at noon and then
from 57th Street to 18th, so time was short." The whole wedding party
raced around Manhattan to get them to the pier on time. Then, with
the Deweys on their way, Evelyn took everyone back to the apartment
at 320 East 72d Street and had a "very nice" buffet lunch.

After the guests left, before starting on her honeymoon, Evelyn
proofread the edited manuscript of her last book, *Children of the New
Day* (1934), written jointly with Katherine Glover. *Children of the New
Day* struck a very advanced modern note. The book gathered together
and extended the reports of the White House conference on Child
Health and Protection, arranged by President Herbert Hoover. In it
Evelyn drew a picture of the "new" child, raised "often with two working parents instead of one," in a home smaller in size and worked by
"push-buttons instead of human energy." Such a child, she observed,
"belongs to the community almost as much as the family." Modern
children are the creation of "change, change, change." What is in the
future? She predicted "a clarification of values, a return of the spiritual motive to life"; a reconciliation between science and religion; continued experiments in education; and a deepening of "awareness" of
order and beauty.

For years thereafter, John Dewey visited her in Missouri at least
once annually. Anytime he was on a train through St. Louis, he would
take a side trip to Kirksville. Evelyn and Granville owned a big cattle
and sheep ranch, and John's "annual joke" was that whenever he
arrived, he carried with him just what they "needed"—a leg of lamb
and a rib roast. When he started to spend winters in Key West, Evelyn

often drove down to join him there. She died at the ranch in 1965, just after her seventy-sixth birthday. But this is far in the future. For John Dewey, it is still 1894.

ANOTHER KIND OF EDUCATION

Shortly after arriving at the University of Chicago, Dewey observed, "The interest & ferment is quite as great . . . as it is in everything in Chicago. This place is the greatest stew house on earth." Like the time of his remarkable, soothing vision in Oil City or those days when he fell in love with Alice, his life again changed in the summer of 1894. He was cut loose from his history. He left Michigan and moved to Chicago; Alice took the two older children to Europe in May; he had lost his emotional tie to organized religion; and his idealistic philosophy had withered and was slowly being replaced by functionalism. Much that had been sacred to him simply disappeared and left him with empty inner spaces into which new concerns and new commitments flowed. He was a grown man with a family and a professional reputation; he remained a dutiful son; and he had accomplished or become all that his early life and times and talents had promised. And now, in only a few months, even though he looked the same on the surface, he underwent another metamorphosis.

Hardly had Dewey accepted Harper's offer when his enthusiasm ran before him and fantasies of travel became real plans. Alice would go ahead of him to Europe, taking Fred and Evelyn with her, while he finished his examinations at Michigan and then taught summer school, followed by the fall semester in Chicago. Finally, in December, he would join his family in Europe. Fred was already seven and Evelyn five by this time, but Morris, who was born in 1892, would not be two years old until October 18. John insisted that Alice would get nothing done in Europe if she were hindered by the infant, and he remained adamant that he and his mother could easily care for Morris until they joined the others.

Accordingly, Alice and their two oldest children departed on May 19. Even before they sailed, John experienced a powerful awakening of his loving emotions. He ended the last letter he could get to her before she left: "I love you dearest one & send you my heart to keep. Good voyage dearest. . . . I wish I were going . . . with you. . . . I love you dear one I love you." Alice assured him, "I love you and love you and love you." For seven months, in letters written on an average of three times a week, this was the main thing that they wanted to tell each other, over and over. John also regularly sent full measures of love to "my dear Freddy boy" and "Dear Eveliny girl"—"Dear boy I love you and send you more kisses than you could count in a week"; "I love you my little sweet heart"—and the children replied enthusiastically in kind.

At first, Lucina stayed in Ann Arbor taking care of Morris, and later she moved to Chicago to join her son. Occasionally she took the little one back to Lapeer and sometimes to Fenton where Alice's grandparents still lived. But John spent an immense amount of time with Morris. More and more he had been focusing his psychological research on child development and early education. Early in 1894 his article "The Psychology of Infant Language" appeared, based chiefly on his observations of Fred and Evelyn, with Morris also providing a few details. Now, with the rest of his family abroad, all of the loving care and attention that John had in limitless store was showered on Morris and reported in letters to Fred and Evelyn three times a week. Convinced that Fred and Evelyn would be interested in the development of their younger brother, he described Morris's doings in detail.

Before Alice departed, while she was still agonizing about leaving her one-and-a-half-year-old son, John told her: "Don't think of taking Morris . . . it isn't right to be so homesick for Morris & at the same time worry lest he be trouble to me. He is the one bright spot here that keeps me from feeling wholly a wanderer on the face of the earth. As long as he is with me, I feel that I still have a home & a place & a belonging." He doted on the boy. Taking Morris by train up to Lapeer to stay there with Lucina for part of the summer, he gave a full account of Morris's delightfully rambunctious behavior. He ran up and down the railway car ("it made me dizzy to run after him"), seizing the passengers' hats. "I think Morris can pretty nearly fly. He stands clear up on the tips of his toes sometimes when he is running around & waves his arms. I think he thinks he is a bird." Soon the bemused father was crooning:

> I think I shall bust with [love of] him. He is so perfectly sweet. . . . I don't believe . . . any young one of his age ever developed such an affection as he did. The lighting up of the traditional lover's eye . . . came over his face whenever I came in . . . & then the way his little finger came up "There's papa, there's papa," in the gentlest most contented tone.

Falling in love so completely with Morris, he even wrote letters to Fred and Evelyn in Morris's voice:

> Dear Freddy brother and Evelyn sister—I'm papa's boy, & mama's joy, & gma's darling, & Sadies' man, & Ella's sweetheart & Lillian's love & Freddy's & Evelyn's little brudder. . . . I fool papa most every time he tries to put me to sleep; I just hurry up & empty my bottle, & then I get up and try to run 'round or else I tell papa to rock me—I can fool him & not have to take a nap at all.

Such rhapsodies continued all through the fall. Morris was nothing less than "the most perfect work of art." "He has a genius for language." Morris was "distinctly himself," and John, knowing Alice's theories about child development, assured her that he was not disciplining Morris or moralizing him. At the end of a tantrum, Morris "looked most angelic. I came over to him & he remarked 'Sweet.' Well, waves of sentiment & self gratulation that I had raised no moral issue with him were upon me." John was especially pleased to report that Lucina herself had evidently adopted a new theory of natural childhood since she had raised John, and she too seemed free from concern about Morris's moral nature. She played with him happily and put aside her concern for his soul's destination. She even ceased to ask John about his own relation to Jesus and now was content merely to urge him to exercise rigorously.

If possible, John was almost equally enthusiastic about the life of Chicago, especially the Pullman strike and his developing relation with Jane Addams's Hull House. By the 1890s the mission house, which had developed decades earlier in New England, had evolved into the "settlement house," disconnected from religious organizations and devoted to the relief and care of the needy and education for all. Hull House was the most famous of the innumerable settlement houses that were soon founded in all large cities in America.

The Pullman strike of unionized railroad workers and their sympathizers among related unions occurred just when Alice was getting settled in Europe and John was moving from Ann Arbor to Chicago. The strike caused a sensation, attracting national attention and initiating the public's awareness of the coming conflicts between capital and labor. It also raised Eugene Debs, the head of the Pullman Car Workers Union, to national prominence as a spokesman for social justice. The strike plunged Dewey into the same messianic populist enthusiasm that had hypnotized him in his association with Franklin and Corydon Ford. After talking to a young railway organizer for a mere fifteen minutes, he told Alice, his nerves were more thrilled than they had been for years:

> I felt as if I had better resign my job teaching & follow him round till I got into life. One lost all sense of the right or wrong of things in admiration of his absolute almost fanatic sincerity and earnestness. . . . I don't believe the world has seen but few times such a spectacle of magnificent, widespread union of men about a common interest as this strike evinces.

On the Fourth of July 1894, Dewey made a point of visiting the strikers and shared with them his utopian hope and belief that a general strike of unions would develop if Pullman didn't give in or arbitrate. Of course, they all recognized the possibility that the strike could be brutally crushed. Potential martyrs became giddy, and Dewey was with them. Conservatives, however, were saying that "Debs ought to be tried for treason" and that labor had "forfeited all public sympathy." Business interests were urging the president to take some forceful action against the strikers. Liberals, including Dewey, were hopeful but also predicted that "the gov't is evidently going to take a hand in & the men will be beaten almost to a certainty—but it's a great thing & the beginning of greater." By July 10, all the city's unions voted to go out on a sympathetic strike, and Chicago was in a furor. Federal soldiers were sent to the city, and Dewey feared that President Cleveland was ready to declare martial law. It was rumored that the strikers had burned thousands of railroad cars. "Of course," Dewey commented,

> the govt can't put up with actual rioting, but a more sympathetic attitude, a discrimination between the strikers and the looting, rioting crowds of bums, and the attempt to bring a little pressure to bear on Pullman instead of all on the strikers w'd have made a vast amount of difference. It is impossible that all the wrong should be on the side of the men.

By now, John felt himself to be "a good deal of an anarchist."

By the middle of the month the strike was broken, Debs was arrested, and capitalism smiled triumphantly at the crippled unions. But Dewey was not persuaded: "If I am a prophet, [labor] really won. . . . The exhibition of what the unions might accomplish, if organized and working together" had been impressive. Even the arrest of Debs "is a mighty good thing," for it exposed the fear of the business class, the impotence of the courts, and the poverty and chaos of both political parties. Dewey condemned both Republicans and Democrats. Still committed to the basic principle of "thought news," he tried to look beneath the surface of events and issues. The "silver question, [the] tariff question & all the rest of it," he concluded, merely reflected "children wrestling at random in the dark"; politicians were playing a "bunco game" with the public. Given the attitude of the "higher classes," he said, it was a "wonder" that "there aren't more downright socialists." He was becoming a socialist himself.

In contrast with his earlier experience with "thought news," Dewey got a lesson in practical politics from the Pullman strike. With a national depression in full force, "thousands out of work," and full of his success in the earlier strike against the Great Northern line, Debs had temporarily overreached himself, but Dewey believed that the "effect of the strike" would eventually be "tremendous." Yet he also recognized the short-term loss: the coming winter, he predicted, would be "harder even than [the] last, & so many of the wealthier people are embittered that it will be harder to get 'charity.' "

Endowed by Rockefeller and imbued with Baptist principles, the University of Chicago, Dewey clearly understood, was not likely to be hospitable to the workers' struggle. "I fear Chicago University is a capitalist institution," he observed. "The University is evidently in bad repute with 'labor,' " he added later. The faculty was conservative. One of the historians commented that "Debs' tyranny [was] worse than the Czar of Russia," and Dewey heard a "minister of the Gospel of Christ" at the university express the hope that the strike would not be settled "before some of the men [were] . . . shot & thus learn a lesson." Those simple days when Lucina could organize the Christian ministers of Burlington to contribute to the amelioration of elementary social problems through the Adams Mission House were over. The unprecedented and wholly unexpected growth of the capitalist economy following the Civil War had overwhelmed the capacity of goodwill in churches to cope with social ills. With thousands out of work, financial schemes were rampant, and depression and poverty were much more widespread than progress. Dewey concluded that organized religion was more likely to support capitalism than to reform it.

When asked in early August to lead chapel exercises, Dewey declined on the grounds "of inability to pray," which merely caused "some surprise." Less than three months after he arrived in Chicago, he accepted an invitation to speak to the University Christian Union on "Psychology and Religion." But his real object was to explain himself: "It seemed as well to make known my heterodoxy first as last—if it isn't already known," he decided. He had expected to shock his audience, but he caused hardly a stir, even among the Baptist ministers, who merely showed "complacency" over Dewey's heterodoxy. Beneath the "offensive and blatant display[s] of piety" at the university, Dewey concluded, lay an attitude of laissez-faire that amounted to indifference to even religious belief. No one cared whether he was right with Jesus as long as he supported capitalism. He reconsidered the paradoxes he had experienced. At Michigan, a state university, "there was freedom as to social questions, but some restraint on the religious side," whereas in the private, Baptist-supported University of Chicago, "complete religious freedom" existed, along with "constriction on the social side." While Dewey still approved of Zola's social critique, he could not accept the conclusion of Zola's new novel *Lourdes* that since science had not solved "the question of human welfare," a "return to the mystical & supernatural, symbolized by Lourdes" was necessary. Zola had written a "simple but great" book, but Dewey no longer believed that religion would solve economic problems. But then what would? He had severed his connection with the Congregational Church when he left Ann Arbor, and now with the Pullman strike foremost in his mind, he rebelled against the tight conservative law-and-order box that he entered in Chicago. He was cut from his earliest roots even more than he had been by Franklin Ford. Now he realized how "anarchistic" his "thoughts and especially feelings" were. But he was not prepared to become an anarchist. Where would he go? With what could he ally?

Hull House became his new church, "justice" rather than "law and order" his watchword, Jane Addams his pastor, and instrumentalism his creed. Political economy shared his mind with philosophy. Workers as much as students evoked his concern. John had visited Hull House while he was teaching at Michigan and had been appropriately impressed. But in the summer and fall of 1894, Hull House was the refrain of his letters. "Hull House is the one natural place in existence, I guess," this professor of logic illogically but passionately asserted. Jane Addams's theory of the social functions of Hull House perfectly matched Dewey's changing mind and emotional needs and filled in the spaces left empty by the withering away of his old allegiances. Indeed, Addams always insisted that "the great awakening of social consciousness in the labor movement was one of the most deeply religious things in modern times." She testified that Pullman believed in "competition for wages & monopoly for rents." John agreed and applauded. She declared that the "special aim" of Hull House was "the unification of the city's life or the realizing of the city's unity." For John this was better than Hegelian organicism. According to Adams, "the only way Hull House could take . . . learning to anyone was by turning it into action so that it could be seen—people were already talked to death and written to death." Dewey himself had arrived at a philosophy of action, and she provided a vehicle for it. Addams's coworker, Ellen Gates Starr, praised "the magnificence of men all over the country throwing away their bread and butter in order that their fellows hundreds of miles away might get their rights." Dewey's admiration was raised as high. He was a Hull House convert.

Dewey's mind came to rest, finally, through a conversation with Jane Addams at Hull House on October 9, 1894, following a lecture that he gave there in a series on social psychology. He was discussing the Pullman strike with her and stressing the dialectics of antagonisms in it, unconsciously falling into the Hegelian perspective on progress, when Miss Addams brought him up short.

"Antagonism," she insisted, "is not only useless and harmful, but entirely unnecessary."

He asked what she meant.

"Antagonism never lies in the objective differences, which will always grow into unity if left alone," she replied, "but arises when a person mixes into reality his own personal reactions."

What was she talking about?

"When one gives extra emphasis to a part of the truth, when an individual takes enjoyment in doing something because it will be unpalatable to others, or when one feels that he must *prove* he is not a moral coward, and in a number of other ways, then emotion, not reality, produces conflict."

She paused but resumed before he could speak. "What is more, *historically* only evil has come from antagonisms. What do you think? Isn't that so?"

He agreed but then "dissented—after the manner of fools—as to past history."

She pressed him with a biblical example. "If Jesus *did* drive the money changers out of the temple, that accounted for the difference between the later years of his ministry and the earlier, as for much of the falsity in Christianity since. If he did it, then he must have lost his faith, reacting so conflictually."

She went on. "We freed the slaves by [the Civil] war, but what benefit did this conflict bring? Now we have to free them all over individually and pay the costs of the war once more, even as we reckon with the added bitterness of the southerner besides."

"But," Dewey responded, "don't you think that besides personal antagonisms, there are genuine antagonisms intrinsic in ideas and institutions? For instance, between Christianity and Judaism, or Labor and Capital, or the Church and Democracy? And isn't it true that a realization of such antagonisms is necessary to an application of the Truth and to a consciousness of growth?"

Jane Addams answered, "No."

Poor Dewey. He was not getting any answers to confirm his beliefs.

But Miss Addams continued: "The antagonism of institutions is always unreal. It may simply be due to the personal attitude and individual reactions, and then, instead of adding to the recognition of unified meaning, it delays and distorts it."

Dewey tried to counter her argument with one of his pet idealist ideas. "Tension itself is central in life: it exists in all natural forces and in growth."

"Of course," she acknowledged, but then she made a nice philosophical distinction that the philosopher himself had missed. "There's stress in action, but mere choosing is an entirely different thing from the unity of reality." She dominated their conversation. She and Miss Starr told Dewey about her antagonistic troubles at Hull House—stones thrown at the building, windows smashed, break-ins—and said "she would give the whole thing up before she would ask for a policeman and increase the conflict." She even told him that "one day a Negro spat straight in her face in the street, and she simply wiped it off and went on talking without noticing it."

Dewey thought about this conversation when he was alone and tried to convey its import to Alice. "If I could tell you the absolutely commonplace and unemotional way in which she said all these things, it would give some better idea of the most magnificent exhibition of intellectual and moral faith I ever saw."

He was, as he wrote to Alice, simply dazed. "When I repeat the conversation to you," he told her," "it seems so natural and common-place now . . . and it didn't impress me as anything wonderful, but I have never had anything take hold of me so. And by the next day it began to dawn on me."

He pondered the implications of the talk for his philosophic point of view. On the one hand, he was resistant, but he was aware that his reaction *was* resistance. "I can't see what all this conflict and passing of history means if it's perfectly meaningless; my pride of intellect, I sup-pose it is, revolts at thinking it's all merely negative and has no func-tional value" as progress. History should not merely be but mean.

On the other hand, he said, in some sense he had been "converted" in a flash. (For Dewey that word still held a lot of meaning.) And so, he reflected, concerning his philosophic position: "I guess I'll have to give it all up & start over again. I suppose that. . . the only reality"—he started to write *ideal* but caught himself—"is unity, but we assume there is antagonism & then it all goes wrong. I can see that I have always been interpreting the Hegelian"—crossed out—"dialectic wrong end up—the unity as the reconciliation of opposites, instead of the opposites as the unity in its growth, and thus translated physical tension into a moral thing." He trailed off on a powerfully hopeful note: "I can . . . see, or rather dream, that maybe . . . it's a mere illusion because we put ourselves in a wrong position & thus introduce antago-nism where . . . it's all one; & that its sole function is to warn us never to think division." He ended in astonishment: "But when you think that Miss Addams does not think this as a philosophy, but believes it in all her senses and muscles—Great God"! It was, and remained, a characteristic of Dewey that he was always receptive to alternative ideas. With professional philosophers he generally held to his own position, but with intelligent women, nonphilosophers, odd thinkers, and ordinary folk, he was a student again. On that October night in 1894, the lecturer got a good lecture, and it stuck.

Addams's lecture was not the only lesson given to Dewey during this time. The next one came from an utterly unexpected source: his own son Fred. Dewey described the Pullman strike and Hull House in his letters to Alice and even in his postscripts to the children. Although he never asked them whether they were right with Jesus, he was concerned that they be right with social justice, and this had a surprising effect. Reacting to his dad's letters, seven-year-old Fred became intensely interested in the plight of poor people that he had seen in America and now saw in France. Alice wrote to John:

> He insists that we shall live down in a poor quarter of the city. He has been much affected by the beggars and the miserables we have seen here. Yesterday at St. Cloud he saw a pathetic looking blind man begging. All at once this afternoon he broke out crying and reproaching me for not giving anything to the man. I tried to explain to him why I did not and this led to a general discussion of the social evils &c &c. I told him what Miss Addams is trying to do in Chicago and that when we get there we would try to help her then. "*No Sir!* you just go yourself and get a house in the poor quarter. We'll live down with the poor people. You see I never knew about this before mama. I thought it was best to give them money but now I do know. I see it is best to give them something to do." Now [Alice said] I will have him write [to you] himself. He is talking very fast and trying to keep back the tears with his lip trembling and keeps coming back to the blind man.

Unable to keep still, Fred took over the letter:

> Dear Papa. I never knew it was so bad to give people money before. Since I saw an old blind man begging for money on the street I cried & cried afterwards. I believe he had somebody write that sign for him because I think he is a man that would tell the truth. I want to live down in the poorest quarter of

Chicago where the poorest people live. I never knew that was the poorest quarter where Miss Addams lives till Mama told me. We are going to do the very same thing if you want to. I think Miss Addams is very nice to do that and I want to. I am going to be very rich & [if] any poor people in that quarter want anything to eat and don't have any more money, instead of giving them money I will give them work to do. But the blind people that can't work I will give them something to eat and a little money. I am going to build a little French school for Morris off my carpenter shop & I am going . . . [to] have Evelyn teach . . . school too for Morris & any poor child can come in & pay nothing at all and if they want to they can pay something.

At this point, Evelyn told Fred that she wasn't ready to be a teacher and besides, "I don't feel so sorry for the poor people as you do." "Well, then," Fred responded, " I won't build you [a] school." At this Evelyn burst into tears!

Back in Chicago, deeply moved, John wanted to applaud Fred for his idealism but also to caution him realistically: "Dear Freddy, there is one trouble about going there to live. Miss Starr said last spring that she didn't think it was a good place for children." "Bad things" happened on the street, he explained, and "bad words" were spoken that little Morris shouldn't hear, "and you and Evelyn aren't *very* big yet." But then Dewey's own idealism—his oldest personal idealism that was being brought to the fore by Jane Addams—emerged, and he wrote to Fred:

But we will try & do something; & remember that we belong to the common people. You must get strong in your bodies as well as in your minds so you can help. There are so many, many things all mixed up together, that it is hard to tell what to do. It is like trying to walk straight in a dark room where everything is scattered around.

Dewey had turned philosophic idealism into a social ideal that was hopeful. But he also was aware of social complications and complexities; he understood tension but looked toward unity. Privately, he expressed to Alice grave fears for the present: "I might continue indefinitely about the difficulties of the social question, but it doesn't seem fair to the young ones." The absolutist enthusiasm he had stimulated in Fred scared him a bit. He continued:

> The misery next winter, in fact already, is going to be frightful they say. They are feeding lots of people from Hull House now—people who were "respectable"—that is, had savings in the bank a year ago, small tradespeople & skilled laborers . . . there was a sort of enthusiasm of charity wave which helped last winter, but things are getting worse all the time & the wave has died down.

For her part, Alice, in France, was bursting with American democratic radicalism. "Over the façade of Versailles," she told John on her first visit there, "is writ—*à toutes les gloires de la France*, which ought to be replaced by this: *à toutes les folies de la France*."

John's concern was mostly with the children. "I was quite touched . . . by Fred's account of the poor people. Poor Fred & poor poor people." But what would become of a boy with such sensitive feelings, so like John's own emotional responsiveness? "Maybe, he'll be a social agitator—and maybe he'll get to belong to the higher classes & be strong on law & order & very weak on justice & liberty."

Dewey's education was coming from all sides. The next lessons came from his brother Davis. Over the years, John's brother Davis had been earning a reputation as an important commentator on social and economic issues in the United States. John read all his books and reports, and they corresponded regularly. What John did not hear about contemporary problems from Jane Addams, Alice, or his children, he learned from Dave.

Davis was undecided about what he should do after his graduation from the University of Vermont. He had difficulty narrowing his interests. He was good in languages. Mathematics interested him much more than it did John, and he was excellent at it. He was also drawn to scientific experimentation. "I spend my odd moments," he wrote to John in 1883, "making apparatus and experiments. I have dabbled considerably in Electricity and worked some very satisfactory experiments and shown more [ingenuity than] . . . I supposed I had." By summer, he decided to join his younger brother at Johns Hopkins University in the fall of 1883. He was admitted to study political economy and history. In contrast to John, President Gilman readily awarded Dave a fellowship, and he studied with Herbert Baxter Adams and Richard T. Ely. He spent the summers as a correspondent for *Bradstreet's Financial Review*. Two years after John completed his dissertation on Kant, Dave finished his requirements for his Ph.D., with a dissertation entitled "History of the Economics Literature Previous to the Time of Henry Carey."

Just before graduation, Dave was recommended to the developing campus of the State University of Indiana at Bloomington. President Angell of Michigan "wrote to Dave . . . [that] he would stand a pretty good chance of getting the place . . . salary from $1600–1800." But Dave was looking hard at a new school, the Massachusetts Institute of Technology, where a department of political economy was being established. "They want Johns Hopkins methods," John told Alice—meaning that the old political economy of the New England school of Frances Wayland was *not* desired. What was wanted was what Dave had—training in scientific, quantitative research, with an emphasis on method. The salary would be only $1,200—but Herbert Baxter Adams promised Dave that if he took that job, he would arrange for him to teach history part time in "the swellest young ladies school in Boston," at $400 a year. About MIT, John wrote to Alice, "The institution is purely scientific and. . . . [it] will be a first class place, if Dave gets it." He got the job, becoming an instructor in economics, political science, history, and statistics, which enabled him to marry Mary Cornelia Hopkins in Madison, Wisconsin, on June 29, 1886. He and Mary just managed to beat John and Alice to the altar.

These two brothers remained close all their lives. Dave never published at the same rate that John did—who else but W. T. Harris could? Still, his first articles, such as "Municipal Revenue from Street Railways" and "A Syllabus on Political History Since 1815" appeared as early as 1887. Dave's 1903 work, *The Financial History of the United*

States, won the John Marshall Prize and established him as the preeminent economic historian in America. The book, published by Longmans Green, went through many editions and stayed in print until 1968. His *National Problems, 1885–1897*, published by Harper & Brothers in 1907 as part of the multivolume American Nation series edited by Albert Bushnell Hart, was reviewed very favorably and became the standard historical work for that period. During World War I, Dave worked in Washington, D.C., for the federal government. Evidence of the recognition that he earned so quickly is that in 1909 he was elected president of the American Economics Association, and he was secretary of the American Statistical Association for nearly twenty years. Dave also had an important position as a quantitative historian of economic practices and theory. His *Employees and Wages* (1902–8) was a pioneering investigation into the working conditions of U.S. labor based on an exhaustive study of the 1900 census. He considered this his best book. Perhaps Davis Dewey's greatest influence on the discussion of economics in America came through his editorship of the *American Economic Review*, which he directed from 1911 to 1940.

Beyond his strictly statistical and historical work, Dave shared John's interest in social reform. He worked actively for the Boston Children's Bureau and the Boston Public School Association. During the depression between 1893 and 1896, Dave toured the Northeast and Midwest, "examining into methods of relieving or dealing with the unemployed." "Dave has been to six or eight cities. . . . Dave says this is the usual conversation with the Charity Organization people: You don't believe in giving relief without work? No. Do you think there is sufficient machinery in existence to deal with relief? Oh, yes. . . . How much work could you find for people last year? Oh, very little." John told Alice that Dave's "intelligence continues to expand all the time, it seems to me, because his sympathies are so open." All through their lives, John and Dave found ways to meet whenever they could. He was a leading member of several investigatory commissions, ranging from employer-employee relations to charitable and reformatory institutions. He was appointed by Presidents Coolidge and Hoover to mediation boards to resolve railway wage disputes. He lived a useful, productive life.

Whereas John moved away from New England to the Midwest and then to New York, following the two great geographical paths of intellectuals between 1880 and 1920, Dave remained in New England and taught at MIT during his whole career. Davis Rich Dewey died in 1942, a good economist and a loving brother.

Dave's investigation in 1894 of the economic depression and the conditions of employment caused mild difficulties for John. With Alice, Fred, and Evelyn in Europe, John and Morris were staying with the Meads until his mother came to Chicago to set up temporary quarters before they could join the others in Europe. Helen Mead wrote to the Dewey children to tell them about an amusing mishap of their father's:

> The other night your Papa went slumming, and was coming home, he said, about eleven o'clock. In the night I heard a child crying . . . [and] after a long time, I said to myself, "that sounds like Morris, & I'll see if Mr. Dewey wants anything," so I went into his room, & voila!—no Mr. Dewey!—and Morris crying piteously, "Papa come by Morris, Papa come by Morris!"— Then I made him all comfortable, and told him it was Mrs. Mead . . . [and Morris] rolled off into dreamland. You see your papa lost the last car, & stayed in town all night.

That was only half the story. Dewey had lost his sense of time because he had visited some of Chicago's best-known brothels and found discussion with the working girls most illuminating.

John faithfully reported his "slumming" adventure to Alice. First he and Dave went to an outdoor gospel meeting, then to the Park Theatre, then to "a ten cent lodging house," "two gambling places . . . & three houses of prostitution." One was a famous Chicago brothel, Carrie Watson's. Here he saw "a sort of imitation of manners on stage"; the girls were "powdered & painted . . . & invited you casually, to go upstairs with them." Another "was a high select place, a house furnished as elegantly . . . [as] 3/4 of the millionaires houses." Here, the girls "weren't even powdered, & offered no invitations whatever." He was fascinated: "I suppose an expert might pick them out, but I shouldn't know them from women you might meet at an evening party anywhere." One "might have been a kindergarten teacher for all I could see in her." One girl told him that for her it was "a profession" and that "she used a certain amount of her income in regular benevolence." He now agreed with Alice that prostitution is "as much a social institution as anything else" and therefore, as Alice always maintained, a component of the question of female emancipation. But, he added, "for these girls, one can only sit down & cry." Alice, he admitted, knew "infinitely more about it than I."

Few husbands would be likely to write at length to wives who were thousands of miles away that they had been investigating brothels. Few would have related such a visit to the question of women's emancipation. But the 1890s were a special time when serious considerations of social conditions were the order of the day. John and Alice were a remarkable couple, with implicit trust in each other's faithfulness. Both knew that who they were was a result of their relationship.

One other teacher advanced Dewey's experience, bringing him into new areas for reflection. This was William Rainey Harper. At the same time that Dewey was deeply affected by the plight of the poor, the unemployed, and the union workers, he was also being drawn by Harper's endless promotional drive to associate with the wealthy trustees of the new university, with the object of raising money for departmental operations. So Dewey was obliged to solicit aid from what he called "the highest classes," the same group that he and his Hull House friends castigated. He sent Alice a sheaf of newspaper articles, along with editorials from *Harper's Weekly* that condemned the strikers and defended conservative business interests. These expressed the attitudes of the very people from whom he was soliciting contributions:

> I don't know when I have seen anything that seemed so hopeless & discouraging. It is hard to keep one's balance; the only wonder is that when the "higher classes"—damn them— take such views there aren't more downright socialists. . . . It doesn't make any difference that I see what the facts are; that a representative journal of the upper classes—damn them

again—can take the attitude of that Harper's weekly & in common with all other journals, think Debs is a simple lunatic or else doing all this to show his criminal control over the . . . criminal "lower classes"—well, it shows what it is to become a higher class.

Only a few days later, Harper brought him to see the wealthy new trustee Charles Ryerson, who had already endowed the physics laboratory. Perhaps he would also support the creation of a state-of-the-art psychology lab? Dewey, there to ask for another endowment, was uncomfortable but impressed, despite his own convictions, with the fruits of Ryerson's wealth: The Ryerson house and "yard" were "out of sight," he said. "I got simply a glimmering impression of about 250 of the best-colored Oriental Rugs." Ryerson, he added, showing both envy and scorn, "was educated in Paris, studied law & 'does' nothing."

Hull House was inclining him toward radicalism even as his ambition to create a strong department was pushing him toward accommodation. "There is some comfort," he wrote to Alice, "in belonging to a Univ. that can raise money enough to do its subsidiary & outside matters in style. You feel all the time that if it took $50 or $100 more, to do it . . . the money would be raised." He felt a surge of triumph when Harper told him that sure enough, for his "labor" in asking for funds, the trustees would give him $200 more for the psychology lab. Dewey's success prompted him to ask immediately for "an extra thousand for the [philosophy] library." He was being sucked into the money game by his wish to create the premier department in the country, an academic version of the same idealism that fed his increasing radicalism socially and politically. As the money flowed in, he concluded: the more requests for apparatus and books "you shower in upon Harper, the better he likes you—he takes it as a sign that you are alive and 'energetic.' Energy is a great thing in this Univ." He couldn't help confessing his admiration of "Harper's own energy and success, especially when he fetches in a million." All around the university was depression, men out of work, lines of hungry people outside the settlement houses. But inside the great mansions, the softly lighted rooms glowed with oriental carpets and gleamed with polished woods. And Dewey was a small part of it. Even against his will he gave in to it. "I'm going to join the boom," he informed Alice,

> & get what I can in the scramble; & work up the students & my own work. There ought to be some compensation for the bigness, & I think the bigness ought to mean at least room to build up your own dept. and no questions asked. . . . A united dept. here ought to forge ahead fast; and a judicious mixture of claret punch & perfecto cigars is in my opinion an excellent cement.

As far as Dewey's work at the university was concerned, Harper requested that he give a series of "University Lectures" on "philosophy—where is she at or what are we here for?" "It seems to be . . . [in] my interest to seize the occasion to boom the department," he said to Alice, and so he would give the lectures, even though he was a "damn fool" for agreeing. His fall class of twenty students was the largest class in the schedule. It would have been still larger, except that "quite ruthlessly" he turned down several students, despite their pleas that they had come " 'expressly to take your work, Professor Dewey & you're not going to be here the rest of the year either.' " He was trying to find time to resume his own writing. He even got Harper to give him a secretary-stenographer. But many things called him away from his philosophic study. In the gap left by the suspension of his usual technical work, new social attitudes were forming. He lectured regularly at Hull House on educational psychology and social issues, to audiences of up to two hundred persons.

Dewey's budding interest in the theory and practice of education was blooming just at the time of his move to Chicago. He talked to President Harper about his vision of a laboratory school in which experiments in early education could be conducted and studied, but he could not have anticipated how far and how fast Harper would enmesh Dewey's scientific ideas in the university's bureaucracy. In November 1894, Harper invited Dewey to dinner and, in one great swoop, "organized the whole department of pedagogy in two hours;

it's going to start next year." Dewey was to create, all at the same time, kindergarten and grammar-school departments for teacher training, for innovations in research and pedagogical theory, and for educational experiments. He had already seen his philosophy and psychology department grow to five faculty before the fall semester was over. But his new expansion into the chair of pedagogy meant that in addition, he would have to create laboratory schools for the training and experiments; he would need to find space and hire new teachers; and he would have to assemble a cadre of reliable staff members. And this was just the start of Harper's plans. This all was to be organized in a "pedagogy" department separate from philosophy, and Dewey was to be in charge of it. Even he was rather overwhelmed. He told Alice that at first he was hesitant and "begged off on the kindergarten & grammar depts." Undeterred, Harper continued to spin out his grand vision, and by the time the dessert was finished, Dewey found himself agreeing that "the college, high school and primary depts. are going to begin next year." Harper filled him with awe: "It's the same thing as looking at a work of art, to see him handle an administrative matter!" Harper was another version of Franklin Ford, albeit from a different philosophical angle. "So," Dewey told Alice, "we are to have a separate department of pedagogy, but I'm to be the headfish."

Soon, in addition to all his other work, Dewey was traveling to nearby Englewood, where Colonel Frances Parker had his training school. For years Parker had been the central spokesman for educational development in the Upper Midwest. Dewey consulted with him during the day and lectured to audiences of more than two hundred teachers in the evening. Soon he was even helping Parker's teachers adapt his *Psychology* to kindergarten teaching.

Before long, Dewey had completely descended to the state of a university administrator engaged in writing "memoranda." In December 1894 he sketched out his rationale and plans for his new administrative charge. This was the kind of work he was now doing instead of philosophy, but he threw himself into it with the same old energy, imitating Harper, and sketched out grand educational visions. The work "planned in psychology and ethics," he began one proposal, "must be closely related to work in pedagogy, [which is] the most . . . promising of any [subject] now offered to a university—especially in the west—it is a practical necessity in order to give practical illustrations of the work in Psychology and Ethics." Working up enthusiasm for his new responsibilities, he noted that "the work thus far done in Pedagogy in this country has been comparatively useless: it has been mechanical and vague because separated from psychology and social ethics." Even in Europe, only the scholars at Jena had begun to realize the "possibilities of work in education. It is possible to go much further in this country than even at Jena." Although Dewey had resisted Harper's plan, he now became its champion, for he saw in it opportunities for public service and personal fame:

> It is my honest and firm conviction that the American University which first sees rightly the existing situation in education and acts upon the possibilities involved, will by that very fact command the entire university situation. I also firmly and honestly believe that Chicago is the most ripe place in America for undertaking this work.

All Dewey needed in order to accomplish this was "an educational museum," a collection of apparatus, a staff of specialists, some control of public-school curricula, advanced students, and an experimental school "such as now exist at Jena and Columbia. Extending ultimately from kindergarten clear up." He assured Harper, for whom this memo was intended as a planning document, that the cost of all this would be modest. It could be started in a small way. But it was a big plan. The "ultimate flower" of the "whole scheme," Dewey asserted, was that the training of teachers would be integrated into the university, not done separately, and so it could be truly scientific.

The president was always glad to hear big plans from his department heads. He embraced Dewey's idea at once. If the philosopher was willing to work at this enormous task, Harper was ready to support him. Harper assured Dewey that he could "organize a complete experimental school under *our* control." He offered other inducements. Alice could, if she wished, be its principal with a salary of $500. Harper "said he'd start the school next year if I wanted," and Dewey added, "If I weren't going far away, I'd do it quick"; maybe "I'd do it anyway." Somehow, Dewey managed to envision a plan for the school that would combine his dual interests in early education and the social improvement of the working class. "Harper thought the school ought to be near the university so as to be convenient of access; I told him I wanted it over on the westside, and that I had no desire to have an aristocratic school or to help train the children of the higher classes." (Eventually, Harper's argument of easy access prevailed.)

Dewey had plenty of energy, considerable ambition, an excellent work ethic, and a strong will, but the strain of all this activity showed. The psychophysiological conversions under stress to which he had been prone since childhood flared up. In 1894, this took the form of eyestrain, ultimately becoming so serious that he "had to give up all reading for a year" and "rest and exercise with prisms daily." This was a first bad sign of the mistake he had made in taking on so much.

Away from his settled life in Michigan, separated from his family, teaching at a new university, living in Chicago in hotels or rooming houses while Alice was in Europe; confronted by a big city, where the distress of the poor was much more evident than it could ever have been in Ann Arbor, reading Alice's somewhat skeptical assessments of Europe's aristocratic remnants, seeking contacts with the wealthy, and making new socially minded friends—especially those connected with Hull House—it is no wonder that Dewey would have been highly susceptible to change, especially the sort of social awareness toward which he had already been tentatively moving.

MORRIS DEWEY

Overwork, eyestrain pointing to internal stress, and yearnings to be with Alice and the children again haunted him all through summer and fall, 1894. As early as August 5 he wrote to Alice, "I think yesterday was the bluest day I have ever spent." Alice replied that she was just as depressed. She even thought of returning home as early as September. Alice had endless difficulties in locating proper lodgings and even more in her uncertainty about where she and the children should go. To make matters worse, she had unexpected trouble with hotel managers and landladies, all of whom constantly objected to what they regarded as the impossibly unruly behavior of the Dewey children.

John's depression was eased by the presence of Morris, who seemed to confirm the importance of all of John's newest conclusions about infant psychology and infant language. "I had a great time from the psychological point of view with Morris yesterday," he wrote. "The training of children," he asserted, "is one of the exact sciences." He was so excited that he wished he could go back and raise Fred and Evelyn all over again. "I hope I shall never forget the lesson I have learned from Morris," he stated. Even when he tried to reassure Alice that Morris had not forgotten her, he soon reverted to his own engagement with him. "Morris shows how much he misses you," he observed, "by the way he clings to me. . . . When I come in he appreciates me and sticks to me like a clam, so that he and I get a good deal of sympathy out of each other."

Partly because he believed that Fred and Evelyn would be interested in their little brother, partly because he had little else to say to the children, but mostly because he was enraptured by Morris and couldn't help himself, he wrote about him in every letter. "Morris has caught up with his physical system, and the stage of signs and symbols and dawning memory and expectation is upon him," he wrote. He described Morris's activities one morning at length: "Morris woke up early this morning and after playing with me a while in bed he climbed out to play outside." Following Morris's departure, Dewey napped, and when he awoke he found Morris washing the windows. "Morris," he observed like a good academic wrapped up in his scholarly subject, "almost converts one to [Josiah] Royce's theory of imitation—save that he is somebody himself." Morris's imitations were "purely plastic."

Finally, the semester was almost over. "It drives me wild to contemplate what I've got to do before I start," Dewey moaned to Alice. He was beset by small details: "I don't get a damn thing done." "When I think of the lectures I've got to give & the writing I've got to finish up . . . my hair turns white in a single night." Worse still, his mother was sick. Lucina, who had helped John care for Morris, had planned to accompany them to Europe. But early in December she fell ill and decided to remain in Lapeer with her sister. This depressed John even as making preparations to leave bolstered his spirits. On December 13, he and Morris left Chicago for New York, and on the fifteenth they sailed. He carried with him a two-page annotated list of places to visit, especially in Switzerland and Germany. In addition, he had a letter of recommendation from W. T. Harris, now U.S. commissioner of education and supervisor of the Bureau of Education, which was still part of the Department of the Interior. Harris wrote: "Any courtesies that may be shown Professor Dewey in the way of furnishing opportunities to pursue his investigations [into early education] will be gratefully appreciated by him and reciprocated by this Bureau when occasion offers." Dewey wanted to do everything—to meet European philosophers, to see sights, to improve his languages, to visit the new experimental schools in Europe, and to watch his children bloom under the civilizing influences of a complex society. Perhaps, too, it would be a relief to remove himself from the social strife so evident in America. So much beckoned his imagination.

He met his family in France. At first, they remained in Paris where Alice and the children had been settled for some time. John attended the philosophical lectures at the Sorbonne, finding in them miracles of orderly exposition. Then they decided to start out for Italy, which turned out to be a bad decision. Passing through Switzerland and Freiburg, Alice, Evelyn, and Morris caught "something." By the time they arrived in Milan, they all were very sick. All three were admitted to a hospital, and Alice and Evelyn soon got better. But suddenly and unexpectedly, on March 12, little Morris died. "Diphtheria" was the cause stated on the death certificate. Two days later Morris was cremated and interred in a Milan cemetery. He had been nearly two and a half.

Both parents were crushed. John had gotten so close to the boy, and Alice had looked forward so to seeing him. But with hardly a warning, Morris was snatched away. All Alice could think of was going home as soon as possible. At the same time she learned that her grandfather had suffered a serious injury, breaking a hip. Writing to her grandmother, she could offer only one item not filled with gloom: at the hospital where Morris died, "the head nurses and Sisters of Charity and everybody there showed a humanity and simplicity which will always make us seem friends and relations of the Italians." But aside from that one positive note, as one of Dewey's daughters wrote years later, "Morris's death was a blow from which neither of his parents ever fully recovered." Back home in Michigan, Lucina received the heartbreaking news that her grandson had died. She too was inconsolable. She went out to Greenmount Cemetery to visit Archibald's grave and, as a comfort to all, proposed that "a tablet of some kind to the memory of Morrisey [be placed] the other side of your father. . . . I can't help wishing it very much."

Not until two months had passed did Dewey recover sufficiently to write to President Harper.

> I presume you have heard that we have had trouble over here. We lost our youngest child of diphtheria in Italy and have been trying ever since . . . to get home, but one after another of the family, with the exception of myself, were taken sick also—we seem to be all over with it now, and are trying to get rested . . . in this little country town [Giverny]. I should have written you long ago had not everything seemed to be against it.

He now expected to sail early in June, and he expressed the hope, in closing, that at least Harper's year had been "a pleasant and successful one."

For Dewey, the year had been hell. On June 10, the family started home, but they went to Michigan and did not start housekeeping in Chicago until the middle of October. Even then John was only just beginning to be able to tell friends and correspondents about Morris's death. In a remarkably interesting letter that he wrote to Harry Norman Gardiner, Dewey started by referring to Morris's passing and then turned to a subject that Gardiner had raised: the tragic emotion. If anyone at that moment might have had thoughts on this subject based on personal experience, Dewey was the person. "There are some few experiences which are so intense as to be wholly painful," he observed, and continued: "I believe pain is as much an element in the highest moral experience. . . . I do not mean as leading up to it, but in it." Here was Dewey passing from a reminder of the death of his child to the beginning of an affective, ethical, and aesthetic theory that would open up new paths for his later psychological-philosophical speculations. Morris's death had certainly left a hole in his heart that he would eventually try to fill, but for now he stepped back into the stream of life and let himself flow forward into the future. In his basically instrumental way, he was already beginning to discover how to convert pain to knowledge and new life, the life of the mind.

OVERWORKING AT THE UNIVERSITY OF CHICAGO

The University of Chicago was growing quickly. President Harper frequently called on his most distinguished professors. Chairpersons were especially burdened. As in any new university, rules and procedures had to be established (then modified); administrative tasks had to be regularized; and all sorts of unanticipated technical irregularities had to be resolved. New faculty had to be hired. New programs must be created. In short, a new bureaucracy had to be devised and accepted. A philosophic scholar, Dewey was now an administrator, and he was soon feeling bombarded by the seeming tons of memoranda that fell on his head.

Dewey had his fingers in all of this and much more. He was chair of one of the three most powerful departments. He was also running the new pedagogical unit. He was centrally engaged in creating a curriculum for the new university elementary school. He had to recruit and hire teachers and staff for all three units. He soon had to report to the dean of education, the provost, the registrar, and so on. He was being called on to give lectures, to attend meetings, to visit schools, and to consult with public-school principals.

Dewey returned from Europe depressed. Months after Morris's death, Evelyn was still sick. Alice herself had not entirely recovered. Fred was uncharacteristically listless. The whole family was in a bad state. Things were so desperate that in July John took Fred and Evelyn to the famous Battle Creek Sanitarium run by the Kelloggs, where Evelyn took the prescribed baths and seemed to be "getting better." Alice was so distraught that instead of going with them, she went on a trip all alone. This didn't prevent her from feeling the depressing ambivalence that often beset her. "I do sometimes think I have no business to be taking such a trip, and that the luxury costs too much in more ways that one," she wrote the children.

There was Grandpa Riggs to care for, including help with the continuing negotiations over sale of his mining claims and help using crutches following his fall. The Deweys had to find appropriate lodgings in Chicago. For the summer they moved to Fenton to be with the Stoners and Riggses, but this only delayed the move until the fall. As if all this was not enough, Lucina was beginning to suffer from Alzheimer's disease, which became so serious that there was talk of confining her to an institution.

In the midst of all this, John was trying to get back to his writing. At Michigan he had been extraordinarily prolific, publishing three books in four years. But now four years had passed since the publication in 1891 of his *Outlines of a Critical Theory of Ethics*, which established him, according to George Herbert Palmer, as "the first man in the country in his subject of ethics." In the meantime Dewey was writing short articles and reviews, which often were worked out first in lectures and then turned into essays. He had been trapped in a complicated life, made still more complicated by the shadows from Morris's death that hung over his inner life.

Dewey's life was made even more complicated by the inundation of administrative work. Perhaps, though, he now embraced it because it provided relief from his personal grief. In addition to his responsibility for several academic units, demands that he court trustees and donors, and solicitations for lectures from all quarters, Dewey had the enormous task in a new university of establishing procedures, fixing lines of communication, learning the rules of authority relations, and engaging in university politics. At first, after his experience at Michigan, Dewey did not realize that at the University of Chicago a business-type administrative bureaucracy would rule, and he took his administrative duties rather casually. Immediately he got into trouble, accused on all sides of not keeping sufficient records, of not consulting before making decisions, and of keeping inadequate financial accounts. His excuse was time constraints: "That in this pressure things may [not] have been done and left undone which would be differently attended to with more leisure, it is too much, perhaps, not to expect." The convolutions in this sentence show his inner confusion. He continued just as awkwardly: "That in this *pressure* ~~some~~ *no mistakes of any kind have been made,* ~~is too much to hope~~; tho I hope none of importance." Then embarrassment set in, and he tried to appease his critics. He confessed to his friend Frank Manny in 1896, "I made some mistakes last year, and consequently . . . tried to have the [President's] Office consulted about everything before making any moves this year. . . . We are probably having to suffer from my remissness last year; however, nobody gave me any instructions, and I had to learn through my blunders." One memo written by the dean of the School of Education to Dewey says it all about Dewey's burdens: "I thought best to submit this whole matter to you before proceeding further since we are without precedent." Written in 1902, several years after Dewey's arrival, this is a perfect example of how much had to be settled when he arrived. Collections of Dewey materials at the Center for Dewey Studies at Southern Illinois University and in the University of Chicago contain thousands of pages of memoranda saved from the even more thousands of pages that crossed Dewey's desk.

Sometimes Dewey's exasperation showed through, especially with people outside the university to whom he could express his feelings of harassment, as when he wrote to his old friend W. T. Harris that he could not only not satisfy a request by Harris at once but "am afraid I shall not find any time to do so in the next two or three years."

Occasionally he became impatient, as when he was surprised by seeing his name on an announcement of a university parents' association meeting and wrote to the dean:

> May I inquire who is responsible for issuing the announcement, and who gave authority for the use of my name? I am not in the habit of having other persons use my name without some authority from me. If such a matter ever occurs again I shall take it upon myself to print and send to everyone concerned a statement that an unauthorized use has been made of my name. If this seems a small point to you, or to whoever is responsible for using it, I think that reflection will enable you to see the matter in another light.

Sometimes Dewey's overburdened feelings leaked through, even to Harper: "I hardly think it wise for me to go upon the Committee of Seven that has to do with elementary work. I have my hands so full of other things that it is a good deal of a divergence of interest to take up the elementary school problem just now."

Soon Dewey began to refuse invitations to write books and articles or to deliver lectures that he would have welcomed earlier. When the economist Richard T. Ely, whom he had known at Hopkins, began editing the Library of Social Issues series, he wrote to ask Dewey to compose a work on education. Dewey answered, "Possibly the time may come in the future when I shall have leisure and ability to undertake it. At present I am too tied up." He formed a plan to teach summers in order to have one or two regular semesters off, but he found himself too busy with administration to take the time. No wonder that in 1897 and again in 1900 he experienced eyestrain all over again and had to turn down invitations to review books or write articles.

More Publications

Still, at no time in his adult life, from the time he sent his first article to the *Journal of Speculative Philosophy*, did Dewey entirely cease writing for publication. Of his writing during his first years at the University of Chicago, W. R. McKenzie commented:

> At first glance, and even after a second look, Dewey's writings of these years seem to represent an alarming diffusion, a scattering of effort in too many directions. They present so many reactions to so many influences on so many subjects expressed in so many forms that one looks almost in desperation for some element which ties them all together.

This is true—but not entirely so. As a professional philosopher, whatever his varied interests might be, Dewey always centered his exposition of any topic in a concept of logic as a theory of inquiry. Whether he looked at a strictly philosophic topic such as ethics, at an applied field such as education, at a psychological concern such as the mechanisms of mental processes or the psychology of numbers, or a social problem such as political justice, Dewey always engaged these primarily as a logical procedure. He was always more interested in a basic point of view than in topics or techniques. His earliest work on the logical theories of Lotze and his reactions against him in an attempt to adumbrate, by way of Hegel, a new logic situated his writings in this concern with logical method and conferred a basic unity on all his works. Educators saw the importance of his work for the innovations in education that it suggested; those readers who had social concerns embraced his progressive ideas relative to social justice; psychologists were instructed and encouraged by his concept of mind; and philosophers were excited by the strains of radical empiricism that emerged in his latest writing. But behind all these, his central effort at logical inquiry informed all his varied interests. Of the many works written after he arrived at the University of Chicago, four stand out for their excellence and their exemplifications of the way that Dewey thought about everything.

Published in 1896, "The Reflex Arc Concept in Psychology" extended Dewey's reputation as the leading exponent in America of a unified concept of mind. With James McKeen Cattell, his friend at Hopkins who was now at Columbia, this article made Dewey the parent of behavioral psychology in America. Written at a time when, as Dewey put it, "all generalizations and classifications [in psychology] are most questioned and questionable," this essay subjected to scrutiny the mechanistic pseudoscientific psychology of stimulus and response theory and experiments. In contrast to the mechanistic psychology then current, he asserted that the dynamic "idea of the reflex arc" came nearer than any other to providing a unifying concept that could withstand logical examination. At the same time he scrutinized and exposed the hidden dualisms of both the old and the "new" scientific psychology: "The older dualism [in psychology] between sensation and idea is repeated in the current dualism of peripheral and central structures and functions; the older dualism of body and soul finds a distinct echo in the current dualism of stimulus and response." Mechanistic psychology, he concluded, "is a survival of the metaphysical dualism, first formulated by Plato." The result is "a patchwork of disjointed parts" rather than an "organic unity." But when function and process replace structure, the "psychical unity" of mind emerges in the *logical consequence of action*. Stimulus and response, he concluded, are not "distinctions of existence" but of teleology. In short, whether regarded physiologically, biologically, or psychically, the mind operates as a circuit of conjoined activities, not as a sequence of call and response. Dewey thus expanded his "reflex arc" concept into the even more dynamic idea of an "adjustive arc," continually active, self-regulating, and unified as one ongoing circuit. The dynamic logic of activity must replace the mechanistic logic of dualism. Dewey was part of the great movement in thought from the mechanistic world of Newton to the dynamism of Darwin—and, in the longest forward-looking aspect of his development—to the relativisitic world of Einstein. Dewey's idea of the adjustive arc put him on this path by taking him well beyond the concept of mental processes that William James had derived from the empiricists.

"Interest in Relation to Training of the Will" was to educators what "The Reflex Arc" was to psychologists: a unifying new idea. Published first in the Herbart Society's *Yearbook* in 1896 and later, in considerably revised form, separately in 1899, this work had a major influence on American education. Again, Dewey discerned a single unifying idea in the concept of attention or interest: "Interest is in the closest relation to the emotional life, on one side; and, through its close relation, if not identity, with attention, to the intellectual life, on the other side." Then the question proposed for logical inquiry must be, how do feeling and knowledge relate to the activity of the will in acting with interest and attention as a single, unified, organic choice by the whole organism?

Dewey chose to locate his inquiry in education, specifically the claims of rival educational theories, one stressing interest and the other effort, as if his inquiry were a legal contest between a plaintiff and defendant, a dispute that originally for Dewey had its roots in the difference between his realistic father and his idealistic mother. He provisionally concluded that each contestant is an effective critique of the other. But what both aim at—and what the child who is the courtroom in which these different life attitudes compete aims at—is *growth*. As Dewey's logic takes the form of inquiry, it drives behind the competing theories of education to stress the child's inner need to develop, to realize its intrinsic potential in the extrinsic arena of the classroom. Dewey had absorbed this idea from Hegel, and now he put it into practice. Education, he stressed, is about the child, not the teacher. In showing that the child is the essential, primary focus of education, Dewey redirected educational attention from what should be taught to what children need to learn:

> The spontaneous power of the child, his demand for realization of his own impulses, cannot by any possibility be suppressed. If the external conditions are such that the child cannot put his spontaneous activity into the work to be done, if he finds he cannot express himself in that, he learns in a most miraculous way the exact amount of attention that has to be given to this external material to satisfy the requirements of the teacher, while saving up the rest of his mental powers for following out lines of imagery that appeal to him.

By concentrating on the fundamental growth needs of the developing organism, Dewey called the attention of educators to internal growth in relation to moral training and habits of obedience; and he placed the discipline of "the deeper intellectual and moral nature of the child" on a level at least equal to education's traditional emphasis on "outward habits of action." While not denying the importance of work habits, he urged the equally important training of inward aspirations and the capacity for "self-expression." Crucial to his argument was the ethical problem of ends and means, on which Dewey focused all his life. If the end of education is growth toward self-expression, then self-expression and not mere habit must inform and direct the means of education. When means and ends are divided, agitation, instead of growth, results.

When Dewey first presented this paper to the Herbart Society in 1896, it resulted in a vigorous discussion, led chiefly by W. T. Harris, who declared it "a very able production [that] . . . deserves several readings, as do all of Dr. Dewey's works." Better than anyone else except Dewey himself, Harris saw that in it Dewey had developed logically the perspective of Hegel's *Philosophy of Right* in centering on "a universe of freedom and evolution" and collapsing "interest" into "self expression." But Dewey had abandoned Hegel's emphasis on "pure being" in making self-activity itself the law of development. Harris remained the conventional Hegelian, discussing "the will of man as related to the will of God, and how far the finite will is a form or expression of the infinite" while Dewey was now using hints from Hegel psychologically in the service of an instrumental logic.

Harris's presence in this debate is a reminder of Dewey's drive to create a philosophic community. He never wholly abandoned any of his mentors, and he never separated from any of his colleagues. As a thinker he was temperamentally attached to evolution, not rebellion. Around him he had gathered Torrey, Harris, George Morris, Peirce, William James, and Colonel Frances Parker as older mentors, along with such new colleagues and coworkers as Tufts, Addison W. Moore, Mead, James Rowland Angell, and Lloyd. He continued to add new influences from his reading, remaining a teacher, but always looking for new sources of instruction.

This was certainly true of a book that Dewey wrote with James A. McLellan. While he was still at Michigan, he had collaborated with McLellan on the second edition of *Applied Psychology*. They then wrote together *The Psychology of Number and Its Applications to Methods of Teaching Arithmetic*, which was published in 1897 by D. Appleton. This book was the result of three years of collaborative work, done at what Dewey called "my usual crablike speed." He saw it as a book suitable for high-school instruction, and he had visions of making a lot of money from it.

Dewey believed that it was numbers, the art of measuring, by which people had subjugated nature, whereas language was a secondary act of preservation, keeping number knowledge from perishing. Together, number plus speech gave humans control of nature. He explained his approach in this book to Alice in 1894: "I'm trying to turn the Hegelian logic of quantity over into psychology & then turn that over into [a] method for teaching arithmetic." To his surprise, he found the investigation "quite fascinating." In this collaboration Dewey was to "furnish" the psychology, and McLellan, the methods: "The teacher drops his nickel in the slot—and the pupil does the rest, as usual. However, it's rather a fascinating thing to work out the psych. of counting, subtracting & dividing." The general editor of Appleton's International Education Series, in which his and McLellan's *Psychology of Number* appeared, was W. T. Harris, who wrote the preface in which he praised the "admirable manner" in which Dewey and McLellan presented "the psychological view of number." Dewey first presented in this book the idea of valuation, which occupied him for the next fifty years. "Number," he wrote, "represents . . . *valuation*; number is the tool whereby modern society in its vast and intricate processes of exchange introduces system, balance and economy into those relations upon which our daily life depends." The psychology of number is thus the web upon which all forms of civilization build:

> Properly conceived and presented, neither geography nor history is a more effective mode of bringing home to the pupil the

realities of the social environments in which he lives than is arithmetic. Society has its form also, and it is found in the processes of fixing standards of value and methods of valuation, the processes of weighing and counting . . . whether in space or time, and of balancing the various resulting values against one another.

The first chapter, written by Dewey, is entitled "What Psychology Can Do for the Teacher." Dewey's contribution to the book is general, his philosophical argument running throughout it. He argues that the psychology of civilization is equivalent to the psychology of measurement and that both are essential to the evolution of educational organization and the minds of each pupil. Here, in an unlikely place—a textbook on teaching arithmetic—Dewey found yet another occasion and medium through which to explain how civilization grows.

This same endeavor is equally apparent in *Studies in Logical Theory* (1903). This volume consists of four essays by Dewey, followed by seven chapters written by scholars who had held graduate fellowships in Dewey's department at the University of Chicago—followers rather than disciples—along with discursive interpolations by Dewey. Dewey's influence on these authors is apparent everywhere. On the first page of her chapter, Dewey's student Helen Bradford Thompson, who became director of the psychological laboratory at Mount Holyoke College, points out that her criticism of Bosanquet's theory of judgment "was influenced by Dewey's lecture course on 'The Theory of Logic.' " The views of Mill, Lotze, Bosanquet, and Bradley—all thinkers once important to Dewey—remain, in this book, only as foci for opposition. Dewey and his school were bent on putting these logicians behind them. The influences of Alfred Lloyd, Dewey's assistant at Michigan, and George Herbert Mead and James Angell, his assistants at Chicago, are evident. Symbolizing Dewey's gathering of a philosophic community about him, he dedicated the book to William James in recognition of the "inspiration and the forging of the tools with which the writers have worked."

Implicit in all the essays is the idea that "judgment is the central function of knowing, and hence affords the central problem of logic." Asserting and attempting to show that knowing—*knowing, not knowledge*—is made up of affection, appreciation, and habit and is illuminated by psychology, Dewey and his colleagues conclude that logic must be open to change, absorptive of experience, mindful of process, and therefore "reconstructive" and "transformatory." Since there is no end to the knowing function, knowing focuses on the readjustment and expansion of judgment. He and his colleagues, Dewey asserts, "all agree that this conception gives the only promising basis upon which the working methods of science and the proper demands of the moral life, may cooperate." Addison W. Moore, who earned his Ph.D. with Dewey and stayed on at Chicago as an assistant professor, ends the collection of essays by stressing the logic of knowing, a participial logic of process: reality consists "in . . . loving and hoping, desiring and willing, believing and working" activities, and a logic and language of process must reflect the character of the indissolubly changeful worlds of fact and idea.

Dewey's four essays, which open the book, describe the general problem of logical theory by holding up thought as "derivative and secondary": it is *about* something, comes "after something and out of something, and [is] for the sake of something." This is as true, Dewey notes, of everyday practical thinking as of scientific thought. Right away, Dewey brings up naturalistic empiricism. Primary, of course, is the relation of thought to its empirical antecedents and the object of thought, the search for truth in relation to reality. He speaks of thought with the excitement of a new explorer:

> We think about anything and everything: snow on the ground; the alternating clanks and thuds that rise from below; the relation of the Monroe Doctrine to the embroglio in Venezuela; the relation of art to industry; the poetic quality of a painting by Botticelli; the battle of Marathon; the economic interpretation of history; the proper definition of cause;

the best method of reducing expenses; whether and how to renew the ties of a broken friendship; the interpretation of an equation in hydrodynamics, etc.

Around the same time as Freud did, Dewey discovered free association, which he called "the madness of this miscellaneous citation." The content of thought is the sum of our past, as all its elements flow into the arc of thought in the here and now and aim in the future at knowing. Logic is the method of this process. In this way Dewey gives James's empiricism a dynamics and method. Logical theory in Dewey's hands became the consideration of the relation of thought to reality and necessarily involved "much psychological material," along with consideration of scientific methods of investigation and verification. "It may busily concern itself [as well] with the differentiation of various types and forms" of thought and judgment, but always with the object of joining experience, thought, and knowing. Dewey announces, "logic is supposed to grow out of the epistemological inquiry and to lead up to its solution." He had discovered Deweyan *impure* logic.

William James not only accepted the tribute of the book; he also greeted it with enthusiasm. Even before the book appeared, James had been praising Dewey's achievement in shaping a philosophic movement on native grounds. For some years James had been thrown off the track in understanding Dewey, misled by the Hegelian panoply in Dewey's *Psychology*, and he had never adequately grasped Dewey's development from Hegelianism to empiricism and experimentalism. When Dewey sent him the proofs of *Studies in Logical Theory* with the request that he accept the dedication, he acknowledged that in reading Addison Moore's article, so heavily influenced by Dewey, he had at last seen Dewey with new eyes:

It humiliates me that I had to wait till I read Moore's articles before finding how much on my own lines you were working. Of course I had welcomed you as one coming nearer and nearer, but I had missed the central root of the whole business, and shall now re-read you . . . and try again a hack at Mead and

Lloyd of whom I have always recognized the originality, but whom I have found so far unassimilably obscure. I fancy that much depends on the place one starts from—you have all come from Hegel and your terminology *s'en ressent*, I from Empiricism, and though we reach much the same goal it superficially looks different from opposite sides.

"It rejoices me greatly that your School (I mean your philosophic school) at the U. of C. is, after this long gestation, bringing its fruits to birth in a way that will demonstrate its great unity and vitality," James added. In reply Dewey graciously wrote that he and the other contributors were "simply rendering back in logical vocabulary what was already your own." James had already written to the British pragmatist F. C. S. Schiller that *Studies in Logical Theory* "is splendid stuff, and Dewey is a hero. A real school & real thought." James famously remarked: "At Harvard we have plenty of thought, but no school; at Yale and Cornell, the other way about."

Then the reviews began to appear. Dewey's teacher Charles Sanders Peirce wrote in *The Nation* that the book exhibited "an impressive decade's work," offering "conclusive proof" that Dewey's effort to ally mind with experience was leading to the fruitful conclusion that logic could become "a natural history of thought." From this time on, Peirce started to claim Dewey as "a pupil of mine, & one of the shining lights of the philosophy of today,—and highly original as most of my pupils have turned out." He added: "I always devoted myself to developing originality in my pupils & am never better pleased than when they attack my position." For his part, Dewey started to read Peirce at around this time and soon recommended that the Carnegie Institution help publish "the contributions of . . . Peirce to the logic of the sciences." This started him on a forty-year study of Peirce that greatly affected his development. He had not understood Peirce at all when he took his class at Johns Hopkins. And then he did understand him and began to see the flaws and deficiencies of Peirce's development of an "objective idealism" as early as 1893 in his article "The Superstition of Necessity." Later, Dewey resumed his study of Peirce, and while avoiding any criticism of Peirce's synthetic argument, he began to develop Peirce's "logic of use." Between 1893 and 1903 Dewey showed how able a logician he himself already was—and might become.

Other reviewers beside Peirce applauded Dewey's *Studies in Logical Theory*. From England Schiller termed *Studies* "a weighty contribution to current logical controversy." Observing what James had alerted him to, Schiller saw that Dewey had developed a logical theory that paralleled and supported James's pragmatism, and he compared this coincidence with the simultaneous discovery of natural selection by Darwin and Wallace. Schiller, who had followed somewhat the same path as Dewey—from Hegel by way of Darwin to empiricism—announced that Dewey's logic had passed beyond absolute idealism through "his admirable proof of the superfluity of an absolute *truth-to-be-copied*, existing alongside of the human truth which is *made* by our efforts." James himself completed the series of positive reviews with his own notice, "The Chicago School":

> Professor John Dewey and . . . his disciples, have collectively put into the world of statement, homogeneous in spite of so many cooperating minds, a view of the world, both theoretical and practical, which is so simple, massive and positive that . . . it deserves the title of a new system of philosophy.

Always on the lookout for a distinctly American culture, James concluded that Dewey's Chicago school was "certainly something of which Americans may be proud."

Dewey was moved by James's review but not surprised, for in early December James had given him advance notice of it in a letter to Dewey as his colleague and coworker in developing a native American philosophy:

> You can't guess the delight with which all this work fills me. It is a glorious thing for you and for the university to have created such a genuine school of original thought. I cannot help

believing that you have struck the *truth*, and that our system
has a very great future. It sorely needs building out, however,
in cosmological, psychological, & epistemological directions.
The ethical buildings-out are already tip-top.

He added that his idealist colleague Royce was "hard hit by your deliv-
erances."

Not all the reviews of Dewey's book were positive, however. A dis-
senting view was voiced by F. H. Bradley. In his own essays, Dewey
had generally exhibited respect for Bradley's *Principles of Logic* while
pointing out the difficulties of Bradley's insufficient appreciation of the
importance of psychology and psychical reality in his analysis of
thought and thought-content. But Dewey's followers were more critical, and Bradley was stung. He turned the tables by pointing out the
difficulties created by *his* critics when they collapsed logical into psychological processes, declaring that if "there is to be no such thing as
independent thought, that is, which in its actual exercise takes no
account of the psychological situation," we must be skeptical of the
very exercise of logic. "On this point, I have so far failed to gain any
assurance from Prof. Dewey." Still, Bradley later told T. S. Eliot of his
admiration for Dewey.

Whether Dewey wrote or lectured about logic, education, psychology, ethics, conflicts between labor and capital, or social change, underpinning these and all that he thought and did were a few unifying concepts—wholeness, growth, and experience. When he considered social
issues, this meant the search for justice; if he reflected on education, it
took the form of interest in knowing; in psychology, the watchword
was the ever expanding circuit; in logic, the indissoluble engagement
between idea and reality; in all, the primacy of inquiry. After preparing for this in Michigan, in his early years in Chicago Dewey had
arrived at a calm philosophic perspective in a unification of experience
and self that gave him a relaxed air that, despite numerous vicissitudes
of life, stayed with him always. He could still, for a time, become agitated by academic busywork, but his philosophic development began
to roll forward smoothly.

Only by achieving a focus and confidence in his basic convictions was Dewey able to do so much during the ten years following his arrival at Chicago. The work that he accomplished in any one field would have sufficed for most person's decade, and he was busy in many fields. His application of philosophy and psychology to education added a whole new aspect to his activities. The years of Dewey's greatest actual involvement in educational experiment were those at Chicago between 1894 and 1904. Hardly had he arrived at Chicago when he was asked to speak at a convocation for the study of child nature on the subject of parents' need to study child psychology. He became a professor of pedagogy and the director of the laboratory school. He became a member of the National Herbart Society and the Illinois Society for Child Study and was in constant demand as a speaker in all parts of the country. An interview with Dewey that appeared in the *Chautauqua Assembly Herald* on July 23, 1896, is typical of the ease with which he had learned to speak on his favorite topics:

> Prof. John Dewey yesterday told me a number of interesting things concerning his work in pedagogy at the University of Chicago. "We have a well equipped psychological laboratory," said he, "which is largely used in connection with our pedagogical department, and our aim is, not so much the drilling of individual teachers, as the development of method in psychological experiment and observation as applied to the child-study movement. For this purpose we have in our charge some fifty children from six to eight years of age." "How do you arrange the children's studies?" "Always by combining practical illustration with their mental work," said he, "and thus we are enabled to observe the correlation of the mental perception and physical activity. We also make experiments adapted to testing the child's senses and motor power." "Can these methods be successfully applied in ascertaining the capabilities of children for different trades?" "The present state of our experimental knowledge does not indicate that possibility, except in

a limited measure." Dr. Dewey expressed his great delight with the children's clubs at Chautauqua. "Your opportunities for child-study here seem to me unbounded," he remarked. "I am especially interested in this phase of Chautauqua life."

PROGRESSIVE EDUCATION

The result of all this activity was a book, *The School and Society* (1899), which became Dewey's most widely read work. He had turned the subject over and over in his mind as he lectured on it, and so the book virtually wrote itself.

The School and Society is built on the psychological theses of "Interest in Relation to Training of the Will," but the theories of child capability and its development barely break the surface of Dewey's extended argument that education contains three primary elements: the school; a dynamic, evolving society; and the children, who can pass through the right kind of school to become a part of the community, contributing their own inner development to the growth of society (as members of a community) and to the progress of politics (as citizens). Many people—including many educators—misunderstood Dewey to mean that instead of a traditionally *institution*-centered aim, education should become *child*-centered. Although this interpretation served the purposes of teachers in a democratic society, Dewey insisted that education be *society*-centered, for children are destined to become not isolated individuals but members and citizens of society. He saw and stated clearly that children's inner nature or mind grows from within but must be completed through relationships. Children naturally encounter a multitude of relations in school, and if school can bring out the children's inner capacities, these can grow into social possibilities in love relations, family activities, social justice, and political discrimination. Dewey's logic was at work here, not a romantic notion that children's impulses were natural and were needed to alter society. Rather, Dewey always focused on progress, not on revolution, but on amelioration, and so his progressivism was basically conservative in philosophy and liberal in activity. Dewey's readers had to learn that his liberalism was his own creation and not an attempt to imitate some abstract "liberal tradition."

His so-called laboratory school—officially named the University Elementary School—itself was organized as a microsociety occupied with unifying the personal and community interests that carry life forward. Dewey chose to organize the school as a reflection of life instead of a curriculum, which is why the school's earliest activities were centered on occupations. Planting, growing, harvesting, and cooking what is produced, weaving to create useful household items, sewing to create and repair garments, woodworking to create socially useful products, writing for communication instead of penmanship, drawing or painting to convey emotions, counting numbers to maintain accounts, reading the stars to learn directions, resting for restoration—these were activities designed to develop the children's talents in relation to their social use. "We must conceive of work in wood and metal, of weaving, sewing, and cooking as methods of living and learning, not as distinct studies."

A child in Dewey's school was instantly a member of a cooperative commonwealth. Learning and creating knowledge were merely two forms of knowing, what Dewey called "methods of life." From occupations, students in Dewey's school proceeded naturally to their correlatives in the so-called disciplines: from production to economics; from cooperation to politics; from experiment to science; from activity in a community to the understanding of other, larger communities through history, social studies, geography, and culture; and from the activities of a civilization to ethics, morals, and manners. Wherever Dewey's students entered an occupation, they came out on the other side in interest-saturated reflection. "You can concentrate the history of all mankind," Dewey wrote, "into the evolution of the flax, cotton, and wool fibres into clothing." "Active occupation" was the route to life, the basis of "the child's habitat, where he learns through directed living" in "an embryonic society" that leads him, as he becomes ready for it, into the larger world in which he must learn to live even as he seeks to improve it. Even though philosophers—Tufts, Mead, Angell,

Moore, and, of course, Dewey himself—were always wandering around the school, no philosophy was taught there. Rather, the school was the *expression* of a philosophy, philosophy itself enacted. The students there did not learn logic, they lived it.

In this work—and indeed in all his future work on education—Dewey assumed that children's need to develop coincided with a democratic culture like America's. Here his divergence from Marxist theory was evident: change would come not through the proletarian class (or any other social class) but through school classes and education in its broadest sense. As the schools in America became more and more laboratories for living, society would progress toward greater and greater democracy and thus grow in social justice. This assumption that child-nature and democracy were parallel separates Dewey from the educational theorists who preceded him or were his contemporaries. Pestalozzi, for instance, was concerned with education for workers. In contrast, Dewey did not think of education in terms of class. His distinctive angle of vision was always focused on the unity of growth of all children in a democracy, along with the growth of democracy through child-education.

"Dewey's Lab School" became a well-known phrase in educational circles during his years at Chicago, and "progressive education" became a household phrase. European educators came to Chicago to teach and to study with Dewey and learn his methods. Articles by and about Dewey were eagerly solicited by editors. His lectures attracted large audiences, and they were regularly reported in the newspapers. In short, he became the most famous educator in America.

Even in Hawaii Dewey was well known. In 1894 the islands became a republic, and four years later the republic voted to cede itself to the United States as a territory. But since the educational system had been established in 1840 by Congregational missionaries, the school system in Hawaii had been organized and conducted on American principles. Indeed, Hawaii's school system was actually ahead of that of several states on the mainland.

By mid-1890 Hawaii was already reflecting the experiments in educational theory and practice conducted by Dewey, Colonel Parker, and others. Parker, in fact, was invited to lecture there in 1896. As part of the resolution aimed at annexation to the United States, a Hawaiian commission declared: "The school system and its methods are particularly American." In 1899, Henry S. Townsend, the superintendent of public instruction, argued for one of Dewey's principles, that all instruction had to be connected "with the experiences of those taught." Townsend then founded a journal explicitly reflecting Dewey's ideas, entitled *The Progressive Educator*, which featured items about Dewey's earliest ideas on education. He had a direct line to Dewey's experiments through Dewey's colleague George Herbert Mead, who was married to Helen Castle, the daughter of one of Hawaii's most prominent business families. In 1898, the family asked Dewey's aid in helping establish a kindergarten in memory of Henry Castle and his daughter and to find an appropriate teacher for it. The teacher would be initially trained in the Chicago Normal School, so that the kindergarten would be a pure "Parker-Dewey school." It wouldn't be "orthodox," Dewey said, but simply "do for the little tots whatever seems best for them." He recommended Flora J. Cooke, one of the best teachers in his school, reminding her that "it is a great chance to do something for primary education in the Islands." Shortly thereafter, in 1899, Townsend invited Dewey to teach his principles directly to the teachers of Hawaii in the summer school for teachers that Townsend had created in 1896.

On sabbatical for the spring semester of 1899, Dewey and his family traveled to California in April. At the University of California at Berkeley, John lectured on "Psychology and the Philosophic Method" to the Philosophic Union. John and Alice kept the younger children, Gordon and Lucy, with them, and Fred and Evelyn stayed with Alice's friend Lucy Moore in Santa Barbara. Late in July, Lucy Moore and another friend, Annie Stevens, took all four Dewey youngsters into their care in Santa Barbara, allowing their parents to go to Honolulu on August 1.

Officially, Dewey was employed by the University of Hawaii's Extension Division. He gave ten lectures, one each Tuesday and Friday, to a registered class of 125 teachers. His topics included "Early Childhood," "Play and Imagination," "Later Childhood and Interest," "Adolescence and Emotions," and "General Principles of Growth."

Besides his official duties, he consulted with school administrators, individual teachers, and city education officials. He even visited and observed a school for native Hawaiian girls. Always fascinated by ancient cultures, John spent his spare time gathering local legends and myths. But mostly he taught, consulted, and talked with everyone who wanted to hear his views on education, especially since Honolulu seemed ripe for the further development of progressive education. When he and Alice left Honolulu on September 19, Henry Townsend summed up the meaning of his visit: "In this [1899] session we "had the very great privilege of the presence of Dr. Dewey himself, not only on the lecture platform but in our daily discussions. He was our Great High Priest."

THE LAB SCHOOL

During these years, Dewey was unbelievably busy. When he had been head of a department at the relatively slow-growing University of Michigan, his administrative duties had been light. But unlike Dewey's faculty in philosophy, into which most of his colleagues in Michigan followed him, the pedagogical faculty had to be trained or retrained for the new educational ventures that he and his colleagues wanted to try. The Lab School soon had twenty-three teachers and 140 pupils. In addition, the members of the philosophy department plus faculty from other departments of the University of Chicago had to be persuaded to join in the experiment. Suddenly Dewey was responsible for three units. Two other factors made this already heavy burden nearly unmanageable. First, he was now directly responsible to another administrative officer, the dean of the School of Education, Wilbur S. Jackman. A man with boundless attention to detail and a well-known educationalist himself, Jackman was soon minutely managing Dewey's every move. Although both men were eminently capable, they were mismatched in their styles of attention, with Jackman stressing details and Dewey, goals.

Second, Dewey's administrative position as head of the Department of Pedagogy and director of the Lab School meant that he soon had to achieve scholarly preeminence in educational theory. Without diminishing his productivity as a philosopher or his duties as a teacher and director of theses in the graduate program in philosophy, he had to become just as famous and influential in the field of education. He accomplished this.

Financial needs and ambition prompted Dewey to take on more and more. In 1901 Dewey agreed to be supervisor of the South Side Academy and also of the Chicago Manual Training School in order to add a $2,000 stipend to his $5,000 salary, which was the University of Chicago's pay ceiling. Also in 1901, the famous training school that had been created by Colonel Frances W. Parker near Chicago well before the University of Chicago was established, was brought by Harper into the University of Chicago through the urging of its wealthy and influential patroness, Mrs. Anita McCormick Blaine. Though ailing, Parker remained its president until February 1902 when he died.

President Harper met with Mrs. Blaine and three other trustees of the Chicago Institute in April 1902. Two persons were proposed to fill the vacancy left by Colonel Parker: John Dewey and Wilbur S. Jackman, to whom Dewey reported and who was the more natural choice. But Mrs. Blaine was a firm supporter of Dewey. She was appointed by the group to consult with the faculty of the School of Education to determine which man would be better. Five days later, she reported back—with Jackman present—that the "consensus of opinion" was that "Mr. Jackman could not be the leader of the school and that it is very much desired for the school to gain Dr. Dewey as a leader of the work." Two days later, Dewey was called to the meeting. Would he accept the directorship of the Parker School? Dewey told the trustees that he shared the "feeling of responsibility with them." Questions arose about maintaining the school's continuity. Dewey replied "that he would be very slow to make changes in the school." What assurances of that could he give? Dewey responded that the assurance was himself. How much time could he devote to it? He "stated that he could not give up his work in Philosophy but he would give all his time that would be given to educational matters to the school." He said that he would not assume the responsibility of the school "in name only but in actuality and would expect to give to it all that it would demand." This last promise, especially, put him out on a limb, with Harper ready to consume all his time and Jackman, who had been passed over, still his supervisor. Dewey's strongest stated motive in taking on this new burden was his high regard for Colonel Parker and a wish to carry on his work; his unstated motive was the extra stipend of $2,500 that the directorship brought.

Dewey was given the job, but by August he was already backpedaling. But the appointment was signed and sealed. So in 1902 Dewey was chair of the philosophy and the pedagogy departments, administrator of the University Elementary School, supervisor of an academy and a manual training school, the director of the Frances W. Parker Institute, and the chief of the teacher-training program.

Now the problems that he had seen earlier in Harper's expansive style of management hit Dewey with full force. Hardly had Dewey arrived in Chicago, in July 1894, when he predicted the problem that he would eventually encounter. He had told Alice this early: "There are . . . suggestions that faculty discussions are all a sham—Pres. does just what he pleases with no consultations . . . etc. It is all as nothing to me—until it hits me." In 1901, it did. Dewey was struggling under impossible administrative and professional burdens. The main problem seems to have been that Harper had "so many schemes on hand" and had become so addicted to "springing schemes on the public"— especially the possible patrons of the university—that he made promises he could not keep and never intended to keep. As Dewey's administrative burdens started to build, he began to displace onto Harper his frustration with not being able to fulfill all his duties and to feel increasingly irritated by what he saw now as Harper's "willingness to embarrass and hamper" his work by making promises that he could not keep and starting Dewey on work that could not be completed.

All this time Dewey was doing his best to meet every expectation that Harper imposed on him. *Studies in Logical Theory* fulfilled Harper's academic aim to have an American school of philosophy emerge in Chicago. He took great pride in that and in the increasing international reputation of his star philosopher, Dewey. Many philosophers regarded Dewey as the person who would soon take William James's place as the preeminent exponent of radical empiricism, pragmatism, or instrumentalism—whatever this new movement was to be called. Similarly, psychologists saw Dewey as one of the great leaders of psychological theory; with many regarding his concept of the reflex arc as the core around which the entire movement in psychology would be built. Dewey had also placed himself at the center of the national movement to reform American education. He was most active precisely at the time that education in America started toward creating a culture that would soon produce knowledge as easily as it previously produced goods.

Harper was delighted at Dewey's spreading fame, but he began to feel that he was neglecting Chicago; so when Dewey announced lectures at Columbia University and the Brooklyn Institute, Harper suggested that he instead increase the number of his appearances in the city where he was employed. "I am wondering," he wrote Dewey, "whether we can persuade you to give six or twelve lectures at one of the Chicago centers next year. It seems too bad that the Brooklyn people can have the pleasure of hearing you, and the same pleasure denied the Chicago people." Dewey's reply was impatient: "Other circumstances will doubtless decide the question of my giving extension lectures. . . . But I can not refrain from stating that Brooklyn pays $200 for three lectures while I think the Extension Department offers $100 for six." Nonetheless, Harper continued to press Dewey for additional contributions.

Soon after his arrival, Dewey had observed with surprise that at the University of Chicago, founded under Baptist influence, there was less call for religious conformity than at the University of Michigan, a publicly founded institution. But then he soon detected the narrow fundamentalist streak that ran through Harper himself. He told Alice:

> Pres Harper has been at some Baptist convention [in the] east; the speech he made . . . is enough to give you the shivers; said "secularism" was dechristianizing universities; no professor ought to be allowed who is an agnostic &c; and . . . if you

wanted the genuine thing with patent Christian attachment and guaranteed agnostic automatic cut-off, you better patronize Chicago University.

As time went by, Dewey perceived in Harper's attitude, which pervaded the school, a fundamentalist emphasis on relentless effort, and Dewey began to resent the unspoken demand for personal sacrifice.

Dewey made one bold attempt to fulfill all the commitments he had made. In 1901 he appointed Alice the principal of the Lab School. Dewey was now accused of making this appointment "without consultation." He immediately wrote to Harper "with reference to Mrs. Dewey's name for Principal":

> I was perhaps overanxious to get as much settled as possible before leaving; we had not found a principal. Mrs. Dewey was suggested—by me, not by Mrs Young—at a late moment, & it was literally at the last moment that Mrs Dewey consented at all. I realize that altho' this was only a few hours before the budget was sent in, I still might & should have found time to consult you with reference to it—I am sure you will recognize that I intended no discourtesy—that because it was Mrs Dewey's name that was sent in, I would have been more than ordinarily anxious to have everything straight—but this was due to my giving way to pressures on my time. . . .
>
> I should add that Mrs. Dewey has not been aware that you were not consulted and that she also is naturally annoyed at the omission—She accepted the position only after protest and with much reluctance, and wishes me to express her desire for a readjustment if you see anything to object to in the matter—.

Harper now supported Dewey and asked him to "assure Mrs. Dewey that there is no desire on my part for readjustment." By this time Harper had probably completely forgotten that in November 1894 it was he who suggested that when a lab school was developed, Alice could run it and later approved a salary of $1,250 for her. So Alice

became principal of the Lab School on a one-year contract. Dewey recommended to the trustees that her contract be extended to three years,
and although this was not accepted, it did not seem to mean that her
appointment was to be for one year only.

Alice took up the job with the greatest enthusiasm and commen-
surate success. She even began to publish, and her article "The Place
of the Kindergarten," appeared in *The Elementary School Teacher*
in January 1903. In it she referred approvingly to Froebel's "great principle of inner development and continuity." She also began to help
John with his responsibilities in the School of Education. While his
administrative commitments were still heavy, this brought some relief
and, moreover, had the benefit that he and Alice could work together
and that she could employ her talents. An assessment of her success
was made by Frank Pierrepont Graves, the president of the University
of Washington, who had taken a leave of absence to come to Chicago
to study educational philosophy. He spoke warmly of the classes he
took from John Dewey and then added:

> In my own case, great as is my debt to Mr. Dewey, amounting,
> I hope, to a complete intellectual revolution in the future, it
> is scarcely . . . more marked than what I owe to Mrs. Dewey
> for the example of self-control, impartial judgment, and in-
> telligent study of child rights which was afforded us in her
> classes.

Alice's students were enthusiastic. But rumblings among the faculty had started, and they continued until Harper decided to take the
matter in hand. On the last day of February 1904, he wrote to Dewey
about the "question of the principalship" and delicately tried to put the
best face on his new policy by claiming it to be an old one. The trustees
believed, he told Dewey, "that the appointment of the present principal of the Elementary School" was inappropriate, not, of course, from
the point of view of the person involved, but because "a fundamental
principle is involved in the employment of the wife of a professor in an
administrative or definite position in the university." He expressed his

hope that "arrangements for the present year will appear to you and to Mrs. Dewey to have met all the demands that were involved in the complication of last spring."

Dewey was bewildered. Neither he nor Alice had believed her appointment to be a merely temporary solution. Indeed, it had resulted in a greater success than either anticipated. Unfortunately, their confusion could not be cleared up immediately, as Dewey was constantly traveling. But Alice was at home and decided to settle the question. While John was away, she arranged an interview with Harper on March 27. The president must have continued to speak indirectly, for both of them came out of the session with different understandings. In summarizing their talk for Harper, Alice remembered that what Harper

> said to me [Alice] in that interview was that you [Harper] . . . understood and you supposed Mr Dewey had understood that my appointment was for one year. Nothing was said about my pleasure at any time during the interview, nor was there any mention either in word or idea that I should "withdraw." On the other hand when I asked you among other questions what you wished me to do your reply was that you were not clear on that point.

Harper, however, believed that he told Alice that "she was going to resign" but that she did not respond to his assertion. Even he must have been a bit intimidated by her. "Mrs. Dewey," he told John when he returned, "is a woman of extraordinary dignity."

The result was that all parties were frustrated. The Deweys felt that Harper was meddling in their eminently successful arrangement. But after John returned and met with Harper, Dewey's mind was made up. As it so often happened, he acted precipitously and then was stuck with his decision. He would resign from the directorship of the School of Education. To his surprise, he realized that as soon as he had decided, he felt tremendous relief, not anger at Harper. On April 6, with great formal dignity, Dewey told Harper that "since the administrative or external side of the work which I undertook . . . has now been accomplished, and since the conditions as you outline them are not favorable to development upon the educational side, I hereby present my resignation . . . to take effect July 1st, 1904." He followed this on the next day with a cordial note to Harper indicating that he wished to take his accumulated leave to go abroad for the next year.

RESIGNATION

Had Harper responded as cordially, accepted Dewey's resignation from the School of Education, and made arrangements to grant his leave even at this late date, the Deweys would probably have gone off to Europe; Tufts would have filled in as chair of philosophy for a year; and Dewey would have returned in the fall of 1905 to resume a productive career in philosophy at Chicago. But Harper, anxious to resolve all questions after he had left so much unclear for too long, now pressed Dewey to be definite on all points. The trustees were meeting on April 12. Before he presented Dewey's resignation from the directorship in the School of Education to them, along with his request for a sabbatical, what assurances could Dewey give that he would continue at Chicago after the conclusion of the next year?

Dewey could not see this as anything other than more interference. He certainly felt pushed, backed into a corner, and now he was angry. The day before the trustees' meeting, he dashed off a terse note to Harper: "I present herewith my resignation as Professor & Head of the Department of Philosophy." He told Harper to present both resignations at the same time, which meant that he would have no further connection whatsoever with the university except that—always financially prudent—he reminded Harper that he expected to be paid for his accumulated vacation time until that was exhausted. (In fact, he did not receive all the money due him until nearly ten years later.)

From Harper's point of view, he had been merely clearing up administrative details and was shocked at the result. Dewey could resign the directorship of the School of Education, and Alice could easily be replaced at the elementary school. But it was unthinkable that he might lose his star philosopher, psychologist, and professor of pedagogy in this manner. He did not present Dewey's resignations on April 12, but instead, on the eighteenth he attempted to make amends. He invited Dewey to meet with him in order to achieve "a fuller consideration of the whole matter than we have yet been able to have." He appealed to Dewey intellectually, reminding him that "as men standing for scientific work," they should not draw conclusions until all the data were "fully in mind." He alluded to new information, "additional light," that had just recently become available, and he suggested that Dewey had misunderstood his "point of view."

Harper's refusal to accept Dewey's complete resignation changed everything. What if Harper refused to let him resign? The only sure thing seemed to be that Alice would not be principal in 1904–5. Alice herself was forced to acknowledge this publicly because W. T. Harris—still the U.S. commissioner of education—had asked her to be a member of one of his educational commissions, and she felt obliged to inform him that "Mr. Dewey and I have severed our connection with the School of Education." She added that they now planned to "go abroad for a number of months," beginning in July. The Deweys' long, friendly relation with Harris now began to push the Chicago contretemps into the open. Harris responded in a concerned but encouraging manner to Alice, which prompted John to explain more fully:

> I have resigned not merely from the School of Education but from the University. It is a long story, with which I will not trouble you. But the gist of it is simply that I found I could not work harmoniously under the conditions which the President's methods of conducting affairs created and imposed.

By making his hitherto confidential resignation public, Dewey was pushing himself in a direction from which no retreat would be possible.

But Harper was still trying to find some sort of favorable resolution. A meeting with Dewey on the twenty-third ended inconclusively, and Harper proposed meeting with both Deweys as soon as possible. He even offered to meet in John's office at the School of Education. Not waiting for a reply from John, he tried to apologize to Alice, saying that he was "very sorry." Then Harper enlisted Mrs. Blaine to try to explain things, since the Deweys had every reason to feel friendly to her, as she had been such a strong supporter of all their efforts.

Mrs. Blaine failed to smooth matters over, since in clarifying matters she had to admit that originally the faculty's opposition to Alice's appointment had been concealed from John. This only made things worse. She gave Harper a copy of her report of her conversation:

> I said to him [Dewey] that the Trustees had not felt at liberty to bring to him the facts of the disagreement with the plan [to appoint Mrs. Dewey principal], on the part of the teachers. . . . Mr. Dewey was greatly surprised at the opposition of Miss [Zonia] Baber and Miss [Emily] Rice [teachers, respectively, of geography and history and literature]. His main feeling in this interview was the injustice which he felt had been done him by not having their position made known to him before on the question of the Principalship. . . . He felt that he was put in a very false position in having been allowed to present the plan to the President and the Trustees of the University with the comment that it was sanctioned by the heads of the School of Education. I brought out to him that this particular nomination had not been laid before Miss Rice and Miss Baber by him for comment and I drew his attention to the many circumstances surrounding this nomination which would make it difficult for them to express their full opinion to him—a natural hesitation which perhaps would be wrong—a feeling of responsibility in evoking a question which might prove one of great trouble—and, on Miss Baber's part, a hesitation in speaking of this matter since she occupied the position of Principal at present herself, etc.

Mr. Dewey did not feel that this explained or excused their not coming to him with their full feeling on the subject. He said that the question had been brought to them by Mrs. Young and that they had not made any objection to this appointment to her.

Mrs. Blaine tried to discuss what could be done to resolve the matter, but the conversation ended without resolution.

Dewey's impatience grew. Immediately after his interview with Mrs. Blaine, he wrote to Harper that in the ten days following Harper's letter, which stated that there were "facts or considerations which you [Harper] thought it important that I [Dewey] should know," he had heard nothing and could no longer share responsibility for Harper's withholding his resignation from the trustees. Dewey was now so frustrated that he even began to tell others about his dissatisfaction. Responding to a letter from the director of the California Institute for the Blind in Berkeley, he explained his resignation:

> Mr. Harper and I did not seem to hit it off very well together, and the difficulties seem to grow more rather than less, and as I do not like the idea of working in an institution when there does not seem to be a reasonable degree of ability to get a mutual understanding I have thought it better to resign.

By now, of course, the Deweys' resignations were becoming common knowledge at the university. By the end of April, grade teachers in the elementary school began resigning; already, three of the best teachers had decided to leave. Dewey, in his usual way, tried to find new positions for them. But finally, on the last day of April, Harper conceded that he had no choice but to submit the Deweys' resignations, which he did at the May 2 meeting.

In announcing his acceptance of their resignations, Harper implied that they were caused by the termination of Alice's principalship. Many shared that view, among them Pearl Hunter, Dewey's secretary, who wrote that "Mr. Dewey left Chicago because of [the president's]. . .

mistreatment of Mrs. Dewey." But this was not accurate, as a full account of the situation shows. Dewey resented Harper's presentation of his motives as a merely disgruntled, cranky husband, and he fired off one last letter to him:

> As you are aware, the construction you put by statement and by implications of context upon my resignation in your letters of April 30th do not represent my own reasons for resigning—a point upon which I am presumably the better informed.
>
> In presenting my resignation to the Board of Trustees, and in recommending its acceptance, I request you to make it clear to the Board that the question of the alleged failure to reappoint Mrs. Dewey as Principal of the Elementary School is in no sense the cause of my resignation, and that this question had never been discussed between us till after our resignations were in your hands. Your willingness to embarrass and hamper my work as Director by making use of the fact that Mrs. Dewey was Principal is but one incident in the history of years.

By this time Harper was sick of both Deweys, and he nursed his annoyance and resentment for years. Some time after the final dissolution of Dewey's relations with Harper's university, the man who was responsible for getting Dewey another job, Dewey's old classmate James McKeen Cattell, met Harper and said that he "hoped he would forgive me for taking Dewey away." Harper sullenly retorted: "I am under great obligations to you for doing so."

For John and Alice in 1904, there was still much left to do after the acceptance of their resignations. Both had to complete their administrative work, make preparations for their trip abroad, say their farewells, and attend a final banquet given to them by their students in June. They had to plan for their future, much of it uncertain. Only one thing was certain. The Chicago chapter was closed.

LUCY DEWEY

Since Morris's death, Alice had given birth to three more children. The oldest, Gordon Chipman, named after Alice's father, was born in the late summer of 1896, about eighteen months after Morris's death. His arrival helped console Alice and John for the loss of Morris; he "replaced" him, and both his parents doted on him. Almost from birth, Gordon seemed unruffled, calm, precociously mature, and self-contained. The two youngest children were girls, Lucy Alice and Jane Mary.

Lucy Alice Dewey was born in Chicago on December 28, 1897. Although Alice was ill off and on during the first six months of Lucy's life, the child thrived. When she was about six months old, her mother described her: "The baby is the same angelic creature as ever. She was awake in the night last night but didn't cry hard tho' we did not feed her till morning. She grows all the time." In her early years she exhibited the most affectionate disposition of all the children. Letters that mention her activities usually refer to her "great glee" and portray her dancing and laughing.

Lucy started her education in public-school kindergarten and first grade and continued at the Ethical Culture School in 1906 where she remained for three years. In the late summer of 1913 Alice, always restlessly traveling, took Lucy and Jane to Europe, where Evelyn met them in Genoa. The two young girls were enrolled in a school in Lausanne, Switzerland, while Evelyn and Alice went on to the Alps and eventually returned to Italy. In the spring of 1914 Lucy and Jane joined Alice in Florence. They traveled to Rome in April and, at the end of the month, sailed for home. In the fall, Lucy enrolled at Barnard College where she majored in history and anthropology and graduated in January 1919.

Just when Lucy was about to complete her degree, John and Alice were making their final plans to visit Japan and China, and Alice was concerned about Lucy. "I worry about Lucy," she wrote to Evelyn, and I think she shows the need of a little more worry on my part than she has had . . . you know she needs a home and mother and all that atmosphere can do rather more than others. I think she will be likely to be confused when put to the stress of too much activity for a good many years to come, perhaps always. It seems to me she shows that pressure now and is less happy than she thinks she is.

Alice urged Evelyn to be a mother to her younger sister. In truth, Alice did not need to worry about Lucy. But by now Alice's anxiety was a fixed habit. She began trying to persuade Lucy to join them in Asia. It was not until July 1919, two months after the Deweys had gone from Japan to China, that Lucy agreed to join her parents. Hardly had Lucy arrived when she came down with typhoid. But she received good treatment in the Rockefeller Foundation's Union Medical Hospital in Beijing and made a complete recovery.

In Beijing, too, the determining event of Lucy's life occurred: She met and fell in love with an Austrian citizen, Wolfgang Brandauer, whose family had been working in Tianjin, where his cousin was the Austrian consul. Wolf was thirty years old and Lucy twenty-four when they met in 1921, and in a very short time, they decided to marry. Alice insisted that they first experience a separation in order to make sure that their decision was sound. Lucy returned to the United States and got a job with the Committee on the Scientific Problems of Human Migration in Washington, D.C. Soon, Wolf was writing to Lucy from remote Kalgan, just south of Inner Mongolia, and from Urga, near the Aral Sea, a remote and primitive area where he had gone to make his fortune. In August 1923 Alice agreed to the marriage. Alone, Lucy started for the West Coast around August 20, stopped in Portland to see her Uncle Charles, and sailed from Seattle for China on August 30. Alice described the departure to her friend Anne Edwards:

She went off in high spirits. . . . The man she is to marry is Wolfgang Carl Brandauer of Vienna. He was [a] prisoner in Russia during four years of the war. Because he had tried to escape he was in Siberia most of the time and after the Armistice he drifted with others down to China, where he has relatives. He is now engaged with an American trading company between Kalgan and Urga. If you wish to imagine how and where she expects to live look up Urga, which is the capital of Outer Mongolia. They go four hundred miles in an automobile if they can. . . . Before the war he had charge of his father's factory in England. The family are now without income from their industries which were of considerable size before. He is of considerable courage as his history shows and Lucy thinks she likes the wild life.

On September 25 Lucy and Wolf were married in Beijing, accompanied by friends that the Deweys had made there, including the American consul. Nonetheless, Alice remained gloomy about Lucy's future. After the brief honeymoon, the couple "go north . . . if they can. The mercury goes down to forty below [in Urga], and during that time they expect to live in Kalgan, which is the gate through the great wall to Manchuria. It is all on the old caravan route and is still followed by camels. . . . Such is life in that old wild land."

Anyone who reads Alice's letter can hear the despondence: she was back in New York after almost three years in China and Japan; Lucy was gone; and she was at loose ends. But Alice's depression was no stranger to her, and she could identify what was below the surface: "It is like waking up dead to have this absence of work and responsibility."

Two years later, on October 23, 1924, Lucy gave birth to a boy at the Rockefeller Hospital in Beijing, and within a few months, she, Wolf, and little Carl Martin Brandauer moved to Vienna where Wolf had gotten a job. Vienna proved to be a poor choice. The economy was very depressed, and in order for them barely to survive, Wolf "had to run hard and fast." John began to try to get them admitted to America, where the economy was still booming; but the quota list for Austria was filled "six or seven years ahead." The State Department unreasonably maintained that when Lucy married an Austrian citizen in China, she had forfeited her citizenship, even though she had visited her family in the United States in 1925 on her American passport. Delay followed delay. Dewey visited Vienna twice, in 1928 and 1931. The reason for the second of these visits was the death of Lucy's two-year-old daughter, Evelyn Jane. "I feel I must go over and be with [Lucy] . . . for a few weeks." On this trip he also made friends with his seven-year-old grandson, Carl Martin. With his fair German combined with Carl's limited English, they got along, and John was soon consulting with his grandson about what toy store they might visit and what could be bought there. Carl chose "a wind-up boat," and he and grandpa were soon sailing it on a pond.

After Hitler came to power and marched into Austria, the Nazis began suppressing the socialists in the workers' district where Lucy lived. By 1936, Lucy and her family were in desperate straits financially and had to ask help from John, who managed to get her American citizenship restored. By 1938, it was obvious they had to leave, and in the fall, Lucy was able to leave with Carl Martin and go to Missouri, to stay with Evelyn on the ranch. Wolf, who was subject to being drafted into the Austrian military, was forced to stay in Vienna. But in July 1939, he was able to get a visa to America through the personal intervention of Frances Perkins, whom Dewey had asked for help. Wolf was able to get a job with Chrysler in Detroit and in 1940 became district manager of a Chrysler servicing plant in Binghamton, New York. Once again, they started over. Lucy died on May 18, 1983.

JANE DEWEY

Jane Mary Dewey was born in Chicago on July 11, 1900, about two and a half years after Lucy. She was something of a "lost" child in the Dewey family.

A few days after Jane's birth, John took the other children with him to Chautauqua, New York, where he had promised to lecture, leaving Alice and the "new little girl" in Chicago. So began the separations from her parents that Jane experienced more frequently and at an earlier age than her siblings. She was separated from her mother before being weaned. John told Mrs. Tufts that Jane "is taking kindly to a bottle," and he weaned her before Alice returned. "Janie clings to me more than ever," Alice wrote when Jane was two. "She knew me and kept saying 'hello mama' all the afternoon." A little later, in September 1902, Alice was away and John was caring for the two-year-old. "Janie doesn't consciously miss you," he told Alice in a double message; "her [excess] . . . of affection for me seems to reveal a void however." No wonder that in her play Jane began to make things disappear and then come back. She was fascinated with hiding a handkerchief somewhere and then making it appear again.

Jane attended the Ethical Culture School with Lucy between 1906 and 1909. When Alice took Lucy and Jane to Switzerland in 1914 and left the girls in school while she and Evelyn went to Italy, Jane was inconsolably lonely. She begged Alice to come to get her. "I don't care where we go as long as we are near you," she pleaded. It was only February, but already she moaned: "I wish it was June now so we could go home." She wrote a barely disguised complaint about her parents: "The horrid old things! Why should they educate people who don't want to be educated, like me. I haven't the slightest wish to be educated & I don't think I should ever go to College if I had any thing else to do, which I unfortunately haven't."

The trouble was that she was the brightest of all the Dewey children. So she seemed doomed to succeed in the very arena she said she cared least about, while failing to achieve the truly consistent loving relations that she craved. Upon her return from Italy, she skipped her freshman year of high school and was enrolled as a sophomore in the Spence School, taking courses in Chaucer, physics, Latin (Caesar), fifth-year French, and independent reading. There was nothing in which she didn't excel, but she stood out in mathematics. In her graduation yearbook, she was memorialized in verse:

Mathematics is our bane,
Mere amusement for our Jane.
What is trig or analyt
To a maid of mighty wit?

In 1918 John and Alice went to California for John to give the Raymond F. West Memorial Lectures, which became the basis for *Human Nature and Conduct*. Jane insisted on going with them. Alice saw that "Jane is far more homesick than I realized." In the summer, when Alice read a melancholic book, Arthur Gleason's *Golden Lands*, she hid it, for she was convinced it was "too sad for Jane to be allowed to read it." A letter from Alice to Evelyn indicates that by the time Jane was eighteen, she had developed the isolating defenses that could protect her against feeling loss too deeply. Alice called Jane's developing aloofness "dignity."

> With that dignity of hers it takes time to figure out what is in her mind. . . . Of course I do need her as she needs me, but there is a tenseness about her that gives me a pain as I see it more and more. She does not seem to expect joy and the sort of fun she used to have . . . and it is a tragic thing to be home-sick.

Alice went on to discuss other matters with Evelyn, but she kept coming back to Jane and as she went on she became more and more diagnostic in her observations: "I am very unhappy when I see that this depression has come to her. . . . I could not stand to have Jane lose herself by this constant repression." Alice acknowledged that she was to blame, since she was now convinced that Jane's evident brittleness had been caused by all the separations, "yet I can not change things now." She didn't know what to do with Jane. Should Lucy come to California? Should she send Jane home? Perhaps Jane could go to art school in San Francisco. But Jane, for whom school was so easy, didn't want to go to art school; she didn't want to go to school at all. She flatly turned down John's suggestion that she study sculpture with Benny Bufano in San Francisco or Statia Eberle in New York. She wanted to work, to earn money, to help with the family's finances. Alice couldn't understand that what Jane wanted was to be needed, and especially to feel herself to be a needed part of the family. All Alice could think about was, who would care for Jane? If Jane went home, would Evelyn let her live with her? By the end of her letter, Alice became concerned that she was dumping all this in Evelyn's lap, and for a brief decisive moment she declared, "I shall not let Jane drift." But Alice soon felt helpless again, and she thought of an alternative plan that would place Jane under the care of F. Matthias Alexander back in New York.

Jane refused any commitment to develop her obvious scientific talents. When her father began teaching at Berkeley, she enrolled in one of his courses, commenting that it was "rather nervy but it gives me three units which I very much need at a good hour." When the term ended, she had finally made a decision. Her intellectual talents and defenses finally won out over her depressive fears of separation, and she decided to go back to New York to be with Evelyn and Lucy and to register at Barnard. She was given a year's advanced standing, and she completed college without interruption in 1922. Immediately she applied for graduate study at the Massachusetts Institute of Technology, where she excelled in several fields—physical chemistry, physics, and mathematics. At MIT she also met the answer to her emotional needs in the person of a handsome, young, exciting southerner, Alston Clark. He had graduated from MIT in 1920, become a graduate student that fall, and in 1921 was a teaching assistant in physics. He took a year off to manage his father's Mississippi plantation in Clarksdale, the town named after his family, and then returned to MIT in 1922. Jane fell in love with him at once. Alston was truly a charming person, as his letters show: warm, bright, lively, and friendly. True, he held personal opinions inherited from his family and his region, especially concerning the need to keep business enterprise unregulated; and these differed so much from John's and Alice's views that they were shocked when he casually expressed them—and Jane took Alston's side! Suddenly, just a few days before John and Alice were to leave on an educational mission to Turkey, Jane announced that she and Alston were going to marry. They did so, "quietly," five days before her parents sailed on May 29, 1924, for Turkey.

Dr. and Mrs. Clark returned to Cambridge. Jane took her final Ph.D. exams in physical chemistry and was awarded her doctorate in 1925. Her research, John Dewey told Mead, was on "some hunt for the fragments of the atom." In 1925, Jane and Alston were the brightest couple in the world of physics. They both applied to the American Scandinavian Foundation for fellowships to do mathematics research in Copenhagen. Acceptance of any sort always brought Jane at least temporary joy; and when she told her family that she had also been appointed a National Research Council Fellow to work with Niels Bohr at the Universitets Institut for Teoretisk Fysik, she declared herself "so excited by it. $1800 a year. Renewable for three years." She started to publish articles while she was finishing her degree. The first, a study of the "Intensities in the Stark Effect of Helium," appeared in the *Physical Review* in 1926. She submitted one of her theoretical papers to Bohr in 1927. Between 1925 and 1930 she published eight articles in major journals, her research focusing on spectroscopy applied to atomic theory. In October 1927 she began delivering a series of lectures on wave mechanics to Bohr's research team. In her customarily tart tone, she remarked: "Nobody understood a damned thing." Back in the United States in 1929, she continued her National Council Fellowship at Princeton's Palmer Physical Laboratory under K. T. Compton. In 1929, to be near Alston, who was at Cornell, she became a research fellow in geology at the University of Rochester.

In 1931 Jane secured a teaching position in the Department of Physics at Bryn Mawr, and she and Alston moved to Haverford, Pennsylvania. She taught a wide array of such courses as theoretical mechanics, optics, and spectroscopy and atomic theory. In her second year she became an associate professor and chair of the department. Around this time she and Alston separated, and thereafter her health deteriorated. She took a two-year leave of absence from Bryn Mawr because of "ill health," during which she traveled with her father to South Africa in 1934 and to Haiti the next year. In 1936 she returned to MIT as a research adjunct in the chemistry department. Then she simply stopped working for three years and lived with her father. In 1937 and 1938 she spent several months in Key West, Florida, with him and was often ill. By 1939, she had not worked for three years, and she was so debilitated that in December she wrote to James McKeen Cattell asking him to help her get a secretarial or copy-editing job. He advised her to resume her scientific work, and she attempted to do so.

In 1940, after surgery, she did some "semi-scientific work on Long Island." She went to scientific meetings in Atlantic City seeking a job and took a position as a lecturer in Hunter College in New York City, where she continued to teach sporadically from September 1940 to mid-1942. For a while in 1941 she worked in Washington, D.C., but she fell ill again and returned to Key West. There, in 1942, she was offered a "technical" war job with the Department of the Navy but turned it down.

Jane's difficulties were confusing and troubling for her father. In 1939, he wrote: "No doctor knows what the trouble is. . . . [we] had a talk—she almost never says anything about herself—she is too undemonstrative for her own good—& she said she couldn't hold a job possibly, there was no use applying, as 3 hours a day was her limit." No one could understand what tortured Jane, even Jane herself. John spoke of her "peculiarities" and was shocked at the "unkind" things she said to Evelyn. But it was Evelyn who paid her the clearest tribute: "Being a scientist she lives in a fierce and remote world of her own."

Then all at once, in 1942 Jane found herself free of the ailments that had so tormented her. The United States was at war, and she was hired as a research physicist by U.S. Rubber as soon as she applied. She continued to publish in such professional publications as the *Journal of Applied Physics* (for example, "The Elastic Constants of Materials Loaded with Non-Rigid Fillers"). After five years she found the job at which she remained until 1970, in the Ballistic Research Laboratory at the Aberdeen Proving Grounds in Maryland. In 1975 Jane moved back to Key West where she lived until her death. Like most of John's other children, Jane lived out a part of her father's interests. As a professor and a scientist, she did brilliantly what he aspired to do in philosophy. Most of all, she had what he had—courage.

COLUMBIA COMES TO THE RESCUE

One reason that John Dewey took so many jobs and gave so many lectures during his Chicago years pertained to the "imperial" tendency of his mind and personality. Intellectually, he was always pushing into unoccupied territory, but another reason for his activity had to do with the need for money, which expanded as the size of his family increased. With Jane's birth in 1900 Dewey found himself with five children to support, and he wanted to nurture them as fully as possible, to take them to Europe, to give them the opportunity to learn languages, to expose them to culture.

On April 11, 1904, when John Dewey resigned all his posts in the University of Chicago, he was forty-four years old, the parent of five living children, a world-famous philosopher, and unemployed. The euphoria of shedding his wearisome administrative duties and the undoubted pleasure of surprising William Rainey Harper in the most unpleasant manner soon faded, and he began to think of the economic realities. True, he could count on pay coming from the University of Chicago for several months yet. But then what? Nothing seemed more important now than beginning work anew.

Dewey wrote letters to three people who knew him well, William James at Harvard, James McKeen Cattell at Columbia, and W. T. Harris in Washington, D.C. James had taken the most interest in his work. Cattell, already one of America's leading psychologists, had been a classmate of Dewey's at Johns Hopkins. Dewey was in frequent contact with him, as Cattell was editor of *The Psychological Review*. Dewey also had supported Cattell in his acrimonious dispute with James Mark Baldwin in 1903. When Dewey gave six lectures at Columbia on "Problems of Knowledge," they had renewed their friendship in person. For his part, Harris early on had encouraged Dewey to make philosophy his career. Each of them saw a different Dewey. James hailed him as a new-style empirical philosopher; Cattell, as a psychologist; and Harris, as a leading figure in the reform of American education. In writing to Harris, Dewey told him he was "not going to burden you with a request to give me advice and suggestions about the future," but "if the spirit moves you to give away counsel, it will be most welcome." He told him that he wished to find a place, if one existed, where "democratic education" could be preeminent. Dewey was mindful that no one knew better than Harris where the educational opportunities in the United States were. Dewey even was considering what, for him, would have been the very worst position—the presidency of a university, involving "a great deal more administrative responsibility," even though the problems of administrative overload had already exhausted him at Chicago.

Dewey's lectures at Columbia had been a great success, and they were hardly concluded when Cattell invited him to give a set of outside lectures in psychology over the next year. "I enjoyed my experience at Columbia wonderfully well," Dewey told F. J. E. Woodbridge, another philosopher at Columbia and the editor of the *Journal of Philosophy*. It was natural that five days after Dewey resigned from Chicago, he should have written to Cattell, chair of Columbia's Department of Philosophy. Dewey said he had been thinking "for two or three years" of resigning his Chicago posts. He knew that Cattell would not be entirely surprised, "as I have talked more freely with you about the situation here, than with anyone else outside the Univ." Besides, he continued, "I have nothing in view and shall have to rely on my friends to let me know of things that might appropriately come within my scope."

Instantly upon receiving Dewey's letter, Cattell went into action. He secured an immediate appointment with Columbia's president, Nicholas Murray Butler, who would want to know, Cattell felt sure, of Dewey's availability. Butler told him at once that he would try to find money for Dewey's salary. Cattell asked Dewey if he would accept a professorship at Columbia, adding, "and, please say 'yes.' "

But the offer came too suddenly, and instead of responding by telegraph, as the excited Cattell asked him to do, Dewey wrote a letter and temporized. "I am not in good shape to decide anything just now—I want a rest," he replied. "The strain of the last two weeks," he added, "make[s] it impossible for me to get my mind thoroughly on your proposition." Cattell's offer had caught him, Dewey realized, at a "depressed moment." In about a week the resourceful Butler found the money and wired Dewey an offer of a professorship at a salary of $5,000.

Dewey now awoke enough from his lassitude, if not his indecisiveness, to inform Harris of the offer. Harris wrote back promptly that a post at Columbia was exactly the idea that had occurred to him and that he saw it as "a tremendous opportunity both for Columbia and for you." If John wanted to seek a presidency, Harris said, he would assist him "to my utmost ability," but he regarded Columbia University to be the best choice.

Even before Harris's letter arrived, Dewey independently arrived at the same conclusion. Upon receiving Butler's telegram, he tentatively decided to accept. Butler urged Cattell to secure Dewey's acceptance immediately, for Dewey was thinking about applying for the presidency of the University of Illinois or even "cutting loose, from institutional connections." Aware that Dewey was considering pursuing a presidency, Cattell appealed to Dewey's philosophic side:

> I think it is your duty to go on with your philosophical work . . . you and James seem to me our two great men in philosophy, and philosophical genius is so much rarer and so much more valuable to the world than executive work that I think you should regard yourself as a kind of public trust.

Two weeks after his several resignations, Dewey's mind turned to how he would be able to support his children in New York City, which, he assumed, was even more expensive than Chicago. He expressed his concerns to Cattell, and again Cattell brought them to Butler. Butler gave him the aid he could: teaching in summer session would bring him $500 more plus a $400 stipend for an annual program of lectures in psychology. The faculty had already nominated Dewey to that post in 1905, to succeed Harvard's Hugo Münsterberg. In addition, Butler said, Dewey could teach in the university's extension department, lecturing to teachers, which would bring up to $1,000 annually. Perhaps, too, if she wished, Alice would be able to teach at the Speyer School in Columbia's Teachers College, roughly equivalent to Chicago's University Elementary School. In short, Butler gave Dewey every encouragement in his power, for he believed that with the addition of Dewey, Columbia's department would be the strongest anywhere. Butler urged him to decide quickly, and at last Dewey did so, wiring his acceptance to the president on April 28. Butler always remained a supporter of Dewey without ever, in any way, trying to exercise control over him, as Harper had done so frequently. Although Dewey acknowledged to Cattell on the same day that he might still wish "to consider the desirability of administrative work" in the future, nothing of the sort was "in view." On May 5 Columbia's trustees approved his appointment to begin, as Dewey requested, on February 1, 1905, at which time he would also take up the lectureship in psychology.

The news was soon out. The president of the University of Washington, himself a Columbia graduate, predicted that the Deweys would receive a warm greeting there but lamented that they would never again find "a more loyal, devoted, and appreciative set of students" than those who had studied with both John and Alice during 1903–4. Another Dewey Ph.D. student and disciple, E. C. Moore, wrote from San Francisco: "We have heard of your appointment at Columbia with mingled feelings of joy and sorrow. . . . I for one will never cease to regret the change if it takes you away from school work permanently." He hoped the rumor that Dewey was to be "a sort of unofficial director of the Teachers College was true." (It was not.)

Meanwhile, Dewey was beginning to make plans for his new life. In the last week of June and the first of July, he lectured to teachers in a summer program in Knoxville, Tennessee, offering a small seminar to selected participants and giving platform lectures to all the attendees. His lectures, he felt, were "ground" out "with obvious creakings and wheezings." He was still exhausted from the nervous strain of the break with Chicago, which may have been the cause at this time of a mysterious "bilious attack or something which may go by that name." But in Knoxville he was alone, and as always, he was lonely. For the extra $400 stipend attached to the one-year lectureship in psychology, he agreed to give nine or ten lectures on "The Psychology of Behavior." James E. Russell, the director of Teachers College, offered him work during the spring 1905 semester in the Extension Division, "fifteen or thirty lectures. . . . Honorarium three hundred fifty or six hundred dollars respectively." This was easy, since the course could be a part of his regular teaching load, with the addition of nonmatriculated students. Russell praised Dewey's contributions to educational theory and practice and expressed the hope that he would regularly "give at least one course of an educational character which might be taken by all students interested in the general problem of education." "Anything that you decide to include will be heartily welcomed," he graciously added. Dewey had already been trying to think about his upcoming courses at the college and had written an uncharacteristically indecisive letter to Cattell about them. Then he thought better of his suggestions and proposed new courses, including "The Development of Logical Theory in England from Locke to Mill," "Logic of Ethics," "Logic Applied to Teaching," and "The Evolution of Educational Ideals Since the Renaissance." Clearly, he was focusing on his philosophical work and letting the psychological side go while tenuously holding onto educational philosophy. As things turned out, this was the direction he would take for the rest of his life.

Back to Europe

But one plan was settled. The family was to sail for Europe. Ten years earlier, Morris had died during the family's European excursion that came between Dewey's departure from Michigan and his arrival at Chicago. There had been little talk of European travel since then. But now the past was repeating itself. He was going from Chicago to Columbia and again planning a European adventure. Alice was still depressed over Morris's death, more now that she had no work on which to focus her thoughts and give form to her feelings. But John's desire to turn a separation into a new start prevailed. With the prospect of six months' release from teaching, supported by vacation pay that he had accumulated while working at the University of Chicago, freedom from all the built-up stresses made Europe once again beckon to them.

They rationalized that such a trip would enable "Fred and Evelyn to get on with their French and German more rapidly than they can in this country," but it was really freedom that that they sought.

With their five children, John and Alice sailed for Europe on July 9, relieved and cautiously joyous at the prospect of a long trip abroad. John looked forward to going to the Science Association meeting in Cambridge in August, where he could meet the European philosophers whom he knew only by their publications. Perhaps more important, he expected to enjoy a rest from the daily grind of teaching, lecturing, and running university programs. Alice planned to investigate the education of women in Europe. She asked W. T. Harris whether he "desire[d] reports on any subject pertaining to women's education," for she intended "to remain abroad long enough to look up quite thoroughly the schools for the training of children . . . with reference to the education of girls and women." She also was committed to write a book on the same subject for a series edited by the psychologist James Mark Baldwin. When they first met at the University of Michigan, Alice had urged John to write on issues concerning women in education. On her own she had been reading about the psychology of women but finding little to satisfy her among the pieces written by men. For instance, after reading Hugo Münsterberg's "Women," she told John, "I thought at first he was pretty clear but one sees . . . that the masculine habit is not to think to the bottom of things when that bottom goes deeper than himself. A little esoteric Buddhism might do well for such souls."

Alice and John expected Evelyn and Fred, their older children, to benefit most from the trip. Gordon, blossoming early, would get much out of the trip, too. All who knew Gordon in Chicago agreed that he was, like Morris, a remarkable child, "a mature personality, without precocity," by the age of six. But again their little boy was struck in a tragic repetition of Morris's illness. Before arriving in Europe, Gordon fell ill during the crossing. By the time the Deweys reached Liverpool, he was very ill. Aboard the vessel, which Alice declared "filthy," the ship's physician diagnosed Gordon as having "food poisoning."

Immediately upon landing in late July, the Deweys took Gordon to the nearest hospital. John remained with him while Alice took the younger children out of danger to the city of Chester, where they were met by friends and the children were taken to Ireland. Alice returned and remained with John in Liverpool.

Gordon got steadily worse. Alice gave the children's nurse, Mary Bradshaw, the first report: "Gordon . . . is pretty sick. About the other children I am anxious to hear. The fever and other trouble they had on the ship is quite enough to be the beginning of typhoid." She warned Mary to watch for symptoms in the other children. When Gordon was definitely diagnosed as having typhoid, her fears for the other children mounted; he, after all, was being taken care of in a good hospital while they might be increasing their danger by "going about."

Within a week they believed that Gordon "has turned the corner in the disease." A specialist in children's diseases advised them that Gordon had a "mild case" of typhoid, although he was still losing weight. His father bought *Gulliver's Travels* and *Hiawatha* and spent days reading to him. John and Alice also amused him by starting a scrapbook with pictures and stories and even a hopeful title: "Gordon's Trip to Ireland." Meanwhile, happy news came from Ireland that the other children showed no symptoms. At last, a little more than three weeks later, Gordon was released from the hospital, and the three proceeded on to Ireland. Gordon wrote a letter to Fred and Evelyn, who had gone to England with Mary, about how much he hoped to be well again. "I hope I will soon . . . go to Dublin with you, and then go to Italy, & catch the lizards & things—catch the oranges off the trees when they are falling down." But even as he wrote this, he had a relapse at Ballinsloe—"mild" at first, then evidently serious. On September 9, Dewey uttered his worst fear, that Gordon was "sicker . . . than he was the other time." Two days later Gordon died of enteric fever before the other children could return. "The nervous strain on Mama," Dewey— himself brokenhearted—wrote the children, "has been great." Years later Jane wrote that "the blow [to Alice] . . . was so serious that she never fully recovered her former energy." Even months later, John was lamenting that with Gordon's death "the light went out" and grieving "how much harder and emptier it gets all the time."

STARTING OVER

Alice bravely continued their plan of keeping the children on the Continent to learn languages while John returned to New York to begin teaching at Columbia. He was inconsolable. At his new post, he told Alice, " I'm minding my own business . . . & not attempting to improve anybody or anything—I'm done with that." News of Gordon's death soon reached the Deweys' friends in Chicago, and a memorial was held at Hull House, where Jane Addams gave the principal address to seventy friends of the Deweys. Addams recalled a moment when Gordon was brought to a car to meet Admiral Dewey and shook hands with him, "restraining his boundless enthusiasm with a quaint sense of the dignity which is befitting one who bears the same great name." When asked what he had said to the commodore, Gordon replied, "I couldn't say much, because I am a Dewey too." Dewey's former colleague, the philosopher James Tufts, wrote that Gordon was "so quaint and original that we always felt we were coming into the presence of a new and fresh personality when we talked with him." On a visit to Cambridge, Addams told William James of the event, and on October 9 James wrote to John: "How sad a beginning of your and Mrs. Dewey's new life. Pray receive the tenderest sympathy of both my wife and myself—there is nothing more to be said in these pathetic situations." Dewey replied with the last and best of his tributes to the dead boy: "Gordon whom we lost is the only person I have ever known—I do not say child—who was at once always serious & always playful in his treatment of life. I shall never understand why he was taken from the world."

In Europe, Alice abandoned her plans to survey women's education in Europe, and John informed Baldwin that there would be no book from her: "Gordon's death . . . interfered of course with that as with everything else." John had been away from the family for little more than a month when he was already begging Lucy and Jane to write "nice letters often" to him: "Tell what you do and what you play & where you go & what you see . . . and anything else." On March 1, 1905, he wrote to Alice, who was in Rome:

> It is four weeks today since I arrived[.]—The first two weeks went fast as I was under pressure of being behind in work and I suppose probably excited by the diversities of change[.]—Now the days drag themselves along and the chief relief is considering how much nearer June it is, & the prospect of either all of us going to the [Adirondack] mountains or my going over there.

He was at loose ends, staying in a Columbia dormitory, and frequently eating with friends or new colleagues, such as the historian James Harvey Robinson and his family. But he was busy. In addition to his teaching, he had to prepare the series of ten lectures on "the psychology of behavior," and as he said when he started planning them just a week before they were announced to begin, "getting these ready takes the spare time I didn't need for my other work."

During the spring semester of 1905, Dewey moped about, interested only in visiting colleagues who had children. He mourned Gordon, and he missed his surviving children. His attitude toward how to live his life had undergone a subtle but permanent change: he moved inward. His practical involvement in education disappeared into his philosophic activities, as did his psychological work, which, disconnected from the experimental laboratory, was absorbed into philosophical reflection. He abandoned any interest in administration, and he seems to have decided to settle permanently into the life of Columbia University. He left the administration to Cattell and Woodbridge. True, he twice was chairman of the Department of Philosophy, but this was only caretaking; he no longer wished to create a school. Once he arrived at Columbia, he never again talked of seeking a university presidency or any other form of administration. Even more dramatic was his declining interest in pedagogy. He never again became deeply involved in original educational research, and although his later writing on the subject clarified and expanded his earlier work, it did not go beyond it. The students at Teachers College eagerly awaited his arrival, but he never involved himself in teacher education as closely as he had at the University Elementary School. Although the students and graduates of Teachers College claimed him as their mentor and inspiration, it was more for his symbolic presence and past work than for his actual involvement. Mostly, they came to Philosophy Hall and enrolled in his regular classes. Eventually they and others evoked the authority of "John Dewey" for their experiments and innovations in education, and in that way they made Dewey seem to be the father of a version of "progressive education" that he neither practiced nor advocated. The same was true of psychology: he did less and less new research work in that field, although the continuing usefulness of his concept of the adjustive arc and his studies of interest and attention made it seem as if his activities in psychology had remained current. It was clear that with the increasing specialization and the amazing growth of American scholarship in the educational and psychological fields, he had to choose among disciplines.

He chose philosophy. Surely, there was a melancholy tone to all these renunciations, partly resulting from the collapse of his many activities in Chicago and intensified by Gordon's death and his loneliness during this spring semester of 1905. "Everything seemed too much for me," he told Alice. In February, he remarked that "it seems more like work" to go to Europe than to remain in America, and besides, "the mountain cottage seems like a haven of rest & peace to me." But he remained undecided, "so shaken" that he couldn't face "alternatives."

His general depression led Dewey to renounce, to pull in, to consolidate his interests, and then to begin to refuse the invitations to give lectures that he had once accepted enthusiastically. Eventually, he built a new life that once again became profoundly satisfying. He grew philosophically as he turned to the world outside the university in his quest to contribute to the varied life of society on his own terms.

Around this time he wrote to Fred, who had gone alone to Jena to study German, giving him the same advice he was giving himself: "I hope you will be able to get a settled life & to lead it regularly—be on the lookout against being carried away by excitement or against being depressed." This was precisely the course he himself followed as he tried to find a path from depression to self-reliance. He described to Alice his daily walks alone along the Hudson River, "at about sunset . . . the lights on the water, the palisades on the other side, the floating ice, the ferry boats . . . the soft coal smoke, drifting from the New Jersey factories," and he seemed as melancholy a figure as the poet Edwin Arlington Robinson's "man against the sky." But he also was determined now to go his own way without depending on others.

Dewey slowly became aware of his altered perspective on the conduct of his life, jogged by a letter from Alice in which she warned him about the unconsidered ease with which in the past he had gotten involved in too many things and with too many people. He responded to her with unusual gravity: "I realize the seriousness of the two points you bring up— . . . I have realized them prior to your letter & . . . have thought a great deal about them. I do not think I am going to be drawn into things & people. . . . I am trying & shall continue to try." He looked instead to a "community of intellectual life" rather than a deep personal involvement in busywork projects. By this seemingly depressive, inward-looking route, he became the clearest, sanest independent thinker in America. He made his way alone, and by doing so, he was eagerly followed by a large audience who trusted him even when they disagreed with him.

As the spring semester was ending, John finally decided that instead of bringing the family home, he would join them in Europe. He asked President Butler for permission to leave before the commencement, and it was readily granted. The day after his last class, he sailed for Italy to meet his family. Alice had spent the spring in Rome, and so now they all went directly to Venice. And there the strangest, yet most predictable event occurred.

All the Deweys were still mourning Gordon. Now that they were back in Italy, John and Alice could not help but think of Morris as well.

The family was having lunch in a Venice pastry shop when John's eye was caught by a handsome young Italian boy playing outside the window. He looked to be about eight years old, Gordon's age, and was full of vim and vigor. But he also limped. Evidently he was poor. Something about him, some grace, overwhelmed the philosopher with a renewed longing for Gordon. As usual, despite his disclaimers that he never did so, Dewey acted impulsively. He and Alice beckoned to the boy, invited him to join them, fed him, and questioned him. Before the afternoon was over, they marched him off to the boy's home. Within a couple of days, the Deweys concluded with the boy's mother and the boy to take him into the Dewey family and raise him back in the United States. And so, the boy—Sabino Piro Levis, soon rechristened "Bino"—became a Dewey. He was about Gordon's age; he had grown up in the country where Morris's ashes lay; and he replaced, in one stroke, both children. John had five children again. Dewey never regretted this sudden decision. Three months later he told Alice: "I am glad I followed my feelings for once": certainly a false self-estimation by a man who found it hard to admit that he was ruled by his impulses all his life.

It is obvious that what led Dewey to adopt an eight-or-nine-year-old Italian boy into his family was his grief and his wish to reverse reality. This led him to the instantaneous and not necessarily conscious conclusion that if he himself had long ago assuaged his parents' grief by replacing a dead boy, John Archibald, and if Gordon had soothed his parents by replacing Morris, then by adopting a child to replace Morris and Gordon he could bring comfort to Alice and himself. Dewey never legally adopted Sabino, but he did better: he simply took him into the family as if he had given birth to Sabino fully formed at eight years of age.

The psychology of the replacement child, as is evident here, provided Dewey with a new child. But it also went beyond that, into his work, giving him a kind of inner experience that gave a distinctive turn to his philosophy that blossomed especially when he constructed a mature critique of social ills and social needs. Readers of Dewey should not confuse the origin of his impulses—always strongly emotional—

with the results of his reflections, which at their best were built on feelings heightened by logic and comprehensive scholarship. The distinctive features of Dewey's philosophy are that logic and philosophic inquiry are instrumental, that is, designed to create and to continue a process of thought; that thought should flow into action; that all thought and action are contingent and life involves continuous risk, not certainty; that thought-turned-into-action naturally flows into social life, experience, and chance-laden activity; that education is the best test of philosophy; and that social change can be its consequence. Following his arrival at Columbia, Dewey turned now more and more to concern with social ills. His experience gave him a special empathy for the second-best, the second-class citizen, the loser in society.

Those who came under Dewey's influence at Columbia were attracted by his personal qualities—warmth, a powerful intellect, and fine scholarship. Walter Pitkin, a new member of Dewey's newly renamed Department of Philosophy, Psychology, and Anthropology, recalled: "My first clear memories of Dewey in those days [fall 1905] had to do with his extraordinary continuous performance as a thinker. The man could not stop thinking." He was "the most relaxed, easy-going . . . philosopher who ever lived . . . like Socrates, with never a pose." Another young colleague, Wendell Bush, told a student that "Dewey has given a new direction to my life." His students were as galvanized by him as his colleagues were.

Many students came from China and Japan to study with him, anxious to bring back his ideas about democracy in education to their own countries. Many became important leaders in their native lands. One of the Chinese students who came around the same time that Dewey arrived at Columbia was P. W. Guo, who became the founder and president of Nanjing Teachers College. A few years later Menglin Jiang also came to Teachers College at Columbia to study with Dewey and later became the chancellor of Beijing University. A third student, Hu Shi, China's leading intellectual and educational reformer during the 1920s, audited Dewey's course "Moral and Political Philosophy."

For a decade Dewey had also been attracting Japanese students to the United States to study with him. One Japanese graduate student was moved to write a poem about his experience of Dewey at Columbia:

> Climbing breathlessly three flights of stairs,
> passing through a dark corridor,
> the door opening on the classroom
> as lit by brilliant candles,
> the faces tense but shining with delight
> all illuminated by the thoughts flowing from him one by one.

Dewey also was anxious to assist émigrés from Europe. One was a young Jewish woman, Nima Hirschensohn, who emigrated to the United States from Paris in 1904 and started classes at Columbia in the fall of 1905. She spoke little English. The chair of the philosophy department, Frederick J. E. Woodbridge, then the department adviser, was surprised to hear that she wanted to take Dewey's "Psychological Ethics" class:

> The choice of studies had to be approved by [Woodbridge, she remembered. And he told her:] "You have had no elementary training in philosophy, and you hit upon the most difficult class, for only advanced and selected students. You can hardly speak English. . . . He laughed heartily. Knowing that Dewey could not possibly admit me, he said smilingly: "Go ask him about it." Dewey said to me, "Attend a few lectures, and if you like them you can stay. It is a little difficult, but it will not remain so if the subject appeals to you."

Destined to become the president of Teachers College and a disciple of Dewey, William Heard Kilpatrick had followed Dewey from Chicago and in 1905 was Nima's classmate. He lent her his notes and told her that Dewey was "the greatest American philosopher and the greatest educator." Many others sought aid. Nima described the "reception room adjoining Dewey's little office . . . filled to capacity long before the appointed [office] hours." When she told Woodbridge of Dewey's kindness to her, he replied: "You are very privileged that for your first entry into the United States you met not only a great philosopher, but also a great American spirit; this is 'America.'"

Dewey's activities at Columbia showed that he had learned a great deal from his overinvolvement at Chicago. His period of restless movement from one university to another was over. When in March 1906 David Starr Jordan, the president of Stanford University, urged him to accept a chair at his school, Dewey responded politely to Jordan's vision of the "green fields" with an unambiguous negative. Dewey continued to turn away a stream of similar offers. What remained was his passionate commitment to involve himself in the causes of social justice. For him, thinking and writing came first, with his family a close second. Whatever emotional force was not expended by his continuing passion for his family was given to American causes, and he had enough energy to give what seemed like a very full life to each of the three.

The Gorky Affair

John Dewey arrived at Columbia University in January 1905, in the middle of his life, to start the last long phase of it. The depressing experience of Gordon's death was mixed with new prospects and expectations. Dewey fell in love with New York City, telling Alice, "Chicago is a country village in comparison." As his grief over Gordon faded somewhat, his concern for the living—in his family and outside it— steadily grew. Encouraged and supported by Alice, he soon saw his commitment to justice and principle tested by a nationally publicized and sensationalized event.

In April 1906, the Russian writer Maxim Gorky visited America, to generate support and raise money for revolutionaries fighting the czar and czarist injustices in Russia. This was a time when Americans were very supportive of any move toward democratization in Russia. The progressive period was in full swing. Within days President Theodore Roosevelt made his famous speech on muckraking, giving a name to the disclosures of public corruption in America itself. Until this time, critics of American business had been called "knockers" and were regarded with disfavor. Now they would be "muckrakers" who were doing the positive job of clearing away corruption, and they bore that designation proudly. As far as Gorky was concerned, New York, along with Chicago, was a center of American socialism. In intellectual quarters, "socialism" and "democracy" were often used interchangeably, so Gorky arrived in New York on a tide of liberal approval and was greeted by a crowd of newspapermen. The reporter for the *New York Times* wrote that "thousands of his countrymen" had waited in the rain "for hours" to greet him. "The novelist was accompanied," the article continued, "by his wife, who is a Russian actress, well known on the stage as Mme. Andreieva." Gorky told the gathered crowd that he would "remain in this country for at least two months . . . chiefly for the purpose of raising funds for the Russian Revolutionists, but partly for the benefit of his health." He declared himself overcome with emotions over his arrival in America, saying that "Columbus could not have been more anxious to discover America than I." His reception committee had planned a fine event for him on the evening of his arrival in a Fifth Avenue club, where such New York luminaries as Mark Twain, William Dean Howells, and Finley Peter Dunne would meet him.

A grand entrance to America indeed, and then it fell flat. Americans could accept and even applaud Gorky's revolutionary fervor; they could donate money to arm the revolutionists; and they could support socialism—especially for Russians. But they could not accept flagrant breaches of conventional morality. Before four days had passed, the newspapers revealed that Andreieva was not Gorky's wife. Gorky's wife and two children were still in Russia. The management of the Hotel Belleclaire, where they were staying, was offended by the revelations. Its manager appeared at their door and demanded that they leave. They moved to the Lafayette-Breevort Hotel, but hardly had they opened their bags when its manager appeared and asked that they leave. The same scenario was repeated in the next hotel to which they moved.

Gorky was shocked. Only two days earlier, Mark Twain had spoken passionately at a fund-raising event for him, reminding reporters that America had sought aid in the revolution from France and now Americans should help the Russians. "Revolutions are conducted with blood and courage alone," Twain told them. The fund-raising had commenced well; Gorky had already raised $8,000. But rumors about Gorky's "companion" circulated rapidly. Those who had initially supported him now turned their backs on him. William Dean Howells and many others begged to be excused from any comment, canceling appearances at any event connected with Gorky. When the news broke, Twain reconsidered his support of incendiary activities in Russia and did not meet again with Gorky. Gorky's indignant assertion that "never was [a] union between man and woman more holy" convinced no one. His supporters in Boston immediately announced that "taken aback by the revelations of his domestic affairs," they had abandoned plans to invite him to their city. A spokesman for President Roosevelt announced that Gorky would not be received at the White House by him or any other official of the U.S. government. Immigration officials declared that had they known about this immoral liaison, the pair would "undoubtedly have been sent to Ellis Island" and been barred from infecting American soil.

Suddenly deserted by all and finding his engagements canceled, Gorky had only one big event scheduled in New York, a speech at Carnegie Hall. Following that, he planned to leave for Chicago where Jane Addams would take him in. She was immediately branded a "Red" by the city's papers. When Gorky returned to New York City in early May, the problem, of course, was that no hotel would receive him. From the first, John Dewey had been a member of the organizing committee for Gorky's visit. Now John and Alice Dewey made a decision. Even Count Leo Tolstoy had invited Gorky and Madame Andreieva to his estate and greeted them warmly. Would no American show the same courtesy?

Alice and John Dewey invited Gorky and Andreieva to move in with them. Would not such a scandalous invitation jeopardize John

Dewey's new job at Columbia? Alice put a determined look on her face and said to Max Eastman and others: "I would rather starve and see my children starve than see John sacrifice his principles." Gorky and his mistress were soon living in the Deweys' apartment. People were scandalized that John and Alice would bring this woman into a house full of children, and, Eastman wrote, "Dewey was violently attacked for this act of magnanimity." On May 4, with John's assistance, Alice invited the students of Barnard College to a party for the couple, with Andreieva as the principal guest.

> Mme. Andreieva, the actress, whom Maxim Gorky brought over from Russia and introduced as his wife . . . was the center last night at an exclusive gathering at No. 431 Riverside Drive, the home of Professor John Dewey. . . . [The Deweys] planned a secret reception for Mme. Andreieva and . . . selected [the] . . . list with great care. [John Dewey] knew that some of the girls at Barnard College who attend his classes at Columbia were interested in the cause Gorky represents, and he thought it would be a good idea to ask them to his house to meet Mme. Andreieva.

About "twenty-five of the most enthusiastic Russian sympathizers" were sworn to secrecy about the upcoming party, as were about a half-dozen other women who were "deeply interested in the plight of the Russians." Alice's hand was everywhere apparent in this reception, with John's approval. When a reporter showed up at the door, he was formally told "by a determined young woman"—very likely Evelyn—that "no outsiders were wanted," and she informed him that "it was nobody's business if Mme. Andreieva was lecturing to the whole of Barnard College."

The actress, speaking in French, told the assembled women that in Russia "the women are fighting for independence as hard as the men," and she added her appreciation "of the charms of American women." Although the party was a success, it had no effect on Americans outside the Dewey sanctuary, and the next day the Y.M.C.A. Hall in Providence, Rhode Island, canceled Gorky's reservation and returned the rent.

John Dewey did not lose his job; it wasn't even threatened. Columbia's Nicholas Murray Butler was a much more humane president than Harper had been and never wavered in his support of Dewey. Many years after arriving at Columbia, in responding to a query about how the authorities there had restricted his academic freedom, Dewey noted: "Doubtless this will surprise you, but . . . no one at Columbia has ever directly or indirectly attempted to influence my teaching or writing or interfered in any way." He added, "This isn't very flattering to me." But because he was never restricted, his work flourished at Columbia.

FIVE ARCS OF ACTIVITIES

Following the Maxim Gorky episode, John Dewey settled into life in New York. In contrast to the hurried tasks of his earlier years, Dewey's activities began to take shape as great arcs extending over several decades. He was just as engaged as ever, and his activities were as varied as they had always been. Life in New York gave him new opportunities, and his own increasing inner harmony led him to form long-lasting associations and to pledge himself to commitments that had a longer duration.

The first of Dewey's commitments was to voluntary organizations, which were central to his work. Dewey agreed that municipal, state, and federal government assistance was desirable and sometimes necessary. Although he believed in individualism, he knew that in the complicated life of twentieth-century America, individuals alone would not be able to institute the changes and improvements that would be required. Organized groups of citizens were needed. Dewey always believed that an essential, always-to-be-preserved institution of American democracy was the voluntary organization, which he saw as the democratic community in action. His own involvement in voluntary organizations grew in New York City. By "voluntary associations," he wrote to Hu Shi, "I was simply trying to describe the method of democratic control of the machinery of the state." Dewey was the leading promoter of social reform through voluntary organizations. The concept of the voluntary organization is a typical American ideal, a group of citizens who join together without professional compensation to ameliorate a social ill or produce a social benefit that governmental agencies or legislation cannot effect. From the first decade of the twentieth century to the 1950s, Dewey founded or played a leading role in many voluntary organizations.

A second arc of Dewey's activities pertained to his worldwide influence as an educator and educational theorist. From 1919 to 1934, he often was abroad, in Japan, China, Turkey, Mexico, the Soviet Union, and South Africa, advising government officials, national groups, and local educators on the reformation of their school systems in relation to the growth of democracy.

A third arc was Dewey's active engagement in politics, public affairs, and public policy. He founded, inspired, led, or joined political groups that were aimed at creating a third party or otherwise represented the political interests of the American people. He led a research team in a sociological study of immigrants and made policy recommendations at the highest government level. He headed an international tribunal; he was pressured to run for office; and he opposed and often publicly castigated the policies of several presidents, from 1919 to 1952. Dewey's participation in national and local politics began shortly after he arrived in New York and continued to his death.

Fourth, in contrast to his writings before he came to Columbia, in New York Dewey was a leading player in several controversies involving educational policy, freedom of speech, and other major social and intellectual issues. Consequently, much of his writing was polemical and controversial. He was attacked and he counterattacked. His activities as a controversialist occurred over a span of several decades. Finally, in his widest and longest arc, his engagement in philosophy, he continued to pour out a steady stream of articles and books. These five arcs of Dewey's activities were parallel. Occasionally, the boundaries between them broke down, met and merged, and influenced one another.

The most important of Dewey's long-term commitments was his continuous promotion of volunteerism. Dewey's experience with the suppression of Gorky's political activities was one event among many others that led him to believe that America had reached a crucial point in the twentieth century: "We are reaching—have reached—a turning point, a critical point," he declared in 1916; "Whatever may have been said in the past in favor of letting things drift and grow along their own lines in their own way, we have now reached a point where we have to take more conscious and deliberate thought respecting these matters." Still influenced by his involvement with "thought news," he understood that as a thoughtful citizen he was obliged to promote organized intelligence, chiefly through voluntary organizations.

The idea of the voluntary organization was, of course, part of his inheritance from Lucina and the American culture that she herself inherited. Many influential voluntary organizations in America, such as the Women's Christian Temperance Union or even Lucina's Adams Mission House and Jane Addams's Hull House, flourished in America before and immediately after the Civil War. American-style voluntary organizations were private, nongovernmental groups of often otherwise unrelated individuals who discerned a social problem and banded together to remedy it. Usually, as Lucina did with the ministers of Burlington, such organizations used publicity or persuasion to solicit financial and moral support from interested groups or individuals. The members were typically idealistic, educated, and reform minded. Too, they regarded their activities in a classless society as substituting for the hierarchical welfare structures built into class society in Europe. For example, they may have helped the poor, but they saw them as unfortunate individuals, not as permanent members of a lower order. When their aims were accomplished, as in the case of temperance or abolitionist organizations, these organizations usually passed out of existence. Their basic aim was to reconstruct society by the progressive amelioration of social ills or the temporary filling in of structural deficiencies in America's loose, individualistic, democratic society.

In early America, schools were a prime example of the activities of voluntary organizations. Dewey spoke favorably of the impulse that had energized private efforts to create local schools based on voluntary association, exemplified in the Vermont Lakeside Seminary in which Dewey himself had taught. Dewey wrote: "These little school houses dotted all over our land represent the fact that parents took the initiative: they did not wait for any government, any state government, much less national government to force an education on them." From his earliest writings on education, he saw the school as the primary institution of democratization in America. He believed that education as organized intelligence would remake the social order through its transformative effect on young people. Dewey assumed that if the schools organized modern intelligence effectively, democracy would be the inevitable result. And if democratic citizens emerged, they would organize education, and in turn education would become more democratic. This is Dewey's self-propelling idea of the adjustive arc in its largest form. Dewey believed that in closing the frontier, announced by the census of 1890, it became the responsibility of education to remedy what history had left undone. "The schools," he declared, "have now to make up to the disinherited masses by conscious instruction, by the development of personal power, skill, ability, and initiative, for the loss of external opportunities consequent on the passing of our pioneer days." It was an often repeated Deweyan trope that educational democracy would replace the democratization process on the frontier: the immigrant and the industrial worker would now learn democracy through educational institutions, whereas several decades earlier, Americanization was supplied by free land, rural work, and historical opportunity. Dewey's early reading of Henry George stood behind and supported this idea. Early education, of course, passed naturally from being organized privately by parents to requiring local and state support and so evolved from the voluntary to the institutional stage; but Dewey dreamed of keeping the voluntary fire alive in it. American education, he argued, could not have, for a long time to come, a high degree of centralized authority without doing harm. His underlying conception was that institutional education is or should be a state of mind, a psychology, local and volunteeristic.

As his theory of voluntary educational organizations developed, Dewey looked to the organization of teachers as well as that of students. In February 1913, along with Charlotte Perkins Gilman and others, Dewey announced a plan for teachers and issued a call "for those teachers who think that something constructive can be done by teachers themselves." Characteristically, in addressing the teachers of New York City in 1913, he started locally. By forming a voluntary organization, he said, teachers could improve working conditions and bring about "better educational results for children." His "call" had two main principles: that teachers should have a voice in the determination of educational policy and they should be included on the board of education with the right to vote. These changes "would inevitably contribute to the development of a strong professional spirit, and to the intelligent use of their experience in the interest of the public. . . . In no more practical way could teachers prepare themselves for training children for citizenship in democracy."

In Dewey's proposal to the teachers can be seen the beginnings of the transition from voluntarily organized education to a full awareness that in the twentieth century, education could no longer entirely be left to individual parents. Modern education would necessarily have to implicate the state and local governments, which alone could "command the most expert educational capacity that there is, and which shall put it at the disposal of every community that wants it, and of every community that needs it." Dewey envisioned "a staff of individuals, advisory experts, actually going out into the communities" to persuade local authorities to organize modern intelligence for the sake of democratic development. Persuasion, not legislation or legal coercion, would be compatible, he believed, with American traditions.

Dewey's notion of the reconstructive importance of voluntary associations resulted in 1913 in the creation of another voluntary group, this time for the benefit of higher education. In 1913 Dewey and Arthur O. Lovejoy began to plan for a national association of university professors. Again, Dewey issued a "call." An organization was needed, he said, that would "facilitate a more effective cooperation among the members of the profession in the discharge of their special responsibilities as custodians of the interests of higher education and research in America" and make collective action possible in maintaining and advancing "the standards and ideals of the profession." Those who wrote to Dewey to raise doubts about the organization received lively replies. He wrote, for instance, to the conservative Harvard professor of English Barrett Wendell: "If I thought an organization would lessen the freedom of individual scholars, I should be heartily opposed to it," but instead, the American Association of University Professors (AAUP) would "assist in the formation of a larger and more reasoned public opinion and promote the growth in the general American public" of understanding the importance of organized intelligence in higher education. "So," he concluded, "I hope you'll join." In his usual manner, Dewey was intensely active from the outset in promoting this cause. He started an aggressive campaign in April 1914. The organization was formed; he was elected its first president; and he was soon writing to all his friends to urge them to become members. Dewey's first annual address as president, delivered on December 31, 1915, spelled out what he believed the organization had achieved in its first year. "We met one year ago with mingled hopes and fears. We meet today with a record of things accomplished and a definite program of things yet to be undertaken—with fears allayed and hopes confirmed." Early in the next year, when a letter written to *The Nation* predicted the imminent demise of the AAUP, Dewey responded. He foresaw its long life "proceeding most vigorously and prosperously." The association, in fact, was vigorous and ready for action; it almost immediately began investigating the dismissal of eight professors at the University of Utah. Eventually the association honored Dewey with a life membership.

Dewey's activities in forming and often leading organizations in the field of education constituted only a small part of his voluntaristic efforts. In 1909, Dewey saw that the time had come when racial antagonism and race prejudice might be effectively challenged not so much through legislation as by the operations of voluntary associations. In an article under the headline "Whites and Blacks Confer as Equals / Plan Civil Equality / Go on Record as Favoring Such a Change," the *New York Times* reported that the socialist William English Walling had called for a meeting of representatives of both races to discuss the means of achieving "civil and political equality" in America. This took place on the last day of May and the first day of June 1909, in the Convention Hall of the United Charities Building in New York City.

New York City Mayor Seth Low, Andrew Carnegie, and Booker T. Washington declined invitations. Three hundred men and women attended. From this meeting the National Association for the Advancement of Colored People was formed. As a founding member of the organization, John Dewey encouraged its growth. Oswald Garrison Villard was soon promoting membership by telling prospective adherents that "Professor Dewey is so much interested" and was on "the side of justice for a downtrodden race." When John was passionate about some aspect of social justice, Alice was likely to be even more active. No sooner had the NAACP been formed than Alice organized a big meeting of a group of African American women at her house, in an attempt to join with them and to join them to the women's suffrage movement. Hearing of this, the owner of the building forbade by letter any further integrated meetings in the Dewey apartment, which led the NAACP to organize a big mass meeting at the Ethical Culture Meeting House to protest against the infringement of citizens' rights. The organization grew in strength. Professor W. E. B. DuBois resigned his academic position to become the NAACP's director of the Bureau of Research and Publicity. For a long time the national offices of the NAACP remained in New York City, and Dewey continued to work closely with this and other organizations promoting the civil rights of African Americans.

This was not the only organization that Dewey joined to promote racial equality. As late as the 1940s he helped create the American Federation of Negro College Students and persuaded Eleanor Roosevelt to chair its Advisory Council. In 1949, on Dewey's ninetieth birthday, the NAACP remembered Dewey's early support. Roy Wilkins, then the acting secretary, recalled Dewey's "immeasurable contribution to the struggle against racial discrimination as a signer of the regional Lincoln Day call which forty years ago marked the birth of the NAACP." Dewey, Wilkins declared, was "universally respected for [his] concern for civil liberties and the rights of man."

In 1916, the American Union Against Militarism (AUAM) was founded by some fifty leading liberal intellectuals to investigate and protest the pervasive suppression of those who spoke against the war and America's possible involvement in it. Dewey was joined by Jane Addams, the socialist political leader Norman Thomas, Felix Frankfurter, Roger Baldwin, and even Helen Keller in founding the organization. When the war was over, the AUAM metamorphosed into an organization with an expanded charge: the American Civil Liberties Union, dedicated to fight against abuses of civil freedom in any sphere. Dewey became a long-standing member of the National Committee, remaining active until the early 1930s. In 1931 he became a member of the new "ACLU National Committee on Labor Injunctions," which fought court orders for injunctions against strikes by laborers, and supported Senator George W. Norris's liberal congressional legislation favoring strikers. Dewey had not forgotten the Pullman strike, and he remained a strong advocate of voluntary unionization. He also helped organize the New York City Teachers Union and remained active until the mid-1930s, when members of the Communist Party infiltrated it as well as the ACLU. Dewey then resigned from both. For his work in organizing the New York City teachers, Dewey was honored by the issuance of a stamp, only the second stamp commemorating the contributions of "trade unionists" to American civilization. (Samuel Gompers was the first so designated.)

A list of all Dewey's memberships in liberal organizations, usually as a founder, would be long indeed. He helped found the League for Independent Political Action; he was vice-president of the American Association for the Advancement of Science; he founded the Committee on Education for International Goodwill; he was chairman of the Organizing Committee for National Aid to Education; he was a member of the American Committee for the Relief of Russian Children; he was a member of the Chinese-American Commission— the list goes on and on. But he did not join automatically. His participation was voluntary, not ideological or automatic. When he did join, he gave wholehearted support. But he was no longer dazzled by pretenders and fast-talking promoters, as he had been by Franklin Ford. In 1923, when Arthur Dunn invited him to join the People's Committee of One Thousand to support the League of Nations, Dewey refused. "I suppose intelligent people may differ about the advisability of the United States entering into the League of Nations. I do not see how they can differ about the claptrap which was sent out in connection with your letter. . . . I decline your invitation." He especially objected to the League's exclusion of Russia, asking, "Is Russia outside your international humanitarianism?"

MORE PUBLICATIONS

Between his arrival at Columbia in 1904 and the beginning of a new phase of his life when the war in Europe began in 1914, Dewey's publications seemed to be somewhat a summing up, a consolidation, and the completion of an evolution in his thought. *Ethics* (1908), written in collaboration with James Tufts, marks the completion of a phase of thought that had begun with his 1891 *Outlines of a Cultural Theory of Ethics*. *Moral Principles in Education* (1909) related his concern with ethics to several earlier articles on education and democracy and was closely related to *Schools of To-Morrow* (1915) and *Democracy and Education* (1916). These brought his concern with education as applied philosophy and with practical democracy to at least a temporary conclusion. *How We Think* (1910) draws on his first book, *Psychology*, but dispensed with the earlier Hegelian framework. *Essays in Experimental Logic* (1916) brings new perspectives to his earlier *Studies in Logical Theory* (1903) and anticipates the underlying thesis of such later works as *Experience and Nature*. While *German Philosophy and Politics* would not have been written without World War I, the book actually originated in his study of German philosophy in his work with Torrey and Morris.

Written in collaboration with James Tufts, *Ethics* (1908) is an important volume. Each author was responsible for his own section of the book, although each "contributed suggestions and criticisms of the work of the other." Tufts contributed a long historical introduction concerning "the beginnings and growth of morality," which was followed by Dewey's section on theory and analysis and the chapters analyzing ethics in relation to the "World of Action." Ethical behavior,

Dewey argued, could be understood only in the context of social organizations, civil society, and the political state. Dewey and Tufts held that their aim was "not . . . to install the notions of a school nor to inculcate a ready-made system, but to show the development of [ethical] theories out of the problems and experience of every-day conduct, and to suggest how these theories may be fruitfully applied in practical exigencies."

Dewey maintained his focus on ethics for the remainder of his career, rewriting this book in 1932 when he was over seventy. How we believe, how we think, and how we act were concerns that always occupied Dewey. Since the publication of *Outlines of a Critical Theory of Ethics*, Dewey's outlook had changed considerably, but even in his earliest work he had concentrated not on a predetermined system of ethics, to be imposed on an individual, but on method and judgment: "how to decide what to do." He continued to be influenced by his psychological investigations, because for him they paralleled his work on ethics. He emphasized the psychological *how* rather than the moral *what* of ethics. Imaginative possibility was thereby joined with reason to produce possible ethical action. He stressed, of course, the transformation from conventional or customary morals to what he called "reflective morals." In accord with this basic principle, Dewey treated all earlier ethical propositions simply as theories, rehearsals of how to think, leading to personal decisions about how to act, rather than propositions that are right or wrong in themselves. Clearly, Dewey was trying to ally moral investigation with scientific research and thus to allow any person "to judge the [complex] problems of conduct for himself." Since his "end in view" was the emancipation and enlightenment of individual judgment, the means to achieve that end must involve speculation, reflection, construction of hypotheses, forecasting of results, and provisional experiments in action—to be followed by the beginning of this whole process anew.

Given Dewey's real involvement in the world of social and political action in Chicago and especially in New York, the initial chapters of part 3 of his *Ethics* are of particular interest. Here he was concerned with the involvement of individual morality in society and its contemporary problems. Dewey's basic conviction comes strongly to the fore, namely, that relations to others and not an individual's desires create and lead to the evolution of morals. On their own, people would "live the life of a brute animal," a life of appetites, but in the "social medium" they discover and then develop their true "needs and capacities":

> The wider and the richer the social relations into which an individual enters, the more fully are his powers evoked, and the more fully is he brought to recognize the possibilities latent in them. It is from seeing noble architecture and hearing harmonious music that the individual learns to know to what his own constructive and rhythmic tendencies, otherwise blind and inchoate, may come. It is from achievement in industrial, national, and family life that he is initiated into perception of his own energy, loyalty, and affection.

As usual, Dewey's ideas interlock. Philosophy needs psychology. Psychology has gone well beyond the physiological to become social psychology. Ethics is intimately related to society and social action. Education is applied philosophy. And when these are allowed freedom to be joined at their highest superindividual level, even more progressive democracy results. In all his books and articles Dewey was writing one book with many facets. This can easily be seen in his 1909 book, *Moral Principles in Education*, which is closely related to *Ethics*, in which the same set of "standards"—psychology, society, morality, and growth—is simply refocused on education. In all his books, *freedom* is the repeated core word as he stresses orderly progress toward more and more freedom.

Not unexpectedly, then, *How We Think* (1910) uses the same materials, this time centering on psychology but equally involving the very same core concerns of morality, society, democracy, and philosophy. In a remarkable revelation of how he worked in tandem, Dewey revised *Ethics* (1908) in 1932 and *How We Think* in 1933. Though seldom as explicit, this procedure was typical of Dewey: every book and article became a building block for later works. Just as civilizations use the materials of earlier structures to construct new buildings, Dewey kept reassembling his older constructions to create new monuments.

The 1910 version of *How We Think* is designed as a guide for teachers determining how to train young minds and thus open them to the ethical instruction of society and the scientific investigation of nature. Children, Dewey writes, naturally love "experimental inquiry," which becomes the basis for developing "that habit of thought, which we call scientific." The title itself points to the book's central assertion: we can think about anything, but *how* we think about it is the important consideration. Thinking, for Dewey, is rethinking, continued thinking, reconstructed thinking, reflection, investigation, experiment, a willing suspension of final conclusions in favor of an extended, perhaps never completed, process of thought. Reflective thinking "involves willingness to endure a condition of mental unrest and disturbance" as one accepts the pain of "further inquiry." Dewey concludes: "To maintain the state of doubt and to carry on systematic and protracted inquiry—these are the essentials of thinking."

"Systematic and protracted inquiry" describes both Dewey's understanding of the process of thought and his own method of philosophical investigation. In both he was influenced by Charles Darwin's work and the broader concept of evolution promulgated by Darwin and his many explicators, disciples, and coworkers. One of Dewey's best essays, "The Influence of Darwinism on Philosophy" (1909), exhibits the pervasive influence of the idea of evolution. For him, the evolution of thought meant continued investigation and experiment, hermeneutic openness, logic as inquiry, provisional conclusions, and social progress. "Evolution" meant philosophy itself, and philosophy meant evolution. Together, philosophy and evolution could be subsumed under the word *instrumentalism*, Dewey's name for what he did. Always interested in experiment and assessment through observation, it was nearly inevitable that Dewey would write a book about experimental schools in America and their contributions to the evolution of democracy. *Schools of To-Morrow* was this book.

The impetus for *Schools of To-Morrow* came to Dewey from Burgess Johnson, the education editor at E. P. Dutton. Once Johnson got Dutton's president, John Macrae, to agree that the house should become a serious publisher of educational books, he was determined to persuade John Dewey to write the initial volume on "progressive" schools. Although Dewey had written several articles on educational subjects, he had not composed a book on education since *The School and Society* (1899) and *The Child and the Curriculum* (1902). In the interim, several new experimental schools had been launched, and in 1913 the public interest in them was high.

By the time Johnson arrived at Dewey's office at Columbia, he already had a title to propose to him: *Schools of Tomorrow*. That was a good title and the subject was good, Dewey said, but he feared he was writing too much and he had vowed to take a break. His ideas about education were in a state of flux, and he didn't want to commit himself on paper until he had solidified them.

Johnson asked whether Dewey would at least help him think of some chapter titles for new educational experiments. "After ten or twelve were written out and lying there before us, I asked him whether he had not completed some of those chapters already in addresses, or articles." With a "little smile," Dewey replied, "Yes, I think that book is about half written already."

At the time, Dewey was defending several of his philosophical positions and was busy replying to his critics. He asked Evelyn to help him with Johnson's proposed book, and with her assistance it was quickly completed. But when Johnson received the manuscript and started to read it, he was disappointed. The first chapter, he thought, "would attract only the educational technician." With a sinking heart, he went on to the second chapter. This was exactly the Dewey he wanted, informative and likely to be popular with parents who wanted information about educational innovations.

Johnson returned to Dewey's office and explained how the book struck him. Could it begin with the second chapter? "He listened to me quietly and then said in his gentle voice, 'What you say interests me greatly. I wrote the first chapter and my daughter Evelyn wrote the second.' " John rewrote the first chapter, making it into a lively survey of the educational themes in Rousseau's *Émile*. Then Evelyn continued by showing how Rousseau's theories had been put into practice by Mrs. Johnson in her school in Fairhope, Alabama. These chapters established the narrative: first the ideas of a renowned theorist are discussed, and then a school that applies them is examined. Using this method, the Deweys described educational experiments in Indianapolis, Chicago, Pittsburgh, New York City, Gary, and a dozen other places. *Schools of To-Morrow* showed that if only we could seize and extend it, the future already existed.

Dewey's early philosophic perspective was, in his own opinion, best summed up in his 1916 book, *Democracy and Education*. Until the publication of *Experience and Education* (1938), this was his most mature consideration of the many roles of education in America's progressive society. It also showed his most mature and subtle use of psychological reflections developed during the previous twenty years, both a provisional summing up and a going forward. Just as Dewey defined education as a process by which students learn to use past and present experiences for intelligent action in the future, so Dewey was a student to himself in this book, looking backward as a vehicle for going forward. Fifteen years after the publication of *Democracy and Education*, Dewey wrote that in it "my philosophy . . . was most fully expounded," for in the subject of education he had located "the supreme human interest in which . . . other problems, cosmological, moral, logical, come to a head."

His announced plan in *Democracy and Education* was twofold: first, "to detect and state the ideas implied in a democratic society" and, second, "to apply these ideas to the enterprise of education." Of necessity, the bridge between "ideas" and action, or application, had to be psychological and instrumental. What ideas can be translated into action? How do we conceive "education" to be "democratic"? Are all experiences educative, psychologically? Is "democracy" a clear and single entity, in both the mind and its practical realization in individuals and in society as a whole? When Dewey started with two simple ideas, they were likely to become complicated and to lead to many questions rather than answers. Like most of Dewey's best books, *Democracy and Education* is itself an education, taking its readers into

Dewey's own thinking and making the readers think with him. Here are some questions that you have probably thought about yourself, Dewey is saying. Perhaps if we do not try at once to arrive at answers, perhaps if we think together, we will find that we first need to devise or discover a method about how to think about these matters. Then let us use this as an instrument with which to think as deeply as possible about the consequences of asking these simple, and therefore important, questions. Right away, Dewey suggests the *method* of investigation that he will employ, and he invites us to follow him. His attitude is that if we choose to follow a different procedure, Dewey will await our answers with interest. If we accept his invitation to follow him, he will be ready to carry us along. His attitude is Whitman-like: "I will stop somewhere waiting for you."

Education, he announces immediately, is "a necessity of life." Sentient life exists in its continuous renewal. Human life in its fullest sense includes renewal by experience: "the recreation of beliefs, ideals, hopes, happiness, misery, and practices" in both the individual and society. Education is the specific activity of renewing experience in an individual with and within a social group. In Whitman's phrasing, the "simple, solitary person" is nourished by education even as the "democratic en-masse" flourishes through the education of numerous individuals, for society continues to grow even as individuals perish. Life is transmission and transformation.

This is true of all societies. Beyond the savage stage, formal education begins to have important effects on society. As civilizations become more complex and the need to transmit morals, knowledge, and skills more urgent, education becomes more necessary; people need to understand how to learn as well as what they must learn. But when the growth of civilizations reaches the stage of democracies, the situation is yet more complex; for in an egalitarian society in which hierarchies and classes are not built into the structure, the problems of education soon become evident. The "aim" or "end" of democracy is produced by "means" that must be democratic and arise from conceptions of equality and freedom. From this point of departure,

Democracy and Education unfolds as Dewey examines appropriate experiences, objects, approaches, and subjects of education in a curriculum.

This book is not a survey of experimental schools, as *Schools of To-Morrow* is. Rather, it is the philosophy of education that concerns Dewey—a theory of knowledge and an ethical theory of a "good enough" democratic education. Appropriately, the book ends with a consideration of morals or, more properly, education-as-moral. Here Dewey's discussion reflects his success in resolving his own struggle with Hegelian dualisms—mind and body, spiritual and physical, thought and activity, and intelligence and character. Dewey worked hard and long to integrate such dualisms and now supplies the reader with the fruits of his own growth. These may be condensed into one unified and unifying statement: without character there is no intelligence, without the physical there is no spiritual, and so on; when one is lacking, both are lacking. Blake's maxim "Without contraries [there] is no advance" is overturned in favor of "Without unity [there] is no progress." Struggle is a factor in learning; effort is essential. But unless these are directed toward unity, inner and outer, they cause only conflict. Means and ends, too, are not separable dualisms but indissolubly one.

> Discipline, culture, social efficiency, personal refinement, improvement of character are but phases of the growth of capacity nobly to share in such a balanced experience. And education is not a mere means to such a life. Education is such a life. To maintain capacity for such education is the essence of morals. For conscious life is a continual beginning afresh.

In 1916, when *Democracy and Education* was published, anyone who looked into the state of the world would have taken, as Herman Hesse put it, a "look into chaos," and might have wondered what Dewey, with his incurable optimism for advance, was talking about. It was a world at war, a world unsafe for democracy. War threatened to reduce education to the effective employment of technology and whatever terror, privation, suffering, pain, and death might bring. But Dewey continued to believe that education would make the future.

DEWEY'S TEACHING STYLE

Dewey was a husband, a father, a philosopher, a promoter of social change, an activist, a political commentator, and perhaps, above all, a teacher. His teaching career began in 1879 in Oil City, Pennsylvania. In 1949, though officially having retired from Columbia University years before, he was still attending Philosophy Club meetings and arguing with graduate students. Although he published many books and articles and delivered hundreds of lectures, he probably spent more time teaching during these seventy years than in any other single activity. His style of teaching altered over time, but consistent through the years was his emphasis on teaching as another form of "systematic and protracted inquiry." Dewey himself did not provide an account of his teaching methods: he simply taught. Consistent with his philosophy, teaching was an inquiry in which teachers and students formed a community of minds that "saw together." There was no dogmatism in this mode of instruction. As he saw it, the meaning of a class session resided in the transaction between production, usually by the teacher at first, and then reception, usually by the students, leading to production by the students and reception by the teacher, and so on in the reflex arc, until the class session or the whole course ended.

Dewey devised different methods to achieve this transactional inquiry in his classes. At Michigan he handed out detailed syllabi and summaries of the "subjects" for each class so that he could allow himself and his students to think freely in the class session itself. In this way he could start anywhere and make the mode and method of thinking his "subject" in any course whatsoever. One Michigan student remembered that on the first day of a particular class, Dewey brought in an alarm clock, put it on the desk, and said:

"Suppose this clock is the universe and there's something wrong inside it. How can it ever be righted?" That was the semester theme and at each meeting he gave general questions for us to ponder and at the next meeting he tried to draw out opinions. I do not recall that there was ever a formal lecture.

I. B. Lipson, who became a distinguished attorney, remembers that in a late afternoon class he took with Dewey, the philosopher would get so wrapped up in thinking things through that eventually Alice would send Fred or Evelyn to the classroom, to "open the door and shout, 'John, are you ready to go home?' " But often, he would simply sit the child on the platform while he finished his thought.

A student at the University of Chicago described a later version of Dewey's teaching style:

When Dr. Dewey made a speech or gave a lecture, he never stood up like an elegant orator. He acted like an ordinary man: . . . [he] turned to the right, leaned sideways on the wall behind him, seemed to be looking off into the distance . . . no gestures, no papers or notes—until he seemed to intuit that some student wished to ask a question. Then he was all eyes to that student. I remember one time I had to ask a question. Then he acted as if he could hardly wait to hear what it was.

Unlike every other course at the university, she notes, in Dewey's class the students did not raise their hands, they simply engaged in conversation.

Even decades later, many students at Columbia described Dewey's mode of teaching there in similar terms. Brand Blanshard portrayed his manner in a 1917 class:

He came shuffling into the room, looking rather absent-mindedly over the top of his spectacles. He sat down on a chair on the rostrum, looked out of the window, began crumbling a single sheet of notepaper which usually served as a sufficiency of notes, and began to talk. . . . [He] looked out the window and lectured on what seemed to me, after my experience of philosophers abroad, a rather mumbling fashion. But I found, when I got home and went over my notes that what seemed in the hearing a rather inconsecutive and rambling discourse, was really very closely knit and carefully thought out.

From the window of the classroom in which Dewey frequently taught, he could look out on Rodin's statue *The Thinker* positioned outside Philosophy Hall. It was an apt symbol of what he, too, was attempting to do.

Many students had exactly the same experiences: the little piece of paper ("he'd fold it and fold it and keep talking"), Dewey's abstracted manner, the talk that seemed disjointed turning out to be closely reasoned. But the theme that is endlessly reiterated in these accounts is that Dewey's way of teaching made him extremely vulnerable, for he exposed the process of his own thoughts. He wasn't teaching; he was revealing his thinking. Ernest Nagel tells what the consequence might be:

Someone in the class raised a question; Dewey stopped to think and finally said, "I do not know the answer, and we might as well dismiss the class until I can think through what the answer is." That is, he wasn't willing to simply give a perfunctory answer and didn't think there was any point in going on until what he thought was a fundamental issue had been at least reasonably resolved.

James Gutmann, first his student and later his colleague, recalled:

I think there was no other teacher I ever had who gave such a sense that for fifty minutes you were watching a man think; and the [symbol of this was] . . . he would take the notes he'd brought along, . . . often on yellow paper [or sometimes on a piece of a brown bag], and crunch them up as though to say, "I've thought it through, now I've said it, and next time I'll think again.

Max Eastman says the same—that Dewey would look out the window or up at the ceiling and "begin to talk, very slowly and with little emphasis and long pauses. . . . He was thinking rather than lecturing."

But as Pearl Hunter Weber said, when a student posed a question or made a comment, Dewey came to attention mentally. He would "draw out of him and his innocent question intellectual wonders. . . . Drawing out was never better done," because in Dewey's "active deference," he gave "unqualified . . . attention to . . . anybody." Blanshard remarked that Dewey "was a very kindly person, very generous, . . . easily approachable," which had an effect on his office conversations with students. Thomas Munro was a student of Dewey's before World War I and a colleague afterward. "He was a great figure," Munro says,

> and I hesitated to bother him [but] . . . I found him always willing to stop what he was doing, even in the midst of typewriting. I often apologized for interrupting him, but he always waved me to a chair and asked me to explain what I had in mind. He would finish with some good, practical suggestion. . . . He was always friendly; he was never pompous . . . he tacitly encouraged a student to talk. . . . He wanted to help the student . . . work out his own problems.

Talk, for Dewey, was the transactional version of thinking; "talking together" or "listening together" was "thinking together."

The casual observer might conclude that Dewey's manner of thinking-as-teaching might simply have been a natural derivative of his gentle and abstracted personality. But we have evidence that he had consciously decided to teach by exposing (as one of his book titles put it) how to think or, more precisely, how he thought and how his students might think. One body of evidence of the deliberate intentions behind his manner are the notes for his lectures that survived the usual procedure of being crumpled and tossed. Often they are extremely detailed and explicitly state the problem to be considered during the hour, indicating what was problematic and why. A method of investigation generally followed, then objections to the method. The problem might then be stated in a different light, which led to hypothesis, questions, and "warrantable assertions," or provisional conclusions. Examples of evidence came next. A new problem would arise, and a "conclusion"—until the next class—would be tentatively reached, but he suggested a list of readings to encourage further thought until the next class meeting.

The second piece of evidence that Dewey's teaching manner was well thought out comes from the experiences of those who heard him lecture as both a professor and a political speaker. As a teacher, Bruce Raup says, "Dewey was in a world of thought." But Raup also listened to a speech by Dewey on behalf of Robert La Follette during the senator's campaign for president in 1924:

> I . . . was never so surprised in my life at anybody as I was at Dewey at that meeting. Came time for him to speak (and he was the principal speaker at that meeting) he stood at the speaker's stand and revealed the man in a different perspective, in a different manner from that which I had become acquainted with in his classrooms. . . . He spoke with wit, he spoke fluently, rapidly, not slow and deliberate. He spoke with zest and zeal for the cause and simply held the audience spellbound. Well that was a Dewey that I never had seen before.

Teaching was thinking and required the manner of reflection. A political speaker performed an act that was meant to lead to a vote; it required the manner of an active transaction. Advising was aimed at understanding, and in it Dewey's manner was empathetic curiosity. His philosophical articles and books, his political journalism, his engagements in social controversy, and his essays on literature and art all required appropriate treatment, Dewey's version of Sullivan's dictum that form follows function. Dewey's teaching was as central to his

life as writing was and, moreover, gave Dewey the experience of lis-
teners that he carried over to his best writing. Talking or teaching
increasingly became the source of his publications.

Dewey was also being taught by the unanticipated changes occurring in America. One of the lessons taught to him between 1895 and
1917 was that America was destined or doomed to become a world
power, which meant that it had to begin to practice at war.

War

The social, economic, and political unrest of the 1890s seemed to many
to result from stresses that had been produced by America's inward-
looking continental expansion just before the closing of the frontier in
1890. After that date, many political and social thinkers began to look
globally, not only because they believed it to be America's manifest destiny to extend itself into the world, but also because such expansion
would ease domestic tensions. In the same year that Frederick Jackson
Turner declared the frontier to be closed, Alfred Thayer Mahan's book
The Influence of Sea Power Upon History appeared. All great nations,
Mahan argued, had relied on sea power. The United States was bound-
ed by two great oceans, but they did not bind America. Far from it:
they were the new wilderness that Americans had to cross and con-
quer. The frontier was not closed; instead, it was opened by the pathways east and west of the Atlantic and Pacific. America's destiny was
its geography. The conquest of the continent was completed. Naval
power would begin the conquest of the oceans.

The expansion of American interests beyond its boundaries had
already begun. Hawaii and Samoa were colonized, and a naval base
was constructed at Pearl Harbor in the late 1880s. In 1893 American
marines helped depose Queen Liliuokalani, and the political maneu-
vers to annex Hawaii as a territory of the United States began.

A sign of America's outward looking drive and the new feeling of
world power became apparent in 1895 when Venezuela and Great
Britain disputed the boundary between Venezuela and the British

colony of Guiana. Backing Venezuela in the recently formed Pan-American Union, the secretary of state, Richard Olney, declared that the dispute must be arbitrated, and he implied that Britain's continued truculence violated the Monroe Doctrine. In oblique but no uncertain terms, Britain was informed that the United States was ready to settle the controversy by military and naval means.

The longest remembered and the most explosive episode in this expansion was the Spanish-American War, which began with the long struggle between the Cubans and the Spanish colonizers. In this instance, President Grover Cleveland saw no reason to evoke the Monroe Doctrine, and so the struggle was confined for a long period to sensational articles in the popular press and agitation by "Free Cuba" organizations operating in the United States. Cleveland's successor, William McKinley, protested, threatened, and then temporized. He sent the battleship *Maine* to Havana harbor, ostensibly to protect the lives of American residents and their business interests in Cuba, but more likely as a token warning. When the ship exploded, causing the deaths of 260 people, the newspapers and pro-Cuban publicists instantly joined in an incendiary battle cry: *"Remember the Maine!"* They demanded intervention by American troops and naval vessels. Still McKinley waited while even little known members of his administration, including Assistant Secretary of the Navy Theodore Roosevelt, called for war. On April 25, the 1898 war—a "splendid little war," as John Hay called it—came in a congressional declaration. With a few exceptions, Americans rejoiced. Part of the national jubilation was that America was beginning its destined rise to global preeminence. Officially, Cuba became independent, but it was now closely allied with U.S. interests. Puerto Rico and the Philippines were annexed as territories. Guam and a few Pacific islands fell into America's lap. The war lasted only three months, but it erased the terrible memory of the Civil War, in which so many had died. Anti-imperialists might carp, but the nation loved the war, gratefully accepted its new island treasures, and elected Colonel Roosevelt vice-president in the election of 1900.

In the Far East, America's growing interest in Asia led to Secretary of State John Hay's declaration of an "open door" policy in China. This meant that along with Japan and a few interested European nations, America would regard China as open to trade through foreign concessions creating "spheres of influence." American troops joined the European imperialists in putting down the Boxer Uprising and helped cut up China into foreign concessions. The United States had had nearly twenty years of practicing for war. Now it was ready for a full-scale adventure. Pacifism had never been popular in America, and it was not popular in 1915. John Dewey was a declared pacifist but a complicated one. No one who grew up during the aftermath of the Civil War could forget the terrible loss of life and the extended period of national mourning following it. Yet in Vermont there had also been general rejoicing at the results of the war, especially the freeing of slaves. Dewey's attitude was that war was an evil but if a war had to be fought to extend democracy abroad and deepen American ideals internally, then Dewey could support it even as he mourned it.

For him war was a moral strategy. By 1915, philosophically, conflict had ceased for him to be a vehicle for social advance. But it could be a necessary action to promote or protect ideals. Toward the end of *German Philosophy and Politics*, he observed: "In and of itself, the idea of peace is a negative idea; it is a police idea. There *are* things more important than keeping one's body whole and one's property intact." In Dewey's pacifist view, the arguments against war must generally prevail, for war disturbs "the fruitful processes of cooperation in the great experiment of living together." Besides, how could the goal of peace be achieved by employing devastating violence as the means to achieve it? How could the goal of extending democracy be realized through the restrictions of freedom that wars always brought? How could democracy be enlarged for Americans by involvements beyond its boundaries? How could imperialism be ended if the United States joined the exploiters and brought the colonizers' psychology home to its own shores?

Dewey described his opinion of the war in Europe to a colleague in Columbia's philosophy department, George S. Fullerton, who had sent his colleagues on the faculty a pro-German circular letter about public opinion in the United States concerning the war. In his reply, Dewey condemned the Germans for violating Belgian neutrality and for their unwillingness to allow diplomatic negotiations to mature. "Germany may emerge victorious," Dewey wrote, but "victorious or defeated, she has suffered an irreparable loss of intellectual and moral prestige." Germany had once achieved social and intellectual "victories in science, industry, commerce, and a civil administration devoted to the amelioration of suffering and poverty," but now the "tragedy of the present war" was that its sole means for victory was "the heaped-up dead on the battle fields." Dewey lamented the failure of German moral philosophy, but he was not ready to go to war.

At first Dewey doubted that the United States would be drawn into the war. Perhaps no logical connection existed between the outbreak of the war in Europe and threats to the fulfillment of the "American Dream," as Dewey conceived of it. But for Dewey, as for numerous other progressives, the danger to American democracy was that if America became involved in fighting Germany, it would have to become like the German state, which was hierarchical, efficient, autocratic, industrialized, and corporate. In short, it was a state perfectly organized for warfare. Dewey understood in 1914 that any nation drawn into the war and hoping to defeat Germany would have to adopt some of its same characteristics and form its own war machine. He also realized that some of these antidemocratic characteristics were already evident, if developed only rudimentarily, in America. War, he believed, would bring them out. Thus, Germany offered America a terrible prophecy of its future, especially if America had to organize for war.

At first, America's involvement seemed only a remote possibility. Dewey was intent on doing what he could with his philosophic tools to alert Americans to the moral and intellectual character and quandaries of the German people. His own immersion in German philosophy and his effort to free himself from it put him in the perfect position to understand the relationship among German philosophy, German politics, German culture, and war. In *German Philosophy and Politics* (1915), he analyzed these connections.

While Dewey developed his own position with regard to the connections between German philosophy and politics, his argument about the important cultural connections between German policy and German philosophy reached far back in his own life to George Sylvester Morris's discussion of the state and his criticism of Kant in favor of Hegel. In *German Philosophy and Politics,* Dewey argued that Kant's separation of nature from natural science bifurcated the German mind. The dualisms that were thereby engendered allowed Germans to split their consciousness of duties, requiring outer obedience to the state, on the one hand, but allowing freedom from obedience to morals privately, on the other hand. Thus, however ostensibly idealistic and even moralistic in appearance, Kant propelled the German people in a direction that led them to separate political and moral duties and to allow the state to rule moral action through politics. It was not Kant himself, of course, that Dewey identified as the germ of the nation's split psychology, but Kantianism as it infiltrated the German character. Kant's separation, in contrast to Hegel's drive toward unity, made Kant and not Hegel, who might have seemed the more obvious choice, the psychological progenitor of Germany's ability to wage war without moral justification. Dewey had already arrived at the position that nothing, even reason, was *pure*; and he located in Kant's concept of purity an escape into psychological isolation from consequences that made Kant the unintended theorist of the German machine state. "Kant still remains the philosopher of Germany," Dewey wrote.

Dewey's critique had no effect on the European theater of war and almost no effect on the way that Americans began to prepare for war, even as they resisted consciously any implication that they were about to enter it. Subtly, American culture altered its historic course. As war seemed more and more likely, the emphasis in American development shifted. Building toward mechanization in preparation for war, industrialization accelerated, which led to calls in America to expand industrial education. Dewey opposed this as the first evidence that Americans were drifting toward war. For him, education should be conducted so as to encourage democracy, not to assist in the growth of industrial power. But other changes kept emerging, until the preparation for war seemed like a hydra-headed monster. No sooner had

Dewey massed his philosophical arguments against one head than several more appeared. As preparations for entry into the conflict mounted, the need to regulate labor to maintain the war effort began to restrict workers' rights. For Dewey, an ardent supporter of workers, this struck a second blow at democracy. The impending war gave capital and management powerful tools to stifle protest, quash strikes, and limit wages. Modern war, too, was a matter of masses, not an individual or even a community battle. Thus, as the need to assemble a war "machine" grew, the American individual faded in value and meaning. Dewey's analysis of these accelerating transformations was lucid. To win a war against Germany could mean to lose the key to democracy, equality, and freedom. To Dewey it was unacceptable to defeat Germany by becoming more German than the Germans.

But in his accustomed way, Dewey also located two reasons for hope among these prognostications. He believed that he and other right progressives might weigh in on the side of America's reluctance to meddle in foreign strife. War might still be prevented by the persuasions of intelligence. If that proved impossible, then Dewey and like-minded thinkers might still alert Americans to the dangers of imitating Germany and thereby keep citizens on the alternative path of increasing democratization in education, expanding workers' rights, and emphasizing the value of the person in a democratic community of individuals even as they engaged in combat. If the war were fought to preserve and expand basic American values, even a descent into fighting could enhance democracy in the United States. But if America fought in order to grow in power, the country would be defeated, whatever the war's outcome.

By the beginning of 1917 the effects of the European war and war preparations on America were evident to Dewey, especially in events at his own university. President Butler was determined that Columbia represent the purest ideals of American patriotism. Practically, this meant opposition to Germany and support for America's allies, including entry into the spreading conflict. When Butler became the first signer of a petition calling on President Woodrow Wilson to demand that Germany cease deporting Belgians, this presented no problem. Four hundred Columbia faculty, including John Dewey, signed their names under Butler's. But the relations between the president and his faculty soon turned acrimonious when Butler saw himself as a possible vice-presidential or even presidential candidate on the Republican ticket to oppose Wilson and the Democrats in the 1920 elections. (He had received eight electoral votes for vice-president on the Taft ticket in 1916.) So far, the Wilson administration had kept America out of the war. Butler, therefore, had to establish for himself a firm line as a war proponent against Wilson's and the Democratic Party's indecisiveness.

NEW RESTRICTIONS

In February 1917, an incident occurred that, it seemed to many, might lead to the beginning of the curtailment of free speech at Columbia. Count Ilya Tolstoy had been invited by a student society to speak at the university. He was well known as an opponent of Russia's continued war efforts in support of the Allies and a proponent of its withdrawal. Then, with the acknowledged support of President Butler, the chair of the Department of Slavonic Languages prevented Tolstoy from lecturing, by withdrawing permission for him to use a university building, explaining that this "was due entirely to my belief that at this critical juncture in American history, when it seems most important to inculcate the principles of sound patriotism . . . any attempt to belittle the importance of nationalism and to denounce patriotism ought not to be associated with the name of the University." As usual, reporters sought Dewey's opinion, since he led the faculty opposition. Dewey asked Butler to rescind the veto, declaring that "freedom of speech and liberty of opinion have always existed at Columbia." But the faculty petition that he helped gather did not move Butler. The students joined the Dewey-led faculty position and papered the campus with posters declaring: "Free speech at Columbia is threatened." An editor of a student magazine was suspended. A student protest meeting was called, and Dewey was named as the main speaker.

Many of the Columbia faculty privately opposed America's drift toward war, and a few expressed their opposition publicly. In March, the anthropologist Franz Boas privately consulted Dewey about a letter opposing America's entry into the war, which Boas considered making public. Boas's proposed letter, Dewey advised him, "is so temperate, . . . [and] its general principles contain so much in which I personally strongly believe that it seems rather quibbling to make any suggestion that it shouldn't be published." But he did counsel delay. Boas's arguments against America's involvement, Dewey acknowledged, were strong, although he was concerned that given Boas's obviously German name, the letter would be "discounted as a natural expression . . . of German sympathies." Boas wavered and replied to Dewey three days later: "What I feel . . . is that everybody who is for peace needs stiffening of the back." Beyond that, he added, intellectuals need "to show that we cannot be intimidated." But Boas continued to waver. So did Dewey.

The most famous of Dewey's essays on the coming war was "In a Time of National Hesitation" (1917). Dewey contended that the hesitation of Americans and their representatives to join the war was a sign that the nation was in full "possession of its senses." Americans were right to hesitate. The fight for democracy on national soil, he argued, has to constitute our major battle, and the United States had not yet fulfilled the promise of democracy. Dewey's was a brilliant parry by right against left progressivism, by those intent on consolidating democracy on native grounds, in contrast to those who wished to promote perhaps paler versions of democracy across the globe. "Not until the almost impossible happens," Dewey wrote, "not until the Allies are fighting on our terms for our democracy and civilization, will that happen." America, he concluded, had at last become separated from Europe. It was no longer a colony but a "new body and a new spirit in the world."

President Wilson seemed to waver, too. In 1916, he had run on the slogan "He kept us out of the war!" against the progressive Republican candidate Charles Evans Hughes, who favored America's entry. But Wilson's campaign literature reflected the necessities of domestic politics; Wilson himself had never been reluctant to commit American troops beyond the borders of the United States. Hardly had he been inaugurated to a second term when on April 2, 1917, he asked a joint session of Congress to declare war. A weak coalition of pacifists, non-interventionists, and anti-imperialists put up a brief fight in Congress and the daily press until, four days later, Congress gave Wilson the declaration he had requested. Now Wilson vowed to pursue the war "without stint."

At Columbia, others' backs stiffened in the opposite way. At the beginning of the 1917 fall term, Professor of English Henry Wadsworth Longfellow Dana spoke out against the war and was instantly fired by President Butler for disseminating doctrines of disloyalty. Soon after Dana's dismissal, there was a much more complicated case of termination. In 1904, as chair of the Department of Philosophy and Psychology, James McKeen Cattell had been instrumental in hiring Dewey at Columbia following his precipitous resignation from Chicago. Now Cattell was threatened with termination. For more than four years, Cattell had constantly been at odds with the administration and was regarded as a troublemaker. The trustees had made a motion to retire him with a pension. But Dewey and others protested, and Cattell was retained with the general understanding that he would be "on his good behavior." But early in 1917, when Cattell sent out a confidential letter to three hundred faculty members protesting a minor decision by the trustees concerning the Faculty Club and suggesting that the faculty take possession of Butler's presidential house as their Faculty Club, the press got a copy of the letter and played up its sensational elements. The matter came before a faculty committee headed by the acting graduate school dean and professor of economics E. R. A. Seligman and including Dewey, and they persuaded Cattell to apologize. He agreed to sign whatever document they drafted. This should have brought the incident to a close, except that Seligman forwarded this letter of apology to all three hundred faculty who had received Cattell's original letter of protest.

At this, Cattell exploded. He dashed off another letter accusing Seligman of bad faith, and it, too, appeared in the papers. Cattell threatened to sue the members of the committee and the trustees of the university. "Owing to his banking affiliations Professor Seligman naturally flocks with the Trustees," Cattell told reporters. By this time the

United States had entered the war, and President Wilson declared that it was America's duty to make the world safe for democracy. Congress enacted an unprecedented flurry of legislation, including compulsory military service. Dewey, who had hoped for idealistic goals if America did enter the conflict, suspended his pacifism and supported America's participation.

But Cattell went in the other direction, writing to many congressmen to assert what he called the "traditional American doctrine . . . that volunteers only should be sent overseas." In a gratuitous slap at Butler, he made a speech on campus in which he declared that his right of free speech had been violated. At this, the trustees voted to terminate Cattell immediately and also to deprive him of a pension. The reason now given was Cattell's "unpatriotic opposition" to the already adopted compulsory service legislation. As Dewey publicly said, this ruse "smeared the whole case over with [claims of] patriotism."

Dewey told the philosopher Robert Mark Wenley, who was sent from the University of Michigan by the American Association of University Professors to investigate Cattell's termination, that Cattell's case possessed all "the elements of tragedy." Dewey, Charles Beard, and the historian James Harvey Robinson protested the termination but were ignored. The only remaining thing that Dewey could think to do to aid his old friend Cattell was to write to Jacques Loeb, president of the Rockefeller Institute, to stress the "services rendered by Cattell to the organization and promotion of science in this country" and to solicit Loeb's support in recommending to the Carnegie Foundation, which was interested in the problem of faculty pensions, that Cattell receive a pension from Carnegie. Aware that the trustees might regard this as outside interference, Dewey quietly organized a group of influential "representatives," like Loeb, from outside the university, to write to the trustees urging this solution. At least in interesting the Carnegie Foundation in funding Cattell's pension, Dewey's campaign proved to be successful.

This affair had not yet been resolved completely when another controversy erupted. Charles Beard, one of the nation's most distinguished political historians, suddenly resigned on October 8, 1917, in

protest over the terminations of Dana and Cattell. As Walter
Lippmann's diary notes indicate, Dewey was a party in advance to the
discussion of Beard's resignation. On October 7, Dewey, Beard, and
Lippmann met at the City Club to plan for the public announcement.
With Lippmann, Dewey had been creating a "public opinion" scheme
vaguely resembling the old "thought news," and they proposed to
Beard that after his resignation, he should "go to Russia for three or
four months, and start that branch of our intelligence organization"
there. "He liked the idea very much," Lippmann noted. Columbia,
Beard told reporters on October 8, had fallen under "the control of a
small and active group of trustees, who, although 'without standing in
the world of education,' 'reactionary and visionless in politics,' and
'narrow and medieval in religion,' had throttled freedom of expression
among the educators." Trouble between Beard and the trustees had
been brewing for months, ever since he had given a speech on freedom
of expression in which he declared that if the nation could not bear to
hear some malcontents say "To hell with the Stars and Stripes!"
democracy in this nation was a failure. In deciding to resign, Beard
first made the announcement to his politics class. "His action was
greeted with applause which lasted five minutes. . . . He was in tears
when he left the room." On that same day, Beard gave his reasons to
President Butler. "We are in the midst of a great war, and we stand on
the threshold of an era which will call for all the emancipated thinking
that American can command," he began. He reminded Butler that his
own position could in no way be construed as pro-German: "As you
are aware, I have, from the beginning, believed that a victory for the
German Imperial Government would plunge all of us into the black
night of military barbarism." However, Beard firmly held to the conviction that the issue of freedom of speech was paramount, and the
opinions of those who did not agree with the war program could not
be "changed by curses or bludgeons." It would be better to lose a war
than lose the First Amendment.

Naturally, Dewey was consulted by the press and forthrightly
declared: "I regard the action of Professor Beard as the natural consequence of the degrading action of the Trustees." In a printed press

release he added that "Beard's wise and courageous resignation has separated the issue of academic freedom from the issue of patriotism." At the end of the spring semester, James Harvey Robinson followed Beard in resigning. According to Robinson's account, he informed President Butler in person, and "Butler it appears made littl[e] effort to disguise his joy." Both Robinson and Beard urged Dewey to join them in forming a new school that would focus on the social sciences and in which sociological fieldwork would be an important part of the curriculum. Late in July Beard told Dewey that the new school had raised enough funds for ten years and would open in the fall of 1919 and that he was "authorized . . . to ask me for my terms if I wanted to go in with them." Alice was steadfastly opposed to John's leaving Columbia. Beard and Robinson's new school appeared to her to be another shaky scheme of the sort that Dewey was so fond of pursuing. This time he refused. Eventually, against all expectations, the new school prospered, becoming the New School for Social Research, and Dewey did occasionally teach a course there.

Dewey and Beard continued to work together on abuses of freedom of speech. In the middle of December 1917, following the dismissal of three New York City high-school teachers for disloyalty, Dewey spoke at the DeWitt Clinton High School on the subject of "Democracy and Loyalty in the Schools." Dewey, who had been one of the founding organizers of the New York Teachers Union, was the natural choice to be the defender of free speech in the schools. In his usual way, he had studied, he said, the minutes of the trial and concluded, "I don't know what this is called in 1917, but I know what it used to be called. It used to be called the Inquisition." Beard agreed with Dewey. In a letter that he sent to the meeting, he observed that the "trial" showed that there was "no little anti-Semitic feeling in the case." Following the meeting, he wrote to Dewey, praising him for his courageous and continuous progressive activity. "There is no one whose commendation I value as highly as yours," Dewey modestly replied, "for you have actually made sacrifices and I can't say that I have done anything." Perhaps, Dewey suggested, with regard to the continuing threats to dismiss New York City teachers, it would be politically

1. Dewey's parents:
Archibald Sprague Dewey and
Lucina Artemisia Dewey,
Ann Arbor, Michigan, c. 1889–1890.

2. *From left to right*:
John Rich (cousin),
John Dewey,
Davis Rich Dewey, and
Charles Miner Dewey, 1865.

3. David Rich Dewey, mid 1890s.

4. Charles Miner Dewey, c. 1900.

5. Alice Chipman (*bottom row, second from right*), *Collegiate Sorosis, 1886–1906*,
University of Michigan, 1884–1885.

6. John Dewey (*second from left*) and the editorial board of "The Inlander," University of Michigan, 1885.

7. At the Glenmore School of Philosophy, Keene Valley, New York, 1893. *Left to right*: sitting on porch, Josiah Royce, Thomas Davidson; seated in chair: J. Clark Murray; standing: John Dewey, Rabbi Max Margolis, W. T. Harris, and Ibn Abi Sulaiman.

8. Lucy Dewey, Jane Dewey, and Frederick Dewey, 1901.

9. John Dewey at
the University of Chicago,
1902.
Photo by Eva W. Schutze.

10. John and Alice Chipman Dewey in China, 1919.

11. John Dewey,
Evelyn Dewey, and
Lucy Dewey
examining records of
China trip, 1922.

12. Sabino Dewey, 1922.

13. Sabino with Elizabeth Anne Dewey
(Frederick Dewey's first child), 1923.

14. Jane Dewey, c. 1930.
Photo by Robert Norwood.

15. Preliminary Commission of Inquiry Into the Charges Against Leon Trotsky.
Commissioners Suzanne La Follette, Ben Stolberg, Otto Rühle, and John Dewey,
at Diego Rivera's Casa Azul, Coyoacán, Mexico, April 1937.

16. Roberta Lowitz and John Dewey
in Florida, c. 1939.

17. John Dewey at Columbia University,
c. 1941.

18. John Dewey at work outside his cabin at Hubbards, Nova Scotia, 1944.

19. John Dewey and Pandit Nehru
at Dewey's ninetieth birthday celebration,
New York City, 1949.
Photo by Alexander Archer.

efficacious to pursue the argument "that nothing could be . . . more harmful to the real war cause in this country than giving the impression that the disloyalty issue was being used as a cloak for private and personal persecution."

Dewey remained active publicly, but privately he was despondent over the sudden upsurge of antidemocratic tendencies brought on by the war. While he supported U.S. participation in the conflict, he continued to fight against restrictions of freedom. For instance, he signed a petition printed in the *New Republic* protesting the arrest of 110 leaders of a radical union, the International Workers of the World, for "conspiracy to obstruct the war."

Coincidentally, during this same period, Dewey himself was offered an opportunity to escape from Columbia and take up a professorship at Harvard where calm still reigned.

THE AFTERMATH

This proposal developed slowly. Dewey's associations with William James had allied him for a long time with Harvard's philosophy department. Recently, in 1914, the secretary of the Harvard Philosophic Club, a young Ph.D. candidate then styling himself Thomas S. Eliot, invited Dewey to address the club. Dewey selected "What Are Minds?" as his topic. On the day following his lecture, he had lunch with young Eliot and Bertrand Russell, who was delivering the series of Lowell lectures on "Our Knowledge of the External World" at Harvard. Russell wrote to Ottoline Morrell that after lunch he and Dewey took a walk: "To my surprise, I like him very much. He has a large slow-moving mind, very empirical and candid, with something of the impassivity and impartiality of a natural force." Russell noted that when he made a philosophic observation about the concept of "I," Dewey saw its importance at once, but Ralph Barton Perry failed to grasp the point. Dewey stayed to listen to a talk by Russell, and as Russell noted, "the most effective criticism was from Dewey, who again impressed me very greatly, both as a philosopher and as a lovable man." Concerning his trip to America, Russell later concluded that "with the exception of Dewey" and one other person, "I have met hardly a soul who had any quality."

After these days at Harvard, Dewey preserved cordial relations with the Harvard philosophy faculty, especially with W. E. Hocking. Early in 1917, Hocking wrote to Dewey to urge him to visit for a semester. "We have not had, since the death of Professor James, any good representative of the pragmatic idea in Philosophy. . . . Our need is certainly very great," and Hocking concluded, "No one else could give the same assistance." This was Dewey's chance, should he choose to take it, to flee the chaos at Columbia. But now he had achieved a substantial inner calm. Almost at once Dewey replied with "my sincere appreciation of the great honor," but he raised many obstacles to the likelihood of his acceptance. In particular, he mentioned that he had made "certain plans" for his next year's sabbatical. Harvard did not take his refusal easily; and in the fall, just when the progressive struggles at Columbia and in New York were most intense, Harvard's chair of philosophy renewed the pursuit, now proposing that Dewey become a permanent member of the faculty, in essence succeeding William James, to whom he owed so much. "It would be a wonderful honor," he began his reply, "to be connected in any way with carrying on the tradition of William James in his own institution." However, he noted, "I am very happily situated here [at Columbia] so far as my colleagues and students are concerned." But he added, "What I can least forgive our anarchistic trustees for is that having a great and free-spirited institution they have succeeded in spreading . . . just the opposite impression about Columbia." Mindful of the turmoil over free speech at Columbia, Dewey did acknowledge "that conditions might arise in which I should have to close my relations here . . . as my part in a protest." Such ambiguity was not characteristic of Dewey and shows how tempted he was to leave the political turmoil and move to Harvard.

Dewey eventually made peace with America's entry into the war. He became convinced that in the person and purpose of Woodrow Wilson, the United States was joining the war effort not to enhance its national power or to support capitalism but to preserve its democratic ideals. At the invitation of Columbia University's *Alumni News*, he explained his position in May 1918:

> The war means to America the establishment in the world at large of the social and political ideals upon which this country has based its development, and . . . the failure to secure a decisive defeat of the German autocracy will render the future of these ideals uncertain . . . not merely in Europe but in this country.

Less than a week later, almost immediately after he arrived in Palo Alto to deliver a series of lectures on "Factors in Human Conduct," he delivered a special lecture, "The Fundamental Issues of the War," on May 29. The entire student body was dismissed from classes at 11:00 a.m. to attend his talk, in which he again stressed the fundamental defense of democratic ideals for which he believed the United Sates was fighting.

With hardly a delay following Dewey's earliest announcement of his support for the war, Randolph Bourne, one of Dewey's recent students and already the leader of many young political intellectuals, published an essay in *Seven Arts* entitled "Twilight of Idols." The chief target was Dewey, and the reason for the twilight of this god was what Bourne regarded as his failure of nerve in deciding to come in on the side of war: "A philosopher who senses so little the sinister forces of war . . . is speaking to another element of the younger intelligentsia than that to which I belong." Dewey was surprised by the vehemence of Bourne's essay but did not reply to it. After the collapse of Wilson's peace plans at the end of the war and thus the end of Dewey's justification for America's entry, he responded to Bourne obliquely when he acknowledged that in retrospect the pacifists had been right and he had been mistaken in his support.

Dewey continued to speak and write on the issues raised by the war. In particular, he urged extreme vigilance in the preservation of freedom of speech. One could be "pro-Ally," he pointed out, without being "in favor of establishing Prussianism in New York City." During 1917 and 1918 he wrote a dozen essays in which war issues figure prominently. "America in the World" (1918) is a good example of Dewey's belief that a gulf still existed between the United States and the rest of the world. The war signaled the end of America's period of isolation, during which the country had been "a laboratory set aside from the rest of the world in which to make . . . a great social experiment." Now the danger of America's global involvement, Dewey believed, could be the loss of the liberating benefits that the American experiment had achieved. We must be determined, he argued, to "see to it that . . . other nations accept and are influenced by the American idea rather than ourselves by European idea."

At Johns Hopkins, Dewey had thought that Woodrow Wilson "could go far" in politics, but Wilson went further than Dewey wished; and Americans were soon crowded into the trenches and dying with the citizens of European monarchies. Dewey was concerned with the decline of democratic freedoms on the home front. He wrote several essays on the psychology of war and its effects on American democratic society. Soon after the United States entered the war, Dewey wrote "In Explanation of Our Lapse" (1917). He saw, and said he saw, the "conscription of mind" occurring in America: the American mind drafted into the war effort and drifting more and more into intolerance, bigotry, passion, and rhetoric.

Dewey's reflections on America's global military adventures did not end with its entry into the war or even with the conclusion of the war. But in 1918, matters other than war concerned him. These came to be tangentially related to the war, and involved politics, but mainly they pertained to a personal crisis in Dewey's life.

THE POLISH PROJECT

In Dewey's graduate seminar and advanced undergraduate-graduate lecture courses on social and political philosophy in the fall of 1917, some of his best graduate students were enrolled: Irwin Edman, Brand

Blanshard, and Frances Bradshaw. All eventually had distinguished academic careers as philosophers. Paul Blanshard, Brand's twin brother, also attended occasionally. Another participant was not a student at all. This was Albert C. Barnes, a wealthy, complicated, eccentric, passionate businessman. Brand Blanshard described him as a "rough and ready type . . . a man with a violent temper and . . . very strong prejudices." Barnes had done graduate work in chemistry at several German universities. He had formulated a product called Argyrol, a preparation that prevented infection in wounds and was used by all sides in the war. Even before the war he had made a lot of money and assembled a fabulous collection of French impressionist art. His other passion was John Dewey. He didn't quite "collect" Dewey the way he did a Renoir, but he gave Dewey his full support and even affection. He was the only person ever to call John Dewey "Jack," and Dewey was the only one allowed to call him "Al." Barnes admired Dewey's work so much that he distributed copies of *Democracy and Education* to all the workers in his Merion, Pennsylvania, factory and even gave them time off to read it. As early as 1916, he attended one of Dewey's seminars, on John Stuart Mill. In the spring semester of 1918 he audited Dewey's "Ethics and Educational Problems." Barnes was deeply— and remained unqualifiedly—impressed by Dewey's thought. "I want to tell you what a rare treat your seminar was to me," he told Dewey after the conclusion of the 1918 seminar.

> It was a delight at the moment, and I feel that my life has been permanently enriched by it. For many years I have had the seminar habit, and the only one I have known that leaves anything near the pleasing memory that yours did is the one with Kuno Fischer, in Heidelberg, in 1900.

Barnes's reading of *Democracy and Education* and his personal participation in Dewey's seminars inspired the always inventive entrepreneur to want to try an experiment in the assimilation and Americanization of recent immigrants that would focus on the practical realization of Dewey's ideas concerning education for democracy.

"The experience of the seminar," he told the philosopher, "has increased my wish to see your philosophy made dynamic in its democratizing possibilities, instead of the present intellectually attractive but, nevertheless, static system." Bertrand Russell was right: Dewey was "empirical" and was always tantalized by the idea that philosophy might be translated into immediate social betterment. When that possibility was packaged by a powerful, persuasive, somewhat hare-brained personality, Dewey tended to fall into line. But what sort of project would be suitable for an experiment arising from *Democracy and Education*? Barnes fastened on four of Dewey's current passions. Three of these—democracy, education, and politics—were continuing passions; one, the assimilation of immigrants, was more recent. Barnes infused these with his own visionary idealism for social improvement.

At this time of crisis in America in 1918, the combination was, for Dewey, irresistible. Like Ford, Barnes told Dewey that he had a project in mind that would offer Dewey "a good chance to put to the pragmatic test some of the principles in . . . [*Democracy and Education*] and determine whether they are what I think, namely, sensible, practical ideas, or whether they are the musings of a mere college professor." Then he sprang his idea. As Brand Blanshard understood the purpose, it was a "simple one; here [in Philadelphia] was a large colony of Poles retaining the ideas and mores of the fatherland and to that extent resisting assimilation [into] . . . their new society. Why?" Barnes was sure that the question could be answered and that, in Dewey's spirit, methods to achieve democratization could be developed. Action would follow to hasten and improve assimilation. Enthusiastically, he told Dewey: "When we finish [the first] . . . job, there are so many similar ones of even greater importance to get busy with that I think it will not take long to do some real, intelligent, and honest work for the advancement of civilization." Barnes was ready to go. His enthusiasm (and a financial stipend) brought Dewey's graduate students into the project. Their initial experiment would be carried out in Philadelphia, beginning in the summer of 1918. In Philadelphia's "Little Poland" there was an insulated group of mostly Catholic Polish immigrants.

They spoke Polish, retained their Polish customs, dressed as they did in the Old World, kept to themselves, and organized their lives around the Catholic Church and the local clergy. Here, then, was a perfect laboratory in which to test Dewey's ideas, by examining the process by which immigrants might be democratized in America. The project also touched directly on Dewey's long-term interest in the work of settlement houses, beginning with Hull House and continuing, in New York, with Columbia University's Settlement House uptown, Mary Simkhovitch's Greenwich House, and Lillian Wald's famous Henry Street Settlement downtown. He had been at home in Hull House and these others, and he expected to feel comfortable in the Polish section of Philadelphia. Dewey's graduate students would be hired at $100 a month each. Daily they would examine the Poles under the microscope. Frances Bradshaw would study the ideas of education held by the residents; Brand Blanshard, their religion; his brother Paul Blanshard, their social customs; and Irwin Edman, their general intellectual, aesthetic, and neighborhood activities. Dewey would choose his own topic for study after he surveyed the scene. The plan was that each of the investigators would work independently but all would be centrally concerned with the education and assimilation of foreign elements. Two local residents were hired as translators. Barnes got busy. When they could not get a house to rent as a base, he simply bought one with six bedrooms to serve as offices. He hired a cook and rented furniture.

A young woman, Mrs. Arnold Levitas, was also hired to act as an adviser. She too had attended Dewey's seminar at Columbia, though she was not a graduate student. The final member of the investigatory group, she was to be chiefly concerned with "conditions affecting family life and women." Herself a fairly recent emigrant, she implied that she spoke Polish and could assist with translation. Her participation had come about accidentally. In December 1917 she had suddenly appeared at Dewey's office to seek his help in securing a permanent, full-time teaching post in the New York City school system. She explained that she had learned to be a vocational teacher of cooking at the Clara de Hirsch Home for Working Girls in New York City and that she had a diploma from Columbia Teachers College. She had taught domestic science three years earlier, but disillusioned with teaching, she had resigned her job with no warning. Possibly, the authorities held this sudden resignation against her and regarded her as unreliable. Possibly, too, her previous frequent absences for sickness or "nerves" had also been recorded. In any event, now that she had reapplied she was refused a regular post and offered only low-paid substitute teaching. The Board of Education, she complained, had treated her prejudicially. Dewey was in the mood to suspect the board of (in Beard's phrase) "no little anti-Semitism," for several Jewish teachers had recently been fired and Mrs. Levitas was Jewish. For her part, she had read about his speech just a week before in support of the three terminated instructors. In his talk Dewey had said, "it is not the teachers who are under indictment; it is the method of administering the public-school system of New York City in relation to the teachers." She believed he would respond to her plea, and he did. She needed a decent job, she explained, to sustain herself while she wrote fiction. In support of her claim, she handed Dewey one of the stories she had already published, "The Free Vacation House," and another about-to-be-published tale, "While Lovers Dream." Clearly, she looked to the great man to be her mentor in the new world, as her later fictionalized and certainly idealized picture of their first encounter shows:

> His noble head and fine gray eyes contrasted . . . with a slip-shod appearance—clothes worn, . . . , pockets bulging with papers, tie crooked. . . . He looked like a small-town lawyer or tradesman, but [my] . . . fanatic idealism made him the symbol of all [I] . . . could never be. He was free of [the] . . . sordid bondage for bread. He was culture, leisure, the freedom and glamour of the "Higher Life."

She appealed to him to follow her downtown, watch her teach, and testify to the board that she was competent in the classroom. Dewey's opinion, she knew, would have some weight.

He agreed. At a downtown elementary school where she was sub-stitute teaching, she improvised a cooking class for a hastily gathered group of girls. At its conclusion, he declared her to be undoubtedly qualified for a regular job. But then he refused to support her for a position. "I wish you well," he said, "but I don't wish you to be a teacher. Something creative, yes, but a teacher, no." He promised to improve upon her request by bringing one of her stories to his friend Herbert Croly, editor of the *New Republic*, and helping start her career. He even gave her a typewriter, the first one she owned, and urged her to devote her energies to writing fiction. Finally, he allowed her to attend a few sessions of his graduate seminar on "Ethics and Educational Problems" during the spring semester.

Dewey gave her the push she needed. Croly published "Soap and Water and the Immigrant," presenting her, in Mary Dearborn's words, as "a genuine immigrant fresh from the ghetto of New York's Lower East Side." With this start, other editors began to accept her stories. When Barnes suggested the Philadelphia project, Dewey naturally thought of Mrs. Levitas: she seemed to have the requisite qualifica-tions, and the study would give her an income and might provide her with additional material for her fiction. At first, in April 1918, Barnes was dubious. Dewey had given him the manuscript of Mrs. Levitas's story "Soap and Water and the Immigrant," and it troubled Barnes. "I would like to meet the Polish woman whose manuscript you gave me," he wrote Dewey, "and try to form an opinion as to whether the abnor-malities she manifests in the article would be against her as one of the workers in Philadelphia." "Please tell Mr. Dewey," Barnes wrote to Alice at the end of April 1918, "that what he has written me about the Polish-Jew makes me think that we most certainly do want her to work here in Philadelphia, and that I hope to see the woman . . . at his office in Columbia." Apparently, Barnes was satisfied by their inter-view in Dewey's office two days later. For the summer of 1918 she lived at their office on Richmond Street and was paid the same $100 a month as the others, courtesy of the Barnes fortune. Barnes actually hired Anzia Levitas in May, in advance of the others to do preparatory work, housing her in temporary quarters near the project house, which would not be available until June 1. She started to work, and Barnes told Dewey with satisfaction that "the ferret and the bee have nothing on Mrs. Levitas."

The Polish study considered as a whole proved or disproved nothing about the pragmatic validity of *Democracy and Education*. It was too loosely organized, each member going his or her own way. When the project began, Dewey was away delivering a series of lectures at Stanford University and helping Alice find a house in San Francisco for the fall semester when he would be teaching at Berkeley. After giving his Stanford lectures, he left California on June 23, went to Portland, Oregon, to see his brother Charles Miner and then rested a while at Glacier House in British Columbia, finally stopping in Detroit to visit Sabino. When he arrived in Philadelphia in early July, he made little attempt to achieve investigatory coherence or to formulate a team plan for the investigators. The group thus continued to function like a graduate seminar rather than an organized study. None of the investigators had the slightest training in field research. Indeed, Paul Blanshard distributed a questionnaire that was so poorly composed that it caused considerable friction. Only one little booklet emerged from the student researchers, Brand Blanshard's "The Church and the Polish Immigrant," but its publication was delayed until the end of the war when his military service was completed, and it evoked no echo in the other workers. Barnes himself published a pamphlet by Dewey, "Conditions Among the Poles in the United States" (1918).

In late June, Barnes, who had been loosely supervising the project, sent a report to Dewey, who was still in San Francisco. He had left the researchers "free," he wrote, "to develop their own methods," meeting with them about twice a week for "a general talk." They were "young and totally without experience." Barnes was deeply suspicious of what he called "academitis," by which he meant thinking without relation to function. He called the graduate students "autistic." Edman, he said, was "far and away the best of the lot," but even he lacked "a clear and comprehensive idea of what we are trying to do." Brand was the next best, but he was too metaphysical. Paul, a minister, was full of "B.S." Frances "can recite what she has read and not see the relations between things." As for Mrs. Levitas, she "is an artist and, as Santayana says, to criticize her would be of the same degree of irrationality as to criticize the color of a child's eyes."

When Dewey at long last arrived on July 8, he found the research project in disarray. He told Alice, who was with Jane in San Francisco, that "there have been personal difficulties—among the 'workers' and between Mr. Barnes and myself. . . . I think Mr. B. now understands where the line is drawn between the work and personalities, and that he will be more subdued." Dewey's way of quieting the chaos was to turn it into a discussion group. In the evenings, Brand Blanshard remembered, Dewey usually typed out an article for the *New Republic* or *The Nation* and then at breakfast read it to his researchers for their criticisms. After breakfast, each would go his own way among the Poles. Dewey typically spent his days interviewing residents concerning the political conflicts in the Polish community. At supper the group might discuss the sociological studies of Polish immigrants by W. I. Thomas and Florina Znaniecki. When they began examining the Poles' group psychology, Dewey recommended Wilfred Trotter's *Instincts of the Herd in Peace and War*, whereas Barnes favored Lyman Wells's *Mental Adjustment*s: "the best compilation of the psychological principles which dominate the unconscious." For their own physical well-being, Dewey suggested F. Matthias Alexander's *Man's Supreme Inheritance*.

ALEXANDER'S INFLUENCE ON DEWEY

It is worth pausing here over the person of Alexander and his place in Dewey's life. From his youth Dewey had been plagued with psychophysiological problems—eyestrain, back pains, a painfully sore neck—which flared up whenever he was under such stress as he had been experiencing recently. In 1916 his friend James Harvey Robinson introduced him to F. Matthias Alexander, with the recommendation that Dewey seek therapeutic relief from him. Alexander's understanding of psychophysiological distress was quite different from Freud's emphasis on unconscious conflicts. Dewey's own psychological experiments in his laboratory and his concept of the adjustive arc made it unnecessary for him to accept the idea of the unconscious and so left him acquainted with but indifferent to Freud. But Alexander's view was congenial to Dewey's own. In a preface that Dewey wrote in 1918 for a reprint of *Man's Supreme Inheritance*, he explained the "Alexander method": "the crisis in the physical and mental health of the individual [is] produced by the conflict between the functions of the brain and the nervous system on the one side and the functions of digestion, circulation, respiration, and the muscular system on the other." Alexander tried to unify these systems in a series of laboratory-like sessions by reeducating the patient's physical system through adjustments of breathing and posture. For Dewey the treatments of 1916–17 were important. He was not only mostly relieved from pain, but also he found in the Alexander method a practical confirmation of his own psychology. For inclusion in the brief biography of Dewey officially composed by Jane, John wrote: "My theories of mind-body, of the coordination of the active elements of the self and of the place of ideas in inhibition and control of overt action required [for confirmation] contact with the work of F. M. Alexander."

Dewey's personal estimation of how much Alexander had helped him was confirmed when he met with Ella Flagg Young in late August 1918. They had not seen each other for more than a decade, but she said at once that physically he "was a radically changed person." Not surprisingly, Dewey referred several of his own children to Alexander for treatment, and he remained committed to him. He had not been overly distressed when Randolph Bourne had excoriated his own politics in 1917, but in 1918, when Bourne, in an oblique attack on Dewey, savaged Alexander's book, Dewey accused Bourne of completely misunderstanding Alexander's thesis. In a private letter to Bourne, Dewey wrote that he was bewildered by Bourne's "almost incredible bias" in his argument against Alexander and tried to explain at length the difference between Alexander's approach and psychoanalysis. When Bourne died late in 1918, the Deweys reflected sadly on his short life. He "gave proof of real talent," Alice told Evelyn, but she also believed that had he lived longer, his life "would have been an experience of increasing bitterness."

A Philadelphia Story

One event occurred that summer that might have produced enough stress to test the efficacy of Alexander's work, except that Dewey expressed his strained emotions through poetry rather than painful posture and eye problems. In 1918 he was a famous philosopher, a renowned educator, a married man of nearly fifty-eight, and the parent of four grown children—and he found himself in love with his coworker Anzia Levitas, who also was married. Intent on a literary career, she had left her husband and daughter, and apparently, in a wholly fantasized way she fell in love with Dewey. In fact, he was such a fantasy to her that it could be said that she loved him before she met him. Clearly, she idealized Dewey as having and being all she could never have and never be. His characteristically generous response to her—the same sort he had given to hundreds of others—cemented her adoration. For Dewey, the immediacy and intensity of his emotional response to her might be thought surprising until we remember the tremendous outrush of emotions that the young instructor in philosophy had had for Alice Chipman, his future wife. In the spring of 1918, away from Alice, separated more than usual from the children, concerned about Fred's military service, worried that Sabino might be drafted, and obviously adored by a young woman, his affections were set afire.

"Mrs. Arnold Levitas" published under her maiden name, Anzia Yezierska. She was soon to become famous. In 1919, the well-known anthologist Edward O'Brien selected one of her stories as the best of the year. The stories that Dewey had helped her place were collected in 1920 in *Hungry Hearts*, published by Houghton Mifflin and reprinted by Grosset & Dunlap. Always on the lookout for new properties, Sam Goldwyn bought the rights to *Hungry Hearts* and quickly produced a successful silent film based on it. Yezierska had one theme in all her works: the confrontation between the hungry heart of the poor immigrant woman and the well-bred but cold intellectualism of the established Yankee man. Even before she knocked on Dewey's door, this was an old story for her, and Dewey neatly slipped into place as a character in her personal scenario. Over and over again, in her earliest stories, written while she was still in contact with Dewey, as well as in her later novels and memoir, she played out the themes of their encounters. Occasionally the scenario reaches a happy conclusion, but mostly the vast differences between the immigrant girl and her ideal lead to disappointment. "The Miracle," written during the summer of 1918, ends positively and probably reflected her hopes at that time. In it Sara Reisel, full of hope, emigrates to America from Poland. She experiences only disillusion until she attends a night-school class. The teacher is "so much above" her, he "wasn't a man to me at all. He was a god," she thinks. She yearns to be like him, cool, composed, and rational: a true Yankee. But as it turns out, he yearns to be like her. "You can save me from my coldness," he tells her. "You can free me from the bondage of age long repressions . . . you are fire and sunshine and desire." The immigrant and the Puritan American meet—and melt into each other.

Her novel *All I Can Never Be* explicitly and closely portrays the Dewey-Barnes Polish project of 1918. The Polish heroine receives a letter from the philosopher Henry Scott, who is the author of a Deweyan book, *The Meaning of Democracy*. One striking passage leaves no doubt that she truly and accurately transcribed what Dewey said to her, for the phrasing and exuberant tone reproduce precisely the same tone and attitude as Dewey's love letters to Alice during their courtship. It is very likely that she was quoting from one of the letters from Dewey that she saved and copied after he asked her to return them. Henry Scott is writing to the heroine:

> You are beautifully communicative in simply being. You are, but you don't yet fully know that you are. You feel as if you wanted to be. You suffer from striving, but it is unnecessary. You are already. And perhaps I can have the great happiness

of helping you to a realization that you are, and what you are. You do not have to reach, or strive, or try to achieve or accomplish. You already are. I repeat it a million times to you, my dear spirit. It only remains for you to do. . . . All things of the spirit are yours, now.

Henry Scott also sends the Polish translator, Tanya Ivanowna, a poem entitled "Generations":

Generations as yet unuttered, dumb, smothered,
Inchoate, unutterable by me and mine,
In you I see them coming to be,
Luminous, slow revolving, ordered in rhythm.
You shall not utter them. You shall be them,
And from out the pain
A great song shall fill the world.

Because Jo Ann Boydston, the general editor of the complete Dewey edition, so expertly edited Dewey's poems, found after his death, we know that this poem was actually written by Dewey and sent to Yezierska. He placed himself in her scenario precisely, and she used his poem expertly. Clearly, their relationship was intense, full of mutual fantasies. Her fantasy was formed before she met Dewey but was suddenly concretized in him: that America—experienced by her as cold, withholding, and aloof—would suddenly embrace her passionately. His fantasy interlocked with hers. His puritanical upbringing, his shyness with women, and his reticence as an academic left him always ready to find a way to allow his own loving emotions to break through. Such a highly charged emotional life was opposite his identity but identical with his desire. He could be fired into passion by Alice; reading a mere report on grueling conditions for workers could inspire him to think about dynamiting capitalists; he could involve himself completely in such daffy schemes as "thought news"; he could resign a distinguished professorship suddenly; he could spontaneously adopt an

Italian boy; and he could be profoundly stirred by the adoration of a passionate woman. Dewey remained a rational philosopher until a flicker of love shimmered on the horizon.

That Anzia herself was passionate—and especially a passionate fantasist—in precisely the way that she describes her heroines to be is clear. After the Polish project had started but before Dewey joined the group, Barnes wrote to him in California:

> Anzia, like the true artist that she is, keeps aloof from the science [of sociological research] which she detests, and spends considerable time in her room building phantasies, some of which she is putting into stories and a novel, and some into my private ear, that she is not appreciated by the others; but her compensation is the statement that you will appreciate the kind of work she is doing.

From a less sympathetic point of view, Brand Blanshard saw her as "something of a flibbertigibbet, full of enthusiasms and repulsions, but lacking steadiness and balance of judgment." He would take any of her claims, he said, "with a good deal of salt," even if made in a "factual report." Apparently, in 1918 Blanshard even made this opinion known to her, for she used it years later in *All I Can Never Be*, when one of the members of the study group complains that Tanya "has no sense of proportion . . . no discrimination." Blanshard was close to the mark. Even Yezierska's daughter remembered her as a "dazzling, stunning volcano of a person. . . . romantic, impatient, childlike, excitable and exciting."

Yezierska fashioned several stories, novels, and an autobiography out of her brief encounter with Dewey; the passion between them was a literary, not a sexual, episode. Yezierska's stories and memoir clearly indicate that nothing physical, not even a kiss, occurred. But in her fantasies, and surely to a degree in his, a romance was ignited. Nearly all Dewey's acquaintances testify to his ready compassion. His empathy allowed him to fall easily into the pattern of her fantasy—seeing her as warm and vibrant and himself as restrained and rule-ridden. In a second Dewey poem, "I Wake from the Long, Long Night," which

Yezierska attributed to another Deweyan character, he refers to himself as "joyless, griefless" and bound by "a silken web" of "duties." While in fact Dewey experienced both joy and grief, he was empathetically writing of himself as he knew she saw him.

Dewey's restraint had, of course, more real and immediate causes than the Yankee aloofness so compelling in Yezierska's fantasies. He was married and devoted to Alice; he had children and adored them; and his own personal morals made anything but a literary expression of sexual love unthinkable outside marriage. But imaginative fantasy was more than acceptable to him, and as he had done before and would do afterward, he composed poetry to express his emotions. He noted approvingly in a later book, *Art as Experience*, that Edmund Spenser had described poetry as "the world's sweet inn from pain and wearisome turmoil." Dewey could as easily have said this of his own poetry. But in the poems to Anzia, Dewey repeatedly made one thing clear: their passion was to have no aftermath. In "Two Weeks," he was apparently responding to an accusation from Anzia that he was resisting the deepening of romantic relations with her because he feared that if his marriage broke up he would suffer a material loss:

Riches, possessions hold me? Nay,
Not rightly have you guessed
The things that block the way,
Nor into what ties I've slowly grown
By which I am possessed.

"Who makes has," he adds. Even in the midst of powerful emotions, Dewey's ethical imperatives were clear. A few lines later he repeats, "What I am to anyone is but a loan / From those who made, and own." Parents, mentors, a wife, children, friends, influences—all those who "made" him—render him unavailable to any new love that would dispossess the old ones. His earliest loves made him and now they own him.

What Anzia owned and made of Dewey was a powerful memory and the creation of a character eminently usable for dramatic fiction. She had concentrated on him so wholly that she seems to have remembered his conversations verbatim many years later. She even quoted one of his addresses to the National Education Association in 1916 as part of President Irvine's comments to Sophie Sapinsky in "To the Stars" (1921) and alluded to several of its passages in the speeches of her characters. And she adapted a poem he sent her, "I Wake from the Long, Long Night," for use in her memoir, *Red Ribbon on a White Horse*.

The summer study broke up at the end of August. Yezierska returned to New York and found temporary work in a restaurant. Dewey went to the farm that he had bought years earlier in Huntington, Long Island. He saw Anzia briefly in the middle of September, at which time he apparently asked her to return his letters. She eventually did so, but not before she copied at least some of them. Then on September 25, Dewey left for San Francisco and never saw or corresponded with her again. When *Hungry Hearts* appeared in 1920, the first person she requested to be sent a free copy was Dewey. When it became clear that there was no possibility of a continuing romantic relation between her and Dewey, Yezierska's passionate devotion to him turned just as passionately adversarial. In 1921, she was able to persuade the review editor of *The Bookman* to let her review *Democracy and Education*, which Dewey had published five years earlier. In her review she wrote that this "giant of the intellect—this pioneer . . . in philosophy has so suppressed the personal life in himself that his book is devoid of the intimate, self-revealing touches that make writing human." Written so long after the book's publication, this review has all the earmarks of a deliberate and gratuitous attack on a person she once believed she loved.

Asked in the 1970s whether there had been some sort of romantic relation between Dewey and Yezierska, Blanshard responded: "This never so much as occurred to me, nor can I recollect any intimation of it from any others of our group." That may well be, for the most intense emotional involvement between the two occurred during late 1917 and the early spring of 1918. Dewey may have written some of the poems to Yezierska as early as December 1917, as hinted at in a letter he sent to the Kentucky poet Cale Young Rice, praising his "metaphysical" sonnets and declaring himself "piqued by the question as to how far poetry can become a medium of expression of ideas which are generally confined to rather arid prose." In the summer of 1918 he showed no special wish to join Anzia, for he did not hurry to join the group in Philadelphia. Anzia had worked there for a month and a half before he arrived. Indeed, during his return from California, when he visited Glacier Park, Alice and his children, not the waiting Anzia, were the persons he wanted to have with him. "If you were with me," he wrote to "Dear Family," " I don't believe we'd get home till everything froze up—and the money gave out." And "I wish we were all here, from west and east." Dewey had already planned to spend the fall term as a visiting professor at Berkeley and then to take a semester's sabbatical from Columbia.

Dewey's Interest in Poland

Shortly after Dewey joined the group in Philadelphia, he became much more involved than he could possibly have anticipated, not with Anzia, but with the political turmoil of the Polish community. He soon was deeply concerned with "Little Poland" as an international problem.

If any doubt existed concerning the depth of passion that Dewey could invest in research, his involvement in the study of the Polish community in Philadelphia would dispel it completely. Even before he arrived, reports from Barnes were calculated to fire his imagination. The local political leaders were not indifferent to the fact that the Columbia philosophers were studying "hot" areas of power and privilege. Hardly had Anzia Levitas started work, Barnes warned Dewey, than she encountered opposition from local Philadelphia politicians. It did not help her with the Catholic Poles that she was a New York Jew who did not speak Polish—they inferred (in a way, correctly) that she was an agent of the opposition. Barnes stormed in to see "the Grand Mogul of the political situation and told him in very unphilosophical language that if the three bastards who are opposing us did not immediately stop, they would be in jail within a week." That undiplomatic outburst cemented the opposition against the study group right at the outset. When the "Grand Mogul" saw to it that no house was available for rental, Barnes stepped in and simply bought one. He bluntly told Dewey that the Catholic Church was attempting to keep the poor immigrants ignorant, in "a condition of intellectual and physical serfdom." Here indeed was a place for Dewey's democratic education. Barnes's wish to see Dewey's philosophy realized in society soon grew into truly grandiose visions. When the study was completed, he told the philosopher, "we shall be in a position to go to President Wilson and say: 'Here's a practical working plan to convert your speeches' " from theory to fact. Shortly thereafter, bursting with pleasure, Barnes told Dewey that the group's research "is proving even more interesting and germane to your philosophy than I thought."

When Dewey arrived in Philadelphia, it was "like living in a whirlpool." He fired Paul Blanshard because his ideas in general and the survey he administered locally seemed likely to "sidetrack the inquiry" into issues of Catholicism. He quickly began his own investigation and soon became more energetic, more enthusiastic in his involvement, and more productive in his writing than any of his much younger students. Somewhat uncertainly, he began to interview leaders in the Polish community, and suddenly his topic opened up before him. Briefly, what he found was that the Polish diaspora contained two social and political parties, and they were at odds. One was Roman Catholic and conservative. Its leader—or at least its figurehead—was the famous musician Ignacy Paderewski who, with his equally influential and perhaps more active wife Helene, shuttled back and forth between America—especially Philadelphia, Chicago, and Detroit—and Paris. This group had strong alliances with the Catholic churchmen in these cities. The other group of Poles was liberal and largely Jewish, and its centers of power were in New York City and London. This second group, socialist in spirit, supported a range of progressive causes, but especially Wilsonian idealism and the Russian Revolution. Dewey perceived at once that the struggle of these two groups for political supremacy would help determine Poland's political direction in the postwar period.

The conservative group was winning the struggle for recognition by the U.S. government concerning which party would represent Poland and become legitimized as the Polish government once the war was over. Dewey quickly concluded that the insulation and isolation of the Polish community they were studying was the result of a deliberate plan by the pro-Paderewski forces, led by the Polish National Alliance, to keep the Poles separated from all that was American— and, by definition for Dewey (and Barnes), progressive. Through isolation, the immigrants could be controlled by the priests and a handful of leaders and thus manipulated to give support to Paderewski and the other conservative leaders who were jockeying for power. The local leaders also delivered the Polish vote to the Republican Party. More and more each day, Dewey's interest turned from the specifics of the local immigrant politics to the larger issues of Poland's postwar political fate. He and Barnes agreed in their disapproval of the reactionary side that had gained control in Philadelphia. In Barnes's words, the Barnes-Dewey group hoped to make the sort of critique that might succeed in eliminating the "forces alien to democratic internationalism and [instead] promote American ideals in accordance with the principles announced by President Wilson."

The local politicians became increasingly suspicious and, Dewey suspected, "frightened by even an appearance of an academic investigation." Based on the clattering of typewriters coming from the house, which was located near the shipyards, a report was made to the U.S. Department of Justice that these strangers might be spies. Barnes, who had studied in Germany and was still associated with German interests, was accused of pro-German activities. Dewey's earlier opposition to the war added to the suspicion and accusation. Both a Secret Service agent and the police came to the house asking questions. Their mail was opened and resealed before it was delivered. Far from restraining his interviews, Dewey forged ahead.

Before he had been back for three weeks, Dewey had seen enough to complete an article on the Polish situation. Entitled "Autocracy Under Cover," it appeared in the *New Republic* on August 24. But he wanted to do more than write articles; he wanted to make sure that in the postwar period American democratic ideals would be extended to

European nations. As a result, Dewey himself asked the editor of the *New Republic*, Herbert Croly, to help him get an appointment with Colonel E. M. House, President Wilson's military attaché, so that he could present the Polish situation to him accurately. Croly wrote to House that certainly Dewey needed no introduction: "His investigation has been so thorough and he himself is a man of such . . . ability (he is certainly the greatest living American philosopher) that what he has to say is entitled to the most careful consideration." House was vacationing in Manchester, Massachusetts, and Barnes was ready to have his chauffeur drive them there.

Events were rapidly unfolding. The Poles were to have a national convention in Detroit on August 26, and Dewey was intent on discovering which party, reactionary or radical, would take control. He believed that the pro-Paderewski group would emerge as dominant and that their intent would be to have Wilson promise to recognize a free and independent Poland and immediately "to constitute a certain committee of Poles in Paris as the official representative of the new gov't ignoring . . . all other factions." Indeed, the reactionary group had already induced one senator to introduce legislation along those lines. In Dewey's view, this would make postwar democracy in Poland impossible, and he gathered as much material as he could in order to persuade House and Wilson that Paderewski and his faction were dangerous. Dewey piled up data at a great rate, trying to leave no stone unturned. He persuaded Lucy in Huntington and Evelyn in New York to do research for him on the international Polish situation, and he wrote to Ella Flagg Young and Jane Addams for information about the Chicago contingent of Poles. In New York City he interviewed the U.S. leader of the Polish radicals. He arranged for Irwin Edman to attend the Detroit convention, and through Edman he made an appointment to see Paderewski on August 14. Suddenly the fate of Polish democracy had become the most important thing in the world to him. No wonder, as he told Alice, it all was "a jumble— . . . bald and simple in outline and yet intensely complicated and obscure in detail."

On August 9 he reported to Alice that he had had his meeting with Colonel House: "After waiting all the afternoon, [we] saw the Colonel for about twenty minutes. He is all his reputation makes him as an effective and affable listener—quick and responsive to points, but giving no more idea of any impression made on him than an oiled sphinx." It was a good thing, John told Alice, that his personal expectations were low, for "I don't think I got anywhere with him," he concluded.

In this Dewey was wrong. House took his report seriously and passed it on to the Army Intelligence Bureau. On August 16, Dewey was handed a telegram from Colonel M. Churchill from the Office of Military Intelligence asking him to come to Washington "immediately." All Saturday and Sunday Dewey spent in interviews, and then on Monday he was given a stenographer to whom he dictated a "confidential report." He spent Tuesday interviewing one representative of the radical faction and one of the conservative group. Both, he judged, were "honest men" and sophisticated intellectuals who spoke "all the known languages." To Dewey's complete surprise, he was asked to accept a captaincy "in the propaganda dept of the Intelligence Bureau." The Intelligence Office obviously had been impressed by his confidential report. Dewey speculated that perhaps the military thought he could be useful since "I [am] . . . in touch with all the dubious socialists in the country and might be able to influence them."

By the time Dewey arrived back in Philadelphia, the Columbia researchers were breaking camp. In the last week of August, only Frances Bradshaw stayed behind, volunteering to dispose of the material left in the house. Dewey sequestered himself at the Long Island farm and, drawing on his earlier dictation, composed a long report on the state of current Polish politics and their implications for the future. The conservative group had indeed won the day at the Detroit convention, and only his own report, he believed, would provide a truthful balance. Evelyn reported to her mother and sister that "Dad is certainly having an exciting time, and it doesnt seem to tire him."

His full report was not completed and printed until the end of September, when he forwarded six copies to Major H. T. Hunt of the Intelligence Office, with additional copies to each of several other officers who had been involved in the discussions during the five days he spent in Washington. A few days later he mailed a copy directly to President Wilson, alerting him to the "object of the project, the report, [which] . . . was to point out wherein the forces operative among Poles in the United States run counter to the American principles which you have so clearly set forth." In turn, Wilson requested a summary, which he received on October 3. The next day Wilson wrote to Dewey thanking him for his report. So after all, Barnes's outrageous speculation had been accurate. Near the conclusion of all this activity, Barnes reiterated his sense of the importance of Dewey's information, calling it "one of the most important contributions made to one of the most urgent of America's problems."

Dewey's relations with the Office of Military Intelligence continued even after he left for California. For instance, on November 6, Churchill, now a general, asked him to assess the Polish National Defense Committee (K.O.N.) meeting held in New York in late October: "We cannot altogether trust the newspaper reports and I am appealing to you to lend your good offices" to getting reliable information. The disappointing result of all of Dewey's labor and passion was not known until January 22, 1919, when the United States gave de jure recognition to the Paderewski government. By generalizing the international Polish situation as based on the local factions in Philadelphia, Dewey had in fact badly misconceived the problem. For he never understood that there was a third faction—the so-called General Pilsudski group—that was pro-German and hoped for a German victory that would allow Poland to ally with Germany and thereby escape Russia's control. Only the Paderewski Catholic faction, not the socialist group that Dewey supported, had enough power in America to swing Polish American efforts and Polish war volunteers to the Allied side against Germany. The independent Polish army, organized by Paderewski with fifteen thousand Polish American volunteers, was the core of the Polish movement for independence. It was no wonder, then, that the U.S. government authorized the Polish National Committee as the only body that could certify individual Poles as loyal to the United States and thus make way for U.S. citizenship for Polish aliens. In the complex swirl of postwar politics, the Dewey position was declared to be idealistic but "impractical."

But by the time this happened, Dewey's eyes were turned away from Europe and Wilson's various capitulations and compromises. He was looking west from Berkeley, California, preparing to cross the Pacific to Japan.

BOOK III

Engagement

Dewey's tentative plan to give a series of lectures in Japan had formed early in 1917 when a Professor Fukusaki of the University of Tokyo proposed to try to get him an invitation to lecture there sometime in 1918–19. Dewey had let the possibility of this plan slip out when he responded to W. E. Hocking's invitation to become a visiting professor at Harvard: "I have laid certain plans . . . which I hope . . . would take me to Japan." A little later, this prospect of a semester lecturing in Japan in the spring of 1919 kept him from moving with Beard, Robinson, and Thorstein Veblen to the New School for Social Research, and it influenced many of his decisions throughout 1917 and the first half of 1918. Dewey asked whether Benjamin Ide Wheeler, president of the University of California at Berkeley, would renew his offer of a term there as a visiting professor. Wheeler was happy to invite Dewey to teach there in the fall of 1918, which also made it possible for him to offer a lecture series at Stanford in May and June 1918. These lectures, which Dewey seemed to take so lightly, proved to be important, for eventually they became the basis for one of his best books, *Human Nature and Conduct*. But in the spring of 1918, he was too hurried to complete the book: he gave the lectures, filed them away for future reconsideration, banked his fee, and rushed back to Philadelphia.

In fact, Dewey was concerned about money. He had always been concerned about money, for the Deweys had always been close to being poor. At a time when every middle-class professional had a maid, the Deweys could not afford one until the birth of their sixth child made a servant almost obligatory. Six children were a constant drain on a professor's salary. For a long time the Deweys did not even have a telephone and had to rely on a neighbor to call them to his phone. A collection was taken up in Fenton to buy the children shoes. Whatever money could be saved was set aside for books or European trips, years apart, not as vacations, but as periodic extensions of knowledge. No wonder John bargained hard for good salaries at Michigan and Chicago. In 1895, he became extremely agitated over the fact that Wahr and Phillips, which had published his *Ethics* syllabus, owed him $73.60. Although he was a distinguished philosopher, he was almost impoverished. The move to Columbia was a financial blow, and even with all his extra teaching, it took him ten years to get back to a salary that had the buying power of his salary in Chicago. Even as recently as 1914, Alice commented to John about his heavy schedule of lecturing: "Of course, the money is always needed. That's the worst of it, and that is what drives you so."

A tour of Japan beckoned. He was on sabbatical with half-pay. How much would the trip cost? Where would the money come from? Always generous where his affections lay, Barnes recognized Dewey's plight and proposed paying Dewey a monthly stipend for him "to make a report on Japan as a factor in the future international situation." Along with a promise from the *New Republic* that he would be guaranteed a monthly stipend for his articles on Japanese culture and politics, added to the royalties that were now coming in regularly, he would be secure financially for four or five months. If Professor Fukusaki or Dewey's old friend from Michigan, Ono Eijirô, were able to arrange for Dewey to get an official invitation to lecture in Japan, that would further help pay expenses. This meant simply that he could go to Japan. But why did he *want* to go to Japan?

True, the children played a part in the idea, for 1919 was the earliest time that he and Alice could get off alone, without the expense or care of the children. Sabino had a job. Fred was in the army. Evelyn was settled in a career in New York. Lucy would graduate from Barnard in December, and in the fall of 1918 his youngest child Jane would be a freshman at Berkeley. After he and Alice stayed near Jane during the semester he spent at Berkeley, she presumably would have settled in. For the first time, the Deweys were free to go away for an extended period. Moreover, he would be away from Columbia and New York where there had been so many difficulties to deal with. He also would not be under pressure to respond daily to the political chaos of the war's aftermath, especially the anticipated restrictions on progressive ideas. By November 1918, Dewey was already disillusioned with Wilson's leadership and very pessimistic about the results of the war. "The situation is disquieting," he wrote to Samuel H. Goldenson, "Wilson's real test of character is yet to come; whether he is already weakening and hedging to get the appearance of victory for his aims, when the reality is being seriously encroached upon, it is hard to tell." But Dewey inclined to believe that at the end, democratic idealism would not be heightened by the war. It was also true, as he recalled for John D. Graves years later, that in 1918 he himself had become depressed: "I had got in a rut or the doldrums." These all counted as minor motives, but none explains why Dewey found the prospect of going abroad so compelling.

The reason was Alice.

Two of the Deweys' children had died in Europe, first Morris and then Gordon, who had in a sense, taken Morris's place. Although John was still sad, Alice was truly depressed, and her depressions determined many decisions in Dewey's life. Thus the decision to go to Asia was at least partly related to Alice's almost unremittingly dark moods.

ALICE'S DEPRESSION

Alice had a lifelong history of depression. Her father mourned himself to death after her mother died when Alice was four years old. As very young children she and her sister watched him fade away, day by day, until he simply took a last breath, died, and made them orphans. All her life Alice kept the few letters she had from her father, which tell a pathetic story. In April or May 1863, Alice's mother, Lucy Riggs Chipman, gave birth to her third child in Fentonville, Michigan. After a month's illness, she died on June 5. Gordon O. Chipman, left with three children, was inconsolable. He managed to hold himself together during the daytime, but when the night fell he became the sort of melancholic that Edward Young and the other "graveside poets" wrote about in the mid-eighteenth century. A hired girl was watching Augusta, Harriet Alice, and the baby. Gordon slept in his office and took his meals at a hotel. Uncared for, the baby, Alice's younger sister, did not thrive and died on August 7, 1863. Virtually abandoned, the two remaining children merely survived. Gordon's melancholy continued unassuaged. Early in 1864, he moaned to his mother: "Tonight after tea the weather being so pleasant I walked out to the home of the Dead. Oh it does me good to visit that sacred spot and there pour out my heart." Alice turned to religion, attending church and Sunday school. She needed some consolation. "She was much pleased with it and wants to go regular," her father mentioned. "Oh I wish she could." But if she prayed for her father's health, neither that nor his incessant visiting of the home of the Dead did him any good, for he died before Alice turned six. She stopped going to church and was taken in by her mother's parents.

Evaline, her grandmother, provided an anchor in her life, but it was her grandfather Fred Riggs whom she idealized. Indeed, just as Fred had been described as a "moody loner" perfectly suited to the life of a solitary frontiersman or miner, so Alice was often similarly described as moody, discontented, and hypercritical. Like him, Alice found solace only in motion.

She was like this even before she met John Dewey. On the surface she seemed strong and her intellectual brilliance seemed to confirm this impression, but there was a brittle part of her that sometimes cracked open and dropped her into depression. When Alice entered the University of Michigan, she found a place and the kind of intellectual work that eased her depressive moods, but even so she attended irregularly and took six years to graduate. Leaving Fentonville when she married made little change in her, although the excitement of having a partner and then children covered over her deeper grief. Although she tried to suppress it, it occasionally surfaced. She loved traveling. But when, for instance, she went to Europe in 1894, her self-recriminations started immediately. John was afraid to see them emerge, but he was more worried about her guilt, and he advised her once: "Don't reproach yourself for letting your troubles ooze out and don't cease to do it in the future."

Morris's death hit her hard, and she barely recovered from it through the distractions of her new work as principal of the University of Chicago Laboratory Elementary School. Then President Harper and she began their acrimonious disputes, which ended her work. Soon thereafter, Gordon died. Dewey's student Max Eastman wrote that after Gordon's death,

> she fell gradually into a habit of resentment. She grew caustic where she had been keen, captious where she had been critical. Her health began to decline. . . . The less she could do herself, the more her perfectionism, her insistence upon everybody's doing his best and doing it just right, turned into a vice of Pironical nagging.

Others diagnosed the cause differently but saw the same result as Eastman did. Adolf E. Meyer referred to the fact that "her resentment at Harper's unjust treatment [of her] never cooled, and gradually her erstwhile wit and charm turned to acid."

By 1896, Alice appeared to be clinically depressed. She wished she were dead. "My whole existence," she wrote, "is passed in screwing my self up to standing the next week. It doesn't pay. There is no telling what may transpire in the next week." By now John was familiar with these dark moods. In 1897 he tried to help her out of her "discouragement" by reminding her not to let it get a hold on her: "As we have frequently discovered, it is the worst of policy to get so deep in a hole that it doesn't seem worth while to get out." Perhaps, he suggested, it would help her to take a little jaunt from their cottage in Keene, where she was so miserable, to Lake Placid, a resort area nearby. He knew that traveling was one of the few things that could cheer her up, and she went. But exactly a month later she was showing new signs of "discouragement," and John gave her the same prescription: "getting off for a good long change and rest."

During the last months of her pregnancy with Lucy, in March 1900, Alice was severely depressed—and once again took the "travel cure." John took care of Fred, Gordon, and Lucy while Alice took Evelyn on a trip to Georgia, Florida, and New Orleans. When her usual guilty recriminations reappeared, John comforted her: "The thing for you to do is to get thoroughly rested . . . from the babies awhile." But Alice got little pleasure from the trip.

From this time on, Alice regularly complained of exhaustion. She had planned to resume teaching once she got to New York, but after her return from Europe it was not until 1907 that she was able to prepare an outline for a course on "Elementary Education . . . Methods: Their Theory and Practice" at the School of Liberal Arts and Sciences for Non-Residents. Alice taught the course only once, however, and fell back into the depression that manifested itself as exhaustion. In 1909 she consulted a doctor about her fatigue, but neither he nor anyone else understood that it was depression that sapped her strength. Concerned, Evelyn wrote from Honolulu: "I'm afraid it has been terribly hard for mother. I don't understand very well about her being run down before, was there anything definite [about] this matter, and is it something which will probably last always?" John's best explanation was that moving from Chicago to New York had damaged her will: "The idea of starting all over again . . . was too much for mamma."

The next year Alice was on the move again, taking Lucy and Jane to Europe, where she found a school for them in Switzerland and then traveled through Italy with Evelyn. But when she got there, she realized that she was making an invalid of herself: "I seem to have cut myself off from the useful life for about three months more," and this depressing thought spoiled the trip and left her more depressed than when she began it. Alice drifted in her life, caring for the children but without her original passion. Occasionally when she was challenged, her old spirit revived, as in the case of Maxim Gorky and in her advocacy of female suffrage. Her phrase to describe her life was "fiddling around in the usual way." Like her grandfather, she traveled restlessly.

By the summer of 1918 she was in a bad way. "I have been through some hard times in my life," she wrote to Evelyn, "but for concentrated dull misery of a fruitless sort this summer goes ahead of anything I can remember." She went to the movies to be entertained but left the theater with the feeling that cinema "is really as stupid as it looks from the outside . . . most of the stupidity is so labored as to be painful." After Dewey had gotten her and Jane settled in San Francisco, hardly a month passed when she was already discontented and restless, thinking of moving to Berkeley. Then she considered moving back to New York. She wondered what to do "in case the present is a failure." When John left California to begin his project in Philadelphia, she "was so depressed at first as to be rather incapacitated." She told John that she was convinced of "the hopelessness of anticipating anything humane from the future." The war also hit her hard, for she obsessed about the mass slaughter of young boys. Such thoughts made her "so depressed . . . as to be rather incapacitated." She dreaded that Sabino was doomed. He would, she imagined, be drafted and slaughtered. She told Evelyn that "my mind has become numb these weeks as the result of constant repressions."

Gordon was still very much on her mind. John and Alice met the San Francisco sculptor Benny Bufano and showed him Gordon's photo and death mask, asking Bufano "to make a good high relief" of his face. Alice also worried about the other children. She feared that Jane seemed hopelessly depressed. When would Fred be released from the service? What would happen to Lucy if Evelyn got a roommate and left her sister all alone in Long Island or New York? Would Evelyn be able to complete her book on her own? Where and how would Sabino live, and would he be drafted? Fred and his wife Elizabeth had had a baby, and she wanted to see it. Confused and indecisive, she thought of simply returning home, even though John was scheduled to teach the fall term in California. "I feel something as if I died," she told Lucy, "and was hearing of these things . . . from another world." John might be blue, but Alice plunged into blackness. Whether she stayed or went, it would look to her like one more instance of "my 'fool impulses.' " Although Lucy was nearly three thousand miles away, she sensed from Alice's letters that her thoughts were "disjointed." In the fall her distress was obvious. Alice spoke of the "collapse of my feelings," and everyone knew what that meant.

All this made Alice wonder whether even John's plan to go to Japan for a term was sound: "One begins to wonder," she confided to Fred and Elizabeth, "why go to a strange and expensive land for troubles we have always with us." The very excursion that he had planned to help ease her discontent now was causing her grief. But he persevered, and at last Alice became reconciled to going, determined to make the best of the trip. In her usual studious way she began to read up on Japanese civilization and especially Japanese art. This was just what John had hoped for, to find something that would engage her personal attention, something besides brooding about their dead children and worrying about their living ones. Alice needed something of her own instead of the reactive life into which she had fallen. And something positive, not the sort of protest that had merely masked her depression as a young girl, even before she had met John. In the fall, John watched with guarded optimism as Alice slowly turned to the task of becoming, as she called it, a "connoisseur" of Asian art. Benny Bufano led her to stores of Asian antiques in San Francisco, and she read all the books that she could find. Periodically, her spirits flagged when she allowed herself to drift into depression in the mornings, but her work brought her back.

ON TO JAPAN

A few days after Christmas, when a cablegram arrived confirming Dewey's invitation to lecture at Tokyo Imperial University, he himself suddenly became regretful, worrying about the children and how they would manage without their parents' constant attention. "The time seems short now and I have sinkings of heart to think we are to be so far away from you all. To wish you a happy new year seems so little in comparison with the love I would send you that it is hard to put it down." He felt that he should leave enough money in the United States for the support of all the children. "If the stock market should have an inflation . . . I'll be all right," he told Barnes. He was particularly worried about Sabino, who had joined them in California, because the boy had never been legally adopted. Now he tried to do so but discovered that California law required a year's residence first. Nonetheless John was determined to go to Japan for a few months, and they left on January 23 for Honolulu.

As early as 1884, when Herbert Baxter Adams brought a speaker into his seminary who had lived in China for forty years, Dewey had been interested in the possible development of democracy in Asia. Indeed, Adams's guest speaker had "called attention [to] the prevalence of democratic ideas among the Chinese." At both the University of Chicago and Columbia, Dewey had attracted a considerable number of students from Japan and China, and from the first, he had shown a special interest in them. Partly because of his worldwide fame but mainly because he was a well-known sponsor of Asian students and the only major American philosopher interested in Asian philosophy, Dewey was warmly greeted in Japan. Upon arriving in Tokyo, he and Alice took a room at the famous Imperial Hotel, but after five days, they moved to Dr. and Mrs. Nitobe Inago's house, as they were soon leaving for France. Alice was very glad to save the astonishingly high hotel expense and then, in addition, to learn that "the University will pay very well for the lectures, so," she told the girls, "you need to have no anxiety about our money and Bino need not send on any money that he may accumulate." In addition, Mrs. Nitobe was an American and a Quaker and gave Alice a quick sketch of Japan's "small feminist movement."

Alice was in for a series of surprises. Everything fascinated her. "It is more exciting than any play ever," she declared. In her second letter home, it was clear that Alice was experiencing great relief from her habitual anxieties and depression. She showed interest, even excitement, about attending a traditional tea ceremony. She looked forward to going to Kyoto in the spring to see the cherry blossoms and temples. Her imagination revived and she even began to think about continuing on to China. "It is even more interesting than we anticipated," she wrote. By March she was speaking Japanese from a phrase book. Dewey's hoped-for travel cure was starting to work. Alice seemed to have left her cares behind.

John was beginning to realize how busy he would be kept in Japan. In addition to his "official" schedule of eight lectures at Tokyo Imperial University, he was invited to talk at four or five private universities as well as normal schools, teacher associations, and so on. He gave several lectures at the private Waseda University, where more than one of his students taught. For his public lectures he drew as many as five hundred persons. For each, he prepared a synopsis of his talk in advance for the benefit of his translators, and the synopses turned out to be helpful when he converted the lectures into his book *Reconstruction in Philosophy*. While in Japan he was constantly visited or was brought to visit distinguished people, and he was a guest of honor at various societies, such as the Concordia Society and the Japan-America Society.

In March, Alice told the children that they would probably stay on and go to China for about six weeks or longer. For some time they had thought about going to China as tourists. Then, "two Chinese gentlemen [two of Dewey's Ph.D. students, Hu Shi, now a professor, and P. W. Guo, president of Nanjing Teachers College] called this afternoon. . . . And they wanted to know if they could arrange it at Columbia [that] I could stay in China next year and divide time between the University of Beijing and some other government institution." They proposed an exchange between Columbia and Beijing University in which the Chinese government would pay Dewey his salary, which would free his salary at Columbia for a substitute. Here was the best evidence that Dewey had been right about the trip's benefit for Alice, for she immediately expressed her desire to accept this plan, and John agreed. Now, for a change, Alice's enthusiasm was running ahead of his, and he tried to catch up. Privately, Dewey was not sure that Columbia would grant him a leave to teach elsewhere. After all, when he had written to Dean Woodbridge for permission to teach at the New School for Social Research, Woodbridge had argued strongly against it on several moral grounds. Surprised at this rejection, Dewey appealed to President Butler, only to find him completely in agreement with Woodbridge and opposed to Dewey's teaching elsewhere on leave. But as should have been clear to Dewey, their opposition was based on the political grounds of denying support to the New School, whereas they had no objection to his educating the whole of China if he wished. And so in April, Dewey received a cablegram instructing him "to accept the exchange if he wants it." Their tourist excursion to China was now transformed into a formal plan to educate the youth of a newly emerging nation.

Dewey's lectures at Tokyo Imperial University were completed around the end of March. He told his Columbia chairman, Wendell Bush, that having given the lectures, he felt compelled to make them into a book so as not to "waste so much good typewriting." But he liked the book a good deal, claiming that its "merit" was that "it is reasonably free from philosophic partisanship, being an attempt to evaluate the modern spirit in general in contrast with that of classic philosophies." He saw this book primarily as a summary of his past thought and therefore as a springboard "for a fresh start." *Reconstruction in Philosophy* was so easily transformed from lectures that it was published before the end of 1920.

During breaks between his formal commitments, John and Alice traveled several times to nearby Kamakura. On many days they were brought to famous sites in Tokyo, made guests of honor at parties, and taken on tours. Alice recorded their adventures in detail for the girls. Evelyn kept all the letters and eventually edited them by removing personal concerns and the names of all persons and in 1920 published them as *Letters from China and Japan* by John Dewey and Alice Chipman Dewey. At the end of March 1919, the Deweys were free to travel around Japan, but of course wherever they went, they were expected in advance and offered special shows, entertainments, and dinners. John was "treated as of the same rank as an Imperial professor" (about the same level as minor nobility) and greeted by high priests, mayors, and other dignitaries.

From Kyoto they went to Kobe where John gave a final lecture in a "beautiful" school hall. He believed that it went off "rather better than the others." And then, finally, they left for Shanghai. They planned to return to Japan in July and to meet Lucy there, for nothing had been decided yet about their staying in China as more than mere tourists. As they sailed away from Japan, Alice's thoughts turned a bit depressive again with the regret of departure. Japanese women, she thought, were unselfish and unappreciated. The men did not see the sadness in the women's eyes, but Alice did, and she carried that thought while she looked backward to Japan.

China and "New Culture"

Alice still was in a low mood when they arrived in Shanghai on the last day of April. At first glance, from her depressed perspective, Shanghai looked like Detroit, but John was excited, impressed at once. Here he was, in Shanghai, the great Chinese city divided up into European, Japanese, and American concessions by John Hay's Open Door policy. He could see for himself what contact with Europe had done to China. John found that he preferred the seemingly easygoing Chinese to the much more formal Japanese, but he usually found something good wherever he went. Alice continued to think about the ill treatment of women in both countries:

> The east is an example of what masculine civilization can be and do. The trouble I should say is that the discussions have been confined to the subjection of the women as if that were a thing affecting the women only. It is my conviction that not merely the domestic and educational backwardness of China, but the increasing physical degeneration and the universal

political corruption and lack of public spirit, which make China such an easy mark is the result . . . of the submission of women.

Whereas Alice focused on the underlying causes of political and public corruption in both countries, John studied its effects. The world war that had already made several Japanese millionaires had also made Chinese revolutionaries, and China was playing with democratic change even as Japan was still theorizing about it.

The Deweys arrived in China just as the New Culture movement was erupting. This movement was an effort to do away with the remnants of traditional Confucian culture and to replace Confucianism with some sort of republican government. The Deweys were seeing, as Alice soon put it, the exciting "birth of a nation." When the dynastic system collapsed in 1911 and Yuan Shikai's attempt to restore Confucianism and the emperor crumbled in 1916, a cultural vacuum was created into which the democratic-socialist revolution of Sun Yat-sen flowed. When the Deweys arrived, change was in the air, fed by the conviction that the initial success of the political revolution could be sustained only by a cultural revolution. This is what the Chinese students meant when they called themselves part of the New Culture movement. Those polemicists who attacked Confucian vestiges; those writers who decried classical Chinese and sought to create a new realism and to use a popular language in literature; those intellectuals who tried to develop—almost to invent—a scientific, rational, positivistic, modernist, nationalistic, skeptical philosophy of life; and those avant-garde thinkers who rejected Chinese national traditions in favor of embracing internationalism in political and social ideas, who looked to the West, they, though hardly a coherent group, were all part of the loose assemblage of the restless discontented that was sending China into turmoil even as Dewey was leaving Kobe. They were all, as the title of their revolutionary journal put it, "the new youth," and almost immediately when he arrived, Dewey found himself in the lead.

In China, Dewey's name was well known, especially in connection with his modernist revolution in democratization through education. In the month before his arrival, Dewey's visit was heralded in many

Chinese newspapers and journals; his photograph appeared; articles by his students were avidly read; and his biography and summaries of his books were widely published. Hu Shi, P. W. Guo, and Menglin Jiang wrote and were interviewed about their former teacher. For the Chinese intellectuals, in educational theory and practice, Dewey offered in his person an instrument that could be at once effective as part of the revolt against traditional values, and he also could lead in creating modern, democratic, experimental, evolutionary values. Dewey's Chinese students were invariably allied with the modernist movement. Most of them had become educators themselves and had created their own Dewey disciples. But many collateral influences were in the air as well. The Russian Revolution had made Marx and Lenin important figures. Comte and his followers in sociological positivism had been fully incorporated. In 1919, the figures at the forefront of intellectual modernism were John Dewey and Bertrand Russell. For different reasons, each filled part of the vacuum left when Confucianism was discredited. Indeed, for Chinese modernists, Dewey took the position Confucius had held for so long. "Dewey," Shiyan Zhui wrote in 1919, "is a great revolutionist in the history of philosophy." The basis of Dewey's thought, Shiyan explained, was that philosophy should be an instrument "for solving human problems. . . . It must enable people to have creative intelligence, . . . envisage a bright future on the basis of present needs, and . . . be able to create new methods and tools to realize the future." The same week that this article appeared Dewey reached Shanghai.

Three days after the Deweys arrived, the famous May Fourth Incident took place in Beijing, when the student riots against the government began. Initially, the government countered with mass arrests until the students *sought* arrests in such numbers that the authorities emptied the jails and apologized to the rioters. In a letter to his children from Hangzhou, Dewey commented on the May Fourth Incident, sensing its possible importance:

> Here is one incident which personally concerns us, and also seems typical. The other day the Peking Univ. students started a parade in protest of the Paris Peace conference action in

turning the German interest in China over to the Japanese. Being interfered with by the police they got more unruly and beat up the Chinese minister to Japan who negotiated the treaties that sold China out. . . . Well, in one sense this was a kind of Hallowe'en students spree with a somewhat serious political purpose attached. In another sense, it *may* be— though probably not—the beginning of an important active political movement, out of which anything may grow . . . some twenty students were arrested . . . it is . . . typical that no one will guess which way things are going to turn, whether this is a temporary excitement or the beginning of the new political movement China needs.

In fact, it was the beginning of the revolutionary movement in China, and especially with Hu Shi as his guide, Dewey could understand the momentousness of the occasion. The underlying theme of the revolt, he said, was "the need of educational change; attacks on the family system; discussion of socialism; of democratic ideals; of all kind of utopias." He had arrived at the very spot and time when his philosophy was burning most brightly as an inspiration for a whole generation. When he stepped to the podium in China, he usually looked out at a full house, an audience of a thousand or more people. Within days of his arrival, he was invited to dinner with Sun Yat-sen. The historian of Dewey's impact on China has put his visit in a remarkable light: "His brief stay was one of the most significant and influential events in recent Chinese cultural history . . . there can be no doubt that China was the one foreign country in which Dewey exercised his greatest influence, particularly in the field of education." After his stay in China, more than a dozen of his books were translated and published there. A volume of Dewey's Chinese lectures sold 140,000 copies in two years and continued to be reprinted until the 1950s.

Dewey thought he had come to China to be a tourist, but he was greeted as a revolutionary. Thousands of Chinese waited anxiously to hear him. Although he believed he would be back in Japan in two months, he ended up spending twenty-six months in China. He published three quick sketches of Japan, the first of which was a comparative commentary simply entitled "Japan and America." But in China he started writing almost as soon as he arrived, and by the time he left, he had delivered 133 lectures and written nearly forty articles on the politics, culture, education, and psychology of China.

Years afterward he described the condition of his mind when he got to China and what the trip had meant to him. In New York, he said, he had been in the "doldrums," but in China

> I had a wonderful two years and a half; . . . I hadn't read up on China and went in a state of blissful ignorance with no opera-tion of culture weighing me down—and it was literally won-derful. . . . I gave lectures on education—that had of course to be interpreted—"interrupted" as they say—with soldiers around the room with their guns in their hands. . . . I spent most of my time . . . telling them about their chance of making a fresh start with a genuinely democratic type of education.

Dewey's first comparison of China and Japan came after a week in China. "Japan," he wrote, "was rather baffling and tantalizing. China is overpowering." Without delay he was lecturing to groups that hasti-ly gathered out of nowhere. His former students traveled from distant parts of China to greet him, and Menglin Jiang, a former student, wrote about his lectures regularly from his editorship of the *New Education* magazine. He translated Dewey's series of lectures on "The Relation Between Democracy and Education," and he was the rector of Beijing University where Dewey gave most of his talks.

Alice was in demand too. In Japan, she had felt that intellectual women were not wanted except, in the case of geisha, as entertainers. But in China, intelligence in a woman was valued, at least in the cities. Women were involved in politics; they were appointed to committees; and their advice was sought. Whereas a Japanese woman who went to the United States to be educated would have difficulty marrying, Western-educated women in China were particularly valued as wives. Accordingly, Alice soon was besieged with invitations. By May 9, she was "speaking to the girls of various schools" while John stayed at home writing letters.

The largest hall that could be found was always booked for talks by the Deweys. Each lecture lasted two hours, an hour for Dewey and an hour for the translation. After Dewey had spoken for a few minutes—sometimes after each sentence—an interpreter, guided by Dewey's outline, would translate. Hu Shi himself interpreted almost all of Dewey's lectures in Beijing and in Shandong and Shanxi Provinces. In Suzhou and Hangzhou, his interpreter was Zong Haizheng, who translated for both Deweys.

For each of his lectures on "The Philosophy of Education," Dewey typed out two pages of notes which he gave to Hu Shi in advance. "On account of the interpretation," he informed Barnes, "I have to write my lecture notes out much more fully than ever before." He gave several talks a week, and, he told Barnes, "I am more than satiated with writing." In addition to his talks he was busy writing what he called "pot boilers" for *Asia* magazine and the *New Republic*, giving numerous interviews, and, as always, keeping a steady stream of letters flowing to his children.

Alice was busy with her own program. Her closer observations soon convinced her that while on the surface women in China were indeed freer than in Japan, China was not yet truly democratic, since women were "left out" as equal agents in the new culture movement. "Now there is no doubt that the greatest need in China is elementary education and schools for small children taught by women. Without that all teaching can do is to perpetuate the old false ideas of education." John's periodic reminders in his lectures of the need to educate women equally with men "as an absolute necessity to a democracy" helped, but Alice saw the male leaders ignoring such promptings by her husband, and she herself spoke forcefully and frequently on this theme. Hardly had the Deweys arrived in China when their hosts urged them to stay for a year, with their salary guaranteed by private societies. But Alice made it clear that she would refuse to remain unless the women educators were given an equal place, and she got her way.

She stayed and found plenty of opportunities to raise the consciousness of young Chinese women. She even began to write again and published several articles in a student magazine at Nanjing.

Lucy decided to join her parents, and after a brief stay in Honolulu to see Sabino and a month spent in Japan, she came and remained until April 1920. Alice immediately drafted Lucy into her feminist program, and soon Lucy too was giving lectures. "You can't imagine," Dewey wrote to those at home, "the enormity of this: a young unmarried woman appearing [as an expert] before a school of young men." In her own way Alice, then Lucy, and later Evelyn did their parts to democratize China.

By July the Deweys' base was Beijing, where the greatest revolutionary agitation was occurring. Sometimes he was giving three lecture series simultaneously, eight talks per week; but he was enjoying the experience so much that he termed this "quite light work." By November 1919 Dewey was certain that he would not be back in New York before the end of June, and he turned down a proposal by the head of Teachers College to offer a summer course. By January 1920, nothing had been decided about their return: "You can never tell, we may decide to go to India and the vale of Cashmir or even Tibet before we return." By the time Evelyn arrived, Dewey had agreed to stay for a second year to work in the educational department at Beijing, and Evelyn, already a published expert on education, was offered a job at Beijing University, and an offer to Lucy came next. Then the Dewey feminist revolution fizzled: Evelyn decided to return to the United States at the end of the summer, and Lucy, who remained with her parents during their last year in China, declined a regular job. But Alice continued to push for the recognition of women in Chinese education, and she made considerable headway. Following a talk she gave at a girls' high school in Shandong,

> she asked the girls to express their wishes and plans, and after
> a while three of them got up and made very interesting speech-
> es on girls' education, the difficulty they had in securing prepa-
> ration for even the few higher schools there were, one of them

almost wept as she told how the men didn't want the women educated. Another said that she and several of her classmates were going to start a primary school after they graduated, as the government schools didn't allow enough liberty and were too subject to interference from officials.

By October, John was writing home that "a sign that some change is occurring," that at long last women were "invited to most of the public functions," and even in a provincial town they met four young women who had been accepted at American colleges. Alice's depression had evaporated in these exciting new experiences and her meaningful activities.

Dewey tried to explain to the current chairman of philosophy at Columbia why he was staying one more year: he wanted "to try to clinch whatever [I] may have gotten started this year" in assisting in the democratic reform of Chinese education. The National University expressed its gratitude to Dewey by awarding him an honorary doctor of philosophy degree in October 1920. Professor Dewey was only the fifth foreigner upon whom that honor had been bestowed in China.

Unexpectedly one day, Dewey was handed a cablegram at the U.S. embassy from a Colonel Drysdale. Dewey's last contact with the Office of Military Intelligence had been in 1918 and concerned the Polish question. But with the unrest in China and the instability of the government, the office now wanted information about the possibility of a Communist revolution in China.

Dewey stated that from May 1919 until this date he had been in nine provinces. He minimized the influence of Bolshevism on "teachers, writers, and students who are sometimes called radicals," although he emphasized that many were surely "quite radical in their social and economic ideas." The students, he said, were "much inclined to new ideas, and to projects of social and economic change. . . . They are practically all Socialists, and some call themselves Communists. Many think the Russian revolution a very fine thing." But "the whole social and economic background of Bolshevism as a practical going concern is lacking." Dewey knew several leaders of the Chinese Communist

Party, but he predicted that it would not become powerful in China.

The Chinese Communist Party was founded in May 1920 by Chen Duxiu and Li Daozhao. Both were supporters of the New Youth movement and friends and associates of Hu Shi and proponents of Dewey's pragmatism. With Hu Shi, in 1919 Chen signed the "manifesto" of the pragmatic *New Youth Magazine*. In economic terms, Dewey was an ally of the socialists and strongly supportive of workers, labor, professional unions, and a cooperative commonwealth. From his earliest days in Chicago, the activities of Eugene Debs in the Pullman strike impressed him, and he later supported Norman Thomas, a perennial presidential candidate on the Socialist Party ticket. Dewey's social philosophy resembled a nativist version of guild socialism. In philosophic terms he rejected the specific ideas of Marxism almost completely, even though he remained interested in observing the Soviet experiment in socialism. His attitude continued to be influenced by George Sylvester Morris, who had taught Dewey idealistic democratic, and spiritual Hegelianism. Dewey's brand of progressivism, which sought to perfect democracy on American grounds, and his opposition to the globalist progressivism of Wilson and others reflected his personal beliefs concerning how American society should evolve. He rejected dialectical materialism in favor of experimentalism; class warfare in favor of cooperation; revolutionary change in favor of evolutionary amelioration; party discipline in favor of freedom of thought; and the separation of means from ends in favor of their unity. Above all, he rejected violence as the chosen instrument of change, in favor of bringing change about through peaceful evolution. In short, he was a contented socialist but a fierce opponent of Marxism-Leninism.

In China, Dewey spoke out explicitly and regularly against Bolshevism, arguing that Marxism did not provide an adequate basis for achieving a just, democratic society. Dewey understood that among the young in China, the idea of "revolution" was paramount, and in the rush toward revolution, he understood, any revolution might do; the most radical might win over the most productive. Therefore it was important, as he saw it, that the Chinese revolution proceed along

Deweyan lines: revolution that was evolution. He made an excellent, concise analysis for Barnes in September 1920:

> The whole temper among the younger generation is revolutionary, they are so sick of their old institutions that they assume any change will be for the better—the more extreme and complete the change, the better. And they seem to me to have little idea of the difficulties in the way of any constructive change. . . .[This] is a wonderful chance to study the psychology of revolutionary idealism. . . . Not having any [long-standing democratic tradition or] background . . . to the liberals here anything is likely to be as true as anything else, provided only it is different.

This inclination, Dewey saw, gave Marxism a chance in China, since its propagandists promoted communism as the most radical solution to China's problems. He was aware that the Soviets were active in China and that "the general influence of the fact of the Russian revolution was great," but he was convinced that in China there was no social or economic basis for "technical Bolshevism." He remained nearly alone among the major American intellectuals between 1920 and 1950 in firmly supporting socialism even as he opposed Marxism.

What Dewey found in China was a fulcrum of unsteady change. Although the overthrow of once revered traditions made any new idea attractive, Dewey counseled continuity with the past. Young Chinese radicals believed that the attack on the Confucian family meant that "the family ought to be completely done away with." But Dewey advocated the evolution of an egalitarian family. The revolt against the Confucian emphasis on "proper" relations between the sexes as an aspect of family stability meant for the radicals that "promiscuous relations between the sexes [should now be] set up." Dewey suggested restraint and responsible freedom. For the radicals, the overthrow of filial piety meant the displacement of parents and the conviction that "all children [should be] cared for by public authorities." Dewey stressed the importance of education.

With Dewey's help, Bertrand Russell came to China while Dewey was there. Dewey was convinced that Russell would have more impact on Chinese intellectuals than he himself could have, simply because Russell's radical reputation made him seem more advanced: "He is the great hero of radical thought in China." Russell even showed up in China with a young mistress, Dora Black, one of his former students at Cambridge, as a sort of symbolic evidence that he was a true radical. But Russell soon astonished the Chinese communists by attacking Bolshevism and distinguishing among different kinds of socialisms. "It's fortunate for China," Dewey wrote home, that "his reaction [against communism] was unfavorable as [the students] . . . will stand things from him on acct of his radical rep they wouldn't from anybody else. They rather idealize the Bolshevists here [in Hunan], especially the radicals among the students. This place seems to be a hot bed." However warmly he was greeted by the Chinese radicals, Russell had miscalculated the effect of Dora's presence on both the American community in Beijing and upper-class Chinese. Both welcomed him but ostracized Dora. Alice took pity on Dora: "If I can accept Bertrand Russell, why can't I accept Dora Black?" she asked.

When Russell became ill and was hospitalized, the Deweys took Dora into their apartment. Meanwhile, John spent several days in the German hospital with Russell. Certain he was dying, Russell dictated his last will and testament to John, naming Dora Black as his sole heir. Dewey remarked when he returned home late that night that he hoped he wouldn't have to go to London when the will was contested by Russell's wife. Both the *Japan Advertiser* and the *New York Times* reported that Russell died on March 28 of pneumonia caused by influenza. But he left the hospital and resumed his lectures. Six weeks later, in May, he and Dora left China. Alice never forgot that in those six weeks, they had no acknowledgment of gratitude from Russell or Dora, only a brief note from the woman saying that she had been "too busy" to contact the Deweys. John seems to have felt no ill will. Even later, when Russell blasted pragmatism or instrumentalism, Dewey never took his opposition personally but, as he told Harold Fries, attributed it to Russell's anti-Americanism and wish to "smear the U.S.

[rather] than a particular philosophical position." He said of Russell: "I think I can hold, with a minimum of prejudice, that he never has made a serious attempt to understand any view that is different from his own" but instead "trusted to his natural brilliancy to improvise." Lucy had a different explanation, believing that "Bertie realized that . . . father was smarter than he was, and this never set right with Mr. Russell." But John didn't agree, and when Russell needed defending years later, Dewey was quick to help.

Finally, at the end of July the Deweys left China and returned to Japan, where he again was received warmly. He had stayed in touch with Japanese intellectuals and sent several articles to the journal *Kaizô*; these which started to appear in April 1921. In one article he argued that the only possibility of peace in Asia was to establish a truly cooperative relationship between China and Japan. This was almost his last word before he left Japan for America after nearly three years.

He gave his best brief summary of what this long adventure had meant to him to his Columbia colleague John Jacob Coss: "Nothing western looks quite like the same anymore, and this is as near to a renewal of youth as can be hoped for in this world." But this was not Dewey's last word on China. Even before Dewey left, Walter Lippmann had urged him to write a book on China, calling the articles he had published in *Asia* and the *New Republic* "models of what political reporting ought to be." Hardly had he arrived back at the university when a reporter for the *Columbia Spectator* interviewed him. The leaders in Chinese education, Dewey said, were Columbia trained and taught "Columbia methods." Then he took up Alice's theme, which he wholly shared: "Women are gradually being recognized by Chinese educational authorities. . . . Within the last year women have been admitted to the national universities at Peking and Nanking."

Dewey continued to stay in contact with Chinese leaders. In 1924 he was appointed to the board of the Boxer Fund and charged with disbursing funds remitted by the United States on the account of the Boxer indemnity. At a memorial service for Sun Yat-sen, Dewey was the principal speaker, and he continued to promulgate his prosocialist, anti-Marxist position to an audience of a thousand people. Dr. Sun, he stated, was the father of "a free, progressive, independent and democratic China." The "little ring" of Communists sitting in the front row broke into applause when Dewey noted that Russia was aiding the Chinese Nationalists, but "they were silent thereafter while Dewey denied that the Chinese movement was Communist and talked about the English and American sources of Dr. Sun's program of progressive democracy. He compared a Soviet effort to enlist the Chinese masses in Communism to that of the fox who had lost his tail to induce other foxes to part with theirs."

Addressing the League for Industrial Democracy in December 1931, Dewey urged the boycott of Japanese goods until Japan withdrew its invasion forces from Chinese territory. In 1938 the Guomindang government awarded Dewey the Blue Grand Cordon of the Order of the Jade for his contributions to Chinese education. Even as late as 1942, after America went to war against Japan, the State Department, convinced of Dewey's still immense influence, asked him to compose a message to the people of China. Thousands of leaflets containing a message from Dewey were scattered all over China by U.S. airplanes in an effort to encourage the Chinese to keep fighting against the Japanese invaders. "Your country and my country," Dewey began, "love peace and have no designs on other nations. We are alike in having been attacked without reason and without warning by a rapacious and treacherous enemy. . . . We are now comrades in a common fight." At his conclusion he predicted the "coming victory of America and China."

Hardly had the Allied victory been assured when Dewey received an invitation from Menglin Jiang, now in the Ministry of Education, to visit China "as a guest of Chinese Universities, [to] . . . make [a] survey of our problems." Travel to China at that time was difficult. Jane said that any thought of his going was "crazy." But he was determined to go, and as Dewey told Edward Lindeman, "my physicians seem inclined to give an OK. I'd like to try." The Chinese embassy wired Dewey in March 1946 that he should "start immediately inoculations for small pox, typhus, typhoid, cholera, yellow fever, tetanus and plague": a heavy dose for an eighty-six-year-old man. In April, Dewey and one "secretary" were granted priority travel on a U.S. Air Force airplane, and the Ministry of Education in Beijing sent him $5,000 for traveling expenses. However, delay followed delay until the end of the year when Menglin Jiang told him that conditions were too "unsettled" for him to take the risk. And so the opportunity passed.

With regret Dewey soon saw a new Communist regime take power in China and achieve the triumph that he had doubted would occur. He immediately predicted what would happen: "Now that they are Bolshevized my name will be mud—the philosopher of Imperialistic bourgeois capitalism." He was right. Those of his disciples in China who could not flee were purged; a few recanted and "acknowledged" that Dewey had corrupted them. Proof of Dewey's great influence was the virulence and volume of excoriation of Dewey and Hu Shi, Dewey's chief proponent in China.

The trip had been a complete success for Alice. She had been made an honorary dean of women at Nanjing Teachers College, and she welcomed the many Chinese students from Nanjing and Beijing who came to Columbia, where she was called their "beloved mother." At Columbia she went to all the seminars and lectures on China, and she often expressed her indignation at the Great Powers' transgressions in China.

By the time the Dewey returned to the United States in October 1921 for the beginning of classes, he was glad to get back to philosophy. "I did no philosophical reading in China at all," he told the British pragmatist F. C. S. Schiller. He had used up his accumulated capital of philosophic ideas, and he was preparing to begin anew.

No League and No War

Following the conclusion of the war and the collapse of left progressivism in Wilson's failure to extend democracy to Europe, Dewey took up two causes closely connected with the war and wrote several essays on each. The first was his complete opposition to America's joining the League of Nations. The second was his support of the movement to outlaw war.

Dewey's opposition to the League of Nations was based on a simple principle, which he had argued in "In a Time of National Hesitation." The League, he insisted, was a European organization created for European ends. If America entered the League, democracy would lose. For Dewey, the League was not only antithetical to the fulfillment of American democracy, it would also mark the beginning of its decline. The truth is, Dewey wrote, that "Europe does not want and will not tolerate our cooperation except on its own terms." The European politicians want America to join the League "for the same reason that they wanted us [to join them] during the war—to add power to *their* policies."

In addition, Dewey gave all his support and considerable publicity through articles and newspaper interviews to the movement to outlaw war initiated by Salmon O. Levinson. A prominent corporate attorney in Chicago, Levinson had married Nellie B. Haire, a former student of Dewey's at Michigan and a classmate of Alice's. In Chicago the two couples established a firm friendship that lasted for decades. Dewey and Levinson worried about the war together; they both opposed the League of Nations. Eventually Levinson devised one of those American utopian schemes that was so simple that it seemed to be the obvious solution everyone else had previously missed. An attorney, Levinson realized suddenly that war had achieved legal status as a mode for settling international conflicts. But suppose that nations agreed that war was illegal? Then all those who began wars would be criminals and subject to criminal penalties. Levinson urged those activists who opposed war not to expend their energies in pacifism or protest but to support what he called "the outlawry of war."

When Levinson's book *Outlawry of War* was published in 1921, Dewey wrote a preface to it connecting his opposition to the League of Nations with his advocacy of Levinson's idea. Those who once favored the League but now opposed it, as he did, "should unite in favoring the plan for a world court based upon world codification of international law having for its major premise the outlawry of war." The League would simply continue the status quo by accepting war as legal and therefore would continue "the old tradition of the lawfulness of war." Levinson's plan, in fact, became an alternative to the League of Nations among opponents to America's entry into it.

With Dewey's preface, *Outlawry of War* was inserted into the *Congressional Record* by Senator William Borah, who supported the plan. He introduced a resolution favoring the outlawry of war and recommended Levinson's plan to the State Department as the principle on which the country's foreign policy should be based. In 1922 Dewey wrote to Borah to thank him for his efforts and explained why Levinson's plan was so appealing to him. As Dewey saw it, the outlawry idea resolved the conflict among globalists. Through it, the United States could express the highest of democratic ideals—world peace—and also satisfy "the need for constructive leadership in international cooperation." Far better than the League, it could allow American ideals global play without compromising them in enmeshments with Europe's nondemocratic practices. But Borah did little more to further the cause.

In addition to his preface, during 1923 Dewey wrote several articles defending the outlawry idea. The most important and most interesting is "What Outlawry of War Is Not," a critique of an article by Walter Lippmann. In this piece, Dewey argues as a controversialist—a posture he took more and more frequently in the 1930s. Lippmann pronounced Levinson's idea to be "confused and sterile" and attacked it precisely on the grounds that Dewey defended it—its simplicity and its refusal to stress the role of diplomacy. "Once more," Lippmann concluded on a note of disillusion with all utopias, "we witness the tragic futility of noble sentiments frustrated by confused ideas." When Dewey was in his controversialist mode, he could be quite uncharacteristically fierce. Lippmann's proposition, he wrote, is "a rival to the most elementary common sense." For this reason, he argued, Lippmann's article would not damage the movement to outlaw war, but by misleading uninformed readers, his article "is likely to damage . . . the cause of peace." Dewey demolished each of Lippmann's arguments, showing him to be merely a covert defender of the League of Nations. One of Levinson's supporters wrote to Dewey after reading his article that it "is one of the most brilliant pieces of controversial writing that I have ever seen and one more evidence that Dewey's mind is . . . unmatched in our world today."

Judged by the legislation it prompted, Levinson's plan was a complete success, as it provided the basis for the Kellogg-Briand Pact, which was signed in Paris in 1928 by fifteen nations, including the United States, Japan, France, Great Britain, and Germany. This agreement condemned war as a legal instrument and pledged the signatories to settling international disputes peacefully. Dewey praised the pact as historic. But the ink was hardly dry on the ratifications when all these nations began dropping bombs on one other, and S. O. Levinson, the outlawry of war proposal, and the Kellogg-Briand Pact all passed into the oblivion of historical curiosities.

Sabino Dewey

Despite being absorbed by the issues of war and peace, Dewey's attention was never drawn entirely away from his family. As much as for any of his own children, his concern for Sabino was both intense and continuous. Although Sabino was not a Dewey by blood, he became one by practice.

Both Deweys doted on the boy and were always worried about his health and his education. Sabino was superb at mechanical tasks, whereas the Dewey children were skilled intellectually. The major issue thus became finding something he really wanted to do. When the Deweys bought an automobile, Sabino liked driving it even more than riding his motorcycle or driving a carriage. Although the car regularly broke down, he was able to fix it and keep it running. "Dad drove it once, but a tree got in his way," he said, so in his teens Sabino became the chauffeur. "My parents understood," Sabino added, "that I was mechanical, not intellectual. . . . Dad called the ability I had to work with my hands 'experience in living.' " Alice brought out one of the few treasured items of her father's that she had saved, his original workbox as a cabinetmaker, and presented it to Sabino.

When the Deweys bought the farm in Huntington, Long Island, it was run down. John and Sabino put in an extensive irrigation system, powered by the gasoline motor from the pumping house that supplied their drinking water. For Alice, Sabino planted an herb garden with brick pathways, modeled in miniature on the Villa Borghese's gardens. John had written much about the value and necessity of mechanical training, and Sabino was a practical example of this. When they went to the summer cottage in the Adirondacks, John bought Sabino a gun and taught him how to shoot. He became an expert shot. In 1916 they sent him to study veterinary science at MacDonald College of McGill University in Montreal, and he stayed for two years. The practical work went well, but the required college courses didn't appeal to him and he withdrew from the school. He then spent two years in an automotive college program.

When the United States entered the war, Sabino was eligible for the draft. He felt worn out by what he called "all my successive failures" and was unwilling to try another college, even though attending college could have exempted him from the draft. He became despondent and seemed to John to have developed "fatalistic resignation." Sabino himself told Alice in 1918: "I can see quite clearly now that my greatest fault [has been] . . . lack of confidence." That state of mind led him to go partway to Japan with his parents in 1919, then get off the boat in Hawaii and stay in Honolulu, working at the College of Hawaii for a year. Eventually, he drifted back to the United States.

John was now convinced that Sabino's preference for "farm and country work" was genuine. He seemed to be doing a good job working a tractor on a drainage project. "Perhaps you can find something out about those small farms the state is preparing in California," John urged him. When the Deweys returned from Japan, Sabino decided he wanted to go back to Italy "to see something of my origin" and "meet my brothers and sisters." When he told his parents, Alice said right away, "You know, I've been longing to go to Europe; if you will take me, I'll pay all your expenses." So they both went. On their way to

Venice, Alice told him something he had not known. She and John had paid for the music education in Italy of one of Sabino's brothers, and he had become a maestro in Venice. They found that he was to play first violin in a concert of the national band just after they were to arrive. Sabino went, but he had forgotten all his Italian and had to talk in French, which he had learned in school; and so his brother couldn't believe it was really he. Finally the confusion was ironed out. They telephoned another brother, "who was in some sort of diplomatic service," and he joined them. Later Sabino went to Verona to meet a sister. Ironic but true, Sabino went to the Berlitz school in Venice and then in Parma to learn Italian. In Parma he found another brother who was a professional wood-carver.

Italy had changed since the last time Alice was there. Black shirts were everywhere, and Fascist demonstrations were a daily occurrence. Alice and Sabino went to Rome and then Sicily. But Alice was worried that Sabino, whose passport indicated that he had been born in Venice, could be drafted. "We must surely go," she told Sabino one day, and they immediately took a train to Naples and from there left Europe.

Sabino went to work in Chicago, where he met Edith Thornton. They married and had a son in October 1925. If it had been a girl, he would have named her Alice, he told his Mamma. When he and Edith had a second child, it *was* a girl, and he did name her Alice. Mamma was convinced that Sabino should be a teacher. "I am desperately interested in your going at teaching," she told him in 1927. "I feel sure you could do it." And in fact, he did get a job as the vocational director at the Columbus Vocational School in Indiana and taught auto mechanics there. But he found it difficult to stay in one place.

Finally, Sabino returned to what he was always destined for. He moved back to Huntington, Long Island, and became the manager of the Old Fields Farm on Greenlawn Road. He became a member of the school board and chairman of the Liberal Party of Suffolk County. The final advice that his father gave him was to watch out for the infiltration of the party by a "fifth column" and to be ready to get out of the American Labor or Liberal Party if it turned communist.

Sabino lived out the side of Dewey's educational theory that was concerned with vocations. He also was the only one of the Dewey children who was interested in political activism. But his daughter Alice continued the intellectual Dewey tradition that skipped Sabino's generation, becoming a professor of anthropology at the University of Hawaii.

Sabino was a real Dewey after all.

Idealism Corrupted

The 1920s, following Dewey's return from Asia, was the first decade in which the American character seemed to be in the process of breaking up. President Woodrow Wilson's moral fervor, purity of purpose, and missionary single-mindedness reflected the democratic dream of virtue in public as well as private behavior. He stood for character. When Wilson told an audience in 1914, "there are some simple things in the world. One . . . is principle," many Americans agreed. When he declared in 1915 that "America . . . will not fight . . . because peace is the healing and elevating influence of the world," he expressed the contempt felt by most Americans for European squabbles. Even when he reversed himself and, on April 2, 1917, asked Congress to declare war, his reasons were utopian and visionary: to make the world "safe for democracy" and to achieve "the liberation of its peoples." Such aims assumed the existence of a vigorously virtuous American character.

But the moral zeal with which Americans entered World War I soon faded. Former President William Howard Taft denounced Wilson as an "autocrat." Many young people labeled the war a hoax and were generally disillusioned with idealism, and this brought about the rapid growth of isolationism. John Dewey had been right about the bad psychological and political effects of America's entry into the war. By 1919, when Wilson toured America to defend the peace treaty and the League of Nations, he had lost the support of Congress. Most citizens, worried by recession, disturbed by labor unrest, and tired of foreign entanglements, were no longer moved by Wilson's utopianism. It was time to find a new goal and to elect a new president who would bring them the benefits of "normalcy."

Warren Harding, elected president in 1920, stated his program clearly: "Prosper America first." He declared himself "old-fashioned and even reactionary on matters of faith and morals" and conducted his campaign from the front porch of his Marion, Ohio, home. Harding's small-town behavior suited a politics of nostalgia, and his running mate, Calvin Coolidge, had much the same appeal. Both men were devoted to programs promising material abundance. Americans listened to their promises and gave them the greatest victory in Republican Party history.

But they might have been wiser to listen to Sinclair Lewis, who showed in *Main Street* (1920) the limitations of an American society that had become narrow and grasping. Harding appointed Herbert Hoover, Andrew Mellon, and Charles Evan Hughes to his cabinet, but he also gave his cronies and political supporters high posts. In creating what historian Frederick Lewis Allen named "the aristocrat of scandals," Teapot Dome, these appointees left a lasting symbol of the misuse of power and wealth. The idealism of the war period had nearly disappeared.

Governmental corruption in the 1920s rested on the popular preference for power over justice and possessions over conscience. Scorn for the law was so pervasive that Smedley D. Butler, a tough general borrowed from the marines to clean up Philadelphia, was dismissed after two years as a public nuisance. "Trying to enforce the law in Philadelphia was worse than any battle I was ever in," he complained. Especially evident was disregard for laws forbidding the sale of alcoholic beverages. Prohibition, "the experiment noble in purpose," as Herbert Hoover called it, started as a reformist ideal. Other American ideals also lay behind the century-old Temperance movement, which became a way of imposing the Anglo-Saxon middle-class values of hard work, abstinence, and thrift on the newly arrived immigrants and the working classes, particularly in the cities.

The social cost of Prohibition was high. It ushered in urban gang-sterism, and the upper and middle classes made a mockery of the very values of restraint and order that were preached to immigrants and workers. No one supposed Harding to be a teetotaler, and some knew that Andrew Mellon, who as secretary of the treasury was responsible for enforcing Prohibition laws, had investments in Overholt Whiskey. If Andrew Mellon was not personally corrupt, his tax revision plans and government spending policies shared at least one assumption with the perpetrators of Teapot Dome, the underworld, and the general public: that virtue resided in the possession of wealth and power. Completed by 1926, Mellon's programs reduced the maximum surtax to 20 percent, lowered the basic income tax, and repealed inheritance and gift taxes while at the same time drastically reducing the government's activities by cutting federal expenditures in half. The effect of these policies was to buttress wealth and wealth making. Neither Mellon nor most Americans seemed to notice that the average yearly income of farmers, miners, and construction workers all fell during the 1920s and that the economic gap between the upper and lower classes was growing.

All through the 1920s Dewey stuck to his own brand of idealism and devoted a considerable part of his writing to preserving a memory of liberal ideals in a people who were doing their best to forget about liberal politics.

Now to Turkey

Before he traveled to China and Japan, Dewey had achieved a definite sense of his own identity and a multifaceted public reputation: first, as the preeminent living American exponent of the first distinctive American philosophy, called pragmatism; second, as the leading theorist of and commentator on educational reform in America; and finally, as the philosopher of American democracy. By the time he returned to the United States in 1921, a subtle change had taken place in him.

He continued to write and speak vigorously on philosophic method and instrumental logic. He remained deeply engaged in the ongoing debate over the kind of education appropriate to democratic development, and he kept on commenting on the conditions of American culture. But he had become a changed person, more precisely, an evolving person. His educational vision and his political understanding had broadened beyond American boundaries to include the world.

China and Japan gave Dewey's international interest intellectual focus, and during the 1920s he traveled on educational missions to several countries. More and more it became clear that he was a man of the world, a person on whom nothing would be lost. Between 1920 and 1935, while he was traveling, he continued to write original works. Once *Reconstruction in Philosophy* was published and a two-year hiatus in philosophic reading had freshened his mind, he started on new voyages, both physically and, more important, intellectually. Now over sixty, he began to understand what he had always been trying to say, and he was able to articulate his newly clarified, clarifying vision.

In turning outward to the world during the 1920s, Dewey did what many Americans were doing. During World War I, many young American men went abroad for the first time, and some stayed. America was experiencing a great boom from the war. The exchange rate of dollars to depressed European currencies was favorable, and American farmers were temporarily reaping great profits from the shortages of food in Europe just after the war. American business was adjusting to global economics and investment. Foreign countries clamored for American products, American aid, and American ideas. They clamored for John Dewey, too.

His articles concerning conditions in Japan and China, the many reports on the educational reforms that Dewey was helping promote in China especially, the hope that he was ready and willing to undertake some similar activities in other countries, and his steady stream of books and articles concerning the relation between education and social progress all led to invitations by foreign governments to inspect their educational systems. The first occurred in Turkey in 1924, and then in the summer of 1926 he traveled to Mexico City to teach a summer course and to assess Mexican education. Two years later he was invited to the Soviet Union to examine school programs and to observe the achievements of socialism there. Finally, in 1934, he went to South Africa, the last of his educational missions abroad.

Intent on modernizing Turkey, on bringing his country into the family of Western democratic nations, the president of Turkey, Mustafa Kemal—later called Atatürk—began a long-term process of wholesale reform. He became the first president of Turkey in 1923, the year that Turkey was proclaimed a republic. Atatürk quickly introduced a series of reforms, making Ankara the capital and easing Turkish law away from strictly Islamic rules and regulations. He reorganized society on a largely democratic basis. Most important, he did away with the rigid class differences in status and power, increasing the middle classes' mobility. He encouraged the growth of native industry, international relations, and cultural interchange. To achieve the last of these, he insisted that the Arabic script of the Turkish language be converted to Roman letters. Eleanor Bisbee declared that this decision was based on the advice of John Dewey, "who advocated the change." Atatürk saw that to accomplish many of these reforms, and certainly to establish them on a lasting basis, education was key. First, he was determined to dispose of the core of Ottoman elementary education—rote learning of the Qu'ran—and to replace it with an up-to-date European-American-style progressive education. Second, he attacked the widespread problem of illiteracy in Turkey and introduced legislation that mandated compulsory education for all children up to high-school age.

It was almost inevitable, then, that Atatürk and his ministers would invite John Dewey to play a role in this reconstruction of Turkish education. In the spring of 1924 Dewey received an invitation from Sefa Bey, then the minister of public instruction, to leave for Turkey as soon as the semester at Columbia ended. John and Alice stayed in New York just long enough to see Jane married to Alston Clark on May 24 and left five days later for Europe.

The Turkish press greeted the Deweys' arrival enthusiastically. As one observer said, the public "seemed to expect a series of miracles of him." As usual, John gave talks to local groups such as the Chamber of Commerce and others organized by the local authorities. In

Constantinople the Deweys consulted with the American administrators and teachers of Robert College and collected statistical material on Turkish education from the Chamber of Commerce, the Turkish Office of Education, and officials at the American embassy. Most of July they spent in Ankara (then called Angora), which they used as a base to travel to outlying areas. Afterward, they began to travel back and forth between Angora and the old capital, Constantinople. While most of the Turkish schools were closed for the summer, this proved to be an advantage, for Dewey was able to avoid some of the ceremonies when he visited a school as a dignitary. John and Alice were able to inspect the facilities, the school buildings, the classrooms, the vocational areas, the equipment, and the like at their leisure. For the same reason, they were able to make a fairly comprehensive circuit of the schools in the Turkish provinces, to interview teachers and administrators and to consult with the local educational organizations. In late July John and Alice returned briefly to Constantinople for a rest and took up residence in a house on the grounds of Robert College.

They visited schools in the old Ottoman capital of Bursa, and they inspected the facilities of Turkey's best school, the Galata-Lycée. But the majority of schools were far below this standard. An excursion into the countryside to see the rural schools came next. Alice was cautioned by the American women at Robert College about the trip beyond Angora that they planned to take in early August. She told Bino: "I [was] . . . warned by some of the foreign women not to go as they say every body comes back sick or nearly so." But she forged ahead, for she defiantly believed she could "stand all that Pa can." After all, she reasoned, she had stayed healthy in China by drinking only "hot tea." But in Turkey that expedient proved ineffective, and Alice became ill. The seriousness of her illness was not immediately apparent, for at first she felt only discomfort and so she did not seek appropriate treatment.

Back in Constantinople in early September, Dewey sketched out a preliminary report on the educational situation in Turkey. By mid-September he handed the draft to Vassif Bey, the new minister of public instruction. Just before he departed, Dewey also gave a copy of his report to the first secretary of the U.S. embassy, Robert M. Scotten, and had a long discussion with him, which Scotten reported in his letter of transmittal with Dewey's preliminary report to the secretary of state in Washington. Dewey, Scotten stated, had been "engaged in studying the Turkish educational system with a view to suggesting improvements." Unfortunately, Scotten sensed, Dewey left Turkey in a rather pessimistic mood, believing that the few funds available for education left little prospect for educational improvement. Not only were the teachers poorly paid, but the teaching conditions were extremely difficult, the school buildings were inadequate, and the school system—if it could be called a system—was entangled in bureaucracy. The country's schools were highly centralized, so local schools were ruled from afar. But Dewey believed that local control was essential. "Professor Dewey," Scotten noted, "was amused by the expectation . . . among Turks that he would at once propose a whole series of *reforms* . . . of the most sweeping and destructive character."

In his preliminary report Dewey confined himself to considering the ways that teaching might be improved, especially by developing the teaching staff. He outlined a systematic plan for providing teachers with up-to-date readings on educational practices and advocated the formation of teachers' study groups. Again and again, he stressed practical solutions, reflecting his sense that the conditions for education in Turkey were still minimal. For instance, he wrote, "No steady development of progressive education is possible without buildings which have proper sanitary toilet facilities, places for manual training, domestic science, drawing and art, library, museum, etc." He suggested that the "first steps" for long-term improvement be applied to elementary education. He made budgetary suggestions. Finally, he rose to the philosophic plane. The ministry should be "the intellectual and moral leader and inspirer . . . and avoid all activities which do not lead to this end."

Dewey filed his preliminary report. Then suddenly, Alice became seriously ill. Evelyn, who got the news first, wrote to Sabino that "Mamma came down with uremic poisoning and malaria, fortunately very mild, only sick for about two days." But she was sicker than Evelyn was told. She spent two days in a hospital shortly before they were to depart. She was so worn out that they delayed their departure for about a week so that Alice could gain strength. This was the beginning of Alice's physical ills, and after returning from Turkey she would never be entirely well again.

When they arrived in New York and John composed his final report, he finished on the same idealistic plane with which the preliminary report had ended. The main goal of Turkey's educational system should be "the development of Turkey as a vital, free, independent, and lay republic in full membership in the circle of civilized States," and therefore the citizens "must be educated for intellectual participation in the political, economic, and cultural growth of the country." Schools should be "centers of community life," foundations for a democratic republic. Written with a broad view, sympathetic and analytic, both demanding and understanding, Dewey's report is a model of its genre. One Turkish scholar, indeed, declared that "few [others] have made, within such a short span of time, a more lasting and substantial contribution to the Turkish nation than Dewey in educational matters."

Dewey seldom let any experience go to waste, and soon he turned to the conditions that he had observed in Turkey as the subject for a series of articles for the *New Republic*. "Secularizing a Theocracy," "Angora, the New," "The Turkish Tragedy," "Foreign Schools in Turkey," and "The Problems of Turkey" appeared in late 1924 and January 1925. As a group, these form Dewey's critique of Turkey's various problems in trying to modernize. As he saw it, Turkey's transformation would involve a basic conflict between the "claims of traditional religion" and those of new nationalism and the state. Dewey arrived at several hopeful conclusions. Patriotism would prove stronger than religious sentiment. The abandonment of Constantinople in favor of Angora as the capital was a forceful symbolic statement of Turkey's new direction. Angora would both symbolize the creation of a new state and be a reminder of the grandeur of Turkey during the Roman Empire. In contrast to the old capital where the caliphs and the religious leaders had reigned, Angora would represent Turkish nationhood and reinforce the "pioneer spirit which the activities of the present create." The mainland, not Constantinople, was to become and provide Turkey's version of the renewal that had occurred on the American frontier. The cost of Turkish nationalism would be high, Dewey warned, for it meant the expulsion of the Greeks and Armenians from Anatolia. Nationalism, which had the capacity to overcome the old religious power, also had its own tendency to become a "virulent disease" of oppression. The role of the new government, Dewey concluded, was to face hard realities and entertain no illusions. Its two greatest needs would be good schools and an uncorrupted civil administration. In the last of his essays, "The Problems of Turkey," Dewey compared China and Turkey. Both, he believed, had the same need for "transformation" through "the struggle for economic development and for culture in art, science and philosophy."

Dewey seemed to swing between optimism and pessimism concerning whether his trip had helped modernize education in Turkey. But in fact, he had had more influence than he realized. Atatürk said later that some of his social reforms had been suggested by the Deweys' visit—the unveiling of Turkish women, for instance, about which Alice certainly had had something to say. One sign of the continuing impact of Dewey's recommendations is that his report was made available to the public; the government reprinted it in 1939 and 1952, and Dewey continued to be cited in Turkish educational journals and conferences for three decades.

THEN TO MEXICO

Dewey spent the summer of 1926 in Mexico City, teaching in the summer program of the National University. He offered two courses, "Contemporary Philosophic Thought" and "Advanced Educational Problems," to the five or six hundred U.S. teachers and students for whom the school was designed. Shortly after the Deweys arrived in Mexico City in late June to prepare for the opening of the term, Alice's health problems flared up, just as they had the year before, in the summer of 1925 when she and John went to Copenhagen to visit Jane. At that time, she was hospitalized for exhaustion, although it seemed that she was "all over" her malaria attacks, "thanks to quinine." During the rest of that summer, they continued, as John termed it, their "sampling of European hospitals." Now in 1926, after arriving in Mexico, she had a mild heart attack and decided to return to New York for medical care. In her customary courageous way, she insisted that she could make the return trip alone. Early in July, back in New York, her physician removed a circulatory obstruction, but that procedure promised "only less discomfort, not any actual change" in the seriousness of her condition. Eventually, she went to stay at the Clifton Springs Sanitarium for a long rest. And so began her heart problems that only increased, never abated. In Mexico City, John missed Alice and resolved to never again lecture abroad.

Mexico itself was unsettled in 1926. The church and the confederacy were at odds. There were rumors that the railways would be closed down. A revolution seemed likely. Of the troubled state of affairs, Dewey observed wryly, everything was quiet enough, "barring political assassinations." Although the summer school program was intended primarily for Americans, Dewey found his classroom full of Mexican teachers who were attending independently of summer school, so he had to prepare lectures for a larger audience than expected. He followed somewhat the same method he had used in China. For each course he prepared a syllabus to be translated into Spanish, and then, for each lecture he wrote out an abstract for a translator. Toward the end of August, Evelyn came down to keep him company and to help him assess Mexican education.

Dewey had made an agreement with the minister of education to investigate the educational resources and to suggest what might be needed for the modernization and improvement of education in Mexico. President Plutarco Elías Calles himself had begun his career as a rural schoolteacher, and so education was one of his priorities. Dewey inquired about the conditions of schools in Mexico City during the week while he was teaching, and the presence of many Mexican teachers in his classes helped his investigations. On weekends, he toured the rural school districts with guides and drivers working for the Ministry of Education. He made a quick excursion to Cuernavaca. As soon as the term ended, the Ministry of Education provided him with a car, driver, and interpreter, and he and Evelyn traveled as far as Guadalajara. He told a former student that he went to the country districts, mingled with the "indigenous" people, and "was impressed both with [their] capacities . . . and what the government was doing for them." John was particularly struck by the "aesthetic capacities of the Mexican people." Dewey's mission to Mexico was so successful in educational terms that a historian of Mexican education declared: "During the 1920s the Mexican curriculum almost gave full sway to the Master of Morningside Heights."

By this time, travel to a developing democracy inevitably meant for Dewey an attempt to tally in print the successes and difficulties of the social and political life that was being transformed. Soon, the first of his four articles about Mexico reached the desk of Herbert Croly. In the first of these, "Church and State in Mexico," Dewey started with the same conflict he had observed in Turkey: the clash of progressive politics and traditional religion. As in China, Dewey's timing was fortunate. Only a few days after the Deweys had arrived in Mexico, on July 3, 1926, President Calles enforced the sweeping provisions of the Carranza constitution of 1917 directed against the church. This led to a clerical strike, attempting to create the impression that the state had forced the churches to close and thus turn popular opinion against the civil authorities. Dewey concluded: "The revolution in Mexico is not completed," but he predicted that the state would win in this historic conflict.

In the second of his articles, "Mexico's Educational Renaissance," Dewey was as enthusiastic about Mexico's schools as he had been pessimistic about similar provincial schools in Turkey. "There is no educational movement in the world," he stated, "which exhibits more of the spirit of intimate union of school activities with those of the community." The brightest spot in Mexican reform was its educational activity, Dewey believed. His essay "From a Mexican Notebook" sketches out Dewey's accumulations of impressionistic observations.

Complicating the Mexican issue internationally, Dewey argued in the last of his articles, was the almost intentionless, habitual inevitability of American imperialism, the economic colonization of Mexico in the interest of the United States. Perhaps Mexico was doomed, since "both economic conditions and political arrangements and traditions combine to make imperialism easy."

LOSING ALICE

During the fall of 1926, after his return to New York, Dewey's forebodings concerning Alice's heart problems were borne out. By the end of September, the doctors made it clear that Alice had no hope of a permanent recovery. By December, John believed that she needed intensive care, and he looked into nursing homes as far away as Portland, Oregon, and Asheville, North Carolina. She failed so markedly in vigor and the doctor's prognoses were so negative that Dewey took a leave of absence from teaching in the spring of 1927 in order to attend to her needs. Briefly she felt well enough to visit friends in Cambridge and Marlborough, Massachusetts, but soon afterward she weakened measurably and generally remained in bed. She was, as Dewey later told a correspondent, "seriously ill all winter . . . needing constant care."

To the last, Dewey wrote a colleague, Alice "never lost her courage," "tho' confinement was very hard on one of her temperament." On July 4 she suffered a minor stroke, caused by worsening arteriosclerosis and hypertension. After this, little time remained before her death. Her physician visited her for the last time on July 13, and then, on the morning of the fourteenth, she died peacefully of a cerebral thrombosis. John and Alice were two weeks short of having been married for forty-one years. That same day Dewey made final arrangements for her burial. He felt "terrible fatigue," he told his family, but he fought on and sent telegrams to his closest friends. George Herbert Mead responded immediately upon hearing the unwelcome news. "I have been thinking," Mead said in a moving telegram, "of the unrecoverable days here in Chicago when she was so large a part of the great adventure of life that we lived together—of how greatly she made the adventure worth while, and of how much we loved her." Mead rushed to New York for the funeral, which was arranged for the sixteenth. John's brother Davis and his wife came down from Cambridge. Addison Moore came. Cables and notes poured in. Dewey's students and colleagues came to his support. An especially heartfelt note came from Dewey's student Sidney Hook. "Dear, dear Professor Dewey," Hook started, "Let me assure you that there is at least one person, the warmth of whose affection for you is more 'filial' than professional—who considers it an honor and delight to be of help to you in any way and at any time." In the years to come, Hook remained faithful to these promises. Dewey's closest friend at Columbia, William P. Montague, spoke at the memorial.

Dewey remained in New York for about a week, answering many expressions of condolence in his usual patient way. His note to S. O. Levinson was typical: "Thank you so much for your beautiful flowers and your message. Mrs. Dewey's many friends were most kind and everything was done that was helpful & consoling that was possible. Of course we had known she could not recover but the end was rapid, unexpectedly so." Fred and Elizabeth had been vacationing with their children in Nova Scotia when Alice died, and they were not able to get back to New York before the funeral. Fred begged his father to join them in Canada as soon as possible after the burial. At the end of July, accompanied by Jane, John started by boat for "that quiet spot," Hubbards, Nova Scotia, where he rested even as he continued to send grief-filled expressions of thanks to friends. "I have been very fortunate," he wrote to the philosopher E. A. Burtt, "in having five children & as many grandchildren, & I realized as I never did before how fortunate I am compared with those who [are] really left alone." Dewey was mindful of "how close knit are the ties which are formed in sharing all the vicissitudes of life" for four decades, even as the outpouring of warmth and affection for his loss really did remind him of how many ties remained. In a tribute to Alice, he told Helen and George Mead: "I do not feel that I have a right to complain. Over forty years we were together & Alice has made my life more than anything else."

Hubbards itself thereafter came to hold a very special place in John's affections. Perhaps it was because it was here that he came immediately after Alice's death. Situated on Lake Sawlor, or Sawley, a pond about a half-mile from the ocean and thirty-five miles southwest of Halifax, Hubbards was a place to which he returned almost every summer for the next twenty-five years.

At the end of September the family returned to New York. Dewey had two years still remaining on his lease at 2880 Broadway. But before he left Hubbards he had already decided to sublet that apartment, and he asked his oldest daughter Evelyn to "find a suitable apartment somewhere near her work" where he could live with her. Upon his return he and Evelyn moved into 125 East 62d Street. His old life with Alice was over.

F. Matthias Alexander, who knew Alice well, said of her in 1921 that she had "the keenest mind and the shrewdest comprehension of men and women and life in general, of any woman he has ever had the privilege of meeting." The editor in chief at E. P. Dutton, John Macrae, had told her that she "owe[d] it to society to write a book" on her reactions to Japan and China. But Alice did not write the book he begged to have from her. It was not to be books but her personality that most forcefully impressed people. She gave to many people just what they needed. Beneath and between the depressions that surfaced all too often, she had a deeply kind nature and an incisive, sane mind. She was, as Henry Castle said, "one of the very few women who had the rare power of pure thought." Genevieve Hodge remembered "her brilliant conversation." James Tufts recalled "her tender affection for our little children." And Dorothea Moore saw her as being "the most richly elemental woma[n] I have ever had the fortune to know." John Dewey said simply: "She liberated me."

The abiding interest in Alice's life was women's rights, as defined by the "new" feminism that emerged in the 1880s. The new feminists split into roughly two groups: a small group of what John and Alice called "professional feminists," like Charlotte Perkins Gilman, and a much larger group of activist women. Alice belonged to the second group, with Mary Simkhovitch and Lillian Wald. Her causes were those that preoccupied the new feminists: equal opportunity in education, which meant coeducation; equal social opportunity, which meant the end of social differentiation; and equal political opportunity, which meant the right to vote.

Alice understood all three of these fundamental concerns in the context of a basic philosophy. A remark she made to Lucy in 1918 is one of many examples of her attitude. When Alice met the Harvard philosopher George Santayana, she said that "he lived in the drawing room and had never seen the kitchen." She had little use for men—especially philosophers—who lived in a solitary masculine world. It was little wonder that an instructor at Columbia characterized her as "filled with high enthusiasms, [and] capable of magnificent scorn for petty and ugly and cruel things." Reflecting on the rise and fall of civilizations, she recommended to her daughter Lucy that she write a book: "There is a great idea and [p]iece of work for someone to do . . . something you might like to take up . . . it is the relations between the success of nations and their treatment of women." Only a few weeks later, in another letter to Lucy, Alice took up the theme of women's work in relation to future American development:

> I am very desirous of knowing how you like your work in this year of great uncertainty for girls. This is still a world of sad revelation for what men do and do not think about women, is it not? With the failure of the suffrage amendment there is added the fact that the universities remain oblivious of the fact that women will have to be as much better prepared for work after the war as they need to be during the war in order to meet the increased responsibilities new work puts over [them]. I wonder if the western universities here in Cal with their two rather Prussian minded presidents have adapted less to the new conditions than have the older institutions that are nearer to the pressure from the facts and incidents of

war. I hope that is so for unless it is war will appear to have set
back rather than pushed on . . . women's progress.

Here, of course, Alice was concerned with women's prospects for a
good education and equal work opportunities, and she brought both
concerns to China and Japan. In Japan, she saw little opportunity for
women: marriage gave women a position in society, but the submission
that went along with it prevented them from using it. In China, the
situation was different, and Alice advised elementary school girls to go
to high school, high-school women to attend college, and college-
educated women to take an equal place with men in society.

The suffrage issue did not apply even remotely to Japan and was
not relevant to Chinese politics when Alice was there. But in the
United States, suffrage was a major focus of her energies. In 1910–11,
Alice was district leader of the Woman's Suffrage Party for the
Twenty-first Assembly District of New York City. She organized a
prosuffrage society in New York, and she got John to use his position
on behalf of the cause. The *New York Times* reported in 1912 that
Professor Dewey had addressed the summer students at Columbia on
that subject: "He was scheduled to speak on suffrage only, and so many
people came to hear him that many could not get inside the doors."
Boys would be better educated by women if women were enfran-
chised, Professor Dewey said. The speech continued:

> "Women are shut out of most important social functions," he
> said. "To have education what it should be[,] we should have
> the educators educated. Education is life and experience. You
> can't have a real democracy where there is caste and cliques or
> sects. Women are shut out from the culmination and zeal for
> full citizenship, the outward and visible sign of the inward and
> spiritual grace which is liberty."

After Dewey's talk, members of the Women's Suffrage Party
waited at the doors to hand the audience announcements of that
evening's meeting. Dewey gave a version of this talk several times. On

October 17, 1917, he delivered it to the Discussion Club of Teachers College. In published articles and in a long, unpublished memorandum that he wrote in 1902 to A. K. Parker, recorder of the University of Chicago, concerning Parker's proposal that men and women be separately educated, John supported the main tenets of the new feminism. Indeed, it is accurate to say that of the men who were associated with the new feminism, "no single male figure's efforts emerge with as much consistent praise as John Dewey's." Alice had educated her husband in feminist issues. He was a serious supporter of new feminism, and Alice's influence led him to cultivate important relations with Jane Addams and other activist new feminists. It was not only that he was willing to cut a comic figure when he marched in a suffrage parade in New York, carrying a sign reading "Men can vote. Why can't I?" Any devoted husband might have done that. But he fully incorporated her thought into his. During his long correspondence with a somewhat scatterbrained scientist, Scudder Klyce, he was led by Klyce's remarks on women to teach him a good lesson. "If you have the good fortune to be able to talk to intelligent women, and listen to them expressing their views about men as a class," he told Klyce,

> you will find that they agree that men are essentially hogs—
> and that the worst of it is they havent the slightest idea of the
> fact, since what they hog are intangible things—in other
> words they assume that *their* work is the really important thing
> in the world. Till my attention was called to it I am bound to
> say I had always assumed that, and I don't think I [have] . . .
> ever met a man who didn't practically say to himself "Why of
> course it is. How funny that anybody should question it." . . .
> [If] that isnt being a hog, I don't know what it is. And you can't
> have such unbalance on one side without having a lot on the
> other. . . . I have never met a man, no matter how much more
> he knew of somethings than I did, that I couldn't see how he
> did it intellectually. . . . Only women have ever given [me] real-
> ly intellectual surprises; I'll be darned if I can see how they do
> it—but they do. Their observations . . . are more honest than

men's—they are much less easily imposed upon . . . [and] more willing to face the unpleasant side of facts. I am not generalizing; I am only reporting what I have seen.

But Alice did not need John to present her feminist case. In 1915, she wrote a letter to the editor of the *New York Times* commenting on an editorial warning that women's voting would lead to the decline of female virtue. Alice regarded the editorial from the lofty vantage point of bemused contempt. "I shall preserve your article," she began, "as it will make excellent propaganda material for women's suffrage." The newspaper, she suggested, was about fifty years behind the times, back in the 1870s, when "gentlemen then [as now, in the *Times* article] spoke for God . . . to protect . . . the order of nature. Their so-called arguments are as whimsical and humorous to the modern reader as the hats and clothes of that day are to the modern dressmaker."

She liberated John Dewey, as he acknowledged. But that was, after all, secondary to the main achievement of her life, the liberation of her own being.

For him, after her death, he had no choice but to go forward. John recovered slowly, believing that he had only a few years left to live. So he did the only thing he had ever known how to do: he returned to work. His way of looking at any sort of work, whether it was philosophy or social protest or merely growing asparagus, brought him back to the world. He got closer to his children. He helped found more social-action groups, and he continued to travel around the world to examine educational and social progress.

DEWEY AMONG THE SOVIETS

Dewey's attitude toward the Soviet Union was complex. He was a fierce critic of Leninist Marxism, but he also suspected that the Russian people, as distinguished from their party leaders, were not so much Bolsheviks as they were engaged in a human experiment to reform society. He wanted to see it for himself, and the chance came. The American Society for Cultural Relations with Russia was founded in

1927 at Lillian Wald's Henry Street Settlement. John Dewey became one of its original directors, along with Edgar Varese, Edward Albion Ross, and Leopold Stokowski. Floyd Dell and Norman Hapgood soon joined the group. Around this time, Stalin was tightening his grip on the revolution, and an effort was being made to influence foreign intellectuals to form favorable impressions of the Soviet experiment. Accordingly, the Soviet minister of education, Anatoli V. Lunacharsky, invited Dewey to lead a group of educators to the Soviet Union during the summer of 1928. Dewey accepted the invitation, and it was soon announced that he would lead a nonpolitical mission of twenty-five American educators to study methods of instruction in Soviet Russia this summer. The group of educators included James McKeen Cattell, now editor of *Science*; the presidents of Carleton College and the University of Minnesota; "Fola" La Follette, Senator Robert La Follette's daughter; Katherine Blake, a public-school teacher in the New York City schools; and Evelyn Dewey. Fred's wife Elizabeth agreed to accompany John, who wanted to leave early to look at art galleries in London, Paris, and Berlin before July 7, when the commission was to assemble in Leningrad.

Publicly, the announcement of this trip was greeted enthusiastically. The *Daily Worker* heralded Dewey's acceptance of the invitation as signifying his approval of the Soviet state. Privately, however, the Office of Eastern Affairs was hurriedly gathering information on the board members of the American Society for Cultural Relations with Russia and those participating in the educational mission. Only a few years earlier, Dewey had been consulted on "Bolshevism" in China; now he had come to be regarded as a possibly dangerous subversive himself. An FBI informant wrote that Dewey "has been very consistently helping the Soviet game," listed numerous past associations that might be deemed supportive of communism, and stressed Dewey's published opposition to military training. "The Communists oppose military training in the United States," the agent noted, "but go in for it in Russia."

Dewey simply kept his own counsel. Anything new was of interest to him. He made little if any distinction between seeing a Titian in the Hermitage and visiting a school for wayward children: both were experience. Both were likely to produce further thought, and such reflection would eventually mean some more material to put into prose and then into print. His trip was thus just one more expression of his omnivorous mind at work.

Dewey could not leave New York before May 16, when he was to be presented with a portrait bust by the famous sculptor Jacob Epstein, for whom he had sat the previous year. A group of Dewey's friends, led by James Harvey Robinson and Joseph Ratner, had formed a committee to commission Epstein to create a portrait bust to be presented to Dewey. After organizing an appeal by mail for funds, Epstein's fee was collected, the bust was completed, and it was presented to Dewey in a modest ceremony at the Henry Street Settlement. One of those who had answered the appeal for contributions was Anzia Yezierska, by now a famous novelist and short story writer. She sent in $25 and then wrote to Dewey. She knew that Alice had died. In her book *All I Can Never Be*, Anzia fashioned a romantic account in which she and John made an appointment. Always the outsider, she had to wait outside his locked office door. When he arrived, he was aloof, but she stammered out her hopes. Then, while he answered a phone call, she found her first book, *Hungry Hearts*, on his shelf and noticed that "the pages were uncut." Sentimental, tragic, and a charming fiction. But Dewey never answered her letter, and they never again met.

Dewey and his daughter-in-law Elizabeth left Hoboken for England, where they arrived eight days later. Liz had friends in England who met them and took them on a motor tour to visit famous architectural sites, mainly cathedrals—Exeter, Salisbury, Winchester—then Oxford, the Ashmolean Museum, and so on during four packed days. Liz had previously gone with Dewey on one of Barnes's summer tours of European art museums, and when they arrived in London they settled into a rigorous schedule of museum visits, occasionally interrupted by social occasions. The English, Dewey said, "were most hospitable and friendly." Still, he was more interested in paintings than in courtesies, and after two weeks in London, they left for Paris to take another look at pictures they had originally seen with Barnes. "Our serious occupation is pictures," Dewey wrote to

George Mead. "In fact I think Im more interested in [paintings] . . . than anything else outside of philosophy." But there were pictures to be seen in Berlin too, and after a week in Paris they left for Germany.

Now time was running short. Dewey was to join Evelyn and the rest of the group on July 7, and he wanted to spend as much time as possible at the Hermitage before the commission arrived. Although the revolutionary Soviet Union seemed rather dreary, the day after they arrived they went at once at the Hermitage. Liz noticed the shabbiness of everything, the poorly dressed people, the run-down facilities. It was not until the next day that they sought out the offices of Vox, the state cultural agency that had handled their arrangements. The president of Vox was much upset at Dewey's unofficial arrival, and he was determined to plan every detail of their visit. They were taken in hand and generally guided around to what the Russians wanted them to see until the commission arrived. Evelyn and the other commissioners arrived on schedule. Evelyn, Liz, and Fola La Follette were all about the same age, and they formed a little group around John Dewey. At once the commissioners were guided on a circuit of the wonders of the new Soviet Union: the "House of Popular Culture" built by workers for study and cultural activities; a restaurant "which was given over to the waiters at the time of the revolution"; Chekhov's *Uncle Vanya* and *The Cherry Orchard*, and Gorky's *In the Depths* at the Moscow Art Theater; the Komsomol center; Peterhof; Russian cinema ("one [movie] of peasants" and "one of the October revolution"); and, of course, children's schools, worker's schools, university schools, pedagogical institutes, a school for tubercular children, laboratory schools, Tartar schools, Dr. Wirtenberg's nature study school ("very scientific work"), the children's village at Detskoye Selo ("150 homeless children . . . very hygienic"), a rest home for scientists, a sanitarium for intellectuals, and a labor commune in the country for criminals ("no walls— no imprisonment—learn trades").

Elizabeth, not yet forty years old, wilted under the regimen. She complained about the poor quality of the bed and the "bum" suppers, and she had intense stomach cramps. She was in a state of complete nervous exhaustion. Evelyn and Fola La Follette also began to skip the evening events; both were ill. But John Dewey, sixty-eight years old, slept soundly, stayed out at parties, gave dinners, visited night clubs, attended every event, and never experienced a day of dysentery. On July 28, all three young women were sick in bed, but Dewey sailed on, full of curiosity. He managed to see as much art as possible, the icons, the folk art, and modern paintings in Moscow. But he also went on every obligatory excursion and found those nearly as interesting. As he traveled around Russia, Dewey exercised the same charm over children that he had in China. One of the group later told

> how, in the villages the delegates visited, little children along the streets ran to hold John Dewey's hands, to cling to his coat-tails and show him their small childish treasures; . . . their parents and teachers knew John Dewey's name, and . . . it served as a password, not only into schools and homes, but into factories and government bureaus.

In Moscow Dewey attended a conference organized by Professor A. G. Kalashnikov of the pedagogical department of Moscow Technical University. Ten days later Kalashnikov sent Dewey a two-volume set of the *Soviet Pedagogical Encyclopedia* for 1927, with a note: "Your works, especially 'School and Society' and 'The School and the Child' have very much influenced the development of the Russian pedagogy and in the first years of [the] revolution you were one of the most renowned writers." At present, he continued, Soviet "philosoph-ico-socialistic" theory differed a bit from Dewey's recommendations, but still, those "concrete shapes of pedagogical practice, which you have developed in your works, will be for a long time the aim of our tendencies."

Dewey's distinguished commission was given special treatment. Armand Hammer entertained the members several times. Madame Kameneff, Trotsky's sister, "one of the ablest women in Russia," made a gracious speech of welcome on behalf of the Society for Cultural Relations with Foreign Countries, an organization of which she was president. Minister of Education Lunacharsky received them in the

Kremlin. "The high red wall of the Kremlin is shut to foreigners with rare exceptions," a newspaperman reported. "But last week it opened to admit the party of educationists led by Professor John Dewey. . . . The authorities are eager to show every courtesy to the Americans." Lunacharsky frankly admitted that in education the Soviets had made "slow, arduous, and incomplete" progress, but he reminded the delegates that the country was still emerging from "chaos . . . [with] everything to be created anew." Russian reporters and American journalists—among them John Gunther—interviewed the group. They were even received by Lenin's widow, Madam Krupskaya, who talked to them about the problems of educating children and peasants. To Dewey, Krupskaya seemed to speak his own language, to share his views: "Her conversation . . . was about incidents of a human sort that had occurred in her contact with children and women, incidents illustrative of their desire for education and for new light and life—evincing an interest on her part that was congruous with her distinctly maternal, almost housewifely type." Like Alice, she was committed to the task of enabling "every human being to obtain personal cultivation. . . . to share to the full in all the things that give virtue to human life."

Even after Evelyn and the rest of the mission left, Dewey and Liz stayed one more day—to see pictures! On the afternoon of August 14, they rushed to the train. Madam Kameneff was waiting on the platform to see them off. At 7:30 the next morning they crossed the Russian border into Poland, and as Liz wrote with considerable relief, they were at last "out of Russia!"

Dewey was not yet ready to go home, for he yearned to see his daughter Lucy Alice, who was living in Vienna. Lucy Jane, his sixth grandchild, was only four months old. He stayed for two weeks and then went for ten days to the baths at Carlsbad that he had enjoyed so much with Alice in 1924. He did not return to New York until early October, but he soon wrote to Sidney Hook that the trip had been "infinitely interesting" and that he felt "a tremendous vitality" in Russia. Even this early he struck the note that was to form the basis of his published commentaries—that the Soviet Marxist-Leninist theories were important only as "symbolic formulations," whereas the true significance of the revolution would be the practical "genuine and significant rebirth of culture" among the people. He predicted a very different outcome than the Soviet theorists anticipated.

When he got home, everyone was curious about Dewey's views on Russia. On November 10 a dinner was arranged at New York's Hotel Astor in honor of Dewey and the delegation. George S. Counts presided over the event, attended by eight hundred people. Dewey was the featured speaker. "Russia," he told the audience, "keeps track of us to an extraordinary degree." He personally believed that the Russians "are more akin to the American people than to any other people. There is, or could be, a strong bond between the two peoples . . . if certain artificial barriers could be removed." This was, of course, music to ears of the Soviets, and Dewey's words were reported in bold headlines in the Moscow press. It was not music to the American government, though, and a member of the audience sent a report to the State Department concerning Dewey's "pro-Communist ties." The agent failed to notice that Dewey tirelessly distinguished between Marxist-Leninist theory, of which he disapproved, and Russia, with which, as Corliss Lamont later said, he had a "love affair." For the rest of his life he maintained this distinction, always favoring the Russian people but remaining critical of Marxist theory and Soviet politics.

Readers of the *New Republic* knew that if Dewey had visited the Soviet Union, articles by him would soon appear in that journal. With little delay, Dewey published five articles about the state of culture, reform, and politics in the Soviet Union. These, with his earlier articles on his visits to the four major revolutionary centers of the postwar world, form a coherent series. His observations of the Soviet Union are constructed and arranged like a drama to answer the question, What is the meaning of this ten-year-old Russian experiment? Dewey's dramatic approach is evident in the opening sentence of the series: "The alteration of Petrograd into Leningrad is, without question a symbol, but the mind wavers in deciding of what." Taken as a whole, Dewey's answer in the five articles is that the revolution of the Russians was immensely more significant than the Marxism of the Bolsheviks.

The revolution that he experienced was of heart and mind, but its economic and political results were far less accomplished and had far less importance than the "liberation of a people to consciousness of themselves as a determining power in the shaping of their ultimate fate." Marxist philosophy and ideology struck Dewey as "outworn, absolutistic metaphysics and bygone theories of straight-line, one way 'evolution,' " compared with the energies that had been aroused "in the minds of the people." Dewey spoke personally, out of his own experience of moving (as he himself put it) from "absolutism" to "experimentalism": "The fanatic of individual capitalistic business for private gain and the Marxian dogmatic fanatic" debate with each other out of closed systems:

> According to the first, the [Soviet] attempt is destined to failure; it is fated to produce, in the words of Mr. Hoover, an "economic vacuum"; according to the latter, the transformation from individualism to collectivism of action is the absolute and inevitable result of the working of laws that as positively known to social "science" as, say, the law of gravitation to physical science. Not being an absolutist of either type, I find it more instructive to regard it as an experiment whose outcome is quite undetermined.

Dewey stressed the experiment-in-progress, a "new world in the making"—not one already completed—in which education was the central problem. Far more than any inspection of specific political and industrial conditions, educational effort was Dewey's guide and key to understanding Soviet society—just as it had been for him in China, Turkey, and Mexico. The revolution that engaged his imagination was not ideological but imaginative; not determined but adventurous and problematic; not political but psychological and moral. Neither the devotees nor the enemies of the Bolshevik regime had it right. The future society that he believed he saw already emerging in the Soviet Union was to be unlike the "western world of private capital and individual profit" but also, he predicted, "unlike the society which orthodox Marxian formulae call for." But who could be truly certain of the outcome? Would the people's revolution or Marxist ideology triumph? "There are too many unknowns in the equation." Dewey kept his eye on the experiment and lived to see an important part of the outcome and to participate in it.

THREE MORE BOOKS

Within a few years after his return from his long stay in Asia, Dewey published three important and related books: *Human Nature and Conduct* (1922), *Experience and Nature* (1925), and *The Quest for Certainty* (1929). In a broad sense, *Human Nature and Conduct,* subtitled *An Introduction to Social Psychology*, is a continuation of Dewey's ongoing concern with ethical values and behavior. It is an advance on Dewey's sections in his collaboration with James H. Tufts in the sense that by 1922 Dewey had worked out a clearer and more flexible understanding of the psychology of impulses, habits, cognition, intention, and custom that form the web of moral behavior. Dewey's last chapter opens: "Intelligence . . . is not ours originally or by production. 'It thinks' is a truer psychological statement than 'I think.' Thoughts sprout and vegetate; ideas proliferate. They come from deep unconscious sources." Habits or social customs "think us" more than we think them. Ideas do not originate with us, nor will they end with us: in short, our intelligence is "bound up . . . with the community life of which we are a part" and is not a solitary act. Psychology, of course, replaces abstract theory, since Dewey was intent on demonstrating that morality can be explained naturalistically, in terms of human habits or repetitious human wishes, human needs, and social functions. He argued that to understand conduct, we must understand human nature, from which alone human conduct proceeds. But human nature itself looks both inward and outward. A person is separate and simple, ineluctably himself or herself. But he or she is also necessarily enmeshed in complicated social groupings, "culture," or civilization— in ideas, assumptions, rituals, and ceremonials shared by others.

Human nature is thus shaped from the inside by the individual's effort to be himself or herself and thus to try to reform or transform society so that it will accommodate self-realization. At the same time, the individual's character and wishes are joined, from the outside, by the traditions, laws, customs and imperatives of communities. There is no possibility that inside and outside, self and society, can be separated, for their interaction forms the unity of human nature, and conduct is its expression. As these two directions, intrinsic and extrinsic, interact, morals are the result. But since the nature and conditions of the interactions are always changing, so are morals. So constituted, human nature *searches* for morals, the action of two opposed impulses as they meet. Not by conscious intent but by the very nature of human nature, morals are in a constant state of flux. Theoretically, a democracy should provide the best setting to unify inner and outer. But for all his love of democracy, Dewey disagreed. No sentimentalist, he declared democracy in the present day to be "still . . . immature." At present, democracy in America has produced little more than a leveling of individuals and "messy confusion." If our democracy were more mature, so would our morals be; if our morals improved, our democracy would mature. Existence in the here and now is all: "Morals are connected with actualities . . . not with ideals, ends and obligations independent of concrete actualities." They *are*, not *ought*. *Human Nature and Conduct* is a book-in-progress, relating to Dewey's earlier examinations of ethics and looking toward further consolidation of the mystery of human behavior, how it is and, possibly, how it might be.

Experience and Nature begins with the question of what makes things true. What happens when old and new truths conflict? Which is to receive priority? While this is a basic epistemological question in philosophy and is so treated in this book, it also has an autobiographical undercurrent; for in *Experience and Nature* Dewey is working on new material with new ideas, starting tentatively on new paths. Dewey's great advance in this book was his expansion of the concept of "experience" to encompass all we have. The various dichotomies between experience and "something other" and the arguments about them that run through the history of philosophy are resolved by

Dewey into parts of a person's single, complex, multifaceted existence, his or her "experience." "The constant task of thought," he says at the outset, "is to establish working connections between old and new subject matters. We cannot lay hold of the new, we cannot even keep it before our minds, much less understand it, save by the use of ideas and knowledge we already possess." True enough—but it is also true of the book he is writing, the book before him, which in order to make it new, he must draw it through the accumulations of his previous ideas. No easy task, for the attempt to achieve originality can begin to disconnect the continuity between the declining old thoughts and the still inchoate emerging ones. "The greater the gap, the disparity . . . the greater is the burden imposed upon reflections; the distance between the old and the new is the measure of the range and depth of the thought required."

As a philosopher and writer, Dewey stressed continuity rather than unanticipated originality. To read his books in order, one after the other, is to get a picture of a mind moving toward deeper insight and sharper refinement. Russell was right in calling Dewey's mind a "natural force." It moved like nature, like the seasons, like the slow but unstoppable advances that Darwin described.

Dewey characterized his approach in *Experience and Nature* as what can best be called critical *empirical naturalism*. The method is "critical" but not negative: it is a commitment to examine nature empirically and thereby to earn the perspective and the courage to build a deeper culture and to envisage a higher aim for humanity. The approach to understanding experience through empirical naturalism, Dewey believed, creates a firmer foundation for people's cherished beliefs than does idealism or supernaturalism. What it saves, what remains after the method has winnowed away the chaff of old prejudices, is a higher vision of individual man and of the prospects for the evolution of culture. "The failures of philosophy," Dewey wrote, "have come from lack of confidence in the directive powers that inhere in experience, if men have but the wit and courage to follow them." *Experience and Nature* exhibits the courage to have and pursue knowledge. Dewey frequently uses such words as *perilous, dangerous, precarious*, and *uncertainty* to remind the reader that this book should be regarded as the philosophical version of the traditional myth of the search.

Because it takes the form of an epic journey, *Experience and Nature* is modeled on one of the books cherished by the young Dewey: Homer's *Odyssey*. Empirical naturalism is the boat that takes the questers on their journey, with the dangers of wishing for "certainty," "security," or "stability," "permanence," "faith," or "universality," paralleling the dangers faced by the classic questing heroes—to stay with the lotus eaters, to embrace the sirens, to be seduced by Calypso's ideal beauty. Many begin the search, but few make it all the way back to Ithaca or understanding. The goal—like the golden fleece or the kingdom to be claimed—is the knowledge of what Dewey termed "the true nature of experience." Just as for Odysseus, the revelation of the quest is that questing never ends. Arrival in Ithaca offers only provisional truth. Nature beckons. Culture and self grow by searching for nature's meanings. Continued growth comes only with continued striving, not with finding and concluding, only with never yielding.

Experience and Nature, then, is both autobiography and epic, a book about how one writes such a book, showing how it is done. It is a book that discovers it can have no conclusion. True to the open nature of experience, this book remained open-ended. Indeed, in 1949 Dewey revised it and wrote a new introduction to it. As Joseph Ratner remarked, the "revisions were more than editorial; they were reworkings resulting in new visions." Dewey even considered changing the title to *Culture and Nature*: "I would abandon the term 'experience.' . . . I would substitute the term 'culture' because . . . it can fully and freely carry my philosophy of experience." He understood that culture itself required and consisted of constant revision. The book he was writing thus needed constant rewriting. It could, in the long run, aim at nothing less than a complete history and philosophic interpretation of human development. Dewey told Oscar Cargill that among his books, *Experience and Nature* was "the one I had the most satisfaction in writing."

It is not surprising, therefore, that in the penultimate chapter Dewey turned to the "culture" that humans make out of artistic expression through their evolving experience of nature, which leads to knowledge and thus to art. For Dewey, art offered a key to understand the self-reflexive character of his book: "Thinking is preeminently an art; knowledge and propositions which are the products of thinking, are works of art, as much so as statuary or symphonies." Later he included science as a work of art. Our time, he declared, is a new epic age. Art has freed itself from magical rites and cults and primitive superstitions, so that all our best efforts of culture can be seen as artistic: "the history of human experience is a history of the development of arts"; science is a "record of the differentiation of arts, not a record of separation from art." As knowledge advances, so does culture; as culture advances, knowledge leads to another advancement of our art. *Experience and Nature* thus looks toward *Art as Experience* (1934).

THE GIFFORD LECTURES

Before Dewey left for Russia, one time period of his own future had already been arranged. In March 1928, he received a letter from Sir Alfred Ewing, principal of the University of Edinburgh, inviting him to accept an appointment there as the Gifford lecturer in natural theology. In philosophic circles, the Gifford Lectureship was internationally esteemed to be a high honor, and William James and Josiah Royce were the only Americans who had been appointed to it. One of James's best books, *The Varieties of Religious Experience*, had come from his Gifford lectures thirty years earlier. Dewey's selection, he was informed, "was unanimous." Almost immediately, Dewey wired acceptance for 1929. His sole concern was to allow adequate "leisure for preparation of the lectures," since "my time for the coming summer is already so pledged." Even while he was in Russia, in a letter to Mead, he expressed concern about having adequate time upon his return to prepare his talks. This was unusual for Dewey, who had lectured so often with scarcely any advance preparation that his worry proved the seriousness with which he took this appointment. To prepare adequately, he requested a leave of absence for the entire spring semester, which was granted by President Butler with his usual generosity toward Dewey. "You may have the leave of absence," he wrote, "but we shall arrange it so that you will need to relinquish only half of the salary for the spring session." Dewey also received an honorarium of about £200 from the Gifford endowment.

He had requested that the lectures be given as late in the spring semester of 1929 as possible, and so from April 17 to May 17, each Wednesday and Friday he delivered a lecture. In between lectures, he continued to work on the talks. "I am hard at work getting my lectures into shape," he wrote to Sidney Hook in the midst of the course, "just rewriting all the time. I suppose I hadn't let it cook long enough." He thought the audience "nice . . . not large, but a good quality, mainly adults, not many students."

A reporter for the *Edinburgh Scotsman* reported on the first lecture: "Extraordinary scenes were witnessed. There was not an available seat in the hall, while the platform at the back was crowded with people standing. Many were unable to gain admission to the hall itself, and stood on the stairway leading to it, where they could have heard little." Dewey began with some casual remarks. His subject, "The Quest for Certainty," was peculiarly interesting to him, he said,

> because it seems to me now that certainty is the last thing that anyone could hope to find. When I was a young man we were all cocksure about most things. But now, all foundations have been shaken, even the elementary facts of physics. I had thought that if anything was certain these were. But physics now remains an elegant superstructure without any foundation.

The audience broke into laughter at that. Here was an American beginning the world's most distinguished lecture series in philosophy in a discursive, homespun way. The audience relaxed. Dewey continued: "Physics is like one of those hotels in America which are shifted from one foundation to another, but keep going." More laughter. It was just like listening to what Emerson famously called "man thinking."

He *was* thinking. Much of his earlier philosophic work was present in these new lectures but tempered by the political lessons he had learned in China, Turkey, Mexico, and, most recently, the Soviet Union. In each he believed he had seen the stirrings of a modern revolution against established institutions and beliefs. He did not have to look back to medieval Europe to see what he was describing; he had seen in person the conflict between the quest for certainty and the wish for security, counterpoised to the pressure of change. Even earlier, he had, as he implied, experienced that same conflict in himself as he moved from his earliest allegiance to Hegelian idealism to adherence to science, the psychological laboratory, and philosophic operationalism. His earliest and his most recent experiences drove these Gifford lectures as Dewey got into his subject. When later revised, these lectures formed the basis for one of his best books, *The Quest for Certainty*. Simultaneously he was writing a history of the search for absolutes, a critique of contemporary revolutionary politics, and an autobiography of his own changing mind.

Still speaking rather casually in his first talk, Dewey reminded his audience that modern science's view of the universe was hostile to many of the most esteemed ideas of western Europe and civilization. For the last three centuries, the task of philosophy had been to adjust evolving scientific ideas to established moral and religious beliefs. His aim in the lectures, he told his audience, was to discuss that conflict between science and values from the standpoint of scientific inquiry as a practical undertaking. But first he would start with a discussion of the way that theory and practice had become separated from each other.

In the earliest stages of human development, Dewey began, people sought an "escape from peril," a refuge in a world full of hazards. They tried two strategies: first, sacrifice and ceremonies to propitiate the powers that seemed to decide their destiny. Next, the "sacrifice of a contrite heart was esteemed more pleasing than that of bulls and oxen," and people came to believe that reverence and devotion were more effective in persuading the powers to come to their aid, so that they could "escape defeat and might triumph in the midst of destruction." The second strategy was controlling nature: people invented arts and crafts to construct a fortress out of the same materials that threatened them. They were attempting to secure themselves through external action as well as internal sacrifice and self-denial. As it developed in the West, philosophy tended to disparage action, to deny activity, and to stress an advanced version of the first strategy, by preferring reflection over action and placing *theoria* over *praxis*. The development of the natural sciences had finally overturned this opposition by fusing theory with experiment and investigation with knowledge. For a long time, the separation of theory and practice held sway, and it produced important consequences for how we regard industry, politics, the fine arts, ethics, conceptions of the good, and so on. But now, Dewey asked, "What would the effect be if the divorce were annulled, and knowing and doing were brought into intrinsic connection with one another?" The consequences for the way we think might be considerable. What revisions of the traditional theory of mind would be required, and what changes in the idea of the office of philosophy would be demanded? "What modifications would ensue in the disciplines which are concerned with the various phases of human activity?" On behalf of humanity's quest for absolute certainty, philosophy had taken the side of absolute and eternal knowledge while it disparaged practice, which is changeable, experimental, and uncertain. When this old alignment crumbles through the operations of science, where does the quest for certainty go?

Such questions, Dewey announced, would form the theme of his talks. The discussion of these issues in these lectures would require him to become a psychologist, historian, sociologist, aesthetician, political analyst, and cultural critic, all of which were subsumed under the grant for the Gifford endowment in the phrase "natural theology." *Natural* theology might indeed be the best way to classify the subject of these lectures. Dewey started his philosophic career under the influence of supernatural theology. Now, forty-five years later, he had become a theologian of the natural. All the varied activities of his life, often pursued and conducted separately, had been brought together in one philosophical synthesis. His answer to the question, Where does the quest for immutable certainty go when the old dichotomy crumbles, was that the quest for certainty would crumble, too; and humanity would become free to enter a new stage of human development in an uncertain, experimental, challenging, operational world of contingent probability.

The Quest for Certainty is in the great tradition of skeptical thought, most immediately connected in Dewey's mind with Hume in philosophy and Montaigne in belles lettres. In his third lecture, Dewey's skeptical challenge to the traditions of philosophy was simple: "Why has modern philosophy contributed so little to bringing about an integration between what we know about the world and the intelligent direction of what we do?" His argument in the remaining lectures was that standards of validity must take form provisionally in activities— artistic, scientific, moral, physical, political, and so on—not in a priori conceptions of correctness. Finally, this claim allowed Dewey to announce and argue for an "uncertainty principle" far broader than Heisenberg's. Uncertainty should become the heart of the sort of values that have "authority over conduct."

Heisenberg's "uncertainty principle" in mathematics had been stated less than two years earlier. Dewey's lectures, drafted in 1928–29, already incorporated into his argument Heisenberg's and other recent developments in physical science. He had followed the evolution of the natural, experimental sciences ever since he had taken G. Stanley Hall's laboratory course in psychology as a graduate student at Johns Hopkins. He had studied Darwin and written a brilliant essay on Darwin's influence on philosophy. And more recently, partly stimulated by his daughter Jane but also as a natural consequence of his close tracking of scientific developments, he had been paying attention to modern physics. His discussion of Einstein in the context of the disappearance of detached absolute objectivity in favor of relativity; of such mathematical-physical thinkers as Bridgman, Eddington, and Heisenberg; or his remarks on the departures from traditional philosophy initiated by Peirce all served his core argument that their work

had made a profound revolution in the philosophic theory of knowledge and the logic of science, namely, that

> what is known is . . . a product of which the act of observation
> plays a necessary role. Knowing is seen to be a participant in
> what is finally known. Moreover, the metaphysics of existence
> as something fixed and therefore capable of literally exact
> mathematical description and prediction is undermined. . . .
> Knowing is, for philosophical theory, a case of specially direct-
> ed activity instead of something isolated from practice. The
> quest for certainty by means of exact possession in mind of
> immutable reality is exchanged for security by means of active
> control of the changing course of events.

In short, the job of the philosopher was not to search for eternal truths
beyond the world of events but to help humankind achieve whatever
security that, moment to moment, through the best intelligence, could
be mustered. It is evident how far Dewey had come from his stabs at
discerning truth through religion, from "thought news," or from
dialectics. Now he was able to transform these earlier methods and to
see in Darwin, China, physics, the Soviet Union, mathematics, and
Peirce the greatest of all revolutions in thought and society. He had
arrived at an integrated conception of knowledge and the values associated with it as activity. Ideas are "intellectual instruments" to be "tested and confirmed." "No ideas but in things," as William Carlos
Williams put it in *Paterson*. No ends but means, Dewey claimed.

Toward the culmination of his lectures, Dewey made the
inevitable move to stress the obligation of philosophers to generate
"large and generous ideas," not fixed systems, in order to deal with
"the confusion of tongues, beliefs and purposes that characterizes present [day] life." Above all, philosophers should assume as their task the
provision of hypotheses by which to connect the facts of the actual
world, generated by the sciences, with the operational realization of
possible values. We need, and philosophy can supply, Dewey insisted,
knowing and value making as necessary human activities, not just by

philosophers and scientists, but by every person. Dewey ended his Gifford lectures with characteristic humility: "I have tried to indicate in outline the nature of the task to be accomplished and to suggest some of the resources at hand for its realization."

The applause in the Music Room rose and subsided. Dewey sat. The presiding chairperson stood to give thanks to the lecturer, and he went directly to the heart of Dewey's achievement. Dewey, he said, had engaged the subject of "the nature, genesis, and validity of knowledge." It was not surprising, he added in a tribute to Dewey's Americanness, that Dewey's thought had a parallel in the "nation which had subdued the mighty American Continent within a few centuries to the uses of man." He concluded that the audience had sat "at the feet of a master worthily handling great themes" and had listened "to a thinker whose sincerity was as conspicuous as his intellectual ability."

It was generous of this Scots philosopher to compare the force and character of Dewey's thought to the push westward of the American nation and to speak graciously of Dewey's contribution. But even in his praise he had underestimated both the profundity of Dewey's epistemological contribution and the international character of Dewey's mind. Beginning with *The Quest for Certainty*, Dewey started to think through and write his best works as a philosopher. He had not simply become a man known to the whole world; he had become a philosopher of the world whose thought reached beyond national boundaries and specific concerns into the farthest reaches of the world, in his time and ours.

ENJOYING LIFE AGAIN

Dewey continued to accumulate international honors. Even during the Gifford lectures he took a day off to attend a ceremony conferring on him the honorary degree of fellow of the Educational Institute of Scotland, as an expression of "appreciation [and] gratitude to him for the many pregnant and fruitful contributions he had made both to the theory and the practice of education, not only in his own country but the world over." In the previous year he had been asked to accept an honorary doctorate of laws at the University of St. Andrews, but since he had planned to be in the Soviet Union then, the university postponed the honor until 1929. The degree was awarded in the middle of May 1929, just before his Gifford talks at Edinburgh were completed.

In 1930, Dewey was also made a doctor *honoris causa* by the University of Paris and proclaimed by the dean of arts and letters as "the most profound, most complete expression of the American genius." At the University of Paris, there was a remarkable and touching moment following the ceremonial awarding of the degree. Dewey had prepared a paper to present to the faculty of the university's philosophy department. During the discussion the social philosopher Marcel Mauss rose to address Dewey. His philosophic master, Émile Durkheim, Mauss began, had given his final lecture on John Dewey. No transcript of the lecture remained, only a few note cards that Mauss treasured. In his talk, Durkheim had expressed a greater a3dmiration for John Dewey than for any other living thinker. To Mauss's great sadness, Durkheim had died—but here was his beloved teacher's ideal, Dewey himself! Although Mauss had no philosophic point to make, merely telling Dewey about this made a more moving point than any of the technical deliberations of the other philosophers.

During most summers Dewey returned to the lakeside cottage in Hubbards, Nova Scotia. There, sitting in front of his typewriter on the little veranda, he revised his Gifford lectures for publication. Summer after summer he continued to compose in this quiet place. He was solitary, with plenty of time to work, but not entirely alone. Alice Dewey had been ill for several years before she died, and for a long time Dewey had curtailed his social activities and turned inward. "During all that time," a friend said, Dewey had "never really opened up with anyone of himself and his feelings." Perhaps, in fact, he had withdrawn as early as the fall of 1918, following his relationship with Anzia Yezierska. Then, when Alice died, he went through a genuine period of fatigue and mourning. But in the fall of 1927, as an old acquaintance remembered, "all of a sudden, J.D. changed. He was like 25 years younger and came to all the parties. It was just terrific. . . . I think that decade between about 1927 and 1940 . . . was the period when he was most just himself." From this time on, he basked anew in the attention and affection of women.

Dewey's daughters and Fred's wife Liz played the largest part. Dewey also flirted a bit with Fola La Follette after the trip to Russia. Myrtle McGraw, a graduate student at Columbia who typed *Experience and Nature* for him, was part of his circle of women and a close friend of his daughters and Liz. In 1929 she traveled with him from London to Inverness and then to Paris before they went their separate ways: he to Carlsbad again, and she to visit Lucy in Vienna. "It was just a very devoted sort of daughter-father relationship. . . . I was closely identified with that . . . family," she remembered. The women friends he acquired after Alice's death gave him pleasure safe from entanglements, and from the point of view of the young women, there was undoubtedly an element of sexual safety too, along with the flattery of attention from a world-famous man. He was full of play, and he could be great fun to be with, although straitlaced people were sometimes discomforted by his playfulness. The philosopher G. E. Moore reported that "once when he was with Dewey in Key West they were solicited by a prostitute. Dewey told the girl, 'Oh, I'm too old for that sort of thing.' " Moore "was very upset that Dewey should make such a reply, since the implication was that if he were younger, he might have entertained her offer."

Dewey had a general spiritedness and joviality that, with few exceptions, attracted people of all ages, genders, and races. The philosopher of science F. C. S. Northrop remembered that he and his family shared a table at dinner with Dewey during a transatlantic voyage in 1930. Northrop's two sons, who were then of grade-school age, "were delighted with him. He participated in their games with the gusto of one of them." Although he was capable of solitary work, he was not temperamentally a loner; he was always seeking out human contact. If he was with a man, he joked or talked philosophy and politics; with a child, he played; with a lively young girl or vivacious married woman, he flirted—or, if the possibility arose, he talked philosophy, art, and politics too.

Dewey Turns Seventy

As regularly as the seasons, honors came Dewey's way. Universities showered degrees on him. He was asked to give talks in many of the world's most distinguished endowed lecture series. Polls invariably named him as one of the most eminent Americans. Foreign countries offered him decorations. Just as regularly, beginning with Dewey's seventieth birthday, Americans held national celebrations every ten years to pay homage to him. His seventieth birthday was on October 20, 1929, nine days before Black Thursday.

One day in the winter of 1928, Henry Linville, the president of the New York Teachers Union and a close friend of Dewey's, was sitting in an associate's office. He noticed a row of *Who's Who in America* on the shelves. On more than one occasion, he and Dewey's friends had wondered how old he might be. He found Dewey's entry. Gradually, Linville says, "a thought took shape, and at the next meeting of our Executive Board I proposed to the members that we start a movement to celebrate [his] birthday." Linville was well acquainted with Dewey's closest friends and associates, and he asked their advice. William Heard Kilpatrick, the president of Teachers College, liked the idea. Oswald Garrison Villard, editor of *The Nation*, argued that the celebrations should be national. Beulah Amidon suggested that the New York celebration be not only a dinner with toasts but also an "institute" with papers on various aspects of Dewey's work. By April an advisory board of about twenty-five persons had been formed and held a meeting at the Town Hall Club. Kilpatrick agreed to be the chair, Linville, the secretary, and an executive committee to sponsor the celebration was created.

All this was to be kept from John Dewey, of course. But when he finally had to be told, what would he think of it? Evelyn was consulted. She talked with the other children, and the family's approval was secured. Dewey was in Europe for the summer, and so it remained only to raise funds and create a program. Raising the money was easy. As Linville later told Dewey, "You are a better risk than I thought . . . for the money came in almost embarrassing amounts with the offer of 'more if you need it.' " The expenses of the speakers and the anticipated bills for printing, postage, and office costs were soon entirely covered. Choosing the speakers and planning the talks proved to be more diffi- cult. What started as a few papers to be delivered at a dinner now turned into a packed two-day celebration.

On Friday night, when the topic would be "John Dewey and Education," the best place for the festivities was the Horace Mann Auditorium. Mann had been the first great educationalist in America, and Dewey had been born on the same day that Mann died. On Saturday morning, when the program would be organized around Dewey's philosophy, what better place could there be than Philosophy Hall at Columbia? Then on Saturday afternoon, there would be a big luncheon. The logical hotel for such an event was the capacious Hotel Astor. "John Dewey and Social Progress" would be the topic of the program there.

Between the end of May and the middle of June, possible speakers were contacted. Kilpatrick wrote to Dewey's former student and current philosophy colleague Herbert Schneider and to George Herbert Mead to form the panel on philosophy, asking each to give a paper of about forty-five minutes. Both accepted. Harvard professor Ralph Barton Perry was asked to preside, and he accepted. For the big luncheon at the Astor, to everyone's astonishment, Jane Addams agreed to travel from Chicago and speak for twenty minutes. James Harvey Robinson completed the panel. Then Kilpatrick wrote to one of Dewey's earliest graduate students at Michigan and later his col- league at Chicago and now the president of Yale, James Rowland Angell.

> We feel very sure that your long-continued and deep rooted friendship with Professor Dewey would make your acceptance deeply pleasing to him. We believe too that your high standing in American education would make this service a suitable symbol to the American people of the worth of Professor Dewey's outstanding contribution to our civilization.

Angell accepted, and on September 10 invitations went out to the peo- ple likely to attend. The proposed national committee included

Eleanor Roosevelt, Walter Lippmann, Alfred E. Smith (Dewey's choice for president in 1928), Clarence Darrow, Senator Borah, Justices Felix Frankfurter and Oliver Wendell Holmes Jr., and Oswald Garrison Villard.

As the number of events proliferated, the details that Linville had to attend to grew proportionally. Only a few days before the event, fourteen issues still needed to be settled; Linville submitted a list of them to the national committee for their opinions. The number of those who sought tickets to the luncheon rose past one thousand. The Saturday event was switched from the Astor's New Ballroom to the Grand Ballroom. Twenty-five hundred registrants were admitted, and Linville was besieged with more requests for tickets. He told Dewey that had they been prepared, "we could have had 10,000 at the celebration . . . you should have heard the begging for places put up by persons who were late in ordering." An organist was hired. A three-tiered birthday cake was baked. They all agreed that the people on the panels should make sure that this celebration did not in any way mark the end of Dewey's career but, instead, should suggest "our unquestioned expectation of yet long-continued contributions from him."

And so the great event came off. Dewey begged not to be seated at the speakers' table but to sit at a "regular seat . . . perhaps toward the front." Linville agreed but privately arranged to have Dewey escorted to the platform by a distinguished group when at the proceedings' conclusion, it came time for him to offer a response. A "stenotypist" would record his impromptu comments. President Angell arose and compared the celebration for Dewey with that for an earlier American thinker:

> I can recall in the history of American life no parallel for this
> distinguished gathering [and its] . . . grateful appreciation of a
> great personality and a great contributor to our national life,
> unless one should go back to the days of Benjamin Franklin
> and to the occasion of his triumphal return from the continent
> and particularly from Paris, where he had left the impress of
> his powerful mind upon all the contemporary thinking of the
> day.

Tributes and awards followed this introduction. Justice Holmes wrote that in his opinion, Dewey's insights had gone "to as high a point as ever has been reached by articulate speech." Justice Frankfurter sent this telegram:

> Every worker in every field of American thought is John Dewey's debtor. . . . Our immediate intellectual debts are heavy. Even more important has been his unflagging devotion to the noble calling of truth-seeker. That he has pursued the paths of truth and freedom by the very nature of his being, quite casually and as a matter of course, makes his endeavors no less gay and gallant. And so we are expressing not merely our affection and gratitude to John Dewey. We are celebrating one of the great sources of the spiritual life of the nation.

The National Education Association, of which Dewey had long been a member, presented him with its first life membership. The American Federation of Teachers, which Dewey had helped found, saluted him with an embossed resolution declaring him "its most distinguished member." Jane Addams, too, spoke with affection and admiration of Dewey and their long association, more as an extended "toast" to him than on a "topic," she explained. And James Harvey Robinson hailed Dewey as "the chief spokesman of our age and the chief thinker of our days."

Finally Dewey came up from the audience to the stage. Applause followed him and lasted until he was ready. Laughter followed his somewhat Benjamin Franklin–like (or Archibald Sprague Dewey–like) remark that although some of the tributes had been "somewhat exaggerated," he had "lapped them up." Still, in common with those auditors who might have been skeptical about them, he said, he also "share[d] their skepticism." The celebration, and especially the joy that he, its beneficiary, had had from it, he continued, naturally led him to think about the "conditions of happiness." For him, these were, in addition to luck, two: first, the choice of a career that allowed him the pleasure of thinking. He loved to think, he told the audience, "and while I am quite regular at my meals . . . I had rather work—and perhaps even more play—with ideas and with thinking than eat." When he mentioned the second source of his happiness, he also had to be thinking of the great losses of Morris and Gordon and, most recently, of Alice, for now he touched on the joy of family: "though I have experienced great sorrows, I can truly say that in my life companion, in my children, and in my grandchildren, I have been blessed by the circumstances and fortunes of life." The human impediment to happiness, he claimed, was fear, an unwillingness or inability to be open before changing experience; for Americans, the main barrier to happiness was the search for it in external possessions. *Face the world with wonder*, he concluded.

Dewey's speech moved the audience deeply. Arthur O. Lovejoy of Johns Hopkins wrote to Dewey that his remarks had given him "especial pleasure." Carleton Washburne went further: "The one thing for which no one praised you was your ability as a public speaker," but "that final talk of yours was one of the best—in its tact, its humor, its soundness and above all its appropriateness—that I have ever heard."

The day after his talk, Dewey went out to Great Neck, Long Island, to stay at Fred's house. His brother Dave had come down for the occasion and was there with his wife. Sabino and Edith had come as well. Naturally, the reporters followed Dewey there, and he was soon giving the sort of quotable interviews for which he was so frequently solicited. One reporter asked him about his criticism of America's money culture in his remarks of the previous day, and now Dewey eased his criticism. Yes, he told the press, money will continue to be an "incentive to human actions," but the beneficial uses to which money may be put will henceforth play a greater role in conduct. He saw hope in the increasing capacity of individuals to find meaning in groups, in the more liberal attitudes of the young, and in the increasing opportunities for aesthetic appreciation. Taken together, these, he thought, could modify or redirect the rapacious drive to make money.

The seventieth-birthday celebration seemed like such a good idea that the Ford Hall Forum wanted to repeat it in Boston. Three weeks later, the MacDowell Club in New York also gave a reception to honor

Dewey. He had to attend parties, respond with thanks to the participants, and read all the newspapers and journals that reported the events. Two of his Columbia colleagues, Irwin Edman and Scott Buchanan, wrote long pieces about him in the *New York Times Magazine* and *The Nation*. The many letters and telegrams pouring in to Linville's office were periodically shipped to Dewey. It took him six days before he was able to write Jane Addams. "I hope you know," he said, "that there is no one in the world whom I would have so much desired to be present and speak." Then finally, even the echoes of the tributes died away, and Dewey happily returned to the work of thinking.

The Stock Market Crash and Its Aftermath

During the 1920s, the dream of material abundance blossomed: one could become rich, it seemed, with little effort, and Americans exhibited an extraordinary passion for wealth. Investment counselors dazzled them with visions of riches; bankers encouraged them with credit; and the steadily rising stock prices strengthened their confidence. In his final message of 1928, President Calvin Coolidge referred boldly to "the pleasing prospect" of "years of prosperity." In short, Americans were determined to have prosperity at any cost. But then on "Black Thursday," the cost became clear: stock values began to slide from a paper value of $100 billion and ended in a crash with a value of $26 billion. That crash and the ensuing depression were incomprehensible. Why did people go hungry? Because modern agriculture produced too much food. Why did they wear rags? There was too much cotton, too many mills. Why was there unemployment? Because of improvements in industry. What had happened to their utopia? It had been realized too fully. It hardly mattered, then, that the economist John Maynard Keynes called their predicament "a crisis of abundance" when it looked the same as a crisis of poverty.

The most pressing question, of course, was how to reverse the downward spiral. Most people took comfort in the traditional theory of depressions, which held that prosperity caused extravagance, reckless spending, and riotous waste, eventually overinflating the economy. Allowed to run its course, the depression would, in theory, cure the ills that created it, renew the virtues of industry and frugality, and automatically return the country to its proper business—business. Thus, Hoover relied on mild measures, such as cutting taxes and easing credit, and on the voluntary cooperation of businessmen to maintain current production, employment, and wage levels. It soon became evident, however, that this policy was not working. By 1932, wages had fallen as much as 35 percent; construction was at a standstill; and employment was steadily decreasing. By 1933, unemployment had risen to 25 percent; industrial production was half its 1929 volume; and farmers were burning crops that they could not sell for enough to cover the cost of harvesting them.

Long before the economic crash, American writers had put together a case against the spiritual poverty of contemporary society. The public had listened to these writers in the 1920s but refused to take their criticisms too seriously. After the crash, however, the prewar literary traditions of muckraking and reform revived in popular esteem. Whether calling themselves Marxists, progressives, historians, or novelists, such writers as John Dewey, Michael Gold, Max Eastman, Edmund Wilson, Matthew Josephson, and John Dos Passos all could be termed social critics, and all agreed that something was rotten in society, as exemplified by the Depression.

Many citizens, of course, were doing their own reflecting and revising their beliefs accordingly. One thing seemed obvious: the crash of 1929 had been caused by remediable factors, including a vastly unequal distribution of income, corporate and banking practices unregulated by law and ripe for abuse, and a mad credit system.

These problems caused doubts about Hoover's belief that the economy would revive without further tampering, and respect for the wealthy and business leaders dropped sharply. "As for leading us out of the crisis," the editor of *The Nation* declared, "the captains of industry have plainly no vision, no plan, no economic program." Attitudes toward the poor also began to shift. Americans had always assumed that poverty was the result of personal inadequacy. But when so many American citizens were living below "the standard of living," this notion of poverty had to be reassessed. When the new president, Franklin D. Roosevelt, announced his concern for the third of the nation that was "ill-housed, ill-clad, ill-fed," he was speaking, as well, for many members of the upper two-thirds.

People are not moved to revolt, the Declaration of Independence says, by "light and transient causes." During the Depression, European visitors to America kept asking, "Will the Americans revolt?" By 1933, when Roosevelt became president, Americans were rejecting many of their traditional beliefs, but they never came close to revolution. Between 1933 and 1941, Americans reexperienced impulses that had diminished during the 1920s: a renewal of confidence in the public realm and a willingness to pursue collectively projects of public improvement. Thus, while several European countries tumbled into political chaos, Roosevelt was able to maintain and even strengthen the basic American institutions of liberty and ownership. Many old habits crashed with the market, but Americans had by no means lost their utopian belief in a better future. They had simply accepted that it would be different from what they had dreamed of.

For John Dewey, the ceremonial honors and casual flirtations were swept aside by the stock market crash, and even he suffered a considerable financial loss, though he never complained of his personal losses. The crash awakened him again to home matters, the disorder in the American economy, and the suffering of uncounted numbers of individual Americans.

In *The Public and Its Problems* (1927), Dewey had already anticipated this return of Americans from personal to national concerns. "Democracy must begin at home," he wrote. Although Dewey had never been an expatriate, he had been out of the country a great deal since going to Japan in 1919, and he had focused most of his attention during the previous decade on the revolutionary world outside the United States. Much of his journalistic writing concerned foreign countries or American foreign policy, and his contributions to the controversy over the United States' participation in the League of Nations had a focus abroad. Many summers he had gone to Europe with

Barnes. In *Human Nature and Conduct*, *Experience and Nature*, and *The Quest for Certainty*, he had examined the large themes recurring in Western thought.

A closer look at Dewey's activism, however, shows several continuous themes and preoccupations spanning his career as far back as his advocacy of Debs and the Pullman strikers and centering him in American concerns, to which he always returned. His issue-based advocacy was almost always connected with an organization or a group enterprise. He seldom started the movements he assisted; he usually joined them. As an advocate he was a tireless proponent of the ideas of others. It was not surprising, then, that as early as 1922, when the Conference for Progressive Political Action (CPPA) was formed as a third political party and nominated Robert La Follette for president, that Dewey immediately supported the newest effort to reform American politics. La Follette received five million votes in the 1924 election but Coolidge won, and support for the CPPA faded. In 1928, Dewey had to choose between Al Smith and Herbert Hoover. He chose Smith, but reluctantly, since he regarded both candidates as equally allied with big business: "The old parties are so firmly entrenched throughout the nation, and the organizations so closely bound up with the business system that unorganized individuals find themselves helpless."

Even as he was planning to vote for Smith, Dewey was helping form a third party. Since neither of the major parties seemed ready to address the urgent need for economic reorganization, Dewey turned his attention to a new organization, the League for Independent Political Action, which was being organized by Paul H. Douglas, an economist from the University of Chicago. Douglas's inspiration came directly from Dewey's 1927 book *The Public and Its Problems*. On September 8, 1929, less than two months before the great crash, Douglas met with a group of progressives to organize the League for Independent Political Action, and they elected Dewey as its first president. The league's core aim was to bring together liberal and radical thinkers to create a new coalition third party. As Dewey said in a radio broadcast, since both major parties had "surrendered abjectly to domination by big business interests and become their errand boys," the league would independently adopt economic and social principles that would bring liberals together in a new party.

The Public and Its Problems had been widely read, and Dewey's endorsement of the league gave the new organization a boost. As president, he sent out numerous letters appealing for support and enrolling members, and in less than a year the membership had grown to 2,500. Moving rapidly, in the 1930 interim elections the league successfully supported several third-party candidates for office, with success in the elections of Farmer-Laborites in Minnesota. These early successes emboldened Dewey to believe that the league had tapped a significant but hitherto unorganized wellspring of alternative belief and political thought in America.

In November 1930, when Dewey was in Paris to receive the highest honor the University of Paris could award a scholar, he warned the international press corps that Americans were awakening to the "blind faith" they had invested in the last two Republican administrations, and now their "sublime trust" in "economic miracles" might have been shattered for good.

The crash and the economic depression that continued to deepen helped strengthen the league and encouraged its leaders to make a public critique of growing insecurity, unemployment, low wages, and "the scrapping of men at forty-five and fifty years of age." Dewey believed that now was the time to form a third major national party. Supported by the National Committee of the League, including Stuart Chase, Oswald Garrison Villard, Harry Laidler, and Reinhold Niebuhr, Dewey, as the league president, began to seek a candidate who could head a ticket in the upcoming national presidential elections of 1932. Dewey timed his announcement of the birth of a new party for a day when most Americans would celebrate a new birth, on Christmas 1930. The new third party would, he said in a press release, "renounce both of [the] . . . old parties and give birth to a new party based upon the principles of planning and control for the purpose of building happier lives, a more just society and that peaceful world which was the dream of Him whose birthday we celebrate this Christmas Day."

Dewey wrote an open letter to Senator George W. Norris urging him to leave the Republican Party and head the new party in time for the 1932 elections: "I urge that you sever forever your connections with that political machine and join with those of us in the League for Independent Political Action and other liberal groups to form a new party to which you can give full allegiance." He predicted that if they made a start immediately, they could "give desperate workers and farmers a constructive vehicle of political expression" that "could win the presidency within the next ten years." The *New York Times* reported rather skeptically on Dewey's invitation in an article entitled "The Professor and the Senator." Dewey, the editorial began, deserves the highest esteem and respect; no one could doubt the sincerity and purity of his motives in becoming chairman of the League for Independent Political Action. But his invitation to Senator Norris "seems to 'smell of the lamp' rather than . . . the hard realities of political life." When Norris learned of the appeal to bolt his party and head a new one, his first response, the *Times* noted, was to say, "Isn't that funny?"

Dewey told Norris: "You do not belong in the Republican Party," reminding the senator that he stood for "social planning and social control," not "rugged individualism." However, Norris declined, asserting that he wanted to stay a Republican in order to purify his party from within. "The scourging of the money-changers out of the temple must be done by one who has the right of entry into it." Dewey was disappointed and uncharacteristically furious when five days after his open letter and Norris's declination, he addressed the New History Society. He denounced Norris and, for good measure, added another Republican maverick senator, William Borah, to his criticism, for "drifting on a tide they can ride without having to take risks. It is too bad they lack courage."

Ironically, only a little earlier in 1930, Dewey had himself been asked to lead a party, and he too had declined. In the summer of 1930,

B. C. Vladeck, manager of the *Jewish Daily Forward*, interrupted Dewey's peace in Hubbards on behalf of the Socialist Party. Vladeck reminded him of the large vote for president polled by Norman Thomas in 1928. The Socialists planned to run candidates in four congressional districts, but "in order to have a real lively campaign, we must have a strong man [running for governor] at the head of our ticket." Then Vladeck promised Dewey the "whole-hearted support of all Socialist and Liberal elements in the state" and hopefully concluded that a Dewey candidacy for governor of New York "would lend our [state] movement a strength which no one else could provide." If Dewey accepted, he would be nominated unanimously at the party convention in Schenectady nine days hence.

Dewey responded that he could not anticipate doing the campaigning necessary to make a showing helpful to party candidates, but he did not definitely refuse. Vladeck walked through the door that Dewey left open and seized the opportunity to try to persuade him. Immediately he cabled back that he believed that 1930 offered a "historic opportunity" for the advance of socialism. Dewey's acceptance, even with a brief campaign of three or four weeks, would be "simply wonderful." Then Dewey did refuse unambiguously. Still, in this instance, he at least departed from his usual practice of not supporting Socialist candidates, and he endorsed Vladeck as a candidate for the Eighth Congressional District in Brooklyn. "Not the slightest hope remains of accomplishing any fundamental change through either of the two old parties," Dewey remarked. In fact, he was occupied with his continuing efforts on behalf of the League for Industrial Democracy, his plans for the League for Independent Political Action, and with one more organization, the People's Lobby.

Shortly after World War I, the People's Reconstruction League had been founded to lobby on behalf of labor unions. Later, its title was changed to the Anti-Monopoly League, and its lobbying activities shifted. In 1929, the board voted to invite John Dewey to assume its presidency. Dewey objected immediately that he was a philosopher and knew nothing of lobbying. But his friend Ben Marsh, the executive secretary, argued with him. This "lobby" was a lobby on behalf of all the people; it was not a parochial organization. It was the one and only lobby that existed to support causes for the people of America as a whole. Dewey yielded on the contingent grounds that if Marsh was correct, the organization must be renamed. And so the "People's Lobby" it became. Dewey assumed the presidency and remained at its head for seven years. All at once, Dewey had another forum for political activity open to him on behalf of his belief in the necessity of change. Events provided the occasion. Not long after he accepted the presidency, the stock market collapsed. Everyone was looking for answers, solutions to the disaster. As president of the People's Lobby, Dewey did not have to wait for the press to come to him. He called press conferences and frequently issued press releases, and journalists were glad to get Dewey's updated "thoughts" on the Depression. He proposed legislation; he supported or opposed bills in Congress; he made recommendations to Hoover; he called for action; he made predictions; he issued dire warnings. The People's Lobby had its own bulletin, and Dewey used it as his personal forum to offer his own solutions for the problems of a government that, in his view, supported maintaining and fostering "the private property of predatory and stupidly selfish interests."

For a brief time after Norris's refusal to head a third party with the support of the new League for Independent Political Action, it seemed that the league would crumble and go out of existence. But Dewey's activities in the People's Lobby had convinced him that its continued existence as an organ of propaganda and opposition would be valuable. Now he was determined to see it continue. He convinced the editors of the *New Republic* to assist the league, and early in 1932 the journal enthusiastically announced its support. Dewey did his part by writing four articles on the league which appeared in the *New Republic* in March and April 1931.

Predictably, Dewey's positions on behalf of the People's Lobby and the League for Independent Political Action were similar. When he wrote or spoke for one organization, he could just as easily have been writing for the other. But in terms of policy, the league held to a consistent aim of finding means and allies with which to create an actual third party. Consequently, much more than the People's Lobby, it found itself constantly seeking alliances with various other liberal political groups, parties, and persons, whereas the People's Lobby remained considerably more confined to identifying the appropriate aims and policies by which social change might be achieved.

Ever since Morton White's *Social Thought in America: The Revolt Against Formalism* was published in 1957, following in the tradition of Randolph Bourne's attack on Dewey in 1918, Dewey has been occasionally charged with offering philosophic critiques of American politics without supplying concrete proposals for reform. As White saw it, Dewey supplied "no particular or specific political position that can be acted upon, only a plea for intelligence." But White was wrong. The astonishing number of political proposals that Dewey made during the Depression shows how involved he was in promulgating actual policies that he believed would ameliorate suffering and enhance social justice. Since in both the People's Lobby and the League of Independent Political Action he was making concrete proposals for reform, these groups do not need to be distinguished in what follows. Beginning in 1929 Dewey proposed and argued for (1) a federally planned economy, involving government control or ownership of natural resources, utilities, power, coal, banking, railroads, and credit; (2) regulation of the radio and press; (3) the taxation of unearned increments in land value; (4) higher taxes for higher-income brackets; (5) the calling of special sessions of Congress to ensure more continuous and more effective government planning to meet people's needs; (6) unemployment insurance; (7) massive outlays for public works; (8) a four-year presidential plan to spend at least $5 million for public works and $250 million for direct relief; (9) taxes on corporations; (10) taxes on inheritance; (11) workers' insurance; (12) old-age pensions; (13) the abolition of child labor; (14) a six-hour workday; (15) aid to farmers, including a reduction in tariffs; (16) recognition of the Soviet Union; and (17) participation in the World Court. Undergirding these policy and legislative proposals was Dewey's unyielding belief that because "financial and business leaders will not make these changes voluntarily," the federal government must take control, since it

> alone has the power to force the wealthy owners of the nation to surrender their control over the lives and destinies of the overwhelming majority of the American people, and the first step is to make them pay taxes commensurate in sacrifice with that of people with very small incomes.

Nothing is clearer than that Dewey's philosophic critiques passed directly and immediately into political and economic policies.

This is even clearer with regard to the organizational aims of the League for Independent Political Action. Consistent with Dewey's personal convictions, he guided the league toward (but not into) the Socialist Party, and at the same time away from the Communist Party. The league's leadership supported socialist candidates but voted not to back any communists. When Norman Thomas's party made common cause with the communists, Dewey led the league against support of the socialists. He consistently opposed any adherence to ideological absolutes and held that a successful American political party must have an experimental temper. Accordingly, he allied the league with the Farmer-Labor Party. Dewey and the league opposed Hoover, arguing that he was unwilling to tax those who had contributed to his campaign. They rejected Roosevelt for much the same reason, that his program was basically an attempt "to bolster and repair" the capitalist system. So Dewey organized a "Continental Congress" for May 1933 in Washington, D.C., aimed at unifying otherwise separated and fragmented radicals. In attendance were the members of the Farm Holiday Association, the Conference for Progressive Labor Action, trade unions, the Non-Partisan League, and the Socialist Party. A second Conference for Progressive Political Action was called for October. At this conference Dewey was named chairman of the newly created United Action Campaign Committee, whose purpose was getting "down into the dirt and dust of the arena and fight[ing] for human rights in a practical, aggressive, realistic manner."

From his leadership positions in three organizations now, Dewey castigated the New Deal for its timidity and wrote an open letter to Roosevelt urging "a reduction in mortgage debts and interest rates . . . proportional to the reduction in prices of farm land." Soon after this, he proposed that the sales tax initiated by Hoover be repealed and the Revenue Act be revised to tax the upper income brackets more heavily. Dewey's support of farmers brought the league into a close alliance with the Farmer Labor Political Federation and the newly formed Wisconsin Progressive Party. All soon joined together to create a regional third party that won legislative control of the state of Wisconsin in 1934. Similar gains were made by the Farmer Labor Political Federation in Minnesota where the socialist Floyd Olson was elected governor. The union leader of the milk strikes, Milo Reno, who was passionately devoted to the creation of a third party, joined these organizations. In July 1935, Dewey and his League for Independent Political Action participated in a convention in Chicago in which all of these groups formed the American Commonwealth Political Federation, realizing Dewey's hope to lead in uniting otherwise isolated progressive groups.

Then it all fell apart. Norman Thomas tried to increase the Socialist Party's power by allying with the Communist Party, and so his large group departed. The communists kept their own counsel, infiltrated the American Commonwealth Political Federation, and so drove Dewey's League for Independent Political Action out of the most promising federation it had formed. Milo Reno, whose support was crucial, died suddenly. Olson and many others began to fear that the creation of a third party at this critical time could swing the undecided vote to the Republicans in the 1936 election. Dewey's league splintered. Paul Douglas and the agrarian leaders swung over to Roosevelt through Henry Wallace. For his own reasons, an important league director, Oswald Garrison Villard, announced his support for Roosevelt. Dewey was left alone as the last person in the League for Independent Political Action still hoping to promote a third party and still opposing both major parties.

In organizational terms, Dewey's League for Industrial Democracy, the People's Lobby, and the League for Independent Political Action failed to bring a new party into power. But in terms of the policies that Dewey introduced, these organizations had a considerable influence on the New Deal. Dewey's own personal activities as a social critic and pragmatic thinker certainly influenced Roosevelt's policies through A. A. Berle and Rexford Tugwell, Dewey's Columbia colleagues and central players in FDR's "brain trust." These and others associated with them in the administration "applied their interpretation of Dewey's experimental method to the problems of New Deal recovery and reform." Tugwell himself acknowledged Dewey's influence on his thought. Although he opposed Roosevelt's ameliorative policies, he soon started to influence the administration, and to his surprise he even began to be invited to White House dinners. Now he wrote increasingly about and for the American public.

DEWEY'S POLITICAL PHILOSOPHY

The books that specifically develop the philosophy underlying Dewey's political activities in the 1930s are *The Public and Its Problems* (1927), *Individualism, Old and New* (1930), and *Liberalism and Social Action* (1935). These are best read in the context of Dewey's concrete political activities between 1928 and 1936. Dewey was a reconstructionist. Since lecturing in Japan, he had seen the role of the contemporary philosopher as reconstructing the ideas bequeathed to him by the traditions of Western thought. Such reconstruction, he argued, was imperative on American grounds because the fulfillment of democracy demanded a new conception of the idea of a "public" suitable for the conditions of democracy.

Following in the tradition of William James's biosocial thinking, Dewey asserted that humans are, by nature, associative and that all social activities have consequences. Some affect only the person causing them and so may be designated "private." But in modern, democratic life, the majority of acts produce consequences that affect others. By doing so, they not only *are* public: they *create* a public. Social acts of this kind continuously bring multiform publics into existence. These publics are dynamic, always changing, because the social acts that create them are themselves in flux. Politics and the organization of politics in the creation of states derive directly from the existence of publics, for some coordination and regulation must exist to care for the consequences of the multiplicity of social, public-making transactions, toward the goal of achieving (in Laurence Gronlund's phrase) a "cooperative commonwealth." The rise of democracy and industrialization has made the problem of the democratic public immensely more complicated than it was in earlier periods of history. Democracy is the consequence of a "large and varied number of particular [democratic] happenings." But a democracy in an industrial age makes the regulation of its public interest more complicated than do most other forms of government, for democracy creates a weak, unruly public, uncertain of what "the public interest" might be and why or how to regulate it. Democracy and industry have combined to make the relations of multiple publics so subtle, so far-reaching, so infinitely extended and interconnected that the varied publics of a modern democracy can no longer easily identify themselves and coordinate their interests. In what way, then, are the officials charged with regulating public transactions to understand the means by which the public can be best represented?

In 1925, Walter Lippmann published *The Phantom Public*, which Dewey reviewed favorably. Toward the conclusion of his review, Dewey called for "a scientific organization for discovering, recording and interpreting all conduct having a public bearing," that is, intelligent, informed understanding of the multiform democratic public. Dewey stated that Lippmann's critique must "suggest the need of further analysis," and in the final sentence of his review he added, "I hope to return to this phase of the matter later." The *Public and Its Problems* (1927) was the result of Dewey's further reflections on the subject of the publics in democratic America. Typically, Dewey found the answers to the complex problems of the new public in the very conditions—

democracy and industry—that created its problems. The aim of the contemporary political theorist should be to forge from democracy and industry the political means whose goal is the clarification and elevation of a truly democratic state. As W. E. Hocking noted, Dewey's "cure for the ills of democracy" was "more democracy." But such a task was far from easy; Lippmann had all but declared it impossible.

In *The Public and Its Problems*, Dewey considers the importance of individual needs, desires, and activities and then reflects on the consequences of individual drives in relation to the needs and desires of others. He describes how the extension of effects from the individual to society creates a public and how the regulation of the public interest makes government necessary. The resulting state "is the organization of the public effected through officials for the protection of the interests shared by its members." The success of a state consists in the "degree of organization of the public [interest] which is attained, and the degree in which its officers are so constituted as to perform their functions of caring for public interests." Of course, for Dewey, no implication existed that there was an absolute ideal form for any such state. Rather, "there is no a priori rule that can be laid down," since "in no two ages or places is there the same public." The state is a derivative of the always-changing public interest. A state is "good" (not best) when it corresponds to and gives expression to public "interest." A state is an experiment:

> The trial process may go on with diverse degrees of blindness and accident, and at the cost of unregulated procedures of cut and try, of fumbling and groping, without insight into what men are after or clear knowledge of a good state even when it is achieved. Or it may proceed more intelligently, because guided by knowledge of the conditions which must be fulfilled. But it is still experimental. And since conditions of action and of inquiry and knowledge are always changing, the experiment must always be retried; the State must always be rediscovered.

In America, democracy and industry combined to produce monumental changes and thus to create a new state. But as Americans approached the mid-twentieth century, they would require a wholly new experiment, a wholesale redefinition of the public, and a consequent reconstruction of the state. In chapter 3 Dewey examines "The Democratic State." He concludes that the development of modern conditions has been so rapid, the examination of them so inadequate, and the experiments in rediscovery so limited, that in what Woodrow Wilson called "the new age of human relationships," there were "no political agencies worthy of it. The democratic public is still largely inchoate and unorganized." In short, the public has been "eclipsed" but not yet reconstructed, and the prospects for the democratic state seem dismal. Dewey's theme of reconstruction, however, gives him a way to hope that the transformation of an inchoate society into a coherent community through communication can reconstruct a public. The public has become, as Lippmann said, a "phantom." Dewey replied: "The prime *condition* of a democratically organized public is a kind of knowledge and insight which does not yet exist." But that was not its end. "Communication can . . . create a great community" in the United States. Undoubtedly, this is the point that Paul Douglas picked up in taking *The Public and Its Problems* as the inspiration for creating the League for Independent Political Action. Communication is an institution of exchange and requires organizations and organs for it to occur; without them it exists only as an idea.

So Dewey worked toward reconstructing signs, symbols, and organized actions capable of unifying a public in America. What he had said about China, Turkey, Mexico, and the Soviet Union he now said about his own country: that by means of evolving education, communication is central, since informed discussion, debate, and persuasion are made possible only by appropriate communicative means and methods, that is, by schooling. The problem of the public, then, is to free and enlarge "the processes of inquiry" and the "dissemination of . . . conclusions." In this process it is not mere intelligence or "expertise" that counts but also the means and desire to investigate, the possession of a judgment free from prejudice, and an inclination to recognize common concerns. "Intelligence is not an original, innate endowment," Dewey explained, but a consequence of the education that social conditions effect, what he called *"embodied* intelligence." The implication of this position is clear, though dynamically circular: intelligent action is the product of social conditions, but social conditions form the context for the development of intelligence embodied in local communities. Dewey's conception is a double helix model of knowledge in which mind and society, knowing and doing, individuals and their neighbors all are spun forward by social evolution, twisting around and lifting one another as they rise. Wrapped in this vision, Dewey's prophetic spirit takes wing at the conclusion:

> There is no limit to the liberal expansion and confirmation of limited personal intellectual endowment[s] which may proceed from the flow of social intelligence when that circulates . . . in the communications of the local community. That and that only gives reality to public opinion. We lie, as Emerson said, in the lap of an immense intelligence. But that intelligence is dormant and its communications are broken, inarticulate and faint until it possesses the local community as its medium.

Nearly all the reviews of *The Public and Its Problems* were favorable. Dewey himself regarded the book as "the best balanced of my writings . . . [and] the most 'instrumental' " in that it defined the state not as an ideal but as a continuously redefined process. It was widely read and remained in print until 1941. Douglas was far from the only person inspired by it to attempt to apply its analysis to social and political institutions.

Published three years later, during Dewey's deep involvement in political activity, *Individualism, Old and New* takes up the other side of his argument for the transformation of the public. In this new book, a companion to *The Public and Its Problems*, he examines the transformation of the individual. He had said earlier that the greatest need of American democracy was to create an informed, unified public. Now

Dewey is looking toward the entity that accumulates and combines to form the public—the acting individual—and contends that the greatest problem is "constructing a new individuality consonant with the objective conditions under which we live." In beginning *Individualism, Old and New* with the Lincoln-Douglas metaphor of the dangers of a house divided against itself, Dewey evokes the central problem of the individual. The older American ideal of "rugged individualism" is still held as a moral, economic, and political goal, but the corporate organization of American life has rendered the traditional myth of America merely "ragged individualism." Our moral culture still clings to "ideals and values of an individualism derived from the pre-scientific, pre-technological age," whereas our material culture is permeated with collective and corporate conditions. What we believe about individuals and what we experience as individuals are at odds. Dewey sees in this conflict the consequences of profound social changes at work in the family and in mental contentment. Divided against himself, the individual is "lost." The conditions and loyalties that supported the "old" individual have disappeared, but even though new, unprecedented conditions now prevail, no new internalized loyalties have developed to foster a suitable unity and identity for the "new" individual to come. The results, as Dewey shows in his fourth chapter, are individuals who are confused intellectually, economically, politically, and morally.

Europeans, Dewey shows with impressive insight, castigate modern American civilization for its emphasis on "quantification, mechanization, and standardization." But these are not phenomena that qualify as "American"; they are the conditions that will arrive just a bit later in Europe, too. Whereas Europe once endowed America with its "culture," now Americans will return the favor because they are ahead of any other nation in the evolution of modernism. Europeans too will now increasingly encounter the imperatives of the only possible future. Because the older idea of the solitary individual has been weakened by the social conditions in which humanity now exists, there has developed a compensating "enrichment of community resources." As the ideal of private profit intrinsic to the conception of the old individual fades, Dewey believed, the idea of social, collective—above all, community—advance can grow in power and issue into the ideal of a new sort of individualism fulfilling its potential in a shared culture.

As Dewey began to write *Individualism, Old and New*, the stock market collapsed, which, for him, was symbolic proof of his argument. As he saw it, the crash provided a useful marker for the beginning of the decay of the old individualism designed for financial profit. But such a decline could also lead to a transformation of the individual through an "inner movement toward integration" along new lines. Dewey did not yet have a suitable name for this new integration. *Socialization* had negative connotations, and *service* and *social responsibility* had become clichés or cant. Thus he said simply that in the new individual, "we are in for some kind of socialism, call it by whatever name we please," for the nature of our collective life must ultimately, for human needs, frame its policies in the social interest. But he also contended that the character and the meaning of an individual must be coordinate with and grow from the realities of the civilization in which it takes form. Americans seemed to be lamenting that the corporate, technological, and mechanistic aspects of contemporary life had destroyed the individual. For Dewey, these conditions were precisely the basis on which a new individualism could—and would—be reconstructed. In 1930, the individual was in a state of transition. The new conditions of society still remained external, outside the individual, which was why society seemed confused and the individual lost. However, "when the corporateness becomes internal, when, that is, it is realized in thought and purpose, it will become qualitative."

In human nature itself, in the social ideals of corporation-as-cooperation, and in the immense increase in technique through technology, Dewey found the vehicles to construct an emergent individualism based on connection, union, and intelligent technical control. Dewey's observations concerning emergent democracies, along with those of his parallel political and economic public policy activities occurring at this same time, all follow the same path. His books and his activities coalesced completely. *The Public and Its Problems* and *Individualism, Old and New* were closely related and in turn fit harmoniously with his political activities and public policy proposals. His other observations during the same years corresponded to his writings and his politics. His favorable impressions of the Russian Revolution, for instance, were based on his conviction that Americans could learn from the Soviets' planned economy while avoiding the "destruction and coercion" intrinsic to Marxist theories of class conflict. He forecast in *Individualism, Old and New* that the new individual would use the taxing power of government to effect the redistribution of wealth and that legislation would mitigate the "scandal of private appropriation of socially produced values in unused land." These are, of course, proposals that Dewey himself actively promulgated in the organizations that he headed. He did not have to describe the new man, as he himself was the man of the future. Such a claim, certainly, would not have been made by Dewey himself; indeed, it is scarcely likely that such a conceit would have so much as crossed his mind. But undeniably for his readers, the connections between Dewey's analysis and Dewey the man were close and made him a model for many young thinkers.

Liberalism and Social Action, which was published in 1935, forms a trilogy with *The Public and Its Problems* and *Individualism, Old and New*. In the preface to this book, Dewey reminds his readers that its three chapters were lectures originally delivered at the University of Virginia and that "three lectures do not permit one to say all he thinks." In the following months, Dewey returned to the themes of liberalism several times in additional essays that were, in an extended sense, part of the work he would have written had he planned the whole as a book. He begins with the puzzling changes in meaning and levels of approval undergone by the concept of "liberal" in America. Only a few decades earlier, to be "liberal" was to be progressive and open-minded. More recently, liberals had been attacked by communists, as radicals in thought but adherents of capitalism in their actions. From the other side, liberals were attacked as dangerous subversives bent on undermining American traditions. When "liberal" is used in such a contradictory manner, what possibility now exists, Dewey asks, for "a person to continue, honestly and intelligently, to be a liberal"?

Another question follows: "What kind of liberal faith should be asserted today"?

"Liberalism" is indissolubly associated with "liberty." But liberty for whom? And for what purpose? Quickly reviewing the rise of liberal concepts beginning with Locke, Dewey exhibits the vicissitudes of meaning that made "liberalism" turn about on itself and come to mean opposite things. The liberals of the present moment "are committed to the principle that organized society must use its powers to establish the conditions under which the mass of individuals can possess actual as distinct from merely legal liberty." The "crisis" of liberalism is always contextual and historical. In some sense, liberalism means equality along with liberty, independence, and freedom of thought, that is, intelligence, but these need to be sought in different ways as new social and intellectual challenges arise historically. So in the present day, the critical question concerning liberalism is, How can contemporary liberals continue to strive for equality, initiative, and intelligence under current conditions and thereby "resolve the crisis, and emerge as a compact, aggressive force"? The crucial problem for liberal theory, Dewey argues, has been the absence in it of historicity, which meant that in liberalism there was no proper recognition that "effective liberty is a function of the social conditions existing at any time." Liberals failed to understand that liberty was not something to be discovered, but something always to be striven toward.

As a fact of life, social change means that liberalism must continue adjusting the operation of intelligence to keep equality and individuality alive. But as Dewey knew, people have always feared change and protected themselves against change "by resorting to what psychoanalysis has taught us to call rationalizations, in other words, protective fantasies." At the other extreme, Marxism's concept of catastrophic change was an equally protective fantasy. Liberalism needs to become historical, to incorporate a concept of continuous change and then respond to life by being ever "renascent," always reforming, always changing with social change. This means, for Dewey, that in the present, liberalism must learn to be truly radical in order to keep pace with the rapid changes in society that have opened up a gulf between social fact and social policy.

In *Liberalism and Social Action* Dewey completes the picture sketched in his two preceding books. An altered "public" is struggling to come into existence, from which a transformed "individualism" must grow; and liberalism—the commitment to intelligence as a method—must supply both the new individual and the new public with usable instruments for social action. In all three books, Dewey's belief is that to reflect the crisis of the present and to transcend the absolutist traps of pecuniary capitalism, fascist conservatism, and Marxist revolutionism, liberalism must find ways "in which the new forces of productivity are cooperatively controlled and used in the interest of the effective liberty and the cultural development of the individuals that constitute society."

The three lectures from which Dewey wrote *Liberalism and Social Action* started him on a course of thought that soon appeared in at least eight other essays centrally on this subject, along with several others that refer to the same concerns. In "The Future of Liberalism" (1934) Dewey stresses the necessity for liberalism to commit to "experimental procedure; for liberalism is not a body of ideas, it is a *method*, the method of intelligence, a mode of analysis. Its object is cultural freedom, the opportunity to share in the resources of civilization." "Democracy Is Radical" (1937) clarifies the title's assertion. The radicalism of democracy consists of the effort to discern a method of inquiry that will uncover the changing forms by which democracy can continue to be vital. Democracy is a "buoyant, crusading, and militant faith" in our common nature and in the power of voluntary action, relying on public, collective intelligence. In "Liberty and Social Control" (1935), Dewey opposes the current tendency to see freedom and restraint as opposites. Instead, he contends, liberty for some can mean the lack of liberty for many; by contrast, social control can result in liberty for all. The struggle for a cooperative economic system is intended to bring about a wider "distribution of liberties" through social control. In a manner similar to Dewey's explanation of why "liberty" and "social control" are not opposites, in "Liberalism and Equality" (1936) he refutes the belief that "liberalism and equality are so incompatible that liberalism is not a possible social philosophy." He invokes Thomas Jefferson's philosophy as one that simultaneously embraces liberal freedom and democratic equality. In "The Meaning of Liberalism" (1935) Dewey presents economic control as the means of increasing liberty:

> The ends which liberalism has always professed can be attained only as control of the means of production and distribution is taken out of the hands of individuals who exercise powers created socially for narrow individual interests. The ends remain valid. But the means of attaining them demand a radical change in economic institutions and the political arrangements based upon them. These changes are necessary in order that social control of forces and agencies socially created may accrue to the liberation of all individuals associated together in the great undertaking of building a life that expresses and promotes human liberty.

In "Liberalism and Civil Liberties" (1936), Dewey identifies these two. Historically, liberalism was that action of ideals meant to displace "the earlier practices of political autocracy, which subordinated subjects to the arbitrary will of governmental authorities." Noting that civil liberties had diminished since World War I, Dewey advocates expanding them in order to protect both the individual and the community.

His final word on his reconsideration of liberalism comes at the conclusion of his 1940 essay, "The Meaning of the Term: Liberalism." In his books and his earlier essays, he had worked through the issue of the value of liberalism. Now, at the brink of another war, he seemed to have reached a calm point at which he could accept and envision the enduring value of his philosophy of action. Liberalism is, he states, the "quiet and patient pursuit of truth, marked by the will to learn from every quarter. Liberalism is humble and persistent, and yet is strong and positive in its faith that the intercourse of free minds will always bring to light an increasing measure of truth."

In *The Public and Its Problems, Individualism, Old and New*, and *Liberalism and Social Action*, with their elaborations in articles, Dewey was trying to preserve and extend a special American way of thinking and behaving. The condition of nations external to America and the internal crisis of America prompted this attempt at restoring the spirit of America and its origin and propelling it, revised and renewed, into the future. Fascism, communism, and individualistic capitalism, at home or abroad, each had different goals. Nonetheless, as Dewey analyzed them, they shared something of the same effort to restrict equality, individualism, and freedom of thought. Now Dewey proposed a fourth way of future development: the continued expansion of American democracy. On an international scale, he implicitly believed that if he could help keep America American at home, its ideals could expand in the world at large. Would Japan, China, Germany, Spain, the Soviet Union, and Italy reverse their nascent development toward democracy and descend toward fascism or communism? Would the United States cease its restless expansion of freedom and constrict into rapacious individualistic capitalism? And would the countries incorporating these powers and ideas battle toward another descent into darkness? Or might the force and ideas of our liberators, Jefferson to Whitman, prevail? That was the path Dewey was tracing in the 1930s, with guarded hope but considerable doubt.

Dewey's Interest in the Arts

Even as Dewey was engaged philosophically in defining liberalism in relation to democracy in a series of books and articles, he found a way of writing about a passion that he said rivaled his love of philosophy: the enjoyment of beauty in art. His involvement with Albert Barnes did not end with the Polish project. Dewey continued to meet with him all through the 1920s and 1930s, but now their association centered on understanding the visual arts.

With the employees of the A. C. Barnes Company, Albert Barnes carried out a bold experiment: Following an idealistic American tradition initiated in the nineteenth century with the factory women in the Lowell, Massachusetts, mills, Barnes gave his workers a break from 12:30 to 2:30 each day in order to advance their education. In the most adventurous utopian manner, he decided to lead them through seminars and discussions of texts that he provided. The main premises of his educational experiment came from Dewey's *Democracy and Education*. Barnes said that if he had not encountered Dewey and his philosophy, he would probably have lived out "the more intelligent life of drinking, yachting, fishing, and indulgence in one of the other favorite indoor sports." Instead, he started his workers reading William James's *The Principles of Psychology, Pragmatism*, and *The Varieties of Religious Experience*. They got through these but then got stuck on *Essays in Radical Empiricism*. John Dewey's *How We Think* got them back on track. They kept going in readings of Bertrand Russell. Then because Barnes was an avid art collector, they turned to Santayana's *The Sense of Beauty* and *Reason in Art*, along with Roger Fry's art criticism. They discussed the important impressionist paintings with which Barnes had decorated the walls of the factory; an artistic environment, too, was part of his educational scheme.

Barnes tried to educate everyone he met, including John Dewey. In two areas their knowledge was far apart. One was applied science, especially chemistry. The other was Barnes's keen interest in paintings. Indeed, he was on his way to assembling the finest privately owned collection of impressionist paintings in the United States. Dewey knew little about chemistry and scarcely more about the visual arts. In Burlington and Ann Arbor, Dewey had had few opportunities to see art, and color printing had not yet developed to the state that art books could offer good reproductions. Popular prints—the sort of chromolithographs that Mark Twain satirized in *Adventures of Huckleberry Finn*—were the best that were regularly available. Even museum collections in the great American cities were still only beginning to be established when Dewey was a young man. Later, when the Deweys lived in Chicago and New York, they had access to good collections of art. But between 1894 and 1925, Dewey spent so much time on his philosophic writing, social issues, and public activities that he had little time for strolling about in galleries.

Still, from a very early time, Dewey had been interested in aesthetics and tried to acquaint himself with visual art. With H. A. P. Torrey at Vermont, he had studied Joseph Torrey's *A Theory of Fine Art* (1874), and he was permanently influenced by the elder Torrey's argument that "the end of all the imaginative arts is to express the truth of things in sensible forms." At Michigan he designed a course on "The Philosophy of Beauty." His "field of inquiry" had three divisions: (1) the conditions of (a) nature and (b) society from which aesthetic satisfaction springs; (2) the nature of aesthetic capacity, including "the psychology of aesthetic experience"; and (3) the objective results of aesthetic activity in the individual, society, nature, and art. Undoubtedly he relied heavily on Kant's *Critique of Aesthetic Judgment* in this course, and he tried to use pictorial art to illustrate his philosophic texts.

Dewey's philosophical interests in aesthetics did not require familiarity with every branch of art. He knew literature quite well. In early America, as in most developing countries, the literary arts, which relied on language, matured much more quickly than the visual or musical arts could do. For this reason, like most Americans born in the middle of the nineteenth century, Dewey identified "art" with "literature." He was a great reader and familiar with British literature, especially with the Romantics and the Victorian novelists and poets. As early as 1891 he addressed the Philosophical Society at Michigan on "The Interpretation of Literature." He often said that as a young man, his favorite British poet "was Wordsworth; in my middle years it was Browning." Lionel Trilling praised his essay on Matthew Arnold. John Herman Randall Jr. recalled that Dewey "often quoted [poetry] . . . in class. He had a good knowledge of English poetry—and . . . of Greek." The poetry he read, and the poetry he wrote, tended to be conventional. But his reading in fiction was expansive. He read novels by Tolstoy, Zola, and Dostoevsky and showed an interest in contemporary literature and experimental writers.

The library that he possessed at the end of his life included plays by Sophocles, Aeschylus, Chekhov, Euripides, Ibsen, Maeterlinck, Moliere, Racine, August Strindberg, and Shaw. Among novelists, he kept a few of the volumes he read, by Balzac, Bellamy, Willa Cather, Conan Doyle, George Eliot, Goethe, Gorky, Hawthorne, Henry James, Robert Louis Stevenson, Mark Twain, Turgenev, and Proust. He also kept several volumes of poetry on his shelves, including all of Browning's works, Chaucer, Dante, George Herbert's *The Temple*, Milton, Shelley, Tennyson, Whitman, and an 1879 edition of

Wordsworth. Among the twentieth-century poets, he had books by Conrad Aiken, Vachel Lindsay, Edgar Lee Masters, Edna St. Vincent Millay, Marianne Moore, Theodore Roethke, and Gertrude Stein, whom he "read with great" interest. At his death he owned more volumes of literature than he did of philosophy. (He kept copies of only a few of the philosophers he read. Most noteworthy are the six volumes of Peirce's *Collected Papers*, *The Literary Remains of Henry James, Sr.*, Ludwig Wittgenstein's *Tractatus Logico-Philosophicus*, and Karl Mannheim's *Man and Society*.)

Dewey had sporadically written on the philosophy of art ever since his first book, *Psychology*, in which one chapter concerned "aesthetic feeling." He reviewed Bernard Bosanquet's *A History of Aesthetic* while he was still strongly influenced by neo-Hegelianism. He examined the function of art in education, making recommendations for the Lab School derived from aesthetic principles. These also turned into an article, "The Aesthetic Element in Education" (1897), and an encyclopedia article, "Art in Education." His periodic studies of aesthetics were allied with his interest in imagination, and in *Experience and Nature* and *The Quest for Certainty*, he touched on issues of art and what he called "consummatory experience," in which the activity or expression of art is itself its final end. This important concept was worked out as early as 1921 in his lectures in China on "Types of Philosophic Thought" and later developed as a year-long course at Columbia in 1921–22. "Artistic-aesthetic experience," he wrote in his syllabus for that course, "is final, consummatory, not instrumental." Art deals with the "ends of ideal goods and illustrates a desirable life," but it does not promote or refer to "objective" reality or "social tradition."

Dewey's friend Barnes was more than a collector; he was a true pedagogue. He scarcely spoke except to joke or lecture. When he joked with those whom he regarded as his enemies, he was bitterly sarcastic. When he lectured his enemies, he tried to run a verbal spear through them. But with friends he joked in a kind way, and he lectured slowly and patiently and, at least in the instance of art, with genuinely informed intelligence. The painter Thomas Hart Benton said of Barnes, "He was the one collector I ever knew who had something of the painter's technical view of painting." Barnes paid Dewey's expenses to accompany him to European churches and art museums during several summer excursions. How he talked and what he talked about on these tours is reflected in his 1925 book, *The Art of Painting*, dedicated to John Dewey. Thomas Munro had been a student of Dewey's between 1915 and 1924, from his Columbia College days through his dissertation, which Dewey directed. In the 1920s he was one of the teachers in the Barnes Foundation, which gave courses in art and aesthetics to students who received credit through the University of Pennsylvania. Munro accompanied Barnes on all his European tours. Dewey, Munro says, "didn't talk very much. He listened. He . . . said frankly that he didn't know much about the visual arts. He had little interest in most types of music. What he knew of art was in literature." But Albert Barnes introduced him to a whole new area of knowledge. Without Barnes's impetus, Dewey would probably never have written a book on aesthetics. Literature was so much a part of his life from the earliest times that he simply took it for granted. Munro's impression was that he

> enjoyed literature without stopping to analyze or theorize about it very much in terms of aesthetic form. With visual art it was different. It was rather new to him and he had to think about it, especially since in Barnes he had a friend who evidently *did* think about it, and insisted that everyone else think with him.

Barnes showed Dewey an approach to artistic productions that stirred his philosophic interest. By temperament, Dewey tended to be interested in naturalistic or realistic literature. But Barnes was not interested in realistic content; rather, he stressed the formal aspects of art. By expanding Dewey's acquaintance with the visual arts and also by emphasizing the power of form in all artistic productions, and finally by focusing on the technical aspects of art criticism, Barnes gave Dewey all the material he needed that, added to his own evident interest in artistic productions, would lead Dewey to begin to think about writing a book on aesthetics.

The book was *Art as Experience*. Based on ten lectures that Dewey gave at Harvard in 1931, it was published in 1934. Dewey's earliest announcement of his interest in writing a book on aesthetics was in 1930. He spoke of it almost as if it had come as a vision, a visitation, telling Sidney Hook: "I . . . feel the desire to get into a field I haven't treated systematically, and art and aesthetics has come to me." From an early time he had regarded art as the highest expression of experience. His first idea for a chapter, "The Artistic and the Aesthetic in Experience," eventually influenced his choice of the title for the book he would write. He already knew what his book would exhibit: "the attempt at an e[m]pirical philos. of art, etc., which is more than *merely* psychological. That is to show why and how experience contains aesthetic and artistic features in itself." The composition of the book simply awaited an invitation to deliver a series of lectures.

Dewey was not going to be a Barnes epigone but went his own way in accordance with his long-standing convictions. Barnes started with an actual painting and moved to principles of art. Dewey started with experience and moved to aesthetic principles and then to a particular instance. For Barnes "art" didn't exist until it was realized in an art object. For Dewey, art resided in experience before any concrete expression of it was created. Whether Dewey "was talking about literature, music, or painting," Munro says, "he liked to think that the best art came out of the daily work, occupations, and interests of common people; that it was not something off by itself in the clouds." Munro was close but did not get it quite right. Dewey's view was simpler: experience is itself aesthetic, and art is the consummation of ordinary experience found everywhere. The best art is the best experience; the best experience is consummated aesthetically. Politics, shoemaking, watching a sunset, counting, buying and selling, or telling a joke are no different from a Cézanne landscape, a Renoir portraying the fullness of experience, a Seurat seeing life in its atomic particulars. Barnes was interested in *form* in art. Dewey was too, but ultimately he was more interested in "what form of satisfaction is most fully entitled to the name aesthetics," as he put it in announcing his early course in Michigan on "Philosophy of the Beautiful." Dewey and Barnes agreed that art did not tell a story, reflect an author's autobiography, or have a moral, any more than experience does. Experience *means in its activity*, and so does art; they are one. Once Dewey had fully developed a psychology of experience in *Human Nature and Conduct* and *The Quest for Certainty*, he was ready for Barnes to point the way to the last perspectives that he needed to write a book on aesthetic experience.

Art as Experience tests Dewey's flexibility. A lesser philosopher would have been tempted to process every subject that he studied through his preordained system. Pragmatism is a theory of knowing and a method of inquiry. The temptation would have been great for Dewey to regard art similarly as a form of knowing and a means of cognitive experimentation. But Dewey started afresh and did not attempt to bring art "within the scope of pragmatic philosophy" or any preconceived philosophy. Indeed, he explicitly rejected any notion that aesthetic subject matter is a form of knowledge or a cognitive insight into so-called reality. He freely acknowledged that in itself pragmatism has little to say about art. There is only one point of connection between the two. His aesthetic theory, like his pragmatic theory, holds that art, like inquiry for the sake of knowing, is an activity of human beings and that art, like knowing, "represents a highly important concern of human life." Philosophy and art have their own modes of conveying an experience of reality, Dewey argued. Art is not a quality of experience; it is qualitative experience itself. It has value and vision as "a frame of reference in the mind which is favorable to integration of experience" and therefore tends to assist in social harmony and "ordered political and economic action."

Dewey considered the first chapter of *Art as Experience*, entitled "The Live Creature," to be a clear description of his aesthetic theory. The task of one writing on the arts, he explained, is to "restore continuity between the refined and intensified forms of experience that are works of art and the everyday events, doings, and sufferings that are universally recognized to constitute experience." He uses an analogy: "Mountain peaks do not float unsupported; they do not even rest upon the earth. They *are* the earth in one of its manifest operations." It follows that art is not "about" experience; it is not an "imitation" of an action; it is not a "reproduction" of history; it is not a "spiritual" experience; it is not a "description" of experience; and it is not—as in the concept of "art for art's sake"—a substitute for experience. Rather, it is "a quality that permeates an experience." If the materials of a building are steel and bricks, the materials of architecture-as-art are reverie, dream, imagination, form, order, rhythm, and integrative vision. Dewey paraphrased Shelley's dictum that "imagination is the chief instrument of the good." The possession of these qualities and the impulse in artists to make them available to others through their art activity make art a life experience that, at its best, nourishes and heightens both social harmony and science. Art is not separate from them; it transmits meaning to them. At the biological substratum where art originates, art may be said simply to be *energy*, experience at its most alive. Dewey does not deny the conclusion that necessarily follows: art is the consummate expression of human life. If art is vibrant and alive, society, economics, thought, and science also can flourish, since art provides the energy through which these activities can come alive. Without art, the world would be a confused flux, "caprice and disorder," change without conclusion, or else a dead, completed world. Art keeps life evolving, not by some special presumed power, such as Bergson's *élan vital* or an intuition of an ideal, as in Benedetto Croce, but in the most naturally vital, biological human way, by fueling further reaches of experience through the qualities that it possesses. Dewey wrote a dozen years later in a speech on the W.P.A. artists who decorated federal buildings: "Creation, not acquisition, is a measure of a nation's rank." "Art" is not the poem, the painting, the building; it is the *perception* that is manifested in these concrete manifestations, and that perception extends beyond the concretized object.

Several commentators on Dewey's career regard *Art as Experience* as the book that best represents his deepest concerns. Certainly, read with Dewey's works that preceded or followed it in the 1920s and 1930s, it may be the only instance in which Dewey treated the qualities of perception as central. In that sense, *Art as Experience* "fills in" a gap, but it is not "central." Trying to find the one core work in Dewey's corpus would be a mistake, as he was always changing. *Art as Experience* is a remarkable instance of the risks he could take, even in arguing with his own philosophy.

The Last Educational Mission

The fifth and final of Dewey's educational missions abroad came in 1934 when he and his daughter Jane went to South Africa from July 2 to July 17, 1934, at the invitation of the World Conference of New Education Fellowship in Cape Town and Johannesburg. The stated theme of the conference, "The Adaptation of Education to Meet the Rapidly Changing Conditions of Social and Economic Life, with Special Reference to South Africa," reflected the dawning awareness of the country's social, economic, and educational problems and expressed an urgent need for remedial measures. Dewey had consistently preached that social change must start with education, and so it was almost inevitable that he would be invited to South Africa at this time. Among the other invited conferees were Lord Eustace Percy, former minister of education in Great Britain; Dewey's friend Edward Lindeman of the New York School of Social Work; and the great anthropologist Bronislaw Malinowski. John's and Jane's expenses were paid by the Carnegie Foundation.

The event was an unusually large one. More than four thousand persons attended, and more than three hundred lectures were given by 145 speakers. Dewey delivered several talks on familiar topics: "The Need for a Philosophy of Education," "What Is Learning?" and "Growth in Activity." He followed the practice that was by now well established with him, mixing educational inquiry with investigations of the local scene and culture. He traveled to the Cape of Good Hope, Durban, Victoria Falls, Pretoria, and Rhodesia (now Zimbabwe) and looked at schools, talked to pupils, and gave lectures to the administrators and teachers. By this time, Dewey's international fame was so great that he could hardly go anywhere without having to undergo some sort of ceremony. On August 3 he accepted an honorary degree from the University of Witwatersrand and delivered a lecture to its philosophy faculty. On the following day, he gave a big public lecture in Pretoria. Not until the end of August did he sail from Cape Town for the long journey back to the United States.

South Africa would have provided an abundance of material for the kind of essays that Dewey had once written for the *New Republic*.

But his relations with the magazine were no longer cordial, and there was no other ready outlet for him in which he could write the kind of reports that he had once sent from Japan, China, Turkey, and Mexico. His only printed comment on the social problems in South Africa came in a talk on "The Need for a Philosophy of Education." His main thesis was that the rapid industrialization of the world was now affecting groups, tribes, and races that had once been able to live in isolation. This was creating a crisis in South Africa and elsewhere, where, he argued, education must have as its social aim the education of the mind and will in the philosophy of cooperation. Dewey quoted a Geneva Commission study of mine workers in Johannesburg concerning the increasing dependency of the native workers on Western investment in South Africa. He remained consistent in his version of globalism. American investment was not enough; without an accompanying increase in democracy in developing countries, investment would be mere exploitation.

His South Africa excursion turned out to be the last time Dewey traveled abroad to investigate the possibility of planting the seeds of American democratic education in a foreign soil. With the Depression deepening at home, the need for social reform there so evident, and with a mounting array of controversies on his hands, Dewey simply decided to remain in the United States and see whether he could educate the citizens of his own country. But to do this, he had to take one last trip abroad, not to develop democratic schools, but to educate his fellow liberals in political judgment. The trip was to Mexico, but the reason for it started in Moscow.

LEON TROTSKY

Dewey's writings and his own activities were inextricably intertwined in the 1930s. His books and the public affairs and policy recommendations and the lobbying into which Dewey put enormous energy went hand in hand. Now, following his writings on liberalism as an idea and ideal opposing the authoritarian absolutes that threatened to dominate the political, social, and economic spheres, Dewey was confronted by a new challenge to his commitment to intelligence-as-action on behalf of freedom and justice. This challenge came in 1937. The events that led to this special experience had begun some years earlier. Lenin's death in 1924 had led to a struggle for supremacy in the Soviet Union between Josef Stalin and Leon Trotsky. Stalin's shaky victory in this contest led to Trotsky's exile, first to the Chinese frontier, then to Turkey, next to France, and finally to Norway, each move an attempt to find some spot safe from Stalin's increasing enmity and its personal danger for him. In Mexico throughout the 1930s, President Lázaro Cárdenas followed the generous practice of granting admission to political refugees, and so Trotsky looked toward Mexico as a possible political haven. Besides, in Mexico the party's Trotskyist wing was fairly strong, and Trotsky received an invitation from Diego Rivera and Frida Kahlo, great painters but naïve Troskyists, to stay at their house in Coyocoán, at the edge of Mexico City. He fled there.

Meanwhile, the Moscow trials had begun. Stalin was consolidating his power, and anyone even tangentially associated with Trotsky became an enemy of the people. Many of these "enemies" were rounded up and tried. Their "confessions" were quickly followed by executions. "It is nineteen thirty-seven now," the poet Delmore Schwartz wrote. "Many great dears are taken away." By the time the trials were over, of those who had once composed the Central Committee of the Communist Party in the Soviet Union, only Stalin and Trotsky were left. Stalin's minister of justice, Andrei Vyshinsky, announced the ultimate charge: Trotsky had plotted to assassinate Stalin and bring Germany and Japan into a war against the Soviet Union.

But Trotsky himself was as full of defiance as ever. Indeed, rather than being crushed by the Soviet charge, his branch of the party was somewhat invigorated, especially now that Trotsky was safe in Mexico. It was ready for a counterattack against Stalin. Almost immediately, the French Trotskyists formed the Comité pour l'enquête sur la procés de Moscou to defend Trotsky, and soon after, Americans formed the Committee for the Defense of Leon Trotsky. Both groups demanded that an international tribunal be formed to "hear" Stalin's charges and allow Trotsky to defend himself while he still remained in the security of exile. Obviously, there was no real thought of his returning voluntarily to Moscow for a trial.

Almost at once, wrangling between André Breton and André Malraux broke out in the French group, and no decision could be reached concerning the membership of an appropriate tribunal. It was left to the American group to offer Trotsky a hearing. The leaders of the American committee included the sociologist Edward A. Ross and George Novack. They realized that a tribunal consisting entirely of Trotsky sympathizers could scarcely achieve credibility on the international stage. What they needed was a group, and especially a chairman, who had an international reputation for fairness and whose integrity could be accepted by liberals, Soviet sympathizers, and intellectuals everywhere. Encouraged by the socialist philosopher Sidney Hook, their hopes soon fastened on Hook's dissertation adviser, the seventy-eight-year-old John Dewey, as the best possible choice for chair. After all, Dewey had been celebrated in the Soviet Union when he went there in 1928 and had been asked by the Socialist Party to run on their ticket for governor of New York. But he was also quoted every week or so in the moderate *New York Times*; he was invited to the White House for dinner; he was the friend of powerful capitalists; he had chaired the philosophy and pedagogy departments at Mr. Rockefeller's University of Chicago; and now at Columbia he was a favorite of President Nicholas Murray Butler.

Hook was joined by James T. Farrell, the leading Trotskyist among prominent American writers, in persuading Dewey to undertake the responsibility of chairing the tribunal, which meant traveling to Mexico where the hearings were to be held at Rivera's house, as well as reading and absorbing a mass of documents. At first Dewey was adamantly opposed. He was intent on finishing his *Logic: The Theory of Inquiry*. This book, which was certainly the crown of Dewey's work in the field of logic and possibly his best book, had been occupying him on and off for the last ten years, and in 1937 he was determined to finish it. Several other people provided him with plenty of reasons why he should not go. His oldest child, Fred, for instance, was fiercely opposed to the trip, fearful of the effect it could have on his father's health. Once the word leaked out that Dewey was being persuaded to go, Dewey's friends and acquaintances in the "common front" of socialism also spent a lot of energy urging him not to support Trotsky, whom they regarded as an enemy of the Soviet revolution. In a letter, Dewey's close friend Alex Gumberg advised him: "John, my friend, don't go. I feel justified in trying to urge you again not to ally yourself with the 'dark forces' of the Counter Revolution." No discredit, Gumberg argued, should be allowed to fall on the Soviet experiment. Malcolm Cowley, the literary editor of the *New Republic*, later wrote to Dewey: "I think American progressives of all shades should stick together— they will have to hang together or hang in some other way.... The evidence is overwhelming that Trotsky is guilty. We must not injure the cause of liberalism and democracy." Dewey also received anonymous death threats, which continued long after he returned from Mexico.

Around this time Dewey's long association with the *New Republic* came to an end. For almost two decades he had drawn a regular weekly salary from that journal while sending his contributions in irregularly. "We never put the slightest pressure on him," its editor Bruce Bliven said, "and ... we never rejected anything he produced." In 1937, however, Dewey believed that the current editors "had given up what I take to be liberalism in order to be ... apologist[s] for Stalinism," and he resigned as a contributing editor. At odds with the *New Republic* now, he was not likely to heed the warnings or advice of Cowley, whom he regarded as a supporter of Stalin.

Besides all the other reasons he had or was given to remain at home and not get involved in a hearing abroad, Dewey had one more special reason not to go to Mexico. He had recently fallen in love with a journalist in her thirties named Roberta Lowitz. Alice had died eight years before, and Dewey had had no serious, sexually intimate affairs before this one. But this one was serious. If all these incentives to refuse did not work, a final one was also destined to fail. One last attempt was made to dissuade him from going. Sidney Hook says that one night he was at Dewey's apartment when a well-known radical, an opera singer, arrived. The man said that he had come as an official representative of the Soviet artistic organization Vox. The Soviets, he said, remembered Dewey's earlier trip with pleasure, and they wanted him to return for a visit, all expenses paid. He stressed the all expenses *paid*, and he out-lined a luxury junket on the Black Sea. Dewey said, "Well, I don't know if this would be an appropriate time for me to visit the Soviet Union because I'm thinking of going to Mexico with the Trotsky Commission." At this point the visitor interrupted, "Trotsky, Schmotsky! We aren't interested in him. We would only like for you to come, to see that wonderful things have happened in the ten years since you were there. But you have to come now. . . . All expenses will be paid by Vox. Yalta, the Black Sea. A wonderful trip." Dewey thanked him, the man left, and Dewey turned to Hook. "Well, that was pretty barefaced, wasn't it?" he asked.

He accepted the chairmanship of the hearing, after all, and he made it clear why he had: it was for his beliefs. According to Agnes Meyer, "John told me he soon realized he had to accept, despite the arduous journey. Wherever the truth might lead, he said, the outcome of the investigation would afford an opportunity for American democracy to reorient itself toward the solution of its own social problems." Nonetheless, Fred kept trying to persuade Dewey not to go, pursuing him all the way to the train platform, still insisting that it was irrational for him to make the journey. Dewey wrote to Roberta Lowitz, "I tried to answer Fred's questions about why I was going and had to tell him that he was too rational and there weren't any rational answers to his questions in a world as irrational as this one."

Thinking of Gumberg and Cowley, he wrote to a friend:

> I have spent my whole life searching for truth. It is disheart-ening that in our own country some liberals have come to believe that for reasons of expediency our own people should be left in the dark as to the actual atrocities in Russia. But truth is not a bourgeois delusion, it is the mainspring of human progress.

When it was learned that in 1937 Dewey *would* go to Mexico, Edward Ross wrote to Novack: "No one in the country could bring so much prestige to the committee as he can." Dewey's presence on the com-mission meant that the major papers would cover the hearing, an extremely important consideration. Upon learning that Dewey had accepted and the hearing was to go forward, Trotsky gave a speech transmitted by telephone to a large audience at the New York Hippodrome, stating: "If this commission decides that I am guilty of the crimes which Stalin imputes to me, I pledge to place myself voluntarily in the hands of the executioner of the G.P.U."

James T. Farrell accompanied Dewey on the train from New York. Dewey carried Trotsky's and Lenin's complete works in his luggage, along with a portable typewriter and a suitcase full of documents. He read and wrote on the train, mastering Trotsky's works and writing letters, sometimes several a day, to Roberta: "Dear Robbie: I love you. . . . What more is there to say? These pages are covered with the words I love you." He was seventy-eight years old, but he had preserved the idealistic romanticism of his youth.

The hearing was held at Rivera's house just outside Mexico City. Preparations were made and precautions organized with the utmost care, for an attack on Trotsky or the commissioners was expected at any moment. Diego Rivera, looking like a figure in one of his murals, wore ammunition belts slung across his chest and carried a carbine. Clothed in a Mexican Indian dress, Frida Kahlo carried a gun too. An official card of admission, personally signed by Dewey, was required for entrance.

The other commissioners were Otto Ruehle, Karl Marx's biographer and a leader of the German communists who opposed Hitler's rise to power; Benjamin Stolberg, a labor advocate and writer; Carleton Beals, a well-known Latin America expert; and Suzanne La Follette, the editor of *The Freeman* and a member of the well-known Progressive family. Other figures in the Progressive movement who were in attendance included Carlo Tresca, the anarchosyndicalist editor of *Il Martello*. John F. Finerty, Tom Mooney's attorney, served as the counsel for the committee. The world press was in attendance, along with representatives of major American papers and the "March of Time" newsreel cameramen. Soviet authorities were invited to send documentary material and representatives to examine Trotsky. The

Soviet ambassador to the United States, Andrei Troyanovsky, was invited to attend, but he refused.

The surviving newspaper photographs and sketches and paintings show that the spacious room in which the hearings were conducted was divided in two. On the one side of a barrier, the commission and Trotsky sat. On the other were seats for the press, Mexican representatives of the labor movement, and other spectators. The room was always full to overflowing. Diego Rivera sketched Dewey's face and then promptly slept through most of the hearings. At 10 a.m. on April 10, 1937, the hearings were opened by John Dewey with these words:

> This commission, like many millions of workers of city and country, of hand and brain, believes that no man should be condemned without a chance to defend himself. . . . The simple fact that we are here is evidence that conscience demands that Mr. Trotsky be not condemned before he has had full opportunity to present whatever evidence is in his possession in reply to the guilty verdict returned in a court where he was neither present nor represented. If Leon Trotsky *is* guilty of the acts with which he is charged, no condemnation can be too severe.

Dewey concluded his opening speech with words that the philosopher John J. McDermott says were "worthy of the famous speech by Socrates in the *Apology* of Plato":

> Speaking, finally, not for the commission but for myself, I had hoped that a chairman might be found whose experience better fitted him for the difficult and delicate task to be performed. But I have given my life to the work of education which I have conceived to be that of public enlightenment in the interests of society. If I finally accepted the responsible post I now occupy, it was because I realized that to act otherwise would be false to my life's work.

With that the hearing opened, and Trotsky made his preliminary remarks:

> Esteemed commissioners. The composition of the Commission and the high authority of its chairman exclude the possibility that the investigation would be anything but objective. . . . My duty is simply to try to help it in its work. I will try to accomplish this duty faithfully before the eyes of the world.

He did not repeat his offer to return to the Soviet Union for trial should he not be exonerated by the commissioners. Albert Goldman, appointed to undertake the legal aspects of Trotsky's defense, said in his initial statement, "We are determined to convince the members of this commission, and everyone who reads and thinks with an independent mind, *beyond all doubt*, that Leon Trotsky and his son are guiltless of the monstrous charges made against them." And so, the hearings were begun. Each of the next thirteen sessions unfolded in much the same way. The commissioners raised various questions about the charges against Trotsky. He answered vigorously, with a remarkable command of detail and a capacity for analysis. Albert Goldman was present to help Trotsky in his defense, but he needed little assistance. Despite his heavy accent, Trotsky spoke with exceptional clarity, sometimes even with wit and beauty, and always with impeccable logic, in his own defense. Dewey showed a particular interest in Trotsky's activities with Lenin during the early stages of the revolution.

A war of words was also going on outside the conference room. The hearing was rapidly becoming a catalyst for the conflict between the unbending supporters of the Russian Revolution and those who were skeptical of it. Stalin's and Vyshinsky's decision to accuse Trotsky of treason so as to render him impotent as a dissenter since he was beyond their reach, was in danger of backfiring. Trotsky's defense was getting unexpected publicity. The American Committee for the Defense of Trotsky was issuing bulletins, press releases, and announcements on behalf of Trotsky. It contacted labor unions; it sent out publicity; and it disseminated the details of Trotsky's defense, which soon turned into a wholesale attack on Stalin as a revolutionary-turned-fascist-dictator. All the defendants in the earlier Moscow trials had made "confessions." Trotsky was unreconstructed. Never before had a prominent member of the revolution condemned so fully, in reports so widely distributed, the revolution's failure.

The Kremlin mounted a virulent campaign against the hearings. Communist papers like the *Daily Worker* in America and many leftist journals heaped abuse on the hearings and its chair. For instance, in the *New Masses*, Marion Hammett and William Smith mocked "the so-called impartial inquiry": "The hearings merely presented a rosy picture of Trotsky while blackening the Moscow defendants who implicated him. The commissioners heard only Trotsky's version. Suzanne La Follette's questions were so biased that even Mr. Dewey had to object." Dewey was attacked as a deluded old man who had once been a friend of the Soviets but now was merely duped by the enemies of socialism. In the Soviet Union, Dewey was charged with being "an enemy of peace and progress." For years after the hearing, Dewey was denounced by the Soviets. Even in response to his ninetieth birthday celebrations, he was ungraciously characterized as "a philosophical lackey of American imperialism" and "a warmongering Winston Churchill of Philosophy."

In the midst of the hearings, a dramatic event occurred: Carleton Beals resigned in protest. It was evident to all that this was a party strategy to shift attention away from Trotsky's defense against Stalin's charges and to make the commission itself the subject of controversy. Naturally, as expected, Beals's resignation itself took over the headlines. His criticism of the committee, rather than the substance of the hearings, briefly became the focus of the news. He was ready with a series of announcements. "Thus far," he told the reporters in an evident attempt to discredit Trotsky's damning testimony against Stalin, "no investigation has been conducted, but merely a pink tea party—with everyone but myself uttering sweet platitudes. Trotsky had wings sprouting from his shoulders." Beals had the party line down pat, with all the available clichés. "By its Czarist methods," he told the press, "the

Commission prevented me from clarifying matters." He alone, he suggested, could question Trotsky effectively and reveal his counterrevolutionary acts, but only if the commission were disbanded. Beals concluded: "Until Trotsky is willing to disavow the stupidities of the Commission, he can twiddle his thumbs so far as I am concerned." Back in Washington, D.C., Soviet Ambassador Troyanovsky was also trying to persuade newsmen that the commission was a "flop"—his words—a "put-up job" to rehabilitate Trotsky. Dewey was not just a dupe but a willing tool of the reactionaries.

So the battle raged, all over the world. Dewey held the hearings together with his own moral integrity and personal intellectual sincerity and impartiality. Bertram Wolfe, who later became well known for his work *Three Who Made a Revolution*, as well as his biography of Diego Rivera and other books, was a young, excited spectator at the hearings. He wrote to another young man, Arthur Mizener, who would eventually be F. Scott Fitzgerald's first biographer: "Here is fine old Dewey, an honest liberal worth all the ultra-revolutionary intellectuals put together, going to school again at the age of 78, and learning all about the worker's movement, reading everything, [and] asking [all of us] for bibliography, etc." Dewey, of course, was merely following his usual habits: spending all day in sessions, reading at night, and then preparing long lists of questions for the next day before he went to bed.

Sometimes a bit of gossip would come up, such as Dewey's report of the revelation made by Carlos Tresca, who was in a position to know, that despite the noble defense of the innocence of Sacco and Vanzetti ten years earlier, the truth was that Sacco was actually guilty of the crimes he was charged with. Dewey was astounded, but it did not make him swerve from his desire to seek justice for Trotsky. Even though he knew that Trotsky was a ruthless revolutionary, who perhaps deserved the most severe penalties for his crimes against humanity, the question here was more narrow and concerned only with whether Trotsky was guilty of the crimes charged against him by Stalin. Unlike others, Dewey never wavered in his focus on this one question.

The sessions continued, one after another, comprehensively covering Trotsky's life, his revolutionary and terrorist activities, his associations with those accused of conspiracy with him, and his activities in France and Norway when he was charged with plotting against Stalin. Much documentary evidence was introduced. Finally, in the last session, Trotsky made a long, impassioned speech in his own defense, accusing Stalin of betraying the revolution. It was the climax of the hearings:

> One can understand the acts of Stalin only by starting from the conditions of existence of the new privileged bureaucracy— greedy for power, greedy for material comforts, apprehensive for its positions, fearing the masses, and mortally hating the opposition. Stalin, who was once a revolutionist, became the leader of the new privileged bureaucracy. The moral authority of the leaders of the bureaucracy and, above all, of Stalin, rests in large measure upon the Tower of Babel of slanderers and falsifications erected over a period of thirteen years. This Tower of Babel is maintained with the aid of more and more terrible repressions. These gentlemen buy human consciences like sacks of potatoes. Fortunately, not everybody can be bought. Otherwise humanity would have rotted away a long time ago. Here, in the person of the Commission, we have a precious cell of unmarketable public conscience. All those who thirst for purification of the social atmosphere will turn instinctively toward the Commission. In spite of intrigues, bribes and calumny, it will be rapidly protected by the armor of the sympathy of broad, popular masses.

At his conclusion he expressed "profound respect to the educator, philosopher and personification of genuine American idealism, the scholar who heads the work of your Commission." The speech lasted an hour. It was followed by a burst of applause and then a hushed silence. The spectators waited for Dewey to speak, Finally, he said softly: "Anything I can say will be an anti-climax . . . the hearings of the preliminary commission of inquiry are now ended."

Of course, they were not ended. The commissioners had to return to New York, sift through the evidence, and make their decision, which would be weeks away. Following the end of the hearings, Trotsky said to Dewey that for him they had proved that American idealism was not a myth but a reality. "I have realized that American Liberalism exists as a fact," Trotsky said to Dewey as he gave him a final embrace in farewell. Dewey responded quickly and graciously: "If all Marxists were like you, Mr. Trotsky, I would be a Marxist." And Trotsky replied, "If all liberals were like you, Dr. Dewey, I would be a liberal."

Dewey boarded the train a few days later, planning to return from Mexico by way of St. Louis. He felt fine despite the long, demanding hearings. In fact, he was the only one of the commissioners who had not become sick in Mexico. Dewey never indulged the thought that he was aged or feeble. As he boarded the train in Mexico City, Albert Glotzer, who had transcribed the proceedings, took his arm to help him up the steps, but Dewey angrily pushed the hand away and skipped ahead.

In St. Louis he had agreed to deliver a lecture on the evening of his arrival to one thousand doctors at the annual meeting of the American College of Physicians. "A bad case has been made out against Russia," he told the reporter for the *St. Louis Star Times*. "If the accused are innocent, we have an example of arbitrary exercise of power by a dictatorship. If they are guilty, we have former leaders betraying the cause for which they fought—an evidence of some sort of rottenness in the system itself." He said little about Trotsky; that person was already behind him, and he never dwelled on the past. He wanted the reporters to know that he had followed the news of the day from Mexico and that he was more interested now in how the Supreme Court could be renovated; he doubted that FDR's court-packing plan could succeed. But Dewey's experience in the Trotsky trial had had an effect, after all. From this time forward, his deep suspicion of the leadership of the Soviet Union was evident. On communism as applied to America, he said definitively to the reporter who interviewed him in St. Louis:

> The surest way to put this country into fascist hands is to try to make it communist. For me, however, I have great faith in the

common sense of the average American and in democracy and education. I look into the future with hope. If recovery lasts, I'll feel easy; if it doesn't, I'll be afraid of Fascism and war.

From around this time, too, his advocacy of socialism cooled. He began to think that the traditional forms of socialism were worn out as a vigorous idea. "The so-called guild socialists once started something," he wrote to James T. Farrell, "but events have left them nearly as much behind as it has the 'old-fashioned' socialists." If he were to remain a socialist, it would have to be as a Deweyan party-of-one. "Liberal" proved to be a good-enough label for him.

The onslaught against him by party members and, more broadly, by those who declared themselves liberals, brought Dewey to the conclusion that American liberalism had become corrupted by the ideology of communism, which above all else stressed loyalty to the party. In early May he wrote that

> unwillingness to face the unpleasant is the standing weakness of liberals. They are only too likely to be brave when affairs are going smoothly and then to shirk when unpleasant situations demand decision and action. I cannot believe that a single *genuine* liberal would, if he once faces the alternatives, hold that persecution and falsification are a sound basis on which to build an enduring Socialist society.

Dewey continued to see himself as a true liberal—but to doubt the claims of professed liberals. On May 10, when speaking to a large audience at Mecca Temple in New York City, and a little later during a radio speech, he expressed his fears:

> One more word. I have spoken thus far of rather political issues. I hope the time is not yet when the cause of elementary justice may not be mentioned. I have all my life, today more that ever, disagreed with the type of political thought represented by Trotsky. I disagreed ten years ago with the political thought of Sacco and Vanzetti. That did not prevent me from

resisting to the last the hounding of those two martyrs who died for a crime never proven against them. As an American who believes that no man shall be convicted without an opportunity to defend himself, I could not, despite my pressing personal duties, refuse when asked to serve on the commission which gave Trotsky, our political and philosophical adversary, a chance to speak in his own behalf. That is a motive which, I feel sure, is as valid today for many Americans as it was in the days of our struggle against the persecutors of Sacco and Vanzetti.

Dewey and his cocommissioners quickly worked through the transcripts of the hearings and prepared a large volume containing the evidence they had examined. When published, the title of the book was "NOT GUILTY!" Dewey received many letters of appreciation for the part he played in the hearing, including two from the great revolutionary Emma Goldman. She wrote that although Trotsky was not guilty of the crimes with which he was charged by Stalin, he was surely guilty of many others and deserved no mercy. "Nevertheless," she wrote, "I rejoice that brave men and women have been found, with you, dear Professor, in the lead, to cry out against the dreadful butcheries going on under Stalin's regime." The evidence of history confirms that Dewey and the commission judged correctly. Trotsky was certainly no innocent, but of Stalin's charges he was not guilty. The materials released from the Soviet archives during Premier Nikita Khrushchev's time and after the breakup of the Soviet Union show conclusively that the Moscow trials were frame-ups. Trotsky was, of course, elated to hear the "verdict" and at once wired Dewey: "Warmest greetings to the Chairman whose firmness, vigilance, and high moral authority assured the success of the investigation. Long life, Dr. Dewey!" Numerous media outlets sympathetic to Trotsky used the verdict to castigate Stalin and his policies anew. But Stalin was not finished. Trotsky's son Sedov died in France under suspicious circumstances in February 1938. Hearing the news, Dewey wired Leon and

Natalia his "deepest sympathy in your terrible bereavement." Trotsky wired back "the warmest wishes for your health and the sincerest admiration for your great personality." In 1940 a flunky for the Soviet Secret Service worked his way into Trotsky's trust and then drove an ice ax into his brain.

Before his death, Trotsky made a mistake with Dewey. Convinced that he had made Dewey a convert to his ideas, or at least a sympathizer with them, Trotsky invited him to comment in the *New International* on a lead article that he himself had just written. It was entitled "Their Morals and Ours" and appeared in June 1938. But he was wrong about Dewey. The "not guilty" judgment that he rendered was based on his concept of justice, not on his political or ideological adherence to Trotskyist logic. At the end of the hearings, Dewey confided to James T. Farrell: "Trotsky's the most brilliant man I've ever heard talk . . . but he needs a guardian." Although he was a persuasive rhetorician, Trotsky lacked the guardianship of values. So, when Trotsky asked Dewey to judge him on philosophic grounds, Dewey was unsparing in his criticism of the improper conflation of means and ends contained in Trotsky's central claim: "A means can be justified only by its ends."

This was favorite Deweyan theme. Dewey began his reply, "Means and Ends," by noting that "the relation of means and ends has long been an outstanding issue in morals." His position was almost directly opposite Trotsky's on this issue. Of course, means and ends are intricately intertwined. In "The Future of Liberalism," Dewey wrote: "The kind of means used, determines the kind of consequences actually reached—the ends in the only sense in which 'ends' do not signify abstractions." But adjusting the balance of operations between means and ends was the question. In Trotsky's essay Dewey had a concrete case, the kind he liked. By placing emphasis on the *means* of revolution, Trotsky, not so differently from Stalin, Dewey argued, would achieve the end of a revolution embodying the means used to achieve it: terror, coercion, control. Such means used would result in a dictatorial society rather than a democratic one. Dewey, by contrast, put the emphasis on the *ends* to be achieved and then reflected on the means that would, when chosen, achieve the desired ends.

In his reply to Trotsky, he arrived immediately at his central critique:

> Means and ends are certainly interdependent, and one would expect that if the liberation of mankind is the end-in-view, there would follow an examination of all *means* that are likely to attain this *end* without any fixed conception of what the means must be. And every suggested means would be considered and weighed and judged on the express grounds of the consequences they are likely to produce. But when Mr. Trotsky finds in the class struggle the "law of laws," the one and only means to human liberation, then the means become the end.

Dewey argued that if one starts with struggle or violence as a means, when the revolution itself is achieved, it will continue the struggle and violence.

> It is tragic to see Trotsky's brilliant native intelligence so completely locked up in an absolute so that means become ends. Orthodox Marxism shares with orthodox religionism and with traditional idealism the belief that human ends are interwoven into the very texture and structure of existence—a conception inherited from its Hegelian origin. Trotsky is an absolutist, and he is unable to escape from the prisonhouse of absolutism.

Dewey's insistence on the interdependence of means and ends is a crucial point in understanding his method of logic. In a seminar that he gave at the University of Chicago in the winter of 1926, his colleague George Herbert Mead referred to the means-ends problem as the "core," the "final statement of Dewey's philosophy." For Dewey, philosophy must be, Mead said, "a criticism of the means in the process [of analysis] which gives us the end of the process . . . philosophy is not *knowledge* as an abstraction—it's a criticism of the methods by which you reach your ends, or results." *How* we think will lead to *what* we think, and what we do.

The Trotsky hearings constituted a central turning point in the history of American liberalism. From John Reed's celebration of the revolution on through the Palmer raids, the well-publicized conversion to communism of Lincoln Steffens, the onset of the Depression, and the announcement of liberals like Edmund Wilson in 1932 that they would vote for the Communist candidate for president, American liberalism had all but merged with Soviet Communism. Only a few liberal thinkers, like Sidney Hook, were anti-Soviet. Stalin's mounting of the Moscow trials, dubious though they were, were held far from America and were easily justified by the claim that any means that saved the revolution were acceptable. But when the most revered of American liberal intellectuals, John Dewey, announced after examining the evidence thoroughly that he had concluded that Stalin's accusations against Trotsky were false and self-condemning, the public— which seldom agreed with Dewey but always trusted his intelligence and honesty—and even American liberals began for the first time to question the Soviet leadership, and this led to an examination of the Soviet experiment. One by one, most American intellectuals began to see the revolution, as Richard Wright later put it, as "the God that failed." It was a great, historic moment for Dewey personally, but an even greater demonstration that intellectual honesty, rather than party loyalty, can alter history.

In the Trotsky "trial," Dewey exhibited the true basis for political choice in rendering a just verdict, unmindful of death threats, attacks on his reputation, pleas from friends and family, or material bribes. Moreover, the trial had a special meaning for Dewey. He told Max Eastman that "it was the most interesting single experience of my life." The episode offers a remarkable revelation of Dewey's character and thought, philosophy, and social activism. In the most vivid way, this event conveyed the character of John Dewey: his personality, his commitments, his ideals, and the way he acted on them.

Dewey's Logic

Liberalism, Dewey had been arguing for a decade, was a never completed quest. The finding of Dewey's committee that Trotsky was "not guilty" was one more instance of Dewey's ongoing effort to preserve freedom by means of liberal intelligence-in-action. When Stalin's charges were refuted, of course, the Soviet Union did not collapse. Only one small stone in the edifice of Communism was loosened. The trial was over. But no one could doubt that both the fascist and the communist authorities meant business, that both accepted the notion that change would take place only through violence. And that meant war.

Dewey was characteristically attentive to the ways in which war always resulted in constraints on freedom. As in his reaction to the approach of World War I, therefore, his inclination in the late 1930s was to hope against informed hope that the United States could avoid being drawn into another conflict. With regard to the Spanish civil war, Dewey declared: "Certainly, the United States must be kept out of any European war." Individual Americans could certainly volunteer to assist the republican cause. Surely, democracy in the Spanish republic should be encouraged against fascist and communist forces. But as a nation, the United States should stay out. Two years later, Dewey participated in a symposium on the question "If War Comes, Shall We Participate or Be Neutral?" Again, the theme he struck was concern for democracy. To reorganize America's industrial, political, and human resources for entry into a war would make for a regression in democratic institutions. The renascent liberalism of the late 1930s would disappear as surely as the Progressive movement had dissolved during World War I. And from the evidence of the Palmer raids in 1919, the restrictions on freedom of speech before and after the war, and the frenzied finance that followed the war in the 1920s, Dewey knew that it would be hard for democracy to recover from wartime mobilization. "It is quite conceivable," he speculated, "that after the next war in this country we should have a semi-military, semi-financial autocracy . . . [and] the suppression of all the democratic values for the

sake of which we professedly went to war." For an American democratic advance, he predicted, war would be "the greatest social catastrophe that could overtake us, the destruction of all the foundations
upon which to erect a socialized democracy." Around the same time he
wrote privately to James Tufts of his fears: "What will become of our
democracy and of our social gains of the last few years"? But what
would happen to democracy, not just in Europe and Asia, but also in
the United States, if totalitarian regimes prevailed abroad? Dewey
waited for more news, and while he waited, he returned to his long-
awaited book on logic.

In early 1938, Dewey met his colleague Herbert Schneider on
the street. "I've just handed the publisher what I regard as my chief
work, . . . my formulation, the best I can do it, of my life's work." More
than any of his other books, *Logic: The Theory of Inquiry* (1938) is an
experiment in the reconstruction of logical traditions, in which Dewey
aims at "bringing logical theory into accord with scientific practice."
For those people who believe that "truth" is the object of logic, logic is
at the heart of the philosophical enterprise. Dewey asserts that the idea
that logic "discovered" truths should be deconstructed in favor of a
search for "warrantable assertions." Finally, he casts doubt on the very
procedures of deduction and induction that had seemed to be the con-
stitutive ingredients of logic itself, and in place of these, he substitutes
a theory of inquiry in which the context of the investigation and the
functions intended for the experiment are the determining factors. He
told Joseph Ratner that the turning point in his philosophical career
came in his understanding inquiry as a "mode of living activity."

The originality and uniqueness of *Logic: The Theory of Inquiry* can
be grasped only against the background of the development of traditional logical theory. For Aristotle and the tradition that flows from his
work, logic consists of the rules of reason which, if the premises are
true and the thinker reasons correctly, must make the conclusion true.
A second stream of logic had begun with George Boole, who allied
logic with mathematics. By Dewey's time, this variant had been picked
up by the logical positivists who used mathematics to analyze the
tautological or synthetic statements that led to scientific propositions.

A parallel stream was developed by Russell and Whitehead, who contended that all of mathematics was derived from logic.

Dewey's way with logic starts from a wholly different point of view and has a different source. Hegel suggested that reason—which was identical with the new, dynamic logic he adumbrated—worked its way into every aspect of the world—history, politics, mechanics, aesthetics, and the like. Logic became, then, the way of understanding what reason created: simply, the ways we live. Starting with Hegel's expansive logic, Dewey invented instrumental logic, an investigation of the ways we live that would not lead to static Truth but to dynamic, provisional assertions. His severe criticisms of Lotze; his wish to construct a logic suitable to support James's pragmatism; the influence of Peirce, who stressed inquiry; Dewey's rejection of the simplistic tautology-synthetic statement continuum; his desire to find logical models that use and illuminate the ways of the world; and his aim of attaching logic and scientific procedures to individual and social life all took him far beyond Hegel, even as the germ of his logic in Hegel's writings is clear in *Logic: The Theory of Inquiry*.

Dewey had studied Aristotelian logic with H. A. P. Torrey at the University of Vermont and Hegel's logic with George Sylvester Morris at Johns Hopkins. During his early career, in his published writing, annotated syllabi, and private letters, Dewey frequently referred to such more recent logicians as Bernard Bosanquet, John Stuart Mill, and Hermann Lotze, who considered logic to be a means of inquiry by which *truth* is discovered. Dewey's initial position, starting with *Studies in Logical Theory* (1903), repudiated the procedures and conclusions of these philosophers and contended that logical inquiry does not achieve fixed truths about life and the ways we live. Rather, it is a method of scientific investigation whose conclusions are always provisional, but this is the best kind of knowledge, for it drives us toward further inquiry, whereas "absolute truth" is static. In *Logic: The Theory of Inquiry*, Dewey went further than he had earlier, with the possible exception of some sections of *The Quest for Certainty*, and argued that truth was not discovered through inquiry, it was *produced* by inquiry. In accord with his own concept of continuing investigation, Dewey reflected for a long time on this problem and made the best statement of his position in "Propositions, Warranted Assertability, and Truth" (1941), an essay correcting Russell's misconceptions concerning Dewey's argument about warranted assertability.

Accordingly, Dewey regarded even his own book as far from a definitive statement about logic and instead as the beginning of a scientific process that others would continue. More than most of Dewey's works, the book itself exhibits a process of accumulating information, insight, and subtlety. It took about a dozen years to complete, nearly preventing Dewey from chairing the Commission of Inquiry into the case of Leon Trotsky. Long as it took to complete this study and difficult as it was to write, *Logic: The Theory of Inquiry* is an expression of the fact that logic was Dewey's "first love and last love." Nor was he finished with his interest in logical theory with the completion of *Logic*. He explicitly said that he considered his work as a hypothesis, and he urged others to continue the examination he had started. Indeed, near the time of his death, he was making plans to revise the book. He told his friend and correspondent Arthur Bentley, "You suggested once I write a condensed version of the Logic; I feel much more like it now than I ever did before."

In *Logic: The Theory of Inquiry* Dewey repudiated what he had learned from Torrey and Morris. As early as *How We Think*, he had made his own way toward the idea that logic was "reflective thinking." His later study of Peirce was not so much an "influence" on him as it was a stimulus to complete his own thinking on the subject. The first reference made to another philosopher in *Logic* is to Peirce, who first pointed out the importance of "the principle of the continuum of inquiry," which, as Dewey used it, allowed him to give an "empirical account . . . of logical forms." Following Peirce's concept of "pragmaticism" as a method of inquiry, Dewey stressed that "pragmatism" is not a thing but a methodological procedure that can examine "the function of consequences as necessary tests of the validity of propositions." One of the inside narratives of *Logic: The Theory of Inquiry* is Dewey's internal dialogue with Peirce.

As early as 1893 Dewey had expressed his opposition to a central element of James and Peirce in his essay "The Superstition of Necessity." William James had posed the problem of "necessary truths" in his *Principles of Psychology*, grounding the psychology of that book in the subjective experience of truths a priori to experience. For all his admiration for James's book, Dewey could not be satisfied with the assumption of a mental structure incorporating necessary truths. Nor could he accept Peirce's transcendental argument for a priori truths. In "The Superstition of Necessity," Dewey articulated the conviction that would rule his philosophic method up to and beyond the *Logic* of 1938. Philosophers, he asserted, could easily fall into the superstition of "clinging to old ideas after those ideas have lost their use, and hence, like all superstitions, have become obstructions." The idea of necessary truths, which Peirce had defended in an 1893 essay, "The Doctrine of Necessity Examined," was one of those superstitions, Dewey believed. Dewey modestly wrote that his own thought would take "a different turn" from Peirce's. Dewey's "turn" was experimental psychology. "When we say something or other *must* be so," he wrote, the "must does not indicate anything in the nature of the fact itself, but a trait in our *judgment* of that fact." "Necessity" is a stage of thought, one of the tools of inquiry into the object of investigation. "Its character," Dewey wrote, "is purely teleological and 'practical.' " Necessity is "neither accidental nor necessary" but a logical construction that functions to produce judgments about "reality" and activity in it. It is one part of the usable instruments of logic that we employ in grappling with "experience."

Dewey separated himself quietly from a basic underpinning of James's *Principles of Psychology*, and he also—just as quietly—rejected the move toward "Synechism" that Peirce started making in 1887, which concluded in Peirce's acceptance of "necessary" transcendental truths that are intrinsic in the cosmic order. Dewey simultaneously rejected James's subjectivist move and Peirce's "objective idealism" and began the logical process that would lead to his own instrumental naturalism. Dewey distinguished between the logical function and meaning of necessity: "The fallacy of the necessitarian theory consists in transforming the determinate sense of the wholly defined, into the determinate in the sense of something made to be what it is." In *Studies in Logical Theory*, Dewey went further. He provided for Jamesian pragmatism the kind of logic, a "logic of use," that could dispose entirely of James's superstition of necessity. Dewey did not need to point this out to James, for James thereafter accepted Dewey's logic and method completely and thus had no more need to assume necessary truths. At this same time, in 1903, Peirce reacted very differently from James. In public, in a review in *The Nation*, he praised Dewey's *Studies*, but in private he was obviously stung by Dewey's 1893 attack on his transcendental, objective idealism. It must have hurt, too, that the centerpiece of Dewey's criticism was his employment against Peirce of the very same logical tools that Peirce had given him in his early article "The Fixation of Belief." So it was not surprising that Peirce struck out at Dewey in a private letter.

First, Peirce wrote, he always followed a basic maxim: "Never permanently bar the road of any true inquiry." He believed that Dewey violated this principle. Second, he called Dewey's method of genetic reasoning "wretched." Third, Dewey's "genetical" premises barred him from studying mathematics, physics, or "physiology proper" and rendered his method "intolerant." Moreover, Dewey's logical procedure of assuming that either he or Lotze was right and then proving Lotze wrong, Peirce correctly claimed, did not make Dewey right: you do not "convince me at all that these are the only alternatives." Besides, Lotze is "rather small game for you," Peirce added, indicating in no subtle way that in his opinion Dewey took the easy way of arguing. In short, he was demolishing Dewey's book.

> Your style of reasoning about reasoning has, to my mind, the usual fault that often men touch on this subject, they seem to think that no reasoning can be too loose, that indeed there is a merit in such slipshod arguments as they themselves would not dream of using in any other branch of science.

Dewey, Peirce also told him directly, had failed to understand the "theory of influence." Dewey and his University of Chicago students, Peirce said, had given themselves over to "a debauch of loose reasoning" or, worse still, "intellectual licentiousness." Only three sciences provide logic with principles, Peirce maintained: mathematics, phenomenology, and ethics. Merely circular or tautological arguments come from "metaphysical philosophy," psychology, linguistics, or history. In a sort of postscript written along the centerfold of his letter, Peirce came down like a hammer on one of Dewey's central assumptions in *Studies*: "The idea that two such elements as Evolution and Function can in the same sense depend upon one another seems to be *absurd*." Still, Peirce concluded, easing his rebuke, he would not write as he had done to "any man with whom I did not feel a very deep respect and sympathy."

In 1931, when Paul Weiss was preparing a biographical article on Peirce, he wrote to Dewey, who admitted that he had "not [been] prepared at the time [he was at Hopkins], either by my dominant interests or previous training, to appreciate the significance of his work. I could see that he was a very learned and original man, but never got further than that." By 1932, when Dewey began reviewing Peirce's *Collected Papers* as they appeared, Peirce was, Dewey now claimed, "the most original philosophical mind this country has produced [in] . . . logical theory, both in the traditional form, as a theory of scientific method and a modern symbolic logic." He was "a philosopher's philosopher." In 1935, when the fifth volume of the *Collected Papers*, dealing with pragmatism, appeared, Dewey reviewed it. This volume, Dewey advised, "should be obligatory for all philosophers." This was a generous assessment, for by this date Dewey had gone beyond Peirce and found his own way in logical analysis. Peirce's ideas, Dewey maintained, augmented his own: "I owe[d] a lot in the way of confirmation and gain in distance to Peirce." Dewey had certainly worked out his own logical theory by 1901–13 before he seriously began studying Peirce. But the "confirmation" that came through Peirce was important.

Perhaps the central critique of *Logic: The Theory of Inquiry* is its antifoundational rejection of Aristotelian logic:

I think the curse of Aristotle hangs more heavily over the world than any other one man. The "semanticists" have attacked his logic, but I don't think they realized sufficiently that his "logic" is just one reflex of his universal substitute of structure for function, form for process, reason for operations.

Dewey was able to move to the antifoundational understanding that logic is simply *continuing* inquiry or, as he put it in *Logic*, "the continuum of inquiry." It was no wonder that a reviewer in *The Nation* concluded that Dewey's *Logic* was a philosophical work of the greatest, revolutionary importance. Had Dewey written nothing else, this reviewer wrote, "it would have been sufficient to earn for him an illustrious place in the history of philosophy."

By two decades Dewey anticipated Ludwig Wittgenstein's solution in grappling with the same problem with Russell's logic in 1913–14 that Dewey had taken up in 1893 with regard to James and Peirce. Wittgenstein's resolution of the problem in the *Tractatus Logico-Philosophicus* (1922) parallels and resembles Dewey's naturalistic treatment of this logical problem. Not surprisingly, the *Tractatus* was one of the few works of philosophy that Dewey still owned when he died. Dewey returned to this theme periodically, often very briefly, as in his own running attacks, starting in 1915, on Russell's logic. The positive assertion of the triumph of Dewey's antifoundational stance culminates, in large measure, in *Logic: The Theory of Inquiry* and in his next work on valuation.

DEWEY AND VALUATION

This closely related work is Dewey's *Theory of Valuation* (1939). Both books are united in the belief that scientific inquiry enables knowing that may arrive at warrantable assertions, the best an investigator can get as part of the process of further inquiry. *Method*, rather than *system*, *inquiry* rather than *knowledge*, or *provisional confirmation* rather than the *truth* were the tools Dewey employed in his version of empirical, instrumental naturalism. He had been interested in the question of valuation for a long time. In several of his books and articles, he had been interested in the questions of value arising from his philosophic commitments. How, he asked, is the concept of "value" to be understood?

Where do values originate? What are their consequences? How is value grounded in experience or culture? Dewey took these up separately in "Logical Conditions of a Scientific Treatment of Morality," "The Objects of Valuation," and other articles. He had last treated the subject directly in 1922 in "Valuation and Experimental Knowledge." But this was a preliminary investigation, for Dewey had not yet arrived at a rounded understanding of the problem. In "Valuation and Experimental Knowledge," he made a definitional advance. By the term *valuation*, he was referring to a "kind of judgment . . . concerned with estimating values not in existence and with bringing them into existence." Such values, he asserted, require the performance of acts so that they may, in this way and this way only, be subjected to judgment. This technical argument led Dewey to insist on the creative activity of the pragmatic method to bring values into existence, and there he let the subject rest.

Dewey had never focused on these axiological questions at length. Perhaps he would not have done so, for his general approach to philosophic method placed questions of worthiness under such other heads as ethics or logic. But in the mid-1930s several Austrian logical positivists who had gathered together to form a circle at the University of Vienna emigrated to the United States and joined with their American counterparts and coworkers to plan an international encyclopedia of unified science, to be compiled by numerous scientists and philosophers, chiefly logical positivists. The whole volume would be edited by the Austrian Otto Neurath; his fellow countryman Rudolf Carnap, the best known of the Vienna circle; and the American Charles W. Morris. As a way of launching this encyclopedia of unified science, the editors planned to commission a series of twenty 20,000-word monographs on the major fields represented in the encyclopedia. These would be issued in two volumes under the title *The Foundations of Science*. One of the topics was valuation. Because Morris had convinced Neurath and Carnap that the project should "include works by pragmatists and logical empiricists," it became an easy next step to try to induce John Dewey to participate and another easy transition to assign Dewey the monograph on valuation. Dewey was the perfect choice of author for the subject of valuation, for in the system of logical positivism there was no real answer to how morals have meaning. Dewey's original contribution has two prongs. First, he looked for a procedure that could validate the discussion of ethics, which he found in the dynamics of means and ends. Second, to test possible values, he asked how they would work by placing each as they arose on the means-ends continuum, thus bringing them into the arena of inquiry. In essence, he constructed a method to reevaluate values.

At first, Dewey was reluctant to write the monograph. He had already expressed serious reservations about the logical positivists, especially with regard to their commitment to the existence of "atomic facts" or "atomic propositions," and he was reluctant to participate in a joint venture with them. Nothing could be done to remove his objection except to arrange a meeting between Dewey and Neurath. It was like a summit meeting between pragmatism and logical positivism, with Dewey's former students Sidney Hook and Ernest Nagel acting as mediators. Nagel, a philosopher who was interested in mathematical logic, epistemology, and the philosophy of science in general, described the meeting:

> Neurath spoke only broken English, and his attempts at explaining his version of logical positivism were not very successful. . . . When he realized that his efforts at explanation were getting him nowhere, he got up, raised his right hand as if he were taking an oath . . . and solemnly declared: "I *swear* we don't believe in atomic propositions."

The ice was broken. Dewey laughed, and probably everyone else breathed a sigh of relief. "Well, we ought to celebrate," Dewey declared, and made drinks. (What liquor he distributed is lost to history, but if he was in an especially good mood, he might have mixed his "Vermont Special": whiskey and maple syrup.)

For the most part, Dewey worked with Morris as his editor to complete the pamphlet on valuation. Necessarily, his approach to the subject would involve him in ethical and logical issues and, centrally, the analysis of value propositions empirically considered. Statements of value, he concluded, were derivatives of desirable human ideals that had been tested in actions, as distinct from desires that proved unworkable as means or undesirable as ends.

Dewey arrived at an unexpected conclusion in *Theory of Valuation*, declaring the issue of valuation to be the crucial question in the present state of knowledge concerning the unity of science, "for at the present time the widest gap in knowledge is that which exists between humanistic and non-humanistic subjects." That breach must and will be bridged when empirical investigation embraces desire "in the framing of means and ends." "Desire" is the defining characteristic that differentiates human from nonhuman behavior. The unity of science must be realized in the integration of "science" with "desire." Lacking such an integration, science, because it is confined to nature, cannot itself be unified. "In this integration not only is science itself *a* value (since it is the expression and the fulfillment of a special human desire and interest) but it is the supreme means of the valid determination of all valuations in all aspects of human and social life." At the most basic level Dewey simply asked humankind to find its morality in its intelligence. *Theory of Valuation* is the culmination of fifty years in which Dewey pondered, more profoundly than any other twentieth-century thinker, ethical principles for the modern person.

Logic: The Theory of Inquiry (1938) and *Theory of Valuation* (1939) were written when Dewey was nearly eighty years old. They came so late in his career and followed so many works defining Dewey's public reputation that they have never received the attention they merit. From Dewey's own point of view, they were expressions of ideas that he had never before understood so clearly. In his life, if not in his public image, they were his defining and culminating works.

DEWEY'S EIGHTIETH BIRTHDAY CELEBRATION

By the time 1939 arrived, questions about the future in America abounded. How long would the economic depression last? Would there be a revolution of any sort in America? What was the likelihood of America's being drawn into the European war? But there was no doubt in anyone's mind that in 1939 the national celebration of Dewey's birthday was to be repeated. Early in the year Horace Kallen began to take the lead in planning for Dewey's eightieth birthday and the summing up of his personal achievements and significance for America during the previous ten years. He consulted a dozen or so people, some of whom had been involved in the previous fete, including Sidney Hook, Albert C. Barnes, Henry Linville, and Kilpatrick, and as a result a "John Dewey eightieth anniversary committee" was formed with Kallen as chair and Dewey's friend Jerome Nathanson, the head of the Ethical Culture Society, as secretary. The others formed the executive committee.

Dewey was extremely reluctant this time to agree to the proceedings. In Key West for an extended period, he viewed a repetition of the previous festival very skeptically. He was convinced that "the one ten years ago was enough for a lifetime." Hook attempted to persuade him that the occasion had national, not merely personal, meaning and that in 1939, with the fascist powers on the march, a big celebration could be used to stress and publicize what Dewey's work had been all about—the meaning and values of democracy, liberalism, and individual freedom. Still, the idea of a birthday circus was "appalling" to Dewey, and even for its extended symbolic value he doubted that he could go through with it. Besides, he explained, he had just completed his big and long-awaited book, *Logic: A Theory of Inquiry*, which had exhausted him. Finally, he had already promised Evelyn that he would spend his birthday month of October with her and her husband at their large ranch in Green Castle, Missouri.

With little delay, Kallen wrote again, urging him to accept and participate in the celebration. "I still don't see how I can go through with it," he insisted. He begged Kallen to understand that "at present I am intellectually pretty much a vacuum," more than at any time he could recall. Was it "old age"? Or that he had put all his ideas into the *Logic*? Or that the "intellectual isolation" of Key West had made him torpid? He wasn't sure, but he did know that he had a definite "aversion" to the idea of giving another lecture to an assembly of well-wishers. Perhaps Kallen himself should give a lecture about Dewey's position on fascism. He admitted the force of Hook's and Kallen's arguments that his point of view about the importance of democracy should be presented on "every legitimate occasion." Suppose, as another alternative, Kallen suggested, Dewey might substitute for his physical presence "something that could be read"? Dewey was quick to agree and promised to send a script "on some phase of democracy" to be read in his absence. A list of guests of honor and possible speakers was submitted to Dewey for his approval, and a group of organizations was assembled to sponsor the coming celebration and support its defense of democracy. A big ballroom at the Hotel Pennsylvania, near New York's Penn Station, was booked.

Next came correspondence with possible speakers. In July Jerome Nathanson wrote to Charles Beard asking him to attend and sit at the "speakers' table." Beard replied that he did indeed plan on attending but that he preferred not to sit at the speakers' table, "so that I can hear what is said. Otherwise I might as well be at home or in the moon!" But did that mean he would speak? Nathanson reminded him that he had also agreed to speak at greater length during one of the daytime sessions organized by the Progressive Education Association as part of the celebration—but that it and the dinner talk were separate speeches. He hoped Beard would "not object to loosing two arrows at once." But Beard did object. "Sorry," he wrote back quickly, "but I just can't stand up and lecture John Dewey to his face on his own works. . . . I am not willing to talk on Dewey to Dewey." Nathanson responded that Dewey himself would not be present. Would Beard "please reconsider" his decision? Grudgingly, Beard responded, "All right. I am willing to do the 2 minute talk at the Dewey dinner."

Beard's acceptance completed the program for Nathanson, and the schedule of speakers was made final. Kilpatrick would speak on "John Dewey in American Life" and then introduce him. Dewey's speech would be piped into the main ballroom of the Hotel Pennsylvania from a radio station in the Midwest as part of a national radio broadcast of the program. Finally, others would speak: Beard; Dewey's friend in Barnard's philosophy department, William P. Montague; Dewey's student Hu Shi, now China's ambassador to the United States;

the economist Wesley C. Mitchell, and Agnes Meyer, wife of the editor of the *Washington Post*. Each would give "Recollections and Reflections."

Dewey had trouble deciding what to talk about. Both Kallen and Hook suggested that he discuss the values of democracy in the context of the rise of fascism in 1939, not just in Germany and Italy and Spain, but in the Soviet Union also, now that the signing of the Hitler-Stalin nonaggression pact had been made public and it was clear that totalitarianism existed on both the right and the left. That sounded like a fine idea, but as late as October 5, two weeks before the celebration, Dewey confessed to Kallen that he was again exhausted after working on four projects all summer "without a let up." He had been preoccupied with preparing and commenting on a volume of selections from the writings of Thomas Jefferson and composing his own contribution to the first volume of Paul Schilpp's "Library of Living Philosophers," devoted to Dewey's work, for which Dewey had to make a detailed commentary on each of the essays concerning his philosophic career, as well as helping Jane, Evelyn, and Lucy prepare a fifteen-thousand-word personal narrative for the book. Finally, he was still working on *Freedom and Culture* (1939), which had to be completed by the end of September. The result was, "I haven't been able to get my thought at work on the speech, I don't even know what line to take."

Dewey's capacity for working rapidly was legendary, but after all, he was nearly eighty. Dewey sent Kallen two suggestions for how he might deal with the theme of democracy: one was a "semihistorical" account of the use and "present conditions" of democracy, and the other was an "analytic" speech, considering "democracy as a way of life." He was so uninspired he asked Kallen to choose. Dewey told Hook that he himself inclined toward the "semihistorical" as the more appropriate subject.

But Kallen chose the "analytic" speech and proposed as a working title, "What We Must Do to Be Free." Aided by a remark that Barnes had made in a recent letter about democracy as the choice of both intelligence and emotion, Dewey accepted Kallen's "analytic" preference and came up with his own title: "Creative Democracy: The Task

Before Us." Dewey wrote his talk in a day, but he begged off going to Des Moines to broadcast the speech, so Kallen had to read the talk to the one thousand people who came to the dinner. It was one of Dewey's best "occasional talks."

In the first paragraph he took a hint from a passage in Jefferson concerning the need to make the new government as strong as possible in creating "the political structure of a self-governing society." During Jefferson's time, when the country's frontier spirit still prevailed, a group of men who were "extraordinarily gifted in political inventive-ness" gave birth to the new nation. But now, Dewey said, "the frontier is moral, not physical," and therefore the "crisis that one hundred and fifty years ago called out social and political inventiveness is with us in a form which puts a heavier demand on human creativeness." Democracy in the present is not a body of political thought or an assemblage of laws but a "way of life" founded on a working belief in the possibilities of human nature and in the capacity of humans for "intelligent judgment and action." Democracy, in short, is a continu-ous, creative experiment in making experience freer and richer with additional possibilities for re-creation and renewal.

After Dewey's talk, the several scheduled speakers gave their rec-ollections. Unexpectedly, Fiorello LaGuardia also rose from the audi-ence to speak. Musing on Dewey's eighty years, the liberal mayor joked, "I didn't think a liberal could live that long," and then he went on to praise Dewey's contribution to American democracy. Many lib-erals were confused these days, LaGuardia said, referring to the Hitler-Stalin pact, but he echoed Dewey's faith that "believers in democracy" would be able to take the right direction "without any leaning on foreign doctrines or theories."

On October 20 and 21, several talks on Dewey and Democracy were presented, including one by Albert Barnes, in sections organized by the Progressive Education Association and a "Conference on Methods." Barnes was as interested as ever in Dewey's well-being, and when he heard in July 1939 that with Dewey's eightieth birthday, his Columbia pension would be cut off, Barnes saw to it that Dewey would receive $5,000 annually "during and for the period of his natural life."

EDUCATION AND FREEDOM

During the 1930s, Dewey renewed his interest in education. Because he had established a reputation as America's leading spokesman for reform in education, he was constantly being asked to lecture or be interviewed on educational issues. So education—education for a democratic society—was never far from Dewey's thoughts. In the 1930s and 1940s, three currents of thought in America brought Dewey back to educational issues. The first was the increasing number of attacks on freedom of expression in the classroom; second was the development of a "humanistic" theory arguing that higher education should be based on classical traditions; and third was the beginning of attacks on progressive education from inside as well as outside the educational establishment. "Progressive education" was a movement and phrase linked inseparably in the public's mind with John Dewey.

For decades, many educators had found their freedom of expression threatened. Since the dismissal of the radical economist Scott Nearing from the University of Pennsylvania in 1915, Dewey had engaged in controversies over academic governance, the importance of unions in education as bulwarks against restrictions by trustees, and academic freedom. When Nearing was terminated, Dewey reminded the editor of the *New York Times* that the public would properly resent trustees' "arbitrary exercises of a legal right based upon the conception [in a university] of a factory employer to his employe[e]." In the same year he published an article in *The Nation* on the violation of the academic freedom of seventeen University of Utah faculty members. Only a short time later, before America's entry into World War I, Dewey defended several New York City high-school teachers who had been dismissed. He continued to oppose the rising tide of public suspicion that godlessness and Bolshevism had been or soon would be introduced into the schools. The curtailment of academic freedom had been the major factor in Dewey's involvement in helping found and organize the American Association of University Professors, the American Civil Liberties Union, and the New York City Teachers Union. All were associated with his communitarian efforts to renew and reconstruct education.

In the 1930s when the great economic boom ended, there was created a vacuum into which a host of radical propositions flew. To the extent that Dewey's ideas had helped radicalize or at least "progressivize" the classroom, educators figured largely in the groups that sponsored new ideas for reform, and not just in education. Accordingly, they were attacked as unwanted troublemakers. Business organizations like the Chamber of Commerce; newspapers, among which the Hearst papers were prominent; and various conservative organizations, such as the American Liberty League, all pressed school boards and legislatures to curtail classroom discussions of social issues. One sign of their success was that twenty-two states and Washington, D.C., enacted legislation limiting free speech in the classroom. Such attacks on education were prompted not only by the increasing gulf between conservative and radical solutions to the economic crisis but also by the fact that economic scarcity and a much smaller tax base had made money for education more difficult to raise. To many people, educational expenses seemed to be one more burden during hard times.

This trend toward retrenchment and conservatism conflicted with Dewey's progressivism, and he started to oppose it, at first obliquely and mildly, then more directly and passionately. In several articles written for the journal *Social Frontier* in the mid-1930s, he laid out his own program for the relationship between education and social awareness. He argued in his radio address "The Teacher and the Public" that as workers, teachers should "ally themselves with their friends against their common foe, the privileged class, and in the alliance develop the character, skill and intelligence that are necessary to make a democratic social order a fact." In "The Teacher and His World" Dewey counseled teachers to immerse themselves in current social movements: "The times are out of joint, and . . . teachers cannot escape even if they would, some responsibility for a share in putting them right." These and other articles by Dewey similar in theme led naturally to his 1936 statement "The Social Significance of Academic Freedom." His arguments in this piece show his evolving thoughts about the role of education in democracy. "Academic freedom," he observed, really means "the freedom to educate and the freedom to learn how to employ citizenship intelligently in the service of "the social reconstructions without which democracy will die." Dewey's logical conclusion was that the restriction of educational freedom is "a crime against democracy."

Dewey regularly entered the public arena as an agent for individual teachers whose rights, as he saw it, had been abused. In 1937, for instance, he helped form a committee to raise funds for legal assistance to Professor Arthur J. Kraus, who had been dismissed by the City College of New York after his hunger strike to protest the persecution of students in Polish universities. In the 1930s, issues of educational freedom came up so frequently that instead of considering them one by one, Dewey decided to form a permanent voluntary group to be a watchdog in this area. The Committee for Cultural Freedom was organized in May 1939 for "the defense of intellectual freedom against the attack of totalitarian forces." Its manifesto was signed by ninety-six writers, artists, and scholars. When the editorial page of the *New Republic* expressed doubt about the committee's usefulness, Dewey composed a long reply that the magazine published two weeks later. Beyond pointing out the numerous misrepresentations in the *New Republic*'s charges, Dewey stated that the Committee for Cultural Freedom held "that it is not enough just to be anti-fascist, but that a positive and aggressive campaign is required against every sort of totalitarian influence in this country."

In October 1939, the committee held its first public meeting, stressing the need for "collective intelligence operating in cooperative action," and it immediately swung into action. The legislature of New York had appropriated $30,000 to investigate the New York public school system while, simultaneously, in Washington, D.C., Representative Martin Dies, chairman of the House Committee to Investigate Un-American Activities, prepared to investigate the subversive political and social activities of textbook writers. Dewey responded. In his article "Investigating Education," written on behalf of the Committee for Cultural Freedom, Dewey pointed out that only a month earlier, Professor Harold Rugg of Columbia Teachers College had seen his textbook branded as subversive and summarily banned from the Binghamton, New York, public schools. Other textbooks had been similarly banned not long before. Dewey wrote that the committee welcomed any thoughtful investigation of American education but was "unalterably opposed" to "prejudice, bigotry, and unenlightenment."

BERTRAND RUSSELL

By 1940, Dewey was again actively participating in educational controversies. He became embroiled in a battle involving Bertrand Russell, a philosopher who stirred controversy wherever he went. When Russell had gone to lecture in China in 1919, at Dewey's suggestion, he had scandalized the Anglo-American community there by bringing his mistress with him. Now, in February 1940 the Board of Higher Education of New York City named Russell to a special visiting professorship of philosophy. He would teach courses on the relationship of philosophy to mathematics and also on advanced logic in the City College of New York and would hold a distinguished chair starting in the spring semester 1941 through the following school year. As a special position, the chair occupied a separate line in the city budget. Suddenly New York seemed about to emerge as a world center of philosophy. With Dewey and his colleagues at Columbia, Horace Kallen at the New School, and Sidney Hook at New York University, the appointment of Russell would have made New York City a preeminent center of philosophy.

In this case, Russell stirred up strife by his previous writings, especially those espousing his views on open marriage, masturbation, religion, and sexual freedom. No sooner had a public announcement been made that Russell had accepted the post than controversy erupted. William T. Manning, the influential, strongly conservative bishop of the Episcopal Church in New York City, immediately sent a letter of protest to the *New York Times*. Russell, he averred, is "a recognized propagandist against both religion and morality" and a profligate who promotes adultery. Manning's letter was buried inside the paper, but it caught the attention of conservative readers. Responses supporting Manning poured in to the papers. *The Tablet*, a paper of the Brooklyn diocese of the Catholic Church, announced that at least eighty-four Catholic organizations had indicated moral outrage at Russell's appointment. Dewey sensed in this, he told Harvard philosopher W. E. Hocking, "the beginning of a movement" by "this old totalitarian institution," the Catholic Church, "to abolish all municipal colleges in greater New York." Harvard had offered Russell a visiting position two years hence, and Dewey was also writing to Hocking to make sure that Harvard would continue to support its appointment. Liberals soon leaped to Russell's defense with characterizations as extreme as the castigations by the conservatives. The journalist Dorothy Thompson dramatized the case, portraying Russell as "a twentieth-century Socrates" and Bishop Manning as offering him a "cup of hemlock."

At this juncture, almost inevitably, the controversy became a legal matter. Jean Kay, a housewife, expressed her concern that her daughter might soon register as a student at City College and feared that she could be adversely influenced by Russell's radical views. A lawyer named Joseph Goldstein "sprang to her aid," and with his assistance, Jean Kay filed a taxpayer's suit in the New York Superior Court to vacate the appointment on the grounds that Russell "was an alien and an advocate of sexual immorality" and that the use of public funds designated for his appointment was illegal as well as an offense to public decency.

The education reporter for *Time* magazine described what happened next: "Big, burly Justice John E. McGeehan, good Catholic, good Democratic 'organization judge' got the case." Goldstein and Mrs. Kay appeared before McGeehan with four of Russell's works in hand (*What I Believe*, *Marriage and Morals*, *Education and the Good Life*, and *Education and the Modern World*) and reviewed a selection of Russell's theses. They maintained that the proposed professor's writings were "lecherous, salacious, libidinous, lustful, venomous, erotomanic, aphrodisiac, atheistic, irreverent, narrow-minded, untruthful, and bereft of moral fiber." As additional biographical evidence,

Goldstein asserted that Russell had run a nudist colony, approved of homosexuality, and liked salacious poetry. Justice McGeehan read the offending volumes, and on March 30, 1940, he returned with a stinging rebuke of Russell and the New York City Board of Education. In making the appointment, the board had, he said, established a "chair of indecency" at City College. He ordered that the appointment be voided on several grounds: That Russell's doctrines would encourage violations of the state's penal laws; that academic freedom cannot "permit a teacher to teach . . . that sexual intercourse between students, where the female is under the age of 18 years, is proper"; that the Board had no right to appoint an alien to a city teaching job; and that the Board should have given Russell a comprehensive examination. Mrs. Kay told reporters: "I am glad that right and decency have triumphed. I have been only a symbol in this great fight. . . . I believe all mothers have a philosophy which is not only comparable to that of some of our greatest savants, but superior in many respects."

At this time Russell was teaching at another public institution, the University of California at Los Angeles, where his appointment had seemingly gone unremarked. Asked by an interviewer for his comment on the New York City hearings, he expressed astonishment: "It strikes me between the eyes," he said. "I don't know what to think or say. I want it understood that I did not seek the position." With uncharacteristic modesty, Russell added: "I am not as interested in sex as is Bishop Manning." Russell indicated that he had authorized the American Civil Liberties Union to appeal in his defense. The battle was joined. Publicity from the New York suit alerted the California public to the presence of an infidel in their midst, and soon a Baptist minister, Ira Wall, filed a new litigation against the California Board of Regents calling for Russell's dismissal from the state university. Russell's views, Wall contended, are "subversive, dangerous, and a menace" to the United States. Interviewed for a response to these charges, Russell stated that in his classrooms he taught philosophy— "never his ideas on sex."

John Dewey had been following the case closely, and within three days, on behalf of the Committee for Cultural Freedom, he, George S.

Counts, Sidney Hook, and Horace Kallen had signed a letter in support of Russell and placed it in the hands of Fiorello LaGuardia, mayor of New York, with copies to Ordway Tead, chairman of the Board of Education; and William Chanler, the city counsel: "With the enlightened citizens of . . . New York," the letter began, they shared the view that Judge McGeehan's decision is "the most serious setback yet sustained by the cause of free education in America," equivalent in its bigotry, they believed, to "the persecution of Socrates and Galileo." To let the decision stand, they argued, "would pave the way for an inquisition." The rhetorical style was probably Kallen's. On the following day, the city press gave widespread attention to this letter and the decision it protested. Dewey himself was active in encouraging positive press coverage and was pleased to see that the chancellor of New York University had written a "courageous" letter to the *New York Times* supporting Russell's academic freedom. An integral aspect of Dewey's involvement in the Russell case was his broader interest in freedom of thought in education. Indeed, he told W. E. Hocking that although he was "extremely sorry for the thoroughly disagreeable position in which the Russells have been personally plunged," he was grateful that the charges had been brought against a well-known philosopher, since the case had attracted "wide attention and protest." Russell, he felt, had taken up a challenge that would benefit many others beyond himself.

Mayor LaGuardia was inclined to wash his hands of the case, and in consultation with Chanler, he decided simply to strike the item line for Russell's salary from the budget while Chanler decided not to appeal McGeehan's ruling. Dewey was not satisfied. Indeed, he proclaimed himself "shocked" that the Democratic mayor had folded under political pressure, and Dewey wrote to remind him that if the decision stood, it would threaten free speech in all higher institutions of learning. At this point, Dewey began to involve his friend Albert C. Barnes. He was more candid with Barnes than with the mayor, telling his friend that the case had "disclosed a yellow streak in LaGuardia." As volatile as ever, Barnes instantly became a fervent supporter of Russell or, rather, a champion of informed intelligence in its fight against ignorance, which this case symbolized for him.

In the meantime, Dewey placed his hopes in and focused his attention on the American Civil Liberties Union, along with further persuasion of the mayor and the education board chairman Tead, whose liberal orientation made action on his part likely—unless, Dewey wrote to Barnes, Tead got "cold feet." Dewey was privately in touch with the national secretary of the ACLU, who promptly sent the mayor a telegram urging "the desirability of taking an appeal" to the New York Supreme Court. The New York chapter of the ACLU followed through and in appellate court challenged the McGeehan order that denied Russell or his representatives the right to intervene in the case. To put further pressure on the mayor, an "academic freedom–Bertrand Russell committee" was hastily formed and sent LaGuardia a legal brief in defense of Russell. Dewey and his colleagues formed the core of the committee; William Pepperell Montague was the president; John Herman Randall Jr., a former student of Dewey's, was secretary, and Franz Boas was on the board. William A. Neilson joined the other protesters.

Ordway Tead proved not to have cold feet. The mayor had written to him suggesting that it would not be "prudent to appeal," but Tead arranged to have the Board of Education's own attorneys, who would serve without pay, seek a judicial review of McGeehan's decision. On April 19 they filed motions in the New York Supreme Court. They attacked the weakest part of McGeehan's decision and questioned, first, "whether professors . . . must in all cases be citizens" and, second, whether the courts could control the appointments made by the board. Mrs. Kay's attorney Joseph Goldstein made a brief reappearance in response and stated he would contest in court the board's right to employ its own counsel.

Emboldened by the progress in the case, Russell wrote an article entitled "Freedom and the Colleges," which appeared in the May issue of H. L. Mencken's *American Mercury*. He argued that academic freedom in America was being threatened by "the plutocracy and the churches," and he predicted that if these have their way, they "would reduce this country to the level of Germany." Denying the charges that he was a communist, he added: "Russia is, for the moment, the most perfect example of a country where ignorant bigots have the degree of control that they are attempting to acquire in New York." These statements were not likely to mollify his opponents but were a clear indication that he and his supporters were taking the offensive.

Dewey seemed to be gaining on all fronts. Next, he turned to Villard's *Nation* for an outlet in which he could air his own views in public. His brief essay "The Case for Bertrand Russell," published in June, focused on the legitimacy of Russell's ability to discuss sexual morals. Dewey examined what Russell had actually written on sexual issues. In the arena of free speech Dewey had a considerable fund of credibility. His interest in ethical theory was long-standing and well known. As recently as 1932, he had published a revision of his sections in his and Tufts's 1908 *Ethics*. In Dewey's analysis, Russell had been arguing for a new sexual ethic, one that more closely allied belief and practice and did not a repudiate sexual ethics. Dewey advised that free discussion, without "dogmatism and intolerance," should be encouraged, not suppressed, and he made it clear that he himself disagreed with many of Russell's views but that his main concern was with freedom of inquiry.

That concern is even more evident in Dewey's private letters. He wrote to Hocking, for example:

> If men are going to be kept out of American colleges because they express unconventional, unorthodox or even unwise views . . . on political, economic, social or moral matters . . . I am heartily glad my own teaching days have come to an end. There will always be some kept prostitutes in any institution.

He added, "I feel strongly on this issue." He sent a copy of this letter to Russell, adding to it in pen: "Sincerely and gratefully yours."

Following Barnes's urgings, Dewey continued the fight in a volume of essays that he edited with Kallen, *The Bertrand Russell Case* (1941). The contributors were selected by the Committee for Cultural

Freedom. Dewey wrote the introduction and also an essay. *Liberalism and Social Action* echoes in his introduction. All the contributors, he maintained, adhered to "the method of intelligence." By contrast, Russell's detractors were trying "to apply the lynch law of popular outcry to settle an issue where enlightened judgment of competent educators . . . was on the other side." The failure of the attempt to silence Russell and the publication of *The Bertrand Russell Case*, Dewey concluded, might in the long run contribute to the eventual achievement of "the freedom of the human spirit and the democratic way of life." The title of Dewey's essay is "Social Realities Versus Police Court Fictions," referring to the dignified and humane treatment of moral issues by Russell in contrast to the salacious, immoral, and lewd characterization of him by Goldstein, McGeehan, and many others.

With the Russell case stalled in the courts, Dewey prepared a second line of support: After he excited Barnes's interest, Barnes turned his outrage into action. At Dewey's prompting, Barnes decided to appoint Russell to be a lecturer at the Barnes Foundation. On May 24, John Herman Randall Jr., as secretary for the Barnes Foundation committee, wrote to Russell's wife indicating that "Mr. Barnes has a plan which, if acceptable to you, would guarantee Mr. Russell's support for life . . . free to do just that work which he wants, and would impose no conditions whatever." A few days later, Barnes's offer, transmitted by Dewey, arrived at Russell's California address. Russell wrote at once to Dewey to acknowledge it: "The proposal that you transmit is . . . all that I could desire." He also told Dewey that concerning Dewey's part in the defense, the Catholic journal *America* had stated that a "crude" Russell was not as dangerous as "an insidious Dewey." By the first week of June, Barnes's offer to Russell of a five-year contract had been accepted.

Barnes actually supported Russell completely for two and a half years, and then on December 28, 1942, Barnes, always combative, dismissed Russell with three days' notice. Russell sued. Barnes issued a press release mocking Russell "for presenting himself to the public as a martyr." Charges were answered by countercharges. But Russell prevailed in the courts and was awarded $16,000 in damages. Barnes had the last word in 1944, however, when he published a pamphlet, *The Case of Bertrand Russell vs. Democracy and Education*, blasting Russell. In any case, Dewey had won the day in 1940. He had galvanized academic, liberal, and moderate public opinion; he had strengthened the resolution of the Harvard administration to appoint Russell if he wished to be so appointed; he had cast doubt on Russell's opponents; and he had almost single-handedly secured Russell's material well-being and eased his anxieties. He had made a spirited defense of freedom of expression, and he had interested the newspapers, as well as many prominent intellectuals, in the issues of freedom. When *The Bertrand Russell Case* was published in 1941, the reviews renewed the discussion of the case. Dewey's victory was unqualified.

More Controversies

Ironically, as Dewey was fighting on several fronts for Russell, his own university launched an attack on the freedom of expression on much the same basis that had earlier led to Columbia's dismissal of Dana and Cattell, followed by Beard's and Robinson's resignations. The cause was the same—President Butler's stand on the war which, in 1940, promised to involve America. Hardly had the Russell case been resolved by Barnes's offer than President Butler addressed the faculty at the beginning of the new semester and stated his conviction that the United States would need to enter the war on behalf of the democratic nations in Europe. He wished to leave "no doubt" concerning "where Columbia University stands in that war." Recalling the earlier unfortunate occasion of faculty dismissals because of war protests voiced in the classroom, Butler announced the university's policy. Although he conceded the faculty's rights, he insisted that "before and above academic freedom of any kind or sort . . . University freedom" was paramount in setting policies by which to support, as an institution, national needs dictated by wartime. Faculty who disagreed with this policy should therefore "withdraw of their own accord from University membership in order that their conduct may be freed from the limitations which University membership naturally and necessarily puts on it."

Butler's remarks were condemned on the floor of the U.S. Senate. Several organizations in which Dewey played a leading role immediately made public protests against Butler's stand, among them being the American Civil Liberties Union and Teachers Union Local No. 5. Dewey, who had good reason to be grateful to President Butler for the many instances of his personal generosity, found a way to praise Butler's ideals while condemning his statement. He began:

> No better statement of the function of the University could be made than that of President Butler. That the University should contribute to "analysis and understanding of the economic, social and political problems involved in the present war" and should do so without emotional excitement, "with calmness, good judgment and full knowledge," is a statement that cannot be improved upon.

Butler's further statements, Dewey observed, do not agree with his admirable opening, which led Dewey to conclude that President Butler could not mean that the university had primacy over the students and faculty, since the university consisted of nothing else but the students and faculty. Besides, to exercise primacy would amount to totalitarianism, and since "President Butler is an opponent of the latter, I am forced to conclude that what he said does not convey his real meaning." Dewey's was the last word on this issue, for Butler took the cue that Dewey's logical juggling afforded him and said no more on the subject. Less than two months later, the Japanese navy attacked Pearl Harbor; America was at once united in the war effort; and Butler's pronouncements were moot.

A second educational controversy in which Dewey became a primary combatant revolved around the conflict between his instrumental philosophy of functional education and the "great ideas" and "great books" programs for cultural literacy advocated by a group of educators who stressed humanistic traditions over social advances. The historical context is important. In the 1880s, when Dewey had begun his work of educational reconstruction, he was reacting against a curriculum and related teaching practices that stressed memorization, verbal intelligence, and drills. In concert with a worldwide reconsideration of the heuristic value of an education so systematized, Dewey—following in the wake of Herbart, Froebel, and Pestalozzi—tried to enlarge learning by liberating students. In America, his ideas took root in the teacher-training programs, in which, through his sustained activity in the cause of society-related education, he served as a guide and model.

In the 1930s, two things happened, one of which was related to the increased radicalism in the decades following the stock market crash. Reform was in the air, and the educational innovations attributed to Dewey were further radicalized and began to drift away from informed intelligence and knowledge to emphasize activity and the sort of liberation that depreciated intellectual discipline. The opposite trend in education was conservative and generated the belief that unanchored activity, so well represented by the shallow and frenzied 1920s, had somehow been the cause of the 1929 disaster. A return to good old-fashioned values and time-tested traditions seemed to offer a way to restore economic soundness.

In university life the movement away from the very narrow, restricted nineteenth-century curriculum eventually led to largely elective curricula. This in turn led to a counterreaction through the creation of foundational courses on the Western tradition of great books and great ideas. The promoters of these courses promised to enlarge education through exposure to the best that has been thought and said. The great books and cultural literacy theorists put their faith in enriching individual minds, not in improving society. The debate between the Deweyites and the traditionalists became unexpectedly bitter. Dewey became actively involved for several reasons. One was that the new stress on traditional education emanated from the two universities with which he had been most closely associated—the University of Chicago and Columbia. Another was that his followers looked to him for leadership in the defense of their position.

Dewey had often criticized the "progressive education" that was being practiced as if it rested on his authority. In 1930, more than ten years after the Progressive Education Association was founded, Dewey assessed the role, value, and purpose of freedom in the schools, such freedom as was often associated with his name. The ostensible purpose of his essay "How Much Freedom in New Schools?" was to evaluate the achievements of progressive education between 1919 and 1929. It was obvious, he began, that there was little apparent consistency from one "progressive" school to another. Innovation was good, but progressive education still showed traces of its counterreaction "against the traditional school." This has had the result that "the watchwords of the progressive movement are capable of being translated into inconsistent practices." By reacting against mass regimentation, many experimental schools had overvalued freedom, and in "extreme cases they represent enthusiasm much more than understanding." The need to revolt against desiccated educational practices was unquestioned, he agreed, but revolt could lead to the mere appearance of freedom even as it actually produced "deplorable egotism, cockiness, impertinence and disregard for the rights of others." Freedom was not the end of education. If education was not a means to acquire intelligence, freedom would be valueless or, worse, injurious. Truly progressive education, Dewey concluded, must connect with society; men and women must be educated to have insight into the character and condition of urban and industrial civilization, or they would possess only a veneer of education.

Few critics of "progressive education" had appraised its current shortcomings so rigorously and justly as Dewey did. But as traditionalist criticisms of Dewey's influence on American education increased, Dewey was forced into the somewhat awkward position of answering his critics. He took the path of defending education for social intelligence as against education for merely refined intelligence. While the general terms of the debate are at least as old as the eighteenth-century contest between the "ancients" and the "moderns," the terms for the debate of the 1930s were set by Dewey, on one side, and Robert M. Hutchins, president of the University of Chicago, on the other. Behind

Dewey were grouped William H. Kilpatrick, Sidney Hook, and Horace Kallen, and behind Hutchins were Mortimer Adler, Mark Van Doren, and Scott Buchanan.

Hutchins's 1936 book, *The Higher Learning in America*, reflected the same spirit that had caused him to tear down the school of philosophy that Dewey had created at the University of Chicago. As president of the university, Hutchins forced the philosophy department to accept the Columbia Ph.D. and neo-Thomist philosopher Mortimer Adler, even though the department voted against his appointment. At this, Dewey's two former colleagues, James Tufts and George Herbert Mead, both resigned their professorships in philosophy. Then Hutchins attacked Dewey's philosophy itself in his book *The Higher Education in America*.

Hutchins might have responded to a question about the meaning of *The Higher Learning in America* in the same way that Dewey answered Louise Romig's question about the meaning of *The Quest for Certainty*: "There isn't any." Hutchins's book critiqued what he saw as the intellectual slackness and disorder in university curricula. For him, the elective system had no underlying metaphysical rationale and therefore no foundation. He urged a coherent system of education that would be informed by Aristotelianism and neo-Thomism, organized concretely through the great ideas of Western humanism but dissociated from concern for the consequences in action of these ideas. For the empirical philosophy of science, he had little regard, even though experimental science played a part in his educational system. By definition, Hutchins argued, vocational and professional training cannot be intellectual, and since by definition, a university must be intellectual, "training for specific jobs cannot be part of the university's work."

For Dewey, learning disconnected from intelligent action was metaphysics without physics. Dewey's understanding of "humanism" was quite different from Hutchins's. In 1930 Dewey had taken up the issue of what was meant by "humanism," calling it a "portmanteau word." For himself, he rejected the versions of such "New Humanists" as Paul Elmer More and Irving Babbitt, who both, Dewey believed, defined humanism negatively, in terms of what it opposed. Moreover,

Dewey argued that for Hutchins and Adler, humanism was dualistic, separating humanity from nature. For Dewey, humanism's "idea of reason and rule that are divorced from all natural basis and natural positive use . . . will terminate, if it follows its own logical conclusion, . . . in the bosom of the church." The "humanism" that Dewey could embrace was essentially naturalism—"an expansion . . . of human life . . . in which nature and the science of nature are made the willing servants of *human good*." In 1940 he told Corliss Lamont, "I have come to think of my own position as cultural or humanistic naturalism—Naturalism, properly interpreted, seems to me a more adequate term than humanism." In answer to a correspondent who somewhat later asked him about his own metaphysics, Dewey replied: "Of course, I have no 'metaphysics.' " Metaphysical thought, he went on to say, "is an enjoyable form of poetry . . . but poetry is a flower, not a rock." The reality of activity in the natural world, along with the scientific method of investigating it, is the foundation of Dewey's thought. "To make any metaphysical 'ism' a foundation for humanism is not only a surrender of the essentials of humanism, but it is to introduce some of the same sectarian divisiveness that has affected the world's historic religions, followed by intolerance."

It was inevitable that Dewey would join in the debate that Hutchins invited. He had ready access to the *Social Frontier: A Journal of Educational Criticism and Reconstruction*, edited by his friend and supporter George S. Counts. In its first year of publication the journal set aside a page, "John Dewey's Page," in which he could write freely on any subject he chose, as well as contributing any longer articles he might wish to write. Shortly after the publication of *The Higher Learning in America*, Dewey commented on the book in an article entitled "Rationality in Education." Hutchins, he observed, undervalues scientific, naturalistic philosophy; he has a static conception of man and human needs; he privileges *theoria* over *praxis* and so denigrates vocationalism of all sorts; and, finally, he holds to an absolutist view of Truth, which is "the same everywhere" and at all times. All of these lead him to the notion of "permanent studies" in his ideal university.

Dewey agreed with Hutchins's criticism on one point only, that "present education is disordered and confused." For Dewey, how education should be reconstructed, not what it should return to, was the crucial question for future consideration.

The "future consideration" that Dewey promised was delivered in the very next issue of *Social Frontier*. Dewey picked up where he left off and praised Hutchins's analysis of the ills of education in American colleges and universities. But, Dewey asserted, Hutchins's remedy of withdrawing by means of higher education from the chaos of contemporary social life into an empyrean of absolute ideals was taking the wrong direction. Instead, for Dewey, "educational reconstruction cannot be accomplished without a social reconstruction in which higher education has a part to play." Perhaps the best way to reform education consisted of an act of foresight by which education could help reconstruct society. Because education helps give society intelligence, the resulting society should in turn reform education. Far from being separated, as Hutchins saw it, learning and society must always be intertwined, reciprocally affecting each other. Without both, no advance of either was possible.

Counts invited Hutchins to reply to Dewey's two articles, which he did in the next issue of *Social Frontier*. His "Grammar, Rhetoric, and Mr. Dewey" starts with a brilliant flash of rhetoric. He had been asked to reply to Dewey's articles, he noted, but "this I am unable to do . . . for Mr. Dewey has stated my position in such a way as to lead me to think I cannot write, and has stated his own in such a way as to make me think I cannot read." Somewhat in the forensic manner of Aquinas, Hutchins denied almost all of Dewey's criticisms and defended himself against the remainder. In conclusion he stated that Dewey had misrepresented him, and he ironically wondered whether Dewey might believe that in his comments on Hutchins, "he is still fighting nineteenth-century German philosophy."

Dewey graciously (but also ironically) replied in the next month's issue of *Social Frontier* that he had regarded Hutchins's book as significant because in clear terms it raised important issues dealing with "the place of experience, practical matters, and experimental scientific method in the constitution of authentic knowledge, and consequently in the [selection and] organization of the subject matter of higher education." But in his reply Hutchins had refused to engage these issues and instead answered with his own defensive, evasive rhetoric. Hutchins's refusal to debate the fundamental issue of knowledge indicated that "I must ask his forgiveness if I took his book too seriously."

Hutchins's withdrawal from direct debate did not end their contention. In 1937 Dewey heard that in a lecture his former student Mortimer Adler, now an ally of Hutchins, had named Dewey "Public Enemy Number One." The debate simmered. In 1943, Hutchins published an article in *Fortune* holding that there existed an immutable human nature outside time or place, "not obliterated by the differing conventions of different cultures." Dewey, a social as well as biological evolutionist, held in contempt the notion that "nothing that can happen to [humankind], or in the physical, biological, and social world of which man is a part, can make any difference to his nature." Dewey replied to Hutchins's article in "Challenge to Liberal Thought" in *Fortune* magazine. Prompted by Hutchins's article and other assaults on "what is modern and new in education," he asked, what "aims and ideals should control our educational policies and undertakings" if we wish our educational philosophy to be a living, not an antiquarian, one? All sides agree that contemporary education lacks unity and focus. One group of critics argues that the defects in the present system "spring from excessive attention to what is modern in human civilization—science, technology, contemporary social issues and problems." The opposite group finds the defect in education in the present time as arising from ineffective representation of those same factors that are "shaping modern culture." The first group holds that liberal education "would require return to the models, patterns, and standards that were laid down in Greece some twenty-five hundred years ago and were renewed and put into practice in the . . . age of feudal medievalism six and seven centuries ago." But, Dewey argued, what was considered a liberal education in Greece reflected the facts of social life then, which assigned vocational, industrial, mechanical, and technological activities to a slave class while those who lived on the fruits of the labor of a servile class could devote themselves to "higher things." In modern times, however, the issue is how to liberalize our scientific, technical, and vocational education, not how to sequester these from other earlier consolidations of a liberal education. Hutchins and his followers glorified the gulf between the "material" and the "spiritual," whereas Dewey aimed to dissolve all such dualisms and bridge the gulf between them. Neither the slave state that undergirded Platonism nor the church state that supported medievalism will succeed in democratic America. According to Dewey, the "chief opportunity and chief responsibility of those who call themselves philosophers are to make clear the intrinsic kinship of democracy with the methods of directing change that have revolutionized science."

Perhaps Hutchins had had enough, so Alexander Meiklejohn stepped in as his defender and replied in the January 1945 issue of *Fortune*. After a long description of his classical program at St. John's College, Meiklejohn tried to mute Dewey's criticisms by asserting that Dewey and he were, by and large, in agreement about many issues, though they approached them from quite different angles. Dewey would have none of that. Meiklejohn, he wrote in the March 1945 issue of *Fortune*, "misconceives my plain meaning ... completely." In fact, he does not appear to understand "what every serious student of my ... writings already knows. The vital problems of philosophy today spring from the need for reconsideration and reconstruction of traditional beliefs about material and spiritual, theory and practice, fact and value." Dualistic separations impede the necessary reconstruction. Meiklejohn's reply was brief. Perhaps, he admits, he had misconceived Dewey; but then, Dewey had also misconceived his article; that is, there had been a "joint failure of communication over a very difficult problem." But Dewey was unyielding: "My reply to Mr. Meiklejohn sought only to set him straight as to my views. He is entitled to admit that he misconceived them. But when he speaks of a 'joint failure' I find him overinclusive. His final words seem to constitute confession by avoidance." At this, the Dewey-Hutchins-Meiklejohn controversy came to an end officially, though of course the debate still continues today, under different terms and with different antagonists.

Because Dewey was attracting so much attention for his progressive ideas, it was not surprising that he also attracted the notice of the FBI, whose agents periodically wrote and updated their own version of a Dewey biography. For instance, on April 29, 1943, the New York Office of the Federal Bureau of Investigation noted the following about Dewey:

Age: 83
Born: October 20, 1859, Burlington, Vermont
Address: 1 West 89 Street, New York City
Build: Tall and thin
Eyes: Black
Hair: Carelessly combed gray hair
Appearance: Disheveled attire
Manner: Retiring, mild manner, gentlemanly
Glasses: Wears spectacles
Speech: Monotonous drawl
Moustache: Drooping moustache

The case agent for the New York Office recommended in 1943 that in view of Dewey's advanced age and the fact that "there is no indication that he is presently engaged in any activity which would be considered inimical to the best interests of the internal security of this country," the case should be closed.

But it was not closed. In fact, the FBI had paid close attention to Dewey's activities for a long time and continued to do so. The confidential reports of the Martin Dies House Committee on Un-American Activities also paid attention to Dewey, even asserting as "a well-established fact" that Dewey was an atheist. Rev. Walter Albion Squires of the Presbyterian Church in Philadelphia added: "Dr. Dewey's influence in public education is a matter of no small concern to the religious interests of America. . . . In Russia, he is recognized as an educational guide."

The U.S. government assembled three files on Dewey "with approximately 500 to 600 See references." A typical entry reads: "It was claimed [by Matthew Woll] that Dewey was doing more for the Soviet cause than all the avowed communists in the country." The summary of Dewey's file initiated by FBI Director J. Edgar Hoover ends with an interesting notation: among the "letters of greetings" that Dewey received on the occasion of his ninetieth birthday, "one of these letters was from President Truman." Since the president of the United States had called Dewey "one of the greatest Americans," it seemed wise to cease investigating him as a subversive.

FURTHER VIEWS ON EDUCATION

Many of the controversies in which Dewey engaged concerned a progressive education. His insistence on the social relevance of education consisted, in about equal parts, of a reaction against the routinized methods of instruction prevalent in his own youth; an effort to introduce the lower social-economic classes, and especially immigrant children, to democracy and openness of thought; a belief that the scientific methods of experimentation could provide a basis for free inquiry in an educational setting; and a conviction that an educated citizenry offered the only effective bulwark against surrender to fascism, communism, or merely money capitalism.

His advocacy left Dewey open to attacks from every side. An attack on Dewey by, say, Rev. Geoffrey O'Connell was typical. Dewey's aims, he told an audience, were "un-American": he and his cohorts at Teachers College had "attempted [the] destruction of Christian aims and ideals in American education." As Dewey often pointed out with regard to his critics, radicals tended to be just as dissatisfied as conservatives were with his philosophy of education. Conservatives were offended by the idea that teachers examine and clarify values.

Religious spokesmen were worried that a Dewey school would be god-less, replacing *divinitas* with *sciencia*. Traditionalists and historicists suspected that a Dewey student would know nothing about the past. Defenders of the status quo were concerned about what Dewey's emphasis on social change might bring. Supporters of basic education worried that if the "three R's" fell from the center of the curriculum, literacy would be doomed to mere subjectivism. Nonscientists feared Dewey's naturalism; scientists wondered whether his emphasis on soci-ety might be antiscientific. Some of his critics were concerned that Dewey's emphasis on intelligence was too intellectual; others saw his ideas as leading toward anti-intellectualism. One group saw his stan-dards for education as being so high as to be unachievable. Another group regarded his standards as hopelessly low. Leftists saw him as too moderate; those on the right feared that he was an extreme radical. Radicals criticized him for persuading students to accept the current system. Supporters of the current social organization were convinced that he was bent on starting a revolution against it. Some saw his edu-cational philosophy as "child centered" and therefore foolishly child-ish. Others saw it as socially purposeful and therefore injurious to the individuality and creativity of pupils. Some thought that he valued the individual too highly; others, that he saw humans scientifically as no more than highly developed animals or else as socially determined machines.

Perhaps not surprisingly, Dewey was the sort of thinker who could agree with all these mischaracterizations, not as applied to himself per-sonally, but, taken as a whole, as an apt description of the many needs that American education was being asked to meet, as well as a portrait of the confusion in educational theory and practice during his time.

That Dewey seriously pondered these problems for a considerable time is evident in the long hiatus of twenty-two years between the pub-lication of *Democracy and Education* in 1916 and *Experience and Education* in 1938. In the interim he wrote numerous articles, reports, lectures, and commentaries concerning educational matters. Of these, perhaps the most interesting is a speech that he delivered at Philadelphia's Central High School in 1932. In his title, "Monastery,

Bargain Counter, or Laboratory in Education?" Dewey offers metaphors to characterize three ways of understanding and organizing education. In early America, an elementary education based on authority and a classical curriculum reflecting British principles of elitist higher education predominated. He called this "monastery training." Such an education, he observed, was appropriate or inevitable for its time; monastery education "was the only avenue to the larger world of the culture of the past." By the second half of the nineteenth century, conditions had changed. "To maintain the idea of democratic equality, schooling was made universal and compulsory." The percentage of students who attended high school and college had risen sixfold. The urbanization of the American population separated people from the practical education that earlier Americans had derived from nature and home industry. Above all, the industrial revolution caused momentous social and economic changes, and education was transformed by these changes.

> While many, perhaps most people, regard the broadening of education to meet the needs of the greater number, and especially the inclusion of a larger amount of the vocational element, as an enrichment of education, there are others who hold a contrary view. . . . [They say] that our education has deteriorated through catering to the needs of larger numbers; that what we now have is a bargain counter education.

That is, sundry bits of learning are spread out on a counter by the storekeeper-teacher, and the customer-pupils can choose those that best suit their taste. Such an education, the hostile critics said, is practical, not cultural. "Some of these criticisms," Dewey acknowledged, "seem to be justified," for contemporary education is "spread out too thin, is too scattered." But the universal access to education that has been achieved can offer a transition to the next stage of learning: the "education of the laboratory," which involves experiment, inquiry, "through testing, through observation and reflection—all processes requiring *activity* of mind." Dewey concluded:

But as yet our education has not found itself; the stream has not yet reached port and the ocean. It has left behind traditional education; it can never return to its source. It has to meet the problems of today, and of the future, not of the past. The stream just now has gathered up a good deal of debris from the shores which it has flooded; it tends to divide and lose itself in a number of streams. It is still dammed at spots by barriers erected in past generations. But it has within itself the power of creating a free experimental intelligence that will do the necessary work of this complex and distracted world in which we and every other modern people have to live.

Many other essays, like "Education and Social Change" and "For a New Education," make similar points, but Dewey's major contribution to the controversies regarding education during the 1930s was *Experience and Education*.

This book had its origin in an invitation by Kappa Delta Pi, a national honor society, to address its annual meeting, as Dewey had first done ten years earlier. He was asked specifically to deliver "a critique of [his] . . . own philosophy of education." Dewey responded by writing a short book of about twenty thousand words and then reducing it to a length suitable for presentation as an evening address. In its full version, the book appeared a few days before the convention and was eagerly read by the participants. During the daytime meetings before his evening lecture, Dewey was told that a group of educational "essentialists," as they termed themselves, chiefly from Teachers College and George Peabody College in Nashville, had attacked William H. Kilpatrick and George S. Counts, both leaders at Teachers College and strong allies of Dewey's, for "perverting" Dewey's teachings. They cited the full text of *Experience and Education* as the source of their accusations, noting that in his new book "Dr. Dewey himself cites several instances in which he thought some progressive schools had applied his theories unwisely."

Clearly, many of the "abuses" of education and the shortcomings of progressive education for which Dewey was attacked can be attributed to the excesses of his followers and not to Dewey himself. Because

Dewey was so well known, his name became a catchall for any abuse that could be found in so-called Dewey progressive schools. Yet it was not easy for Dewey to dissociate himself from the excesses of either theory or practice that his followers—often ardent disciples—absorbed from his writings. In *Experience and Education* he tried to clarify his own position as the best way to separate himself from his supporters. As philosophical in character as *Democracy and Education*, this new book had the added dimension of being a reply to his critics in the controversies that had arisen over the "progressive education" that had become, whatever it was actually, synonymous with "Dewey."

In the first words of his talk at Kappa Delta Pi, Dewey struck a note of controversy: "All social movements involve conflicts which are reflected intellectually in controversies. It would not be a sign of health if such an important interest as education were not also an arena of struggles, practical and theoretical." But it is the duty of the philosopher—his only duty—to go beneath the claims of the contending parties and examine the causes of the conflicts and then to cast aside any "isms"—"even such an 'ism as 'progressivism' "—to gain access to the "larger and deeper" issues involved. For his disciples, who had enthusiastically championed "progressivism" on his behalf, Dewey warned: give up the rallying cry and the name, and look deeper.

At once Dewey plunged into the conflicts between progressive and traditional theories and the modes of organization and teaching arising from each side. Neither theory as a theory provides solutions concerning instruction; rather, each generates problems for instruction to study. Either can become dogmatic; either can be slack and uninformed. "Traditional" education can flounder in its emphasis on the "past," "guidance," and "authority." "Progressive" education can be smashed on the rocks of the "present," "doing," and "freedom." These are not solutions, but problems to be solved. Thought cannot seek solutions before the problems are identified. Dewey advised patience. By yoking "experience" and "education" in his title, Dewey was warning the reader that he was not offering a solution. In the first place, these two terms cannot be equated: some experiences are "mis-educative" and arrest "the growth of further experience." Rather, by joining "experience" to "education," Dewey was asking, in what way can "experience" and "education," being and learning, be positively linked in human becomingness? Dewey's aim in *Experience and Education* was to free education from any ideology and then to reopen it to experience without slogans. In *Experience and Education* and again in "Education, Democracy, and Socialized Economy," an article written later in the same year, Dewey entered the controversies at a problematic level, with the advice: clarify, clarify—then, again, clarify. Controversies can never be solved by contention, only by clarification.

Some controversies may be treated by action. In the case involving Bertrand Russell and educational freedom, Dewey eventually helped mediate an economic solution that led to resolution. Other controversies might be treated by debates over fundamental issues. Refusal to engage debate at that level, as Dewey said of Hutchins, would lead only to polemics. Most basically, controversies must seek their resolution by clarifying issues that, when murky, dispose the contenders to clash. Dewey certainly did not "win" all the controversies in which he engaged during the 1930s. But he was not trying to win; he made his goal intelligent analysis and informed action.

After the War

In 1942, as the University of Chicago Press was preparing to publish John E. Stoner's *S. O. Levinson and the Pact of Paris*, Dewey was invited to supply a foreword. Levinson, he wrote, attempted to "invent" peace. However, Dewey added, Levinson's "immediate purpose was defeated as the second World War so tragically testifies." Still, Dewey predicted, humankind's wish for peace was undying, and Levinson's movement to outlaw the "war system" had to be "recovered."

The whole world was at war when Dewey wrote this. Most of the history that Dewey had lived and helped make was obliterated by the fighting on the battlefields and the consequences of the war for the home front. Progressivism seemed ready to become a historical relic. The Great Depression disappeared with the war effort, and government regulations penetrated every aspect of life. Any thoughts that

American democracy could be matured at home before global involvement became unthinkable now, as Americans were dispersed all over the globe and would obviously need to continue to occupy foreign lands even after the war ended. Dewey had opposed America's entry into the League of Nations after World War I. Now, the United States was a leading force in the creation of a United Nations.

By 1945, at the war's end, Americans were ready to begin history anew—with unprecedented resources, unbounded hopes, an enormous increase in world power, and every prospect of realizing a broadly distributed prosperity such as the world had never before seen. But hardly had the treaties of surrender been signed than the world created a new kind of war and invented a name for it: a "cold war." The democratic China that Dewey had envisioned soon crumbled. The victory of communism that he had considered extremely unlikely came in 1949. Most of Dewey's allies and followers in China fled to Taiwan or the United States; those who stayed were soon removed unless they repudiated Deweyism as a tool of capitalism. But where one conduit of Dewey's influence closed with the end of the war, others opened. In Japan, where the civilian government and the U.S. occupying forces believed that the democratization of the schools was important, all of Dewey's major books on education and educational philosophy were translated into Japanese. A generation of Japanese teachers was trained with Dewey as an influence. In Italy, too, Dewey's books were also being broadly disseminated, especially his works on political philosophy, liberalism, and aesthetics.

Was it a brave or broken new world in which Dewey and other Americans lived during the 1940s and early 1950s? What America had seemed to be building toward all Dewey's life, what he had supported to see realized in society, all seemed to collapse. Dewey's optimism would have encouraged him to take a positive view, but his disappointments, multiplying with each new restriction, disposed him to doubt and disillusion.

Something of the conflict between these two attitudes emerged in the introduction that the University of Chicago philosopher and former Dewey student and colleague Richard McKeon asked Dewey to write to *Democracy in a World of Tensions: A Symposium*, prepared by UNESCO in 1949. For personal and public reasons, Dewey was the natural choice to introduce the volume. UNESCO stood for the United Nations Educational, Scientific, and Cultural Organization, and Dewey was certainly the best-known commentator in America on the relation of democracy, education, science, and culture; it was a virtual description of his career. Personally, too, McKeon told Dewey that his own growing concern for "social-moral matters had brought him much nearer to [Dewey's] . . . position." Within a month Dewey completed the introduction and sent it to McKeon. His emphasis on the "responsibilities of the western democracies, and particularly the United States" delighted McKeon, who called the piece "very forceful."

After consulting with the UNESCO officers, however, McKeon had to backpedal. Politics made an appearance. The concern was raised that if Dewey's essay introduced the volume, the Soviets might consider the whole enterprise to be anticommunist and take reprisals against the contributors who resided behind the Iron Curtain. Then, too, Dewey's emphasis on the duty of the United States to see that UNESCO carried out its mandate to support "the traditional political type of democracy" would provoke further conflict. McKeon had to outline the required changes to Dewey. Without argument, Dewey agreed to the changes. But now his piece was no longer thought to be acceptable as an introduction and instead became chapter 5. Dewey also allowed the deletion of two sentences that seemed to stress too much the role of America as a leader in the world. He stated to McKeon, "I was quite aware of writing from a Western and American point of view; in fact . . . that was the reason d'etre of the whole essay." In the two offending sentences and in his chapter in general, Dewey maintained his usual position on American democracy. But by 1950 the history that had stood behind his position had been transformed, and Dewey's Americanist position was no longer desirable, even in America.

Nonetheless, Dewey's contribution to *Democracy in a World of Tensions* stands as one of the best expressions of his commitment to the preeminent humanistic value of American democracy, along with his awareness of how thoroughly American democratic traditions had been altered, if not wholly rejected. "No argument is required," he begins, "to convince an observer that the peoples of the world are now in such a state of division as merits the name 'Cold War.' " The only effective countermeasure to such a condition is "organized intelligence" aimed at achieving "a common understanding." But the rise of communist states had created a crisis of democracy for America in 1950, and Dewey ended the chapter with the same sentiment that he agreed to delete earlier:

> Responsibility . . . now rests most directly upon democracies of the older political type [as in the United States]; they are the peoples with the longest experience of industrialization. Among the political democracies it rests with particular weight upon the peoples of the United States. For . . . [in contrast to communist "democracies"] they are organically committed to a type of democracy in which political activity is determined by freedoms of discussion, conference, and communication in which all citizens have the right and the duty to participate.

Dewey came down, after all, on the side of optimism. If the history that Dewey had helped make seemed to have been obliterated, it still existed at a deep level in the American psyche and could still reinvigorate the new energies of freedom. For Dewey, America was not erased, only dormant and temporarily rivaled by the new "democracies" of world communism. But, he believed, democratic progress in America could be revived.

JOHN AND ROBERTA

When Roberta Lowitz came to New York in 1930, she called on John Dewey. Her father, Joshua Lowitz, had become friends with Dewey while he was teaching in Oil City and Joshua and his wife lived in nearby Pittsburgh. Roberta was born in 1904. During her childhood, her parents briefly went to China as missionaries, and she spent some of her early years in Asia. Now grown, she was an attractive woman, creative and active. She wrote travel articles for the *Pittsburgh Press*, but she was no ordinary reporter. As early as 1931, she began to organize "travel clubs" in the Pittsburgh public schools. In 1934 Augustus Thomas described what she was doing: "Miss Estelle R. Lowitz, an experienced newspaper woman . . . has one of the most interesting travel features for newspapers that I know. She takes young people on an imaginary journey through various countries and presents the human side of those countries. . . . Her project is higher educational." Traveling to various countries, from them she sent back letters and picture postcards to the children as a special supplement to their education. She toured South America on this program in 1934.

In 1936 Roberta moved from Pittsburgh to New York City and got in touch again with Dewey. At first she solicited his help, which he gave by writing a general "To Whom It May Concern" letter of recommendation for her: "Miss Roberta Lowitz has developed a method for making the teaching of geography in the upper grades or the elementary school both interesting and vital. . . . It will arouse curiosity about and interest in other countries." He urged administrators and school boards to introduce her work into their curricula. But their relationship this time was not merely flirtatious; in late 1936 she and Dewey became intimate. In the first week of January 1937, Dewey went to Passagrille Beach for the winter. "Perfect if you were here," he wired her. He sent her a newspaper cartoon drawing of St. Augustine, who was an avowed sinner before his conversion, with the caption: "Lord, make me pure and chaste—but not quite yet." All during the time he was involved in the Trotsky hearing, he was sending her love letters. At the close of the first day of hearings, he gave Roberta an account of the trial and then spoke of "my new life that began with you." In June he went to the University of Cincinnati to give a summer course. It seemed to him to be "the most successful course I ever gave." But he was lonely. His letters had exactly the same ecstatic style that he had used in writing to Alice and Anzia:

I have a conundrum. . . . Do you love *me*? I know you *love* me
but the emphasis is on me. I shan't blame you if you dont, I
dont love myself an awful lot, though I think better of myself
when I think that you love me and let me love you.

Anticipating a reunion with Roberta as soon as he had finished his lectures at Cincinnati and spent some time with Evelyn in Missouri,
Dewey, seventy-seven years old, was as excited as a teenager. "Oh, to be
seventy again," he wrote in a postscript to the thirty-two-year-old
Roberta. He had already made plans that when he went to Hubbards
in mid-July he would take Roberta with him, and he was simultaneously worried and excited about what his neighbors would say when
they found out that Roberta was sleeping in the little cottage with him.
But there was no fuss, and after ten days there, Dewey wrote to James
T. Farrell: "I have a shack by the lake; life is rather primitive as to conditions; the lake is our only bathtub. We go to the hotel near the bay or
ocean for noon time dinners and Robby cooks breakfasts and suppers
and I help eat them." Dewey's children and young female friends like
Myrtle McGraw were happy for him: "In the beginning, both Liz and
I," Myrtle explained, "we all were delighted that J.D. has someone who
could go with him" on trips.

At the same time, Roberta was carrying on a long-distance love
affair with a mining engineer named Roy Grant, who had been seeking his fortune all over the world. He sent her love letters from the
American West, England, Belgium, Nigeria, and Angola. In
September 1939, she married Grant by proxy while he was still abroad.
Fourteen months later Grant became seriously ill and died on the
Pacific Coast. Dewey's old Chinese student Hu Shi, who was also a
good friend of Roberta's, wired her to express his "shock" at her "great
loss," following with "You are quite right in your own self-analysis";
you were "becoming a woman, a lover, a wife and a widow—all within so short a period in your life!" She and Hu Shi flirted briefly. Loss
followed loss, and in October, Roberta's mother died after a long illness. From Key West, John and Jane sent their "love and sympathy."

Roberta continued her journalism career. In 1939 she was the press representative of the Kingston (Jamaica) *Jamaica Standard* to the World's Fair in New York. During the war, she volunteered for several civilian organizations. In January 1946, Roberta's brother, Herman Lowitz, died, and she inherited 25 percent of the assets of his estate of $1.066 million, chiefly in stock of the American Glass Corporation. Litigation ensued, and in the final distribution Roberta inherited about $200,000 in equities.

At this point she started the process of adopting a four-year-old boy named Lewis Robert Hume, who had been born in Halifax, Nova Scotia, near Hubbards. Although difficulties arose because she was unmarried, she had already taken little Lewis to live with her at the end of the summer of 1946. What could be simpler than to solve this by marrying—John Dewey! On December 10, 1946, John wrote to his doctor,

> I am marrying tomorrow a.m., before leaving for Florida, Miss Roberta Grant. She is a very old and very dear friend. We *decided* on the marriage only a few days ago. No announcement has been made and I hope none will be made . . . the difference in age is so great—and I am afraid she will have some unpleasant publicity. However, she is willing to take the risk, including the comparatively short time we are likely to be happy together.

Jerome Nathanson performed the ceremony, and Roberta and John made their vows and exchanged rings. Then a small celebration took place, after which the newlyweds departed for Key West. Jane moved out at once. Even with their marriage, the adoption process took much longer than expected and was not completed until 1948. Roberta then decided that she wanted to rename Lewis as John Dewey Jr. and also to adopt his sister, who was a year and a half older.

No one ever knows precisely when trouble in a family begins. It starts and then just keeps growing until someone notices it. When Roberta insisted on renaming the boy, Fred's wife Liz was hurt, for that was the name she and Fred had given to their son who had died so early and had left both parents and grandfather John crushed. It seemed to them insensitive of Roberta to go out of her way to make another John Dewey, as if now John Dewey and his name were her possessions. Roberta indeed began to seem possessive. After the marriage, when Evelyn asked Roberta to give her a few of Alice's possessions that were still in the apartment in order to leave a remembrance to each of John's grandchildren, Roberta refused without explanation.

The issue of Alice's will also played into this complex situation. John's bequest of the use of the interest from Alice's estate as long as he remained unmarried meant that as of December 11, 1946, the principal reverted to the children who had been designated his heirs; and between 1927 and 1946 the principal had grown significantly. The Dewey children accepted the principal and divided it among them, except Fred who was deemed to have adequate financial security without any inheritance. John made no protest whatsoever, but Roberta may have harbored some resentment. Possessiveness, entitlement, a strain of narcissism—it is impossible to judge which part of Roberta's personality appeared in her demands, deceptions, and histrionics. Before the marriage, at Dewey's eightieth birthday celebration in 1939, she had complained that she had been slighted by the planners and had not received an invitation to the dinner. When she picked a fight with John over this, he sternly rebuked her: "Robby, you are evidently much offended with me—you know that if one is inclined to be, one can pick out a phrase to justify it." He knew that Roberta was closely in touch with Kallen and the other planners, and she did receive an invitation. In 1942, she felt slighted by Dewey's most loving and attentive disciple, Joseph Ratner, who hoped to write Dewey's biography and was giving John unstinting aid with several of his projects. He usually signed his letters to Dewey "With love," and Dewey's closing was usually "Affectionately." Roberta woke up Ratner one night with a telephone call to demand, "Have you ever said any unkind things about me?" He asked her what it was he was supposed to have said and to whom. But she would not answer, and only repeated the same question over and over for ten minutes. Then she told Ratner: "Don't you know that anything you say to hurt me, hurts Dewey?" This was of course a threat, for above all else in the world, Joseph Ratner treasured his relation with his mentor. Agitated beyond measure, he wrote long letters to Dewey, trying to remember every person he had ever spoken to about Roberta and to exonerate himself of any charges against him. He even suggested that it may have been *Sidney* Ratner who spoke negatively of Roberta and concluded rather pathetically, "I never said to Robbie or anyone else that she attached herself to you."

There was also a histrionic element in Roberta's makeup. Everyone close to the family knew that the two children had been born in Halifax. But in public, Roberta told everyone that she and John had adopted "two Belgian [war] . . . refugees." She informed George Axtelle that John had some friends in Belgium who were killed in the war and that he adopted their two children. On another occasion, she loudly objected to a section in a collection of Dewey's *Wit and Wisdom* concerning his present "marital relation." She made Dewey demand of the publisher, Beacon Press, that the first edition be suppressed and a new one issued without the offending passage. As late as 1950 she continued to check bookstores to see if this had been done, and that year she found two copies of the first edition in Doubleday's bookstore. The same objectionable edition was found in the Columbia University bookstore. Roberta was outraged, and Dewey made his editor apologize and promise speedy amends. On another occasion after Dewey's death, she demanded of Dewey's editor, Charles Madison, that he delete a letter from Corinne Frost from a Dewey book. Jealous possessiveness was certainly a factor here.

Myrtle McGraw commented on what had happened to Dewey's relationship with his family even before the marriage:

> Another time [when] he was sitting in my office . . . he said, "You know we've never had a quarrel." I wondered whatever under the sun made him say it, it never dawned on me that you would quarrel with John Dewey about anything. Then, I went to California in the summer. He was in Nova Scotia, and his letters didn't come and I couldn't understand it. When I got back I discovered somehow Liz and I had

offended Robbie. That began a kind of cleavage . . . that was a very peculiar thing, and . . . I didn't understand it.

Then came the marriage, and things got worse.

> When he . . . married, Liz called me up horrified and said that he and Robbie had decided to get married, and for God's sake I should stay away. It seems that there were these two children, these Belgian children, and she persuaded him to [marry in order to adopt them] . . . his behavior certainly changed. I thought maybe it changed toward me, I didn't know until I got with Evelyn and the girls and I found out it was with all of us.

Things kept getting worse. In May 1948, Liz and Roberta had a big fight. John was ill and Liz came to visit him. For Liz it was like the old days; she was having a chatty good time with him just as they had done in Russia and on other trips. Then Roberta came into the room and tempers flared. In a letter dated May 2, John berated Liz for her "aloof and unkind superiority" and defended Roberta without qualification.

In 1949, at Dewey's ninetieth birthday celebration, Dewey seemed to be a different man. He had sat in the audience at the seventieth and sent a message for the eightieth; but at the ninetieth, there was a great display, a grand entrance. Myrtle McGraw says:

> I sat with the family at the 90th birthday dinner, and to us who had known him, this kind of display that went on was . . . out of keeping with the man that we'd known . . . he didn't appear . . . [until] they came making this big stage entrance, and there were all these children, a whole lot of little children. I said to Evelyn, "Who in the devil are all those children?" And she said, "I wish I knew. I don't know." All that sordid display . . . came into his life. . . . It was a little sad for us, but at the same time, as Liz said to me on the plane, "Well, we had him at his best."

Roberta had staged a theatrical entrance with Dewey surrounded by children. It was a photo opportunity. Perhaps it was narcissism that she had the children call her "Mommy" and call Dewey "Grandpa," as if she were not married to an old man.

The tensions between Roberta and Dewey's family and friends never eased. In 1951, Joe Ratner was ousted from contact with Dewey again. He complained to Evelyn, his closest friend among Dewey's children. Evelyn commiserated with him, assuring Joe that she knew that "gigantic attempts must have been made to knife you." She was bitter and ventured to say that now that her father was really sick, Roberta might find it "pretty hard . . . to do her duty if he continues so ill that he cannot feed her the flattery she demands so constantly or furnish her an ear into which she can pour her evil fantasies." Sidney Hook labeled Roberta a "paranoiac" and a "liar." Evelyn had already concluded that there would be no use in trying to negotiate visits with her father through Roberta. Better, she declared, "to turn up at his side without any preliminaries, and if things get to the point where he asks for it or where her neglect becomes so great that help is needed in seeing that his care is adequate I'll be more than glad to do my share." In 1966 Morris Eames summed all this up in one sentence: Roberta "alienated so many people who were friends of Dewey's and of hers at one time." Eventually, Roberta cut off Ratner completely. Hurt, he suspended his proposed biography of Dewey and then never wrote it. Yes, Kallen added, "he [Ratner] thinks that . . . [Roberta's] dishonest; hates her guts; and she hates his."

John Dewey gave little sign that the rifts between himself and his family that Roberta had caused troubled him very much. He defended Roberta against others' accusations, taking her side. Once he and Robbie were married, he gave his allegiance to her. During his long marriage to Alice, Dewey seems to have learned how to accept and support his wife completely, even when she was as difficult a person as Alice often was. In 1947 he told a Chinese student to whom he was very close that he was writing another book, one about "general philosophy." The book "isn't about love" he mused, "though I am sure that volume . . . will be broadened by the deepened and brightened experience and horizon due to women such as my wife is." Anyone who said, as Joe Ratner was accused of saying, that Robbie attached herself to John would be wrong. It was hard for those who regarded him as a great man and Robbie as a shallow, possessive, jealous woman to realize, but it seems that when they married, he attached himself to her. For her part, she became Mrs. John Dewey, mother of John Dewey Jr., destined guardian of the Dewey legacy, and illustrious keeper of the Dewey flame, even after it would be extinguished.

The Last Birthday Celebration

By 1949, America's world was now a global one, and appropriately, Dewey's ninetieth birthday celebration became an international occasion. Salutations arrived from all over the world. Programs of speeches about Dewey's importance were organized in Canada, Denmark, England, France, Holland, Israel, Italy, Japan, Mexico, Norway, Sweden, and Turkey. Waseda University in Tokyo, where Dewey had lectured in 1919 and 1921, held a three-day symposium of lectures on Dewey's work. In Mexico, the Fondo de cultura economica publishing house marked the occasion with speeches, a radio address, philosophical articles, and a translation of *Art as Experience*. Ömer Celal Sarc, president of the University of Istanbul, wrote to tell Dewey that his birthday would be celebrated by a "special ceremony" there.

In the United States, the main occasion was celebrated over a three-day period, concluding with a dinner at the Hotel Commodore above Grand Central Station in New York City. Outside New York, more than one hundred schools and learned societies held programs of tribute to Dewey. Dewey recorded a tape to be played at the College of the Pacific. Asked which of his ideas had been most misunderstood, he replied that "pragmatism" was an unfortunate label, because "it became identified with a very narrow view of practical utility." He insisted again, as he always did, that pragmatism was a method, not in itself a program of reform or a commitment to a particular cause. To think either, he said, would be "a complete misunderstanding."

A ninetieth birthday fund committee was established with the aim of raising $90,000, one thousand dollars for each year of Dewey's life, so that he could use the fund to contribute financially to causes of his choice. William Kilpatrick served as chair, heading a very large committee of sponsors including people as different as Justice Hugo Black and Eddie Cantor, cartoonist Al Capp and president of Harvard James B. Conant, union leader David Dubinsky and entertainer Jimmy Durante, and Albert Einstein and Douglas Fairbanks Jr. Roberta Dewey was the treasurer of the committee.

To organize the main celebration in the Hotel Commodore, Kilpatrick was the chair, and Nathanson the secretary. A "partial list" of more than five hundred sponsors appeared in the program. Dewey swept into the Grand Ballroom surrounded by children and listened to scheduled greetings and brief addresses by nine dignitaries. The first message read was from President Truman: "Dear Dr. Dewey: Blessed is the man who arrives at fourscore [years] and ten rich in human experience and the love of friends—and endowed with the unconquerable and unconquered spirit of youth." Felix Frankfurter, now associate justice of the U.S. Supreme Court, spoke. At the last moment, the prime minister of India, Jawaharlal Nehru, rushed to the Commodore from another meeting in *his* honor and gave an impromptu speech concerning the significance of Dewey for his country and him. The greetings went on for two hours. Many more speakers than expected claimed the floor. Then Harry Laidler, Dewey's longtime friend and the executive director of the League for Industrial Democracy, stood to introduce the guest of honor. Dewey, he noted, referring to the international outpouring, "has more profoundly affected the educational life of our modern world than any other single man." Finally, Dewey rose and spoke extemporaneously from a few notes. What he wanted to say was that he had spent his life "in the vocation of philosophy," not as an admission reluctantly wrung from him but "as a boast." And in being a philosopher and looking into the need and reasons for thought and action, he said, he dared to hope that Alvin Johnson, president of the New School, had been right in declaring on this evening "that I have helped to liberate my fellow human beings from fear." Harking back to a theological question that had been important in his youth and turning it now to an obligation to truth, Dewey continued: "When we allow ourselves to be fear-ridden and permit it to dictate how we act, it is because we have lost faith in our fellowmen—and that is the unforgivable sin against the spirit of democracy."

One of the speakers at the dinner remarked that this "was undoubtedly the most important dinner ever tendered to a private individual in the United States." He was right. Yet in his response, Dewey turned the occasion from a celebration of a private individual to a promise of the triumph of democracy in America even in a time of crisis. The celebrations at Columbia University lasted for a week. At the end, the president of Columbia—soon to be the president of the United States—Dwight D. Eisenhower, said that he himself had been called "the soldier of freedom" and that Dewey was certainly "the philosopher of freedom." He also spoke of Dewey as "the brightest star in Columbia's firmament."

A reporter for the *New York Times* showed up at Dewey's apartment to interview him on the day after the birthday dinner. Dewey admitted that he had been a bit disturbed by all the "fuss and bother" about his birthday, that he would rather have had a family dinner or taken his two adopted children for a walk in Central Park. The reporter observed genially that if one met Dewey on the street, "you would think he was little more than 70. His bushy hair is tinged with silver, and his heavy mustache, clipped at the edges, has begun to gray." Dewey didn't hesitate to express himself on several issues: Loyalty oaths for teachers will do more harm than good. Public school education should receive federal aid. The Russian system will collapse because "the Soviet imposes its rules . . . without any participation by the people." When the reporter mentioned Dewey's motto "learning by doing," Dewey made a correction: "I don't believe people learn merely by doing. The important things are the ideas that a man puts into his doing. Unintelligent doing will result in his learning the wrong thing." At this point in the interview, Dewey's adopted son, obviously restless, interjected to Roberta, "I betcha Grandpa's sorry he went and got himself 90 years old. Everybody's flashing lights in his face and asking questions and everything when we could come to the park and roll the hoops he bought us and have fun."

Very probably, he did get to the park with the children soon after the interview was concluded. He had had his fill of festivities for a while. The events, he told John Graves, "left me flat as a bottle of fizzy water after the cork is out." Festivities based merely on age were giving him "chron-itis." He wanted to get back to philosophy, and he picked up his ongoing philosophical correspondence with Graves as if there had been no interruption at all. Still, two birthday events at which he had not been present genuinely moved him. He learned that a group of fifty students in a history of philosophy class at Ohio Wesleyan College spontaneously broke out in song, "Happy birthday . . . John Dewey," at their class meeting on October 20. They sent a photograph of themselves addressed to "Dear John." Amused, Dewey wrote back that best of all was the friendly attitude of the students who addressed him so warmly. But the letter that he liked most was from the kindergarten-to-grade 6 students at the Newton School in Massachusetts:

> We wish you a very happy birthday today. When our principal told us about you this morning we decided to write you a note to tell you how much we appreciate what you have done to help improve our schools. . . . If you were here we could give a nice party but since that is not possible we will all try to be good citizens.

THE END

On the occasion of Dewey's ninetieth birthday, Horace Kallen remarked to Dewey: "I do not recall any philosopher alive or dead who has retained so long the fullness of his powers." Kallen was certainly right. Dewey's first article was published in 1882. By 1949 he had been philosophizing for sixty-seven years and had published about a thousand essays, books, reviews, and works in other forms, and he had not yet written his last work. But from the mid-1940s on, his health began to fail. Certainly, as he told Joe Ratner, he now was "paying more attention to medicines than to ideas." Writing to Evelyn in 1950, Ratner summed up the situation: "He never recovered from the celebration last year . . . he has had one relapse after another." Although Dewey showed no diminution of mental clarity, he was so weak that he became reconciled to not writing anything more. However, when his strength returned, even for a few hours, he was back at the typewriter and wrote "solid stuff."

In 1949 he published a book with Arthur Bentley entitled *Knowing and the Known*, which was Dewey's attempt to carry forward into new ground the hypotheses of his own *Logic: A Theory of Inquiry*. He had, in fact, already acknowledged in his preface to *Logic* his indebtedness to Bentley's *Linguistic Analysis of Mathematics* (1932). Bentley's book had helped him see that not just Aristotelian logic but recent formalist mathematical logic "assumes control by meanings fixed outside the operations of inquiry," whereas inquiry requires a logic that depends on itself in the practice of inquiry. The known could function only in the knowing. Such issues had also preoccupied Bentley. If Dewey came to his philosophic position by way of Kant, Hegel, James, and Peirce, Bentley arrived at his via Hegel, Georg Simmel, Wilhelm Dilthey—and John Dewey. In 1895 he had audited Dewey's seminar on logic at the University of Chicago and watched Dewey as he began his movement from Hegel, Bosanquet, and Lotze to pragmatism and the *Studies in Logical Theory*. Among the notes he took in Dewey's class, one lingered until it became the title of their book: "Dewey urged students . . . to ask . . . 'What is the act of knowing itself?' " Both Dewey and Bentley were trying to use the natural sciences to create a science of humanity. Approximately the same age, Dewey and Bentley grew up intellectually under the same general cultural influences in America: a utopian, hopeful, transcendental, evolutionary, naturalistic, organic, idealistic, practical belief that some new segment of history was starting to unfold on American shores. They believed that it was the duty of every American to assist in its development and join with it; it would be democratic and egalitarian but also excellent, in politics, social life, art, and the activities of intelligence.

In *Knowing and the Known* they set out to describe a small but crucial segment of this American vision, a theory of linguistic signs that would be intelligible, "firm," unambiguous, and suitable communicatively to carry pragmatism forward to the next phase of intellectual and social reformation. Dewey's *Logic* would provide the foundation; Bentley's *Linguistic Analysis of Mathematics* was the lever; their examination of the relation of linguistic signs, thought, and behavior was the mode; their exposure of the defects of the formalist logic and foundationalist assumptions of Carnap, Morris, and the other logical positivists was the by-product; and their establishment of Deweyan instrumentalism or "naturalism" on solid communicative underpinnings was the consequence.

In their preface, the authors call the reader's attention to a letter contained in the appendix from Dewey to a "philosopher friend," A. G. Balz. They remark, as if pointing to a basic test, that "he who fails to grasp the viewpoint therein expressed may find himself in the shadow as respects all else we have to say." This cautionary word sent most readers at once to the appendix. "As I see the matter," Dewey wrote, "what marks the scientific movement that began a few centuries ago and that has accomplished a veritable revolution in the methods and conclusions of natural science are its *experimental* conduct and the fact that even the best established theories retain *hypothetical* status." These two convictions go hand in hand and define the Dewey-Bentley project: experimental, not foundational; hypothetical, not positivistic.

In several letters written after the publication of *Knowing and the Known*, Dewey began to speak of his new, visionary idea that modern civilization, especially in America, had entered a new phase of history. The American New World would transform the global world, not by military or expansive business adventures in Europe or Asia, not by opening economic doors, not by making the world safe for democracy, but by remaking civilization through communication and community. In 1949 he wrote the French political philosopher Sebastian de Grazia, commenting appreciatively on his *The Political Community* and sending his own new preface to a reprint of *Reconstruction in Philosophy*.

"The references to our present state of uncertainty, confusion and unsettlement," he remarked,

> are written with reference to the collapse of philosophy at present and its need of facing the human situation with a radically new start. . . . I believe . . . that we are at the beginning of a new period of history, the Modern, and that the centuries since what is called the end of the Medieval period [are] only the time of transition. . . . [Our] crisis is the fact that the new has attained a state of development when its undermining of the old has created its unsettlement but has not reached the point of constructive organization of what is new. . . . [We] may be living in the greatest crisis men have been through . . . certainly greater than that of "The Fall of Rome." . . . Diagnosis is at least the first need.

Nearly a year later, Dewey wrote about his vision of the "years of the Modern" in a letter to Read Bain. "I even wonder if we are in for a change in the make-up and processes of human relations." The next year he returned to the theme for the benefit of a young graduate student in philosophy, whom he admonished to carry on the work: "We are at the beginning of . . . [an epoch in] world history" that began with the Fall of Rome.

Dewey was mostly content to turn the task of reconstruction over to others. But on his good days when his energy revived, he felt that he had one more book, one last book, to write that would summarize his own development, reflect on the history of Western thought, and start the work to be done by others in consolidating the new stage of history. He began this book as early as 1941, telling Corinne Frost that he would write a "sort of" summation of the history of philosophy to show "how much of our present confusion is due to retention of old ideas after their base and function are gone." It would be a pragmatic methodological critique of where thought had failed to adapt to the news of the day. The main title would be, simply, *Naturalism*. It would deal with "the endeavor of man to come to intellectual terms with the world in which he lives." Dewey was making progress on the book, and then a terrible calamity occurred. He explained this to a reporter: he had a "big undertaking" on his hands, writing a book that was to be the summation of his philosophical beliefs through the years. But he had lost the manuscript! He was "inconsolable." According to several accounts, he had nearly completed a draft by working as hard as he could on it all during the summer of 1949 in Hubbards. As Corliss Lamont tells it, John and Roberta returned to New York,

> and pulled up in front of their apartment house at Fifth Avenue and 97th Street. They left their bags with the doorman to bring up, and went upstairs in the elevator. When the door- man had brought up the baggage, Dewey looked around and said to Roberta, "My heavens, my brief case isn't here." Mrs. Dewey immediately rushed downstairs. The brief case *had* been taken out of the car, they knew; but it had disappeared. And in that brief case was the manuscript of Dewey's almost completed book.

There was no carbon copy. He would have to start over—at nine- ty! Joe Ratner tried to console him: "The loss of Mss was quite a blow," he said, but Dewey had struck "a rich philosophic vein" and could write a newer version parallel to the ideas he had recently touched on in his new preface to *Experience and Nature*. Dewey's ideas for this book, after all, Joe said, were "big enough to occupy several genera- tions," and "there is no one can do this job but you." After a few days, Dewey's old optimism returned and he started to think it was good for- tune that he had lost his manuscript: "In a way this has given me new ideas, starting over afresh again. I think I have better ideas now." In an interview that fall, he was so optimistic that he even joked about the Siberians who lived to the age of 120. "If they can live that long, why can't I?" he asked. Plenty of time to write a long book.

The book was to be organized genetically as the history of a phase of thought beginning with the Greek "discovery" of humane morals, which opened up the possibilities of democracy and its further development through education in rationality and logical method. The period from the Greeks to the opening of the Renaissance was devoted, as Dewey saw it, to creating a supernatural version of the Greek synthesis, in which the discourse of salvation replaced the method of rationality. Beginning with the Renaissance, humankind had wandered between two worlds of "imperfect secularization" until the present day. Now a new theory of knowledge based on "adaptations of logic" was growing from the natural and human sciences: psychology, economics, art, linguistics, physics, and mathematics. Dewey envisioned a new epoch in which the theoretical would be identical with the practical.

With such a vision, Dewey could not be satisfied with the philosophy—or humanity—of the present day. He was desperate to finish the book, but he felt so weak on so many days he despaired of doing so. He told a correspondent, "I'd like to finish my new book. [But] . . . maybe I'll never finish it." He tried to preserve his energy, sometimes even to revivify it. He sailed to Montego Bay, Jamaica, in search of a restorative climate. He consulted Ferner Nuhn about whether Tucson might be a possible place to make a long stay. "We've been going to Key West, Fla. but it is often damp there." But Roberta wanted to settle some real estate problems in Florida, and so they went there anyway. He tried to live on Roberta's Pennsylvania farm, Maple Lodge, and he liked getting his own milk and eggs again, but it drained his energy for the book. In late 1950 he, Roberta, and the children flew overnight to Los Angeles and spent several weeks "at a family hotel in Santa Monica." Ever in search of some better place, in January 1951 they sailed to Hawaii. They intended to stay for a month and settled into the Halekulani Hotel on Waikiki. He enjoyed the sunshine in Hawaii but didn't get "as much improvement in health as he or the doctors hoped. Still, he was able to work on an article "How, What and What for in Social Inquiry." He left Honolulu at the end of February and, immediately after docking, checked into the Good Samaritan Hospital in Los Angeles.

Five days of rest and care in the hospital brought back his strength. Dewey's hopefulness could never be crushed for long, and soon he was fantasizing that *this* time the doctors would diagnose and remedy all his physical problems. For a ninety-one-year-old man, his disclaimer in writing about this to Boyd Bode barely conceals an almost grandiose belief in the possibilities for one more new life. "I can hardly hope," he wrote to Boyd from his hospital bed, "to be a 'new man' completely but I am confident I shall have a renewed lease on life in the way of increased vigor as well as increase of freedom from pains and aches." Already his thoughts were turning to "fairly aggressive" new ventures in philosophy and social action. As he contemplated his discharge from the hospital in the second week of March, New York City was still locked in winter and was out of the question as a destination. The Deweys decided on Tucson, where they remained until the middle of May. Roberta wrote to Bob Rothman, one of Dewey's students in the 1930s and now a professor at Wayne State University, to describe the situation: "For months he has not been free for one moment from pain in his temples." He was in no condition to work. Then news came that Albert Barnes had died. Depression followed physical pain, and physical pain followed depression.

Back in New York, Dewey needed daily nursing care. "He was not acutely ill," the nurse who attended him wrote, "but rather, his whole body and vital organs particularly, were showing signs of impairment." Roberta went to work at the U.S. Customs Office. In the evenings after Roberta came home, she wove romantic stories for the nurse's entertainment. "Her earliest childhood memories ever reflected the presence of John Dewey in their hospitable home. . . . She could not recall a time in her childhood when John Dewey was not a frequent and welcome visitor in [her parents'] . . . home. It seemed right and natural that she should become the second Mrs. Dewey." Even more romantic and fantastic was Roberta's story about how she and John came to adopt the two orphans.

It was during the Second World War, while traveling in Europe, that this couple could not turn their eyes and hearts away from the scene of Europe's miserable little war waifs who played in the filth and rubble of the blasted buildings, begging bread and pennies from the passerby; these were externally separated by the injustices of war from the families and everything once held dear. Rescuing them from their plight, the Deweys made all necessary arrangements which could permit them to bring the children to America. Here they were to become legal members of the Dewey family and were soon absorbed in children's activities and enrolled in New York's notable private schools.

Dewey continued to write his big book. In mid-1951 he told a *New York Times* reporter that he was "working on a new book that may be the most comprehensive outline of his educational philosophy that has yet appeared." But the amount of time he could devote to the book grew smaller every week. His sketches, notes, outlines, and fragments remained in a tangle that he would never put together.

Meanwhile, during many months of selfless devotion, Joe Ratner was doing his best to remain in close association with Dewey, to make sure that he was not in need. Of the children, only Fred maintained contact with his father. The others were all "in complete darkness" and felt powerless. Each had a somewhat different individual attitude toward the situation. Liz was completely alienated. Evelyn was bitter. She mused: "I tried for years to make friends and overlook all [Roberta's] tantrums and lies." But what if John needed their help? "I can't believe that anything short of father's asking for us, or her breaking down would bring us in without more trouble afterwards." Perhaps if "father were obviously so terribly weak and ill that she got it through her noggin that every day might be the last, then possibly some sort of visiting or reconciliation might be brought about." But Evelyn doubted even that. She was completely embittered toward the two adopted children, calling them "the brats" and even "the monsters." Fred, who had handled his father's taxes and looked after his investments since the 1920s, learned from Roberta that at her request John had signed his stocks over to her in joint tenancy, and when he attempted to discuss it, he was thrown out of the house.

Toward the end of May, Joe Ratner was so worried about Dewey's latest medical report that he sent a copy to Dewey's daughters. The prognosis was very bad. The worse Dewey's health became, the more Evelyn obsessed about Roberta; Evelyn was tormented by being separated from her father when he was clearly dying. In a letter to Ratner she lashed out at Roberta, unable to turn her anguish anywhere else:

> I am sure your diagnosis of what is going on now is right, and that she probably actually is not getting worse, but as you say just living such an isolated life that her venom cannot spread itself out thin enough to seem on the whole just mostly ridiculous as it did before usually. Perhaps it's wishful thinking but I always console myself with the thought that she is so scatterbrained and lacking in powers of attention that she is unlikely to pull off her law suits or her steps to put us all where we belong. Now that father is really sick she probably has practically no "old friends" at all to even talk dirty to as she used to, we can only hope that the stored venom will not generate enough energy so she actually takes steps. By now nearly everyone must be on to her. I have stopped being noble and holding my tongue, and when anyone asks in . . . the ways that used to cause me to lie or misrepresent I answer truthfully.

Less than two weeks later, on June 1, 1952, John Dewey died. Roberta called John's physician and immediately following his certification of John's death, she contacted Donald Harrington, senior pastor of the Community Church of New York. Harrington came to the house, and they wrapped Dewey's body in a blanket, put it in an automobile, and took it to the Fresh Pond Crematory in Queens, where he was cremated the following day. Only then were the children informed that their father had died and that his ashes were in an urn in the Community Church. Columbia University requested that there be a memorial at the university, to which John Dewey had brought so much distinction and where many remembered him. But Roberta decided to keep the service private and quickly arranged a memorial service at the Community Church. Pastor Harrington read several passages from Proverbs, Ecclesiastes, Corinthians, Dewey's *A Common Faith*,

Matthew Arnold's poem "Rugby Chapel," George Eliot's "The Choir Invisible," and Coleridge's "Ode to Dejection." Two traditional hymns were sung by Arthur Davis. Harrington termed Dewey a "philosopher-saint" and compared him with Socrates. One of Dewey's two closest living friends, Max Otto, gave an address, after which Rev. Harrington led the singing of John Aldington's hymn, "These things shall be, a loftier race / Than e're the world hath known shall rise," and closed with a benediction. Roberta took the ashes home. Jane Dewey, who attended the service, wrote to Max Otto with gratitude for his tribute.

> I am the daughter who lived with him in the latter years of his life. . . . His life was so largely his profession that most of the things said in the press seem largely irrelevant to it, but your contact was with what he cared about and what made him important as a person as well as a public figure.

Evelyn wrote to Harrington that he had arranged a "wonderful service."

Just when the family started to forget Roberta, Evelyn reported the most recent outrage. The Dewey children had no part in the will. Roberta publicly stated that they had gotten their inheritance from Alice when John remarried. All the children believed that the will that Roberta presented for probate was "spurious"; it was dated only in February 1952, after John had broken his hip. And, Evelyn said, "there is some cock and bull story about its being a duplicate of a lost one. Lucy's lawyer says it is full of obvious flaws and a perfect suspicion arouser." Roberta's lawyer even questioned Sabino about whether he had ever been legally adopted and "wanted to know what his legal family status was in case of a 'compromise.' "

A month later, Evelyn was still agitated over Roberta, even as she knew that this was keeping her from mourning properly for her father. Sabino had reported to her that he believed father had an estate of $180,000. Each of the children had a lawyer now. But no one could decide how or if to challenge the will, and each in turn gave up because it seemed best to get on with their lives. The will was swiftly probated on July 24, and that was the end of it.

Or not quite the end. In the summer of 1969, when Neil Armstrong and Edwin "Buzz" Aldrin became the first humans to walk on the surface of the moon, Roberta called the newspapers to say that on his deathbed her husband predicted, "In your lifetime . . . we'll be going to the moon—a year or two short of 20 years from now." He had died seventeen years earlier. Dewey was still newsworthy and his extraordinary "prophecy" was duly reported. Roberta was in the news again, briefly. The next year she died in Miami Beach, after which John Dewey's ashes, along with Roberta's, were sent to the University of Vermont and interred under a granite headstone on which was engraved:

> The things in civilization we most prize are not of ourselves. They exist by grace of the doings and sufferings of the continuous human community in which we are a link. Ours is the responsibility of conserving, transmitting, rectifying and expanding the heritage of values we have received that those who come after us may receive it more solid and secure, more widely accessible and more generously shared than we have received it.

Last Words

Like all biographies, my biography of John Dewey is a mixed form. Obviously, no biography is identical with the life itself; all biographies are inquiries into a life. My book aims at giving a single, unified but complex portrait of Dewey. But to attain that end, I have had to follow two separate paths rather than trying to make them one. On the one hand, in common with philosophical or scientific investigation, I have aimed at *knowing*, knowing John Dewey. A biography that does not accurately render its subject's empirical reality will have little value.

This means searching for "facts," starting with where and when Dewey was born and ending with his death. Far more than this, biographers must know the manner and goals of their subjects' lives, their loves and aversions, their participation in the life of their community and the history that unfolds during their time—the larger life that encloses them and gives meaning to the facts of their existence. On the other hand, in common with the aims of art, a biography must create for its subject a narrative *portraying* the drama of existence. Dewey *constructed* and was constructed by the life that he lived. His biography must be a *reconstruction*. Aiming simultaneously at knowledge and representation, biographers create a new being that freshly represents the life that has ended.

But this is not all. Life is conducted in the web of *culture*. Biography is a cultural form. The "self" that biographers strive to know and to portray arises in a densely packed cultural context, connecting an individual's life with his or her family, work, community, and society. Individuals grow and change within their culture; they are made by it even as they make it. American life would not have been what it was in the late nineteenth and the first half of the twentieth century had Dewey not been a part of it. He would have been a different person had he lived at any other time. Accordingly, as Dewey's biographer, I have tried to participate knowingly and imaginatively in Dewey's culture, even as I recognize that I am also situated in the culture of which I am a part.

Knowledge. Representation. Culture. To these must be added an awareness of the nature of *experience*, Dewey's and my own. Dewey's experience was constituted by the complete sum of his life. As his biographer, my experience again is mixed, for in the context of an inquiry into Dewey's life, I must live provisionally in his experience while maintaining an awareness of my own. His experience is his life; mine as his biographer is my research and the narrative representation into which it grows. His life was his assertions. My life as a biographer consists of my warrantable representational assertions about his life. In some sense, I have been fortunate in my personal experience as a preparation for representing his. I went to a Dewey progressive school in

New York City and then to Columbia College, where I studied under Dewey's students and colleagues. He was still a live presence there.

The mixed nature of the biographical enterprise, which attempts to describe a unified but always changing person, subjects biographers to criticism from every side. Those readers who are interested only in Dewey's writings, seeing these as his life's paramount activity, will regard his other, more mundane life activities as having only an incidental connection with his philosophic importance and existence and will conclude that I have devoted too much space to the insignificant. Conversely, those who regard political activities as equal in importance to the drama of daily strivings will be disappointed that I have omitted some potentially interesting detail. Philosophers who read this book will wonder why I have failed to represent Dewey's career as a philosopher in more detail. Those who regard him as a political activist will be concerned that I have neglected to treat his politics more fully. Those who believe that his educational theories or practices are the most important aspect of his life, for good or ill, will be dissatisfied that I have neither defended nor blamed him. Radical thinkers are likely to express surprise that I have not censured Dewey for his moderate liberalism. Others who are disposed to conservatism may similarly be unhappy that I have not exposed the dangers of his liberal emphasis. All of them may be discontented with my biographical inquiry, which attempts to give the messy, unsystematic narrative of Dewey's various experiences of his own existence. My biography is constituted by and brought into being as a search for John Dewey and the many faces he turned toward the light in the experience of liberating his life.

When Dewey was in his mid-eighties, Professor Herbert Schneider invited him to his apartment for a party with the undergraduate philosophy majors at Columbia. Dewey had some advice to offer to these young students of philosophy: "He remarked that Hegel accused Schelling of changing his mind over and over again through the course of his career and carrying on his philosophical education in public. . . . Then he paused for a moment, and said slowly, 'Where else would one carry on one's philosophical education?' " For Dewey, philosophy, no differently from the rest of life, had a public existence and a public function, as both act and transaction. That his philosophy may change, as Dewey's did, is expected as he learned and grew yet remained himself. A biography of Dewey must be about what he thought and how that thought became public; as well as what he did and how his doing affected others. Like life, every biography is a work in progress, which the reader must try to complete.

Life after death exists for every person in the memories of others. A person like Dewey, who had so profound an influence on so many aspects of cultural life, lives after his death in the continuing drama of cultural transmission. No interment is ever complete until oblivion has had its triumph. In the twenty-first century, which Dewey never saw, scholars, journalists, and commentators of all sorts are still busy keeping him alive in cultural memory. His works or other activities continue to be studied, explicated, interpreted, and reinterpreted.

Dewey's life after death is not the province of individual biography but is part of the life of our culture, the province of cultural biography. In the following, I sketch out the continuing life of Dewey in contemporary culture. Others have been and still are busy in attacking or defending him. Dewey welcomed his attackers and remained wary of his followers. I am concerned with supporting neither, only with locating those elements of his life that continue to be relevant to the life of our times.

Considered as what Emerson called a "representative man," Dewey left in modern culture traces of his courageous life. At Dewey's last public appearance, Ernest Nagel remembered that his "advice to the young men and women [graduate students] in his audience was: 'You must have the courage to try new ideas.' . . . He made clear his conviction that while learning is fine and important, learning is not a substitute for the great adventure of exploring ideas and developing them. . . . he was speaking from the heart." He was not recommending himself as a hero or suggesting that he be imitated. He was saying that all of us should live our lives to the full, not in the shadow of the thoughts of others except as we make these our own and advance beyond them. In a quite Emersonian way, Dewey was saying: "Socrates, or Washington, or Raphael, or Beethoven, or Sir Isaac

Newton, are to you only what they can reveal of your own capacity and circumstance to yourself." His courage resided in the optimism for which Dewey has often been mocked. Skepticism without optimism is fashionable and always easy. Optimism takes hard work to sustain in the face of a world that is always brutal, but it has a necessary function in the continuance of culture. President Lyndon Johnson said as much to James T. Farrell when he remarked, "For myself, I find a deep and lasting significance in Dr. Johnny's belief that the greatest sin of all is to lose faith in one's fellow man." Johnson took the phrase "The Great Society" from Dewey's book *The Public and Its Problems*.

But perhaps the greatest dimension of Dewey's courage was singled out by Clifford Geertz. Reflecting on what "above all else" he had learned from Dewey, Geertz arrived at the

> chilling doctrine that thought is conduct and is to be judged as such. . . . [The] reason thinking is so serious is that it is a social act, and that one is therefore responsible for it as for any other social act. Perhaps even more so, for, in the long run, it is the most consequential of social acts. In short, Dewey brings thinking into the public world where ethical judgment can get at it.

Geertz was pointing to the reason why Dewey's work on ethics and valuation is so valuable: its strength is its rigor in assessing the moral relation of the individual to the social world. Dewey's was the sort of courage that must remain a residue in contemporary culture because there are so few sources of such moral clarity in our own time, and we need reminders of what courage can be and mean. George Herbert Mead expressed the value and the difficulties of Dewey's pragmatism in remarking that it "is a philosophy which comes with something of the effect of a cold shower, and it depends somewhat upon the vitality of the man . . . whether it leaves him with a chill or a glow." To be a philosopher *does* take guts, the very virtue we need most today.

Considered as a thinker, Dewey's continuing importance has several components. Our own time is dominated by imitation, collective thinking, party loyalties, groupthink, and unconsidered or ill-considered allegiances. Dewey's refusal to create and consolidate any system is part of his personality but also part of his triumph as a thinker. Almost all who knew him commented on his continuous preoccupation with thinking. His thinking has a special cast: he was interested in postulates not absolutes, in the tools of thinking rather than in settled convictions, in learning far more than in knowledge. He said that very early he saw "the superficiality of all formulas and statements which approach creeds," and he sought no disciples, only asking "students to use their own minds and have their own method for seeing things for themselves." Much of his writing centers on the idea of continuous reconstruction. All of it points toward what he called "transactional knowing," that is, "knowing together," not in isolation, but knowing in company with others. He resembles Benjamin Franklin in that he scarcely ever rejected ideas with which he disagreed but always at least considered them. Dewey remarked that when his contemporaries "ran across something with which they didn't agree the one interest they displayed—if any at all—was rejecting it. I found by contrast . . . [that I would] wonder why an intelligent person would hold and say such a thing, and I decided my policy was the better of the two." His students uniformly reported that when they turned in papers to him, he would invariably say, "You've got something here. Develop it." He was a true hermeneutic thinker, always ready to dispute with himself. "I was arguing with myself," he told the psychologist Roderick Chisholm, referring to his whole career. He kept inventing new names for what he did because he could not accept that complex thought could be circumscribed by a single name. Dewey wrote that to a certain point he envied those who had a single theme. But for himself, by contrast, "I seem to be unstable, chameleon-like, yielding one after another to many diverse and even incompatible influences; struggling to assimilate something from each and yet striving to carry it forward." Pragmatism, instrumentalism, functionalism, operationalism, radical empiricism, idealistic empiricism, naturalistic empiricism, and transactionalism: these are the changing names he gave to what he did. Of *pragmatism*, he said as early as 1905: "I have never known a myth to grow so rapidly as 'pragmatism.' To read its critics one would think it was a positive system set forth for centuries in hundreds of volumes. . . . But I object root and branch to the term 'pragmatism.' "

Perhaps Dewey's ability to think freshly was a psychological derivative of his personality, which was suffused with independence. After he finally freed himself to become himself, he was never again captured by either the pole of egotism or its opposite, conformity. He was always prepared for change. "When I complete a book," Dewey told Scudder Klyce, "it is launched on the sea and its further fortunes concern others. I hope it will get to port [,] naturally. If it doesn't . . . I try to learn something so I can do a better job next time." Dewey was never content with one mode or meaning. Typically, he criticized Henry Adams's comment in the *Education* that "his education was the search for some meaning and law of life and the world." A much better aim, Dewey remarked, would have been "to have tried to get as many meanings out of as many things as he could." The law of life is that there is no one law. There are lasting truths and basic principles, but to last and to remain basic, they must be always in the process of reconstruction. Dewey's work continues to instruct us about how to endure modernity, with its unstopping change. His respect for experience forces him—and can teach us—to recognize the centrality of inquiry and thus to accept the problematic character of existence. He recognized that in individuals and no less in the cultural community, there is an almost unconquerable "dread and dislike of any change which seriously disturbs the habits . . . to which men are accustomed." He devoted most of his career to confronting this hatred of change, and he can still help men and women of the present day face change as challenge instead of catastrophe.

Dewey consistently stressed the importance of both intelligence and imagination, not as personal capacities, but as methods of inquiry. He once said that he liked Bergson's observation that homo sapiens is also homo faber. He kept pondering Bergson's suggestion until, a few weeks later, he improved on it: "I have been amusing myself trying to see what adjective would most characteristically replace 'sapiens' in homo sapiens. . . . Homo fabricator—better than Bergson's homo faber; because it includes man the make-believer, the play-actor, stage performer, etc." People are responsible for making their world. Their instruments, first, are intelligence, which aims at knowing what they are making and, second, imagination, which represents to them what they can make. Today, when intelligence is confused with elitism, and imagination is downgraded to fantasy, we need to learn again that without those currently despised tools, no other means of making a suitable world will do.

Of the concepts with which Dewey was most preoccupied as a thinker, democracy was certainly one of the most important. Dewey knew that democracy was fragile, stronger as a critique of other political and social systems than it was in its own operations. Dewey made a profound shift, which we have not yet begun to absorb, in understanding democracy not as a political system, or a body of rights, or as the excrescence of such documents as the Declaration of Independence or the Constitution, or as a system of legislation or legal authorities, but as a way of life. He was explicit about this. In "Democracy and Educational Administration" (1937), he wrote: "The key-note of democracy as a way of life may be expressed, it seems to me, as the necessity for the participation of every mature human being in formation of the values that regulate the living of men together." Formation is the key word in the idea that democracy is a way of life. Democracy consists in the "formation" of values, not in preestablished values. We do not hold to democratic values; we experimentally strive toward them and then live them. James Gouinlock rightly says that Dewey created "the most innovative and elaborately developed philosophy of value to appear in modern history." When the majority of even professional philosophers are today sunk in the linguistic intricacies of ethical theory and appear unaware of Dewey's achievement, it is no wonder that the contemporary public has yet to discover Dewey's achievement in reconstructing the idea of democratic values as a core for life. His work still waits for us to arrive at it.

One of the most enduring clichés in contemporary culture is that Dewey is the father of progressive education and the source of our current condition of educational decadence and decline. Both parts of this cliché are false. The truth is that Dewey's educational theory has yet to be understood and his practice has yet to be tried. As early as 1938 in *Experience and Education*, Dewey tried to make clear how what passed for "progressive education" was far from his own conception. Toward the end of his life he complained frequently about the misapprehension of his theories by the general public as well as educators and schools of education. Such public figures as Admiral Hyman Rickover or such historians as Arthur Bestor and Richard Hofstadter who attacked Dewey for intellectual slackness or anti-intellectualism seemingly made no effort to inform themselves better than the public or the educational establishment by reading his work. Dewey's famous Lab School in Chicago was an organized research unit "to exhibit, test, verify, and criticize theoretical statements and principles." Its special mission was to achieve new educational "conditions," and the means were "to create new standards and ideals" for education. Every child, in some sense, was turned into a researcher whose duty was to discover and satisfy his or her own capacities and needs and then, also, to discover how this had been done. The curriculum in the Dewey school scarcely matched the clichés about the "freedom" of progressive education. There was not a single elective in it; it was as systematic as any scientific investigation. Education in Dewey's hands was the means to achieve a democratic end. But to be of any value, this was to be done through scientific rigor and constant experiment. Educational theory would be tested constantly in practice. We speak of the desirability of "accountability" today as if that could be achieved by periodic tests. In Dewey's true educational laboratory, accountability would be relentlessly examined through daily participant-observation. Dewey believed that a society could be judged by how it educated its children; for him, American education had to fashion and further American democracy.

While he continued to write on educational issues, Dewey's original research on education was concluded when he left Chicago for Columbia in 1904. His later writings on education are refined expressions of his early research. Ellen Lagemann has shown that the truncation of the educational research that ended when Dewey left Chicago doomed his educational ideas to fail to be implemented, even though he remained the educational thinker best known to the public. The result was that the professional educationalists who followed him used his name and some of his phrases, such as "progressive education," but pursued their own modes of educational practice under the Dewey banner while departing widely from his ideas. The "progressive education" for which Dewey has been condemned for the last sixty or more years is not his creation at all. It is the product of two men, Charles Hubbard Judd, Dewey's replacement in the School of Education at the University of Chicago, and Edward L. Thorndike, Dewey's contemporary at Teachers College, Columbia University, assisted by William Heard Kilpatrick, Dewey's student at Chicago and Columbia. For Dewey, education was a scientific experiment that tested his philosophic method, and he tried to develop education as a science. For Judd, education was a field in which to professionalize teachers and attach students to them. With Judd's arrival at Chicago, the Department of Education severed its connection with the Department of Philosophy. Judd introduced such courses as "Methods of Teaching" and "Educational Administration." He dropped George Herbert Mead's course, "Philosophy of Education" and replaced it with "Principles of Education." In Judd's department, Dewey's name was always uttered derisively. The university faculty who had participated in Dewey's Lab School were banished. Judd was far more intent on creating the school as an effective institution than with developing a science of education.

Thorndike's career at Teachers College spanned forty-two years, from 1899 to 1941, during which time he instructed thousands of teachers. He published hundreds of articles, too, that reached far beyond the Columbia University campus. His views on educational issues were often sought and widely quoted. He was an expert on "school surveys, curricula, tests, and laws of learning." Lagemann writes about these two influential educators: "Not concerned as Dewey had been with the significance of education as a source of social renewal and social change, Judd and Thorndike both saw education as a technique for matching individuals to existing social and economic roles." For them, education was applied work, not scientific learning. Between them from 1915 to 1960, they dominated the most influential graduate training schools in education. They let Dewey have the name of "the father of progressive education" while they created the education that bore his name and eventually left him to bear the blame for it. Even Robert Maynard Hutchins, with whom Dewey had fierce debates, recognized that "Dewey's followers are to blame for many misconceptions about his work." Dewey himself complained to Bob Rothman in 1950, "Why do writers and teachers insist on saddling me with the 'child centered' school? Anyone who has read me knows that it is the socially centered school that I have sought." The trouble was, his name was well known, but his books often remained unread—even by historians.

By "the time of World War I," Lagemann writes, "it was evident that Thorndike had won and Dewey had lost." The baleful results of the educational activities promulgated by Judd and Thorndike are manifest today. When we can learn that these results cannot be traced to Dewey and that his goals for education were suspended in 1904, then perhaps we may go back to the rigorous, experimental education he did sponsor and take it up where it was dropped nearly a hundred years ago. It too, as part of Dewey's unfinished legacy, waits for us.

Dewey was the last philosopher to claim attention from the public and to hold it over a long period of time. Perhaps culture can do without philosophers, but it cannot do without philosophy. How do we judge a society? Perhaps the standard is what we find in its schools. Perhaps, as Dewey once noted, a society can be evaluated by those whom we find in its jails. Perhaps, too, a culture may be judged by the activity of its philosophers. Philosophy, Dewey once said, is "fundamentally nothing but a contribution to the imaginative life of humanity." Its province is not ideas, categories, thought, syntax, mathematics, puzzles, or symbols. For Dewey, philosophy arises from and deals with culture and its problems.

> The principal task of philosophy is to get below the turmoil that is particularly conspicuous in times of rapid cultural change, to get behind what appears on the surface, to get to the

soil in which a given culture has its roots. The business of philosophy is the relation that man has to the world in which he lives, as far as both man and the world are affected by culture.

Without philosophy, then, culture shrivels. Dewey provides a reminder that philosophers can educate the public, but when philosophers shirk from this task, then the citizens at large must make philosophy public. Today we all must be philosophers. Dewey and James and Peirce became philosophers at a time when American philosophy was concerned with dying questions, and they gave new vitality to questioning and new life to philosophy. After all, as Dewey remarked, the same materials and powers in philosophizing also reside "in buying and selling, marrying and giving in marriage, ruling and obeying in the state, tilling the soil and enjoying its fruits, painting a picture, investigating the properties of radium, [and] setting the fallen on their feet." If men and women are capable of these, they have already begun the work of philosophy. Dewey alerts us, and indeed obliges us, to become the philosophizers of culture that culture needs. He himself served as a lifelong model of how this could be done.

Perhaps Dewey's most seminal contribution focuses directly on the chief malady of our time, the separation of facts and values, or of sense and sensibility. Dewey knew that although these are not the same, in our experience we must find a way to unify them. He connected them through the instruments of method, inquiry, intelligence, imagination, and activity. So must we. For to allow fact and value or action and thought to remain separate is to doom our world to functioning without intelligence. Dewey's lifework was dedicated to confronting that divorce and unifying our experience.

As a representative man, a thinker, and an educationalist, Dewey became a philosopher. His works remain repositories of the sort of philosophy that we still need, and his career beckons us to the future so that we can continue to enlarge what he began.

A vast, intelligent literature concerning John Dewey's philosophy already exists and is constantly being augmented by excellent books and articles. It is generally agreed that central to Dewey's thought and to pragmatic philosophy in general is the concept of "experience." Any person's thought is related to his or her experience, "lived experience," in himself or herself, in culture and in nature. "Experience is an affair of doing-undergoing," Dewey wrote in his "Types of Philosophic Thought" syllabus (1921–22).

Absent, then, from the abundance of studies of Dewey's thought is a full account of his "life experience," what he did and what he underwent, that is, his biography considered internally and externally. Mortimer Adler's detailed notes for "Types of Philosophic Thought," a class he took with Dewey, show that Dewey himself recognized the importance of biography to the study of any philosopher's works. Biography is even more crucial to the study of a pragmatist. Dewey's personal life is what has been missing in our engagement with the life of Dewey's work. In Dewey's introductory lecture, on October 3, 1921, to "Types of Philosophic Thought" he turned to this subject again and again, as recorded by Adler:

> Philosophy, when sincere, presents a personal commentary on life; it expresses the way in which the world impinges on some personality. In this sense it is affiliated with literature. . . . Every commentary—literary or philosophic—is a version and a criticism of life. . . . The taste and preferences of the artist . . . [are] in his productions though they may be the most reproductive of portraits. . . .
>
> Thus in literature, as a commentary on life, we have at least the elements of philosophy, firstly the idealization of experience, and secondly, a criticism.
>
> All philosophies are responses to problems of life on the part of people who have a peculiar sensitiveness to problems of life. A man to be a philosopher must possess this sensitiveness, just as a man to be a poet must possess a certain sensitiveness to form and color.
>
> The biographic element must be stressed if we are to study motives and interests of philosophers. We must know his temperament, his personal problems, times, biases, etc.

In attempting a critical interpretation of historic philosophies we have to pay attention to biography and temperament
and the experience of the philosopher. . . . We must also take
the cognizance of the particular social environment of the
philosopher.

One hundred years from now when present day philosophy will be seen in historical perspective, the old truth that no
man can think in a vacuum will be again confirmed.

Compared with every one of the major persons contributing
to American life during Dewey's time—indeed, compared with
most of the minor ones—Dewey has been accorded almost no biographical attention. George Dykhuizen, Dewey's only biographer, wrote
the best kind of biography that could be written in 1973 before the
large collections of personal papers became available that are now
housed in the Center for Dewey Studies and the Special Collections
Division of the Morris Library, both at Southern Illinois University,
Carbondale. For a long time, scholars had to rely on Dykhuizen's
work, noble in its intention but limited in its execution and deficient
in the resources available to its author. In recent years, several excellent books have made use of some of the hundreds of thousands
of manuscript pages and other materials assembled at Southern Illinois
University, but as a general rule each has used these materials—
and often used them brilliantly—in the service not of biography,
a continuous account of Dewey's lived experience, but to support
one or another particular philosophical conception of Dewey and his
significance.

Dewey himself emphasized that a major entry to philosophy is
through biography, the daily life of a man-who-thinks. A wise Dewey
scholar, Ralph W. Sleeper, more recently made the same observation:
"using a biographical approach is sometimes a necessity for understanding pragmatism, especially in regards to Dewey's . . . sense of
'lived experience.' "

Dewey's experience, the subject of my biographical inquiry, is
today, I believe, the crucial portal of entry by which the many people

interested in pragmatism can enter an understanding of Dewey's thoughts and activities. In 1950, Henry Steele Commager proclaimed pragmatism to be "almost the official philosophy of America." For a time it seemed that Commager might be proved wrong, for pragmatism seemed to go into decline. Perhaps, some predicted, it was headed toward oblivion. But starting in the late 1980s, pragmatism emerged anew, in Europe, Australia, and Japan as well as the United States. Today, a broad, informed movement sweeps pragmatists of all sorts across the cultural scene. Pragmatist historians like John Diggins and James T. Kloppenberg; political pragmatists like Robert Westbrook and Gary Bullett; philosophical-cultural pragmatists like Larry Hickman, John J. McDermott, Louis Menand, and Giles Gunn; philosophical-critical pragmatists like Richard Rorty, Richard Bernstein, and Hilary Putnam; pragmatists concerned with race, like Nancy Fraser and Cornel West; pragmatists of religion, like Steven C. Rockefeller and Henry Levinson; comparative philosophical pragmatists like Roger Ames; feminist pragmatists like Joan Scott and Jane Duran; legal-theory pragmatists like Margaret Jane Radin and Richard Posner; literary pragmatists like Mark Bauerlein, Morris Dickstein, and Richard Poirier; and, I am sure, many other versions of pragmatism and pragmatists not listed here, are beginning to form and consolidate a body of method and thought that must and will leave a permanent pragmatist deposit in the American mind for decades to come.

For the foreseeable future we Americans, along with most of the rest of the world, will be deeply engaged in a ceaseless "war against terror." We are now, and will long continue to be, plunged into uncertainty, indeterminacy, and ambiguity. John Dewey speaks profoundly to this condition, for he counsels us constantly to live without the comfort of preconceptions, but instead to investigate and examine our world as it daily presents its surprising alarms to us. Quest must be our condition, no more than warranted assertability our aim. Dewey's philosophy equips us to strive and not to yield in dangerous, dark times. His vision insists on ever-new revision, then new and better visions. He is the indispensible philosopher for our twenty-first century. Drawing on him, we may just barely be able, tentatively and tenuously, to bear the world of terror that is ineluctably our fate but may also become our triumph.

Those who have read my biography of John Dewey have passed through the portal of his "lived experience" into its consequences. Dewey is not dead so long as his life vibrates in us. He deserves further thought, he has still untapped resources for reflection, he beckons to us. How can we be content with our current culture when his vision for its future still lies before us?

Acknowledgments

Anyone who wonders whether scholarship is alive and well in the United States should pay a visit to the Center for Dewey Studies at Southern Illinois University, Carbondale, where the founding director of the center, Jo Ann Boydston; her successor, Larry Hickman; and a group of remarkable editors—Barbara Levine, Diane Meierkort, Ann Sharpe, and Harriet Simon—all have pursued and upheld the highest standards of scholarship, equaled only by the graciousness and generosity of their assistance to Dewey scholars. I am immeasurably indebted to them.

In the Morris Library of Southern Illinois University, David Koch, the curator and director of the Special Collections Library, assisted my research in every possible way, with a continuous spirit of friendly collaboration.

As in the past, I have relied on friends to read my manuscript and to help me turn it into a book. Myron Simon of the University of California at Irvine and Roger T. Ames of the University of Hawaii performed this act of friendship for me. At the Dewey Center, Larry

Hickman took time from his busy schedule to read the book with care. In her constant, extraordinary way, Barbara Levine sent me a detailed portfolio of suggestions. Jo Ann Boydston read several versions and made each one better.

Edith Kurzweil, editor of the *Partisan Review*, encouraged me by printing a section of this book, as did Robert Fogarty, editor of the *Antioch Review*. My colleagues at Claremont McKenna College listened to a part of it. Similarly, my colleagues in American Studies and Philosophy at the University of Hawaii invited me to give colloquia on parts of this book during the year I spent there as Dai Ho Chun Distinguished Visiting Professor. At a conference on biography in Puerto Vallarta, Mexico, I was privileged to discuss the book, completed in draft, with two distinguished biographers, Jerome Loving and Robert D. Richardson.

I am indebted to many university research libraries for permission to quote some of the nearly twenty thousand John Dewey letters and thousands of other manuscripts and letters that I have examined. These libraries are aknowledged inthe following:

LIBRARY RESOURCES:
ABBREVIATION AND ACKNOWLEDGMENTS

The abbreviations used in referring to libraries holding unpublished letters or manuscripts follow. Permissions for and locations of manuscripts which I have used are also indicated in this listing. "Fair use" provisions for the quotation of unpublished manuscripts are observed in accordance with the copyright laws regulating the use of manuscripts in scholarly research. In instances where I have made extensive use of unpublished materials I have obtained permission both from the authors' estates and the libraries possessing the original papers.

Ca OHM: McMaster University, Hamilton, Ontario, Canada. Bertrand Russell Archives.

CDS: Center for Dewey Studies, Southern Illinois University, Carbondale, Illinois.

CLSU: University of Southern California, Los Angeles, California. Archival Research Center Collection 184: William Torrey Harris Papers.

CLU: University of California, Los Angeles, California. F.C.S. Schiller Papers.

CST-Ar: Stanford University, Stanford, California. Archives, David Starr Jordan Papers (SCO58).

CtY: Yale University, New Haven, Connecticut. University Library Manuscripts and Archives, James Rowland Angell Papers, Thomas Davidson Papers, Walter Lippmann Papers.

CU-Banc: University of California, Berkeley, California. Bancroft Library, Manuscript collections, Warring Wilkerson Papers.

DHU: Howard University, Washington, D.C. Moreland-Spingarn Research Center, Joel Spingarn Papers.

DLC: Library of Congress, Washington D.C. James McKeen Cattell Papers, Scudder Klyce Papers, Agnes Meyer Papers.

DNA-I, II: U.S. National Archives Library, Washington, D.C.

IaU: University of Iowa, Iowa City, Iowa. Special Collections, Ruth Suckow Papers.

ICarb S: Southern Illinois University, Carlondale, Illinois. Special Collections, Morris Library. John Dewey Papers, Sidney Hook Papers, Joseph Ratner Papers, Sidney Ratner Papers.

ICHi: Chicago Historical Society, Chicago, Illinois. Manuscripts Division, Flora J. Cooke Papers.

ICU: University of Chicago, Chicago, Illinois. University Archives, William Rainey Harper Papers, John Dewey Papers, S.O. Levinson Papers, James H. Tufts Papers.

InU-Li: Indiana University, Bloomington, Indiana. Lilly Library.

IUCIU: University of Illinois, Chicago Circle, Illinois. Manuscript and Special Collections.

KyBgW: Western State College, Bowling Geen, Kentucky. Manuscript Department of Library, Special Collections.

MdBJ: The Johns Hopkins University, Baltimore, Maryland. Daniel Coit Gilman Papers, Ms. 1, Special Collections and Archives.

MH-Ar: Harvard University Archives, Cambridge, Massachusetts. Archives of the Department of Philosophy.

MH-H: Harvard University, Houghton Library. William James Papers, Barrett Wendell Papers, Lev Trotskii Exile Papers, C.S. Peirce Papers.

MH-L: Harvard University, Law School. Manuscript and Special Collections.

MiU-H: University of Michigan, Ann Arbor, Michigan. Historical Collections, James B. Angell Papers, Henry Carter Adams Papers, Frank B. Manny Papers, George Herbert Mead Papers, Reed Bain Papers.

MNS-Ar: University of Minnesota, Minneapolis, Minnesota. University Archives, Harry Norman Gardiner Papers.

Nhd: Darthmouth College, Hanover, New Hampshire. Adelbert Ames, Jr., Papers.

NiP: Princeton University, Princeton, New Jersey. Woodrow Wilson Papers

NIC: Cornell University, Ithaca, New York. Special Collections.

NLS: National Library of Scotland, Edinburgh, Scotland. Patrick Geddes Papers.

NN: New York Public Library, New York, New York. Manuscripts and Special Collections.

NNC: Columbia University, New York, New York. General Manuscripts, Rare Book and Manuscript Library, *Journal of Philosophy* Papers, John Dewey Papers, E. R. A. Seligman papers, John Jacob Coss Papers, Herbert Schneider Papers.

NNC-Ar: Columbia University, New York, New York. University Archives, Nicholas Murray Butler Papers.

NNYi: Yivo Institute for Jewish Research, New York, New York. Horace Kallen Papers.

NNYU: New York University, New York, New York. Manuscripts and Special Collections.

OCH: Hebrew Union College, Cincinnati, Ohio. Jacob Rader Marcus Center of the American Jewish Archives, Jewish Institute of Religion.

OU: The Ohio State University, Columbus, Ohio. Rare Books and Manuscripts Library, Joseph Denny Papers.

PPAmP: American Philosophical Society, Philadelphia, Pennsylvania. Franz Boas Papers

PPBf: The Barnes Foundation, Merion, Pennsylvania.

TNJ: Joint University Libraries, Nashville, Tennessee. University Archives, Vanderbilt University.

UVt: University of Vermont, Burlington, Vermont. Special Collections, Bailey/Howe Library, John Dewey Papers, George Dykhuizen Papers, John Williston Cook Papers.

UVt-Ar: University of Vermont Archives, Burlington, Vermont. University Archives Collections, Matthew H. Buckham Papers, Elias Lyman Papers, H. A. P Torrey Papers.

VtHi: Vermont Historical Society, Barre, Vermont. Historical Society Library, Collections Misc 363.

ViU: University of Virginia, Charlottesville, Virginia. Albert and Shirley Small Special Collections Library.

Whi: Wisconsin Historical Society, Madison, Wisconsin. Archives and Special Collections.

WiU: University of Wisconsin, Madison, Wisconsin. Manuscripts and Rare Books Library, Max C. Otto Papers, Merle Curti Papers, Richard T. Ely Papers, Anita McCormick Blaine Papers, Horace Fries Papers, Haskell Fain Papers.

Assistance with research expenses was provided by a fund connected with my chair when I was Leo S. Bing Professor of English at the University of Southern California and by a grant from the Emeriti College of the University of Southern California through the Kenneth T. and Eileen L. Norris Foundation. Claremont McKenna College also provided research funds through my chair as Edward S. Gould Professor of Humanities and Government, as well as indispensable secretarial aid. Through Dean Anthony Fucaloro of Claremont McKenna College, I received a summer research grant.

From the first, William Strachan, director of Columbia University Press, expressed an enthusiasm for the book that inspired me to complete it. In different ways, Suzanne Ryan and Anne McCoy took care to keep me and the book moving forward. I am grateful to my copy editor, Margaret B. Yamashita, for the skill and empathy with which she brought the book to its final shape. What better could any scholar hope for from the editors of a press? What good fortune that my agent, John Wright, brought this book to Columbia University Press.

A battalion of others assisted me: Connie Bartling, Miles Clark, Richard Drake, Starr Griffin, Cindi Guimond, John Kurtz, Blenda Long, Gaylene Rice, and Linda Tuthill. The index was compiled by Do Mi Stauber.

Nearly twenty years have passed since I contemplated writing a biography of John Dewey, then began to read through the hundreds of thousands pages of unpublished manuscripts and printed works, and finally began to write in the summer of 2001. As usual, my wife Helen; my children, Helen, Laura, and Jay; and even my grandchildren, Megan, Camille, Alexandra, and Margaret, have had to bear hearing a great deal about John Dewey from me and have sustained me by their love.

My oldest and sweetest debt is a reminiscential one—to Columbia College. I entered college the same year that Dewey died, and I heard about him, now fifty years ago, from such of his colleagues or students as John Herman Randall Jr., Mark Van Doren, Lionel Trilling, and Ernest Nagel. This earliest contact with Dewey wove itself into the fabric of my life as a teenager, and now the threads have formed a pattern, and lo and behold, here is a book!

Jay Martin

Notes

WRITINGS

The abbreviations used in references to John Dewey's writings:

EW (followed by the volume and page): *The Early Works,
    1882–1898* (Carbondale: Southern Illinois University Press,
    1969–72), 5 vols.
MW: *The Middle Works, 1899–1924* (Carbondale: Southern
    Illinois University Press, 1976–83), 15 vols.
LW: *The Late Works, 1925–1953* (Carbondale: Southern Illinois
    University Press, 1981–90), 17 vols. plus index.

One abbreviation is used in citing newspaper articles:

NYT: *New York Times.* Most of the articles cited from the
    New York Times are clippings located in the files of the
    Center for Dewey Studies, Southern Illinois University,
    Carbondale, Illinois.

People

The abbreviations of names used in referring to John Dewey's correspondence:

Dewey Family
AC: Alice Chipman
ACD: Alice Chipman Dewey
ASD: Archibald Sprague Dewey
CMD: Charles Miner Dewey
DRD: Davis Rich Dewey
ED: Evelyn Dewey
Eliz. D: Elizabeth Dewey
FD: Frederick A. Dewey
Gordon D: Gordon Dewey
Jane D: Jane Dewey
JD: John Dewey
LD: Lucy Dewey
LRD: Lucina Rich Dewey
RD: Roberta Dewey
SD: Sabino Dewey

Others
ACB: Albert C. Barnes
JB: Jo Ann Boydston
JDG: John D. Graves
GD: George Dykhuizen
GHM: George Herbert Mead
HAPT: H. A. P. Torrey
JR: Joseph Ratner
RL: Roberta Lowitz
RLG: Robert A. Lowitz Grant
SH: Sidney Hook
WJ: William James
WRH: William Rainey Harper
WTH: W. T. Harris

CITATIONS OF SOURCES

DEDICATION PAGE

JD >AC, 12/22/1885, ICarbS.

EPIGRAPH PAGE

Mortimer J. Adler, notes on Dewey's lectures in course, "Types of Philosophic Thought" 10/3/21, ICarbS; Jack C. Lamb, "John Dewey: A Look Back" typescript, 1959, ICarbS.

BOOK I: EMERGENCE (P. 1)

Childhood (p. 5)
Burlington (Vt.) *Daily Free Press*, 1/18/1859; JD > Mrs. Porter, 7/29/33,VtHi; ASD > Editors, *Daily Free Press*, 6/17/1862; JD > Louise Romig, 4/2/31, ICarbS; MW 1:7–8; JD > JR, 11/19/46, ICarbS; LW 6:102; JD > ACD, 9/14/1894, ICarbS; JD > AC 8/6/1885, ICarbS; JD > RL, 6/15/37, ICarbS; Margaret Buckham > Jo Ann Boydston, 7/28/68, ICarbS; JD > Merrit P. Allen, 11/5/45, ICarbS; ASD, 5/26/1860, ICarbS; ASD > JD, 10/21/1885, ICarbS; Ruth Noble Warren > JR, 4/5/47, ICarbS; JD > Dear Girls, 6/1/18, ICarbS; RD > George Axtelle, 3/9/61, ICarbS.

The Christian Influence (p. 19)
Typescript, ICarbS; JR > T. R. Powell, 11/30/46, ICarbS; LRD > JD, 2/2/1883, ICarbS; SH, "Some Memories of John Dewey 1859–1952," *Commentary* 14 (1952), 46; GD, *The Life and Mind of John Dewey* (Carbondale, Ill., 1973), 7; JD > Bertha Aleck, 11/11/36, ICarbS; JD > Scudder Klyce, 7/5/15, DLC; M. F. P., *Adams Mission Monthly* 1, no. 1 (April 1899), 1; M. F. P., *Adams Mission Monthly*, 1; *The Hundredth Anniversary of the Founding of the First Congregational Church* (Burlington, Vt., October 1905), 63–64; JD > Louise Romig, 4/2/31, ICarbS; *Records of First Congregational Church of Burlington,*

vol. 3, 1871; JR > Professor Becker, 12/7/46, ICarbS; EW 1:91; JD > Max C. Otto, 10/19/41, WHi; Lewis O. Brastow, *The Work of the Preacher* (Boston, 1914), 188, 25; LW 5:149.

The Beginning of John Dewey's Education (p. 25)

This section relies on Jay Martin, *Harvests of Change: American Literature 1865–1914* (Englewood Cliffs, N.J., 1967), 2–24; quoted in Sylvia Bowman, *The Year 2000* (New York, 1958), 74; Mrs. E. F. Ellet, *The Court Circles of the Republic* (Hartford, 1869), 550; Arthur M. Schlesinger, *The Rise of the City* (New York, 1933), 57; quoted in Don M. Wolfe, *The Image of Man in America* (Dallas, 1957), 130–31; Thomas Wentworth Higginson, *Contemporaries* (Boston, 1899), 276; William Dean Howells, *Literary Friends and Acquaintance* (London, 1900), 135; Stow Persons, *American Minds* (New York, 1958), 241; Henry Holt, *Garrulities of an Octogenarian Editor* (Boston, 1923), 49–50; Minot J. Savage, *The Religion of Evolution* (Philadelphia, 1886), 43; Elbert Hubbard, *The Romance of Business* (Aurora, Ill., 1917), 12; Washington Gladden, *Working People and Their Employers* (New York, 1876), 15; GD, *The Life and Mind of John Dewey* (Carbondale, Ill., 1973), 2; Irwin Edman, "America's Philosopher Attains an Alert 90," *New York Times Magazine*, 10/16/49, 17; SH, *John Dewey: An Intellectual Portrait* (New York, 1939), 5; quoted in Ray Bearse, ed., *Vermont*, 2d ed. (Boston, 1966), 2; Burlington City Council Records, 4/3/1865; Samuel N. Thayer, "Report of the Health Officer," 80, 81, 93; Eldridge Mix, Burlington City Documents, 1866, 103, 106, 104; L. G. Ware, Burlington City Documents, 1868, 59; "Annual Report of the [Burlington] City Government," 1869–70; Joseph Auld, *Picturesque Burlington* (Burlington, 1896), 92; Matthew H. Buckham, "Burlington as a Place to Live In," *Vermont Historical Gazetteer* 1 (1867), 724; L. G. Ware, "Report of the Superintendent of Common Schools," Burlington City Documents, 1868, 59; *Vermont School Register*, 1867–68; JD > GD, 10/15/49, UVt; JD > Mrs. Porter, 7/29/33,VtHi; RD > Pearl H. Weber, 9/13/67, ICarbS; JD > Mrs. Porter, 7/29/33,VtHi; M. Buckham > JB, 7/28/68, CDS; JD > JR, 10/2/46, ICarbS; JD > GD, 10/15/49, UVt; DRD, in *"Delta Psi* Goodrich Memorial, Burlington," 1925, 22; Lewis S. Feuer, "John Dewey's Reading at College," *Journal of the History of Ideas* 19 (1958), 415–21; Jane D, "Biography of John Dewey," *The Philosophy of John Dewey*, ed. Paul Arthur Schilipp (Evanston, Ill., 1939), 11; JD > JR, 10/2/46, ICarbS; JD > GD, 10/15/49, UVt;

JD > JR, 10/2/46, ICarbS; LW 5:147; James Marsh > Samuel Taylor Coleridge, 3/23/1829; quoted in Fred N. Scott, *The Castalian* 6 (1891), 21; JD > AC, 12/31/1885, ICarbS; James Marsh, "Preliminary Essay," *North American Review* 15 (1822), 107; LW 5:179; JD > Warring Wilkerson, 8/8/03, CU-BANC; quoted in GD, *The Life and Mind of John Dewey* (Carbondale, Ill., 1973), 332; Herbert Schneider, "Reminiscences About John Dewey at Columbia, 1913–1950," typescript, box 6, folder 66, 3, ICarbS; Joseph Torrey, *Memoir of the Life of James Marsh, D.D.* (Boston, 1843), 79; JR > Professor Becker, 12/7/46, ICarbS; LW 5:148–49; JD > HAPT, 11/17/1883, VtU; JD > JR, 10/2/46, ICarbS; JD > JR, 10/17/46, ICarbS.

A Career in Teaching? (p. 46)

Charles Babcock, *Venango County, Pennsylvania* (Chicago, 1919), 138, 199; *The Derrick*, Oil City, 7/14/80, 1; JD > AC, 12/23/1885, ICarbS; Max Eastman, "John Dewey," *Atlantic Monthly* 168 (1941), 672; John W. Maguire, "John Dewey, Vermont Teacher," *Journal of Rural and Small Schools* 2 (1987), 38–39; Eastman, "John Dewey," 673; EW 1:4; EW 1:4–5; JD > Merle Curti, 7/1/50, WiU; JD > WTH, 5/17/1881, CLSU; Clarence Pelag, "John Dewey Started His Career in Oil City," *The Derrick*, clippings file, CDS; JD > WTH, 10/21/1881, CLSU; LW 5:148; JD > WTH, 10/22/1881, CLSU; JD >WJ, 6/3/1891, MH-H; JD > WTH, 12/17/1886, CLSU; LW 5:150; JD > WTH, 12/17/1886, CLSU; Herbert Kleibard, *The Struggle for the American Curriculum 1893–1958* (Boston, 1986), 35; JD > WTH, 9/12/1890, CLSU; *Gazeteer and Business Directory of Chittenden County, Vermont, 1882–3* (Syracuse, N.Y., 1882), 166; quoted in the University of Michigan *Argonaut 3* (1885), 292; HAPT > G. S. Morris, 2/11/1882, MdBJ; EW 1:20–21; WTH's notes on bottom of JD > WTH, 7/1/1882, CLSU; JD > Daniel Coit Gilman, 8/11/1882; JD, "Application," 9/20/1882, MdBJ; LRD > JD, box 48, folder 5, ICarbS; JD > D. C. Gilman, 9/4/1882, MdBJ.

Or a Career in Philosophy? (p. 58)

LRD > JD, 9/22/1882, ICarbS; CMD > JD, 2/23/1883, ICarbS; LRD > JD, 1887, ICarbS; DRD > JD, 12/7/1882, ICarbS; Aunt Sarah > JD, 9/7/1882, ICarbS; LRD > JD, 9/22/1882, ICarbS; ASD > JD, 9/22/1882, ICarbS; The Girls > JD, 9/22/1882, in a P.S., ICarbS; Fragment, LRD > JD [n.d., 1882], ICarbS; LRD > JD, 2/2/1883, ICarbS; DRD > JD, 12/1882, ICarbS; LRD >

JD, 2/2/1883, ICarbS; DRD > JD, 2/6/1883, ICarbS; CMD > JD, 2/23/1883, ICarbS; CMD > JD, 5/13/1883, ICarbS; ASD > JD, 5/2/1883, ICarbS; ASD > JD, 10/16/1882, ICarbS; JD > HAPT, 10/5/1882, VtU; JD > HAPT, 10/5/1882, VtU; G. S. Morris, "The Fundamental Conceptions of University and Philosophy," paper read at Johns Hopkins Metaphysical Club, 12/12/1882, Johns Hopkins *University Circulars* 2 (1883), 59, 54, MdBJ; JD > HAPT, 10/5/1882, VtU; Morris, "The Fundamental Conceptions," 54; JD > HAPT, 2/14/1883, VtU; *University Circulars*, 2/1883, 63, "Remarks at a dinner given by the Aristogenic Society at the University Club," 5/17/35, "to mark the selection of Professor Dewey as one of the ten living Americans who have been the greatest service to the world," DLC; *University Circulars*, 4/1883, 54; JD > HAPT, 2/4/1883, VtU; JD > WTH, 1/17/1884, CLSU; LW 5:151; LW 5: 153.

Dewey's Philosophic Influences (p. 68)

Neil Coughlan, *Young John Dewey: An Essay in Intellectual History* (Chicago, 1975), 32; LW 5:152; Robert Mark Wenley, *The Life and Work of George Sylvester Morris* (New York, 1917), 128, 228; EW 3:17; G. Stanley Hall, *Life and Confessions of a Psychologist* (New York, 1923), 215; G. S. Morris > D. C. Gilman, 5/15/1884, MdBJ; Herbert Kleibard, *The Struggle for the American Curriculum 1893–1958* (Boston, 1986), 35; JD > HAPT, 2/14/1883, VtU; LW 5:152; JD > WTH, 1/17/1884, CLSU; EW 1:60.

Becoming a Philosopher (p. 74)

JD > WTH, 12/29/1882, CLSU; JD > WTH, 3/29/1883, CLSU; JD > T. R. Ball, 5/28/1888, MdBJ; EW 1:42; D. C. Gilman > Matthew H. Buckham, 3/30/1883, VtU; Matthew H. Buckham > D. C. Gilman, 4/3/1883, MdBJ; HAPT > D. C. Gilman, 4/15/1883, MdBJ; Arthur Yager, "Minutes of the Seminar of Herbert Baxter Adams in History and Political Science," Johns Hopkins University, 10/31/1884, 4–9, MdBJ; *University Circulars*, 6/1884, 118; JD > WTH, 5/15/1884, CLSU; JD > WTH, 1/17/1884, CLSU; G. S. Morris > D. C. Gilman, 5/15/1884, MdBJ; EW 1:48, 49, 50–51, 56, 56–57; JD > WTH, 1/17/1884, CLSU; EW 1:58, 59–60, 60; G. S. Morris > D. C. Gilman, 5/21/1884, MdBJ.

Finding Both a Philosophic Niche and a Job (p. 80)

JD > S. O. Levinson, 11/1/32, ICU; William Dean Howells, *Prefaces to Contemporaries, 1882–1920*, ed. George Arms et al. (Gainesville, Fla., 1957),

38; LW 5:153; JD > James B. Angell, 7/19/1884, MiU-H; University of Michigan *Argonaut*, 12/17/1884; JD > AC, 11/22/1885, ICarbS; JD > Dearest Family, 11/9/19, ICarbS; *Argonaut*, 10/1883, 23–24; *Argonaut*, 11/1883, 83; JD > HAPT, 2/28/1886, VtU; University of Michigan *Chronicle* 17 (1886), 155; University of Michigan *Palladium*, 1884; *Monthly Bulletin* 6 (October 1884), 1; EW 1:61, 63, 62; quoted in John Q. Axelson, "John Dewey," *Michigan Educational Journal* 43 (May 1966), 13–14; *The University*, 1884, 7; "The Inclusiveness of Science," *The University*, 1884, 2; "Minutes and Constitution of the Philosophic Society of the University of Michigan," 1884; *Argonaut* 3/1884, 1–2; JD > WTH, 12/23/1884, CLSU.

Dewey in Love (p. 91)

JD > AC, 12/24–25/1885, ICarbS; *Argonaut*, 4/1885; S. F. Weston > JD, 7/21/27, ICarbS; Linda Robinson Walker, "John Dewey at Michigan: The First Ann Arbor Period," *Michigan Today*, Summer 1997, 4–5; *Fenton Independent*, 11/23/01; JD > Horace Kallen, 12/17/17, OHC; Linda Walker to Jay Martin, 3/4/99; Walker, "John Dewey at Michigan," 2; Alice Lethbridge, *Flint Journal*, 11/13/71, 16; Walker,"John Dewey at Michigan," 4; AC > JD, 4/6/1886, ICarbS; *Argonaut*, 5/22/1886; JD > Corinne C. Frost, 8/11/37, NNC; JD > AC, 6/25/1885, ICarbS; John Chipman, Chipman Genealogy, Burton Historical Collection, Detroit; Sarah M. Churchill > AC, 5/30/1881, ICarbS; JD > ACD, 8/6/1885, ICarbS; JD > AC, 9/15/1885, ICarbS; JD > AC, 12/31/1885, ICarbS; EW 1:64; EW 1:80 (emphasis his).

Dewey's Philosophy Expands (p. 99)

EW 1:81–89; Ann Arbor *Register*, 12/11/1884; EW 1:151; JD > HAPT, 2/16/1886, VtU; JD > John Williston Cook, 1/16/1892, VtU; Harper & Bros. > JD, 12/11/85, ICarbS; JD > AC, 12/22/1885, ICarbS; JD > AC, 12/24–25/1885, ICarbS; AC > JD, 12/24–25/1885, ICarbS; AC > JD, 12/20/1885, ICarbS; JD > AC, 12/22/1885, ICarbS; JD > AC, 12/23/1885, ICarbS; JD > AC, 12/23/1885, ICarbS; AC > JD, 12/24/1885, ICarbS; CMD > JD, 1/30/1886, ICarbS; ASD > JD, 1/6/1886, ICarbS; JD > AC, 4/8/1886, ICarbS; JD > AC, 4/11/1886, ICarbS; EW 2:4; James A McLellan, *Applied Psychology* (Toronto, 1888); James Rowland Angell, 1936, CtY; HJ > Croom Robertson, 3/15/1887, MH-H; G. S. Hall, *American Journal of Psychology*, 1 (1887), 156, 157; JD > ACD, 8/5/1894, ICarbS; JD > Frederick T. Gates, 6/15/03, CDS; Linda Robinson Walker, "John Dewey at Michigan: The First Ann Arbor Period,"

Michigan Today, Summer 1997, 4; quoted in GD, *The Life and Mind of John Dewey* (Carbondale, Ill., 1973), 57; Walker, "John Dewey at Michigan," 5; *Detroit Free Press*, 7/1886, 3; JD > AC, 3/31/1886, ICarbS; JD > AC, 3/31/1886, ICarbS; JD > AC, 4/1/1886, ICarbS; AC > JD, 4/2/1886, ICarbS; JD > AC, 4/8/1886, ICarbS; JD > AC, 4/12/1886, ICarbS; LRD > JD, 8/1?/1886, ICarbS; JD > AC, 4/1/1886, ICarbS; review of Tilden: *The Christian Union* 33, no. 12 (1886), 22.

Dewey's Reputation Builds (p. 108)
JD > AC, 3/29/1886, ICarbS; *Argonaut* 4 (May 1886), 224; EW 1:246; Report of talk, "The Rise. . .," *Argonaut* 4 (1886), 224; EW 1:237; *Argonaut* 5 (March 1887), 140; *Argonaut*, 6/29/1887; Johns Hopkins *University Circulars*, 1883, 81; JD > HAPT, 1/3/1889, UVt; quoted in Hugh Hawkins, *Pioneer: A History of Johns Hopkins University 1874–1889* (Ithaca, N.Y., *1960), 203.*

Fred Dewey (p. 111)
Lillian W. Johnson > JR, ICarbS; Frances Browne Rogers > Editor, *Michigan Today*, Spring 1998, 17; James B. Edmundson > JD 10/17/29, ICarbS; Pearl Hunter Weber > JB 5/13/67, CDS; JD > ACD, 11/27/1894, ICarbS; JD > ACD, 10/16/1894, ICarbS; FD > JD, 6/19?/02, ICarbS; FD > JD & ACD, 6/19?/02, ICarbS; FD > JD, 9/21/02, ICarbS; FD > JD, 3/1/05, ICarbS; FD > ACD, 3/20/09, ICarbS; FD > ACD, 3/22/09, ICarbS; JD > ACD, 8/31/18; NYT, 12/30/34, 17; JD > Bertha Aleck, 1/3/37, ICarbS; JD > S. O. Levinson, 9/1/27, ICU; JR > Francis Davenport, 4/4/46, ICarbS.

To Minnesota and Back to Michigan (p. 117)
JD > HAPT, 3/28/88, VtU; GD, *The Life and Mind of John Dewey* (Carbondale, Ill., 1973), 58; ibid.; *Ariel*, 4/27/1889; ibid.; JD > James B. Angel, 4/19/1889, MiU-H; *Ariel*, 5/21/1889; S. C. Griggs > JD, 12/27/1889, ICarbS; JD > WTH, 1/29/90, CLSU; James B. Angell > James B. Tufts, 7/1/1889, ICarbS; University of Michigan *Calendar, 1889–90*, 54–55; University of Michigan *Monthly Bulletin*, March 15, 1891, 92.

Writing About Ethics (p. 120)
Dewitt H. Parker and C. B. Vibbert, *University of Michigan: An Encyclopedia Survey* (Durham, N.C., 1998), 674; JD > WJ, 5/10/1891, MH-H; EW 3:239;

EW 3:290; EW 3:345, 345–46; EW 4:221; EW 4:361; JD > Thomas Davidson, 3/14/1891, CtY (emphasis his); "Comte's Social Philosophy," *The Christian Union* 33, no. 13 (1886): 22; Mr.Tilden's Political Philosophy," *The Christian Union* 33, no. 12 (1886), 22.

A Utopian Deception (p. 124)

JD > ACD, 6/6/1891, ICarbS; JD > ACD, 6/12–14?/1891, ICarbS; JD > ACD, 6/6/1891, ICarbS; JD > ACD, 6/6/1891, ICarbS; JD > Henry Carter Adams, 4/29/1889, MiU-H; Enclosure in JD > H. C. Adams, 4/29/1889, MiU-H; JD > WJ, 6/3/1891, MH-H; EW 3:139; JD > James Rowland Angell, 3/11/1892, CtY; JD > T. Davidson, 3/8/1892, CtY; (University of) *Michigan Daily*, 4/16/1892; *Michigan Daily*, 4/8/1892; *Detroit Tribune*, 4/8/1892, 4/18/1892; Corydon Ford, *The Child of Democracy* (Ann Arbor, Mich., 1894); JD > James Rowland Angell, 4/25/92, CtY; JD > J. R. Angell, 4/22/92, CtY; William L. Lawrence, "Scholars Forms 'Court of Wisdom' to Guide World," NYT, 9/20/36; JD > WJ, 6/3/1891, MH-H (emphasis his); JD > WJ, 11/22/91, MH-H; JD > Joseph Denney, 2/8/1892, OU; JD > J. R. Angell, 3/11/1892, CtY; Speech files, Hull House, 1/21/1892, CDS; *Michigan Daily*, 1/27/1892, 1.

Family Life (p. 132)

Quoted in Linda Walker, "John Dewey at Michigan: The Birth of Pragmatism 1889–1894," *Michigan Today*, Fall 1997, 17; JR > Francis Davenport, 4/5/46, ICarbS; Bertha Wolfe Levi > JD, 10/20?/29, ICarbS; *Springfield Republican*, 6/19/1890; *Hampshire County Journal*, 6/21/1890; JD > ACD, 9/2/1892, ICarbS; JD > ACD, 8/16,19/1892, ICarbS; JD > ACD, 8/25/1892, ICarbS; JD > ACD, 8/16/1892, ICarbS; JD > ACD, 8/31/1892, ICarbS; ACD > JD, 6–7?/1893, ICarbS; Corliss Lamont, ed., *Dialogue on Dewey* (New York, 1959), 30; *Sociological Theory and Social Research: Selected Papers of Charles Horton Cooley* (New York: Holt, 1930), 6; Friends of the Elementary School > President Harper, 5/31/1899, ICarbS.

Harper and the University of Chicago (p. 137)

James H. Tufts, "Memorandum," ICU; JD > WRH, 2/15/1894, ICU; JD > WRH, 3/5/1894, ICU; JD > WRH, 3/19/1894, ICU; JD > ACD, 7/9/1894, ICarbS; JD > WRH, 4/10/1894, ICU; Tufts, "Memorandum," ICU; JD > WRH, 4/10/1894, ICU; *University of Chicago Weekly*, Fall 1894, 7; JD > ACD,

6/13/1894, ICarbS; ACD > JD, 6/24/1894, ICarbS; ACD > JD, 6/15/1894; ACD > JD, 6/22–24/1894; JD > ACD, 6/13/1894, JD > ACD, 5/10?/1894, ICarbS; JD > ACD, 10/9/1894, ICarbS; JD > ACD, FD, ED, 9/14,16/1894, ICarbS; JD > ACD, FD, ED, 10/25/1894, ICarbS; ACD > JD, 9/6?/1894, ICarbS; JD > ACD, 9/30/1894, ICarbS.

Book II: Experience (p. 145)

LW 9:57; Ruby M. York > JD, 5/10/48; JD > York, 5/12/48, ICarbS; LW 5:153.

Wealth and Poverty (p. 149)

My account draws on my *Harvests of Change*, 240–44; Thorstein Veblen: *The Portable Veblen*, ed. Max Lerner (New York, 1948), 271; W. T. Stead , *If Christ Came to Chicago* (Chicago, 1894), passim; quoted in Wayne Andrews, *Architecture, Ambition, and Americans* (New York, 1955), 220; Stead, *If Christ*, 115; quoted in Joseph Dorfman, *Thorstein Veblen* (New York, 1935), 100; Donnelly, "St. Louis Platform," quoted in John D. Hicks, *The Populist Revolt* (Minneapolis, 1955), 436; Donald McCurry, *Coxey's Army* (Boston, 1929), 37–39.

Evelyn Dewey (p. 154)

JD > ACD, 10/16/1894, ICarbS; JD > William Wirt, 5/10/14, InU-Li; MW 8:207; Evelyn Dewey, *New Schools for Old* (New York, 1919), 336; *The Dalton Laboratory Plan* (New York, 1922), vi, v; JD > ED, 5/15?/1894, ICarbS; ED > JR, 1/8?/34, ICarbS; Katherine Glover and Evelyn Dewey, *Children of the New Day* (New York, 1934), 5, 6, 313; JD > RL, 10/13/39, ICarbS.

Another Kind of Education (p. 158)

JD > ACD, 10/18/1894, ICarbS; JD > ACD, 5/17/1894; ACD > JD, 5/18/1894, ICarbS; JD > ACD, 5/10/1894, ICarbS; JD > ACD, 6/19/1894, ICarbS; JD > FD & ED, 11/22/1894, ICarbS; JD > ACD, 7/9/1894, 8/21/1894, 9/20/1894, ICarbS; JD > ACD, 7/2/1894, ICarbS; JD > ACD, 7/2/1894, ICarbS; JD > ACD, 7/9/1894, ICarbS; JD > FD & ED, 7/14/1894, ICarbS; JD > ACD, 7/14, 16/1894, ICarbS; JD > ACD, 7/23/1894, ICarbS; JD > ACD, 11/18/1894, 7/20/1894, ICarbS; JD > ACD, 7/28,29/1894, ICarbS; JD > ACD, 8/7/1894, ICarbS; JD > ACD, 8/23/1894, 8/28/1894, 8/7/1894, 7/4,5/1894, ICarbS; JD >

ACD, 8/18,19/1894, ICarbS; JD > ACD, 11/18/1894, ICarbS; JD > ACD, 11/18/1894, ICarbS; quoted by JD to ACD, 10/19/1894, ICarbS; quoted by JD to ACD, 7/5/1894, ICarbS; JD > ACD, 10/10/1894, ICarbS; I have arranged Dewey's letter into a dialogue, but I quote all statements in it without change; ACD, FD > JD, 7/30/1894, ICarbS; JD > ACD & Children, 8/5/1894, ICarbS; JD > ACD, 8/5/1894, ICarbS; JD > ACD, 7/20,21/1894, ICarbS; DRD > JD, 2/6?/1883, ICarbS; JD > AC, 4/11/1886, ICarbS; JD > ACD, 9/23/1894, ICarbS; Helen Mead > FD & ED, ICarbS; JD > ACD, 9/23/1894, ICarbS; JD > ACD, 7/20/1894, ICarbS; JD > ACD, 7/16/1894, ICarbS; JD > ACD, 7/16/1894, ICarbS; JD > ACD, 7/19/1894, ICarbS; JD > ACD, 7/16/1894, ICarbS; JD > FD, ED, ACD, 10/27/1894, ICarbS; JD > ACD, 10/9/1894, ICarbS; JD > ACD, 12/8 or 9/1894, ICarbS; JD > ACD, 11/22/1894, ICarbS; JD > James T. Farrell, 9/9/41, ICarbS.

Morris Dewey (p. 179)
JD > ACD, 9/20/1894, ICarbS; JD > ACD, 12/8 or 9/1894, ICarbS; JD > ACD, 12/3, 4/1894, ICarbS; JD > ACD, 11/22/1894, ICarbS; WTH letter for JD, 12/7/1894, ICarbS; LRD > JD & ACD, 6/29/1896, ICarbS; JD > WRH, 5/16/1895, ICU; JD > Harry Norman Gardiner, 10/27/1895, MNS-Ar.

Overworking at the University of Chicago (p. 183)
ACD > JD & LRD, 7/28, 29?/1895, ICarbS; George Herbert Palmer > James B. Angell, 5/22/1895, MiU-H; JD > WRH, 1/11/1896, ICU; JD > Frank A. Manny, 9/4/1896, MiU-H; Wilbur S. Jackman > JD, 11/7/02, ICarbS; JD > WTH, 4/14/03, CLSU; JD > Wilbur S. Jackman, 2/21/03, ICarbS; JD > WRH, 4/24/03, ICarbS; JD > Richard T. Ely, 2/18/03, WHi; JD > WRH, 12/22/03, 1/19/04, ICU; JD > Macmillan, 5/12/1897, NN; JD > Thomas McCormick, 11/19/1900, ICarbS; JD > W. S. Jackman, 6/4/02, ICarbS.

More Publications (p. 186)
EW 5:xiv; EW 5:96, 104, 97, 104; EW 5: 113, 119, 121; EW 5:147, 148; JD > JR, 10/7/46, ICarbS; JD > ACD, 5/22/1894, ICarbS; JD > ACD, 8/18, 19/1894, ICarbS; JD > ACD, 8/25, 26/1894, ICarbS; John Dewey and James A. McLellan, *The Psychology of Number* . . . (New York, 1897), vii, xiii; John Dewey, *Studies in Logical Theory*, Decennial Publications of the University of Chicago, 2d series, vol. 11 (Chicago, 1903, 1909), 86, 382; MW 2:296, 298, 302; WJ > JD, 10/17/03, MH-H; JD > WJ, 1/20/04, MH-H; WJ > F. S. C. Schiller,

11/15/03, MH-H; C. S. Peirce, *The Nation* 76 (1904), 220; Handwritten on bottom of JD > C. S. Peirce, early 1904, MH-H; JD > C. S. Peirce, 1/19/03, MH-H; F. S. C. Schiller, "In Defense of Humanism," *Mind* 13 (1904), 529–30; WJ, "The Chicago School," *Psychological Bulletin* 1 (1904), 1; WJ > JD, 12/3/03, NNC; F. H. Bradley, "On Truth and Practice," *Mind* 13 (1904), 309; *Chautauqua Assembly Herald*, July 23, 1896, 1.

Progressive Education (p. 199)

MW 1:10, 15, 12; Henry S. Townsend, "Educational Progress," *Hawaiian Almanac and Annual* (Honolulu, 1899), 163; JD > Flora J. Cooke, 8/16/1898, ICHi; JD > Flora J. Cooke, 9/1/1898, ICHi; quoted in Benjamin O. Wist, "The Influence of John Dewey upon Education in Hawaii," typescript, ICarbS.

The Lab School (p. 203)

"Minutes of the Meeting of the Three Trustees of the Chicago Institute," 4/30/02, ICU; ibid., 5/5/02, ICU; ibid., 5/7/02, ICU; Robert McCaul, "Dewey's Chicago," *School Review* 67 (1959), 279ff.; Robert McCaul, "Dewey and the University of Chicago," part 1: July 1894–March 1902," *School and Society* 89 (1961), 152–57; part 2: April 1902–May 1903, 179–83; part 3: September 1903–June 1904, 202–6; JD > ACD, 7/16/1894, ICarbS; JD > ACD, 8/5/1894, ICarbS; JD > WRH, 7/16/04, ICU; WRH > JD, 4/7/04, ICarbS; JD > WRH, 4/11/04, ICU; JD > ACD, 6/13/1894, ICarbS; WRH > JD, 8/2/01, ICU; JD > WRH, 7/22/01, ICU; WRH > JD, 8/2/01, ICU; WRH > JD, 4/30/04, ICU; ACD, "The Place of the Kindergarten," *The Elementary School Teacher*, January 1903, 273; see also "Written by Mrs. Dewey," Teachers College Library Archives, 15 pp. typescript, 1; Frank Pierrepont Graves > Miss Carr et al., 6/6/04, ICarbS; WRH > JD, 2/29/04, ICU; ACD > WRH, 5/5?/04, ICarbS; Max Eastman, "John Dewey," *Atlantic Monthly* 168 (1941), 679; JD > WRH, 4/6/04, ICU; JD > WRH, 4/7/04, ICarbS.

Resignation (p. 210)

JD > WRH, 4/11/04, ICU; Wallace Heckman > JD, 11/27/12, ICU; WRH > JD, 4/18/04, ICU; ACD > WTH, 4/21/04, CLSU; JD > WTH, 4/25/04, CLSU; WRH > JD, 4/26/04, ICU; WRH > ACD, 4/30/04, ICU; Anita McCormick Blaine> S. R. McCormick, 4/27/03, WHi; JD > WRH, 4/27/04, ICU; JD > Warring Wilkerson, 4/28/04, CU-BANC; JD > Frank A. Manny,

4/29/04, MiU-H; T. W. Goodspeed > JD, 5/17/04, ICU; Pearl Hunter Weber, ICarbS; JD > WRH, 5/10/04, ICU; James McKeen Cattell: "Remarks at a dinner given by the Aristogenic Society at the University Club," 5/17/35, DLC.

Lucy Dewey (p. 215)
ACD > JD, 7/17/1900, ICarbS; ACD > ED, 11/28/1918, ICarbS; JD > ACD, 9/25/02, ICarbS; Wolfgang Brandauer > LD, 7/20/22, ICarbS; ACD > Anne C. Edwards, 9/5/23, NIC; ACD > A. C. Edwards, 9/25/23, NIC; JD > S. O. Levinson, 1/27/28, ICU; JD > Ruth Levinson, 7/24/31, ICU; JD > Louise Romig, 6/7/33, CDS; JD > Bertha Aleck, 11/11/39, 2/23/43, ICarbS.

Jane Dewey (p. 218)
JD > Anita McCormick Blaine, 7/19/1900, WHi; JD > Mrs. James H. Tufts, ICU; ACD > JD, 7/15/02, ICarbS; JD > ACD, 9/20/02, ICarbS; Jane D > ACD, 2/7/14, ICarbS; Jane D > SD, 2/9/14, ICarbS; ACD > LD, 8/23/18, ICarbS; ACD > ED, 7/26/18; ACD > ED, 1/2/19, ICarbS; JD > ED, 10/8/18, ICarbS; "Notes from Sidney Hook's Visit," 4/21/83, CDS; JD > GHM, 1/4/26, ICarbS; *Physical Review*, 12/28/26, 1108–24; Jane D > Dearest Family, 1, 2?/27, ICarbS; JD > RLG, 4/11/39, ICarbS; Jane D > James McKeen Cattell, 12/13/39, DLC; Cattell > Jane D, 12/15/39, DLC; JD > RLG 7/5/40, 2/1/40, 3/1/42, ICarbS; JD > Bertha Aleck, 10/6/40, ICarbS; JD > RLG, 2/28/39, 1/25/41, ICarbS; ED > JR, 1/8/34, ICarbS; *Journal of Applied Physics*, 6/47, 49.

Columbia Comes to the Rescue (p. 223)
JD > WTH, 4/25/04, CLSU; JD > F. J. E. Woodbridge, 4/4/04, NNC; JD > Cattell, 4/12/04, DLC; Cattell > JD 4/13–15/04, DLC; JD > Cattell, 4/16/04, DLC; WTH > JD, 4/30/04, CLSU; JD > Cattell, 4/21/04, DLC; Cattell > JD, 4/26/04, DLC; JD > Cattell, 4/28/04, DLC; Nicholas Murray Butler > JD, 5/2/04, NNC-Ar; F. P. Graves > Miss Carr et al., 6/6/04., ICarbS; E. C. Moore > JD, 5/22/04, ICarbS; JD > Dewey family, 7/1/04, ICarbS; JD > Dewey family, 7/1/04, ICarbS; JD > ACD, 3/1,3/05, ICarbS; James E. Russell > JD, 5/3/04, ICarbS; JD > Cattell, 5/27/04, DLC.

Back to Europe (p. 228)
JD > Warring Wilkerson, 4/28/04, CU-BANC; ACD > WTH, 4/9/04, CLSU; JD > ACD, 3/16/05, ICarbS; ACD > JD, 7/15?/02, ICarbS; ACD >

Mary Bradshaw, 7/22?/04, ICarbS; 8/2/04, ICarbS; JD > FD & ED, 9/1/04, ICarbS; JD > Patrick Geddes, 9/9/04, NLS.

Starting Over (p. 231)

JD > ACD, 2/16, 17?/05, ICarbS; Jane Addams: GHM > JD, 10/1/04, ICarbS; "Eulogy on Gordon," ICarbS; Jane Addams, *The Excellent Becomes the Permanent* (New York, 1932), 61–72; JD > WJ, 11/21/04, MH-H; JD > ACD, 3/16/05, ICarbS; JD > LD & Jane D, 2/19,20/05, ICarbS; JD > ACD, 3/1, 3/05, ICarbS; JD > ACD, 3/1, 3/05, ICarbS; JD > ACD, 3/13/05, ICarbS; JD > ACD, 2/16, 17?/01, ICarbS; JD > FD, 3/13/05, ICarbS; JD > ACD, 3/1, 3/05, ICarbS; JD > ACD, 3/6–10/05, ICarbS; Walter Pitkin > JR, 3/2/47, ICarbS; quoted by Nima H. Adlerblum, "A Tape-Recording on John Dewey," typescript, box 71/3, 12, ICarbS; ibid., 2–3, 3, 4; David Starr Jordan > JD, 3/19/06, 3/23/06, CSt-AR.

The Gorky Affair (p. 238)

JD > ACD, 2/20/05, ICarbS; "$8,000 for Revolutionists," NYT, 4/15/06, 3; "Mark Twain's Position," NYT, 4/15/06, 1, 3; "Gorky and Actress Asked to Quit Hotels," NYT, 4/15/06, 3; "Boston Will Snub Them," NYT, 4/15/06, 3; "Not Asked to White House," NYT, 4/15/06, 3; quoted in Max Eastman, "John Dewey," *Atlantic Monthly* 168 (1941), 684, *New York World*, 5/5/06, 1; JD > Upton Sinclair, 8/24/22, InU-Li.

Five Arcs of Activities (p. 242)

JD > Hu Shi, 10/27/39, ICarbS; "Organization in American Education," MW 10:405; "Federal Aid to Elementary Education," MW 10:125–26; "Nationalizing Education," MW 10:208; "A Call to Organize," *The American Teacher* 2 (February 1913): 27; JD and Arthur O. Lovejoy, form letter 11/17/14, TNV; JD > Barrett Wendell, 12/7/14, MH-H; JD > Editor of *The Nation*, 3/30/16, ICarbS; "Memorandum of Professor John Dewey, for John A. Kinneman via Constance Roudebush," ICarbS; Oswald Garrison Villard > Joel Springarn, 10/17/10, DHU; Bessie Breuer Papers, box 3/9, ICarbS; O. G. Villard > Joel Springarn, 2/28/11, DHU; Eleanor Roosevelt > JD, 11/13/45, ICarbS; Roy Wilkins > JD, 10/19/49, ICarbS; Donald O. Johnson, *The Challenge to American Freedom: World War I and the Rise of the American Civil Liberties Union* (Lexington, Ky., 1963); NYT, 1/5/31, 2; JD > Arthur Dunn, 2/12/23, ICU.

More Publications (p. 250)

Ethics (1908): MW 5:6, 4; EW 4:56; MW 5:4; MW 5:388, 389; MW 6:179, 191; Burgess Johnson, *As Much as I Dare: A Personal Recollection* (New York, 1944), 186–87; LW 5:156.

Dewey's Teaching Style (p. 258)

Marion B. White > JR, 4/3/47, ICarbS; Pearl Hunter Weber > JB, "Reminiscences," ICarbS; Brand Blanshard, "Interview," 5/18/67, ICarbS; E. A. Burtt, "Interview," 4/13/67, ICarbS; Ernest Nagel, "Interview," 10/10/66, ICarbS; Corliss Lamont, ed., *Dialogue on Dewey* (New York, 1959), 41; Max Eastman, "John Dewey," *Atlantic Monthly* 168 (1941), 682; Thomas Munro, "Interview," 4/26/67, ICarbS; Bruce Raup, "Interview," 7/24/67, ICarbS.

War (p. 263)

In the ensuing account I draw some details from Alan Brinkley, *The Unfinished Nation: A Concise History of the American People*, 2d ed. (New York, 1997), 562 ff.; MW 8: 203; JD > George S. Fullerton, 12/4/14, ICarbS; MW 8:198.

New Restrictions (p. 269)

NYT, 2/14/17; NYT, 2/14/17; JD > Franz Boas, 3/19/17, PPAmP; F. Boas > JD, 3/12/17, PPAmP; MW 10:257; James McKeen Cattell, "Memories of My Last Days at Columbia, Confidential Statement," printed privately at Garrison-on-Hudson, N.Y., 1928, 24 pp.; Robert Mark Wenley, "Report of My Recollections of My Conversation with Dewey on the Cattell Case," 2/28/17, MiU-H; Diary notes for 10/7/17, CtY; Columbia *Spectator*, 10/11/17, 1; JD > ACD, 7/26/18, ICarbS; JD > ACD, 7/26/18, ICarbS; MW 10:1–6; NYT, 12/16/17; JD > Charles Beard, 12/17/17, CDS; "Never Mind What You Think About the I.W.W.," *New Republic*, 6/22/18, 242.

The Aftermath (p. 275)

JD > Thomas S. Eliot, 1/6/14, 3/5/14, MH-H; W. E. Hocking > JD, 2/3/17, 2/6/17, MH-Ar; JD > Professor Hoernle, 11/16/17, MH-Ar; Columbia *Spectator*, 5/22/18; Palo Alto *Daily*, 5/28/18, 1; *Seven Arts*, October 1917, 688–702; reprinted in Randolph Bourne, *History of a Literary Radical* (New York, 1956), 242; MW 11:180–85; MW 10:159; MW 11:70–71; MW 10:292.

The Polish Project (p. 278)
Brand Blanshard, "Interview," 5/18/67, ICarbS; ACB > JD, 5/14/18, ICarbS; ACB > JD, 4/20/18, ICarbS; B. Blanshard > JB, 7/5/74, ICarbS; ACB > JD, 5/15/18, ICarbS; ACB > JD, 4/20/18, ICarbS; Louise Levitas Henricksen, *Anzia Yezierska: A Writer's Life* (New Brunswick, N.J., 1988), 4–5; MW 10:162; Anzia Yezierska, *All I Could Never Be* (New York, 1932), 28; Mary V. Dearborn, *Love in the Promised Land* (New York, 1988), 141; ACB > JD, 4/26/18, ICarbS; ACB > JD, 5/24/18, ICarbS; ACB > JD, 6/28/18, ICarbS; LD > Jane D, 7/8/18, ICarbS; JD > ACD, 8/1/18, ICarbS; ACB > JD, 4/20/18, ICarbS.

Alexander's Influence on Dewey (p. 285)
MW 11:350; F. Matthias Alexander, *Man's Supreme Inheritance* (London, 1918), xx–xxii; Jane D, "Biography of John Dewey," *The Philosophy of John Dewey*, ed. Paul Arthur Schilipp (Evanston, Ill., 1939), 44–45; JD > LD & ED, 8/20/18, ICarbS; MW 11:253–55; JD > Randolph Bourne, 5/22/18, ICarbS; ACD > ED, 1/2/19, ICarbS.

A Philadelphia Story (p. 287)
Anzia Yezierska, *Hungry Hearts* (1920) (New York, 1920, 1985), 135, 141; JB, ed., *The Poems of John Dewey* (Carbondale, Ill., 1977), 4–5; ACB > JD, 6/12/18, ICarbS; B. Blanshard > JB, 7/5/74, ICarbS; Anzia Yezierska, *All I Could Never Be* (New York, 1932), 96–97; Louise Henricksen > JB, 3/4/75, ICarbS; JB, ed., *Poems*, 5; LW 10:285; JB, ed., *Poems*, 14; JD > ACB, 9/6/18, ICarbS; Anzia Yezierska > Ferris Greenslet, 10/25/20, MH-H; Anzia Yezierska, "Prophets of Democracy," *The Bookman* 52 (1921), 496; B. Blanshard > JB, 7/5/74, ICarbS; JD > Cale Young Rice, 12/5/17, KyBgW; JD > Dear family, 6/28/18, ICarbS.

Dewey's Interest in Poland (p. 293)
ACB > JD, 5/24/18, ICarbS; ACB > JD, 6/7/18, ICarbS; ACB > JD, 6/12/18, ICarbS; JD > Jane D, 7/12/18, ICarbS; JD > ACD, 7/13/18, ICarbS; JD > Dear Family, 7/21/18, ICarbS; quoted in Howard Greenfield, *The Devil and Dr. Barnes* (New York, 1987), 58; JD > ACD, 8/1/18, ICarbS; Herbert Croly > E. M. House, 8/3/18, CtY; JD > ACD, 8/3/18, ICarbS; JD > ACD, 8/3/18, ICarbS; Col. M. Churchill > JD, 8/15/18, DNA-I; JD > ACD & Jane D, 8/18/18, ICarbS; JD > Dear Daughter, 8/20/18, ICarbS; Louis L. Gerson,

Woodrow Wilson and the Rebirth of Poland 1914–1920 (New Haven, Conn., 1953), 90–93; ED > ACD & Jane D, 8/14/18, ICarbS; JD > H. T. Hunt, 9/20/18, DNA-I; JD > Woodrow Wilson, 9/25/18, DLC; W. Wilson > Joseph Tumulty, 9/30/18, DLC; W. Wilson > JD, 10/4/18, Ni P; ACB > JD, 8/15/18, ICarbS; Col. M. Churchill > JD, 11/6/18, Military Intelligence Division, RG 165, "Records of the War Department, General and Special Staffs," DNA-I; "Memorandum for Major Hunt, Subject: Polish Affairs," War Department, 9/3/18, DNA-I.

BOOK III: ENGAGEMENT (P. 301)

JD > W. E. Hocking, 2/16/17, MH-Ar; JD > B. I. Wheeler, 10/9/19, ICarbS; ACD > JD, 3/26/14, ICarbS; JD > ACD, 7/13/1898, ICarbS; JD > S. H. Goldenson, 11/21/18, ICarbS; JD > JDG 6/20/49, ICarbS.

Alice's Depression (p. 306)

Gordon O. Chipman > Mother, 2/2/1864, ICarbS; Leo Weigant, "Women of Fenton," typescript, CDS; JD > ACD, 10/7/1894, ICarbS; ACD > JD, 12/1896, ICarbS; JD > ACD, 7/4/1897, ICarbS; JD > ACD, 8/4/1897, ICarbS; JD > ACD, 3/22/1900, ICarbS; ACD > JD, 5/23/06, ICarbS; ED > Dearest Family, 8/15/09, ICarbS; JD > ED, 9/14/13, ICarbS; ACD > JD, 3/26/14, ICarbS; ACD > ED, 8/10/18, ICarbS; ACD > ED, 7/21/18, ICarbS; ACD > ED, 7/26/18, ICarbS; ACD > JD, 8/11/18, ICarbS; ACD > JD, 8/11/18, ICarbS; ACD > ED, 1/2/19, ICarbS; ACD > ED, 7/30/18, ICarbS; ACD > Eliz. D & FD, 11/18/18, ICarbS.

On to Japan (p. 310)

JD > Dearest Family, 12/28/18, ICarbS; Arthur Yager, "Minutes of the Seminar of Herbert Baxter Adams in History and Political Science," Johns Hopkins University, 10/31/1884, MdBJ; ACD > Children, 2/11/19, ICarbS; Jane D, "Biography of John Dewey," *The Philosophy of John Dewey*, ed., Paul Arthur Schilpp (Evanston, Ill., 1939), 40; JD > SD, 2/11/19, ICarbS; JD > N. M. Butler, 1/10/19, NNC-Ar; N. M. Butler > JD, 1/17/19, ICarbS; LD > ED, 4/26/19, ICarbS; JD > Wendell Bush, 8/1/19, NNC; JD > John Jacob Coss, 4/22/20, NNC.

China and "New Culture" (p. 314)

JD > Kids, 5/12/19, ICarbS; Letters 161,162; ACD > SD & Family, 6/1–5/19, ICarbS; quoted in Chow Tse-tsung, *The May Fourth Movement: Intellectual Revolution in Modern China 1915–1924* (Cambridge, Mass., 1960), 175; Barry Keenan, *The Dewey Experiment in China* (Cambridge, Mass., 1977), 11; Kazuko Tsurumi, ed., *John Dewey: A Critical Studyof the American Way of Thinking* (Tokyo, 1950), 186; Hu Shi, ed., *Collection*, vol. 1, 320; see also *Hsin Ch'ng-nien* 6 (April 1919), 342–58; JD > Dear Children, 6/10/19, ICarbS; JD > Dear Children, 5/19/19, ICarbS; Chow, *The May Fourth Movement*, 182–83; W. Theodore de Bary et al., eds., *Sources of Chinese Tradition*, vol. 2 (New York, 2000), 151–73; Robert W. Clopton and Tsuin-chen Ou, *John Dewey: Lectures in China 1919–1920* (Honolulu, 1973), 1; JD > JDG, 6/20/49, ICarbS; JD > Dear Children, 5/9/19, ICarbS; Tsung Hai Cheng, "Memoirs of a Seer's Visit to Our Land 1919–1921," written c. 1932, typescript, ICarbS; Notes, box 67, folder 14, ICarbS; JD > ACB, 1/15/20, ICarbS; J. J. Coss, 11/15/19, NNC; ACD > ED, 5/26/19, ICarbS; JD > Wendell Bush, 8/1/19, NNC; ACD > Eliz. D, 7/16/20, ICarbS; JD > Dearest Family, 11/9/19, ICarbS; JD > Dearest Family, 4/11/20, ICarbS; JD > ED, 1/8/20, ICarbS; JD > Dewey Family, 7/25/21, ICarbS; JD > Dearest Children, 10/26/20, ICarbS; JD > J. J. Coss, 4/22/20, NNC; NYT, 10/19/20, 10; JD > Col. Drysdale, 12/2/20, no. 2702, Service Report, DLC; JD > ACB, 9/12/20, ICarbS; JD > ACB, 9/12/20, ICarbS; T. Fu > Professor Muirhead, no date, 1920, ICarbS; JD > ACB, 9/12/20, 12/5/20, ICarbS; JD > Dearest Children, 10/26/20, ICarbS; Kenneth Duckett, "Interview with Lucy Dewey and Jane Dewey," Report of the Field Trip, 11/4/66, CDS; JD > Horace Fries, 3/8/51, WHi; JD > Roderick Chisholm, 10/23/45, 10/15/45, ICarbS; JD > J. J. Coss, 1/13/20, NNC; Walter Lippmann > JD, 6/14/21, CtY; Columbia *Spectator*, 10/14/21, 2–3; Columbia *Spectator*, 10/15/21; NYT, 9/20/24; NYT, 3/15/27; Hu Shi > JD, 6/29/39, ICarbS; Robert W. Clopton and Tsuin-chen Ou, *John Dewey: Lectures in China 1919–1920* (Honolulu, 1973), 305–6; T. V. Song and Menglin Jiang > JD, 11/15/45, ICarbS; JD > JR, 3/25/46, ICarbS; JD > Edward Lindeman, 3/25/46, NNC; Chinese embassy > JD, 3/26/46, ICarbS; T. Y. Wang > JD, 7/20/27, ICarbS; Ardelia Ripley Hall > JD, 7/25/27, ICarbS; JD > F. S. C. Schiller, 7/18/22, CLU.

No League and No War (p. 327)

MW 15:82; S. O. Levinson, "The Legal Status of War," *New Republic*, 3/9/18, 171–73; MW 13:411; JD > Hon. William E. Borah, 3/6/22, DLC; Walter Lippmann, "The Outlawry of War," *Atlantic Monthly* 132 (1923): 245–53; MW 15:119, 115; John Haynes Holmes > S. O. Levinson, quoted in Levinson > JD, 10/4/23, ICU.

Sabino Dewey (p. 330)

The following account is based on two interviews with Sabino Dewey, one by Sylvia Smith Ashton and the other by Kenneth Duckett, 2/10/67, both in CDS; SD > ACD, 8/10/18, 7/6/18, 7/9/18, ICarbS.

Idealism Corrupted (p. 333)

In this historical commentary, I follow my own article, "Crises and Continuity in the Twentieth Century: Ideals and Other Deals in the 20s," *In Search of the American Dream*, ed. Robert C. Elliott (San Diego, 1974), 26–27.

Now to Turkey (p. 335)

Eleanor Bisbee, *The New Turks: Pioneers of the Republic, 1920–1950* (Philadelphia, 1951), 28; Robert M. Scotten, first secretary of the U.S. embassy > U.S. secretary of state, 9/23/24, ICarbS; MW 15:418–20; ACD > SD, 8/2/24, ICarbS; MW 15:418, 420; MW 15:303, 307; MW 15:275; Ernest Wolf-Gazo, "John Dewey in Turkey: An Educational Mission," *Journal of American Studies of Turkey* 3 (1996), 23; LW 2:193; ACD, box 71, folder 23, ICarbS.

Then to Mexico (p. 341)

American consulate general, Mexico City > U.S. secretary of state, 6/10/26, DNA-II; ACD > Dear Children, 8/29/25, ICarbS; JD > ACD, 7/7/26, ICarbS; JD > ACD, 8/12/26, ICarbS; JD > ACD, 8/12/26, ICarbS; JD > Nima Adlerblum, 11/4/44, ICarbS; George C. Booth, *Mexico's School-Made Society* (Stanford, Calif., 1941), 86; LW 2:198, 202, 162.

Losing Alice (p. 344)

JD > Scudder Klyce, 7/27/27, DLC; JD > E. R. A. Seligman, 10/3/27, NNC; Department of Health, City of New York, Certificate of Death no. 17087;

GHM > JD, 7/14/27, ICarbS; JD > Mrs. Thomas, 7/27/27, ICarbS; JD > E. A. Burtt, 8/14/27, MiU-H; JD > Helen Mead and GHM, 7/27/27, ICarbS; John Macrae > ACD, 10/3/21, CDS; Mabel Castle > JD, 9/18/27, ICarbS; Dorothea Moore > JD, 7/15/27, ICarbS; Max Eastman, "John Dewey," *Atlantic Monthly* 168 (1941): 678; JD > W.R. Houston, 5/21/44, ICarbS; B. Anderson > JD, box 102/8/4, ICarbS; ACD > LD, 8/2/18, ICarbS; ACD > LD, 10/10/18, ICarbS; *Notable American Women 1607–1950*, ed. Edward T. James et al. (Cambridge, Mass., 1971), 467; NYT, 8/9/12; see JB, "John Dewey and the New Feminism," *Teachers College Record,* 441–48; JD > A. K. Parker, 7/25/02, ICU; James Giarelli, "Dewey and the Feminist Successor Pragmatism Project," *Free Inquiry* 13 (1992–93), 30–31; JD > Scudder Klyce, 7/5/15, DLC; ACD > Editor, NYT, 2/14/15.

Dewey Among the Soviets (p. 350)
Frances Ralston Welsh > U.S. Office of Eastern Affairs, 5/19/28, DNA-II; James Harvey Robinson & JR > S. O. Levinson, 12/8/27 (form letter), ICU; Anzia Yezierska, *All I Could Never Be* (New York, 1932), 230–31; Eliz. D, "Europe and Russia, 1928, 'Casual Notes,' " passim; JD > GHM, 6/20/28, ICarbS; *The Survey,* 12/15/28, 348–49; A. G. Kalashnikov > JD, 7/20/28, ICarbS; News clipping in "Places" file, 7/29/28, ICarbS; Walter Duranty, "Russians' Entertainment for John Dewey," NYT, 7/22/28; LW 3:243; JD > SH, 7/25/28, ICarbS; NYT, 11/11/28, 22; Corliss Lamont, "Interview," Dewey Project, 5/20/66, 11, CDS; Advertisement in *New Republic*, 2/6/29.

Three More Books (p. 358)
LW 3:203, 204, 205, 243–44, 223; JD > Oscar Cargill, 11/12/47, ICarbS; LW 1:283, 290.

The Gifford Lectures (p. 362)
Sir Alfred Ewing > JD, 3/12/28, ICarbS; JD > A. Ewing, 3/23/28, ICarbS; N. M. Butler > JD, 4/18/28, ICarbS; JD > SH, 5/10/29, ICarbS; *The Scotsman*, 4/18/29, 7; LW 4:3, 5, 58, 163, 221, 248, 250; *The Scotsman*, 5/18/29, 3.

Enjoying Life Again (p. 368)
The Scotsman, 5/6/29, 12; NYT, 11/8/30; Myrtle McGraw, "Interview," Dewey Project, 2/6/67, 5, 6, 8, CDS; "Memo to be filed with Brand Blanshard typescript," CDS; F. S. C. Northrop > JR, 7/23/46, ICarbS.

Dewey Turns Seventy (p. 371)

Henry R. Linville > JD, 10/20/29, ICarbS; William H. Kilpatrick > Herbert Schneider, 5/25/29, NNC; H. Linville > National Committee to Honor John Dewey, 10/15/29, ICarbS; H. Linville > J. R. Angell, CtY; in *John Dewey: The Man and His Philosophy: Addresses Delivered in New York in Celebration of His Seventieth Birthday* (Cambridge, Mass., 1930), 136–37; Oliver Wendell Holmes Jr. > H. Linville, 5/2/29, ICarbS; Felix Frankfuter > H. Linville, 10/15/29, ICarbS; J. H. Robinson, *Vermont Alumni Weekly* 9 (1929): 89; LW 5:418, 420; Arthur O. Lovejoy > JD, 11/2/29, ICarbS; H. Linville > JD, 10/20/29, ICarbS; JD > Jane Addams, 10/26/29, UVt.

The Stock Market Crash and Its Aftermath (p. 376)

I follow my own article, "The Crash," in *In Search of the American Dream*, ed. Robert C. Elliott (San Diego, 1974), 28–29; LW 2:368; "Dewey Aids La Follette," NYT, 10/23/24; "Why I Am for Smith," *New Republic*, 11/7/28, 320; "The Need for a New Party, I: The Present Crises," *New Republic*, 3/18/31, 115; Arthur M. Schlesinger Jr., *The Age of Roosevelt* (Cambridge, Mass., 1957), 147; "Liberals Here Plan an Opposition Party," NYT, 9/9/29, 1; "John Dewey Assails the Major Parties," NYT, 10/14/29, 2; Edward J. Bordeau, "John Dewey's Ideas About the Great Depression," *Journal of the History of Ideas* 32 (1971), 70; "Dewey Declares America Forgoes Faith in Prosperity," *Herald Tribune* (international ed.), 11/1930; *Bulletin of the League for Independent Political Action*, 11/30, 3; NYT, 12/26/30; "The Professor and the Senator," NYT, 12/27/30, 12; "Norris Declines to Head New Party," NYT, 12/27/30, 12; "Dewey on Norris' Rejection," NYT, 12/31/30; B. C. Vladeck > JD, 7/10/30, ICarbS; Benjamin C. Marsh, *Lobbyist for the People* (Washington, D.C., 1953), 87 ff; NYT, 10/26/30, 21; "The Need for a New Party, I: The Present Crises," *New Republic,* 3/18/31, 115; "The Need for a New Party, II: The Breakdown of the Old Order," 3/25/31, 150; "Lobby Asks Special Session on Debts," *People's Lobby Bulletin,*" October 1933, 1; *People's Lobby Bulletin*, November 1933, 1; John Dewey, *People's Lobby Bulletin*, MAY 1932, 1 (emphasis his).

Dewey's Political Philosophy (p. 387)

LW 2:217; LW 2:220, 219–20, 256, 303, 339, 365, 366 (emphasis his), 371–72; W. E. Hocking, *Journal of Philosophy*, 6/6/29, 329; LW 11:6, 21, 22, 27, 41–42, 40; LW 11:295; LW 11:299; LW 11:362; LW 11:367; LW 11:372; LW 14:254.

Dewey's Interest in the Arts (p. 398)

Quoted in Howard Greenfield, *The Devil and Dr. Barnes* (New York, 1987), 65; Joseph Torrey, *A Theory of Fine Art* (New York, 1874), 43; Michigan *University Record* 1, no. 4 (1891): 58–59; Michigan *University Record*, September–November 1891; Lionel Trilling > JD, 1/11/39, ICarbS; John Herman Randall Jr. > George Eastman, 7/10/64; Stored in Morris Library, Southern Illinois University, Carbondale, Special Collections; JD > Gertrude Stein, 2/19/32, CtY; Paul Monroe, ed., *A Cyclopedia of Education* (New York, 1911); MW 6:375–79; MW 13:362; quoted in ibid., 106; Thomas Munro, "Interview," 4/26/67, CDS; JD > JR, 3/24/31, ICarbS; JD > SH, 3/10/30, ICarbS; Munro, "Interview," 9; Michigan *University Record* 1, no. 4 (1891): 58; JD > Leo Stein, 2/22/26, CtY; John Dewey, "A Comment on the Forgoing Criticisms" [made by Benedetto Croce], ICarbS; LW 15:98; LW 6:332, 333; LW 10:9; LW 10: 329, 350, 25; LW 14:255–56.

The Last Educational Mission (p. 406)

Jane D > GD, 3/5/67, UVt; GD, *The Life and Mind of John Dewey* (Carbondale, Ill., 1973), 265; LW 9:203.

Leon Trotsky (p. 407)

Exchange of telegrams between President Cardenas and the American Committee for the Defense of Leon Trotsky, signed by John Dewey et al., ICarbS; Delmore Schwartz, "For Rhoda," *In Dreams Begin Responsibilities* (Norfolk, Conn., 1938), 94; JD > SH, 4/4/37, ICarbS; Alex Gumberg > JD, 5/11/37, ICarbS; JD replied, 5/11/47, ICarbS; NYT reported 2/17/37 that committee members reported pressure to resign ("Trotsky Inquiry Under Fire Here," 4); Cowley > JD, 6/4/37, ICarbS. JD > Cowley, 6/12/37, ICarbS; Bruce Bliven > George Eastman, 6/22/64, ICarbS; JD's resignation from the *New Republic* is JD > Bliven, 5/26/37, ICarbS; JD > John T. Flynn, 3/21/41, ICarbS; SH, "Interview," 4/6/73, 345, CDS; JD > Agnes Meyer; JD > RL, 4/3/37, ICarbS; Dewey also told Novack about his family's opposition to his going to Mexico: Lev Trotskii Exile Papers, MH-H; E. A. Ross > George Novack, 3/24/37, handwritten fragment, Ross Papers, UWi; JD > RL, 4/3/37, ICarbS; Trotsky's account of the hearings is in *Writings of Leon Trotsky: 1937–38* (New York, 1970), 62–129; LW 11:306–9; also "Preliminary Statement by Dr. Dewey," 4/10/37, CDS; McDermott, LW 11:xxvi; Albert Glotzer, reporter,

Transcript of the Proceedings of the Preliminary Commission of Inquiry (New York, 1937), 617 ff. and xiii–xiv; Marion Hammett and William Smith, "Inside the Trotsky 'Trial,'" *New Masses*, 4/27/37, 6; *Pravda*, 11/20/50; NYT, 10/23/49, 62; "Trotsky Trial Was 'Pink Tea,' Beals Asserts," *Brooklyn Eagle*, 4/19/37, 2; Dewey's response to Beals is in JD > RL, 4/20/37, ICarbS; "For Immediate Release": Statement to the Press by John Dewey, Chairman, Commission of Inquiry into the Charges Made Against Leon Trotsky in the Moscow Trials, 222 West 23d Street, New York City, photocopy, CDS; Bertram Wolfe > Arthur and Rosemary Mizener, Friday–Sunday, April 1937, ICarbS; Suzanne La Follette later wrote: "Dr. Dewey is marvelous–unperturbed, and is as full of fight as if he were half his age. He does not hesitate to take the offensive and to take it with a vigor that is truly amazing. He is truly admirable. La Follette > Leon Trotsky, 12/16/37, MH-H; SH, "Interview," 4/6/73, 345, CDS; Trotsky's closing speech is in Glotzer, *Proceedings*, 459–585; ibid., 585; Alice Rühle-Gerstel, "Trotsky in Mexico," *Encounter* 58 (1982), 36; JD > RL, 4/25/37, ICarbS; quoted in Jean van Heijenoort, *With Trotsky in Exile* (Cambridge, Mass., 1978), 110; Albert Glotzer, *Trotsky: Memoir & Critique* (Buffalo, N.Y., 1989), 272; "The Unity of Man," LW 13:322–26; "Dr. John Dewey Here; Tells of Trotsky 'Trial,'" *St. Louis Star-Times*, 4/21/37; "Dr. Dewey Discusses Roosevelt, Trotsky," *St. Louis Post Dispatch*, 4/21/37; JD > J. T. Farrell, 11/8/48, ICarbS; JD, "For Release in Morning Papers of May 10, 1937; Speech by Dr. John Dewey at Mecca Temple, Sunday evening, May 9," WiU-H; JD's first draft with SH corrections and JD's alterations are in ICarbS; see p. 3; JD et al., *Not Guilty: Report of the Commission of Inquiry into the Charges Made Against Leon Trotsky in the Moscow Trials* (New York, 1938); Emma Goldman > JD, 1/10/38, NN; JD > Emma Goldman, 2/21/38, Institute of Social History, Herengracht, 262, Amsterdam; JD > RL, 1/31/38, ICarbS; Leon and Natalia Trotsky > JD, via Anita Brenner, 10/3/37, Western Union, CDS; JD et al. > Leon Trotsky, 2/16/38, Compania Telegraphica Mexicana, via Western Union; Leon Trotsky, *The New International*, June 1938, 163–73; JD > J. T. Farrell, "Interview," Dewey Project, 11/5/65, 12, CDS; LW 11:259; GHM, Seminar Notes, 1926, ICU; JD > Max Eastman, 5/12/37, InU-Li; see also SH, "Interview," 4/6/73, 30, CDS; and JD > RL, 4/15/37: "It has been one of the most interesting experiences intellectually of my life–and it is not without emotional traits," ICarbS.

Dewey's Logic (p. 424)

LW 11:528; *Common Sense* 8 (1939), 11; JD > J. H. Tufts, 2/2/39, ICarbS; Herbert Schneider, "Interview," Dewey Project, 18–19, CDS; LW 12:5; JD > JR, 6/23/49, ICarbS; JD > ACB, 11/30/34, ICarbS; JD > Arthur Bentley, 1/8/49, ICarbS; JD > Haskell Fain, 4/26/49, WHi; LW 12:3, 4; C. S. Peirce > JD, 12/8/03 MH-H; JD > H. H. Peirce, *1/19/03*, MH-H; JD > C. S. Peirce, 12/23/03, MH-H; JD > C. S. Peirce, 1/11/04, MH-H; C. S. Peirce > JD, 12/24/03, MH-H; JD > Paul Weiss, 10/1/31, MH-H; LW 3:314, 315; LW 6:273; LW 11:421; Peirce, *Collected Papers* (1908), vol. 6, 482; JD > Emmanuel G. Mesthene 10/2/45, ICarbS; LW 15:72; JD > JR, 3/25/46, ICarbS; JD > Haskell Fain, 4/26/48, WHi; JD > A. Ames Jr., 7/2/47, NhD; William Gruen, "The Naturalization of Logic," *The Nation*, October 22, 1938, 427; EW 4:19, 20, 29, 33, 21; C. S. Peirce, *Monist*, April 1893; R. W. Sleeper, "Dewey's Attack on Peirce and Wittgenstein's Dilemma," unpublished typescript, box 27, folder 13, ICarbS.

Dewey and Valuation (p. 431)

MW 13:10; C. W. Morris > S. Morris Eames, 2/6/65; Corliss Lamont, "Interview," Dewey Project, 5/20/66, 11, CDS, 11–12; LW 13:250.

Dewey's Eightieth Birthday Celebration (p. 434)

JD > SH, 3/22/39, IUCIU; JD > SH, 3/25/39, ICarbS; JD > Horace Kallen, 3/30/39, NNYU; Jerome Nathanson > Charles Beard, 7/13/39; Beard > Nathanson, 7/20/39; Nathanson > Beard, 9/13/39; Beard > Nathanson, 9/17/39; Nathanson > Beard, 9/19/39; Beard to Nathanson, 9/22/39, Jerome Nathanson Papers, CDS; JD > J. Nathanson, 6/27/39, Nathanson Papers; JD > H. Kallen, 10/5/39, OCH; ED > JD, 5/26/39, ICarbS; JD > H. Kallen, OCH; JD > SH, 10/5/39, ICarbS; JD > ACB, 10/7/39, ICarbS; LW 14:224, 225, 227; NYT, 10/21/39, 19; "Proceedings of the Annual Meeting of the Trustees of the Barnes Foundation," 12/6/39, ICarbS; JD > RLG, 1/16/40, ICarbS.

Education and Freedom (p. 439)

MW 8:408, 409–10; GD, *The Life and Mind of John Dewey* (Carbondale, Ill., 1973), 274; LW 11:161; LW 11:340; LW 11:378; LW 11:530; LW 14:488; MW 14:366; LW 14:368; LW 14:372.

Bertrand Russell (p. 442)

NYT, 3/1/40, 23; JD > W. E. Hocking, 5/16/40, MH-H; John Herman Randall Jr. > Dora Black Russell, 5/24/40, CaOHM; in Horace Kallen, "Behind the Bertrand Russell Case," *The Bertrand Russell Case*, ed. John Dewey and Horace Kallen (New York, 1941), 28; JD et al. > Fiorello LaGuardia, 4/2/40, CaOHM; JD > W. E. Hocking, 5/16/40, MH-H; NYT, 4/6/40, 1, 15; JD > Fiorello LaGuardia, 4/6/40, CaOHM; JD > ACB, 4/6/40, ICarbS; JD > ACB, 4/6/40, ICarbS; J. H. Randall > F. LaGuardia, 4/14/40, CaOHM; NYT, 4/20/40; ibid.; LW 14:233–34; JD > W. E. Hocking, 5/16/40, MH-H; LW 14:358–59; J. H. Randall Jr. > Mrs. Russell, 5/24/40, CaOHM; Bertrand Russell > JD, 5/30/40, ICarbS.

More Controversies (p. 449)

NYT, 10/4/40, 14; ibid.; LW 14:374; ibid.; LW 5:319, 323, 325; Robert Maynard Hutchins, *The Higher Learning in America* (New Haven, Conn., 1936), passim; LW 5:265, 266; JD > Corliss Lamont, 9/15/40, ICarbS; JD > Edwin H. Wilson, 7/16/40, ICarbS; LW 11:395; LW 11:399; LW 11:592, 597; LW 11:403, 407; Donald A. Piatt > JD, 8/2/39, ICarbS; *Fortune*, June 1943, 159–60, 194, 196, 198, 201–2, 204, 207; LW 15:267, 261–62; "A Reply to John Dewey," LW 15:474–85; LW 15:332, 335; LW 15:486; LW 15:337; FBI New York Office file no. 100–25838, 4/29/43, CDS.

Further Views on Education (p. 459)

NYT, 10/27/39; LW 6:102; LW 6:105, 106, 109 (emphasis his), 110–11; LW 13:410, 3, 11; NYT, 3/2/38, 8.

After the War (p. 464)

LW 15:301–2; JD > SH, 12/18/49, ICarbS; Richard McKeon > JD, 1/23/50, quoted in LW 16:556; McKeon > JD, 3/20/50, quoted in LW 16:557; JD > McKeon, 3/24/50 quoted in LW 16:557; LW 16:339, 406.

John and Roberta (p. 467)

Melvin Arnold > JD, 10/20/49, ICarbS; Augustus Thomas > Charles H. Lake, 4/16/34, ICarbS; JD > Letter of Recommendation, 11/22/36, ICarbS; JD > RL, 1/7/37, ICarbS; JD > RL, 4/10/37, ICarbS; JD > RL, 6/17/37, ICarbS; JD > RL, 6/13/37, ICarbS; JD > RL, 6/14/37, ICarbS; JD > James T. Farrell,

7/29/41, ICarbS; Myrtle McGraw, "Interview," Dewey Project, 2/9/67, CDS; JD > Max Otto, 4/10/46, WHi.; RLG > Roy and Mazlia Peabody, 12/19/40, ICarbS; Hu Shi > RLG, 2/8/41, ICarbS; JD > RLG, 10/6/41, ICarbS; JD > W. R. Houston, 12/9/46, ICarbS; Cyrus S. Eaton > Charles J. Burchell, 5/2/48, ICarbS; JD > Burchell, 4/28/48, ICarbS; JD > Ferner Nuhn, 9/30/47, IaU; JD > RL, 11/2/39, ICarbS; Horace Kallen > RL, 6/26/39, ICarbS; JR > JD, 1941, ICarbS; Harold Taylor, "Interview," 4/8/66, typescript, CDS; "Interview with Horace Kallen, George Axtelle, and Morris Eames," 10/6/66, CDS; Melvin Arnold > JD, 5/18/50, ICarbS; McGraw, "Interview," CDS; JD > ED, 5/2/48, ICarbS; McGraw, "Interview," CDS; ED > JR, 12/9/51, ICarbS; Kallen, Axtelle, Eames, "Interview," 10/6/66, ICarbS; JD > Seng-nan Fen, 2/15/47, ICarbS.

The Last Birthday Celebration (p. 475)
Ömer Celal Sarc > JD, 10/3/49, ICarbS; Columbia University Oral History, tape "Presented by Professor Oliver Reiser," Vertical file, 104, 4, ICarbS; Harry S. Truman > JD, 10/6/49, in Harry W. Laidler, ed., *John Dewey at Ninety* (New York, 1950), n.p.; Laidler, *John Dewey*, "Introduction, Remarks"; LW 17:84, 86; Laidler, *John Dewey*; NYT, 10/23/49; NYT, 10/19/49; JD > JDG, 11/29/49, ICarbS; Loyd D. Easton > JD, 12/28/49, ICarbS; JD > Easton, 1/4/50, ICarbS.

The End (p. 478)
JR > ED, 12/18/50, ICarbS; Sidney Ratner and Jules Altman, eds., *John Dewey and Arthur F. Bentley: A Philosophical Correspondence, 1932–1951* (New Brunswick, N.J., 1964), 27–28; LW 16:5, 292; JD > Sebastian de Grazia, 1/25/49, ICarbS; JD > Read Bain, 10/25/49, MiU-H; JD > Matthew Lipman, 10/24/50, ICarbS; JD > Corinne Frost, 9/1/41, ICarbS; Edward C. Lindeman > JD, 11/29/50, ICarbS; Manuscript II, "The Story of Nature," ii, 35, Dewey Collection, box 61, folder 12, ICarbS; Corliss Lamont, ed., *Dialogue on Dewey* (New York, 1959), 50: JR > JD, 7/6/49, ICarbS; *Washington Post*, 10/23/49; JD > Bob Rothman, 10/22/50, ICarbS; JD > Ferner Nuhn, 1/7/50, ICarbS; James T. Farrell, 10/5/50, ICarbS; JD > Boyd H. Bode, 2/15/51, CDS; RD > Bob Rothman, 5/11/51; "Good Morning, Professor," typescript, box 77, folder 16, 1951, 2, 4, ICarbS; NYT, 6/12/51; ED > JR, 12/1/51, 5/21/52, ICarbS; Ed > JR,

5/21/52, ICarbS; David Miller > JB, *3/10/82*, ICarbS; GD, *The Life and Mind of John Dewey* (Carbondale, Ill., 1973), 321; Jane D > Max Otto, 6/8/52, WHi; ED > JR, 6/26/52, ICarbS.

Last Words (p. 488)

James Gutmann, "Interview," Dewey Project, 5/19/66, 16, CDS; Ernest Nagel, "Interview," Dewey Project, 10/10/66, 13, CDS; fragment from a philosophical club address, ca. 1900, box 51, folder 6, ICarbS; Lyndon B. Johnson > James T. Farrell, 11/30/66, ICarbS; Clifford Geertz, *Available Light: Anthropological Reflections on Philosophical Topics* (Princeton, N.J., 2000), 21; GHM, "The Philosophy of John Dewey," unpublished typescript, ICarbS; JD > Scudder Klyce, 3/24/27, DLC; JD > JDG, 7/26/49, ICarbS; Vertical file 99, ICarbS; LW 5:155; JD > Wendell T. Bush, 1/6/39, NNC; JD > Scudder Klyce, DLC; JD > RL, 4/5/40, ICarbS; JD > Agnes Meyer, 7/13/51, DLC; JD > Sterling Lamprecht, 7/24/40, NNC; Adelbert Ames Jr. > JD, 7/27/49, quoting JD > A. Ames Jr., 7/20/49, ICarbS; JD > JDG, 7/27/49, ICarbS; LW *11:217*; James Gouinlock, *John Dewey's Philosophy of Value* (New York, 1972), 359; JD, "The University School," typescript, 10/31/1896, ICarbS; EW 5:436–37; EW5:437; ACD, "Education Along the Lines of Least Resistance," typescript, 12/31/1893, ICarbS; Ellen Condliffe Lagemann, " The Plural Worlds of Educational Research," *History of Education Quarterly* 29 (1989), 212; Hutchins > Pearl Hunter Weber, 1/16/68, ICarbS; Bob Rothman > JD, 10/22/50, ICarbS; JD > George Santayana, 3/9/11, OCH; JD, "The Future of Philosophy," typescript of a talk to the Graduate Department of Philosophy, Columbia University, 11/13/47, ICarbS; LW 17:466–70; JD, "Philosophy and Reality," typescript, box 51, folder 6, 13, ICarbS; JD, "Types of Philosophic Thought," syllabus, 1921–22; MW 13:360; Mortimer J. Adler, notes on course, "Types of Philosophic Thought," notes for 10/3/21, 1, 2, 4; R. W. Sleeper, "What Is Metaphysics?" *Transactions of the Charles S. Peirce Society* 28, no. 2 (1992): 186; James T. Kloppenberg, "Pragmatism: An Old Name for Some New Ways of Thinking," *Journal of American History* 83 (June 1996): 100–38; Morris Dickstein, ed., *The Revival of Pragmatism: New Essays on Social Thought, Law, and Culture* (Durham, N.C., 1998); Mark Bauerlein, review of Dickstein in *Philosophy and Literature* 23 (1999), 424–28.

Note: I have deposited a much fuller and more detailed account of Dewey's life, with complete documentation, in the Center for Dewey Studies, Southern Illinois University, Carbondale, Ill.

Index

This index, following standard practice, provides entries for topics and people that are treated substantively in the text. It does not include names or other information that is mentioned only in passing.